Mergers, Acquisitions & Corporate Restructuring

Text and Cases

Second Edition

Edited by

Chandrasekhar Krishnamurti

Vishwanath S.R.

PUBLISHERS & DISTRIBUTORS (P) LTD

PUBLISHERS & DISTRIBUTORS (P) LTD

7/22, Ansari Road, Darya Ganj, New Delhi
Tel.: +91-11-4077 5252, 2327 3880
E-mail: orders@atlanticbooks.com
Web: www.atlanticbooks.com

This edition published in 2024 by Atlantic Publishers & Distributors (P) Ltd.

Previous edition published by Sage Publications in 2018

Reprinted in 2025

Printed & bound in India by Atlantic Print Services

Contents

Teaching Cases

Detailed Contents

List of Figures, Tables, and Exhibits

Figures

Tables

Exhibits

List of Abbreviations

Chapter 1

M&A	mergers and aquisitions
ABG	ABG Shipyard Limited
BSL	Bharti Shipyard Limited
FDI	foreign direct investment
FMS	flexible manufacturing
GOL	Great Offshore Limited
IPO	input, process and output
JIT	just-in-time
P/L	profit-and-loss
SBU	strategic business units
SEBI	Securities Exchange Board of India

Chapter 2

ADR	average daily rate
ARRs	average room rates
BCG	Boston Consulting Group
CAGR	compound annual growth rate
DPCO	Drug Price Control Order
EBID	earnings before interest and taxes
EBITDA	earnings before interest, tax, depreciation and amortization
FMCG	fast-moving consumer goods
GE	General Electric
LBO	leveraged buyout
M&A	mergers and acquisitions
ORs	occupancy rates
PAT	profit after tax
ROCE	return on capital employed
WMV	Watermill Ventures

Chapter 3

APIs	active pharmaceutical ingredients
APV	adjusted present value
CAP	capital asset pricing
Capex	capital expenditure
CAPM	capital asset pricing model
CCF	capital cash flow
D/E	debt/equity
DCF	discounted cash flow
E/V	equity-to-value
EBIT	earnings before interest but after taxes
EBITDA	earnings before interest, tax, depreciation and amortization
EPS	earnings per share
LBO	leveraged buyout
M/B	book-to-market
NOPAT	net operating profit after tax
NPV	net present value
OTC	over-the-counter
P/B	market-to-book
P/E	price-earnings
PV	present value
ROE	return on equity
ROIC	return on invested capital
WACC	weighted average cost of capital

Chapter 4

BV	book value
CAPM	capital asset pricing model
D/E	debt/equity
DCF	discounted cash flow
EBITDA	earnings before interest tax depreciation and amortization
ECF	equity cash flows
EV	enterprise value
IPO	initial public offering
IRR	internal rate of return
NOPAT	net operating profit after tax
OLS	ordinary least squares
P/BV	price-to-book value
P/E	price-earnings
P/S	price-to-sales

Chapter 5

CAR	cumulative abnormal returns
DCF	discounted cash flow
KT&G	Korean Tobacco and Ginseng Company
SG&A	Selling, general and administrative expenses
NPV	net present value
WACC	weighted average cost of capital

Chapter 6

BSE	Bombay Stock Exchange
CAPM	capital asset pricing model
EPS	earnings per share
P/E	price-earnings
RIL	Reliance Industries Ltd
RPL	Reliance Petrochemicals Ltd

Chapter 7

VAT	value-added taxes

Chapter 8

ARPU	average revenue per user
CAPM	capital asset pricing model
DCF	discounted cash flow
EBIDTA	earnings before interest, taxes, depreciation, and amortization
IPO	initial public offerings
LIBOR	The London Interbank Offered Rate
MVA	market value added
NPV	net present value
PV	present value
SPV	special purpose vehicles
WACC	weighted average cost of capital

Chapter 9

B/M	book-to-market
B/P	book/price
CAPM	capital asset pricing model
CAR	cumulative abnormal return
CRSP	Center for Research in Security Prices

DHRT	Dong, Hirshleifer, Richardson, and Teoh
EBITD	earnings before interest, taxes, and depreciation
EPS	earnings per share
FFJR	Fama, Fisher, Jensen, and Rol
M/B	market-to-book
MS	McConnell and Servaes
MSV	Morck, Shleifer and Vishny
NPV	net present value
NYSE	New York Stock Exchange
P/E	price-earnings
ROE	return on equity
SDC	Securities Data Company
SEC	Securities and Exchange Commission
V/P	valuation to price
WSJ	Wall Street Journal

Chapter 10

ATP	anti-takeover provisions
IPO	initial public offerings

Chapter 11

CFO	chief financial officers
DCF	discounted cash flow
EVA	economic value added
PMI	post-merger integration
PMO	project management office
TSR	total shareholder returns

Chapter 13

GM	General Motors
OTC	over-the-counter
LDC	less developed countries
NPV	net present value
CDR	corporate debt restructuring
DCA	debtor-creditor agreement
ICA	inter-creditor agreement
EG	empowered group
LOA	letter of approval
MDA	multiple discriminant analysis
EBIT	earnings before interest but after taxes
WACC	weighted average cost of capital

MV market value
CCF capital cash flows
NOL net operating loss

Chapter 14

ESOP employee stock ownership plans
SIP share investment plan
AESOP all-employee share ownership plan
ESA employee shareholder association
SAR stock appreciation rights
ERISA Employee Retirement Income Security Act
ISO incentive stock options
GAO General Accounting Office
NCEO National Center for Employee Ownership
ESPP employee stock purchase plans
IRS Internal Revenue Service

Case 1

ADR American depository receipts
BT British Telecommunications
BVQI Bureau Veritas Quality International
CMM Capability Maturity Model
D&B Dun & Bradstreet
DBSS Dun & Bradstreet Satyam Software
EOI expression of interest
ERP enterprise resource planning
ICAI Institute of Chartered Accountants of Indi
IT information technology
L&T Larsen & Toubro
NASSCOM National Association of Software and Service Companies
NSE National Stock Exchange
NYSE New York Stock Exchange
PwC PricewaterhouseCoopers
SAP systems, applications and products
SEBI Securities Exchange Board of India
SEI Software Engineering Institute

Case 2

BRIC Brazil, Russia, India, and China
CARS cumulative alternative reference securities
CSN Companhia Siderúrgica Nacional

EBITDA	earnings before interest, tax, depreciation and amortization
ECA	Export Credit Agency
FCCB	foreign currency convertible bond
FDI	foreign direct investment
FPO	follow-on public offer
GDR	global depository receipts
JV	joint venture
LBO	leveraged buyout
NCD	nonconvertible debentures
NML	New Millennium Capital Corporation
SAIL	Steel Authority of India Limited
SPV	special purpose vehicles
SSI	Sahaviriya Steel Industries
TCP	Teesside Cast Products
TSL	Tata Steel Ltd
WSA	World Steel Association

Case 3

ATF	air turbine fuel
CAGR	compound annual growth rate
CEO	chief executive officer
EBITDAR	earnings before interest, tax, depreciation, amortization and rentals
LCC	low-cost carrier
UBL	United Breweries Ltd
USL	United Spirits Ltd

Case 4

ARPU	average revenue per user
CDMA	code division multiple access
CAGR	compound annual growth rate
DoT	department of telecommunications
EBITDA	earnings before interest, tax, depreciation, and amortization
ERP	enterprise resource planning
FCCB	foreign currency convertible bond
GSM	global system for mobile communication
ILD	international long-distance
IDC	Internet data center
NLD	national long-distance
RTIL	Reliance Telecom Infrastructure Ltd
STD	subscriber trunk dialling
TRAI	Telecom Regulatory Authority of India

Case 5

NYSE	New York Stock Exchange
PCMM	People Capability Maturity Model
SEI CMM	Software Engineering Institute Capability Maturity Model

Case 6

AGL	Australia Gas & Light
CFO	chief financial officer
CDR	corporate debt restructuring
DCA	debtor-creditor agreement
EPS	earnings per share
EG	empowered group
FX	foreign currency
GDRs	global depository receipts
ICA	inter-creditor agreement
LOA	letter of approval
SBI	State Bank of India
TECHNERIA	Technogias Energeticas

Preface to the First Edition

In recent years, the worldwide mergers and acquisitions (M&A) volume has been averaging US$2 trillion. Deals running into several billion dollars are not uncommon. In 2006, Mittal Steel of the UK, for example, made a US$23 billion bid for Arcelor of France, creating the biggest steel company in the world accounting for 10% of the world's steel production. The rise in volume and size of deals has increased the need for sound practical frameworks for the analysis and structuring of transactions. This book focuses on the purchase and sale of equity, and the design of consideration in M&A. The book comprises modules on searching for acquisitions, value drivers and target valuation, design of consideration, a real options perspective of M&A, accounting and tax factors, cross-border acquisitions, and the restructuring of equity and debt contracts.

This book is intended for students with an interest in the financial, strategic, and business issues surrounding corporate restructuring. Far from being a rare event, corporate restructuring has become a permanent affair in the corporate landscape. Corporate restructuring is the process by which a firm renegotiates contracts and claims that it has entered into with its various constituencies such as stockholders, creditors, employees, suppliers, customers, and governments. The book will show students how to deal with and profit from the acquisition or restructuring opportunities that they will encounter in their careers.

The specific kinds of restructuring presented in the book include corporate spin-offs, equity carve-outs, targeted stock offerings, bankruptcy, reorganizations and workouts, and downsizing programs.

EDUCATIONAL OBJECTIVES

The aim of this book is to provide a rigorous understanding of valuation in a variety of settings. Though the book considers the perspectives of all participants in an acquisition/restructuring, the focus is on the managers of the company being restructured. After going through this book, a reader should be able to value and structure an acquisition or a restructuring opportunity.

In particular, the book tries to answer the following questions:

- When does it make sense to restructure a firm's operations?
- What kind of restructuring is most appropriate for addressing particular problems or challenges facing the firm?
- How much value will the acquisition or restructuring create?

TARGET AUDIENCE

This book is meant to be used in a standard mergers, acquisitions, and corporate restructuring course in an MBA program, although students of other professional programs such as CFA, CA, and ICWA would also find it useful. Moreover, this book is suitable for those who are seeking a career in investment banking, general management, strategy consulting, securities analysis, turnaround management, commercial banking, and investment management. The book can also be used in executive education programs such as acquisitions and alliances as well as corporate restructuring.

ACKNOWLEDGMENTS

No book is the result of individual effort. Over the years, we have taught in many universities all over the world. Our thinking has been shaped by discussions with colleagues. This book belongs as much to them as to us. We thank our colleagues and students who have helped us in bringing out this volume. Special thanks are due to the contributors who have made this book possible.

Preface to the Second Edition

In recent years, the worldwide mergers and acquisitions (M&A) volume has been averaging US$5 trillion. Deals running into several billion dollars are not uncommon. In 2006, Mittal Steel of UK, for example, made a US$23 billion bid for Arcelor of France, creating the biggest steel company in the world accounting for 10% of the world's steel production. The rise in volume and size of deals has increased the need for sound practical frameworks for the analysis and structuring of transactions. This book focuses on the purchase and sale of equity, and the design of consideration in M&A. The book comprises modules on searching for acquisitions, value drivers and target valuation, design of consideration, a real options perspective of M&A, accounting and tax factors, cross-border acquisitions, and the restructuring of equity and debt contracts. In this enhanced, revised edition, we have incorporated seven brief cases and six full-length teaching cases that instructors can use for classroom discussion.

This book is intended for students with an interest in studying the financial, strategic, and business issues surrounding corporate restructuring. Far from being a rare event, corporate restructuring has become a permanent affair in the corporate landscape. Corporate restructuring is the process by which a firm renegotiates the contracts and claims that it has entered into with its various constituencies such as stockholders, creditors, employees, suppliers, customers, and governments. The book will show students how to deal with and profit from the acquisition or restructuring opportunities that they will encounter in their careers.

The specific kinds of restructuring presented in the book include corporate spin-offs, equity carve-outs, targeted stock offerings, bankruptcy, reorganizations and workouts, and downsizing programs.

EDUCATIONAL OBJECTIVES

The aim of this book is to provide a rigorous understanding of valuation in a variety of settings. Though the book considers the perspectives of all participants in an acquisition/restructuring, the focus is on the managers of the company being restructured. After going through this book, a reader should be able to value and structure an acquisition or a restructuring opportunity.

In particular, the book tries to answer the following questions:

- When does it make sense to acquire or restructure a firm's operations?
- How does the structure of the deal affect the value creation potential?
- How much value will the acquisition or restructuring create?

- What are the accounting and tax issues in M&A?
- What are some of the post-merger integration issues facing managers?
- What kind of restructuring is most appropriate for addressing particular problems or challenges facing the firm?

TARGET AUDIENCE

This book is meant to be used in a standard mergers, acquisitions, and corporate restructuring course in an MBA program, although students of other professional programs such as CFA, CA, and ICWA would also find it useful. Moreover, this book is suitable for those who are seeking a career in corporate finance, investment banking, general management, strategy consulting, securities analysis, turnaround management, commercial banking, and investment management. The book can also be used in executive education programs such as acquisitions and alliances as well as corporate restructuring.

ACKNOWLEDGMENTS

No book is the result of individual effort. Over the years, we have taught in many universities all over the world. Our thinking has been shaped by discussions with colleagues. This book belongs as much to them as to us. We thank our colleagues and students who have helped us in bringing out this volume. Special thanks are due to the contributors who have made this book possible. In particular, we would like to thank Vijaya Narapareddy (University of Denver), Durga Prasad (T. A. Pai Management Institute), Rajesh Haldipur (PricewaterhouseCoopers), Jaskiran Arora (BML Munjal University), and Kulbir Singh (Institute of Management Technology, Nagpur) who wrote the cases that appear in this edition.

About the Editors and Contributors

EDITORS

Chandrasekhar Krishnamurti is a Professor of Finance at the School of Commerce, University of Southern Queensland, Australia. He has held teaching positions at the National University of Singapore, Nanyang Business School (Singapore), Monash University, Auckland University of Technology, and the Indian Institute of Science (Bengaluru). He has a PhD in finance from the University of Iowa, USA. He has published in major international journals such as *Financial Management, Journal of Banking and Finance, Journal of Corporate Finance*, and *Journal of Financial Research*. The areas of his research interest are market microstructure, corporate governance, emerging markets, international finance, and carbon finance.

Vishwanath S. R. is a Professor of Finance at the School of Management and Entrepreneurship, Shiv Nadar University, Gautam Buddh Nagar, UP. He has held academic positions at S. P. Jain Institute of Management; T. A. Pai Management Institute; Emirates Institute for Banking and Financial Studies, Sharjah, UAE; and the Institute of Management Technology, Nagpur. He was a consultant with the Tata Management Training Center in Pune, India, during 2006–07.

He is the recipient of the Ruth Greene Memorial Award, the Best Workshop Case Award and the Jonathan Welch Award from the North American Case Research Association, and the Unilever-Dewang Mehta Best Professor in Financial Management Award. He has been nominated to Marquis Who's Who in the World and Madison's Who's Who in the World.

He is the author of 6 books and 80 cases in corporate finance, investment management, and mergers, acquisitions, and corporate restructuring for various publications. His research examines trading mechanisms at stock exchanges, performance and risk taking by family firms, the value of certification and analyst recommendations of IPO firms, the effect of taxes on investor and corporate behavior, and the role played by anchor investors in the market for IPOs.

He has presented his research at major global conferences such as the European Financial Management Association Asian Conference, Asian Finance Association Annual Meeting, Journal of Corporate Finance Special Emerging Markets Conference, Financial Markets and Corporate Governance Conference, and the North American Case Research Association (NACRA) Annual Meeting.

CONTRIBUTORS

Jaskiran Arora is a Professor of Accounting at BML Munjal University, Gurgaon. She has published over 20 scholarly articles on accounting, finance, and education.

Sharon Hannes is the head of the Tel Aviv Berkeley Executive LLM program—a joint program of Tel Aviv University and UC Berkeley for advanced lawyers, legal advisors, and judges. Sharon teaches corporations, law and economics, US securities regulation for foreign issuers, a workshop in law and economics, a workshop on markets, firms, and the law, and a seminar in corporations at Tel Aviv University School of Law. In the fall of 2003, he was a Visiting Professor at Northwestern University School of Law. He holds an SJD from Harvard Law School, where he was a recipient of the Byse Fellowship. He holds an LLB and a BA (Accounting) from Tel Aviv University and an LLM in Corporate Studies from New York University Law School, where he was a recipient of the Hauser Global Fellowship.

Pitabas Mohanty is a Professor at XLRI (Xavier School of Management), Jamshedpur, India. He is a fellow of the Indian Institute of Management, Bangalore. His research has won awards at the national level in conferences like the UTI Institute Capital Markets Conference. He has won the best research paper award and the best young teacher award from the AIMS in 1999 and 2002 respectively. He is a coauthor of the Indian edition of the popular Investments text by Bodie, Kane, and Marcus published by Tata McGraw Hill.

Durga Prasad is an Associate Professor at T. A. Pai Management Institute, Manipal. He has 19 years of teaching experience in some of the best management institutions. He is the author of numerous articles and cases published in a variety of journals.

Raghavendra Rau holds the Evelyn de Rothschild Chair at the Judge Business School, Cambridge University, UK. He was an Associate Professor at the Krannert Graduate School of Management, Purdue University, USA. He has a PhD in finance from INSEAD, France. He has published in all the major finance journals such as *the Journal of Finance*, *Journal of Business*, *Journal of Financial Economics*, and *Review of Financial Studies*. Professor Rau's current research areas are in the fields of empirical finance and the economics of information. His research is centered on the acquisition and utilization of information by participants in a market framework. In some of his recent papers, he has investigated the valuation effects of corporate name changes in the dotcom bubble, expropriation in publicly listed firms in China and Hong Kong, valuation effects of mutual fund closures, and changes in market shares of investment banks when their star analysts move. Professor Rau's primary teaching interest is corporate finance.

Corey Rosen is the Executive Director and Cofounder of the National Center for Employee Ownership (NCEO), a private, nonprofit membership, information, and research organization in Oakland, CA, USA. The NCEO is widely considered to be the authoritative source on broad-based employee ownership plans. He cofounded the NCEO in 1981 after working for five years as a professional staff member in the US Senate, where he helped draft legislation on employee ownership plans. Prior to that, he taught political science at Ripon College, WI, USA. He is the author or coauthor of numerous books on employee ownership and over 100 articles.

He coauthored (with John Case) *Equity: Why Employee Ownership is Good for Business* (2005). He was the subject of an extensive interview in *Inc.* magazine in August 2000, has appeared frequently on CNN, PBS, NPR, and other network programs, and is regularly quoted in *The Wall Street Journal*, *The New York Times*, and other leading publications. He has a PhD in political science from Cornell University, NY, USA, and serves on the advisory board of the Certified Equity Professional Institute.

Kulbir Singh is an Associate Professor at the Institute of Management Technology, Nagpur. He is the author of several papers and cases published in the *International Research Journal of Applied Finance*, *Asian Case Research Journal*, and *The CASE Journal*. He has received several awards for case writing from the North American Case Research Association.

K. Sankaran is the Director of Justice K. S. Hegde Institute of Management at Nitte, Karnataka. He holds a BTech from Indian Institute of Technology Kharagpur, PGDM from Indian Institute of Management Bangalore, and PhD from Kent State University, Ohio, USA. He has several years of experience in the USA, East Asia, and India. Some of the institutes that he has worked for include the UK-based Strathclyde University, the University of Sharjah, IMI, New Delhi, S. P. Jain Institute of Management, Mumbai, and T. A. Pai Management Institute, Manipal. Besides academia, he has several years of experience in project management and management consulting.

CHAPTER 1

Diversification via Acquisition

K. Sankaran and Vishwanath S. R.

Learning Objectives

- Provide a rationale for diversification as a strategy
- Highlight the different types of synergy in an acquisition
- Summarize research on diversification

An acquisition is the purchase by one company (the acquirer) of a substantial part of the assets or securities of another (the target company). The purchase may be a division of the target company or a large part (or all) of the target company's voting shares. The purchase can take on two forms: a merger proposal or a tender offer. A merger proposal involves negotiation with the target company's managers (directors). If the managers approve the proposal, the shareholders then vote on the proposed deal. A tender offer, in contrast, involves making a direct offer to the target company's shareholders. The shareholders can decide whether to tender or not. Since tender offers do not require the approval of the target company's managers, they are termed hostile takeovers.

The aggregate value and number of worldwide transactions have risen dramatically in the 2000s, with the value of transactions reaching US$4.67 trillion in 2015 (Exhibit 1.1). The total number of transactions reached 45,000 in the same year, out of which 14,353 were completed in Asia Pacific. Exhibit 1.2 lists out the top M&A deals done during 1998–2015. Until recently, corporate acquisitions have played a much less prominent role in Asia and Europe than in America. Indeed, a large fraction of acquisition activity is concentrated in the USA. The trend is changing now. Several factors are responsible for the increase in acquisition activity in the rest of the world. Many countries in Asia and Europe had restrictive takeover regulations that discouraged foreign companies from acquiring. Lately, foreign companies have been allowed to acquire controlling stakes in many countries. The ceiling on foreign shareholding in South Korea, for example, has been increased from 55% to 100%. Likewise, Indonesia has eased restriction on foreign shareholding in banks. India allows FDI in most sectors, including defense manufacturing. Conglomerates that diversified into unrelated areas where they had no unique skills dominate many countries in Asia and Latin America. Competition and increased expectations from customers and investors are forcing these companies to shed noncore businesses. The chaebol in Korea, for example, were forced to scale down operations in the late 1990s. Many of these countries are also dominated by public sector undertakings that are usually less efficient than their private sector counterparts. The governments in these countries do not have the financial capacity to fund these companies. Consequently, privatization programs are underway in many countries. The privatization of a company can be achieved by a "strategic sale" to a private party.

WHY ARE TAKEOVERS NEEDED?

The market for corporate control or the takeover market is a market in which alternative owners (bidders) compete for the rights to manage (underperforming) companies. The shareholders of the target company can exercise the choice of selling their shares to the highest bidder. Managers in many large corporations do not own significant fractions of shares because of which they do not have the incentive to act in the interest of shareholders.[1] Further, large companies are typically owned by a large number of small investors who do not have the incentive to monitor managers' performance because of which managers may get away uncontested. In the absence of a control mechanism, managers waste resources.

Exhibit 1.1 *Worldwide M&A Activity, 1985 to 2015*

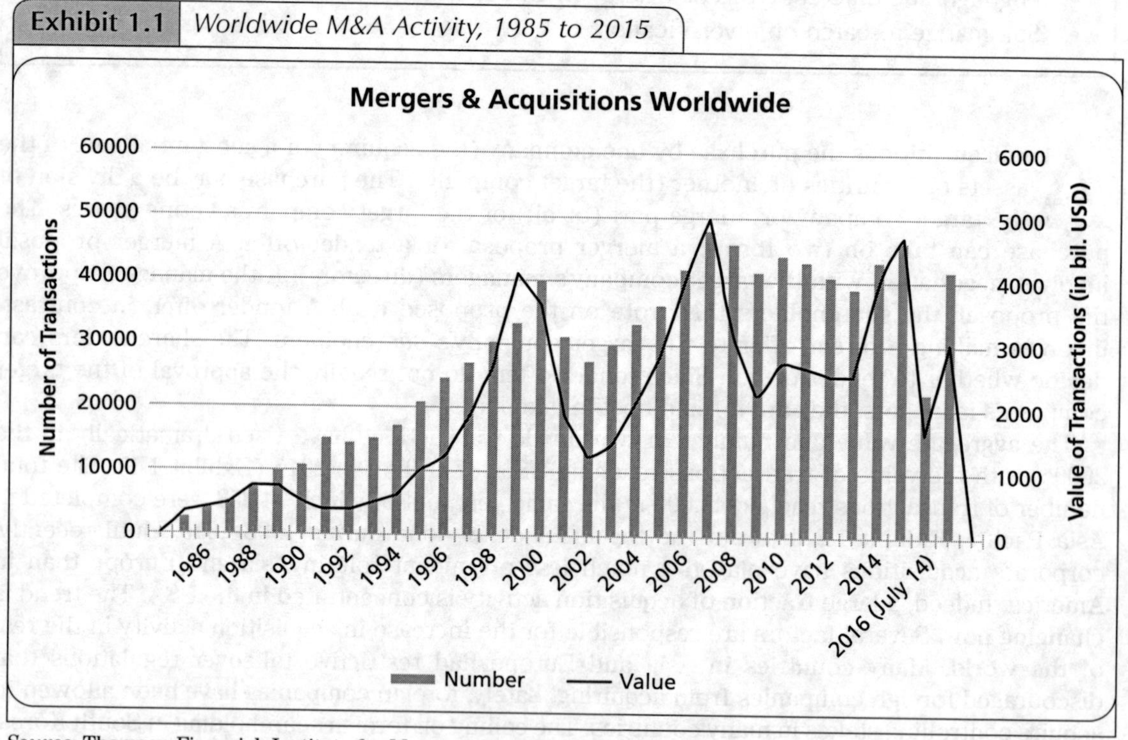

Source: Thomson Financial, Institute for Mergers, Acquisitions, and Alliances.

[1] In addition, the link between pay and performance is apparently weak in US companies. See Jensen and Murphy (1990).

Exhibit 1.2 *Top M&A Deals Completed During 1998–2015*

Year of Completion	Acquiring Company	Acquired Company	Value (US$b)
1999	Vodafone Airtouch	Mannesmann AG	202.79
2000	America Online	Time Warner	164.75
2013	Verizon Comm.	Verizon Wireless	130.3
2015	Anheuser Busch	SAB Miller	109.28
2007	RFS Holdings	Royal Bank of Scotland	98.19
1999	Pfizer	Warner Lambert	89.17
1998	Exxon	Mobil	78.95
2000	Glaxo	Smithkline Beecham	75.96

Source: Thomson Financial, Institute for Mergers, Acquisitions and Alliances.

The job of the market for corporate control is to discipline erring managers. Acquisitions are often viewed as a convenient means to growth. Many academics allege that managers pursue acquisitions at an unfair cost to the shareholder. According to this view, it is the shareholder, and not the manager, who is better placed at investing capital in alternative businesses. They argue that reckless managers aggrandize themselves with extravagant acquisitions, a result of breakdown of agency trust that the shareholders repose with managers.

While there is some merit in this argument, there is no evidence to prove that bidding company managers are systematically harming shareholders to build empires. Indeed there is evidence to the contrary. The stock price increase to target companies comes from the value obtained by putting the target company's assets to better use. Acquisitions are an important vehicle by which managers grow companies or enter new lines of business. Consider the example of Viacom. The company increased its revenues from less than US$1 billion in 1986 to over US$11 billion in 1995; a huge 1,000% growth in less than 10 years! This colossal task would not have been possible in such a short time but for acquisitions, given the time it takes to nurse new projects from scratch, create brand awareness, form networks and information links, and internalize the soft skills of innovation and service delivery.

In this book, we ask the question, "What can companies do to enhance the combined value of acquiring and target companies?" In the rest of this chapter, we discuss the internal and external factors that drive takeovers.

TRADITIONAL VIEW OF DIVERSIFICATION

For several decades in corporate boardrooms as well as in academic circles, the "portfolio" framework dominated the corporate strategy analysis. The term "portfolio," borrowed from the finance literature, represents in this approach the mindset of the corporate planner: Businesses are like securities (e.g., stocks) that could be strategically traded in the market for corporate control. In such a situation, business units are independent and clearly separate, providing no place for anything like cooperation and synergy between them.

Under this view, the corporation would act as a central bank to optimally utilize cash flows among strategic business units (SBUs) while simultaneously minimizing risk from "having all eggs in one basket." Besides the financial control that the "bank" metaphor presupposes, there is also management control that the corporate office exercises over the business units. According to Porter (1987), these controls include evaluation of performance of the business units in a dispassionate manner and appointments of key top management including, but not restricted to, the business head. As opportunistic as the firm is, the corporate office would be specialized in scanning the environment for identifying the right takeover targets and subsequent premerger activities such as negotiations. Financial and management control provides the rationale for a portfolio-type corporate strategy.

Another rationale for acquisitions is that superior performance can be created by a strategy of clever entry in new product-market segments that provides a fit between the firm and its new product market. This argument followed disappointment with conglomerate diversifications of the 1960s that proved to be less fulfilling than anticipated. This leads to the question: What type of diversification leads to superior performance? Early research found that related diversification provided better performance than either unrelated or narrowly focused diversification. This confirmed that diversification strategy is an important decision variable impacting performance.

The resource-based view of the firm offered another rationale for the firm to diversify. The resource-based view of the firm seeks not only lower costs due to better production processes but also the capability to combine and apply resources and internal strengths into unique strategic assets. This required firms to look inward as well as outward for survival and growth. Inter-firm heterogeneity offers the answer to firm performance, and acquisitions should seek such advantages that could help build up inimitable and immobile resources.

SYNERGY: THE KEY TO IMPROVED PERFORMANCE

According to many researchers, the notion of synergy offers the explanation. It captures the creation of additional value through a cooperative process between two entities, over and above the value that existed prior to such a process. What is represented by the cliché "two plus two equals five" offers an idealized alternative to the individualistic pursuit of profits by narrowly focused SBUs. Still, notwithstanding the concept's popularity, conceptualizing the full range of potential synergy types has been extremely elusive, both from the theoretical and empirical viewpoints.

Defining Synergy

Although synergy is theoretically purported to be the intervening variable between diversification strategy and post-merger performance, it is not generally treated as such by academics for lack of a proper definition. They have generally defined synergy as contiguous with diversification strategy, thus, providing little additional information. Chatterjee (1986) examines the performance of acquiring and acquired firms based on synergy types. He correctly points out that there has been a tendency among researchers to connect certain type of M&A with a synergy type on a one-to-one basis. Alluding to this tendency, he writes: "The equivalences imply that there is no difference between the type of mergers and the type of synergy. Unfortunately, mergers, in general, are unlikely to fit into such a classification."

Matching synergy types on a one-to-one basis with diversification types is trivial and provides little or no new information. Seemingly aware of the problem, Chatterjee attempts to match diversification and synergy types on an a priori, nontrivial, basis by defining them as *collusive*, *operational*, and *financial* synergies. However, he neither clearly defines the underlying general concept of synergy nor clearly distinguishes synergy from resources. He further undermines the strength of his study by dropping one type of synergy (collusive synergy) in trying to clean up the sample for empirical evaluation, thus, reducing it to a comparison between operational and financial synergies only.

Notwithstanding these problems, Chatterjee's research was a starting point in the empirical measurement of synergy. It is interesting to note that he called into question the rationale for empirically correlating diversification/acquisition type and performance without questioning the underlying causes for the match.

COMPONENTS OF SYNERGY

What are the perceived sources of additional value the firm(s) would potentially enjoy following a merger or acquisition? Or "What are the rents available to the combined corporation following the merger due to the complementarities of the assets?" There are five levels of synergy:

- Level A: Economies of scale
- Level B: Economies of scope
- Level C: Economies due to competitive positioning
- Level D: Economies due to corporate positioning
- Level E: Economies due to financial strategy

These five levels correspond to different theoretical perspectives that justify mergers. The broader theoretical and practical underpinnings of so conceptualizing synergies are summarized in Exhibit 1.3.

The first two levels are typically related to the enhancement of efficiency. The role of the environment is minimal according to these perspectives. On the other hand, the next two levels relate to striving for greater effectiveness, which automatically posits a dynamic environment. And finally, the last level relates to a portfolio approach to corporate strategy.

Before we go on to explain the various levels, it is pertinent to point out that the strength of the approach would be enhanced by incorporating a second defining dimension for the basic components we seek to describe. This dimension comes from a central consideration of systems theory and operations management and refers to the three basic stages of any process. The idea is implicit in Porter's (1985) notion of "value chain," and has been occasionally suggested by management scientists. On the basis of this suggestion, we differentiate between *input* activities, *process* operations, and *output* activities. This stage-wise differentiation (or the input, process, and output [IPO] framework) provides us with the second defining dimension to cross-classify mergers against the five synergy levels.

Having uncovered five synergy levels and three stages within each, there would be 15 possible synergy subtypes or *components* available for examining synergies available in acquisitions. A summary of synergy components is shown in Exhibit 1.4.

Exhibit 1.3 *Levels of Synergy*

Synergy Levels	Characteristics					
	Underlying Discipline	**Theoretical Thrust**	**Root Metaphor of Organizations**	**Tactical Objectives**	**Main Resource Entailed**	**Tactical Use in Planning**
Economies of Scale	Microeconomics	Perfectly contestable markets	Agglomeration of machines	Maximize efficiency	Machines and equipment	Materials and resource planning
Economies of Scope	Industrial organization	Theory of the multiproduct firm	Group of professionals/ knowledge workers	Maximize efficiency	People and knowledge	R&D planning (in a more comprehensive sense, knowledge management)
Economies due to Competitive Positioning	Competitive strategy	Game theory	Deployment of functional combat units	Maximize effectiveness	Market position & intelligence	Competitive analysis of industry
Economies due to Corporate Positioning	Corporate strategy	Transaction cost theory	Nexus of contracts	Maximize effectiveness	Contractual arrangements and credible commitments	Org. environmental analysis
Economies due to Financial Strategies	Finance	Portfolio theory	Collection of near-liquid assets	Optimize use of near-cash assets	Liquid assets	Analysis of industry & SBU prospects

Source: Author.

Exhibit 1.4 *Synergy Modes and the IPO Framework*

Synergy Mode	Stages of the IPO Framework		
	Input Stage	**Process**	**Output Stage**
Economies of Scale	Economies of scale in sourcing	Economies of scale in operations	Economies of scale in distribution and marketing
Economies of Scope	Transmission of knowledge in sourcing	Transmission of knowledge in operations/ technology	Transmission of knowledge in distribution and marketing
Economies due to Competitive Positioning	Increasing bargaining power over suppliers	Erecting barriers to entry in operations	Increasing power over existing buyers and customer outreach
Economies due to Corporate Positioning	Greater control over suppliers through backward integration and so on	Internal strength due to corporate integration	Greater control of markets through integration
Economies due to Financial Strategies	Availability of Capital	Decreased cost of capital	Smarter retention of cash

Source: Author.

A. Economies of Scale

A major benefit of diversification is the economies of scale. Economies of scale come from two sources. The first source is found in oversized production facilities: the excess capacity permits a reduction in average cost when fixed overhead is spread over additional units. The second source of economies of scale appears when the capacity of the production unit (or infrastructure) is expanded in such a way that the larger one is more intrinsically efficient than the smaller one. This latter form of potential savings is often explained in terms of the more restricted notion of "economies of size." It is apparent that M&A may often give rise to the savings due to the two sources of economies of scale, especially the former.

Exhibit 1.4 provides the summary details of the economies of scale. Under the classical equilibrium condition of perfectly competitive markets, the firm is assumed to be operating in a market with constant returns to scale, implying no economies of scale. The perfectly contestable market accommodates a restricted number of suppliers, unlike the perfectly competitive markets with innumerable suppliers. Under this view, though the firm can achieve advantages over the competitors through economies of scale, there is precious little it can do to influence the environment. In this situation, the major assets of the company are its productive assets. Plant and machinery become the key resource of the company with maximization of efficiency as the key organizational goal. The firm's planning function would concentrate upon material resource planning.

Given the fact that economies of scale could arise at various stages of the IPO framework, the following synergy components can be identified.

(INPUT) Economies of scale in sourcing: Following a merger, when the combined corporation buys any input material(s) in quantities larger than what the units had purchased singly earlier, there is the potential for realization of economies of scale in sourcing. The argument is that buying in larger quantities helps the firm reduce the unit cost of warehousing, storage, and purchasing administration. Any savings thus achieved require that there exist centralized purchasing, warehousing, and storage facilities following a merger. Mergers among retail chains provide a common example.

(PROCESS) Economies of scale in operations: Economies of scale in operations are achievable when the merged corporation is able to reduce its unit cost of any intermediate/final product or service, following a merger, due to increased quantity being produced. Theoretically, economies of scale in operations are achievable in the main activity of production, as well as in the support activities such as engineering, prototyping, product testing, and quality control. Economies of scale are available to a large number of industries (Carlino 1978).

(OUTPUT) Economies of scale in distribution and marketing: Economies of scale in distribution are achievable when unit costs of transportation, warehousing, and insurance are lowered with respect to the output(s) of the corporation after the merger. Consolidation of firms can potentially ensure that larger lot sizes can be shipped out, thus, saving money on a per unit basis. If the unit cost of market planning, market research, advertising, and so on is lower for the corporation following a merger (at the same level of overall marketing involvement), the corporation has achieved synergy due to economies of scale in marketing. As an example, corporations benefit from such synergies when they undertake "corporate" advertisements following a merger, the idea being to promote a number of products through a single ad copy.

B. Economies of Scope

Another form of savings the combined corporation may potentially enjoy is grouped under the category of economies of scope. Cost advantage occurs to the firm when it is cheaper to produce a number of different products together rather than separately by different firms. In other words, joint production often reduces the unit cost. The notion is that economies of scope could spring from the opportunity to exploit advantageous features unused in some subsets of the production systems of one or the other of the merging firms, or that some intermediate function is shared by two or more product lines without complete congestion.

This points to the economies of scale for an intermediate function. In an expanded sense, the intermediate function may be intangible in essence (such as knowledge) that could potentially enhance the innovative ability of the combined firm.

The notion of economies of scale is also closely linked to the theory of the multiproduct firm. A discussion of opportunities for potential economies of scope in corporate strategy at the IPO-stages of production follows:

(INPUT) Transmission of knowledge in sourcing: If one of the merging firms involved in a merger is able to benefit from the other in the system(s) adopted for purchasing input materials, there is transfer of sourcing knowledge. This could manifest itself in improved negotiations with suppliers and material-ordering procedures or any other increased overall efficiency in the purchasing function.

(PROCESS) Transmission of knowledge in operations/technology: Following a merger, if either of the merging firms is able to transmit know-how in operations to the other, there arises synergy. This could be in manufacturing technologies such as just-in-time (JIT) or flexible manufacturing (FMS) technologies, product design, benchmarking, prototyping, testing, or quality control.

(OUTPUT) Transmission of knowledge in distribution and marketing: When the merger results in either of the firms being able to gain knowledge about distribution practices from the other firm, resulting in cost savings, synergy is realized. Following a merger, this could manifest itself in actions such as realignment of market channels, rezoning the markets, and so on. Following a merger, if one of the firms is able to draw upon the expertise of the other in terms of market segmentation, consumer tastes, advertising prowess, and so on, there is a realization of synergy due to transmission of know-how in marketing.

C. Economies due to Competitive Positioning

Diversification can be an effective means of competitively positioning the firm in the market place. There are three major players in the worldview of the business organization: buyers, suppliers, and competitors (including potential entrants). Although primarily a tool of "corporate" strategy, diversification may also enhance the combined firm's position with respect to any of these players. These are likely to be collusive and may be concentric or related diversification. Economies due to competitive positioning could lead to greater bargaining power to make more favorable decisions on production levels and pricing, leading to higher profits or profitability.

The metaphor "competitive positioning" is marked by opportunistic behavior by the firm. In the scale/scope-based efficiency paradigm, organizational environment is assumed to be

Exhibit 1.5 *Chronology of Events*

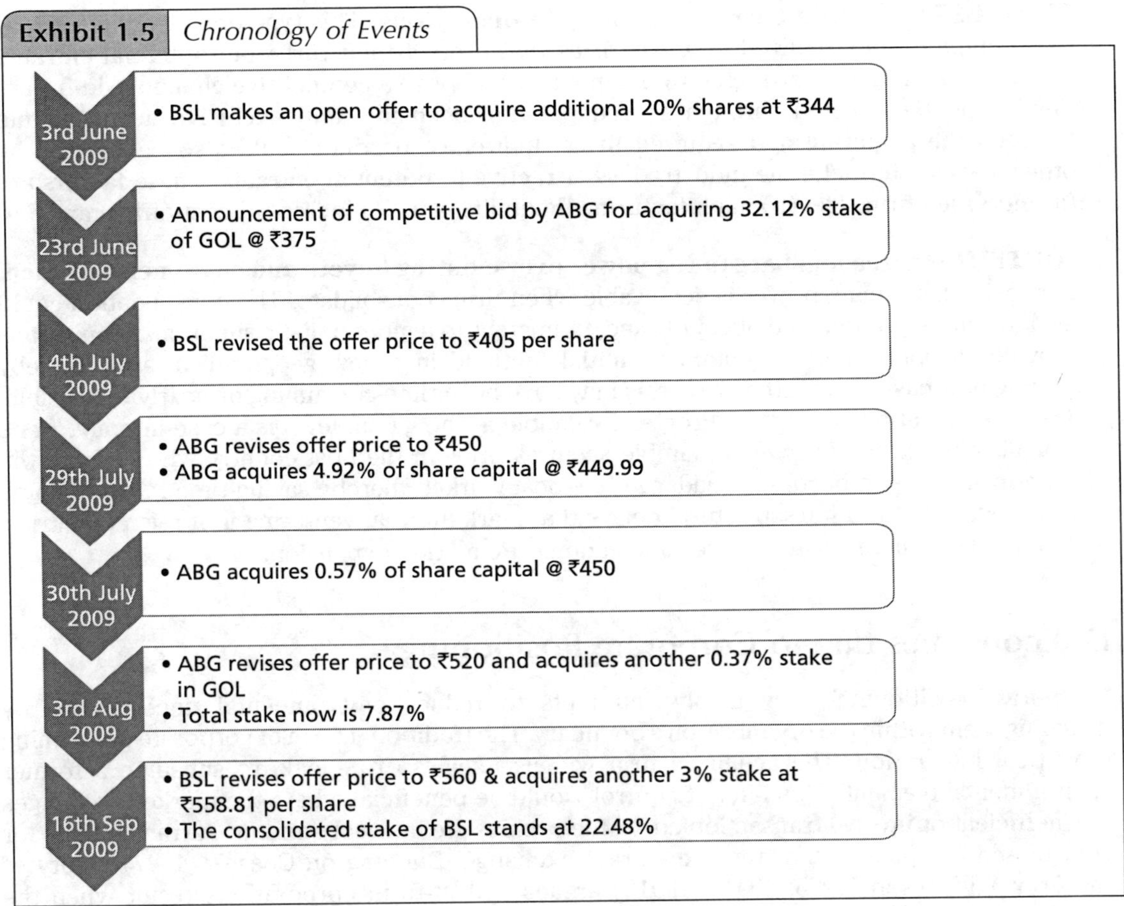

Source: Case writer.

largely placid, and actions by the firm are deterministic in the quest for efficiency. The principal actions there could be characterized as economizing rather than strategizing. In "competitive positioning," the firm is characterized by opportunistic behavior in a dynamic environment. Moves and countermoves by the protagonists could result in positioning benefits to the firm. Exhibit 1.5 provides a link between competitive positioning and Game Theory.

The following definitions describe the three IPO stages of value creation with respect to the synergies associated with competitive positioning:

(INPUT) Increasing bargaining power over suppliers: Increased bargaining power over suppliers is possible when firms consolidate. Such mergers have the effect of rendering the existing suppliers having to deal with one larger, combined firm rather than two separate firms. The consolidated firm offers better bargaining vis-à-vis the suppliers due to size effects. For instance, Kuhn (1986) reports how General Motor's size allowed it to enter into a "requirements contract" with its suppliers. This meant that the company did not have to buy specified quantities; it had to buy only what was needed to maintain current production.

(PROCESS) Erecting barriers to entry in operations: This type of synergy is seen as the economic rents realized by those firms that protect their turf from potential entrants who may otherwise be attracted to the industry and pose a competitive challenge in future. This could be effected through shared patents, licensing, and exclusive arrangements between the acquiring and acquired firms. Indirectly, barriers could also be erected by other means that make the industry less attractive to potential entrants. These factors are (a) increased firm size, (b) manufacturing flexibility, and (c) increased cost-efficiency.

(OUTPUT) Increasing bargaining power over existing buyers and customer outreach: Increasing bargaining power is achievable when firms consolidate. The consolidation could lead to a more pronounced oligopoly and, ultimately, to a monopolistic situation. Acquisitions provide an opportunity to obtain an initial foothold in a new geographical area, thereby gaining new customers; otherwise, this may have been time-consuming or nearly impossible. The diversification strategy of Procter & Gamble at the global level is a case in point. In its globalization thrust, Procter & Gamble acquires firms in the host country who offer all the support it needs to become a leader in the local market, thereby saving time in overcoming local regulatory and infrastructural delays that mark internal venturing in foreign countries. This kind of synergy is also achievable in domestic market expansion.

D. Economies due to Corporate Positioning

"Corporate positioning" may involve attempts to reduce environmental uncertainties by including them within the organization's boundary. The traditional form of corporate positioning is vertical integration. The acquiring firm widens itself, so to speak, to subsume a former environmental element. This kind of control would be beneficial where the market exchanges are inefficient or involve transaction costs: hierarchies are internal structural arrangements for control and compliance that replace market exchange. Building on Coase's (1937) theory of the firm, Williamson (1975, 1991a, 1991b) argues that *M*-form corporations result when the transaction costs exceed those associated with the internal hierarchy. The degree to which the various stakeholders are "included" within the organizational boundary will be a critical issue; also important are decisions as to which units are to be acquired and which divested.

Yet there are other cases where the inclusion is partial, such as joint ventures, licensing, and so on. The emphasis is on the analysis of the trade-offs between the cost of creating and maintaining the hierarchy and the cost of transacting with its environment. The major objective of the firm is to be effective through deals and contracts. For diversifying firms that seek advantages of corporate positioning, contractual arrangements and commitments become the most sensitive resource that can be acquired or harnessed through a merger. Metaphorically the firm could be viewed as a "nexus of contracts." The IPO stages are used to express the possibilities of synergy here too.

(INPUT) Greater control of suppliers through *backward* integration: This form of synergy is best understood by explaining what happens during vertical integration. A firm vertically integrating backward is adopting a "make" decision in preference to a "buy" decision; this results in the firm sourcing materials at a point further up the value chain.

(PROCESS) Internal strength due to *corporate* integration: This is the most difficult of all the synergy components to conceptualize in Western-style corporations. It seems as if some of the Japanese conglomerates have been able to create structures and processes that enhance the internal strength of the corporation via this type of synergy. Synergistic interlinkages could potentially be exploited by corporate integration.

(OUTPUT) Greater control of markets through *forward* integration: Just like the make-or-buy decision, the firm also faces a "sell" or "add value" decision when it comes to its outputs. The traditional forward integration gives rise to this form of synergy. Besides full-fledged forward integration, there are other variations possible. Arrangements such as exclusive dealing, resale price maintenance, exclusive territories, and so on offer alternate forms of partial forward integration. This also includes the acquisition of firms that enable the corporation to offer the customer a more comprehensive basket of products/services that would enhance a firm's value to the customer.

E. Economies due to Financial Strategy

Economies due to financial strategy do not quite fit into the continuum that can be observed in the synergy levels developed so far. However, this is an important element of diversification strategy in its quest of synergy. This type of synergy is transparent in corporate strategy analysis using the portfolio matrix or its variants. The individual businesses are considered stand-alone units that can be traded in the market for corporate control. This market provides an arena where those SBUs with liquid-asset qualities could be shuffled around for maximum cash returns following an acquisition. The corporate office will monitor the performance of the divisions and make funding and other resource allocations. In comparison to the external market, the internal market of an *M*-form corporation is likely to result in higher constitutional powers to conduct audits and access to the firm's incentive and allocation machinery. Therefore, diversification has the potential to provide synergistic gains following a merger. Not only is there a possible lowering of the cost of capital due to reduced monitoring costs but there is also a chance of greater availability of capital for one of the merging firms from the other firm. Acquisitions also offer the potential for smarter retention of cash through lesser tax outflow and so on. These aspects lead to the next three potential components of synergy provided by the IPO stages:

(INPUT) Availability of capital: Diversification could possibly give one of the participating firms access to capital. This is especially true when a cash-rich unit invests in a cash-strapped firm. This type of synergy provides one of the participant's financial resources otherwise not available. The combined firm may also be in a position to leverage the assets to a greater degree, enhancing its debt capacity. Diversification can also lead to changes in risk; this could lead to greater availability of funding.

(PROCESS) Decreased cost of capital: At an overall level, following a merger, there is likely to be a reduction in the cost of capital to the combined firm: there is potential for the transfer of funds from a cash-rich unit to its partner that is currently deficient. Such flexibility and the benefit of *coinsurance* between divisions offer a decrease in the cost of capital.

(OUTPUT) Smarter retention of cash: Diversification could provide opportunities for the retention and growth of cash within the firm. For example, there are a number of M&A that result in lesser tax outflow. Typically, the profits of one of the partners could be offset against the losses of another. Other financial benefits that fall within this category include advantages due to joint investment of cash proceeds.

CONCLUDING COMMENTS

In this chapter, we described different theories of and rationale for mergers; why takeovers are needed and the sources of value in an acquisition. Takeovers can enhance value if there is synergy between the merging entities. There are five levels of synergy. They are:

- Economies of scale
- Economies of scope
- Economies due to competitive positioning
- Economies due to corporate positioning
- Economies due to financial strategies

To make mergers successful:

- Define merger objectives
- Decide what tasks need to be accomplished in the post-merger period.
- Choose managers from both the companies (and from outside).
- Make them a part of the solution rather than the problem.
- Establish performance yardstick and evaluate the managers on that yardstick.
- Put them on an attractive profit-and-loss (P/L) incentive compensation plan.

The following chapters present a framework to screen, value, and integrate potential domestic as well as cross-border acquisition candidates.

Case Study

Bharti Shipyard: The Battle for Great Offshore Limited

The Role of Market for Corporate Control

In June 2009, ABG Shipyard Limited (ABG) and Bharti Shipyard Limited (BSL) were pitched in a takeover battle to control Great Offshore Limited (GOL). BSL was a leading private shipyard and owned six strategically located shipyards. ABG was the largest private sector shipbuilding company with orders in excess of ₹150 billion. GOL was a prominent integrated offshore oilfield services provider and offered a broad spectrum of services to upstream oil and gas producers to carry out offshore exploration and production activities.

The seeds of the clash were sown in 2008. The offshore division of GE Shipping was spun off into Great Offshore in 2005. Mr Vijay Sheth, vice-chairman and managing director of GOL, held 3% equity stake in GE Shipping and GOL respectively. To tighten his grip on GOL, Mr Sheth sold his 3% stake in GE Shipping to his cousins and paid ₹850 per share to GOL to increase his stake. However, he required another ₹3,000 million to increase his stake to 15%. With this started a series of events leading to the takeover of Great Offshore.

IL&FS and Motilal Oswal provided Mr Sheth a loan of ₹3,000 million by keeping his shares in Great Offshore as collateral. Mr Sheth pledged 14.89% of GOL's shares to raise the loan. However, with the global stock market crash in 2008, the shares of GOL corrected by more than 65%. Mr Sheth was required to bring in additional shares as collateral, which he failed to do. IL&FS and Motilal Oswal threatened to sell the shares in the open market in December 2008. As a desperate measure, Mr Sheth took the aid of BSL, a long-term business associate. BSL cleared the debt by taking the 14.89% stake in GOL as a fresh pledge. BSL lent ₹2,000 million to Mr Sheth while the value of the collateral shares was then worth only ₹1,540 million (market price of share was ₹274).[2] Mr Sheth defaulted on his interest commitments to BSL owing to market crash and poor performance of GOL. BSL invoked the pledge and acquired the 14.89% of Mr Sheth's stake on May 6, 2009, at ₹310 per share. BSL had to make an open offer to the public to comply with SEBI's (Securities Exchange Board of India) guidelines. The chronology of events is presented in Exhibit 1.5. The evolution of stock price of GOL through the entire period is shown in Exhibit 1.6.

Rationale for Acquisition

In the previous fiscal year, GOL had made a profit of ₹2,110 million on a top line of ₹9.5 billion. Thus, it had very high profit margins. Indian shipyards were facing a sharp decline in new orders on account of a general economic slowdown. The offshore drilling sector was a booming industry. GOL had floating assets of more than 40 vessels, of which 50% were up for replacement in the next 3–5 years. Thus, GOL offered attractive captive business to anyone who had a control. GOLs vessels also offered repair business opportunities.

The acquisition was of strategic significance for BSL as its order book would last only 2–3 years. The replacement order for 50% of GOL's fleet could be worth around ₹25–30 billion over the next 5 years. GOL was already an important client for BSL. Its order book included a rig and a multipurpose vessel for GOL worth ₹12 billion. This order accounted for more than 20% of BSLs order book.

ABG naturally felt uneasy about the prospect of BSL acquiring GOL, which offered substantial captive business. It was a golden opportunity for ABG to eliminate competition by acquiring a key client of BSL. ABG could also have participated in the takeover contest only to make the acquisition for BSL a costly affair. ABG had an order book of ₹110 billion to be completed by 2014 vis-à-vis BSL's order book of ₹50 billion to be completed by 2012. The market cap of ABG was almost 2.5 times BSLs and, therefore, it would find it easier to arrange financing.

Events after September 16

- On October 8, BSL increased its stake to 23.17%
- On December 1, BSL increased the open offer to ₹590
- Two open offers approved by SEBI
  - ABG offer at ₹520 for 32.12%
  - BSL offer at ₹590 for 20%
- On December 2, ABG sold its entire stake of 8.29% in GOL in the open market to ECL Finance and Carmona Investment and Finance at an average price of ₹570 and made a profit of ₹500 million!
- ABG made significant gains over its purchase price and held only 517 shares of GOL!
- On December 4. SEBI summoned ABG for selling its stake before the commencement of open offer
- ABG explained that it found the deal too expensive. It is also likely that ABG never wanted to buy GOL
- BSL acquired 44.26% stake in GOL for almost ₹8 billion
- It used ₹2,250 million of cash reserves and raised a significant amount of short-term debt to fund the acquisition
- Debt on BSL's book rose by more than 279% after the acquisition of GOL
- Unplanned acquisition leading to substantial short-term liabilities at high interest rates adversely affected the profitability
- BSL underwent a ₹28.5 billion corporate debt restructuring package in February 2012 to convert the short-term debt into long-term debt
- All vessels of GOL remained deployed in 2011–12. However, charter rates remained low due to the economic slowdown, which affected the profitably margin
- As a result, Great Offshore had to slow down on its replacement program
- Net income of BSL and GOL was reduced by 20% and 52% respectively
- The market capitalization of both companies fell by more than 70%!

[2] See http://www.livemint.com/Companies/K2EvM0r3QwiW0lAwSUm0nK/How-Sheth-lost-the-company-he-helped-create.html, accessed August 29, 2017, and http://www.livemint.com/Home-Page/6QBvPFnhIfmOc0ikimBZ5N/Vijay-Sheth-loses-control-of-Great-Offshore-to-Bharati-Shipy.html, accessed August 29, 2017.

Exhibit 1.6 *Stock Price Evolution of GOL*

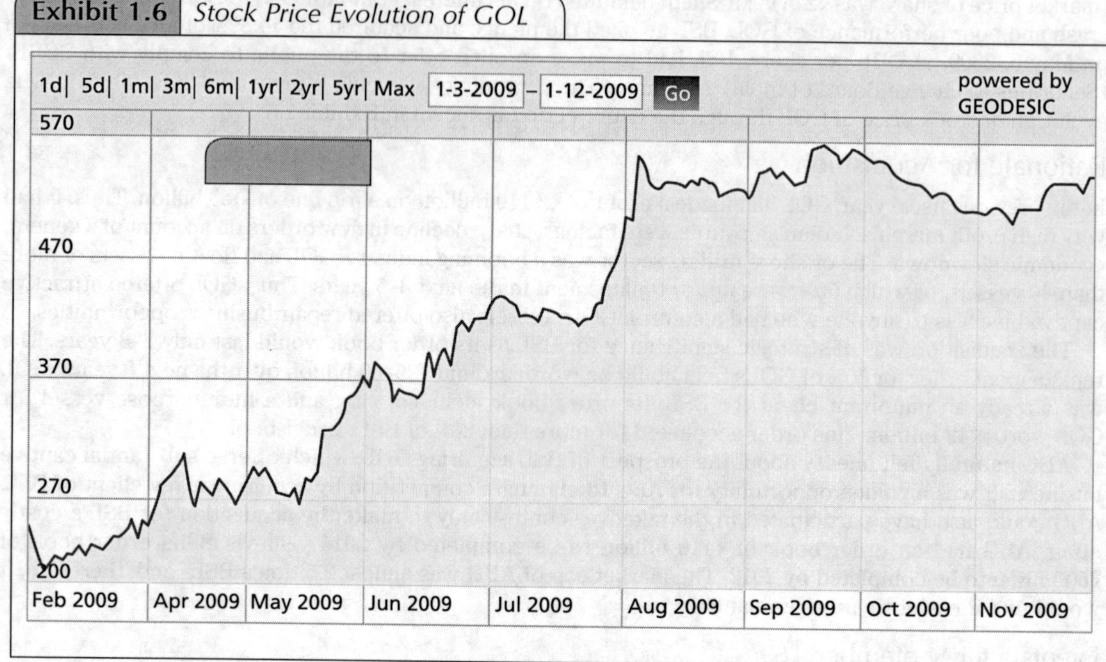

Source: Created by case writer using data available in www.moneycontrol.com

REFERENCES AND SUGGESTED READINGS

Amit, R., and P. J. H. Shoemaker. 1993. "Strategic Assets and Organizational Rent." *Strategic Management Journal*, 14 (1): 33–46.

Ansoff, H. I. 1965. *Corporate Strategy*. New York, NY: McGraw-Hill.

Barney, J. B., and E. J. Zajac. 1994. "Competitive Organisational Knowledge: Toward an Organisationally-based Theory of Competitive Advantage." *Strategic Management Journal*, 15 (1 S): 5–19.

Baumol, W. J., and A. S. Blinder. 1982. *Economic Policy and Principles*. New York, NY: Harcourt Brace Jovanovich.

Baumol, W. J., J. C. Panzer, and R. D. Willig. 1982. *Contestable Markets and the Theory of the Industrial Structure*. New York, NY: Harcourt Brace Jovanovich.

Bergh, D. D. 1997. "Predicting Divestiture of Unrelated Acquisitions: An Integrative Model of *Ex Ante* Conditions." *Strategic Management Journal*, 18: 715–31.

Bowers, E. L., and R. H. Rowntree. 1938. *Economics for Engineers*. New York, NY: McGraw-Hill.

Carlino, G. A. 1978. *Economies of Scale in Manufacturing Location: Theory and Measure*. Leiden/Boston, MA: Martinus Nijhoff Social Sciences Division.

Chase, D. 1987. "P&G: A Global Comeback." *Advertising Age*, 20 (August): 142–46, 212–14.

Chatterjee, S. 1986. "Types of Synergy and Economic Value: The Impact of Acquisitions on Merging and Rival Firms." *Strategic Management Journal*, 7 (2): 119–39.

Chung, K. S., and J. F. Weston. 1982. "Diversification and Mergers in a Strategic Long-Ranging-Planning Framework." In *Mergers and Acquisitions: Current Problems in Perspective*, edited by M. Keenan and L. J. White. 315–47. Lexington, MA: Lexington Books.

Coase, R. H. 1937. "The Nature of the Firm." *Economica*, 4 (16): 386–405.

Collis, D. J., and C. A. Montgomery. 1997. *Corporate Strategy: Resources and the Scope of the Firm*. Chicago, IL: Irwin.

Darter, M. E., W. Acar, and W. J. Amadio. 1988. "A Method of Diagnosing the Right Problem." *Mid-American Journal of Business*, 3: 33–39.

Dyer, J. 1996. "Does Governance Matter? *Keiretsu* Alliances and Asset Specificity as Sources of Japanese Competitive Advantage." *Organization Science*, 7 (6, November–December): 649–66.

Finkler, S. A. 1985. "Mergers and Consolidation: The Motives Behind Healthcare Combinations." *Healthcare Financial Management*, 39 (2): 64–74.

Gerlach, M. L. 1992. *Alliance Capitalism: The Social Organization of Japanese Business*. Berkeley, CA: University of California Press.

Godfrey, P. C., and C. W. L. Hill. 1995. "The Problem of Unobservables in Strategic Management Research." *Strategic Management Journal*, 16: 519–33.

Gold, B. 1981. "Changing Perspectives on Size, Scale, and Returns: An Interpretive Survey." *Journal of Economic Literature*, 19 (1): 5–33.

Hart, S. L. 1995. "A Natural-Resource-Based View of the Firm." *Academy of Management Review*, 20 (4): 986–1014.

Hill, C. W. L. 1988. "Differentiation Versus Low Cost or Differentiation and Low Cost: A Contingency Framework." *Academy of Management Review*, 13 (3): 401–12.

Jensen, M. C. 1984. "Takeovers: Folklore and Science." *Harvard Business Review*, (November–December), 109–121.

———. 1986. "Agency Costs of Free Cash Flow, Corporate Finance, and Takeovers." *American Economic Review*, 76 (2, May): 323–29.

Jensen, M. C., and Kevin J. Murphy. 1990. "CEO Incentives: It's Not How Much You Pay, But How." *Harvard Business Review*, 68 (3, May–June): 138–53.

Kono, T. 1992. *Long Range Planning of Japanese Corporations*. Berlin and New York, NY: Wlater de Gruyter.

Kuhn, A. J. 1986. *GM Passes Ford, 1918–1938: Designing the General Motors Performance Control System*. University Park, PA: Pennsylvania State University Press.

Lewellen, W. G. 1971. "A Pure Financial Rationale for the Conglomerate Merger." *Journal of Finance*, 26 (2): 521–37.

Lubatkin, M. H., and P. J. Lane. 1996. "Psst...The Merger Mavens Still Have It Wrong!" *Academy of Management Executive*, 10: 21–39.

Liebeskind, J. P., 1996. "Knowledge, Strategy, and the Theory of the Firm." *Strategic Management Journal*, 17 (Winter Special Issue): 93–107.

Mahoney, J. T. 1992. "The Choice of Organizational Form: Vertical Financial Ownership Versus Other Methods of Vertical Integration." *Strategic Management Journal*, 13 (8): 559–84.

Maremont, M. 1990. "Can Ford Make a Tiger out of Jaguar?" *Business Week*, October 29, 71–74.

Montgomery, Cynthia. 1994. "Corporate Diversification." *Journal of Economic Perspectives*, 8 (3): 163–78.

Morck, Randall, Andrei Shleifer, and Robert Vishny. 1990. "Do Managerial Objectives Drive Bad Acquisitions." *Journal of Finance*, XLV (1): 31–48.

Mowery, D. C., J. E. Oxley, and B. S. Silverman. 1996. "Strategic Alliances and Interfirm Knowledge Transfer." *Strategic Management Journal*, 17 (Winter Special Issue): 77–91.

Nadler, G. 1970. *Work Design: A Systems Concept*. Homewood, IL: Irwin.

Nonaka, I. 1990. "Managing Globalization as a Self-Renewing Process." In *Managing the Global Firm*, edited by C. A. Bartlett, Y. Doz and G. Hedlund. London and New York, NY: Routledge.

Penrose, E. 1959. *The Theory of the Growth of the Firm*. New York, NY: Wiley.

Peteraf, M. A. 1993. "The Cornerstones of Competitive Advantage: A Resource-Based View." *Strategic Management Journal*, 14 (3): 179–91.

Porter, M. E. 1980. *Competitive Strategy: Techniques for Analysing Industries and Competitors*. New York, NY: Free Press.

———. 1984. "Strategic Interaction: Some Lessons from Industry Histories for Theory and Antitrust Policy." In *Competitive Strategic Management*, edited by R. Lamb. Englewood Cliffs, NJ: Prentice Hall.

———.1985. *Competitive Advantage: Creating and Sustaining Superior Performance*. New York, NY: Free Press.

———. 1987. "From Competitive Advantage to Corporate Strategy." *Harvard Business Review*, 65 (3, May–June): 43, 17.

Rumelt, R. P. 1974. Strategy, Structure and Economic Performance. Boston: Division of Research, Graduate School of Business Administration, Harvard University.

Sankaran, K. 1993. Synergy in Mergers and Acquisitions: Cluster-analytically Derived Diversification Strategy Archetypes and Performance Implications. Unpublished PhD dissertation. Kent State University, Ohio.

Shleifer, A., and R. W. Vishny. 1988. "Value Maximization and the Acquisition Process." *Journal of Economic Perspectives*, 2 (1): 7–20.

———. 1991. "Takeovers in the '60s and the '80s: Evidence and Implications." *Strategic Management Journal*, 12: 51–59.

Spender, J. C. 1996. "Making Knowledge the Basis of a Dynamic Theory of the Firm." *Strategic Management Journal*, 17 (Winter Special Issue), 45–62.

Stapleton, R. C. 1982. "Mergers, Debt Capacity, and the Valuation of Corporate Loan. In Mergers and Acquisitions: Current Problems." In *Perspective*, edited by M. Keenan and L. J. White. Lexington, MA: Lexington Books.

Teece, D. J. 1982. "Towards an Economic Theory of the Multiproduct Firm." Journal of *Economic Behavior and Organization*, 3 (1): 39–63.

———. 1987. "Profiting from Technological Innovation: Implications for Integration, Collaboration, Licensing, and Public Policy." In *The Competitive Challenge: The Strategies for Industrial Innovation and Renewal*, edited by D. J. Teece, 285–305. Cambridge, MA: Ballinger Publishing Co.

Wernerfelt, B. 1984. "A Resource-Based View of the Firm." *Strategic Management Journal*, 5 (2): 171–80.

Williamson, O. E. 1975. "Markets and Hierarchies: Analysis and Antitrust Implications." New York, NY: Free Press.

———. 1991a. "Comparative Economic Organization: The Analysis of Discreet Structural Alternatives." *Administrative Science Quarterly*, 36 (2): 269–96.

———. 1991b. "Strategizing, Economizing and Economic Organization." *Strategic Management Journal*, 12 (S 2): 75–94.

REVIEW QUESTIONS

State whether the statements are true or false. Explain the rationale.

1. Mergers increase the debt capacity of a firm.
2. Cost of capital reduces after a merger.
3. Scope refers to manufacturing several unrelated products under one roof (rather than separately).
4. Mining type of firms have continued economies of scale.
5. Tender offers do not require the approval of target company managers.
6. The acquisition of Jaguar by Tata Motors is a related diversification.
7. Backward and forward integration (as in the case of integrated oil and gas companies) can reduce risk.

From the perspective of an investment bank, prepare a pitch book for the possible M&A transaction:

1. Acquisition of Air India by Tata-Singapore Air JV
2. Acquisition of Bharti Airtel by Singtel with a simultaneous sale of Bharti's Africa business to Etisalat of UAE
3. Acquisition of Tata Global Beverages by PepsiCo
4. Merger of IDBI Bank with ICICI
5. Merger of Flipkart with Future Group (Pantaloons/Big Bazaar)

CHAPTER

2 Searching for Acquisitions

Vishwanath S. R. and K. Sankaran

Learning Objectives

- Provide a framework to search for acquisition candidates
- Highlight the types of analyses involved in acquisitions
- Highlight the stages involved in acquisitions
- Discuss strategy development at the target company
- Provide a framework for entering foreign markets through acquisitions

Academic studies indicate that success in creating value through acquisitions in a competitive market is extremely difficult. Jensen and Ruback (1983) highlight this point by summarizing results from mergers and acquisitions (M&A) over a period of 11 years. They found that in case of a merger, the average return—around the date of announcement—to shareholders of the acquired company is 20%, whereas the average return to the acquiring company is 0%. Another study by McKinsey indicates that 61% of the 116 acquisitions studied were failures and only 23% were successes. Yet another study suggests that more than half the deals—amounting to US$1.5 trillion—fall short of the value creation targets. Despite such statistics, why do companies acquire? What should managers do to ensure success in acquisitions? To answer this question, it is important to understand why firms acquire in the first place and who the sellers are. Takeovers can be broadly classified as friendly and hostile. The purpose of hostile takeovers is to discipline the underperforming management of target companies. Hostile takeovers address the tendency of managers to waste free cash flow. Friendly takeovers, on the other hand, are aimed at realizing synergies in operation, marketing, and R&D. Synergistic takeovers may also lead to a decrease in the cost of capital because the combined entity may be able to borrow at lower rates than stand-alone entities, or the combination may increase the debt capacity or reduce systematic risk.[1]

[1] The systematic risk (beta) of the Merrill Lynch Conglomerate Index comprising of companies such as Martin Marietta, Esmark, and 40 others is 0.91, which suggests that conglomerates are less risky than the broader universe of stocks. See Fridson and Jonsson (1997). One of the earliest studies by Salter and Weinhold (1978) suggests that diversification does not reduce systematic risk.

Hostile takeover targets are often poor performers compared to the acquiring company or other companies in the industry group. They are also less likely to be run by the founder or founder's family. Given here is a list of characteristics of friendly and hostile takeover targets (Morck, Shleifer, and Vishny 1987).

	Friendly	**Hostile Takeovers**
Board ownership	High	Small
Run by founder or founder's family	More likely	Less likely
Growth/performance	Comparable	Poor
Tobin's q[2]	Comparable to the target	Low

THE BCG APPROACH TO STRATEGY DEVELOPMENT

To decide where to invest, companies typically review the performance of different business units (or products) and invest in those units or products where the growth potential is the highest. The product portfolio analysis pioneered by the Boston Consulting Group (BCG) includes the construction of a growth/market share matrix. Products are plotted in the matrix, with each product represented by a circle whose diameter is proportional to the dollar sales for that product. The matrix has four quadrants as shown here:

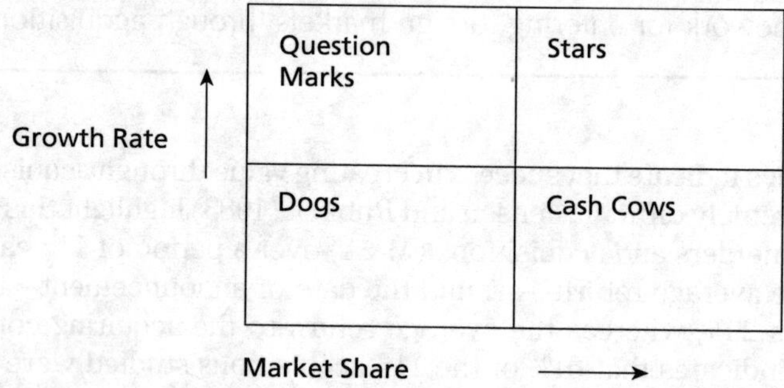

Cash cows are products that have slow growth but high market share because of which they generate large amounts of cash.

Dogs are slow growth, low market share products that neither generate nor require substantial amounts of cash. These products require little additional funds to maintain the market share.

Question marks are high growth but low market share products that require large amounts of cash to maintain the market share.

Stars are high growth, high market share products that are capable of generating large amounts of cash.

---

[2] Tobin's q is a measure of firm performance. It is the ratio of market value of assets and replacement value of assets.

The BCG approach to strategy development involves analysis of the cash flow generation potential of each product and an evaluation of strategy for each product. For example, a company may use cash generated by cash cows to turn question marks into stars, which in turn become cash cows of the future.[3] To grow a particular product or business, one may put up new plants or acquire companies in the same industry group or diversify into related or unrelated areas. In his sample of 33 large diversified corporations, Porter (1987), for example, finds that between 1950 and 1986, the firms entered an average of 80 new industries each and that over 70% of this diversification was accomplished through acquisition, which suggests that growth via acquisition is popular (Porter 1987, as quoted in Shleifer and Vishny 1988).

Buying a business involves the following steps:

- Making the initial decision to buy a business
- Educating oneself on the type of business one wants to buy
- Determining how much one can afford to pay
- Searching for potential acquisitions
- Engaging advisors
- Evaluating the target
- Placing a bid on the business in which one is interested
- Negotiating with the seller
- Executing a letter of intent with the proposed seller
- Performing due diligence
- Structuring and completing documentation for the purpose
- Obtaining a contingent financing commitment
- Signing the purchase agreement
- Closing the purchase

The entire process can be split into five phases:

Deal Flow

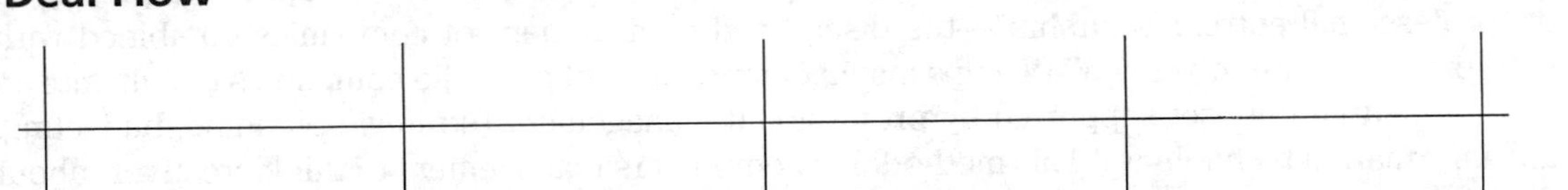

[3] The BCG approach allows managers to circumvent the discipline of capital markets in the sense that the managers get to decide where to invest on behalf of the investors. In reality, managers may spend money on dogs and starve question marks. Some point out that it is better for the cash cows to return cash to shareholders who will in turn decide where to invest, and the question marks should directly access capital markets on their own merit.

DEAL SOURCING THROUGH THE INTERNET/INTERMEDIARIES

Many companies realize that disciplined acquisition search is the key to success. Allied Signal Corporation, for example, surfaced 550 attractive potential businesses to acquire in 1996–97. Of these, 190 targets were selected. Further screening reduced the sample to 52 firms, from which Allied Signal made an offer on 28. Detailed due diligence research was conducted on 17 firms, and Allied Signal consummated 10 of these deals. Perhaps the all-time record for acquisition search was Ciba-Geigy's acquisition of Airwick Industries in 1974, which was preceded by a review of more than 18,000 companies (Bruner 2000)!

One of the most important sources of deal flow for an acquirer (at least a large acquirer) is an investment banker. Investment banks have M&A advisory practice to assist buyers in potential target identification, valuation, legal, tax, financing, and other such matters. Because of their research base and contacts with the business community, they maintain a tab on potential sellers.

Companies seeking to buy or sell businesses are increasingly turning to the Internet for research and advertising. Before the advent of the Internet, finding industry information involved poring through industry databases and articles and undertaking costly, time-consuming research. Now, with the proliferation of the Internet, companies can get access to industry data, gather intelligence, and locate buyers/sellers with minimal cost.

Valuation criteria include a company's assets, industry position, financial status, reputation, management, trade secrets, technology, name recognition, and so on. The Internet is a useful source of such information. There are websites developed exclusively for companies wishing to buy and sell their businesses. These websites provide a variety of information such as selling prices, as well as articles and advertisements. For instance, one website[4] contains a list of more than 10,000 buyers and sellers that can be searched by location, industry, and other criteria.[5]

Watermill Ventures (WMV) is a private investment firm that invests in middle-market companies experiencing strategic, operational, or financing challenges.[6] Watermill provides access to capital and other resources through its strategic investment partners and its hands-on approach to helping management teams further develop their strategic and operational practices. WMV was formed in 1992 through its affiliate HMK Enterprises Inc. founded in 1978. The company provides strategy development expertise and other value-added services. Founded upon the principles of "professional entrepreneurship"—the disciplined management of companies combined with entrepreneurial initiatives—WMV helps management teams of portfolio companies to cultivate an entrepreneurial mindset supported by professional management (strategic planning, budgeting, and information technology). This methodology empowers management to think creatively about their businesses and to explore growth avenues without taking too much risk. WMV's approach is to buy companies, fix them, grow for 4–7 years, and then sell the company or take it public. To source deals, the company has established a website.[7] Watermill has been successful largely because of disciplined screening of industries and businesses and identification of attractive opportunities, combined with strategic and operating attention to portfolio companies. WMV invests in companies in a variety of industries, with a preference for medium-growth industries

---

[4] See www.usbx.com

[5] Also see www.acquisitionadvisors.com

[6] Much of the details on WMV is from its website.

[7] See www.watermill.com

that are experiencing structural change due to new competitive dynamics, new technologies, consolidation, or shifts in demand. The company has the following investment criteria:

Sales	Mid-market
Characteristics	Moderate industry growth Reasonable industry margin Market or segment leadership potential Underperforming vs potential Over-leveraged Status of management

Although the Internet is useful for researching and reaching out, many sellers and buyers prefer to work with a business broker who can guide them through the process. These brokers charge commissions ranging from 10% to 14% of the sale price for their services. Business brokers usually restrict themselves to small deals (up to US$10 million).

Other intermediaries such as leveraged buyout (LBO) firms are also a potential source of deal flow. LBO firms such as Clayton, Dubilier & Rice and Kohlberg Kravis Roberts (KKR & Co. L.P.) assist companies go private. Such firms might be interested in selling a portfolio company if it has satisfied the investment objectives.

A FRAMEWORK FOR DECISION-MAKING

Acquisition opportunities arrive in a random sequence, which implies that a decision-maker will not have the luxury of comparing it with another deal. Further, it is not possible to value all potential candidates before taking a decision. So decision-makers need a useful first-cut screening device, which could be any of the following:

- **Size of the target:** Companies often have a range of size (in terms of sales or assets) in mind. The target size depends on the investment budget of the acquirer. Large acquirers can afford to pay large amounts of money, whereas mid-market companies cannot, usually, afford to purchase big companies. A company, for instance, may specify a sales range of US$250–300 million. Moreover, all acquirers cannot afford to target companies that figure in everybody's hit list.
- **Target company's competence:** The current management fad is to view a firm as a portfolio of skills, and the general prediction is that those firms that align their businesses along those skills will win. Prahlad and Hamel (1990) define core competencies as the collective learning in the organization, especially how to coordinate diverse production skills and integrate multiple stream of technologies. Core competence is not to be confused with core business. Core competence is communication, involvement, and a deep commitment to working across organizational boundaries. It is about harmonizing streams of technology. Sony's competence is in miniaturization, Philip's expertise is in optical media, and Wal-Mart's expertise is in logistics management. Companies need to stop viewing themselves as portfolios of businesses. The successful

companies, even while holding seemingly unrelated businesses, are integrated by a set of common skills. This suggests that companies should acquire strategic capabilities rather than businesses.

- **Profitability/solvency:** It is not enough if a company meets the size requirement; it should also be sufficiently profitable. Buying a big but bankrupt company is obviously not a good idea, unless the acquirer is a vulture investor who specializes in turnarounds. Profitability may be specified in terms of absolute or a range of earnings before interest and taxes (EBIT) or profit after tax (PAT).
- **Asset composition:** Companies derive their value from two sources: assets-in-place and future growth opportunities. Software companies, for instance, derive much of their value from intangible assets such as brand name, patents, and employee quality. Some acquirers (e.g., bio technology and pharmaceuticals) look for the research capabilities and patents, whereas others may look for liquidity of assets (e.g., receivables and cash balance to use it in its business).
- **Nature of the industry and the company's position:** Companies and industries go through a life cycle just like products. The (future) growth rate of the company depends on the state of the industry and the company's competitive position. In other words, a growth rate of 15% for a company itself does not tell us much unless we compare it with that of the industry as a whole. Likewise, growth rates are unlikely to be sustainable if the industry is in a declining phase. Acquirers should also find out if the industry is cyclical.

A typical industry life cycle is shown in Exhibit 2.1.

Exhibit 2.1 *Industry Life Cycle*

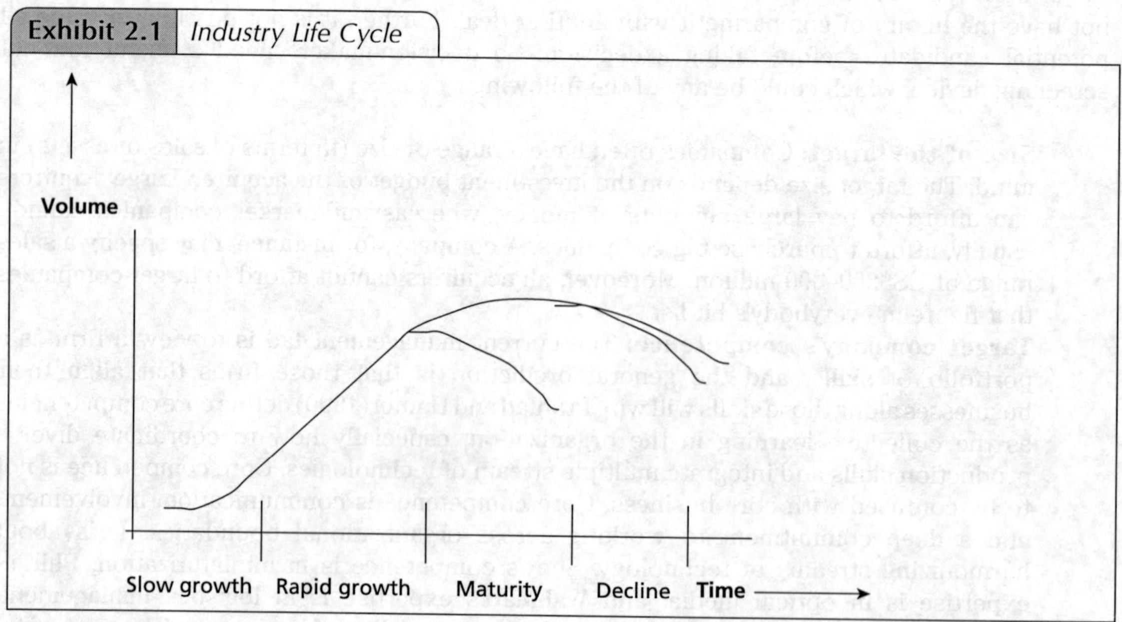

Source: Author.

The life cycle has four phases beginning with a period of slow growth, rapid acceleration, maturity, and decline. When a company reaches a particular point on the life cycle, it may revitalize product lines, giving rise to a new life cycle. Acquirers should be clear about the position of a company in its life cycle, which is hard. WMV, for instance, concentrates on companies in the third and fourth quadrants that present turnaround opportunities.

FINANCIAL ANALYSIS

As a starting point, acquirers may use relative market share and sales data of the company and peer companies and rank them accordingly on a scale of, say, 0–5, where 0 is the worst and 5 is the best. Such a ranking may be used to screen candidates. For example, one might concentrate on companies in the range of 3–5. But concentrating on highly profitable and well-managed companies will limit the upside potential in the sense that there is nothing much one can do with such companies. If, on the other hand, one were to acquire a company ranked 0 or 1, there might be upside potential but also a downside. In sum, one's aggressiveness depends on one's wealth endowment and risk tolerance.

The financial analysis involves analysis of income statement, balance sheet, and cash flow statements to gauge how the company has performed in the recent years. More specifically one can answer such questions as:

- How did the company finance its operations?
- Does the company pay too much or too little in dividends?
- Is the company generating enough cash to support operations?
- Is the company adequately liquid?

This is both an ex post analysis of past performance and a rough estimate of how the company is likely to perform. The analysis ends in what the company can earn under various states of the world, what the acquirer can pay, what changes (if any) should be made in capitalization, how the acquisition is to be financed, and how much and whether the target can meet interest payments. Typically, acquirers may put a floor above the company's debt service, which the target has to meet under all scenarios.

STRATEGIC ANALYSIS

Once the target clears this hurdle, one might begin with the strategic analysis. The strategic analysis, in contrast with financial analysis, is supposed to throw light on the current state of the strategy and what's wrong with it. The analysis leads to the possibilities for repositioning the company and the resources required to implement a strategy. It suggests new segmentation opportunities (i.e., segments with maximum growth opportunities) and sources of cost and revenue improvements. It is important to involve the heads of all functions in this phase so that everyone knows what one is getting into and the underlying assumptions behind the acquisition. The story takes shape as one goes through the remaining phases of the transaction.

Site visits and letter of intent: For the story to take concrete shape, acquirers pay visits to the target's plants and offices to get a firsthand feel of what's right and what's wrong with the company. The site visits serve the following purposes:

- To understand the target company's management and operations better
- To make sure that the assumptions and forecasts that guide the purchase are reasonable
- To make sure that the company's assets are in good condition

To elicit information, the acquiring company's officials may meet all the key executives of the target company. If the site visits are satisfactory, the next step in the process is to sign a letter of intent, which provides the acquirer some time to conduct additional research before concluding the deal. Once the letter of intent is signed, one cannot back out of the deal unless under exceptional circumstances. The due diligence comes next.

Due diligence: Due diligence is a systematic process of acquiring and analyzing information that help a buyer or a seller determine whether to proceed with a transaction. The information obtained relates to all aspects of the business to be purchased. Due diligence includes both quantitative information such as sales, cash flows, and other financial data and qualitative information such as location, quality of management, internal control systems, and so on.

The first phase in the process is the preliminary negotiation, which leads to the execution of letter of intent. The second phase is due diligence. The third phase is the negotiation and signing of the definitive agreement. The final phase is the closing of the transaction. The due diligence phase is the most critical in the sequence. If the due diligence is not handled properly, there can be costly surprises including broken deals.

Due diligence involves analysis of public and proprietary information related to the assets and liabilities of the company being purchased. The information encompasses legal, tax, and financial matters. The due diligence provides the buyer an opportunity to verify the accuracy of the information provided by the seller. The process helps determine whether there are potential concerns such as questionable asset quality, title of assets, government approvals, and so on. For instance, one of the fiercest takeover battles in Europe was fought between Nestlé and the Agnellis over the control of Perrier, a French mineral water company (Sundaram and Dau 1998). Nestlé ultimately won the battle, but, to its dismay, discovered that at least one of the springs that it thought was included in its purchase was not owned by Perrier to begin with (it was leased from the town)! When asked, Perrier officials noted that they did not hide the fact; Nestlé had not asked for it! To conduct due diligence, companies typically form a team comprising of personnel from finance, sales and marketing, human resources, and tax/legal areas. The personnel review and revise the due diligence checklist before sending it to the seller. The seller's team conducts an in-house review of all available information and lets the buyer know when, what, and how any information will be provided. A typical M&A transaction involves preparation of a number of agreements and documents between (by) the buyer and the seller. The most prominent being:

- Nondisclosure agreement
- Letter of intent that was described earlier
- Due diligence

The Nondisclosure agreement spells out the definition of "evaluation material" (any material or information furnished to the recipient) and use of such material. The agreement prevents the buyer from using that information in an inappropriate manner such as public disclosure of the information (even the fact that an agreement has been signed), and it provides for return of all the material to the seller upon request. The process ends with the closure of the deal.

STRATEGY DEVELOPMENT AT THE TARGET COMPANY

Having completed the deal, the acquiring company has to quickly put in place a business plan for the target company. This becomes trickier, especially when the target company operates in product markets different from that of the parent company.

It is useful to start this process by asking the question: "Which stage of industry life cycle does the business belong to?" As pointed out earlier, a business would fall into any of the four stages: (a) embryonic, (b) consolidation, (c) maturity, and (d) decline.

The embryonic stage is characterized by a large number of players who have entered the market recently. Unless the product or service is characterized by high research spends by specialized individual companies (such as highly specialized pharmaceutical companies), the embryonic stage of markets would be characterized by industry fragmentation (e.g., solar cell manufacturing and installation, wind turbine fabrication, and organic fertilizer manufacturing). These industries will continue to have a large number of players or will be fragmented until dominant technological and commercial designs emerge when these industries would start consolidating.

In fragmented industries, the firm can best follow focus strategies (Porter 1980). The focus may be based on customer group, customer need, or geographic region. The examples for these three bases would respectively be (a) expensive vintage wines for connoisseurs, (b) geriatric care hospitals, and (c) rural markets in South America. Focus strategy does not mean that the businesses that follow it remain small. Fragmented industries may not remain fragmented for long. There are numerous examples. Banking is one such industry. In theory, there would be a tendency toward consolidation in case high level of product/service standardization is possible, existing/expected economies of scale are significant, and unit transportation cost as a percentage of total unit costs is low.

This brings us to growth strategies. In case the target company is at a stage ready for growth, the following generic strategies are available for growth.

1. **Chaining:** This is usually found in retailing. This is particularly suitable when there are high economies of scale in purchasing, and the company is able to create networks of linked warehouses and merchandizing outlets characterized by flexible inter-unit stock transfers.

2. **Franchising:** This would apply when a certain level of standardization is possible, which has not been exploited until now. Franchising allows for a large number of local units that have individually low investments but collectively high investment outgo.

3. **Horizontal Mergers:** The other growth strategy is horizontal mergers where the acquiring company does not stop at acquiring the target company but also its competitors to corner greater market share.

Many target companies may fall at the next stage of the industry life cycle, namely, the mature stage. Here the prime objective of the target firm would be maintaining own competitive position and preserving minimum industry profitability. In many cases, the target company may not be performing up to industry standards. In any case, the strategies available to the firm, whether to maintain existing competitive position or to improve, are:

1. **Identifying Product Segments that are Unoccupied:** In other words, find out niche markets that the industry is not offering the customers. An example would be the cement industry that traditionally offered only dry cement. One way to add value and create competitive advantage was to offer pre-mixed concrete.
2. **Managing Rivalry:** Rivalry in mature industries can be managed by a combination of price-based and non-price-based measures. Price measures include price signalling and price leadership. These measures would usually apply to businesses that are dominant in their respective markets. Nonprice measures include selective divestment of upstream and downstream activities on the value chain. This happens when the transaction costs are less than holding costs with respect to activities located at the ends of the value chain; this is not unusual for firms in the maturity stage.

The last of the phases is the declining stage. Depending upon factors discussed earlier, an acquiring company may target a firm that is situated at the declining phase of the industry life cycle. In this case, the available options left open to the acquiring firm are (a) market concentration, (b) asset reduction, or (c) liquidation. Market concentration leads to narrowing of customer groups served or product range. This leads to exiting of marginal niches where the extent of resource freed are significant, existing profit contributions are insignificant, or both. Resources are now concentrated on certain selected niches where the firm can concentrate upon.

Asset reduction refers to harvesting. There will be a freeze on all significant capital expenditure. Immediate profits are sought at the cost of future investments. Those following low-cost strategy are likely to pursue such an approach where new investments in plant and machinery would be frozen and the existing equipment "milked" for minimum production. And finally, the last option is liquidation.

PARENTING STRATEGIES

The previous section dealt with crafting the business strategy of the acquired firm taking into account the industry life cycle, characteristics of the industry (particularly the life cycle stage of the industry in which the firm is located), and competitive dynamics. This is only a part of strategy-making. Even more fundamental is the corporate strategy of the acquiring company. The business strategy of the target firm and corporate strategy of the acquiring firm have to match. The full value of acquisition can be realized only if there is a match. In other words, a good acquisition presupposes clarity of corporate strategy and, by virtue of it, the nature of the parenting support given to, and controls exercised upon, the target firm.

Goold, Campbell, and Alexander (1994) suggest that there are four types of corporate parenting strategies that a modern business could follow. They are stand-alone influence, linkage Influence, central functions and influence and corporate development. These are shown in Exhibit 2.2.

1. **Stand-alone Influence**

   Here the corporate office will be involved in agreeing and monitoring the performance of business units, approving major capital expenditure, and in selecting and replacing of heads of business-units. Some may exercise greater influence in product-market

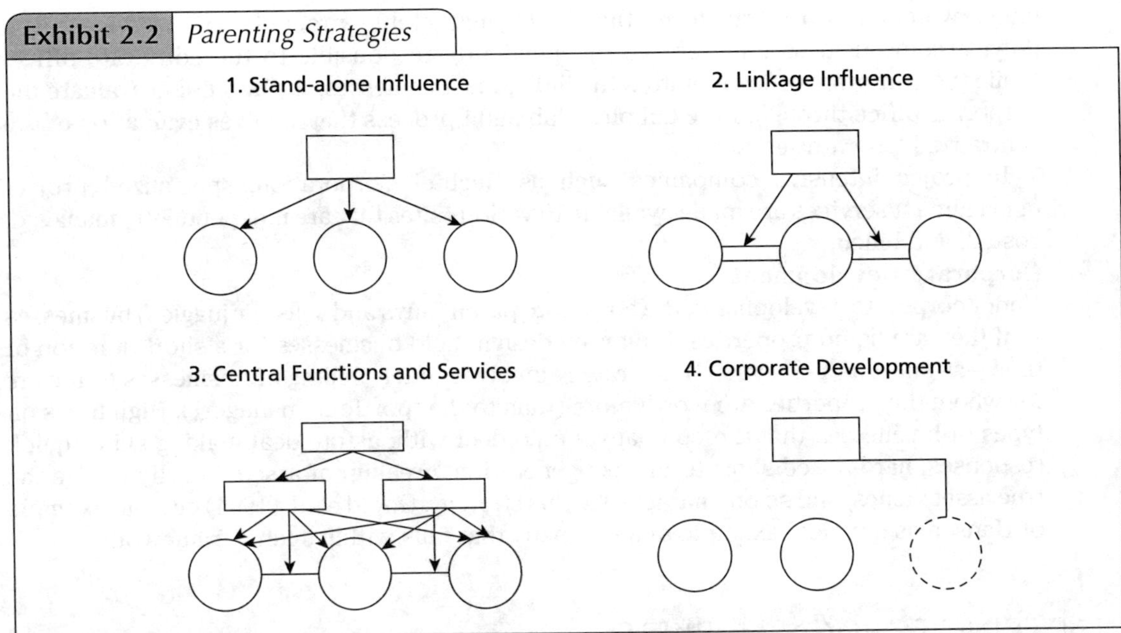

Source: Author.

strategies, pricing decisions, overall HRD policies, and so on. While this kind of control should ideally offer management expertise and dispassionate control, corporate parenting should not result in pressing for wrong targets, starving businesses of resources for worthwhile projects, appointing inappropriate managers, and so on. A textbook example of a successful stand-alone corporate strategy would be that of General Electric (GE) as fashioned by Jack Welch. Each of the businesses under the GE umbrella is a separate entity, or a "strategic business unit," with its own autonomy and performance targets.

2. **Linkage Influence**
   Through linkages such as transfer pricing mechanisms, personal pressure, lateral appointments, and so on, relationships are fostered or mandated between businesses that would not occur if the businesses were stand-alone independent entities. Structural mechanisms and mandates link the businesses to generate synergy. This kind of interlinkage has proved effective in sectors such as banking and retailing. In the case of the banking sector in the USA, for example, various regional banks have consolidated in the recent years. Synergy is realized by standardization and centralization of back-office processing, sharing of information on banking instruments, and so on. Similarly, in the retailing sector, there synergy has been realized in common sourcing and savings in costs due to improved logistics.
3. **Central Function and Services**
   Under this arrangement, the parent provides cost-effective functional (or services) leadership and support to different product-market entities (business units). The functional structure that commonly existed decades ago in many organizations resembled this form of corporate parenting. In more contemporary organizations, such centralized support is provided with respect to other functions such as R&D or specialized project management services.

   A typical example would be that of 3M. Through a central laboratory, the results of high quality innovation management are made available to a large number of business units, which in turn transform them into marketable products and services. The downstream business units are all independently responsible to the corporate office. While the corporate office monitors the individual businesses, the latter also evaluate the corporate office through, for example, a lab audit process that involves evaluation of the centralized laboratories.

In project-intensive companies such as Bechtel Corporation, specialized project management services are made available to various sites that are independently managed, costed, and billed.

4. **Corporate Development**
Under corporate development, the corporate parent buys and sells (or juggles) businesses as if they are liquid properties. It may, by design, hold businesses for a short duration of time—as short as 1–2 years. This strategy involves timely selling of businesses to buyers for whom the properties are worth more (than to the "portfolio manager"). High focus on types of businesses that the company would deal with, astute deal making skills, quick responses, hard-nosed short-term cash generation, breakup of assets to fully realize the true asset values, and so on characterize this strategy. Goold et al. (1994) cite the example of Hansen as a typical example of a company that falls within such a framework.

ENTERING FOREIGN MARKETS

When a company is extending its operations to other countries, the decision on where to locate the plant (either a greenfield project or an acquisition) is not always carefully made partly because of lack of information regarding all the candidate countries or time or potential cost or lack of an analytical framework. Assume that a company has 10 products and is intending to reach out to foreign countries. Since there are more than 100 countries in the world, the decision-maker has to deal with at least 1,000 deals, assuming that one company is evaluated in any country. To add to the complexity, one can combine products and countries in numerous ways. Since the costs associated with gathering and analyzing data is not trivial, there is a need for a framework to simplify the analysis. Four country-related variables are useful in the analysis: size of the market, investment climate, availability of technology, and distance from producers (and other markets).

One of the obvious parameters is the size of the market needed to support a profitable operation. Because of difficulties in estimating market size and growth rates, often investment decisions are made on the basis of guesswork. Further, proxies for market size such as GNP or per capita income do not tell us anything about the size of the market for the product in question because of differences in lifestyles, tastes, and so on. The fast-moving consumer goods (FMCG) companies typically go to developing countries with the expectation that a soft drink, for example, that is acceptable in the USA, say, would be acceptable to consumers in other parts of the world as well. What these companies do not take into account is the differences in lifestyles between countries. While there are many success stories, there are also spectacular failures. The second parameter is the investment climate. To compare the investment climate in different countries, one may construct a rating scale with the factors shown in Exhibit 2.3 (See Stobaugh 1969). Further, a company should also establish a methodology to assign points within each category. Exhibit 2.4 presents a sample categorization and the range of points under the category Capital Repatriation Allowed.

Exhibit 2.5 presents the description of investment climate in India as an example.

Exhibit 2.3 *Rating Scale for Determining a Country's Investment Climate*

Item	No. of Points
Capital repatriation allowed	0–12
Foreign ownership allowed	0–12
Discrimination and controls	0–12
Stability of prices	0–14
Political stability	0–12
Availability of local capital	0–10
Stability of currency	0–20

Source: Author.

Exhibit 2.4 *Range of Points in Category "Capital Repatriation Allowed"*

Item	No. of Points
No restrictions	12
Restrictions based only on time	8
Restrictions on capital	6
Heavy restrictions	2
No repatriation possible	0

Source: Author.

Exhibit 2.5 *Investment Climate in India*

Openness to foreign investment	Post 1991, as part of the liberalization program government promoted foreign investment
	Tax Incentives for investment
	Allows repatriation of investments
Political risk	Reasonable stability in the government
	Long standing problems of corruption
Infrastructure risks	Insufficient, unreliable power supply
Economic risk	High Fiscal Deficit
	Currency depreciates frequently against major currencies
Expropriation risk	Risk is low except for 1 or 2 stray incidents

Source: Author.

The Economist Intelligence Unit publishes useful country reports, which could be used in gathering intelligence. In case of takeovers in foreign countries, it is necessary to understand the local takeover regulations.[8]

[8] The chapter on cross-border acquisitions deals with these issues in greater detail.

Often multinational companies get into a strategic alliance with a host country company and expand later on by buying out the partner. A strategic alliance involves an explicit long-term agreement between two or more firms to exchange goods or services and information. Strategic alliances make sense when the internal resources of either firm are insufficient or deemed risky to invest.

CONCLUDING COMMENTS

In this chapter, we outlined the characteristics of takeover targets, a systematic way to search for potential targets and some generic strategies available to enable lost companies find their way. Companies often merge in the fear that the bigger competitors have economies of scale and may destroy them by exercising stranglehold on raw material supply, distribution, and so on. What they do not realize are the drawbacks of being big (Levinson 1970). The acquiring company's executives would have drawn up elaborate plans for the target without consulting its executives, which leads to resentment and managerial attrition. This can be avoided by honest discussions with the target company's executives. Most companies merge with the hope that the benefits of synergy will be realized. Synergy will be realized only if the merged entity is managed better after the acquisition than it was managed before. It is the quality of the top management that determines the success of the merger. Quite often, the executives of the acquiring company lose interest in the target company due to its smallness (Kitching 1967). The small company executives get bogged down preparing vision and mission statements, budgets, forecasts, and profit plans that were hitherto unheard of. The elaborateness of the control system depends on the size and culture of the company. Once a company is acquired, the acquirer should decide whether the target should be "left alone" or adhere to the acquiring company's culture and control system. This is not an easy question to answer. If the target is a broken company, the answer is yes. If the target is a successful company and the acquisition motive is getting a foothold in other markets or some such thing, one should exercise one's judgment in changing existing systems because the exercise may destroy the unique culture & systems that contributed to the success of the company.

Case Study

ABX Holdings Entry into Hospitality Industry

Assessing the Attractiveness of the Industry and Valuing Targets

In the summer of 2010, ABX Holdings was evaluating options for entering the hospitality industry by setting up four and five star hotels around the country.[9] The company planned to operationalize close to 10 hotels in 5 years. These hotels would be managed by international hotel chains. The group had diversified interests in retailing, hotels and resorts, financial services, and real estate. It operated a fine dining restaurant, a franchise for a Middle East-based restaurant chain, a quick service restaurant, and an upmarket restaurant in Delhi. The group believed that there would be scope for personalized luxury hotels catering to high net worth travelers and "surprising luxury" hotels catering to the budget traveler.

[9] The identity of the company has been disguised to preserve confidentiality. The group also considered several potential acquisitions.

Hospitality Industry

The industry had a capacity of 110,000 rooms with a shortage of 150,000 rooms. CRISIL Research estimated room demand for five star and five star deluxe hotels to increase at a compound annual growth rate (CAGR) of 10% over the next 5 years on the back of increased business travel and foreign tourist arrivals. Supply of rooms was expected to grow at a CAGR of 11% over the next 5 years and occupancy rates (ORs) were likely to decline to 59% in 2015–16 from 62% in 2010–11.

Demand Dynamics

Cyclicality: The hospitality sector is cyclical in nature. During the upswing, the industry witnessed periods of sustained growth, healthy average room rates (ARRs) and ORs. Occupancy rates begin to decline when a recession sets in. This is followed by a decline in ARRs. Revenue growth of the hospitality industry is sensitive to macroeconomic indicators such as nominal GDP growth. Statistics relating to market size is presented in Figure 2.1 and the sensitivity of revenue growth to economic growth is graphically shown in Figure 2.2.

Seasonality: Demand for hospitality is seasonal. The peak season for both business and leisure destinations is the same (January–March). Business destinations experience relatively flat ORs from April to November. Leisure destinations have low ORs during May–October, while occupancy is good (above 70%) during the December holiday period.

Classification of Hotels

The hotel industry displayed considerable diversity in the nature and type of services provided. Airport hotels targeted business customers, airline passengers with overnight travel layover, and airline personnel. Business hotels catered primarily to business travelers and were usually located in downtown or

Figure 2.1 *Hotels Industry: Market Size*

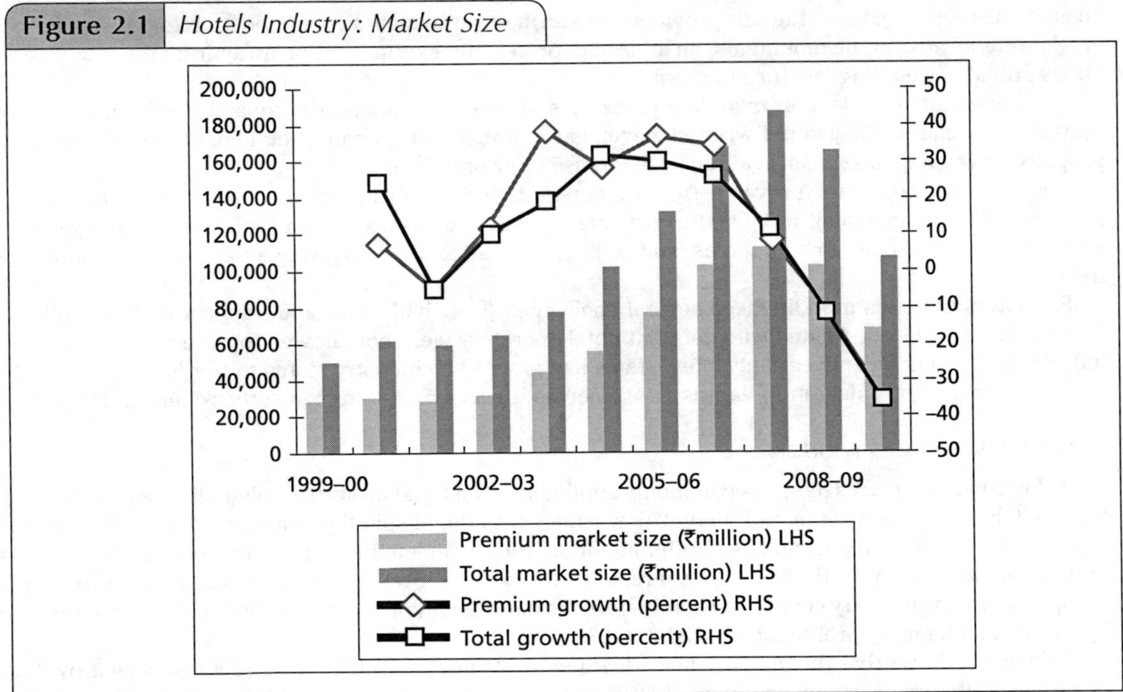

Source: CRISIL Research.

Figure 2.2 *Sensitivity of Hotels Industry to Macroeconomic Growth*

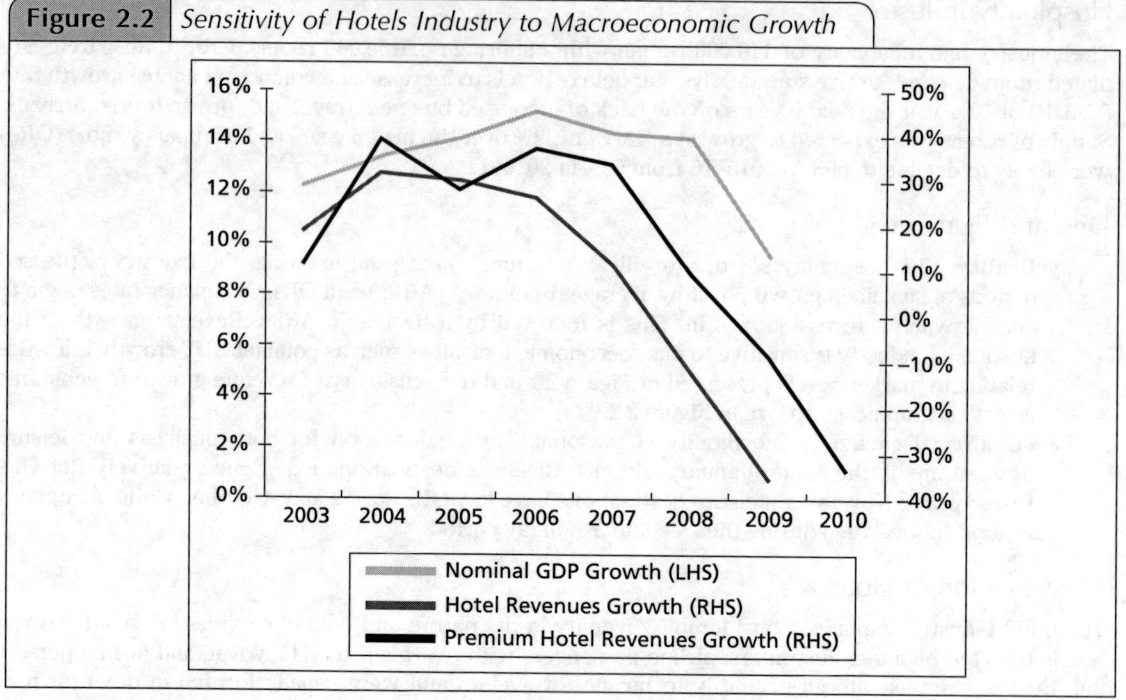

Source: CRISIL Research.

business districts. Apartment hotels provided long-term or permanent accommodation for guests. Resort hotels were located in the mountains, on an island, or in some exotic location away from the city. Casino hotels provided gambling facilities to guests.

Hotel operators could either own their properties or lease it to another party and receive a fixed proportion of revenues. They could write management contracts with luxury hotel chains to manage their property. They could also license a franchisee to use their brand name.

Hotels derived 50% of their revenue from room rentals and 35% from food and beverage. Other services accounted for the remaining 15%. On the cost side, operating costs accounted for 50% and employee cost accounted for 27%. Fuel, raw materials, and selling, general, and administrative expenses accounted for the rest.

Promoters of hotels in India faced several challenges. They had to get 100+ approvals from multiple bodies. Capex had to be funded with debt but hotel operators were not allowed to raise debt abroad. The industry had no tax incentives. Only a few states had granted an industry status to tourism.

The average cost of debt in India was 14%, whereas it was 6.5%–8% in many other countries.

Porter's Five Forces Model

Michel Porter's five forces model is commonly applied in industry analysis to explain differences in industry profitability across sectors. In Exhibit 2.6, we apply it to the hospitality industry in India. The analysis suggests that the industry is unlikely to offer abnormal returns due to high bargaining power of customers and competitive rivalry. At the same time, threat of substitutes is low and threat entry is moderate. Overall, it appears that the industry could offer good returns to a few well-known chains. Our analysis is reinforced by the data on industry profitability in Exhibit 2.7.

Exhibit 2.7 shows that the industry has a low net profit margin of 6.6% despite a net sales growth of close to 20%. Return on capital employed (ROCE) too is not very encouraging (5.5%). However, historically, the industry has been very profitable, with an EBITDA (earnings before interest, tax, depreciation, and

Exhibit 2.6 *Porter's Five Forces Analysis*

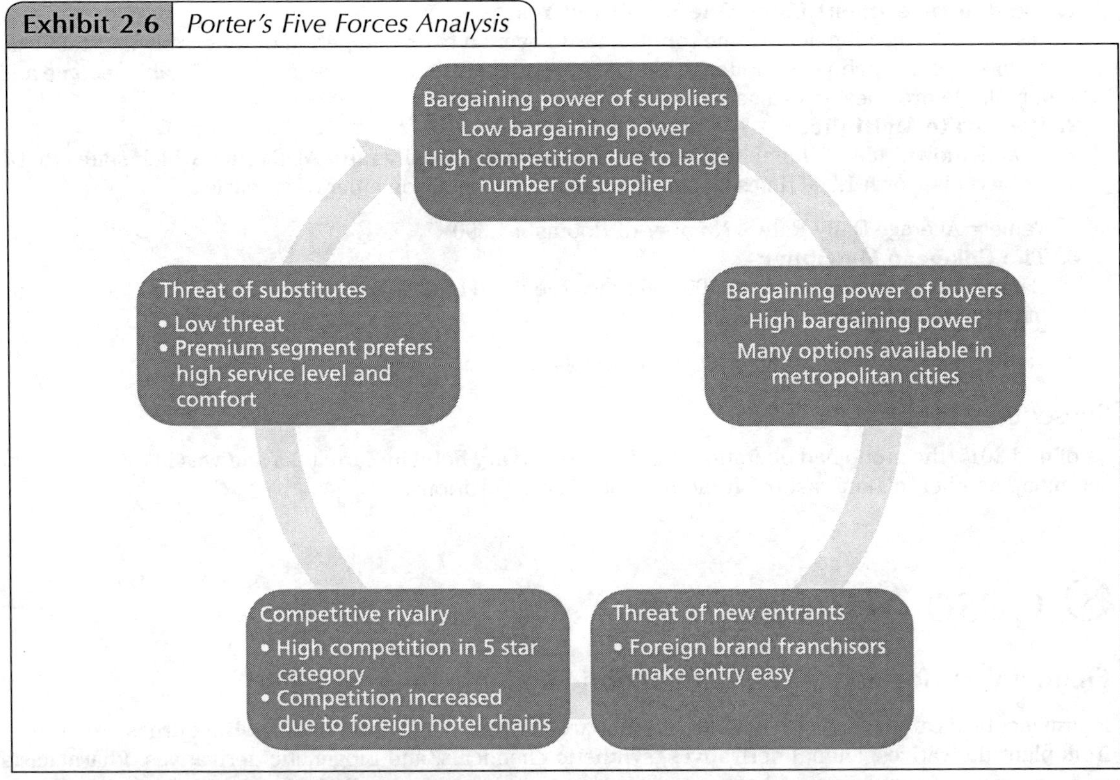

Source: Author.

Exhibit 2.7 *Financials of Hotels Industry (aggregates, in ₹million)*

	2010–11	2009–10	2008–09	2007–08
Net sales	32,155	26,821	29,419	34,205
EBITDA	8,450	7,803	10,667	14,139
Net income	2,143	–1,261	4,894	6,860
Net sales growth%	19.9	–8.8	–14	19.4
EBITDA margin	26	27.5	33.7	40.8
Net profit margin %	6.6	–4.4	15.5	19.8
ROCE	5.5%			

Source: Prowess Database.

amortization) margin of 40.8% and a net profit margin of 19.8%. Increasing competition and the 2007–08 global financial crisis have adversely affected industry profitability.

Valuation Approaches

ABX considered a few potential acquisition candidates apart from greenfield projects. Besides standard discounted cash flow methods, it is a common practice in the industry to use some unconventional rules of thumb to value hotels. We outline three approaches here:

1. **Band of Investment Using One Stabilized Year**
   Instead of projecting net income (or cash flow) over an extended period of time, a single, stabilized estimate of net income is capitalized at an appropriate rate, that is, the product of stable income and a multiple provides an estimate of value.
2. **Room-rate Multiplier**
   A well-known rule of thumb is the known as the average daily rate (ADR) rule, which states that a property is worth 1,000 times its average daily rate (rental) on a per-room basis.

   Value = Average Daily Rate × Number of Rooms × 1,000
3. **The Coke-can Multiplier**
   Each room of a hotel is worth 100,000 times the price of a Coke can found in the on-floor vending machine or the in-room mini-bar!

   Value = Coke price × Number of Rooms × 100,000

Subsequent Events

As of mid-2015, the group had operationalized its first luxury hotel in Karnataka and was in the process of setting up another in Maharashtra. It did not consider acquisitions.

Case Study

Financial Performance of Pharmaceutical Companies in India

Pharmaceuticals are chemicals (bulk drugs) that are converted into formulations. Bulk drugs are derived from plant derivatives, animal derivatives, synthetic chemicals, and biogenetic derivatives. Pharmacists disburse certain formulations only upon medical prescription (the so-called ethical drugs) whereas others are obtained over-the-counter.

The pharmaceutical industry is segmented into two types of firms: those that carry out basic research to manufacture products that are patent protected and those that manufacture generic drugs. Manufacturers of generic drugs manufacture and market pharmaceutical products that are not subject to patent protection. Manufacturers of generic drugs may also manufacture patented products even when the patent expires. Generic drugs are less expensive than the patented products because they these companies would not have spent money on R&D, all else being equal.

In 1995, India became a signatory to the Uruguay Round Agreement—Trade Related Intellectual Property Rights that requires the signatories to enforce product patents. It came into effect in 2005.[10] Historically, drug prices in India were controlled by the Central Government. The Drug Price Control Order (DPCO) established in 1985 enabled the government to control drug prices for 143 basic drugs. The number of drugs covered under DPCO was brought down from 90% to 50% and was reduced further. The aim of the DPCO was to ensure that certain drugs were available at affordable prices to all. The obvious disadvantage of the system is that it does not provide adequate incentives to manufacturers to invest in R&D to produce new molecules because the prices of the end product are low. Indeed, the prices of many drugs in India are among the lowest in the world.

The composition of the global pharmaceutical market is given in Exhibit 2.8. The relaxing of the DPCO, economic liberalization, and increases in health care spending had a favorable impact on the pharmaceutical industry. The total turnover of Indian pharmaceutical companies was estimated at US$21 billion in

[10] The Indian Patents Act recognizes only process patents. Parts of the pharmaceutical industry background are from India Infoline.

Exhibit 2.8 *Global Pharmaceutical Market, 2014*

Country	Sales (US$ billion)
North America	322.5
European Union	213.8
Japan	70.5
Latin America	63.1
Asia, Africa, and Australasia	246.8

Source: www.staista.com

2009. The domestic market size was estimated at US$13.8 billion in 2013. The domestic formulation market has the following segments:

- Analgesics that relieve pain
- Antacids
- Antibiotics
- Antituberculosis products
- Antiparasitic and antifungal products
- Cardiovascular drugs
- Corticosteroids that cure skin problems, asthma, and so on.
- Antirheumatic products that relieve joint pain
- Vitamins

The Indian pharmaceutical industry, like the global counterpart, is highly fragmented with no company holding a substantial market share. In 2015, Sun Pharmaceutical, Lupin, Dr Reddy's Lab, Cipla, and Aurobindo Pharma were the top five pharmaceutical companies in India by market capitalization.

Exhibits 2.9 to 2.14 present the financial statements and relevant financial data of these companies.

- Evaluate each company in terms of growth in total assets, long-term debt, stockholders equity, sales, operating profit, pre-tax income, and net income for 2015.
- See the common size balance sheets. Compare 2014 to 2015. Why do current assets vary across firms? Why does borrowing vary from 0.49% to 37.9% across firms in 2015?
- See the common size income statements. Compare 2014 to 2015. Which firm is the most profitable? Why does net income vary from −18% to 24.35% across firms?
- See the cash flow statements.[11] Did all firms experience an increase in cash flow from operations? If not, why not? Is the cash flow from operations more or less than the cash flow from investing activities for these firms? If yes, why? If not, why not? Compare the cash flow from operations with the cash flow from investing activities. How did the firms finance the investment? Can this situation continue indefinitely? Repeat the analysis for both the years.
- Look at the financial ratios for these firms. Which firm has the most (least) liquidity as of 2015? Can a firm have too much liquidity? Which firm is best (worst) at managing assets as of 2015? Which firm is the most (least) financially leveraged as of 2015? Do you expect pharmaceutical firms to be highly leveraged? Why? Can a firm have too much or too little debt?
- What were the factors that caused the change in return on equity for each company? Perform a DuPont analysis.
- Academic studies suggest the takeover candidates are often firms with low leverage and poor operating performance. Are any of these firms good takeover candidates? Why?

[11] ₹10 million = ₹1 crore.

Exhibit 2.9 *Balance Sheets of 2014 and 2015 (₹crore)*

	Aurobindo	Cipla Ltd	DRL	Lupin Ltd	Sun	Aurobindo	Cipla	DRL	Lupin	Sun
	2014	2014	2014	2014	2014	2015	2015	2015	2015	2015
SOURCES OF FUNDS:										
Share capital	291.5	1,605.80	851	896.8	2,071.20	292	1,605.90	852	899	2,071.20
Reserves total	39,832.40	99,310.60	92,439.00	68,893.60	72,007.60	53,303.40	109,296.00	105,488.00	89,378.40	225,308.00
Equity application money	0	0	0	0	0	0	0	0	0	483.8
Total shareholders funds	40,123.90	100,916.00	93,290.00	69,790.40	74,078.80	53,595.40	110,902.00	106,340.00	90,277.40	227,863.00
Secured loans	20,700.60	8,769.10	17	500	88.1	18,840.10	6.7	14	209.5	2,816.30
Unsecured loans	8,551.00	4.9	26,645.00	944.7	24,002.00	14,007.20	13,799.50	31,247.00	242.6	65,290.50
Total debt /Loan funds	29,251.60	8,774.00	26,662.00	1,444.70	24,090.10	32,847.30	13,806.20	31,261.00	452.1	68,106.80
Other liabilities	83	1,039.90	382	864.3	25,255.70	226.5	2,044.10	753	1,116.20	24,368.80
Total liabilities	69,458.50	110,730.00	120,334.00	72,099.40	123,425.00	86,669.20	126,752.00	138,354.00	91,845.70	320,338.00
APPLICATION OF FUNDS:										
Gross block	30,088.20	53,947.20	48,997.00	30,892.20	19,735.30	35,075.40	59,450.80	58,156.00	33,104.50	59,950.70
Less: Accumulated depreciation	19,379.40	35,241.90	27,483.00	21,794.60	12,671.70	21,900.10	35,936.20	32,494.00	20,356.00	31,852.70
Net block	19,379.40	35,241.90	27,483.00	21,794.60	12,671.70	21,900.10	35,936.20	32,494.00	20,356.00	31,852.70
Capital work in progress	2,038.90	3,766.90	5,761.00	2,670.50	4,804.60	2,271.90	3,607.10	4,883.00	4,899.60	10,905.90
Producing properties										
Investments	8,726.20	35,871.30	28,065.00	11,636.60	70,157.30	10,127.50	44,211.00	38,623.00	34,442.30	258,762.00

Current Assets, loans & advances										
Inventories	17,118.10	25,111.60	15,921.00	13,722.40	9,183.80	21,450.50	32,892.00	17,233.00	17,395.10	21,892.50
Sundry debtors	29,701.20	17,281.00	45,615.00	28,599.20	9,801.50	37,089.40	20,523.80	47,117.00	25,152.10	18,028.20
Cash and bank balance	97.2	460.4	6,651.00	1,462.80	1,414.80	111.3	827.6	9,014.00	593	4,164.60
Loans and advances	3,895.00	5,538.20	10,227.00	4,906.50	27,994.30	4,833.20	7,500.50	9,647.00	4,841.30	9,478.20
Total current assets	50,811.50	48,391.20	78,414.00	48,690.90	48,394.40	63,484.40	61,743.90	83,011.00	47,981.50	53,563.50
Less: Current Liab. & Prov.										
Current liabilities	13,182.50	12,957.00	18,700.00	11,052.90	11,410.70	12,626.00	18,544.30	19,521.00	11,384.00	33,450.30
Provisions	1,061.80	2,440.70	4,795.00	2,358.00	6,880.30	860.2	3,316.20	5,395.00	4,955.20	20,666.90
Total current liabilities	14,244.30	15,397.70	23,495.00	13,410.90	18,291.00	13,486.20	21,860.50	24,916.00	16,339.20	54,117.20
Net current assets	36,567.20	32,993.50	54,919.00	35,280.00	30,103.40	49,998.20	39,883.40	58,095.00	31,642.30	–553.7
Deferred tax assets	185.6	0	231	591.5	115.1	285.5	0	357	665.7	3,893.10
Deferred tax liability	2,238.10	3,112.00	1,483.00	3,070.80	2,043.50	2,388.90	3,305.90	1,647.00	2,557.90	3,893.10
Net deferred tax	–2,052.50	–3,112.00	–1,252.00	–2,479.30	–1,928.40	–2,103.40	–3,305.90	–1,290.00	–1,892.20	0
Other assets	4,799.30	5,968.70	5,358.00	3,197.00	7,616.00	4,474.90	6,420.00	5,549.00	2,397.70	19,371.80
Total assets	69,458.50	110,730.00	120,334.00	72,099.40	123,425.00	86,669.20	126,752.00	138,354.00	91,845.70	320,338.00
Contingent liabilities	2,311.00	3,561.50	16,052.00	3,517.80	7,686.60	5,589.20	4,146.50	12,319.00	3,624.00	20,163.20

Source: Capitaline Databases.

Exhibit 2.10 *Income Statements (₹crore)*

Company Name	Aurobindo	Cipla	DRL	Lupin	Sun	Aurobindo	Cipla	DRL	Lupin	Sun
Year	**2015**	**2015**	**2015**	**2015**	**2015**	**2014**	**2014**	**2014**	**2014**	**2014**
INCOME:										
Sales turnover	82,448.40	102,247.00	100,939.00	98,459.80	81,687.40	72,695.30	95,560.20	98,100.00	90,198.60	29,282.50
Excise duty	1,497.40	929.4	829	935.1	1,403.00	1,588.20	991.2	820	804.8	994.6
Net sales	80,951.00	101,318.00	100,110.00	97,524.70	80,284.40	71,107.10	94,569.00	97,280.00	89,393.80	28,287.90
Other income	672.2	1,479.10	2,228.00	1,806.30	2,115.80	748	2,802.80	1,515.00	4,153.80	1,777.60
Stock adjustments	1,590.90	3,490.50	289	1,708.00	–3,181.00	357.5	1,581.20	1,706.00	762.1	145.3
Total income	83,214.10	106,287.00	102,627.00	101,039.00	79,219.20	72,212.60	98,953.00	100,501.00	94,309.70	30,210.80
EXPENDITURE:										
Raw materials	39,360.90	43,301.50	28,488.00	31,818.20	31,953.30	35,192.30	39,187.40	26,608.00	29,611.90	10,796.60
Power & fuel cost	3,401.30	1,981.90	2,971.00	3,363.90	3,825.20	3,357.10	1,918.40	2,728.00	3,093.60	1,158.00
Employee cost	6,687.50	14,996.30	14,909.00	10,525.50	14,876.50	5,142.10	12,847.50	14,199.00	8,443.20	2,796.30
Other manufacturing expenses	4,414.70	7,152.10	8,480.00	6,659.10	7,377.20	3,301.60	5,042.90	7,949.00	5,614.20	3,436.60
Selling and administration expenses	5,004.70	15,221.00	19,386.00	12,077.40	19,576.40	4,016.80	14,353.60	16,685.00	13,002.60	4,912.20
Miscellaneous expenses	1,168.60	2,542.40	2,254.00	1,056.10	5,081.00	1,260.00	2,905.10	3,200.00	1,267.10	33,918.80
Total expenditure	60,037.70	85,195.20	76,488.00	65,500.20	82,689.60	52,269.90	76,254.90	71,369.00	61,032.60	57,018.50
Operating profit	23,176.40	21,092.20	26,139.00	35,538.80	–3,470.40	19,942.70	22,698.10	29,132.00	33,277.10	–26,807.70
Interest	1,321.40	1,360.50	638	49	5,512.50	2,888.40	1,278.60	783	209.9	183.8
Gross profit	21,855.00	19,731.70	25,501.00	35,489.80	–8,982.90	17,054.30	21,419.50	28,349.00	33,067.20	–26,991.50
Depreciation	2,451.50	4,332.00	4,902.00	3,367.90	6,606.80	1,859.70	3,236.10	3,805.00	1,676.30	1,019.40
Profit before tax	19,403.50	15,399.70	20,599.00	32,121.90	–15,589.70	15,194.60	18,183.40	24,544.00	31,390.90	–28,010.90
Tax	4,106.80	3,187.80	3,767.00	8,455.10	1,080.00	2,100.60	4,000.00	4,901.00	8,101.10	0

Deferred tax	133.2	401	38	−306.7	−1,928.40	1,373.10	300	315	47.6	274.3
Reported Net Profit	15,163.50	11,810.90	16,794.00	23,973.50	−14,741.30	11,720.90	13,883.40	19,328.00	23,242.20	−28,285.20
Extraordinary items	−19.4	284.2	453.9	−25.4	860.1	−14.1	8.1	59.1	−69.6	−27,690.10
Adjusted net profit	15,182.90	11,526.70	16,340.10	23,998.90	−15,601.40	11,735.00	13,875.30	19,268.90	23,311.80	−595.1
Adjst. below net profit	−196.4	−401.9	13	−610.8	158,792.00	0	0	2	304.2	0
P & L Balance brought forward	28,278.40	53,299.70	56,599.00	46,646.60	160.6	18,752.20	42,695.00	43,614.00	28,539.20	32,080.50
Appropriations	1,563.20	1,932.80	5,787.00	4,058.10	8,689.20	2,194.70	3,278.70	6,345.00	5,439.00	3,634.70
P & L Balance carried down	41,682.30	62,775.90	67,619.00	65,951.20	135,522.00	28,278.40	53,299.70	56,599.00	46,646.60	160.6
Dividend	1,312.80	1,605.90	3,408.00	3,371.20	7,219.50	874.1	1,605.80	3,062.00	2,690.10	3,106.70
Equity dividend %	4,500.00	1,000.00	4,000.00	3,750.00	3,000.00	3,000.00	1,000.00	3,600.00	3,000.00	1,500.00
Dividend per share (₹)	45	20	200	75	30	30	20	180	60	15
Earnings per share-₹	510.7	143	944.8	518.1	0	397	169.5	1,105.10	512.8	0
Earnings per share(Adj) ₹	255.35	143	944.8	518.1	0	198.5	169.5	1,105.10	512.8	0
Book value ₹	1,835.50	1,380.10	6,240.60	2,008.40	1,097.80	1,376.50	1,255.80	5,481.20	1,556.40	357.7

Source: Capitaline Database.

Exhibit 2.11 *Common Size Balance Sheets (₹crore)*

Company Name	Aurobindo Pharma	Cipla	Dr Reddy's Labs	Lupin	Sun Pharma. Inds.	Aurobindo Pharma	Cipla	Dr Reddy's Labs	Lupin	Sun Pharma. Inds.
Year	**2015**	**2015**	**2015**	**2015**	**2015**	**2014**	**2014**	**2014**	**2014**	**2014**
SOURCES OF FUNDS:										
Share capital	0.34	1.27	0.62	0.98	0.65	0.42	1.45	0.71	1.24	1.68
Reserves total	61.5	86.2	76.24	97.31	70.33	57.35	89.7	76.82	95.55	58.34
Total shareholders funds	61.84	87.5	76.86	98.29	71.13	57.77	91.1	77.53	96.8	60.02
Secured loans	21.74	0.01	0.01	0.23	0.88	29.8	7.92	0.01	0.69	0.07
Unsecured loans	16.16	10.9	22.58	0.26	20.38	12.31	0	22.14	1.31	19.45
Total debt/Loan funds	37.9	10.9	22.59	0.49	21.26	42.11	7.92	22.16	2	19.52
Other liabilities	0.26	1.61	0.54	1.22	7.61	0.12	0.94	0.32	1.2	20.46
Total liabilities	100	100	100	100	100	100	100	100	100	100
APPLICATION OF FUNDS:										
Gross block	40.47	46.9	42.03	36.04	18.71	43.32	48.7	40.72	42.85	15.99
Less: Accumulated depreciation	25.27	28.4	23.49	22.16	9.94	27.9	31.8	22.84	30.23	10.27
Less: Impairment of assets	0	0	0	0	0	0	0	0	0	0
Net block	25.27	28.4	23.49	22.16	9.94	27.9	31.8	22.84	30.23	10.27
Capital work in progress	2.62	2.85	3.53	5.33	3.4	2.94	3.4	4.79	3.7	3.89
Investments	11.69	34.9	27.92	37.5	80.78	12.56	32.4	23.32	16.14	56.84
Current assets, loans, & advances										
Inventories	24.75	26	12.46	18.94	6.83	24.65	22.7	13.23	19.03	7.44
Sundry debtors	42.79	16.2	34.06	27.39	5.63	42.76	15.6	37.91	39.67	7.94
Cash and bank balance	0.13	0.65	6.52	0.65	1.3	0.14	0.42	5.53	2.03	1.15
Loans and advances	5.58	5.92	6.97	5.27	2.96	5.61	5	8.5	6.81	22.68

Total current assets	73.25	48.7	60	52.24	16.72	73.15	43.7	65.16	67.53	39.21
Less: Current Liab. & Prov.										
Current liabilities	14.57	14.6	14.11	12.39	10.44	18.98	11.7	15.54	15.33	9.25
Provisions	0.99	2.62	3.9	5.4	6.45	1.53	2.2	3.98	3.27	5.57
Total current liabilities	15.56	17.3	18.01	17.79	16.89	20.51	13.9	19.52	18.6	14.82
Net current assets	57.69	31.5	41.99	34.45	–0.17	52.65	29.8	45.64	48.93	24.39
Deferred tax assets	0.33	0	0.26	0.72	1.22	0.27	0	0.19	0.82	0.09
Deferred tax liability	2.76	2.61	1.19	2.79	1.22	3.22	2.81	1.23	4.26	1.66
Net deferred tax	–2.43	–2.61	–0.93	–2.06	0	–2.96	–2.81	–1.04	–3.44	–1.56
Other assets	5.16	5.07	4.01	2.61	6.05	6.91	5.39	4.45	4.43	6.17
Total assets	100	100	100	100	100	100	100	100	100	100
Contingent liabilities	6.45	3.27	8.9	3.95	6.29	3.33	3.22	13.34	4.88	6.23

Source: Capitaline Database.

Exhibit 2.12 *Common Size Income Statements (₹crore)*

Company Name	Aurobindo	Cipla	DRL	Lupin	Sun	Aurobindo	Cipla	DRL	Lupin	Sun
Year	2015	2015	2015	2015	2015	2014	2014	2014	2014	2014
INCOME:										
Sales turnover	100	100	100	100	100	100	100	100	100	100
Excise duty	1.82	0.91	0.82	0.95	1.72	2.18	1.04	0.84	0.89	3.4
Net sales	98.18	99.09	99.18	99.05	98.28	97.82	98.96	99.16	99.11	96.6
Other income	0.82	1.45	2.21	1.83	2.59	1.03	2.93	1.54	4.61	6.07
Stock adjustments	1.93	3.41	0.29	1.73	–3.89	0.49	1.65	1.74	0.84	0.5
Total income	100.93	104	101.7	102.6	96.98	99.34	103.6	102.5	104.6	103.2
EXPENDITURE:										
Raw materials	47.74	42.35	28.22	32.32	39.12	48.41	41.01	27.12	32.83	36.87
Power & fuel cost	4.13	1.94	2.94	3.42	4.68	4.62	2.01	2.78	3.43	3.95
Employee cost	8.11	14.67	14.77	10.69	18.21	7.07	13.44	14.47	9.36	9.55
Other manufacturing expenses	5.35	6.99	8.4	6.76	9.03	4.54	5.28	8.1	6.22	11.74
Selling and administration expenses	6.07	14.89	19.21	12.27	23.97	5.53	15.02	17.01	14.42	16.78
Miscellaneous expenses	1.42	2.49	2.23	1.07	6.22	1.73	3.04	3.26	1.4	115.8
Less: Pre-operative expenses capitalized	0	0	0	0	0	0	0	0	0	0
Total expenditure	72.82	83.32	75.78	66.52	101.2	71.9	79.8	72.75	67.66	194.7
Operating profit	28.11	20.63	25.9	36.09	–4.25	27.43	23.75	29.7	36.89	–91.55
Interest	1.6	1.33	0.63	0.05	6.75	3.97	1.34	0.8	0.23	0.63
Gross profit	26.51	19.3	25.26	36.04	–11	23.46	22.41	28.9	36.66	–92.18
Depreciation	2.97	4.24	4.86	3.42	8.09	2.56	3.39	3.88	1.86	3.48
Profit before tax	23.53	15.06	20.41	32.62	–19.08	20.9	19.03	25.02	34.8	–95.66
Tax	4.98	3.12	3.73	8.59	1.32	2.89	4.19	5	8.98	0
Deferred tax	0.16	0.39	0.04	–0.31	–2.36	1.89	0.31	0.32	0.05	0.94
Reported net profit	18.39	11.55	16.64	24.35	–18.05	16.12	14.53	19.7	25.77	–96.59
Extraordinary items	–0.02	0.28	0.45	–0.03	1.05	–0.02	0.01	0.06	–0.08	–94.56
Adjusted net profit	18.42	11.27	16.19	24.37	–19.1	16.14	14.52	19.64	25.84	–2.03

Adjst. below net profit	−0.24	−0.39	0.01	−0.62	194.4	0	0	0	0.34	0
P & L balance brought forward	34.3	52.13	56.07	47.38	0.2	25.8	44.68	44.46	31.64	109.6
Appropriations	1.9	1.89	5.73	4.12	10.64	3.02	3.43	6.47	6.03	12.41
P & L balance carried down	50.56	61.4	66.99	66.98	165.9	38.9	55.78	57.7	51.72	0.55
Dividend	1.59	1.57	3.38	3.42	8.84	1.2	1.68	3.12	2.98	10.61
Equity dividend %	5.46	0.98	3.96	3.81	3.67	4.13	1.05	3.67	3.33	5.12
Dividend per share (₹)	0.05	0.02	0.2	0.08	0.04	0.04	0.02	0.18	0.07	0.05
Earnings per share ₹	0.62	0.14	0.94	0.53	0	0.55	0.18	1.13	0.57	0
Earnings per share (Adj)-₹	0.31	0.14	0.94	0.53	0	0.27	0.18	1.13	0.57	0
Book value ₹	2.23	1.35	6.18	2.04	1.34	1.89	1.31	5.59	1.73	1.22
Book value (Adj) ₹	1.11	1.35	6.18	2.04	1.34	0.95	1.31	5.59	1.73	1.22

Source: Capitaline Database.

Exhibit 2.13 *Cash Flow Statements (₹crore)*

2014 Cash Flow Statements					
Company Name	**APL**	**Cipla**	**DRL**	**Lupin**	**Sun**
Year	**2014**	**2014**	**2014**	**2014**	**2014**
Net cash flow from operating activities	3,280.3	17,851.9	9,055	15,262.1	–24,930.6
Net profit before tax and extra ordinary income	15,194.6	18,183.4	24,546	31,390.9	–28,010.9
Adjustments for depreciation in cash flow statement	1,859.7	3,236.1	3,805	1,676.3	1,019.4
Adjustments for interest payable in cash flow statement	770.5	1,278.6	783	209.9	183.8
Adjustments due to proven for contingencies					
Adjustments due to foreign exchange gain or loss	909.7	–356.1	4,151	595.5	813.7
Adjustments due to add back of amortizations	4	275.4	86		0.2
Adjustments due to add back of other provisional adjustments	840		2,374	269.4	97.7
Adjustments due to profit or loss on sale of investments	0.1	–80.1	–47	–5.5	–813.2
Adjustments due to profit or loss on sale of assets	20.3	69.5	–28	99.6	21.1
Adjustments for interest income	–59.5	–139.2	–1,022	–63.5	–890.6
Adjustments for dividend income		–714.1	–12	–3,045.4	–0.2
Adjustments for other expenses or income		157.1	472	211	
Adjustments due to provision or liabilities written back	–87.5		–82	–7.3	0
Operating cash flow before working capital changes	19,351.9	21,910.6	34,726	31,330.9	–27,579
Cash flow due to change in trade & other receivables	–13,348.3	–1,780.3	–18,274	–11,054.4	–27,198.8
Cash flow due to change in inventories	–2,800.8	–1,677.8	–1,974	–414.1	–496.2
Cash flow due to change in trade & other payables	3,467.9	2,525.4	746	1,620.6	32,711.1
Cash inflow or (outflow) due to deposits by banks					
Cash flow due to advances					
Cash flow due to others			–739		
Cash flow generated from operations	**6,670.7**	**20,977.9**	**14,485**	**21,483**	**–22,562.9**
Cash outflow due to direct taxes paid	–3,390.4	–2,853.1	–5,430	–6,201.7	–1,487.7
Cash outflow due to dividend tax paid		–272.9		–19.2	–880
Cash flow before extraordinary items	3,280.3	17,851.9	9,055	15,262.1	–24,930.6
Cash flows from extraordinary items					
Cash outflow due to miscellaneous expenditure					

Net cash flow from investment activities	**−4,014.4**	**−14,672.1**	**−8,808**	**−4,465.1**	**5,191.4**
Cash outflow due to purchase of fixed assets	−1,486.5	−5,020.3	−8,718	−3,941.5	−4,343.2
Cash inflow due to sale of fixed assets	103.1	25.5	273	22.9	20.6
Cash flows due to change in capital wip					
Cash flow due to acquisition merger or hiving off					
Cash outflow due to purchase of investments	−2,486.3	−207,277.2	−35,810	−3,024.7	−200,700.9
Cash inflow from sale/maturity proceeds of investments	0	197,504.2	31,069	5.5	204,610.1
Cash flow due to loans to group companies	−213	−829.2	539		
Cash flow due to loans to other companies	0				3,101.9
Cash inflow due to interest received	37.4	157.4	886	63.5	1,056.4
Cash inflow due to dividend received		714.1	12	3,045.4	0.2
Cash inflow/(outflow) due to other income or (expenses)	30.9	53.4	2,941	−636.2	1,446.3
Cash flows due to disbursements					
Net cash flow from financing activities	**−314.4**	**−3,770**	**282**	**−8,425.5**	**18,301**
Cash inflow due to proceeds from share issues	34.5		2	239.4	
Cash outflow due to redemption or buyback of capital					
Cash inflow due to cash subsidy					
Cash inflow from borrowings	10,13.9	0	44,395		24,002
Cash inflow from long-term borrowings	2.1		9,089		
Cash inflow from short-term borrowings	1,011.8	0	35,306		
Cash outflow due to repayment of borrowings	−70.3	−1,129.4	−40,308	−5,316.2	−343.2
Cash outflow due to repayment of long-term liabilities	−70.3	−1.3	−5,078	−1,204.7	
Cash outflow due to repayment of short-term liabilities		−1,128.1	−35,230	−4,111.5	−343.2
Cash outflow due to issue expenses					
Cash outflow due to interest paid	−697	−1,034.8	−828	−221.7	−182.4
Cash outflow due to dividend paid	−595.5	−1,605.8	−2,979	−3,127	−5,175.4
Net cash flow due to net changes in cash and cash equivalents	−1,048.5	−590.2	529	2,371.5	−1,438.2
Cash flow cash opening balance	**1,145.7**	**1,050.7**	**561**	**181.6**	**2,218.1**
Cash flow cash closing balance	**97.2**	**460.4**	**1,156**	**2,553.1**	**763.2**
Cash inflow due to working capital changes	3,467.9	2,525.4	746	1,620.6	32,711.1
Cash outflow due to working capital changes	16,149.1	3,458.1	20,987	11,468.5	27,695
Funds generated or (lost) in operations	13,473.9	17,149.5	21,751	25,353.8	1,876.2

(continued)

Exhibit 2.13 (continued)

2015 Cash Flow Statements

Company Name	APL	Cipla	DRL	Lupin	Sun
Year	**2015**	**2015**	**2015**	**2015**	**2015**
Net cash flow from operating activities	5,626.5	10,241.2	17,861	28,286.5	957.9
Net profit before tax and extra ordinary income	19,403.5	15,399.7	20,601	32,121.9	–15,589.7
Adjustments for depreciation in cash flow statement	2,451.5	4,332	4,902	3,367.9	6,606.8
Adjustments for interest payable in cash flow statement	495.7	1,360.5	638	49	5,512.5
Adjustments due to proven for contingencies					
Adjustments due to foreign exchange gain or loss	343	–7.6	–2,348	–182.9	–5,771.1
Adjustments due to add back of amortizations	0	102.3	208	22.4	
Adjustments due to add back of other provisional adjustments	582.7		3,664	2.5	1,151
Adjustments due to profit or loss on sale of investments		–450.7	–699	–4	–988.9
Adjustments due to profit or loss on sale of assets	25	80.1	120	38.6	64.8
Adjustments for interest income	–128.6	–59.8	–941	–29.2	–849.8
Adjustments for dividend income		–210	–105	–686.9	–0.2
Adjustments for other expenses or income		363.7	519	676.8	205
Adjustments due to provision or liabilities written back	–9.1			–157.1	–70.3
Operating cash flow before working capital changes	23,163.7	20,910.2	26,559	35,219	–9,729.9
Cash flow due to change in trade & other receivables	–7,828	–5,034	–472	4,140.2	30,606.5
Cash flow due to change in inventories	–4,332.4	–7,780.5	–4,020	–3,672.7	4,242.7
Cash flow due to change in trade & other payables	–840.1	5,902.5	–1,272	812.5	–21,698.6
Cash inflow or (outflow) due to deposits by banks					
Cash flow due to advances					
Cash flow due to others			1,858		
Cash flow generated from operations	**10,163.2**	**13,998.2**	**22,653**	**36,499**	**3,420.7**
Cash outflow due to direct taxes paid	–4,259.1	–3,484.1	–4,792	–7,983.8	–1,934.8
Cash outflow due to dividend tax paid	–277.6	–272.9		–228.7	–528
Cash flow before extraordinary items	5,626.5	10,241.2	17,861	28,286.5	957.9
Net cash flow from investment activities	**–6,236**	**–11,942.8**	**–20,165**	**–11,779.9**	**26,407.4**
Cash outflow due to purchase of fixed assets	–5,440	–5,326.3	–9,625	–5,069.8	–10,279.8
Cash inflow due to sale of fixed assets	20.4	80.5	84	21.2	148.4

Cash flows due to change in capital work-in-progress					
Cash flow due to acquisition merger or hiving off					4,879.3
Cash outflow due to purchase of investments	–1,975.4	–209,524.6	–35,946	–8,012.1	–103,608.1
Cash inflow from sale/maturity proceeds of investments		202,777.2	26,096	4	121,912.6
Cash flow due to loans to group companies	996.1	–250	1,308		
Cash flow due to loans to other companies	–10				11,031.8
Cash inflow due to interest received	172.9	59.7	732	29.2	892.6
Cash inflow due to dividend received		210	105	649.8	0.2
Cash inflow/(outflow) due to other income or (expenses)		30.7	–2,919	597.8	1,430.4
Cash flows due to disbursements					
Net cash flow from financing activities	**623.6**	**2,068.9**	**1,894**	**–1,982.5**	**–26,212.9**
Cash inflow due to proceeds from share issues	67.6	0.1	5	413	748.7
Cash outflow due to redemption or buyback of capital					
Cash inflow due to cash subsidy					
Cash inflow from borrowings	3,775.1	5,029	27,370		78,687.4
Cash inflow from long-term borrowings	8.3				
Cash inflow from short-term borrowings	3,766.8	5,029	27,370		
Cash outflow due to repayment of borrowings	–1,103	–0.1	–21,220	–992.6	–99,224.4
Cash outflow due to repayment of long-term liabilities	–1,103	–0.1		–50.5	
Cash outflow due to repayment of short-term liabilities			–21,220	–942.1	–3,391.3
Cash outflow due to interest paid	–589.1	–1,354.3	–687	–58.4	–3,319.8
Cash outflow due to dividend paid	–1,527	–1,605.8	–3,574	–1,344.5	–3,104.8
Net cash flow due to net changes in cash and cash equivalents	14.1	367.3	–410	14,524.1	1,152.4
Cash flow cash opening balance	**97.2**	**460.4**	**1,156**	**2,553.1**	**763.2**
Cash flow cash closing balance	**111.3**	**827.6**	**600**	**17,077.2**	**1,932**
Cash inflow due to working capital changes	0	5,902.5	1,858	4,952.7	34,849.2
Cash outflow due to working capital changes	13,000.5	12,814.5	5,764	3,672.7	21,698.6
Funds generated or (lost) in operations	17,433.6	16,711.3	20,871	27,564.9	179,022.7

Source: Capitaline Database.

Exhibit 2.14 *Key Ratios*

Aurobindo

Year	2015	2014
Key ratios		
Debt–equity ratio	0.66	0.82
Long-term debt–equity ratio	0.18	0.3
Current ratio	1.49	1.36
Turnover ratios		
Fixed assets	2.53	2.46
Inventory	4.28	4.63
Debtors	2.47	3.09
Interest coverage ratio	15.68	6.26
EBIDT margin (%)	28.11	27.43
EBIT margin (%)	25.14	24.88
EBDT margin (%)	26.51	23.46
PAT margin (%)	18.39	16.12
ROCE (%)	26.55	28.53
ROE (%)	32.36	33.72

Cipla

Year	March 2015	March 2014
Key ratios		
Debt–equity ratio	0.11	0.1
Long-term debt–equity ratio	0	0
Current ratio	1.66	1.81
Turnover Ratios		
Fixed assets	1.81	1.84
Inventory	3.53	3.94
Debtors	5.41	5.67
Interest coverage ratio	12.32	15.22
EBIDT margin (%)	20.63	23.75
EBIT margin (%)	16.39	20.37
EBDT margin (%)	19.3	22.41
PAT margin (%)	11.55	14.53
ROCE (%)	14.13	18.56
ROE (%)	11.16	14.66

Dr Reddys Laboratories Ltd

Year	2015	2014
Key ratios		
Debt–equity ratio	0.29	0.28
Long-term debt–equity ratio	0.09	0.05
Current ratio	1.78	1.69
Turnover ratios		
Fixed assets	1.88	2.15
Inventory	6.09	6.29
Debtors	2.18	2.61
Interest coverage ratio	33.29	32.35
EBIDT margin (%)	25.9	29.7
EBIT margin (%)	21.04	25.82
EBDT margin (%)	25.26	28.9
PAT margin (%)	16.64	19.7
ROCE (%)	16.42	23.08
ROE (%)	16.83	22.59

Lupin

Year	2015	2014
Key ratios		
Debt–equity ratio	0.02	0.01
Long-term debt–equity ratio	0	0
Current ratio	2.72	2.66
Turnover ratios		
Fixed assets	3.16	3.08
Inventory	6.23	6.33
Debtors	3.22	3.66
Interest coverage ratio	265.25	656.55
EBIDT margin (%)	37.12	36.09
EBIT margin (%)	34.44	32.67
EBDT margin (%)	36.99	36.04
PAT margin (%)	25.34	24.35
ROCE (%)	36.8	39.25
ROE (%)	27.98	29.95

(continued)

Exhibit 2.14 *(continued)*

Sun Pharmaceuticals Industries Ltd

Year	2015	2014
Key ratios		
Debt–equity ratio	0.31	0.16
Long-term debt–equity ratio	0.04	0
Current ratio	0.67	1.35
Turnover ratios		
Fixed assets	2.05	1.58
Inventory	5.26	3.28
Debtors	5.87	3.41
Interest coverage ratio	−1.83	0.74
EBIDT margin (%)	−4.25	3.95
EBIT margin (%)	−12.3	0.47
EBDT margin (%)	−11	3.32
PAT margin (%)	−18.0	−2.03
ROCE (%)	−4.54	0.13
ROE (%)	−9.76	−0.78

Source: Capitaline Database.

REFERENCES AND SUGGESTED READINGS

Bruner, Robert F. 2000. "Searching for Acquisitions." Technical Note No. UVA-F-1295. Darden Graduate School of Business Administration, University of Virginia.

Clark, Peter J. 1991. *Beyond the Deal: Optimizing Merger and Acquisition Value.* New York: Harper Collins.

Copeland, Thomas, Timothy Koller, and Jack Murrin. 2000. *Valuation: Measuring and Managing the Value of Companies*, 3rd Edition. New York, NY: John Wiley.

Fridson, Martin, and Jon G. Jonsson. 1997. "Contingent Claims Analysis." *Journal of Portfolio Management*, (Winter).

Goold, M., A. Campbell, and M. Alexander. 1994. *Corporate Level Strategy: Creating Value in the Multi-business Company*. New York, NY: John Wiley & Sons.

Jensen, M. C., and R. S. Ruback. 1983. "The Market for Corporate Control: The Scientific Evidence." *Journal of Finance*, 11.

Kitching, John. 1967. "Why do Mergers Miscarry?" *Harvard Business Review*, 45 (November–December): 84–101.

Levinson, Harry. 1970. "A Psychologist Diagnoses Merger Failures." *Harvard Business Review*, 44 (2, March–April): 139–47.

Morck, Randall, Andrei Shleifer, and Robert Vishny. 1987, June. "Characteristics of Hostile and Friendly Takeover Targets." NBER Working Paper No. 2295. Cambridge, MA: National Bureau of Economic Research.

Ohmae, Kenichi, 1989. "The Global Logic of Strategic Alliances." *Harvard Business Review*, (March–April): 143–54.

Palepu, Krishna. 1986. "Predicting Takeover Targets: A Methodological and Empirical Analysis." *Journal of Accounting and Economics*, 8 (1): 3–35.

Porter, M. 1980. *Competitive Strategy: Techniques for Analyzing Industries and Competitors.* New York, NY: The Free Press.

Porter, Michael. 1987. "From Competitive Advantage to Corporate strategy." *Harvard Business Review*, 65 (3, May–June): 43–59.

Prahlad C. K., and Gary Hamel. 1990. "The Core Competence of the Corporation." *Harvard Business Review*, 68 (3, May–June): 79–93.

Salter M., and W. Weinhold. 1978. Creating Value via Diversification. *Harvard Business Review* (July).

Shleifer, Andrei, and Robert Vishny. 1988. "Value Maximization and the Acquisition Process," *Journal of Economic Perspectives*, 2 (1, Winter): 7–20.

Stobaugh, Robert B. 1969. "Where in the World Should We Put That Plant?" *Harvard Business Review*, 47 (1, January–February): 129–36.

Sundaram, Anant, and Hans Dau. 1998. "Perrier, Nestle and the Agnellis." Thunderbird Case No. A06 -98-0016. Glendale, AZ: Thunderbird School of Global Management.

REVIEW QUESTIONS

1. Explain the steps in acquiring a company.
2. What are the different parenting strategies?
3. Apply Michael Porter's five forces model to the Indian two wheeler automotive industry.
4. Develop an investment rank (scale) for China. You may use data available in economist intelligence unit and other sources.

CHAPTER 3

Value Drivers and Target Valuation

Vishwanath S. R. and Chandrasekhar Krishnamurti

Learning Objectives

- Provide a link between growth and shareholder value
- Highlight the role of three value drivers in value creation
- Introduction to alternate valuation frameworks such as free cash flow to firm, adjusted present value, capital cash flow valuation, and relative valuation
- Provide a framework for estimating the value of synergy in acquisitions

In recent years, the worldwide M&A volume has been averaging US$4 trillion. The last few decades have witnessed major waves of acquisitions. Increased regulation and increased uncertainty about the economy coupled with the belief that undervalued companies with strong fundamentals are available for purchase make internal growth relatively unattractive, because of which acquisitions are increasingly becoming an important aspect of growth strategy. Companies acquire for a variety of reasons such as gaining synergy, acquiring undervalued assets, increasing sales and asset growth, increasing market share, and adding new products. Despite the good intentions, few acquisitions actually create value. A number of academic studies around the world have documented neutral or negative announcement day returns to bidding company's shareholders. Despite such statistics, more and more companies are resorting to growth through acquisitions. It is important to understand that only a limited supply of acquisition candidates is available at an attractive price. A well-designed financial evaluation program is necessary to avoid costly mistakes. The purpose of this chapter is to provide a rigorous understanding of the determinants of equity value.

Value-based management assumes that value creation should be the key consideration in managerial decision-making. To make intelligent acquisitions, acquirers need to know what creates value and why, as well as translate that knowledge to measure value creation potential of an acquisition. Value is created when the net present value (NPV) of a strategy is positive at the time of implementation.

Value created by strategy = Present value (PV) of incremental cash flows due to new investment – PV of investment in fixed assets & working capital + PV of residual value.

VALUE DRIVERS

Modern capital budgeting suggests that NPV is a function of valuation parameters or *value drivers* such as sales growth rate, operating profit margin, tax rate, fixed capital investment, working capital investment, cost of capital, and the duration of the project. These value drivers are affected by operating decisions such as product mix, promotion, advertising, distribution, customer service, investment in inventory, capacity expansion, and so on. Value is enhanced if the same returns are achieved for lower level of investment or higher returns for the same level of investment. The value of the strategy can be enhanced by:

- Acceleration of cash flows (leads to higher NPV).
- Increase in level of cash flows.
- A reduction in risk associated with cash flows (volatility) and, hence, indirectly, the firm's cost of capital.
- Increasing the residual value of the business.

Total shareholder value is the sum of the NPVs of all projects undertaken by the firm. Thus, whenever a firm acquires another firm for a price greater than the present values of the expected cash flows, the value of the firm drops (and vice versa). Consider two companies. The first company has an investment opportunity with 25% return on equity (ROE) in amounts sufficient to produce 10% sustainable growth rate[1] in sales for 10 years. The second company has an investment opportunity with 10% ROE in amounts sufficient to produce 10% sustainable growth rate in sales for 10 years. Both the companies have 20% cost of equity. The market value of the two hypothetical companies is shown in Exhibits 3.1 and 3.2.

At the end of 10 years, the stock is expected to sell at the book value of ₹2,593.70. In other words, ROE equals cost of equity. The second company retains all the profits it generates (i.e., retention rate is 100%) to produce a growth of 10% p.a. The theoretical market price for the second company is shown in Exhibit 3.2.

The present value of cash returned to stockholders ₹1,290.5 is ₹290.5 more than the initial investment of ₹1,000 for shareholders in Company A. Hence, the M/B (book-to-market) ratio of Company A is greater than 1. The present value of cash returned to stockholders ₹418.9 is lower than the initial investment of ₹1,000 for shareholders in Company B. Consequently, the M/B ratio of Company B is less than 1. The moral of the story is that how fast a company *can* grow and how fast a company *should* grow are two different things. Growth is desirable if expected ROE is greater than cost of equity and if the spread can be maintained. If not, growth destroys value.

- Market price/Book value = 1,290.5/1,000 = 1.29 for Company A
- Market price/Book value = 418.8/1,000 = 0.42 for Company B

The value creation model shown in Exhibit 3.3 depicts the concept. This value creation model has three components, namely, profitability, advantage horizon, and reinvestment.

---

[1] Sustainable growth rate = Retention rate × [PAT/Sales] × [Sales/Assets] × [Assets/Equity] = ROE × Retention. This analysis is based on a series of articles by William Fruhan in the *Harvard Business Review*. See Fruhan (1984) and Fruhan and Piper (1981).

Exhibit 3.1 *Market Price of Company A*

Beg. of year of inv.	BV	ROE	PAT	RR*	Retained Earnings	Div.	PV@20%
1	1,000	25%	250	40%	100	150	125
2	1,100		275		110	165	114.6
3	1,210		302.5		121	181.5	105
4	1,331.0		332.8		133.1	199.7	96.3
5	1,464.1		363		146.4	219.6	88.3
6	1,610.5		402.6		161.1	241.5	80.9
7	1,771.6		442.9		177.2	265.7	74.2
8	1,948.7		487.2		194.9	292.3	68.0
9	2,143.6		535.90		214.4	321.3	62.3
10	2,357.9		589.5		235.8	353.7	57.1
11	2,593.7					2,593.7	418.8

* RR = retention rate. Total = 1,290.5

Exhibit 3.2 *Market Price of Company B*

Beg. of year of inv.	BV	ROE	PAT	RR*	Retained Earnings	Div.	PV@20%
1	1,000	10%	100	100%	100	0	0
2	1,100		110		110	0	0
3	1,210		121		121	0	0
4	1,331.0		133.1		133.1	0	0
5	1,464.1		146.4		146.4	0	0
6	1,610.5		161.1		161.1	0	0
7	1,771.6		177.2		177.2	0	0
8	1,948.7		194.9		194.9	0	0
9	2,143.6		214.4		214.4	0	0
10	2,357.9		235.8		235.8	0	0
11	2,593.7					2,593.7*	418.8

* Market price at the end = Book value.

Profitability

In any industry group, more profitable firms—those able to generate higher earnings per rupee of earnings—should have higher M/B ratios. Conversely, firms that are unable to generate positive abnormal returns should sell for lower M/B ratios.

Exhibit 3.3 *Value Creation Model*

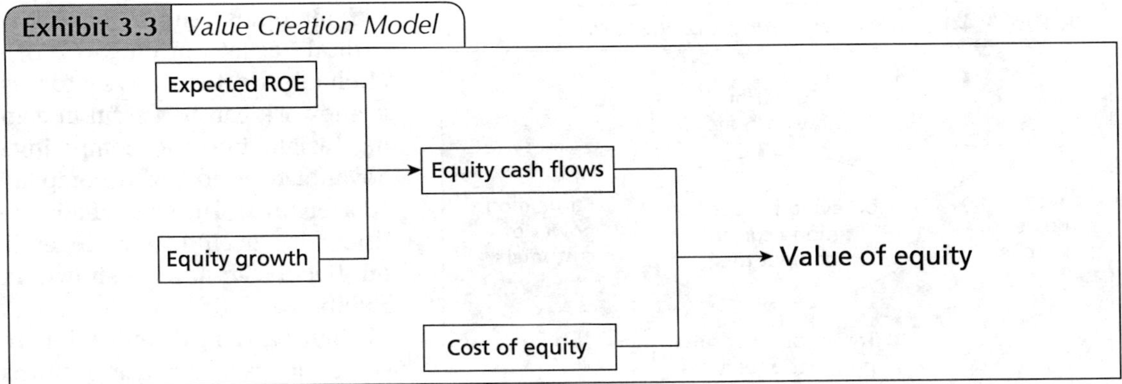

Source: Author.

$$ROE > K_e,\ M/B > 1$$

$$ROE < K_e,\ M/B < 1$$

$$ROE = K_e,\ M/B = 1$$

ROE is a function of profit margin, asset turnover, and leverage.

$$ROE = PAT/Equity = [PAT/Sales] \times [Sales/Assets] \times [Assets/Equity]$$

Increasing any of the components (profit margin, asset turnover, or leverage) increases ROE. Increasing prices or reducing costs, for example, may increase the profit margin. Similarly, decreasing the asset base for the same level of revenue would increase the asset turnover (e.g., by reducing inventory or book debt). If the model is right, we would expect a positive relation between M/B ratios and ROE, keeping cost of equity constant. One of the earliest tests of the model is by Fruhan (1979). He found that higher M/B ratios are indeed associated with high ROEs in a wide range of industries.[2]

Advantage Horizon

The period for which a firm can maintain a positive ($ROE - K_e$) spread is called the advantage horizon. The greater the abnormal return, the longer the advantage horizon; the sooner the abnormal returns, the higher the M/B ratio (Fruhan 1979). Over time, competitive pressures drive returns to the cost of capital. Although a company's competitive advantage period is affected by a multitude of internal and external factors, only a few key factors such as current return on capital, rate of industry change, and barriers to entry have a significant bearing. Companies with high (return on invested capital [ROIC] and hence) price-earnings (P/E) multiples tend to have a long competitive advantage period, and those with low

[2] Since companies in any industry group would be expected to have similar capital structures and, hence, costs of capital (a somewhat restrictive assumption), we can test for association between M/B and ROE for companies in the same industry group.

Exhibit 3.4 *Forces Governing Competition*

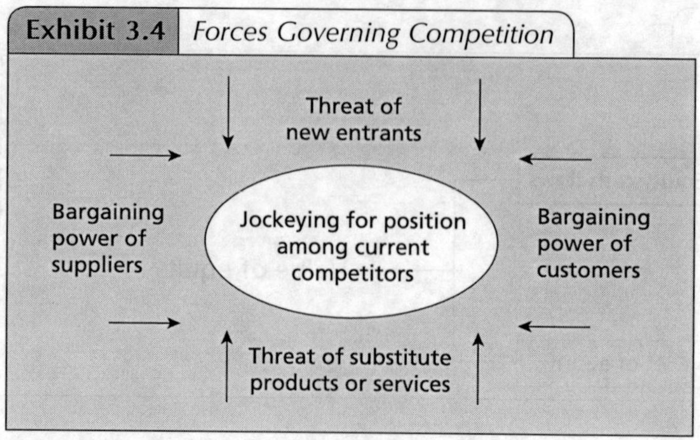

Source: Porter (1979).

P/E multiples tend to have low capital asset pricing (CAP). Michael Porter's five forces framework can be useful in gaining insight into the competitive advantage period of a company (Porter 1979). The state of competition in an industry depends on five basic forces shown in Exhibit 3.4.

High barriers to entry, for instance, locks in increasing returns to the company, making it difficult for competitors to wrest it away. Some of the major sources of barriers to entry are economies of scale, product differentiation, capital requirements, and access to distribution channels. Economies of scale force an entrant to enter the industry on a large scale or accept a cost disadvantage. Economies of scale may be present in production, purchase, or marketing.

The competitive advantage period can range from 0–20 or more years depending on the competitive position of the company. Highly successful companies such as Coca-Cola and Microsoft have relatively long advantage horizons. It is to be understood that the CAP may not remain constant—it may increase or decrease. Whenever the CAP of a company increases, we would expect the stock values to go up. Further, CAP is finite. In other words, companies that earn abnormal return may not continue to do so forever. Returns fall to normal levels and the spread between ROE and cost of equity shrinks.

Reinvestment

A firm can either retain its earnings or pay it out as dividends to shareholders. Intuitively, we would expect value to increase when firms reinvest in projects (acquisitions) that generate abnormal returns. The example of the two firms in Exhibits 3.1 and 3.2 can be generalized as follows.

The value of equity is the present value of dividends

$$= \frac{[(1-r)\times ROE \times E_0]}{(1+K_e)} + \frac{[(1-r)\times ROE \times E_0(1+rROE)}{(1+K_e)^2} + \ldots$$

where r is the retention ratio, E_o is the value of equity at time = 0, ROE is return on equity, and K_e is the cost of equity.

$$= \frac{[(1-r)\times ROE \times E_0]}{(1+K_e)}\{1+\frac{(1+rROE)}{(1+K_e)}+\frac{(1+rROE)}{(1+K_e)^2}+\ldots\}$$

This is a growing perpetuity with growth rate equal to the sustainable growth rate. It can be written as

$$\text{Equity value (market)} = \frac{(\text{Payout})(\text{ROE})(E_0)}{(K_e - g)}$$

Dividing both sides by E_0, the book value of equity,

$$M/B = \frac{(\text{Payout})(\text{ROE})}{(K_e - g)} = \frac{(1 - r)(\text{ROE})}{(K_e - r \times \text{ROE})}$$

where use is made of the fact that sustainable growth = retention ratio × ROE

If the retention ratio is zero, that is the firm pays all its earnings as dividends,

$$M/B = [\text{ROE}/K_e]$$

Those firms that generate returns in excess of cost of equity will sell at higher M/B ratios.

THE ECONOMICS OF A MERGER

Since acquisitions are an alternative to internal growth, the framework presented so far can be applied to mergers as well. The task of enterprise valuation is to estimate the magnitude of (present value of) future benefits to shareholders in relation to the purchase price. The first step in merger analysis is to identify the economic gains from the merger. There are gains if the combined entity is more than the sum of its parts, that is, combined value > (value of acquirer + stand-alone value of target)

The difference between the combined value and the sum of the values of individual companies is usually attributed to synergy.

Value of acquirer + stand-alone value of target + value of synergy = combined value

There is also a cost attached to an acquisition. The cost of acquisition is the price premium paid over the market value plus other costs of integration. Therefore, the net gain is the value of synergy minus premium paid.

Suppose,

$$V_A = \$100$$
$$V_B = \$50$$
$$V_{AB} = \$175$$
$$\text{Synergy} = V_{AB} - (V_A + V_B) = 25$$

If premium is US$10, $\text{Net gain} = \$25 - 10 = \$15$

To illustrate, the sharing of synergy between Daimler and Chrysler is given as

	Daimler	Chrysler	Combined	(US$ billion)
Market value				
Before the deal	52.8	29.4	82.2	
Synergy			18.0	
Merged value			100.2	
Shareholders get	57.2%	42.8%	100%	
Which is now worth	57.3	42.9	100.2	
Share of the gain	4.5	13.5	18	

Exhibit 3.5 *Merger Gains*

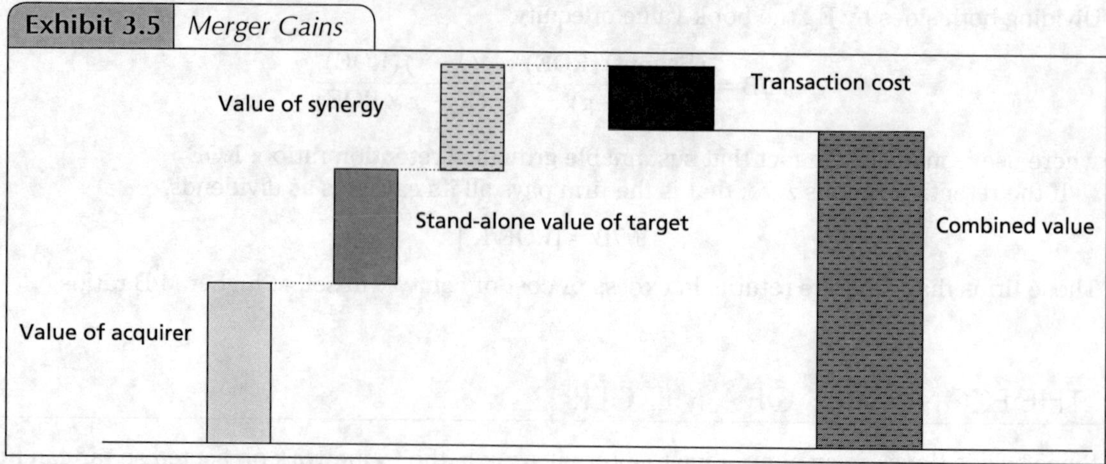

Source: Author.

Exhibit 3.5 depicts the synergy equation. Companies may add value to the target by increasing its profitability or advantage horizon. Acquisitions need not be made with synergy in mind. It is possible to make money from nonsynergistic acquisitions as well. Indeed leveraged buyout (LBO) firms such as Clayton, Dubilier & Rice and companies such as Thermo Electron and Phelps Dodge generate returns of 18%–35% p.a. through nonsynergistic acquisitions. As can be seen from Exhibit 3.6, operating improvements are a big source of value creation. A firm is essentially a collection of capabilities that when applied to business opportunities create competitive advantage for the firm and generate returns to shareholders. The ability to create value depends on the firm's ability to mobilize an organization to form new combination of capabilities. Better post-merger integration could lead to abnormal returns even when the acquired company is in an unrelated business. Managerial talent is one of the most important instruments in creating value apart from other sources such as cost reductions, revenue enhancements and improvements in operating profit margin, cash flow position, and so on. Many a time, executive compensation is tied to the changes in cash flow in the post-merger period. Providing equity stake in the company induces executives to think and behave like shareholders. Some nonsynergistic acquirers offer up to 20% equity stake in the company.

FREE CASH FLOW VALUATION

One of the essential steps in mergers and acquisitions (M&A) is determining the value of the target company. There are several approaches for measuring the value of the target firm. One of the popular methods is the discounted cash flow (DCF) methodology. In the DCF approach, the value of the business is the future expected cash flow discounted at a rate that reflects the riskiness of the projected cash flows. This methodology is used to value companies since firms are essentially a collection of projects. The DCF methodology is founded on the principle that it is inappropriate to capitalize earnings per se. One must also take into account the investment required to generate those earnings. Consequently, cash flows are obtained by deducting net

Exhibit 3.6 *Value Creation in Acquisitions*

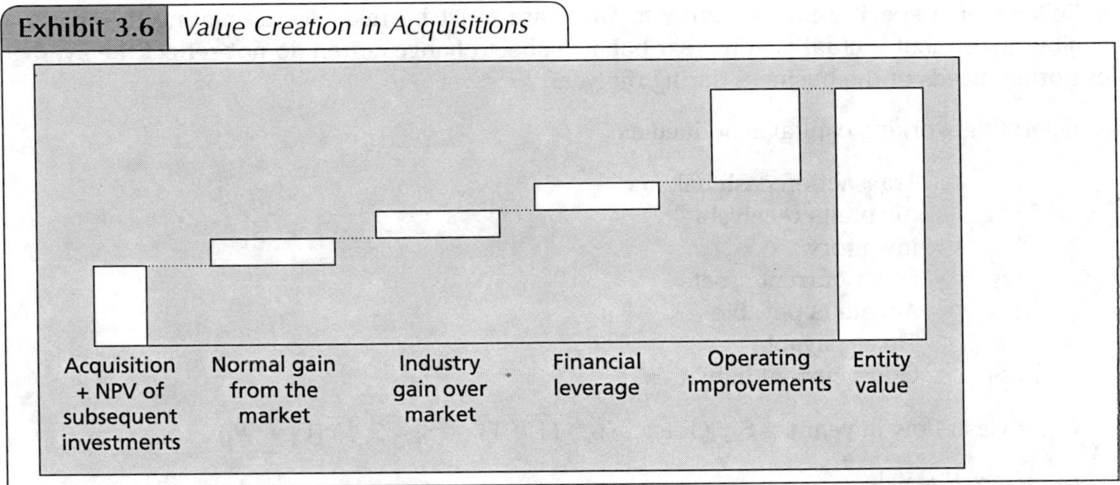

Source: Anslinger and Copeland (1996).

capital expenditure (Capex) and incremental working capital investment from net operating profits after taxes. The steps involved in the valuation are as follows:

Step 1: Determine free cash flow
Free cash flow is the cash flow available to all investors in the company—both shareholders and bondholders—after consideration for taxes, Capex, and working capital investment.

> Free cash flow = NOPAT + Depreciation – Capital expenditure –/+ Increases (decreases) in working capital investment

where NOPAT = Net operating profit after tax = Earnings before interest but after taxes
= EBIT (1 – Tax rate) and
EBIT = Revenue – cost of goods sold – operating expenses – depreciation

Estimation of cash flows requires NOPAT (net operating profit after tax, capital expenditure), and net working capital. In calculating NOPAT, interest is not deducted because the discount rate, the weighted average cost of capital (WACC) incorporates after-tax cost of debt.

The physical assets of a company depreciate and need to be replaced to maintain a certain level of growth in sales. Usually, Capex is estimated as a constant percentage of revenues. Capex can be either positive or negative depending on whether the company is making or liquidating investments. If Capex is negative, it is a source of funds. To gain an estimate of capital investment required per dollar of sales increase, take the sum of all capital investments less depreciation over the last 5 or 10 years, and divide this total by the sales increase from the beginning to the end of the period.

The working capital investment should not include cash and other equivalents, that is, noncash working capital is to be taken into consideration. Free cash flows thus obtained can be either positive or negative depending on whether the business is generating a surplus or a deficit under a specific plan of growth. Due care must be taken in estimating the working capital investment. Actual year-to-year balance sheet changes often do not reflect the average or normal needs of the business during the year.

Operating working capital is defined as

	Transaction cash balance
Plus:	Accounts receivable
Plus:	Inventory
Plus:	Other current assets
Less:	Accounts payable
Less:	Taxes payable
Less:	Other current liabilities

CF_t = Cash flow in year t = $S_{t-1}(1 + g_t)(p_t)(1 - T) - (S_t - S_{t-1})(C_t + W_t)$

where S = Sales
p = Profit margin = EBIT as a percentage of sales
T = Income tax rate
C = Capital investment required (net of depreciation) per dollar of sales increase
W = Net working capital per dollar of sales increase
g = Growth rate

Estimate the most likely incremental cash flows to be generated by the target company with the *acquirer as owner* (and not on an as-is basis). Note that financing is not incorporated in the cash flows. Suitable adjustments for the specific financing of the acquisition will be made in the discount rate. The forecast of free cash flows requires the following inputs:

1. Initial sales before the starting of the forecast period.
2. Growth rate in sales for the entire forecast period. The growth rate may remain constant or change.
3. The ratio of EBIT/Sales (profit margin) for the entire period.
4. The ratio of total operating capital (i.e., Capex + working capital investment) to sales for the period.

Thus,

$$\text{Sales}_t = \text{Sales}_{t-1} \times (1 + g_t)$$
$$\text{EBIT}_t = \text{Sales}_t\,(p_t)$$
$$\text{Asset requirement} = a_t = [(FA + WC)/S]_t$$
$$(FA + WC)_t = \text{Sales}_t \times [(FA + WC)/S]_t$$

Step 2: Estimate a suitable discount rate for the acquisition

The acquiring company can use its weighted average cost of capital based on its target capital structure only if the acquisition will not affect the risk of the acquirer. If the acquirer intends to change the capital structure of the target company, suitable adjustments for the discount rate should be made. The discount rate should reflect the capital structure of the company after the acquisition. To calculate the discount rate:

- Estimate the asset beta for the target using the relationship.
- $\beta_A = \beta_E$ (E/V), where E/V is the equity-to-value ratio and β_E is the equity beta The asset beta may also be obtained by taking the average asset betas of comparable firms in the industry.
- Relever the asset beta at various debt ratios (say, from 0% to 60% using the same relationship and find levered equity beta for the target.
- Estimate cost of equity at various debt ratios.
- Similarly, estimate cost of debt at various debt ratios.
- Calculate WACC as the weighted average of costs of debt and equity, the weights being target, market value, debt-to-value, and equity-to-value ratios.

Step 3: Calculate the present value of cash flows

Since the life of a going concern, by definition, is infinite, the value of the company

= PV of cash flows during the forecast period + terminal value (TV)

We can set the forecast period in such a way that the company reaches a stable phase after that. In other words, we are assuming that the company will grow at a constant rate after the forecast period. The period of high growth can be anywhere from 3 to 20 years (may be even more for some computer software firms) depending on the type of business, size of the market, entry barriers, availability of substitutes, number of players in the market, and so on.

Step 4: Estimate the terminal value

The terminal value is the present value of cash flows occurring after the forecast period. If we assume that cash flows grow at a constant rate after the forecast period, the TV is calculated as

$$TV = [CF_t\,(1 + g)]/k - g$$

where CF_t = cash flow in the last year
g = constant growth rate
k = discount rate

Step 5: Add present value of terminal value

Step 6: Deduct the value of debt and other obligations (say, restructuring charges) assumed by the acquirer.

An Illustration

The forecast of free cash flow for a company is shown in Exhibit 3.7. The acquiring company's management expects the company to grow at 15% p.a. The cost of capital for the target is 14.62%. The present value of cash flows amounts to US$39.09 million, assuming that the acquiring company will not achieve any operating improvements or make changes in the capital structure. The cash flows are expected to grow at 10% forever after 2004.

PV of free cash flow during forecast period = US$39.09 million
Enterprise value = Value of the company during forecast period + TV

Exhibit 3.7 *Free Cash Flow Forecast*

	Year						(Figures in US$million)	
	1	2	3	4	5	6	7	8
Sales	162.13	204.69	235.39	270.7	311.31	358.01	411.71	473.46
NOPAT	10.62	11.22	11.72	12.72	14.41	16.21	18.13	20.11
Depreciation	3.14	2.13	2.68	2.82	2.96	3.11	3.26	3.42
Less:								
Capital exp.	0	0.63	2.36	1.79	1.88	1.97	2.07	2.17
Increase in WC	0	6.44	4.12	6.1	9.45	11.67	12.97	14.32
Free cash flow	13.76	6.28	7.37	7.65	6.04	5.68	6.35	7.04

PV of FCF US$39.09 million

Approach 1: Terminal Value Is a Growing Perpetuity

$$\begin{aligned} TV &= FCF_t\ (1 + g)/(k - g) \\ &= 7.04\ (1.10)/(0.1462 - 0.10) \\ &= \$167.6 \text{ million.} \\ \text{PV of TV} &= 167.6 \times \text{PVIF}\ (14.62, 7) \\ &= 167.6 \times 0.384 = \$64.46 \text{ million} \end{aligned}$$

Total value = $(39.06 + 64.46) million = $103.52 million

Since we are interested in buying only the shares of the firm, the value of outstanding debt should be deducted from the value of the firm to arrive at the value of equity. Assume that the company has debt amounting to US$7.92 million.

Value of equity = 103.52 – 7.92 = $95.60 million.

As is evident, much of the target company's value comes from terminal value, which is sensitive to the assumption made about the growth rate of cash flows in perpetuity. There are three other ways in which terminal value can be estimated.

Approach 2: Terminal Value Is a Stable Perpetuity

If there is no Capex or if Capex exactly equals depreciation after the forecast period, meaning that the total capital does not grow anymore, cash flow equals profit after tax. In other words, when we assume that the company earns a rate of return on capital equal to the cost of capital, irrespective of growth in sales,

$$\begin{aligned} TV &= [\text{free cash flow/discount rate}] = FCF/k \\ &= [7.04/0.1462] = \$48.15 \text{ million.} \end{aligned}$$

Value of the firm = 39.09 + 48.15 = $87.24 million. The difference in value is almost US$16.28 million.

Approach 3: Terminal Value as a Multiple of Book Value

The TV can also be estimated by multiplying the forecasted book value of capital by an appropriate market-to-book ratio (P/BV). Often, the current M/B ratio is taken as proxy for future.

Consider the following example.

		(Figures in US$million)	
	Market Value	**Book Value**	**M/B**
Debt	8.0	8.0	1.0
Equity	15.0	10.0	1.50
Total capital	23.0	18	1.28

The current M/B ratio is 1.28. If the book value of capital at the end of forecast period is US$30 million, the TV = 30 × 1.28 = $38.40 million.

Approach 4: Terminal Value as a Multiple of Earnings

The terminal value under this method is established by multiplying the forecasted terminal year profits by an appropriate Price – Earning multiple. As usual, the current P/E multiple can be used as proxy for future.

Current P/E multiple = Current market value of company/Current profit after tax

To illustrate, if the current market capitalization is US$57.62 million and profit after tax is US$8.23 million, P/E = 57.62/ 8.23 = 7

TV = Last year profits × P/E multiple

If the last year profits are US$20.11 million,

$$= \$20.11 \times 7 = \$140.8 \text{ million}$$

Obviously, the method adopted affects the final value placed on the company's equity. These four methods might give four different answers. The DCF approach can capture the value of assets-in-place. Some components of the acquisition are hard to quantify. Consequently, the final price paid by the acquirer might be much higher than the DCF value obtained. But the premium paid for the synergy should not be out of proportion.

A sensitivity analysis may be conducted for pessimistic and optimistic values of key financial variables such as sales growth rate, profit margin, working capital investment, Capex, period of high growth, and so on. The end product of such an analysis is a range of prices within which the acquisition price may lie. Obviously, the acquirer would want to lower the price as much as possible, and the opposite is true for the target. The most important message is that the acquirer should consider not only what the target may be worth to the buyer but also what the target's next best alternative is likely to be. For example, suppose that when valued as a stand-alone, a target is worth US$100, whereas, due to synergies, the target is worth US$150 as part of the buying firm. A key element in the negotiation process is the value of target to *another bidder.* If the synergy is unique to the buyer, the buyer may purchase the company for one buck more than the stand-alone value (US$101). On the other hand, if the synergy is available to other bidders as well, the buyer may have to raise the bid closer to US$150. In other words, the valuation must take into account the uniqueness of synergy and the likely range of prices affordable by other bidders. To sum up, valuation has three elements: estimation of cash flows, estimation of discount rate, and sensitivity analysis.

We could think of the target company's value as

Value to buyer = Value to seller + Value added by buyer + Change in value to buyer if target firm is acquired by competitor.

The first component is the DCF value of the target firm in its current form with the current growth rate, current financial plan, and so on. The second component, value added by acquirer, comprises of synergy to acquirer, cost savings, value of new strategy after the acquisition, proceeds from sale of redundant assets adjusted for taxes, benefits from improvement in credit rating, and other financing side effects. The third component is the gain or loss to the acquirer if the competition manages to acquire the target. The sum total of these three components gives the maximum value of the target.

ESTIMATION OF THE VALUE OF SYNERGY

Assume that a company has forecasted gains in operating income that arise due to acquisition. The gains in operating income can come from two sources: revenue enhances and cost reductions. Revenue may increase due to better pricing or volume gains (i.e., increase in market share) or better differentiation/segmentation. Reducing head count, overheads, and purchase costs are some generic strategies for reducing costs. Given here is a (hypothetical) forecast of gains estimated by an acquirer.

		Year			**(Figures in US$million)**
		1	**2**	**3**	**4**
Gain in operating income due to					
■ Revenue increases	20	50	100	150	
■ Cost reductions		30	100	200	300
Total		0	150	300	450

Assume a terminal growth rate of 2%

$$TV = \frac{450\ (1.02)}{(k - g)}$$

The gains in operating income and cost reductions result in higher profit after tax (after *adjusting* for taxes). The blended cost of *equity* for the combined entity should be used to discount the stream of changes in profit after tax due to acquisition because synergy will flow to shareholders of both companies.[3]

The blended cost of equity for the combined entity = $R_f + \beta_{E,\ blended}$ (Risk premium).

$$\beta_{E,\ blended} = \beta_{A,\ weighted}\ (V_{total}/E_{total})$$

[3] The appropriate discount rate is the cost of equity and not the cost of capital because the numerator in the series is changes in profit after tax, which shareholders receive.

Weighted asset beta for the combined entity

$$= \beta_{A,\ acquirer}\ (V_{acquirer}/V_{total}) + \beta_{A,\ target}\ (V_{target}/V_{total})$$

$$V_{total} = V_{acquirer} + V_{target}$$

where value, V = Book value of debt + Market value of equity respectively
Market value of equity = No of shares × Pre-announcement stock price
Further β_A (either for the acquirer or target) = β_D (D/V) + β_E (E/V)
where β_D = beta of debt (a small number, say, 0.1)

β_E = beta of equity
D = Book value of debt
$V = D + E_{market\ value}$

To estimate the cost of equity for the combined entity:

- Estimate asset beta for both the companies given β_E, D, E, and, hence, V.
- Estimate asset beta for the combined entity (weighted asset beta) with respective values of companies as weights.
- Estimate equity beta for the combined entity by using the weighted beta calculated earlier.

$$\beta_{E,\ blended} = \beta_{A,\ weighted}\ (V_{total}/E_{total})$$

Cost of equity for the combined entity = $R_f + \beta_{E,\ blended}$ (Risk premium).

As pointed out earlier, a company may lose market share and, hence, revenues (profits) if the competition acquires the target. Assume that the stream has been forecasted for the next 4 years and is expected to grow at 2% in perpetuity.

	Year			
	1	**2**	**3**	**4**
Loss in operating income (US$ million)	(0)	(50)	(100)	(175)
TV				$\frac{175 \times 1.02}{(k - g)}$

The appropriate discount rate for this stream is the *acquirer's* cost of equity.

The sum of the present values of the two streams, namely, revenue enhances + cost reductions and loss in operating income, represents the value of synergy. Dividing it by the number of target company shares gives the present value of synergy/share

The value of target = Base value + synergy

where base case value = Pre-announcement stock price[4]

If pre-announcement stock price of the target is US$50; the present value of revenue enhances and cost reduction per share is US$30; the present value of loss in operating income if the target is acquired by a competitor is US$20, then the value of target is US$100 (=$50 + 30

[4] Market value is the best basis for establishing base case (stand alone) value, as long as the stock price has not been bid up in anticipation of a takeover bid, as it provides a compromise measure of investors' estimates of an asset's present value. If there is run-up in stock price just before the announcement, one can infer that the price already incorporates the value of synergy partly or wholly.

+ 20) per share. This is the maximum price that the acquirer can afford to pay without making a loss, assuming that the forecasts are accurate.

ADJUSTED PRESENT VALUE

Discounting free cash flow at WACC works reasonably well when the company targets a constant debt-to-value ratio. The corporate WACC used in many valuations is based on the assumption that the cash flows of the target are about as risky as that of the acquiring company, and the target company will maintain a similar capital structure as that of the acquiring company. Both are restrictive assumptions.

The adjusted present value (APV) approach is a good alternative when companies target an absolute amount of debt. A transaction can be treated as though it is all equity financed and then this base case value can be adjusted to account for financing effects such as interest tax shield, bankruptcy costs, and so on.

APV unbundles all the components of NPV and analyses each one separately. Whereas WACC bundles all financing side effects into the discount rate.

	Base case value		Value of financing side effects
APV =	Value of firm if all-equity financed	+/–	Interest tax shields/Bankruptcy costs

The first step in calculating APV requires the calculation of present value of target company's cash flows assuming all equity financing.

Consider a hypothetical example. The cash flows of a company are as follows.

(Figures in US$million)

Year (1)	NOPAT (2)	Capital Exp (3)	Dep. (4)	ΔWC (5)	Net Cash Flow (6) = 2 + 4 – 3 – 5
1.	60	30	20	20	30
2.	70	32	22	22	38
3.	75	35	24	23	41
4.	80	37	26	25	44
5.	85	40	28	27	46

Cash flows are expected to grow at 7% forever thereafter.

$$\text{PV of TV} = \frac{46\,(1.07)}{(K - 0.07)\,(1 + K)^5}$$

The unlevered value is obtained by discounting all the cash flows at the *unlevered* cost of equity.

$$= R_f + \beta_u \text{ (risk premium)}$$

where β_u = unlevered beta or asset beta.

The asset beta is the weighted average of betas of debt and equity. That is,

$$\beta_A = \beta_D\,(D/V) + \beta_E\,(E/V)$$

If we assume that the beta of debt is zero,

$$\beta_A = \beta_E \, (E/V)$$

A problem arises when the target company is unlisted. Since unlisted companies, by definition, do not have stock market data, one cannot estimate either equity or asset betas directly. One can, however, estimate asset beta by looking at comparable companies. Assume that the target, an unlisted company, has four "comparable" firms in the same industry group (similar line of business and size). Their betas and debt/equity (D/E) ratios are given:

Firm	Beta	D/E
1.	1.0	0.50
2	0.6	0.0
3	0.8	0.4
4	0.9	0.45

Company 2 has no debt. The cost of equity for this company can be taken as proxy.

Assume the following capital asset pricing model (CAPM) parameters

R_f = 7%,[5] $\beta_A = 0.60$, market premium = 7.5%
Cost of unlevered equity = 7 + 0.60 (7.5) = 11.5%

The present value of cash flows = [30 × PVIF (11.5%, 1) + … + 46 × PVIF (11.5%, 5) + PV of TV]
PV of cash flows during forecast period = $142.62 million

$$TV = \frac{46\,(1.07)}{(0.115 - 0.07)} = \$1{,}093.77 \text{ million}$$

$$\text{PV of TV} = \frac{1{,}093}{(1.15)^5} = \$543.80 \text{ million}$$

All equity value = $142.62 + 543.80 million = $686.40 million.

The acquisition price of US$600 million will be financed with US$300 million of debt. It will be brought down to US$200 million in 5 years. The indebtedness is expected to remain at that level forever.

End of Year	Debt (US$ million)
0	300
1	280
2	260
3	240
4	220
5	200

Present value of interest tax shields = PV of tax shields during the first 5 years + PV of perpetual tax shields after year 5.

[5] This could be the 10-year *T*-bond rate.

Tax shield = interest rate × amount of debt outstanding × tax rate
Assume a tax rate of 35% and interest rate of 14%.

$$\text{PV of tax shield during first 5 years} = [0.14 \times 300 \times 0.35 \times \text{PVIF}(14,1)] + \ldots + 0.14 \times 220 \times 0.35 \times \text{PVIF}(14,5)] = \$44.89 \text{ million}$$

$$\text{TV of tax shields} = \frac{0.14 \times 200 \times 0.35}{0.14\,(1.14)^5} = \$36.84 \text{ million}$$

The cost of debt is used as discount rate on the assumption that tax shields are about as uncertain as debt payments generating them. If tax shields are considered riskier than interest payments, a higher rate may be used.

Present value of tax shields = 44.89 + 36.84 million = $81.73 million

APV = Base case value + PV of tax shield – Acquisition price

APV = $686.40 + 81.73 – 600 million = $768.13 – 600 = $168.13 million

Adjustment for incremental bankruptcy cost can be made either subjectively or by taking suitable proxies. The acquisition price of US$600 million compares well with the base case value (US$686 million). An acquirer should look for making money from incremental improvements in operations rather than from good financing. If tax shields evaporate or the bankruptcy cost exceeds tax shields, the value will never be realized.

CAPITAL CASH FLOW VALUATION

In free cash flow valuation the WACC is used to discount cash flows. The WACC is supposed to capture the tax advantage of debt (WACC incorporates post-tax cost of debt); the cost of debt and cost of equity are both opportunity costs, each consisting of time value and risk-premium. WACC is a catch-all for risk and tax advantage of debt. The common practice is to increase the discount rate if the project is more risky. The methodology assumes that a company targets a debt-equity blend. Because WACC changes when debt capital structure changes, the free cash flow method cannot be easily implemented in many situations, such as LBOs. Since the debt ratio changes every year, it is inappropriate to use a single discount rate (WACC) for all the cash flows (in all the years). Intuitively, we would expect the discount rate to fall when leverage falls because the cash flows to equity investors become less risky. In short, one should come up with a different cost of equity for each of the years.

We know that

$$\text{Assets} = \text{Debt} + \text{Equity}$$
$$A = D + E$$
$$\beta_A A = \beta_D D + \beta_E E$$

Ignoring the systematic risk of debt,[6] we get

$$\beta_A A = \beta_E E$$

or

$$\beta_E = \beta_A [A/E]$$

where A is firm value, D + E.

Using this relationship, one can come up with values of beta and, by extension, the cost of equity for all the years based on the leverage in existence in that year (A/E essentially measures leverage). These discount rates may be used to discount equity cash flows to estimate the value of the company's equity.

An algebraically equivalent, yet superior method is the capital cash flow (CCF) valuation (Ruback 2002). Free cash flow valuation excludes interest tax shields because the discount rate, WACC, incorporates the tax advantage of debt. In CCF valuation, free cash flows plus interest tax shields are discounted at *pre-tax* WACC (expected asset return). Since the asset return does not change when capital structure changes, it is easier to implement CCF valuation.

CCF = Net income + Depreciation – Capital expenditure – Δ Working capital + Cash interest

Or

= EBIT (1 – T) + Depreciation – Capital expenditure – Δ Working capital + Interest tax shields

It is easier to implement the former approach because it incorporates corporate estimates of taxes that reflect the special circumstances facing the firm rather than mechanically finding the product of tax rate and taxable income.[7]

The appropriate discount rate is a before tax rate because the tax benefits of debt are already included in the CCFs. The correct discount rate is the pre-tax WACC.

Pre-tax WACC = Weighted average costs of debt and equity = (D/V) K_D + (E/V) K_E

D/V and E/V are debt-to-value and equity-to-value ratio, respectively, K_D and K_E are costs of debt and equity.

Cost of debt = $K_D = R_f + \beta_D$ (risk premium).

Cost of equity = $K_E = R_f + \beta_E$ (risk premium).

$$\text{Pre–tax WACC} = \frac{D}{V}(R_f + \beta_D \times R_P) + \frac{E}{V}(R_f + \beta_E \times R_P)$$
$$= R_f + (D/V\ \beta_D + E/V\ \beta_E)\ R_P$$
$$= R_f + \beta_A (R_P)$$

Since $\beta_A V = \beta_D D + \beta_E E$

Or $\beta_A = \beta_D D/V + \beta_E E/V$.

Note that the discount rate depends on R_f, β_A, and risk premium and does not incorporate D/V or E/V. That is, the pre-tax WACC is independent of capital structure and, hence, can be applied to all cash flows regardless of the capital structure in existence. In other words, pre-tax WACC, which is a function of asset beta, is constant. Both free cash flow valuation, and CCF valuation provide the same answer. CCF Valuation, however, is easier to implement.

[6] The beta of debt is assumed to be zero. This is a restrictive assumption when leverage is high.

[7] In other words, in many instances, it does not reflect the actual tax paid.

An Illustration

Clariant is in the process of purchasing Synergon. Forecasting cash flows for Synergon under Clariant's management involves suitable assumptions regarding sales growth rate, profit margin, Capex, and net working capital for every dollar of sales increase. The relevant assumptions for the forecast period are given.

	Year	
	1–5	6–10
Sales growth rate, g %	15	10
Profit margin, EBIT/Sales, %	0.18	0.15
Tax rate %	36	36
Capex per dollar of sales increase (C)[8]	0.30	0.15
Working capital per dollar of sales increase (W)	0.15	0.10

The company's value is expected to be stable after the forecast period when the company enters a stable phase. The current financial details of Synergon are given in Exhibit 3.8.

The cash flow in any year = $CF_t = S_{t-1}(1 + g_t)(p_t)(1 - T_c) - (S_t - S_{t-1})(C_t + W_t)$.

Exhibit 3.8 *Recent Financial Statements of Synergon*

Income Statement	**(Figures in US$million)**
	Synergon
Sales	350
EBIT	32.16
Interest @ 12%	12.86
Net Income	24.12
No. of shares Outstanding (m)	16.08
Balance Sheet	
Debt	107.20
Equity	160.80
	268.00
Fixed Assets	
Less: Accumulated Depreciation	216.00
Net working capital	50.00
Other Assets	2.00
	268.00
WACC	12%

[8] Net of depreciation.

Exhibit 3.9 *Forecast of Cash Flows for Synergon (figures in US$ million)*

Year	Sales	EBIT	Pt	NOPAT	St-St-1	C + W	Capex + WC	FCF	PV-Factor	PV
0	350									
1	402.5	72.45	0.18	46.368	52.5	0.45	23.625	22.743	0.893	20.309499
2	462.875	83.31	0.18	53.3184	60.375	0.45	27.16875	26.14965	0.797	20.84127105
3	532.3	95.8	0.18	61.312	69.425	0.45	31.24125	30.07075	0.712	21.410374
4	612.15	110.18	0.18	70.5152	79.85	0.45	35.9325	34.5827	0.636	21.9945972
5	703.97	126.71	0.18	81.0944	91.82	0.45	41.319	39.7754	0.567	22.5526518
6	774.37	116.15	0.15	74.336	70.4	0.25	17.6	56.736	0.507	28.765152
7	851.8	127.77	0.15	81.7728	77.43	0.25	19.3575	62.4153	0.452	28.2117156
8	937	140.55	0.15	89.952	85.2	0.25	21.3	68.652	0.404	27.735408
9	1,030.7	154.6	0.15	98.944	93.7	0.25	23.425	75.519	0.361	27.262359
10	1,133.75	170	0.15	108.8	103.05	0.25	25.7625	83.0375	0.322	26.738075
									Total	245.82

where p = EBIT/Sales
S = sales
T_c = tax rate

Thus, cash flow in year 1 = 350(1 + 0.15) (0.18) (1 – 0.36) – (402.50 – 350) (0.30 + 0.15)
= $46.368 – 23.625 million
= $22.743 million.

The projections for the first 10 years are shown in Exhibit 3.9.[9] Assume that the WACC for the company based on a long run capital structure is 12%.

If we assume that the company generates normal returns from year 10, that is, the company's value is unaffected by growth, the terminal value can be estimated as a perpetuity.

$$TV = \frac{FCF_{10}}{\text{Discount rate}} = \frac{83.03}{0.12} = \$691.90 \text{ million}$$

PV of TV = TV × $[1/(1 + k)^{10}]$ = $171.26 million

Total PV, that is, firm value (US$ million)	317.08
Synergon's debt assumed (US$ million)	107.2
Value of Synergon's equity (US$ million)	209.88
Value per share (US$)	13.05

[9] The sales growth rate and the assumptions regarding margins, Capex, and working capital investment are usually extrapolated from the current year (as base year) based on the assumption that the current year is a normal year. One might take the average of past 2 or 3 years if there is a reason to believe that the current year is too good or too bad so that the trend is not unrealistic.

Clariant may pay a price higher than US$13.05 if cash flows can be enhanced for the same level of investment or reduce investment for the same level of cash flows.

CONCLUDING COMMENTS

This chapter outlined some sensible reasons for mergers, action areas, and valuation approaches. There are essentially two ways of valuing targets: the DCF approach and the relative value approach, which makes use of multiples (see Appendix 3A and 3B). The final price is often a product of negotiations between the concerned parties and the pre-announcement stock prices of the companies involved. Acquisitions work only if:

- There are operating and financial improvements.
- The acquisition price is not too high.
- The incumbent management is competent.
- There is top management involvement in the process.

Many companies do not recognize the need to evaluate the target company's marketing strengths, although the acquisition itself is intended to increase sales growth or market share. Particular attention should be paid to the company's brands, pricing policy, distribution, product development capabilities, and promotion.

The DCF methodology captures the value of assets-in-place. Often the option component embedded in acquisitions could be substantial. The DCF methodology ignores managerial flexibility to time the purchase or new business opportunities that may arise due to a "platform acquisition" in a country or a market. This is the subject of the next chapter.

Case Study

Daiichi Sankyo's (DIS) Acquisition of Ranbaxy Laboratories

Discounted Cash Flow Valuation

On June 11, 2008, Ranbaxy Laboratories announced that DIS, Ranbaxy, and the Singh family (the promoters of Ranbaxy) had entered into a binding share purchase and share subscription agreement, pursuant to which DIS would acquire the entire holding of the Singh family in the company at ₹737 per share. DIS was to further seek to acquire majority of shares of Ranbaxy at the same price. This valued Ranbaxy at US$8.5 billion. The negotiated price of ₹737 represented a premium of 31.4% over the market price of Ranbaxy on the day of the announcement. Additionally, DIS acquired shares issued by Ranbaxy on preferential basis and also through an open offer (to comply with regulatory requirements). Further, 23,834,333 warrants were allotted to DIS with each warrant representing one share that could be converted at ₹737 per share at any time between 6 to 18 months from the date of allotment. In this respect, ₹73.70 per warrant was to be paid by DIS.

Company Backgrounds

Ranbaxy was incorporated in 1961 and went public in 1973. For the year 2009, the company recorded sales of US$1,519 million. The company derived 54% and 39% of revenues from emerging and developed markets. In 2009, North America, the company's largest market, contributed sales of US$397 million.

Europe and Asia generated US$269 million and US$441 million respectively. Ranbaxy was focused on increasing the momentum in its generics business through organic and inorganic growth.

Daiichi Sankyo was founded by Sankyo Shoten (financed jointly by Matasaku Shiobara, Shotaro Nishimura, and Genjiro Fukui) and was involved in R&, manufacturing, import, and sales and marketing of pharmaceutical products. Daiichi Sankyo's goal was to establish itself as a "global pharma innovator." The company had 2,300 overseas medical representatives in 33 locations, mainly in Europe and the USA.

Motives for the Acquisition

The acquisition would pave the way for creating a new and complementary hybrid business model that provided sustainable growth by diversification that spanned the full spectrum of pharma business.

Growth: While DIS grew at 4.7% in 2007 to US$7.12 billion, Ranbaxy grew at over 10% to US$1.6 billion. While the world pharma industry grew at 6%, the generics segment was growing at 11%. The pursuit of a dual business segment strategy would help DIS to improve its growth rate substantially. Jointly, the two companies would rank 15th in the global pharmaceutical market, whereas independently, Ranbaxy stood at 50th and DIS at 22nd.

Reach: DIS would be able to extend its reach to 56 countries (especially emerging markets) from 21 countries where it currently operated. DIS would get the front-end infrastructure. The combined business would have a significant position in India, Eastern Europe, and Asia and a big presence in Africa, Mexico, and Russia.

Cost savings in manufacturing, sales, and R&D: The most important benefit would be the low-cost manufacturing infrastructure and supply chain strengths of Ranbaxy. DIS would be able to bring in efficiency in its operations by sourcing Active Pharmaceutical Ingredients (APIs) and finished dosage products from Ranbaxy's nine manufacturing plants in India and many more in four other countries. One of the products DIS makes was Ofloxacin. Its sales in 2007 were ¥108.7 billion. The average cost of goods sold for DIS was about 30%. Mr Kurosawa of Daiichi believed that by sourcing it from Ranbaxy, DIS would save ¥6.52 billion. Capitalizing the savings at a 6% cost of capital, and based on 373 million share capital of Ranbaxy in 2007, the cost savings generated by outsourcing just one product would be ₹146 per share. Additionally, there will be cost savings for conducting clinical trials and collaborating on research and sales across the world.

R&D to speed-up new development: Ranbaxy would benefit from Daiichi's product pipeline and research facilities. Ranbaxy, after the acquisition, would get access to the proprietary drug portfolio of Daiichi.

Infusion of capital: Under the deal, Daiichi would infuse US$1.2 billion in equity by subscribing to securities issued by Ranbaxy. This would enable Ranbaxy to retire its debt. Ranbaxy expected to have a cash surplus of around ₹30 billion, which would further strengthen its balance sheet.

Valuation

As per Mr Kurosawa's estimate, cost savings (synergy) from one product would be ₹146 per share. The market price per share before the announcement was ₹561. So the fair value is ₹707 (i.e., ₹561 + 146). The price paid by Daiichi is higher than the intrinsic value. Of course, our valuation does not capture the value of other value-enhancing opportunities. Alternatively, one may estimate the intrinsic value by DCF valuation. Exhibit 3.10 presents the free cash flow to equity.

The intrinsic value can be estimated by discounting the forecasted free cash flow to equity. Assume the following CAPM parameters.

Risk-free rate = 7.5%
Beta = 0.8934

Exhibit 3.10

Panel A: Historical FCFE

	2002	2003	2004	2005	2006	2007
Net income	647.76	760.89	701.11	264.24	515.36	786.75
Depreciation	66.12	76.31	85.09	109.32	149.44	172.16
Capex	23.54	38.08	68.27	152.97	97.49	46.57
Change in working capital	0.00	476.12	–79.84	178.90	518.66	–7.49
Net borrowing	0.00	189.22	267.74	1,151.54	1,951.35	185.96
FCFE	690.34	512.22	1,065.51	1,193.23	2,000.00	1,105.79

Panel B: Forecasted FCFE

	2008E	2009E	2010E	2011E	2012E	2013E
FCFE	1,215.05	1,335.1	1,467.03	1,611.98	1,771.26	1,946.27
Total outstanding shares	45.9 million					

Market risk premium = 9%.
Cost of equity = 7.5% + 0.8934 (9%) = 15.54%.

Assume a terminal growth rate of 8%. Estimate the intrinsic value of the stock.

Case Study

Abbott's Acquisition of Piramal Healthcare

Multiples and DCF Valuation

On May 22, 2010, Abbott Laboratories of the USA announced the acquisition of Piramal healthcare for US$3.72 billion (₹17,500 crores or ₹837 per share). The compensation included an upfront payment of US$2.12 billion, with an additional US$400 million annually for the next 4 years.

Miles D White, chairman and CEO, Abbott[10] said:

> This strategic action will advance Abbott into the leading market position in India. The deal will complement our market-leading proprietary pharmaceutical offerings and pipeline in developed markets.

It would catapult Abbott from a negligible position to the top in the Indian pharmaceutical market, with a market share close to 7%. In terms of total turnover, it would be among the top 10, with a turnover of around ₹30 billion. Abbott would add 350 branded generic drugs from the Piramal portfolio. Abbott estimates the growth of its Indian pharmaceutical business with Piramal to approach 20% annually, with expected sales of more than US$2.5 billion by 2020. The Indian market was expected to more than double by 2015 to US$16 billion.

[10] "Abbott buys Piramal's pharma arm for US$3.7bn". See https://timesofindia.indiatimes.com/business/india-business/Abbott-buys-Piramals-pharma-arm-for-3-7bn/articleshow/5960176.cms, accessed September 7, 2017.

The Indian pharmaceutical market had witnessed a compound annual growth rate of 20% with significant growth in exports. Industry forecaster IMS Health had predicted that leading emerging markets would show annual pharmaceuticals sales growth of 14%–17% through 2014, against just 3%–6% a year in the developed markets.[11] Rising income levels, growing elderly population, increased awareness, and a shift from chronic diseases to lifestyle diseases such as diabetes and obesity were driving industry growth.

Piramal Healthcare was founded in 1988 by Ajay Piramal. Piramal Healthcare has the following businesses:

- Domestic formulations
- Custom manufacturing
- Critical care
- OTC consumer products
- Diagnostic services

"The India story is an attractive growth story, but globally and in emerging markets, there is a new way of selling drugs (patented products), which we would not have been able to do on our own," Ajay Piramal, chairman of the Piramal group said in a press meet. "The company's business will get an impetus with Abbott acquiring it."

Abbott is a global pharmaceutical and healthcare products company that operated in more than 130 countries. It employed around 90,000 employees. It was engaged in discovery, development and marketing of pharmaceuticals, hospital products, nutritional products, presence in both over-the-counter (OTC) drugs, and formulations. It had three main divisions: pharmaceuticals, medical products, and nutritional products.

The average share price of Piramal over the previous 6 months was ₹470. Glaxo was supposed to have bid US$1.5 billion for Piramal healthcare while Pfizer bid over US$1.7 billion. Given the valuations of competitors, US$3.7 billion was considered an awfully high price. We can verify whether Abbott overpaid

Exhibit 3.11 *Multiples of Piramal Healthcare*

	2010	2009	2008	2007	2006	Mean	Median
Price Earning (P/E)	20.87	15.59	22.23	29.31	34.27	24.454	22.23
Price to Book Value (P/BV)	5.9	3.41	6.23	5.04	5.93	5.302	5.9
EV/EBIDTA	13.09	8.67	14.32	16.55	20.94	14.714	14.32
Market Cap/ Sales	3.27	1.7	3.17	3.01	3.61	2.952	3.17
EPS	20.31	12.46	13.64	8.38	7.58	12.474	12.46
EBITDA	725.84	578.98	475.23	332.68	268.04	476.154	475.23
Sales	2,650.94	2,316.26	1,913.87	1,604.24	1,413.17	1,979.696	1,913.87
Book Value	71.8	56.89	48.63	48.71	43.83	53.972	48.71
No. of Shares	209,013,144	209,013,144	209,013,144	209,013,133	209,013,133		

Source: CMIE PROWESS Database.

[11] See http://timesofindia.indiatimes.com/business/india-business/Hinduja-buys-Luxembourg-bank-for-1-7bn/articleshow/5960182.cms, accessed September 7, 2017.

by performing multiples and DCF valuation outlined in the text. Exhibit 3.11 presents the data on multiples for Piramal.

Given an (initial) offer price, we can estimate how much Piramal is worth using trading multiples and discounted merger synergies. In undertaking a valuation we should decide:

- Which multiples are appropriate?
- Which firms are most comparable (if data on comparable acquisition transactions are being used)?
- How much is Piramal worth using multiples and discounted synergies?

Which Multiple?

Investment bankers and acquirers use a variety of pricing metrics such as price-to-earnings, market-to-book, sales, cash flow, and market capitalization. Exhibit 3.11 presents the trading multiples of Piramal. While there is a tendency to use certain multiples in certain industries, there is an opportunity to make a general point. In general, the following may be kept in mind while using multiples:

- Asset multiple (market-to-book ratio) generates more precise and less biased estimates than do the sales and earnings multiple.
- The earnings before interest, tax, depreciation and amortization (EBITDA) multiple generally yields better estimates than does the EBIT multiple.
- The accuracy and bias of value estimates vary greatly by company size, company profitability, and the value of intangibles.

Price may be estimated as a multiple of any of the following:

- Sales
- EBITDA
- EBIT
- Net income
- Book value (retained earnings)

This is essentially a simplified income statement. As you move down from sales to book value, accounting choices and distortions become more relevant due to income and cost recognition, depreciation rules, interest expense, and so on. While sales are the least affected, book value is the most affected (due to accounting distortions). But as you move down, you incorporate the effects of greater capital and operating efficiency. So the trade-off is between incorporating accounting distortions and recognizing operating efficiency. That is, as you move down, you are closer to cash flow—the driver of value. Why and when to use equity multiples (e.g., P/E or M/B) versus total enterprise multiples (e.g., EBITDA)? In choosing a multiple, find the one that has the lowest variance across all comparable company stocks. If none of the multiples do a good job of explaining transaction pricing, then it can help to triangulate using a variety of multiples as well as DCF analysis.

Piramal's average earnings per share (EPS) is ₹12.47. Multiplying it with the average P/E multiple of 24.45 yields a per share price of ₹305 (see Exhibit 3.12). Replacing the average EPS with the 2010 EPS yields a price of ₹496. Piramal's average EBITDA multiple was 14.71. Multiplying it with the average EBITDA yields a firm value of ₹106.8 billion. Subtracting the book value of debt (₹6.6096 billion) results in an equity value of ₹100.1904 billion (or ₹479 per share). This price is quite close to the average price that prevailed in the previous 6 months. Likewise, M/B and sales multiples yield per share values of ₹380 and ₹345 respectively.

We can supplement multiples valuation with DCF valuation of synergies by discounting synergy components at suitable discount rates. This calculation is shown in Exhibits 3.13, 3.14, and 3.15. Our DCF analysis suggests that Abbott could afford to pay a maximum premium of ₹172 per share or a total of about ₹540.

Subsequent Events

- The stock market reacted positively to the acquisition. The share price of Abbott increased from ₹956 on May 17, 2010 to ₹1,430 on November 19, 2010.
- The share price of Piramal Healthcare fluctuated between ₹542 on May 18, 2010 to ₹449 on November 18, 2010.
- Abbott's top line grew at 33% in 2011 and 48% in 2012. Before the acquisition, Abbott grew at an average of just 10% over the past 7 years.
- Even though the top line grew at 33% and 48% over the next 2 years, the EPS remained constant at about ₹46.

Exhibit 3.12 *Multiples Valuation of Piramal Healthcare*

Price/Earnings Multiple	
Piramal EPS (Average) ₹	12.474
Average EPS multiple	24.454
Equity value per share ₹	305.039196
Market capitalization	63,757,201,399
Piramal 2009 EPS ₹	12.46
Average EPS multiple	24.454
Equity value per share ₹	304.69684
Market capitalization	63,685,644,495
Piramal 2010 EPS ₹	20.31
Average EPS multiple	24.454
Equity value per share ₹	496.66074
Market capitalization	103,808,622,769

EBITDA Multiple		**Sales Multiple**	
Piramal EBITDA ₹cr	725.84	Piramal sales 2010 ₹cr	2,650.94
Average EBITDA multiple	14.714	Average sales multiple	2.952
Firm value ₹cr	10,680.00976	Firm value ₹cr	7,825.57488
Debt value ₹cr	660.96	Debt value ₹cr	606.96
Equity value (₹crores)	10,019.04976	Equity value ₹cr	7,218.61488
Equity value per share (₹)	479.350225	Equity value per share	345.3665517
Market capitalization (₹)	100,190,497,600	Market capitalization	72,186,148,800
Market/Book multiple			
Piramal BV (₹ crores)	71.8		
Average multiple	5.302		
Equity value per share (₹)	380.6836		
Market capitalization (₹)	79,567,876,105		

Source: CMIE PROWESS Database.

Exhibit 3.13

Outstanding Shares of Piramal (in million)	209
Shares (in million) of Piramal with	
Promoters	108.68
FII	54.758
Institutions	18.392
Private corporations	11.913
Public	15.257
NPV of total deal (US$ million)	3,334.9
No of shares brought (in million)	108.68
Dollar paid per share (US$)	30.68549871
Assuming exchange rate at 47 ₹/ US$ (₹)	1,442.218439
Average price of Piramal during the last 6 months (₹)	470.00

Source: CMIE Prowess and Casewriter.

Exhibit 3.14 *DCF Valuation of Synergy*

	2008	2009	2010	2011E	2012E	2013E	2014E	2015E
Sales of Abbott India	705	800	1,042	1,177	1,331	1,503	1,699	1,920
Sales of Piramal	1,997	2,383	2,708	3,141	3,644	4,227	4,903	5,688
Net profit of Abbott India	61	77	60	82	93	105	119	134
Net profit of Piramal	300	270	443	440	510	592	686	796
Total net profit	361	347	503	522	603	697	805	931
Expected additional net profit (synergy component)				182.77	211.14	243.95	281.88	325.73
Terminal value								4,621.90
Present value				$162.61	$167.13	$171.79	$176.60	$2,757.82
NPV of synergy	$3,435.96							
Income lost if competitors would have taken over	9.15	11.55	9	12.36	13.97	15.78	17.83	20.15
Terminal value								264.5748433
Present value				$10.90	$10.86	$10.83	$10.79	$151.84
NPV of income loss	195.21							

	2008	2009	2010	2011E	2012E	2013E	2014E	2015E
Total (crore)	3,631.17							
No of outstanding shares (crore) of Piramal	20.90							
Max premium that can be paid above 470 ₹	173.74							

Source: Author.

Assumptions:

1. Abbott sales are expected to grow at 13% and that of Piramal at 16%.
2. Net profit margins of Abbott and Piramal are assumed to be 7% and 14%.
3. Synergy (additional profits) is assumed to be 35% of total net income of the combined entity.
4. Terminal growth rate is assumed to be 5%.

Exhibit 3.15 *Estimation of Cost of Equity*

Risk-free rate	7%
Risk premium	8%
Beta levered (Abbott India)	0.8
Beta levered (Piramal)	0.6
Beta unlevered (Abbott India)	0.80
Beta unlevered (Piramal)	0.42
BV of equity (Abbott)	305.00
MV of equity (Abbott)	3,098.0
BV of debt (Abbott)	0.00
Total value (Abbott)	3,098.00
BV of equity(Piramal)	1,500.00
MV of equity (Piramal)	11,495.00
BV of debt (Piramal)	660.00
Total value (Piramal)	12,155.00

Weighted asset beta = Acquirer's asset beta (Value of acquirer/Total value) + Target's beta (Value of target/Total value) = 0.494.

Weighted equity beta = Weighted asset beta (Total value of the combined entity/Total value of equity) = 0.675.

Cost of equity of Abbott	13.4000%
Blended beta	0.675348
Blended cost of equity	12.40%

Source: Author.

REFERENCES AND SUGGESTED READINGS

Anslinger, Patricia L., and Thomas Copeland. 1996. "Growth through Acquisitions: A Fresh Look." *Harvard Business Review*, 74 (1, January–February): 126–35.

Arzac, Enrique R. 1996. "Valuation of Highly Leveraged Firms." *Financial Analysts Journal*, 54 (2, July–August): 42–50.

Bierman, Harold, Jr. 2002. "The Price-Earnings Ratio." *Journal of Portfolio Management*, (Summer): 57–60.

Copeland, Thomas, Timothy Koller, and Jack Murrin. 2000. *Valuation: Measuring and Managing the Value of Companies*, 3rd Edition. New York, NY: John Wiley.

Dodd, Peter. 1983. "The Market for Corporate Control: A Review of the Evidence." *Midland Corporate Finance Journal*, 1 (2, Summer): 6–20 .

Esty, Benjamin, and Mathew Millett. 1998, December. "The Acquisition of Consolidated Rail Corporation (A)." Harvard Business School Case Study No 9-298-006.

———. 1997, April 7. "Note on Value Drivers." HBS Case Study No, 9-297-082. Boston: Harvard Business School Publishing.

———. 2001, May. "The Acquisition of Consolidated Rail Corporation (B)." Harvard Business School Case Study No 9-298-095.

Fernandez, Pablo. 2001, June. "Valuation Using Multiples: How Do Analysts Reach Their Conclusions?" IESE Research Papers D/450. IESE Business School.

Fruhan, William F. 1979. *Financial Strategy: Studies in the Creation, Transfer and Destruction of Shareholder Value*. Homewood, IL: Irwin.

Fruhan, William, Jr. 1984. "How Fast Should Your Company Grow." *Harvard Business Review*, 62 (1, January–February): 84–93.

Fruhan, W. E., Jr., and Thomas R. Piper. 1981. "Is Your Stock Worth Its Market Price?" *Harvard Business Review*, (May–June): 125–26.

Haspeslagh, Philippe C., and David B. Jemison. 1991. *Managing Acquisitions*. New York, NY: The Free Press.

Hise, Richard T. 1991. "Evaluating Marketing Assets in Mergers and Acquisitions." *The Journal of Business Strategy*, 12 (July–August): 46–51.

Inselbag, Isik, and Howard Kaufold. 1997. "Two DCF Approaches for Valuing Companies under Alternative Financing Strategies and How to Choose Between Them." *Journal of Applied Corporate Finance*, 10 (1): 114–22.

Kaplan, Steven N., and Richard Ruback. 1995. "The Valuation of Cash Flow Forecasts: An Empirical Analysis." *Journal of Finance*, L (4, September): 1059–53.

Kopelin, John, Atulya Sarin, and Alan C. Shapiro. 2000. "The Private Company Discount." *Journal of Applied Corporate Finance*, 12 (4, Winter): 94–101.

Luehrman, Timothy A. 1997 "Using APV: A Better Tool for Valuing Operations." *Harvard Business Review*, (May–June): 145–54.

Mauboussin, Michael, and Paul Johnson. 1997, January 14. Competitive Advantage Period CAP: The Neglected Value Driver. New York, NY: CS First Boston Research.

Myers, S. C. 1983. "Evaluation of an Acquisition Target." *Midland Corporate Finance Journal*, (Winter): 39–46.

Palepu, Krishna, Victor L. Bernard, and Paul Healy. 1996. *Business Analysis and Valuation Using Financial Statements*. Cincinnati, OH: South-Western College Publishing.

Porter, Michael E. 1979. "How Competitive Forces Shape Strategy." *Harvard Business Review*, (March–April): 137–45.

Rappaport, Alfred. 1979. "Strategic Analysis for Profitable Acquisitions." *Harvard Business Review*, (July–August).

———. 1986. *Creating Shareholder Value: The New Standard for Business Performance*. New York, NY: The Free Press.

Ruback, Richard S. 1995, January. "A Note on Capital Cash Flow Valuation." Harvard Business School Case No. 9-295-069.

———. 2002, March. "Capital Cash Flows: A Simple Approach to Valuing Risky Cash Flows." *Financial Management* 31: 85–103.

Stapleton R. C. 1975. "The Acquisition Decision as a Capital Budgeting Problem." *Journal of Business Finance and Accounting*, 2 (2): 187–201.

Weaver, Samuel C., Robert Harris, Daniel W. Bielinski, and Kenneth F. MacKenzie. 1991. "Panel Discussion on Merger and Acquisition Valuation." *Financial Management*, (Summer).

REVIEW QUESTIONS

1. Refer to the data given.
   Beta = 1.40, market premium = 10%; Long-term *T*-Bond rate = 12%; Pre-tax cost of debt = 13.5%; Tax rate = 35%; and Target debt-to-value ratio = 0.45. The working results for the past 3 years are given as follows:

			(figures in US$ million)
	1995	**1996**	**1997**
Sales	9.0	9.9	11.0
EBIT	4.5	4.95	5.5
Depreciation	0.72	0.72	0.72

   The company has made Capex of US$0.72 million each year in the last 3 years. It is expected to grow at 10% for the next 3 years and drop to 5% thereafter in line with growth in sales. Working capital is expected to be 15% of sales. Additional depreciation for the next 3 years on the new equipment will be provided on straight-line basis. Free cash flows are expected to grow at 5.5% in perpetuity after 3 years. Determine the value of the company.
2. The APV approach and the WACC approach should yield same results. Can you think of a situation when they diverge?
3. The executives of Nova Chemicals are evaluating a potential acquisition candidate, Reddy Chemicals. The forecast of free cash flow under the current management is given.

	Year				(figures in US$ million)		
	0	1	2	3	4	5	6
Revenues		455	551	800	1,080	1,195	1,255
COGS		341.3	414.9	596	811.10	893.9	941.3
SGA exp		110.4	130	219.2	251.6	280.3	287.4
= NOPAT							
+ Depreciation		19	21	21	46.3	48.1	50
– Capex	100	8.1	9.5	13	16	16.3	17
– Working Capital	25	4.1	5.5	6.0	7.1	8	9.7
Free cash flow							

Cash flows are expected to grow at 6.5% after year 6.

The executives of Nova believe that NOPAT margin can be improved by 8% and working capital investment can be cut by 20%. Reddy chemicals has a strong marketing network that could be used to sell Nova's existing products. The arrangement is likely to generate savings of US$1 million per annum for 8 years.

	for Nova	for Reddy
Cost of equity 20%	22%	
Tax rate	35%	35%
Cost of debt	12.5%	13.5%
Target D/V	30%	20%

a. Estimate the value of Reddy under current management.
b. Estimate the value of Reddy for Nova.
c. Can Nova's cost of capital be used to discount cash flows of Reddy? If yes, when? If not, why not?
d. Nova intends to increase debt by US$2.5 million. What is the value of interest tax shields to Nova? Assume that debt is permanent.
e. Conduct a sensitivity analysis.

4. ABC Ltd is considering the acquisition of XYZ Ltd. The management of ABC believes that cost of goods sold could be reduced by 1.5% over the next 3 years (due to purchasing economies) and Administrative expenses could be brought down by 3%. The forecast of income statement of XYZ under ABC is given: (figures in US$)

Year	1	2	3
Sales	60,000	63,000	66,000
COGS	30,000	31,000	33,000
Depreciation	4,000	4,200	4,300
SGA	21,000	22,000	22,500

Assume that cash flow increases at 7% after year 3. ABC needs to incur expenditure on fixed assets and working capital to make operational improvements to XYZ, the details of which are given as:

Year	1	2	3
Capex	4,900	5,100	5,300
WC	(510)	(540)	(550)

At a discount rate of 13% what is the maximum price that ABC should pay?

APPENDIX 3A: VALUATION USING MULTIPLES

In valuing targets, decision-makers often use multiples in conjunction with the DCF methodology. Several multiples are popular.

The P/E multiple is the ratio of stock price and earnings per share for the most recent four quarters or market capitalization and net income. The (average) P/E multiple commanded by comparable transactions when multiplied by earnings per share (of the target) yields a per share price for the target. Alternatively, one may estimate price using DCF methodology and, hence, P/E multiple for the acquisition and compare it with those of comparable transactions.

The Gordon valuation model suggests that

$$P = \frac{D}{k - g}$$

where P is the stock price, D is the annual dividend, k is the firm's cost of equity, g is the firm's growth rate.

This can be rewritten as

$$P = \frac{(1 - b)E}{k - g}$$

where b is the retention ratio and E is earnings.

Dividing both sides by E,

$$P/E = \frac{(1 - b)}{k - g}$$

Thus, P/E multiple is a function of retention ratio, cost of equity and growth rate.

The price-to-sales multiple is the ratio of stock price and sales per share or market capitalization and sales. The P/S multiple implied by the DCF valuation may be compared with P/S multiples of comparable transactions.

The price-to-book value multiple is the ratio of market capitalization to book value of shareholders' equity.

The enterprise value to EBITDA multiple is the ratio of E/V (i.e., market value of equity plus book value of debt) and EBIDTA. Applying this multiple yields *firm* value not *equity* value.

APPENDIX 3B: ESTIMATING GROWTH RATES

A company's equity value is largely determined by the growth in sales, earnings, and dividends. Growth rates can be measured in several ways:

Arithmetic Versus Compound Growth Rates

The arithmetic average of growth rates in sales for the past 10 years, say, is simply the sum of annual growth rates for the period divided by 10. Compound average in contrast measures the rate at which the sales has grown for the entire period using the equation:

$$S_n = S_o (1 + g)^n$$

where S_n is the sales in the 10th year, S_o is the sales in the current year, g is the growth rate, and n is the number of years. One can solve for g given the value of all other variables.

Moving Average

A moving average is simply the average of growth rates for a specified period of time. Assume that the following data is available. You are required to calculate 3-month moving average.

Growth Rate for Each Time Period (%)	3-month Total	3-month Moving Average
5		
6		
5.5	16.50	5.50
6.5	18.0	6.0
7	19.0	6.33
7.5	21.0	7.00
8.0	22.50	7.50

The moving average may be calculated for any other period (say 6 months or 1 year). The moving average depicts the basic trend after removing seasonal fluctuations.

CHAPTER

Valuation of Privately Held Companies

Pitabas Mohanty

Learning Objectives

- Highlight the issues involved in the valuation of private companies
- Provide an overview of alternate valuation approaches
- Suggest a methodology for estimation of cost of capital for unlisted firms

Valuation of private companies is very similar to the valuation of any other economic asset. The free cash flows of the private company are forecasted and then discounted at a risk-adjusted discount rate to get the value of the company. Though the valuation of a private company is similar to that of a public company, an analyst faces some additional constraints in estimating the inputs required for valuation.

WHY IS VALUATION OF PRIVATE COMPANIES DIFFICULT?

First, a sizeable number of the private companies are in their early stages of development and generate negative free cash flows. In the initial stages of the life of a company, the set-up costs in the form of capital expenditure, R&D expenditure, and so on are high. Since the gestation period is long, the net operating profit after tax (NOPAT) of a company itself would be low. The valuation of the company in such cases would be sensitive to the assumption that an analyst makes about when free cash flows turn positive. The problem is similar to the valuation of distressed firms.

Second, while valuing a private company, one usually does not have access to the past financial performance of the company. The problem gets manifested in two ways. A sizeable number of private limited companies are new because of which there is a limit on the number of years' data that one can get while analyzing the financial performance. The information disclosure requirements for private companies are less stringent compared with those for listed companies. In many countries, private companies are not required to file their income statements with the concerned authority, although they may have to file the balance sheet every year. This makes it difficult to analyze the past financial performance of a private company. Consequently, forecasting free cash flows is problematic.

Third, if the purpose of valuation is to take the company public, certain adjustments to free cash flows are to be made. One adjustment involves top management compensation. In private companies, withdrawal of profits by promoters is treated as dividend payment. However, when the company becomes public, the expense is treated as salary paid by the company.

Fourth, estimation of beta of a private company is difficult due to lack of availability of stock price data. Usually, analysts estimate the beta of a public company by regressing the historical stock returns of the firm against that of a market index such as the S&P 500. Because private companies are not listed, analysts estimate the beta of other "comparable" companies (or the average of comparable firms) and use it to estimate the cost of equity of a private company.

Fifth, the capital asset pricing model (CAPM) assumes that investors hold diversified portfolios and, hence, demand compensation for bearing systematic risk. Since the shareholders of a private limited company usually do not hold a diversified portfolio, they demand a premium for bearing unsystematic risk as well. Consequently, CAPM underestimates the true cost of equity for such firms.

Finally, the cost of capital used in valuation is a function of market value leverage ratio. Since the securities issued by private companies are not traded, it is not possible to estimate leverage.

ALTERNATE VALUATION APPROACHES

Though the discounted cash flow (DCF) method is the most scientific method used in the valuation of a private company,[1] some analysts also use the multiplier method to value private companies. In this section, we will briefly discuss the two methods and see how they can be used to value a private company.

Multiplier method (relative approach to valuation): In multiples valuation, multiples such as price-earnings (P/E) or price-to-book value (P/BV) of publicly traded firms are used to value the private company.

Selection of a comparable company is a difficult exercise because of differences in size, risk, and business of companies that are being compared. However, one must keep the following factors in mind while selecting a comparable firm. Assume that an analyst has decided to use the *P/E method* to value the company. From the Gordon valuation model we know that:

$$P_0 = \frac{D_1}{r-g} = \frac{E_1 * \text{Payout\_ratio}}{r-g}$$

$$\Rightarrow \frac{P_0}{E_1} = \frac{\text{Payout\_ratio}}{r-g} \tag{1}$$

From the equation, it is clear that we can compare the P/E ratio of the two companies only if we can also compare their "payout ratios," "cost of equity," and "g."

[1] Assuming there are no real options to value.

Payout ratio and growth rate: We know from basic corporate finance that the product of retention ratio and the return of equity equals growth rate.[2] That is

$$\text{ROE} * \text{Retention\_ratio} = \text{Growth\_rate}$$
$$\Rightarrow \text{ROE} * (1 - \text{Payout\_ratio}) = \text{Growth\_rate}$$

Therefore, we must ensure that both companies have similar profitability ratios and a similar growth profile. It is important to understand that a company can finance its growth through debt or external equity and that the derivation of the growth rate formula assumes that the company does not finance its growth through external debt or equity.

Cost of equity: If one uses the CAPM to estimate the cost of equity, one must select a comparable firm in such a manner that the betas of two firms are equal. The beta of a levered firm can be written as:

$$\beta = \beta_U\left(1 + (1-t)\frac{D}{E}\right) - \beta_D\frac{D}{E} \tag{2}$$

We can see from the equation that beta is a function of debt-to-equity ratio (financial risk).

From the discussion it becomes apparent that while selecting a pure-play company, we must ensure that the following factors are comparable for the two firms.

1. Profitability ratio
2. Growth opportunity
3. Business risk
4. Financial risk

Analysts usually estimate the median P/E ratio of all companies in the same industry and use that as a proxy for the P/E of the company being valued. This approach may not be appropriate for the following reasons.

1. It is not necessary for all companies to have similar profitability ratios and growth profiles. If a private company is new, then it is likely to have a below-median profitability ratio and above-median growth rate.
2. It is also possible for a private company to have a higher debt ratio than a typical company in the industry.

Two other multiples, P/BV of a stock and price-to-sales of a stock, are also popular.

Price-to-book value (P/BV) method: P/BV is estimated by dividing the stock price by the accounting book value per share. In this method, analysts multiply the P/BV ratio of a comparable firm with the book value (BV) of the company being valued. The Gordon's Valuation Model can be manipulated to derive the following relationship.

$$P = \frac{D}{r-g} = \frac{E * b}{r-g} \tag{3}$$

where "b" stands for payout ratio.

[2] Here we are assuming that the company is financing growth through internal accruals.

We know that ROE $= \frac{E}{BV}$

Therefore, E = ROE × BV. Substituting this in the Gordon model, we obtain:

$$P = \frac{ROE * BV * b}{r - g}$$

$$\Rightarrow \frac{P}{BV} = \frac{b * ROE}{r - g} \quad (4)$$

That is, P/B ratio is a function of payout ratio, return on equity, cost of equity, and growth rate. While selecting a pure-play company, we must ensure that these factors are comparable for the two firms.

Similar analysis could be done for the price-to-sales (P/S) multiple.

Price-to-Sales (P/S) Ratio: P/S ratio is defined as the ratio of total market capitalization and total sales. Equivalently, it can be defined as the ratio of stock price and sales per share.

$$P = \frac{D}{r - g} = \frac{E * b}{r - g} = \frac{Sales * Operating\_Margin * b}{r - g}$$

$$\Rightarrow \frac{P}{Sales} = \frac{Operating\_Margin * b}{r - g} \quad (5)$$

The multiplier approach is often supplemented by DCF approach.

DCF Approach: The DCF approach is based on sound economic principles and is universally acclaimed as one of the most scientific methods to value a company.

The value of a company is given by

$$Value = \sum_{t=1}^{\infty} \frac{FCF_t}{(1 + WACC)^t} \quad (6)$$

Although the methodology is similar to that of valuing a listed company, there are some additional problems in applying the DCF approach to unlisted companies. These are discussed below.

DETERMINATION OF COST OF CAPITAL

The cost of capital can be written as

$$WACC = \frac{\text{Market value of equity}}{\text{Value of company}} * \text{Cost of equity} + \frac{\text{Market value of debt}}{\text{Value of company}} * \text{Cost of debt} * (1 - \text{tax rate}) \quad (7)$$

Therefore, we need estimates of market values of debt and equity, costs of debt and equity, and the cash tax rate to estimate the cost of capital of a company. The problems one encounters in estimating these parameters for a private company are discussed further.

Estimating Market Value of Equity

The market value of equity of a private company is unavailable because the stock is not traded. Further, cost of capital is based on target market value capital structure. Quite often, the current book value leverage is taken as a proxy for target market value leverage. According to modern finance theory, investors demand returns based on market values and not book values. The two values rarely coincide. Unfortunately, measuring market value of equity is difficult. The market value of equity is the present value of equity cash flows (ECFs), but the discount rate used to discount ECFs itself is supposed to be based on market value of equity, that is, there is a circularity problem.[3] This problem could be overcome by estimating the value of equity using book value proportions and a series of iterations.

The following example illustrates the problem.

Assume the following figures (Table 4.1) for a hypothetical company.

Assume that the market value of debt and the book value of debt are equal, that is, the pre-tax cost of debt and the coupon on the bond are equal.

Also assume that we know the cost of equity for the company. Of course, cost of equity itself is a function of the financial leverage of a company. However, analysts usually estimate the cost of equity independently without explicitly bringing the debt/equity (D/E) ratio into picture. Since we discuss the issues relating to cost of equity separately, let us assume that this figure is known to us.

Table 4.1 *Determination of Market Value of Equity Using Iterative Method*

	US$million
Book value of equity	200
Book value of debt (= Market value of debt)	100
Cost of debt (also equal to the coupon rate on bond)	5%
Cost of equity	10%
Cash tax rate	20%
Return on equity	15%
Growth rate	5%

Table 4.2 *Determination of Cost of Capital*

	US$million
Expected net income	30
Expected dividend[4]	25
Value of equity	500
Value of debt (assumed)	100
Value of company	600
True cost of capital	9%

[3] For the mathematical derivation of the results, see Mohanty (2003).

[4] Here since it is a growth company, we must increase debt by 5% as well to keep the market DE ratio constant. This has been factored into our calculation while estimating the dividend. Secondly, it can be verified that to support a growth of 5%, the net investment for the next year will be US$10 million.

The other figures used in the Table 4.1 could be obtained directly from the financial statements of a company. The intrinsic value of the company is US$600 million (see Table 4.2). For a private company, only the book value of equity (and debt) would be known. The cost of capital and the market value of equity can be estimated through a series of iterations.

Iteration 1: Estimate the cost of capital using the book leverage weight. Suppose the cost of capital equal is 8%. The value of the firm (after considering the net investment to support a continuous growth of 5%) is US$800 million and the value of equity turns out to be US$700 million.

Iteration 2: Now that we have an estimate of the value of equity, we can re-estimate the cost of capital by using US$700 million (rather than US$200 million) as the value of equity. This gives us a revised estimate of 9.25% as the cost of capital. The revised values of the firm and equity are US$565 million and US$465 million respectively.

Iteration 3: We can continue with this procedure till we reach a point of convergence. In this example, we try to solve the problem in nine iterations. Table 4.3 and the accompanying charts (Figures 4.1, 4.2, and 4.3) explain the details.

Figures 4.1 and 4.2 suggest that the values converge after three iterations. In this example, we started our first iteration by using the book value leverage to estimate the cost of capital. Book

Table 4.3 *Cost of Capital and Value of Equity in Different Iterations*

Iteration	WACC	MV of Equity
1	0.08	700.00
2	0.09	464.70
3	0.089	509.52
4	0.09	497.66
5	0.089	500.58
6	0.09	499.85
7	0.089	500.03
8	0.09	499.99
9	0.09	500.00

Figure 4.1 *Graphical Depiction of the Value of Cost of Capital in Different Iterations*

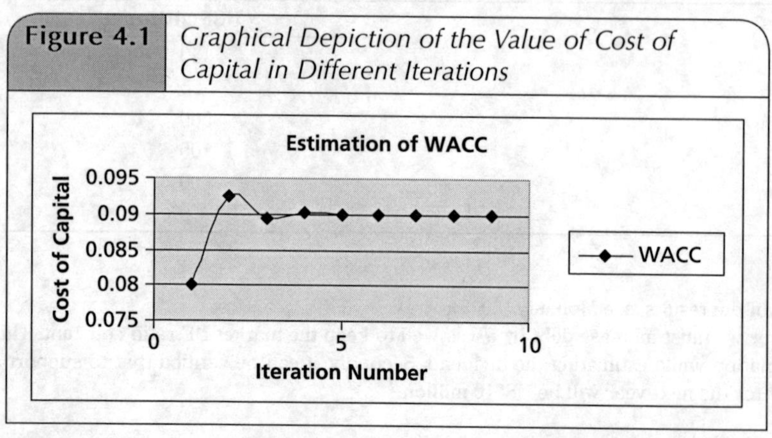

Figure 4.2 *Graphical Depiction of the Value of Equity in Different Iterations*

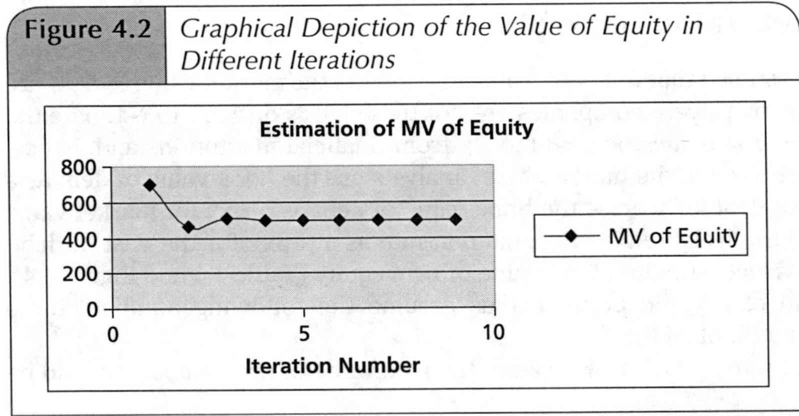

values suffer from credibility problems. Accountants can manipulate earnings, which has an impact on leverage ratios. It can, however, be shown that we get the correct value of cost of capital and the value of the firm (or equity) even by using any arbitrary value of the D/E ratio. To justify our claim, we show that we get the same values of equity and cost of capital by assuming a debt-to-equity ratio of 7/3.

In Table 4.4, the second column provides estimates of the cost of capital assuming 7/3 as the debt-to-equity ratio. The third column gives the cost of capital if one were to use book-leverage.

Table 4.4 *Cost of Capital with an Arbitrary Starting Value*

Iteration	WACC-Arbitrary	WACC-Book Value
1	0.058	0.08
2	0.098	0.09
3	0.088	0.08
4	0.09	0.09
5	0.089	0.08
6	0.09	0.09
7	0.089	0.08
8	0.09	0.09
9	0.089	0.08

Figure 4.3 *Cost of Capital in Different Iterations*

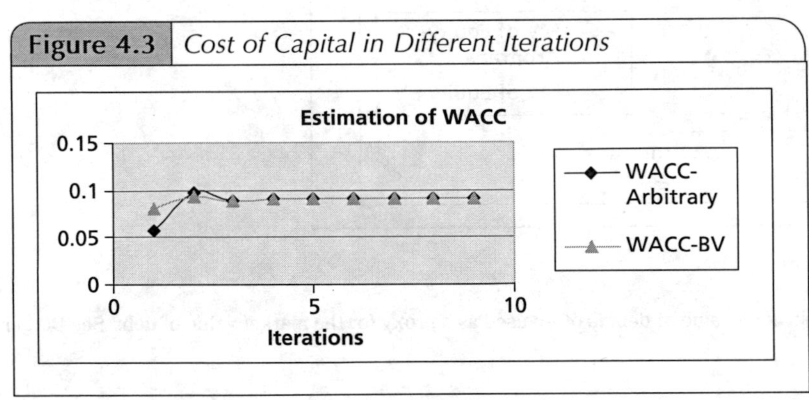

Estimating the Market Value of Debt

In the previous section, we assumed that the book value of debt and the market value of debt are equal. Since securities issued by private companies are not traded, it is difficult to estimate the market value of debt. Private companies borrow money from financial institutions and, hence, such debt instruments do not trade in the market. Most analysts use the book value of debt as a proxy for the market value of debt.[5] If we use the book value of debt as proxy for market value of debt, then one has to use the weighted average coupon rate as a proxy for the cost of debt. Otherwise, we would get a wrong estimate of the value of firm/equity (Table 4.5 and Figure 4.4).

A simple example would clarify the point. Let us assume the following numbers for a hypothetical private company (Table 4.6).

Assuming that the growth rate in cash flow is zero, the true value of the company would be US$520 million.

Sometimes we may know a firm's pre-tax cost of debt (using statistical models) but not its market value of debt.

Table 4.5 *Equity Values Through Iterations*

Iteration	MV of Equity-Arbitrary	MV of Equity-BV
1	2,900	700
2	400	464
3	531	509
4	492	497
5	501	500
6	499	499
7	500	500
8	499	499
9	500	500

Figure 4.4 *Equity Value in Different Iterations*

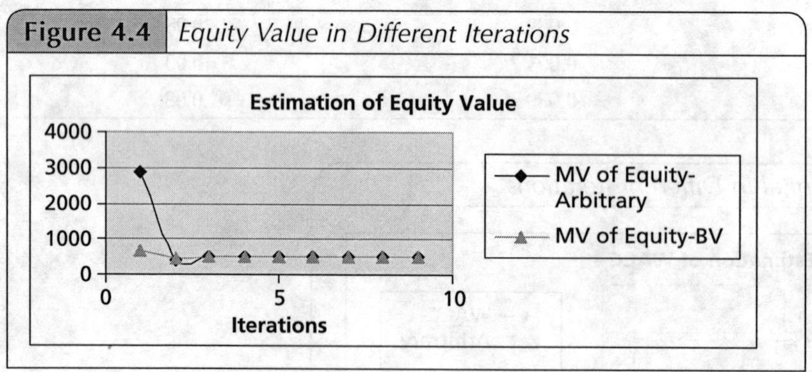

[5] Even in empirical research work, book value of debt is often used as a proxy for the market value of debt. See Berger and Ofek (1995) for an example.

Table 4.6 *A Hypothetical Example*

Net Operating Income US$Millions	**100**
Coupon	10%
Face value of bonds US$	100
Pre-tax cost of debt	12%
Market value of bonds US$	83.33
Tax rate	30%
Net income US$ millions	63

We have the following choices.

- Use the book value of debt as a proxy for the market value of debt. However, use the true cost of debt to estimate the value of firm and equity.
- Use the book value of debt as a proxy for the market value of debt. Use the coupon rate (weighted average coupon rate if there are more than one issue) as a proxy for the true cost of debt.[6]

The first method results in a cost of capital of 13.73% and a value of the firm of US$509.8 million. Since the value of debt is assumed to be US$100 million, the value of equity is US$409.8 million. This is about 2.5% less than the true value of equity, which is US$420 million.

The second method yields a wrong estimate of cost of capital—13.46%—as opposed to a true cost of 13.91%. However, this method yields a correct value of equity because the value of firm under the second method is US$520 million, which gives us the true value of equity as US$420 million (see Table 4.7 for details).

If the objective of the entire valuation exercise is to find the true value of the equity, then the second method will always be preferable. One should not, however, jump to the conclusion that the market value of debt is irrelevant if the weighted average coupon rate is known. Although the second method gives us the correct value of equity, it still gives us the wrong value of the firm. If we are interested in finding the optimum debt-to-equity ratio of a company or in knowing the contribution of total debt to the total firm value, then we should know the true cost of debt and the true value of debt.

In sum, if one were to use the book value of debt as a substitute for the market value of debt, then it is preferable to use the weighted average coupon rate as the pre-tax cost of debt, for this is the only way one can get the correct value of equity.

In the previous discussion, we assumed that the growth rate of the firm is zero. This is an unrealistic assumption. Growth companies pose one more problem in valuation. Since the equity value grows at a particular rate, the market value of debt must also increase at the same rate to ensure that the debt-to-equity ratio remains constant.[7] Therefore, it matters whether we increase the book value of debt or the market value of debt at a particular rate. This also

[6] The second method is better than the first method. The first method invariably gives an inaccurate value of equity.

[7] For a detailed theoretical discussion, see Miles and Ezzel (1980).

Table 4.7 *Value of Equity Under Two Different Assumptions*

Wrong Method 1: Assume that BV of Debt = MV of Debt, True Cost of Debt	
WACC that one will obtain	0.137307692
Value of Company	509.803926
Less: Value of Debt	100
Value of Equity	409.8039216
Wrong Method 1: Assume that BV of Debt = MV of Debt, Cost of Debt = Coupon Rate	
WACC that one will obtain	0.134615385
Value of Company	520
Less: Value of Debt	100
Value of Equity	420

has a bearing on the market value of equity since this directly affects the free cash flow to equity.

ESTIMATING THE COST OF DEBT

To estimate the cost of debt, we suggest the following pecking order be used.

Pecking Order 1: Find the yield-to-maturity of the bond

If the debt instrument is traded in the market, it is easy to estimate the cost of debt. The cost of debt is just the internal rate of return (IRR) of the bond. In the following equation, "y" is the pre-tax cost of debt.

$$\text{Market\_price} = \frac{\text{Coupon}_1}{(1+y)^1} + \frac{\text{Coupon}_2}{(1+y)^2} + \dots + \frac{\text{Coupon}_T}{(1+y)^T} + \frac{\text{Facevalue}}{(1+y)^T} \quad (8)$$

As private companies may not have issued bonds traded on exchanges, market values are unavailable. Therefore, the above method cannot be used to estimate the cost of debt for a private company.

Pecking Order 2: Ask someone who knows

If a company has borrowed from commercial banks and financial institutions, it can elicit from them the rate of interest they would charge if they were to lend now. The philosophy behind this method is: "*If you do not know something, ask someone who knows.*"

Pecking Order 3: Use the credit rating of the company

Given the credit rating of a company, it is possible to estimate the cost of debt for a company by observing the prevailing rates in the same rating class. Thus, for example, if a company has an AAA rating and another company with an AAA rating pays 12% to issue new bonds, then 12% is the pre-tax cost of debt for the first company. Credit rating agencies regularly publish updates of ratings of all rated companies. Therefore, it is possible to use these ratings to obtain the pre-tax cost of debt. The logic behind this method is that the market treats all bonds with similar ratings alike as far as fixing of interest rate is concerned and, therefore, if one AAA-rated company is paying 12% now, then all companies with the same rating would pay 12% (*if they borrow now*).[8]

Pecking Order 4: Rate the bonds yourself

Not all companies get their instruments rated. In some countries instruments with maturities less than a specified number of years need not obtain a rating. Further, no rating would be available if a company were to borrow from private sources. In such situations we will have to rate the instrument.

One can develop a credit rating model using discriminant analysis. Alternatively, one can use the median-ratios of different rating classes to estimate the rating of a firm. One can, for example, use Panel A of Table 4.8[9] to find the tentative rating that S&P would give to a company. In Panel B of Table 4.8, we present median ratios for bonds rated by Moody's.

Table 4.8 *Median Ratios of Some Selected Accounting Ratios for Different Credit Ratings*

Panel A: S&P Median Ratios

Adjusted Key Industrial Financial Ratios
US Industrial Long-term Debt
Three Year (1998–2000) Medians

	AAA	AA	A	BBB	BB	B	CCC
EBIT int.cov. (x)	21.4	10.1	6.1	3.7	2.1	0.8	0.1
EBITDA int.cov. (x)	26.5	12.9	9.1	5.8	3.4	1.8	1.3
Free oper. cash flow/total debt (%)	84.2	25.2	15	8.5	2.6	–3.2	–12.9
FFO/total debt (%)	128.8	55.4	43.2	30.8	18.8	7.8	1.6
Return on Capital (%)	34.9	21.7	19.4	13.6	11.6	6.6	1
Operating Income/Sales (%)	27	22.1	18.6	15.4	15.9	11.9	11.9
Long-term debt/Capital (%)	13.3	28.2	33.9	42.5	57.2	69.7	68.8
Total Debt/Capital (including STD) (%)	22.9	37.7	42.5	48.2	62.6	74.8	87.7
No of Companies	8	29	136	218	273	281	22

Panel B: Moody's Median Ratios

	Aaa	Aa	A	Baa	Ba	B	Caa
EBITA/Average assets	15.3	15.6	12.5	10.1	9.6	7.3	2
Operating margin	14.9	17	13.8	12.6	12.2	8.5	1.6
EBITA margin	14.8	17.5	15.2	13.9	13.4	9.4	2.4
EBITA/Interest expense	17	13.7	8.2	5.1	3.4	1.5	0.3
(Funds from Op + Interest expense)// Interest expense	15.5	15.5	9.6	6.6	4.7	2.6	1.5

Source: Moody's Corporate Finance.

[8] Credit rating agencies rate the instrument and not the company. Some complications may arise due to this.

[9] Can be downloaded from www2.standardandpoors.com/spf/pdf/fixedincome/corpcrit2003r.pdf (accessed on March 31, 2006).

Estimating Cost of Equity

To estimate the cost of equity, analysts usually use the CAPM, which states that the expected return of a stock is directly related to its systematic risk.

$$E(R_i) = R_f + \beta(E(R_m) - R_f) \quad (9)$$

where E (Ri) is the expected return of the stock

R_f is the risk-free rate of return,

Beta is a measure of systematic risk and is defined as:

$$\beta = \frac{\text{Covariance}(R_i, R_m)}{\text{Variance}(R_m)}$$

E (R_m) is the expected return on the market portfolio.

Estimation of Beta

The CAPM could be used to estimate the cost of equity for a listed firm. An unlisted firm, by definition, would not have stock market data. In such a situation one can resort to the "pure play" approach. Since the beta of a private firm is unobservable in the market place, a proxy beta derived from a publicly traded firm whose operations are similar to the firm in question is used as a measure of the firm's systematic risk. The pure play approach attempts to identify firms with publicly traded securities that are solely engaged in the same line of business as the private firm. These comparable firms are called pure play firms. A firm should satisfy the following characteristics to qualify as a pure play firm:

- The firm should have only one business line and no miscellaneous revenue.
- The pure play should be in the same industry or business line as the firm in question.
- The revenues of the pure play should be roughly the same as those of the unlisted firm.
- When more than one firm can be identified as a potential pure play, the firm with the median beta could be chosen as the pure play.

In addition, one must make sure that the private company and the pure play company are comparable in terms of the operating and financial leverage.

The levered betas of comparable companies are unlevered using the following relationship and are used as proxy asset beta (unlevered beta) for the private company.

$$\beta_A = \beta_E \, E/V$$

where E is the market value of equity, V is the value of firm, and β_A and β_E are asset and equity beta respectively.

This approach works well if the firm has a single product line but is difficult to implement if the firm is diversified. After all, there is no rule that private companies have to operate in a single line of business. In such a case, it might be difficult to identify pure play companies. To illustrate, assume that we are valuing a private company that has interests in cement, textile garments, and soda ash. If we want to use the pure play approach, then we must identify companies that are in cement, textiles, soda ash, and nothing else. Not only that, if the private company obtains 50% of its revenue from cement, then our pure play company must also obtain approximately 50% of its revenue from cement. The same rule applies for garment and soda ash.

An alternative method is available that can help us doing precisely what the pure play approach does, but without having to identify pure play companies. This method uses multiple regression to estimate the beta of a company. This method is based on the simple premise that the portfolio beta is just a weighted average of the betas of stocks comprising the portfolio.

$$\beta_{\text{portfolio}} = \sum_{i=1}^{n} w_i * \beta_i \tag{10}$$

Here there are n stocks in the portfolio, and

$$w_i = \frac{\text{MC}_i}{\sum_{i=1}^{\text{n}} \text{MC}_i}$$

where MC is the market capitalization of the stock.

Thus, the beta of a company with interests in steel and real estate is the weighted average of betas of steel and real estate divisions. That is,

$$\beta_{\text{company}} = w_{\text{steel}} * \beta_{\text{steel}} + w_{\text{real\_estate}} * \beta_{\text{real\_estate}}$$

Suppose we have the beta estimates of "m" number of companies. Assume that we also know their product lines. If we can find the W's, we can estimate the beta of different segments by regressing the company beta on the W's. Suppose, the total number of divisions (or segments) that all the "m" companies is "n." A meaningful regression is possible if we ensure that "m" is far greater than "n," that is, m>>n.

We have not yet discussed how to obtain the W's in the above regression. These are the portfolio weights and represent the percentage contribution of each division to the total market value of the company. Thus, for example, if the total market value of a company is US$100 million and the cement division is contributing US$50 million toward the market capitalization, then

$$\text{W}_{cement} = 0.5$$

But we do not know the market value of equity of the cement division itself. In fact, we may be doing this very exercise to find the market values of the different divisions in the first place. In practice, therefore, analysts use the total sales of the division rather than its market capitalization. Thus, for example, suppose the sales of the cement division and the total turnover of the company are US$40 million and US$80 million respectively, thens

$$w_{\text{cement}} = \frac{\$40 \text{ million}}{\$80 \text{ million}} = 0.5 \text{ million}$$

We must resolve another issue before running the multiple regression,[10] Should we use unlevered beta as the dependent variable? Since we do not know the market leverage ratio of private companies, it makes more sense to run the regression using levered betas. Research studies show that in the multiple regression approach, it does not matter whether we lever or

[10] See, for example, Erhardt and Bhagwat (1991), and Wood, McInish, and Lawrence (1992).

unlever the beta. We get a similar answer in both the cases. Therefore, we will use levered beta directly as the dependent variable.

Now we run the following multiple regression equation:

$$\beta_i = w_{i,1} * \beta_1 + w_{i,2} * \beta_2 + \ldots + w_{i,n} * \beta_n \,\forall i.$$

It is to be kept in mind that we are running a regression by forcing the intercept to equal zero. This adjustment is necessary. Otherwise we will not be able to interpret the exact meaning of the intercept. We may be led to a silly conclusion that a company that does no business, has no sales, and so on still has a positive (or negative) beta.

In the above regression equation,

β_i is the levered beta of the ith company

$w_{i,k}$ is the percentage contribution of segment-K to company i

β_k is the beta of segment K, K = 1,…, n

Not all companies would be manufacturing all the products. If a particular company is not manufacturing, say, steel and suppose segment-2 stands for steel, then in our regression, $W_{i,2}$ would be zero.

Most consultants do maintain beta-books that contain beta for individual segments such as steel, food, health care, and so on. The beta book needs to be revised periodically as betas fluctuate over time.

Empirical research shows that portfolio beta is always more stable than individual equity beta. Therefore, it is better to use industry beta if there is a significant difference between individual equity beta and industry beta.[11]

Estimating beta using accounting variables: Some academics observe that beta can be estimated on the basis of certain fundamental factors such as the dividend payout, asset growth, leverage, liquidity, asset size, earnings variability, and the accounting beta. Since these values can be easily estimated for private companies, one can directly estimate the beta of private companies by using a simple ordinary least squares (OLS) regression approach.

Should we worry about unsystematic risk? CAPM assumes that the market prices systematic risk alone because unsystematic risk can be diversified away by holding a portfolio of assets.[12] A risk-averse investor with a concave utility function would gain by diversifying away unsystematic risk. Therefore, it makes sense to assume that rational investors do bear systematic risk alone and, hence, expect compensation for bearing systematic risk.

However, private companies are owned by investors who do not hold well-diversified portfolios. The reason is that a substantial part of the total wealth of the owners of any private company is correlated with the value of the private company. The owners, therefore,

[11] The weighted average of betas of stocks in the same industry group, say, Pharma, is called industry beta; the weights are market capitalization (number of shares outstanding multiplied by market price) of individual companies.

[12] Estimation of the CAPM parameters is discussed in great detail in Damodaran (1994), Copeland, Koller, and Murrin (1994), and Ehrhardt (1994).

bear both systematic and unsystematic risk. Cost of equity, as measured by the CAPM, therefore, underestimates the return expected by the shareholders of the company.[13]

If the private company is likely to go public or expected to be taken over by a listed company the shareholders of which are already well diversified, then we do not need to worry about the premium for unsystematic risk.

DETERMINATION OF CASH FLOWS

While valuing a private company, we need to keep certain facts in mind while estimating free cash flows. In particular, one has to adjust for the following:

Some top managers prefer to receive their remuneration in the form of dividends rather than salaries. This is done deliberately to artificially increase the net income reported by the company, especially before an initial public offering (IPO). Due care must be taken in forecasting the salaries of the company.

Taxes: Private companies (particularly those in the nascent stages of their development) get some favorable tax treatment. However, they lose this favored treatment once they go public. Therefore, the cash tax rate increases after the company goes public.

Other expenses: Public companies are required to maintain a detailed record of their transactions for a certain number of years. They also need to make periodic disclosures of accounting information to the shareholders and the general public. A private company does not incur any of these expenses.

CONCLUDING COMMENTS

Theoretically, there is no difference between the valuation of a private and a listed company. In real life, however, one faces certain constraints, as some of the inputs required for valuation are usually not available for private companies. In this chapter, we discussed the constraints that an analyst faces while valuing a private company and the possible solutions to these problems.

The valuation of private companies is a difficult and often subjective process because a private company has no stock (market) price to serve as a benchmark. Several multiples are in vogue.

The *P/E multiple* is the ratio of stock price and earnings per share for the most recent four quarters (or market capitalization and net income). For example, if a competitor has sold his or her business at a price of five times its net income, then the same P/E multiple may be applied.

Likewise, the *price-to-sales multiple* is the ratio of stock price and sales per share or market capitalization and sales.

The *P/BV* multiple is the ratio of market capitalization to book value of shareholders' equity.

[13] Fama and Jensen (1985), for example, observe that an undiversified owner will demand a higher risk premium before investing in risky assets.

The *enterprise value (EV) to earnings before interest tax depreciation and amortization (EBITDA)* multiple is the ratio of EV (i.e., market value of equity plus book value of debt) and EBITDA. Applying this multiple yields *firm* value, not equity value.

It must be understood that it is not easy to either find comparable transactions or apply the "right" multiple because of differences in risk, growth rate, capital structure, size, and timing of cash flows between the comparable transaction and the company in question. Often companies apply a discount to comparable public transactions to account for lack of marketability of private company shares. A recent study in the USA compared the valuation ratios paid for the private and public companies and found that private companies are acquired at an average 20%–30% discount relative to similar public companies when using earnings multiple as the basis for valuing the transactions (Kopelin, John, Sarin, and Shapiro 2000).

Private company discount = 1 – (private company multiple/public company multiple). One may look at similar transactions and infer a private company discount.

REFERENCES AND SUGGESTED READINGS

Berger, P. G., and E. Ofek. 1995. "Diversification's Effect on Firm Value." *Journal of Financial Economics*, 37 (1): 39–65.

Copeland, T., T. Koller, and J. Murrin. 1994. *Valuation: Measuring and Managing the Value of Companies*, New York, NY: John Wiley & Sons, Inc.

Damodaran, A. 1994. *Damodaran on Valuation*, New York, NY: John Wiley & Sons, Inc.

Ehrhardt, M. C. 1994. *The Search for Value*. Boston, MA: Harvard Business School Press.

Ehrhardt, M. C., and Y. Bhagwat. 1991. "A Full Information Approach for Estimating Divisional Betas." *Financial Management*, (Summer): 60–69.

Fama, E. F., and M. C. Jensen. 1985. "Organizational Forms and Investment Decisions." *Journal of Financial Economics*, 14 (1): 101–19.

Kopelin, John, Atulya Sarin, and Alan C. Shapiro. 2000. "The Private Company Discount." *Journal of Applied Corporate Finance*, 12 (4, Winter): 94–101.

Miles, J. A., and J. R. Ezzel. 1980. "The Weighted Average Cost of Capital, Perfect Capital Markets, and Project Life: A Clarification." *Journal of Financial and Quantitative Analysis*, 15 (3): 719–30.

Mohanty, P. 2003. "Note on the Estimation of the Cost of Capital." Unpublished Paper: X L R I, Jamshedpur, India.

Wood, R. A., T. H. McInish, and K. D. Lawrence. 1992. "Estimating Divisional Betas with Diversified Firm Data." *Review of Quantitative Finance and Accounting*, 2(1): 89–96.

REVIEW QUESTIONS

Mechanical Equipment Ltd is in the process of acquiring Vishy Corp, a small privately held machine tool manufacturer. The pro forma projections for Vishy are presented in Exhibit 4.1.

Since Vishy is unlisted stock market data is not available. So the executives of Mechanical Equipment decided to examine comparable companies. The financial data for comparable companies is presented in Exhibit 4.2.

Other data:

- Yield of 10 year treasury bonds = 7.5%
- Interest on debt = 10%
- Tax rate = 35%
- The company has no debt.

Exhibit 4.1 *Pro-forma Projections for Vishy*

	(US$ '000)				
	2012	2013	2014	2015	2016
Net sales	9,000	14,000	32,000	42,000	50,000
COGS @37% of net sales					
SG&A @ 45% of net sales					
Current assets @ 32% of net sales					
Net fixed assets @ 2% of net sales					
Current ratio = 2.3					

Exhibit 4.2 *Comparable Company Data*

	(US$m)							
	Company A				**Company B**			
	2008	**2009**	**2010**	**2011**	**2008**	**2009**	**2010**	**2011**
Sales	80	75	60	55	150	185	230	300
Debt	5	6	7	8	2.5	5	7	7
Equity	15	16	17	18	55	68	130	200
Beta (levered)				1.4				1.3
Market value				103				850

	Company C			
	2008	**2009**	**2010**	**2011**
Sales	18	18.5	18	19
Debt	0.5	0.6	0.6	0.7
Equity	3.0	2.4	2.5	3.5
Beta (levered)			1.1	
Market value			70	

Estimate:

1. Free cash flow
2. Unlevered beta for comparable companies and Vishy Corp
3. Levered beta for Vishy Corp
4. Cost of equity for Vishy
5. How does your answer change when the beta is estimated as sales or market value weighted?
6. The value of the firm when:
   a) The company has no debt
   b) The company borrows US$3 million, US$4 million, and US$5 million for 3 years starting from 2012 and remains at that level forever. Use capital cash flow valuation.

Assume that the company grows at 5% in perpetuity after 2016.

CHAPTER 5

Real Options Analysis in Mergers and Acquisitions

Vishwanath S. R. and
Chandrasekhar Krishnamurti

Learning Objectives

- Introduce real options analysis as an alternative to the discounted cash flow (DCF) methodology
- Outline the different types of real options
- Highlight the types of real options encountered in M&A

An option gives the holder the right, but not the obligation, to buy or sell a designated asset at a predetermined price. A *call* option gives the holder the right to buy the underlying asset by a certain date for a certain price. A *put* option gives the holder the right to sell the underlying asset by a certain date for a certain price. The contract price is known as strike price or exercise price; the date in the contract is known as expiration date. *American* options can be exercised at any time up to maturity, and *European* options can be exercised only at maturity. Options can be further classified into financial and real options. When the underlying asset of the option contract is a stock, a stock index, a foreign currency, a debt instruments, or a commodity, it is termed as a financial asset. The underlying asset in the case of real option is a real asset.

Most companies implicitly hold real options. The example of a business that has the option to defer the investment is one type of real option. The first account of a real option is found in the writings of Aristotle (Copeland and Keenan 1998a). Thales, a Sophist philosopher, divined from some tea leaves that there would be a bountiful olive harvest in the next season. He bought the right to rent olive presses from the owners of olive presses for a normal rent. When the bountiful harvest arrived, others did not have pressing capacity. So Thales rented the presses to them at above-market rates and pocketed a profit. What Thales had purchased is an option, but not the obligation, to rent the press. If the harvest were to be poor, he could walk away by losing a small "premium."

REAL OPTIONS IN CORPORATE FINANCE

The term "real options" was coined by Professor Myers of MIT in an article published in 1984. In his words:

> Strategic planning needs finance. Present value calculations are needed as a check on strategic analysis and vice versa. However, standard discounted cash flow techniques will tend to understate the option value attached to growing profitable lines of business. Corporate finance theory requires extension to deal with real options. (Myers 1984)

Real options are widely prevalent in corporate finance. We discuss the identification and valuation of real options in this section. Subsequently, we focus on real options in M&A. We believe that a thorough understanding of the application of real options in corporate finance will facilitate our appreciation of the real options framework in M&A.

There are six categories of real options commonly used in corporate finance. They are:

- Timing option
- Growth option
- Abandonment option
- Option to expand scale
- Option to switch inputs and outputs and
- Option to contract scale.

The first step in real options analysis is to recognize them. Exhibit 5.1 presents a partial listing of real options by sector.

Timing Option

Capital projects are like call options in the sense that both involve the right, but not the obligation, to acquire an asset at a specified price on or before a certain date. The analogy between project characteristics and call option is given in Exhibit 5.2.

The amount spent on the project is the exercise price. The present value of cash flows from the project is the stock price. The length of time the company can defer the investment decision

Exhibit 5.1 *Typical Real Options by Sector*

Aerospace	Valuing options in customer contracts
Banking and Securities	Valuing real estate leases
Automotive	Decisions to modify new car designs
Chemicals	Timing of investment
Energy	Timing the development of oil and gas fields switching inputs
Pharmaceuticals	Growth options embedded in R&D projects

Source: Copeland and Keenan (1998b).

Exhibit 5.2 *Project Characteristics and Option Variables*

Project Characteristic		Call Option
Expenditure required acquiring the asset	X	Exercise price
PV of cash flows	S	Stock price
Length of time decision may be deferred	t	Time to expiration
Riskiness of underlying operating assets	σ^2	Variance of stock returns
Time value of money	r_f	Risk-free rate of return

without losing the investment opportunity corresponds to time to maturity. The uncertainty in the project's cash flows corresponds to the standard deviation of returns. The cash flows lost due to competitors who have fully committed corresponds to dividends.

The impact of an increase in each of options variables on the value of the option is shown in Exhibit 5.3. Like financial options, the value of timing option can be found using the option value tables.[1]

Recall that the net present value (NPV) of a project = PV of cash flows – Initial investment

$$= S - X$$

Timing options enable managers to defer investment for a certain period of time without losing the opportunity. In other words, managers would always want to spend later rather than sooner. If an investment can be deferred for 1 year, one could deposit the money in a bank for 1 year and withdraw it when the time is ripe to invest, that is, the proceeds of X would be available after 1 year. Since the money was deposited at r_f for 1 year, the present value of X discounted at r_f represents the amount to be deposited now.

$$PV(X) = X/(1 + r_f)^t$$

Since our objective is to refine NPV to incorporate other options, variables such as r_f, t, and, σ let us redefine NPV as S – PV (X). As with financial options, this can be expressed as a ratio.

$$NPV = S/PV(X)$$

And cumulative variance = $\sigma^2 t$ (cumulative volatility is the square root of cumulative variance).

We can use these two values to estimate the value of the option as percent of value of the underlying assets. An illustration follows.

An oil company has an investment opportunity to develop some reserves. The PV of future cash flows is currently US$100 million. The firm can lock in the investment now by incurring an expenditure of US$80 million. Alternatively, it may wait for 2 years by paying an up-front fee of US$6 million and then making an investment of US$90 million to develop the reserves. Based on the volatility of price of oil, the annual standard deviation of returns for the oil field is 35%.[2] Interest rate is 8%.

[1] See any standard corporate finance text.

[2] It is not correct to estimate the volatility of the cash flows from the oil project on the basis of volatility of oil *prices*. It can at best give a first-cut measure. Estimating volatility will be discussed later.

Exhibit 5.3 *The Impact of Changes in Option Variables on the Value of Real Option*

Variable	Value of Real Option
Increase in the PV of the Project	Increase
A higher investment cost	Decrease
A longer time to maturity	Increase
Increase in uncertainty (Volatility of cash flows)	Increase
Increase in risk-free rate	Increase
Increases in cash flow lost	Decrease

The value of the first alternative is US$20 million. That is NPV = $20 million.

The value of the second alternative is

X = 90, S = 100

PV (exercise price) = $90/1.08^2 = 77.16$

Value of operating assets/PV (X) = 100/77.16 = 1.296

$$\sigma(\sqrt{t}) = 0.35 \times \sqrt{2} = 0.50.$$

Look for the corresponding row and column from the option pricing table. The option value is 31% of asset value = 0.31 × 100 = $31 million.

NPV = $31 million – fees = $31 million – $6 million = $25 million.

The value of flexibility, therefore, is $25 million – $20 million = $5 million. It obviously makes sense to wait and then invest.

Timing options are important in all natural resource extraction industries, real estate development, farming, and paper products.

Growth Option

A growth option is characterized by an early investment (say in R&D), which leads to a chain of interrelated projects opening up future new-generation products and processes, access to new market, oil reserves, and so on. Any investment that creates new investment opportunities can be characterized as a growth option. Companies derive their value from two sources: assets-in-place and present value of growth opportunities. Stock markets realize it when pricing securities. Just as a package of bond and warrants are valued separately, the option component embedded in projects should be evaluated separately and then added to the value obtained from the DCF methodology. Assume that a project is expected to lead to a second-generation investment. The NPV of the entire proposal may be written as:

$$\text{NPV} = \text{NPV (Phase 1)} + \text{Call value of Phase 2.}$$

Traditional NPV analysis does not account for further expansion opportunities.

To evaluate growth options embedded in projects:

- Segregate discretionary expenditure and its associated cash flows of Phase 2 project from Phase 1.
- Find the NPV of Phase 1 using the traditional DCF approach.

- Discount the discretionary spending to the present using an appropriate *risk-free rate*. If the discretionary spending that leads to Phase 2 project is to be made in the third year, discount it to the present by using a 3-year risk-free rate. This constitutes X.
- Find the present value of cash flows (net of inflows and *routine* expenditure on working capital and fixed assets) using weighted average cost of capital (WACC). This is S.
- Find S/PV(X).
- Estimate cumulative volatility ($\sigma\sqrt{t}$); t is 3 years in this case. Estimation of σ is discussed at a later stage.
- Find the value of the call option and add it to the NPV of Phase 1.

Most capital investments are phased investments, and phased investments are compound options, that is, an option on an option. When there are multiple stages in expansion, each stage represents an option on the next stage as given.

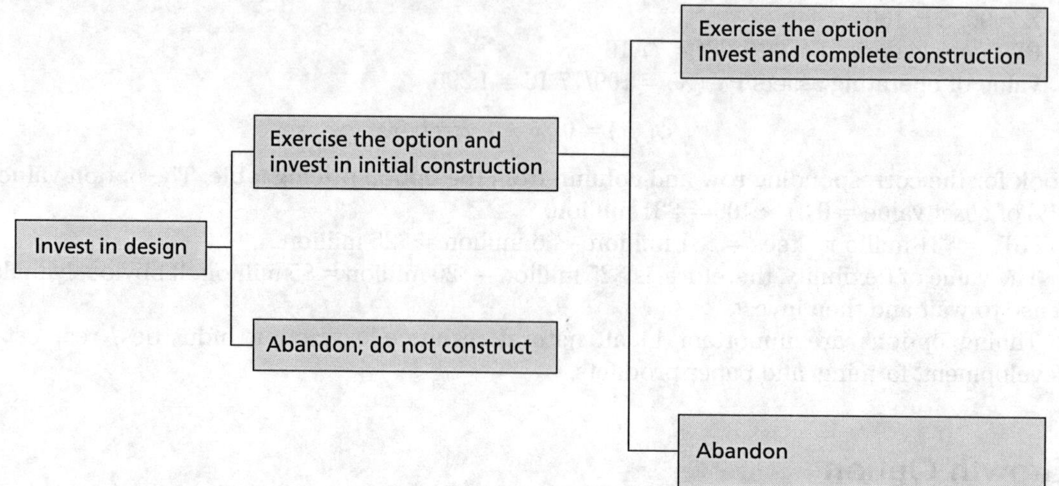

So it is inappropriate to treat projects with multiple stages of expansion as simple call options. These are call options on call options, call options on put options, or put options on put options and so on. Since compound options are more complex, we do not discuss them here.[3]

Abandonment Option

If market conditions deteriorate severely, management can abandon operations and realize the resale value of project assets in second-hand markets. Abandonment options are important in capital-intensive industries, financial services, and new product introduction in uncertain markets.

In a competitive industry with overcapacity, management has to continuously consider whether to stay or get out. The actual decision depends on the value of the project below which management may choose to abandon and the value above which extension could take place. Consider an example. A mining company is considering opening up a gold mine for 2 years. If

---

[3] Interested readers may refer to Rubinstein (1992).

gold price goes up, revenue would go up; whereas if gold prices go down, revenues would go down. The NPV analysis is based on the assumption that the company will continue digging even if revenues are down (thereby incurring a loss). The company might choose to abandon if gold price goes down in both the years. The NPV calculation does not recognize this possibility.

Abandonment options exist in most businesses and are more valuable when uncertainty is high. An option to abandon is a *put* option. The value of the put option can be found by replicating the payoff from the put option. It is possible to construct a portfolio consisting of a fraction of the project (Δ) and lending an amount B at the risk-free rate r that replicates the payoff on the put.[4] Let the payoffs from the project be $V_{1,1}$ and $V_{1,2}$, and those from the replicating portfolios be $P_{1,1}$ and $P_{1,2}$ in the two states of the world.

The payoffs from the replicating portfolio are:

$$P_{1,1} = \Delta V_{1,1} + B(1 + r)$$
$$P_{1,2} = \Delta V_{1,2} + B(1 + r)$$

Solve for Δ and B.

$$\Delta = \frac{(P_{1,1} - P_{1,2})}{(V_{1,1} - V_{1,2})}$$

$$\text{and } B = \frac{P_{1,1} - \Delta V_{1,1}}{(1 + r)}$$

Since the payoffs from the portfolio are identical to the payoffs on the put, the current price of the put must be equal to the current value of the portfolio.

$$P_0 = (\Delta)(V_0) + B$$

Natural Resource Investments: A Special Case

Natural resource investments such as mining and oil exploration are uniquely suited for real options analysis. The owner of a mine, for example, has the option to defer exploration, close or reopen, or even abandon a mine. The owner of the mine has the right to acquire the output of the mine (e.g., copper) at a fixed exercise price (the variable cost of production). When output prices are low and the fixed costs of operating the mine are high, it might be prudent to shut down the mine, at least temporarily till output prices bounce back.

Assume that you have a 2-year right to mine a copper deposit. The mine is known to have eight million pounds of copper.[5] The development of the mine involves a cash outlay of US$1.25 million, and the development itself is expected to take 1 year at the end of which the owner can mine or subcontract extraction to a third party by paying an extraction cost. Assume that the extraction costs are 85 cents per pound. The owner can then sell the output to another party at the spot price 1 year from now. The sequence of activities is shown in a following time line diagram:

[4] This is based on Sachdeva and Vandenberg (1993). Also see Robichek and Van Horne (1967), Courtadon and Merrick (1983), Mason and Merton (1985), and Cox, Ross and Rubinstein (1979). Any standard text on options/ derivatives would discuss the binomial model in great detail.

[5] This example is based on an unpublished note by Professor Campbell Harvey, Duke University.

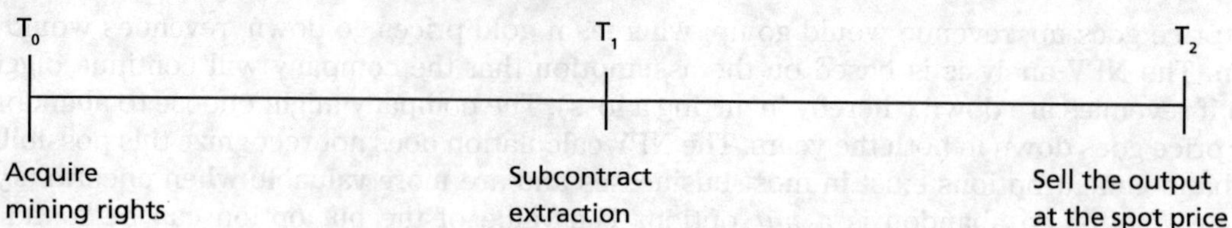

Percentage changes of copper prices follow a normal distribution with a mean of 7% and standard deviation of 20%. The current price of copper is 95 cents per pound. The required rate of return for the project is 10% and the risk-free rate is 5%.

$$\text{The NPV of the project} = -1.25 + \frac{8\,[E(S_1) - 0.85]}{1.1}$$

Where $E(S_1)$ = expected spot price of copper 1 year from now.

The expected spot price $E(S_1) = S_0\, e^{\mu T} = 0.95\, e^{0.07} = 1.0189$.

NPV = –0.022. This analysis ignores the fact that the owner can abandon the project after the development if the spot price is less than 85 cents. This is a 1-year call option on copper with a strike price of 85 cents. The value of the call option can be estimated as:

Value of call $= S_0\, N(d_1) - K\, e^{-rt}\, N(d_2) = 0.95\, N(d_1) - 0.85\, e^{-0.05}\, N(d_2)$

where

$$d_1 = \frac{\ln(S_0 \div K) + r_f + \sigma^2/2}{\sigma\sqrt{t}} = \frac{\ln(0.95 \div 0.85) + 0.05 + .02}{0.20} = 0.906$$

$$d_2 = d_1 - \sigma\sqrt{t} = 0.706$$

Call option value = 0.162.

The "true" NPV = –1.25 + (8) (0.162) = 0.046 million or US$46,000.

In many natural resource investments like oil exploration, there are two sources of uncertainty: the quantity of oil in the ground and the price of oil. Options that derive their value from two or more sources of uncertainty are called rainbow options. Using the simple option-pricing model to value such options can lead to biased estimates of value.

Other Options

If price or demand changes, management can change the output mix of the facility. Such options are termed option to switch (output). These are important in those cases where the good is sought in batches or is subject to uncertain demand. Examples are consumer electronics, toys, and specialty paper. Likewise, management may have the option to switch inputs as in the case of oil, electric power, and agricultural crops. In case of power projects, for example, management can choose the technology in such a way that the flexibility to switch between alternate fuels is retained. This flexibility though comes at a price and can be advantageous depending on the relative prices of fuels and their volatility. Management can switch to the cheaper alternative when the situation warrants.

ESTIMATING VOLATILITY

One of the inputs to the option-pricing model is the variance of returns. In case of equity options, the standard deviation of stock returns in the immediate past (say, 6 months or 3 months) is used to estimate the value of volatility. Another approach is to estimate the volatility "implied" by past option prices. That is, given all parameters and the option price, one may find out volatility by trial and error. In case of real options, the underlying asset is the project. How should volatility be estimated since the project's returns are unobservable? There are many alternatives:

1. Estimate the volatility of a stock market index and take it as proxy for volatility of project returns. Companies can have higher or lower volatility than a broad-based index. Further, cash flows from projects within companies are probably more volatile. What's more, volatility of an index gives the value of volatility of *equity prices*. What we need is the volatility of project returns. In sum, the volatility of a stock market index is only a rough estimate.
2. Calculate the implied volatility of the options on the company's stock and take it as proxy for the project's variance.
3. Use spreadsheets (or sophisticated packages like Crystal Ball) to simulate project's cash flows and estimate the standard deviation of the project's returns.

MANAGING REAL OPTIONS

The value of the real option depends on the underlying variables such as present value of operating cash inflows, outflows, time to maturity, volatility of cash flows, risk-free rate of interest, and cash flow lost due to competition. The value of the option can be (and should be) managed by increasing the present value of cash inflows, decreasing the PV of cash outflows, increasing the uncertainty in cash flows, extending the opportunity's duration, and reducing the value lost by waiting to exercise. One may reduce the value lost by waiting, for example, by erecting entry barriers to competitors (e.g., locking in key customers). Likewise, the present value of cash inflows can be increased by raising prices or reducing expenses.[6] As mentioned earlier, the value of an option can be expressed as a function of two metrics S/PV (X) and $\sigma\sqrt{t}$. The value of option increases if either (or both) increases. A company may classify projects on an option space as shown (see Luehrman 1998a, 1998b).

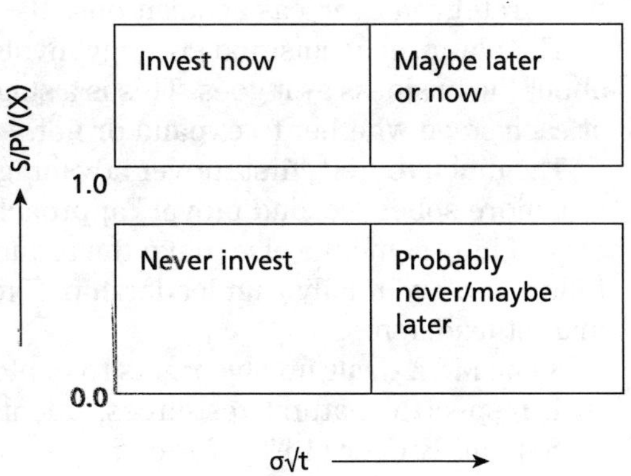

Those projects that have low volatility but high S/PV(X) should be exercised immediately, that is, the company must invest immediately. Those projects that have low volatility *and* low value-to-cost ratio should never be exercised. Those projects with moderately high volatility and value-to-cost ratio may be harvested now, and those with negative NPV, positive value-to-cost ratio, and

[6] It might not be possible to increase prices unless the product has unique features. To add unique features, one may have to invest in capital equipment, marketing and so on. This raises X. That is, altering one variable may have an impact on others. So one should ascertain the *net* impact on the option value.

moderately high volatility may be exercised at a later date when conditions improve. In sum, a manager is required to proactively cultivate a company's projects. Proactive cultivation needs constant monitoring and support to promising projects. Assume that a company has a portfolio of projects of which some have negative NPV. Conventional capital budgeting suggests that they should be discarded. That is incorrect. The principal insight gained from real options analysis is that these projects should be actively cultivated if they have high cumulative volatility.

APPLICATIONS OF REAL OPTIONS IN MERGERS AND ACQUISITIONS

Real options framework is invaluable in the analysis of M&A. It can be gainfully employed in all phases of M&A such as strategic planning, deal design, and post-merger integration.[7]

Real Options in Strategic Planning

When managers discuss M&A plans from a strategic perspective, they tend to use terms such as "rights," "flexibility," and "commitments." These are veiled terms denoting optionality. Some acquisitions tend to create flexibility, while others destroy them. Flexibility is an option and should be treated as such in financial analysis. Flexible investments can be altered as conditions change. Examples of flexibility options include the holding of excess cash, inventory, or manufacturing capacity.

Some M&A involve strategic actions that can hedge a firm's exposure to risk. Insurance works like a put option and should be included as such in the analysis.

Several strategic acquisitions are motivated by the creation of strategic competencies. Gaining more know-how creates strategic competencies and engenders a more flexible workforce. This flexibility constitutes a valuable real option.

Several multinational firms value learning about an unfamiliar market before jumping in fully. Some acquirers obtain first-hand knowledge about the firm by acquiring an interest in the firm and taking a board seat before completing the full acquisition. Anheuser-Busch followed this strategy in overseas acquisitions.

The platform acquisition strategy involves a series of acquisitions that allows a firm to learn about the business as it goes. This is a staged investing process that permits the buyer to decide at each stage whether to expand or not.

The much touted "first-mover advantage" and "winner takes all" approaches have given way to a more sober "second mover" approach in recent years. This perspective has the advantage of watching someone else make the arduous market discovery and then make a quick move to follow and eventually gain leadership. Excel followed Lotus and Visicalc but eventually gained market leadership.

Some M&A deals involve rights to exploit an uncertain resource. This is especially important with respect to natural resources, talent, and intellectual property. Weatherford and Bodily (1988) and Bruner (1988), for example, value the right to drill in a natural gas field using real option techniques. Real option theory can offer a useful framework for identifying attractive

---

[7] We do not discuss real options approach to post-merger integration here.

targets that are undervalued as well. Rappaport and Maubossin (2002) follow this approach in determining buy and sell strategies.

Real Options in Deal Design

Real options are rampant in deal design. The formal contract in many instances is structured as a contingent right. If terms and conditions are satisfied, then the buyer is allowed to acquire the target. In many cases, a buyer typically approaches target shareholders with an offer to buy the shares at a stated price within a stipulated period. The buyer has effectively granted a put option to the target shareholders.

Many M&A deals include topping fees and penalties for not completing the deal. These are rights to payments in the event of nonperformance by one party or another. Since these are contingent payments, they are like options.

The ability to sell an asset on demand is like a put option. Control works like holding a call option on future strategy.

M&A sometimes involve the use of contingent payments such as earnouts. These contingent payments are call options on future performance.

Both buyers and sellers face transaction risks in concluding M&A transactions. This risk can be mitigated by the use of caps, collars, floors, and contingent value rights.

Takeover defenses such as poison pills, lock-ups, and control rights are options.

LIQUIDITY AS AN OPTION

Liquidity and control are rights, and their value must be estimated in terms of their option value. Liquidity discounts have been modeled using option pricing theory. Alli and Thomson (1991) compute the value of liquidity as the value of a put option with a strike price equal to the share price at the date of the issue. Longstaff (1995) estimates the upper and lower bounds of the value of liquidity as the price of a look back option. A subset of his results is reproduced in Exhibit 5.4.

It is seen that the discount due to illiquidity is driven by two major factors: uncertainty and time. The greater the uncertainty in the value of the underlying stock, the greater will be the discount for illiquidity. Furthermore, the longer the delay in exiting from an investment, the greater will be the discount for illiquidity.

Exhibit 5.4 *Upper Bounds for Percentage Discounts Due to Lack of Marketability (Percentage Discounts from Marketable Values)*

Marketability Restriction Period	Volatility = 10%	Volatility = 20%	Volatility = 30%
180 days	5.768	11.793	18.082
1 year	8.232	16.984	26.276
2 years	11.793	24.643	38.605
3 years	19.128	40.979	65.772

Source: Longstaff (1995).

Finnerty (2002) applies this option-based view to a cross-section of letter stock discounts. He found that the discount was predominantly determined by volatility, the length of the restriction period, the riskless rate, and the stock's dividend yield. Furthermore, he documents the finding that dividend payments tend to moderate the size and variability of the discount. When he used the options-based model to assess the actual discounts, he found that it performed well for volatility values in the range of 30%–70%.

CONTROL AS AN OPTION

Control is a call option on the alternate strategies and policies of the firm. Control bestows the right to direct the strategies and activities of the firm. Furthermore, the right to allocate resources and to distribute the economic wealth of the firm also ensues from control. We should emphasize the two key characteristics of control that have option-like features: contingency and volatility. The value of control is contingent on the success of current strategies. If the current strategy works well, the option to switch strategies is out of the money. If the existing strategy works inadequately, then the option to switch is in the money. Furthermore, the value of control depends on the volatility of the values of the firm under current and alternate strategies. The value of control also depends on the uncertainty of those values. Control will be worth more in situations of greater uncertainty.

Thus "control premium" that is frequently mentioned in M&A transactions is the price of the control right. This term is not to be confused with "purchase premium." This is because purchase premium incorporates the value of both control and the expected synergies. In situations where one shareholder has controlling power and the others do not, the value of the dominant shareholder's equity interest will reflect the control premium. Accordingly, the value of minority shareholders will suffer a discount.

A naïve view of controlling power is the ability to command at least 50.1% of the votes. But in most cases, no single owner holds more than 50% of the shares. This is because most ownership is widely dispersed in most listed firms. Thus, effective control may be achieved with as little as 20% of the shares. Another view of controlling power holds that voting power is contingent, that is, votes are relevant only in the context of some game. Lloyd Shapley came up with an insightful breakthrough in developing the process for computing the *Shapley value*. The Shapley value is the ratio of the number of combinations of voting groups in which a given investor j is pivotal to the outcome, divided by the number of all possible combinations. The pivotal shareholder decides the outcome of a voting contest. Quite clearly, the larger the shareholding of investor j, the more powerful investor j is, due to the larger Shapley value. Thus, we can see that controlling power arises from holding relative rather than absolute power in most cases.

Consider the case when two competing raiders are seeking proxies for a takeover target. The power of the mass of atomistic shareholders depends on the relative power of the two powerful raiders. Exhibit 5.5 presents Shapley values for the mass of atomistic shareholders for a range of scenarios. It is seen that atomistic shareholders are relatively powerful in the absence of relatively powerful voting blocks. As the two proxy contestants gain more votes, the power of the atomistic shareholders declines. In general, it is true that the power of atomistic shareholders increase as their collective votes increase. An exception is found in the southeast corner of the table where even with modest holdings, the atomistic shareholders are quite powerful.

Exhibit 5.5 *Sensitivity Analysis of Shapley Values of Atomistic Shareholders in a Hypothetical Proxy Contest*

Votes of Control Shareholder #2	Votes of Control Shareholder #1			
	10%	20%	30%	49%
10%	0.78	0.65	0.50	0.05
20%	0.65	0.56	0.48	0.06
30%	0.50	0.48	0.50	0.09
49%	0.05	0.06	0.09	0.50

There are two divergent views regarding the potential beneficiaries of control. One school holds that control is valuable because it presents an opportunity for majority to expropriate the wealth of the minority. The other school posits that control confers the option to direct the strategy of the firm in ways that benefit all shareholders. We elaborate on these two views further.

The phenomenon in which controlling shareholders expropriate the wealth of minority shareholders is called "tunneling." Empirical evidence on the private benefits school of thought is provided by Dyck and Zingales (2004). They examined a large sample of M&A transactions from 39 countries and found that the premium paid for control is higher in countries that protect their investors less and facilitate extraction of private benefits. A recent and emerging body of research confirms that cross-shareholding arrangements and pyramiding are widely prevalent in countries with poor protection for minority shareholders. Bebchuk, Kraakman, and Triantis (1998) show that for a relatively small investment in a pyramidal firm, the controlling shareholder gains control rights that are disproportionately greater than the cash flow rights. Marco and Mengoli (2001) find that pyramidal firms in Italy are associated with wealth transfers to controllers. The recipients of wealth transfers reported significantly positive CARs (cumulative abnormal returns), while minority shareholders faced losses. Similar evidence regarding expropriation is found in Korea and India.

The alternate view of the benefits of controllership posits that control confers the rights of steering the firm strategically in the right direction. Magrabe (1978) has explored the valuation effects of switching options in industrial settings. Myers (1984) and Kester (1984) examined the value of rights in resource allocation decisions. Celebrated investors such as Warren Buffet and T. Boone Pickens have been able to use their enormous clout in redirecting firm strategies in ways that enrich all shareholders including the minority. A recent example of an activist-investor influencing strategic behavior is the case of Carl Icahn's 6.6% stake in the Korean Tobacco and Ginseng Company (KT&G). Using his clout, Icahn has urged top management at KT&G to divest their real estate assets, spin off their ginseng unit, and pay more dividends.

Research on the premium commanded by dual-class shares quantifies the value of control. Dual-class share structures are a common form of anti-takeover defense employed by a founding family with a large shareholder base. Exhibit 5.6 indicates the value of the control premium when firms have dual-class structures. Dual-class shares are widely prevalent in countries such as Sweden, Italy, and Israel. Hauser and Lauterbach (2000) found that reversions of dual-class firms back to one-share-one-vote structures were associated with positive excess returns. Bruner (1999) documents that in the case of Renault's attempted takeover of Volvo, Volvo's voting premium fell from 46.6% to 2.3% when Renault acquired a significant block of Volvo's stock.

Exhibit 5.6 *Control Premiums of Senior Voting Shares over Junior Voting Shares in Dual-class Share Structures*

Study	Country	Average Premium (%)
Rydqvist (1996)	Sweden	12.0
DeAngelo and DeAngelo (1985)	United States	5.0
Doidge (2003)	Foreign Firms Cross-listed in United States	8.0
Biger (1991)	Israel	74.0
Megginson (1990)	United Kingdom	13.3
Smith and Amoako-Adu (1995)	Canada	10.4
Zingales (1994)	Italy	80.0
Kunz and Angel (1996)	Switzerland	18.0

OPTION-LIKE CONTINGENT PAYMENTS IN M&A

Contingent payments frequently occur in many M&A transactions and take several forms. Some of these are listed and described in the following paragraph:

- Earnout Plans
- Targeted Stocks
- Stock Options
- Bonus Payments
- Escrow Funds
- Holdback Allowance

Earnout plans: In an earnout plan, the trigger on payment may be determined by complicated formulas and agreements for measuring progress. The earnout plan is usually a legally binding contract.

Targeted stocks: The buyer can issue target's shareholders shares of stock whose dividends are pegged to the performance of the target. Esty (2001) contends that targeted stock creates value by facilitating acquisitions.

Stock options: These are rights to acquire shares of the buyer. The exercise price is normally set above the buyer's stock price at closing.

Bonus payments: Bonus payments are made to sellers, especially managers of the selling firms, if they agree to stay on with the target firm.

Escrow funds: In some transactions, a part of the total payment is set aside in an escrow account to be released to the seller on satisfactory completion of some stipulated condition.

Holdback allowance: This is similar to escrow funds with the exception that no escrow account is created.

For ease of exposition, we will refer to all the contingent payments listed earlier as earnouts. Earnouts perform a very vital economic function—they resolve disagreement about the future and create incentives for the target company management.

POTENTIAL BENEFITS OF EARNOUTS

There are three major advantages of using earnouts in an M&A transaction.

1. The most commonly mentioned rationale for employing an earnout is to bridge the valuation gap. Let's assume that a seller is optimistic and values the target firm at US$60 million. The buyer is somewhat pessimistic and values the deal at US$40 million. No deal is possible with this gap in valuation. Now both parties can agree to an immediate payment of US$40 million and a US$20 million contingent payout if certain performance targets are achieved. Thus, earnouts serve to bridge the valuation gap and serve to expedite closure of an M&A transaction.
2. Earnouts serve to facilitate retention of key managers with the combined firm. If a portion of the purchase price is contingent on performance goals after the closure of the sale, target firm managers have an incentive to remain with the firm in order to participate in potential future payments.
3. Earnouts also motivate target's managers and shareholders to continue aggressive growth strategies even after closing the sale.

Despite the substantial theoretical benefits of earnouts described previously, earnouts are not that common. Exhibit 5.7 summarizes the trends in volume and number of deals employing earnouts in deals. Earnouts are employed in only between 0.4% and 2.5% of all deals conducted during the 1985–2002 period in the USA. Over the years, the absolute volume of the deals utilizing earnouts has risen. During periods of robust M&A activity, the volume of deals making use of earnouts rises, and it tends to fall as M&A activity ebbs. In deals employing earnouts, they account for a substantial portion of the deal consideration. Earnouts account for between 19% and 88% of total consideration paid.

Kohers and Ang (2000) conducted a comprehensive study of 938 acquisitions in the USA that used earnouts. Their research covered the 1984–96 period. They conclude that earnouts have two major advantages. First, they help to manage buyer's risk. Second, earnouts aid in retaining management. Some of their principal findings are summarized in the form of snippets:

- Earnouts are predominantly employed in two kinds of deal situations: privately held targets and divestitures of corporate subsidiaries.
- Small buyers are more likely to utilize earnouts. Also, buyers from common law countries are more likely to make use of earnouts than those from civil law countries.
- Earnouts are typically more likely when the buyer and the seller are from different industries.
- In about two-thirds of the deals with earnouts, target managers continued with the firm. Furthermore, the retention of management was highly correlated with the size of the earnout period.
- The size of the earnout component averaged about 45% in private transactions as compared to 33% in divested subsidiaries.
- Acquisition premiums were larger in the case of deals with earnouts than in straight cash or stock offers. Once again, the premium was higher for private targets than for divested subsidiaries.
- The market viewed earnouts positively, as evidenced by positive abnormal returns (1.4%) on announcement as compared to other comparable transactions.

Exhibit 5.7 *Occurrences of Earnouts by Year in the USA*

	Earnout Deals				
Year	**Total Value (US$ million)**	**% All Deals**	**Number**	**% All Deals**	**% Payment Due to Earnout**
1985	447.4	0.4	8	1.3	51
1986	2,081.6	0.9	15	1.2	26
1987	1,697.3	0.9	15	1.1	44
1988	1,795.3	0.7	26	1.5	54
1989	2,774.9	0.9	52	2.4	24
1990	1,438.5	0.8	53	2.6	21
1991	2,254.4	1.8	55	2.8	30
1992	1,272.6	1.1	61	2.7	40
1993	4,332.0	2.5	89	3.4	21
1994	1,990.1	0.7	92	2.7	88
1995	7,150.4	1.8	86	2.3	27
1996	8,831.7	1.5	85	2.0	19
1997	11,711.1	1.7	144	3.1	29
1998	9,845.1	0.8	167	3.5	28
1999	13,562.4	0.9	163	1.7	21
2000	26,028.3	1.6	174	1.9	23
2001	15,644.7	2.2	151	2.4	27
2002	8,089.3	2.1%	150	2.6	29

- The average horizon of earnout payment is between 2 to 5 years. Earnouts are mostly structured based on the profits of the target firm.
- Target firms are likely to be organized as subsidiaries during the earnout period.
- In almost 90% of the cases, some payment was made under the earnout arrangement. In about 50% of the cases, full payment was made.

Several notable acquisition deals included earnouts as part of the consideration. Seagate included an earnout deal in its acquisition of Quinta Corporation in 1998. Seagate paid US$230 million at closing and included a contingent payment of an additional US$95 million over the next 3 years subject to Quinta meeting some technological milestones. In December 1996, Unocal sold its subsidiary 76 Products Company to Tosco Corporation in a deal involving US$2.05 billion in cash, common stock, and an earnout.

Despite the professed advantages of employing earnouts in acquisition deals, their relative infrequency needs to be addressed. We offer some potential explanations based on perceived disadvantages of earnouts.

1. Complexity of Definition: Effective earnout formulas are difficult to build. Objective numerical definitions can at times become too complex for all parties to effectively comprehend.

2. Excessively Aggressive Performance Goals: In order to maximize its valuation, the target firm's management may state overly aggressive goals. If it appears likely that the target would miss the performance goals, then it is likely to demotivate the target firm employees.
3. Post-acquisition Integration: Earnouts are likely to be least effective if the target firm is fully integrated. This would be the case, if the main goal of acquisition is synergy. It is then difficult to segregate the performance of the target from the rest of the firm.
4. Managerial Ownership of Earnouts: If target managers do not receive a sizable chunk of the earnout claim, then are unlikely to be motivated to achieve high levels of future performance.

Given some of these practical difficulties, several buyers would choose not to employ them.

STRUCTURING AND VALUING EARNOUTS

Earnout provisions are call options on the future performance of the firm. They are more complicated than financial options because they are unstandardized and not exchange traded. However, an options framework is likely to be most useful in understanding the implications of using an earnout and for structuring and valuing it as well. Earnouts are likely to be valuable even if they are out of the money now. Valuation of an earnout depends on the likelihood of the option becoming in the money sometime during its remaining life. Earnouts are costly to the buyer and are not at all free. It is not a costless bauble given away to appease the seller. Earnouts are especially appropriate under conditions of great uncertainty regarding the value of the underlying asset. It is especially useful in settings involving high technology and rapid growth, and in turbulent economic environments. Earnouts are highly appropriate when the buyer and seller exhibit highly divergent outlooks. Earnouts will be helpful in bridging the differences in outlook between an optimistic seller and a pessimistic buyer.

The key elements to consider while structuring an earnout are earnout amount, earnout period, performance goals, payment schedule, and operational integration. We discuss each one of these elements further:

Earnout amount: In any acquisition deal with an earnout, both parties must agree on the portion of the deal amount to be paid at closure and the portion that will be subject to earnout. The earnout percentage is usually a function of the negotiation "price gap." Ideally, both parties should strike a proper balance between the payments at closing and the amount at the earnout. The proper balance depends upon the strength of the target's position, the total risk in the earnout, and the parties' objectives. If the earnout ratio is too small, there may be little incentive effect. On the other hand, if the earnout percentage is too large, the target may be subjecting itself to too much risk. In reality, most earnouts are structured in the range of 20% to 70% of the total purchase price.

Earnout period: Typically, most earnouts last between 1 and 5 years, the average being 3 years. The earnout period is mostly determined by the earnout ratio; the larger the earnout ratio, the longer the earnout period. What are the incentives of the seller and the buyer in setting the optimal earnout period? Contrary to the discounted cash flow view, the option view dictates that the seller should desire a longer earnout period, since the longer the time to maturity the more valuable the option is. Thus, the buyer should want shorter earnout periods.

Performance goals: For earnout plans to be effective, payments should be based on clearly defined, mutually understandable, attainable, and easily measurable performance goals. The common performance criteria in vogue include revenues, gross margin, pre-tax profit, cash flow, EBITDA, or nonfinancial milestones. Before selecting the most appropriate measure to use, one must consider the pros and cons of the various performance goals in vogue. Sometimes more than one performance criteria is incorporated into the earnout formula. A mathematical formula must be built that determines the exact amount of cash or shares to be distributed to the target's shareholders.

Payment schedule: There are various ways to structure the payment schedule of an earnout. In order to balance risk and reward, the earnout should provide significant rewards for partial fulfillment of the performance targets. In some instances, the target may exceed the performance goal. In such cases, additional bonuses may be awarded. Alternately, the target may be allowed to use any excess performance in a given year to offset any periods in which it fails to attain the goals. In some cases, buyers may cap the total payment in an earnout. In such instances, it makes sense for targets to demand a minimum payment.

Operational integration: The target and the buyer should make it clear at the beginning whether the target's operations will be integrated with the buyer's operations, and if so, would the revenues from the other divisions be included in the computation of performance goals for the earnout. Also, it needs to be made clear if the target will have operational control in order to fully achieve its goals. Ideally the earnout must be structured in such a way that the strategic as well as the financial objectives of the acquisition are met.

Other issues: The earnout agreement should specify the accounting policies to be followed in measuring the target's performance. The buyer should provide the target with either the funds to ensure that the target will meet the performance goals or the authority to procure the funds from external sources. Both parties should agree on how the target will conduct the business after the closing. The earnout should also specify the risk faced by the seller in the advent of a change in control of the buyer. Some earnout agreements contain provisions that permit the earnout instrument to be sold, assigned, or transferred. These additional features impart liquidity to the earnout instrument and enhance its value. Earnouts are usually disclosed in footnotes of financial statements like other contingent liabilities. It is possible that earnouts increase the financial leverage of the buyer, and it should be taken into account for assessing the debt rating and creditworthiness of the buyer.

Besides being useful in deal design, the real options framework is also suitable for risk management in M&A (particularly collars such as contingent value rights are frequently used). Real options also find a place in takeover defense and attack.

CONCLUDING REMARKS

In this chapter, we have surveyed the use of real options in M&A. Real options may lurk in unexpected corners in any takeover deal where flexibility is being granted or taken away. The right approach of the decision-maker in such cases is to value flexibility and use it in negotiations. Clearly, the discounted cash flow approach in itself is insufficient and, therefore, the options framework is a valuable toolkit not only for analysts but also for the decision-makers in the top management of the firm.

REFERENCES AND SUGGESTED READINGS

Alli, K. L., and D. J. Thompson, II. 1991. "The Value of the Resale Limitation on Restricted Stock: An Option Theory Approach." *Valuation*, 36 (1): 22–24.

Amram, Martha, and Nalin Kulatilaka. 1999a. "Disciplined Decisions: Aligning Strategy with Financial Markets." *Harvard Business Review*, (January–February).

———. 1999b. *Real Options: Managing Strategic Investment in an Uncertain World*. Boston, MA: Harvard Business School Press.

———. 1999c. "Uncertainty: The New Rules for Strategy." *Journal of Business Strategy*, 20 (3, March): 25–29.

———. 2000. "Strategy and Shareholder Value Creation: The Real Options Frontier." *Journal of Applied Corporate Finance*, 13 (2, Summer): 15–28.

Biger, N. 1991. "Market Recognition of the Value of Control." Unpublished Manuscript, University of Haifa.

Bebchuk, L., R. Kraakman, and G. Triantis. 1998. "Stock Pyramids, Cross-ownership, and Dual-class Equity: The Creation and Agency Costs of Separating Control from Ownership from Cash Flow Rights." Working Paper Social Science Research Network.

Brennan, Michael J, and Eduardo Schwartz. 1992. "A New Approach to Evaluating Natural Resource Investments." In *The Revolution in Corporate Finance*, edited by Joel Stern and Donald Chew Jr. Oxford, UK: Basil Blackwell.

Bruner, R. 1988. "Sprigg Lane (B)." Darden Case Collection (UVA-F682) and Associated Teaching Note (UVA-F682TN), University of Virginia.

———. 1999. "An Analysis of Value Destruction and Recovery in the Alliance and Proposed Merger of Volvo and Renault." *Journal of Financial Economics*, 51 (1, January): 125–66.

Colwell, David, Thomas Henker, and John Ho. 2002. "Real Options Valuation of Australian Gold Mines and Mining Companies." Working Paper. University of New South Wales.

Copeland, Thomas. 2001. "The Real-Options Approach to Capital Allocation." *Strategic Finance*, 83 (4, October): 33–37.

Copeland, Thomas, and Philip Keenan. 1998a. "How Much is Flexibility Worth." *The McKinsey Quarterly*, (2).

———. 1998b. "Making Real Options Real." *The McKinsey Quarterly*, (3).

Copeland, Thomas, and Vladimir Antikarov. 2001. *Real Options: A Practitioner's Guide*. New York, NY: Texere LLC.

Courtadon, G. and Merrick J. 1983. "The Option Pricing Model and the Valuation of Corporate Securities." *Midland Corporate Finance Journal*, 1 (3, Autumn): 43–57.

Damodaran, Aswath. 2000. "The Promise of Real Options." *Journal of Applied Corporate Finance*, 13 (2): 29–44.

DeAngelo, H. and L. DeAngelo. 1985. "Managerial Ownership of Voting Rights: A Study of Public Corporations with Dual Classes of Common Stock." *Journal of Financial Economics*, 14: 33–69.

Dixit, Avinash. 1992. "Investment and Hysterisis." *Journal of Economic Perspectives*, 6 (1, Winter): 107–32.

Dixit, Avinash, and Robert Pindyck. 1995. "The Options Approach to Capital Investment." *Harvard Business Review*, 73 (May–June): 105–15.

Doidge, C. 2003. "U.S. Cross-listings and the Private Benefits of Control: Evidence from Dual-class Shares." Working Paper. University of Toronto.

Dyck, Isaac John Alexander, and L. Zingales. 2004. "Private Benefits of Control: An International Comparison." *Journal of Finance*. 59: 537–600.

Edelson, Michael. 1994, March. "Real Options: Valuing Managerial Flexibility." HBS Case No. 9-294-109.

Esty, B. C. 2001. "The Information Content of Litigation Participation Securities: The Case of CalFed Bancorp." *Journal of Financial Economics*, 60 (2–3, May): 371–99.

Fernandez, Pablo. 2015, November 19. "Valuing Real Options: Frequently Made Errors." Available at SSRN: https://ssrn.com/abstract=274855 (Accessed on October 30, 2017).

Finnerty, J. D. 2002. "The Impact of Transfer Restrictions on Stock Prices." Working Paper. Analysis Group/Economics Cambridge.

Grenadier, S and A Weiss. 1997. "Investment in technological Innovation: An Option Pricing Approach." *Journal of Financial Economics*, 44 (3): 397–416.

Gompers, Paul. 1999, April. "Penelope's Personal Pocket Phones." HBS Case No.9-299-004.

Hauser, S., and B. Lauterbach. 2000. "The Value of Voting Rights to Majority Shareholders: Evidence from Dual-class Unifications." Working Paper. Bar Han University.

Imai, Junichi, and Mutsumi Nakajima. 2000. "A Real Option Analysis of an Oil Refinery Project." *Financial Practice and Education*, (Fall/Winter): 78–91.

Kemna, Angelien, G. Z. 1993. "Case Studies on Real Options." *Financial Management*, (Autumn): 259–70.

Kester, Carl W. 1984. "Today's Options for Tomorrow's Growth." *Harvard Business Review*, (March–April): 153–60.

Kohers, N, and J. A. Ang. 2000. "Earnouts in Mergers: Agreeing to Disagree and Agreeing to Stay." *Journal of Business*, 73 (3): 445–76.

Kulatilaka, Nalin, and Venkataraman N. 2001. "Strategic Options in the Digital Era." *Business Strategy Review*, 12 (4): 7–15.

Kunz, R. M., and J. J. Angel. 1996. "Factors Affecting the Value of the Stock Voting Right: Evidence from the Swiss Equity Market." *Financial Management*, 24: 7–20.

Lander, Diana. 2000. "Do Foregone Earnings Matter When Modeling and Valuing Real Options?: A Black-Scholes Teaching Exercise." *Journal of Financial Practice and Education*, 10 (2, Fall/Winter): 121–27.

Leslie, Keith, and Max Michaels. 1997. "The Real Power of Real Options." *The McKinsey Quarterly*, (3).

Longstaff, F. A. 1995. "How Much can Marketability Affect Security Values?" *Journal of Finance*, 50 (5): 1767–74.

Luehrman, Timothy. 1988. "Investment Opportunities as Real Options: Getting Started on the Numbers." *Harvard Business Review*, 76 (4, July–August): 51–67.

———. 1995, March. "Capital Projects as Real Options: An Introduction." Harvard Business School Case No. 9-295-074.

Luehrman, Timothy, and Barbara Wall. 1994, November. "M W Petroleum (A)." HBS Case No. 9-295-029.

Luehrman, Timothy, and William A. Teichner. 1992, June. "Arundel Partners: The Sequel Project." HBS Case No. 9-292-140.

———. 1998. "Strategy as a Portfolio of Real Options." *Harvard Business Review*, 76 (5, July–August): 89–99.

Magrabe, W. 1978. "The Value of an Option to Exchange One Asset for Another." *Journal of Finance*, 33 (1): 177–86.

Marco, B., and S. Mengoli. 2001. "Sub-optimal Acquisition Decisions under a Majority Shareholder System: An Empirical Investigation." Working Paper. Bologna, Italy: University of Bologna.

Mason, Scott, and Robert C. Merton. 1985. "The Role of Contingent Claims Analysis." In *Recent Advances in Corporate Finance*, edited by Edward Altman and Marti Subrahmanyam. Homewood, IL: Richard D. Irwin.

Mauboussin, Michael. 1999. "Get Real: Using Real Options in Security Analysis." *C S First Boston Research*, (June).

McDonald R., and D. Siegel. 1986. "The Value of Waiting to Invest." *Quarterly Journal of Economics*, 101: 707–27.

Megginson, W. L. 1990. "Restricted Voting Stock, Acquisition Premiums, and the Market Value of Corporate Control." *Financial Review*, 25: 175–98.

Meulbroek, Lisa. 2001, March. "Real Options Valuation when Multiple Sources of Uncertainty Exist." HBS Case No. 9-201-106.

Moel, Alberto, and Peter Tufano. 2002. "When are Real Options Exercised? An Empirical Study of Mine Closings." *Review of Financial Studies*, 15 (1, Spring): 35–64.

Myers, S. 1984. "Finance Theory and Financial Strategy." *Interfaces*, 14 (1): 126–37.

Nichols, Nancy. 1994. "Scientific Management at Merck: An Interview with CFO Judy Lewent." *Harvard Business Review*, 72 (1, January–February): 89–99.

Paddock, J., D. Siegel, and J. Smith. 1988. "Option Valuation of Claims on Physical Assets: The Case of Offshore Petroleum Leases." *Quarterly Journal of Economics*, 103 (August): 479–508.

Rappaport, A. and M. J. Mauboussin. 2002. *Expectations Investing: Reading Stock Prices for Better Returns*. Boston, MA: Harvard University Press.

Robichek, A. and J. Van Horne. 1967. "Abandonment Value and Capital Budgeting." *Journal of Finance*, (December): 577–89.

Rubinstein, M. 1992. "Double Trouble." *RISK*, (January): 53–56.

Rydqvist, K. 1996. "Takeover Bids and the Relative Prices of Shares that Differ in their Voting Rights," *Journal of Banking and Finance*, 20: 1407–25.

Sachdeva, Kanwal, and Pieter Vandenberg. 1993. "Valuing the Abandonment Option in Capital Budgeting: An Option Pricing Approach." *Financial Practice and Education*, 3 (2, Fall): 57.

Smit, H. T. J. 1997. "Investment Analysis of Offshore Concessions in the Netherlands." *Financial Management*, 26 (2): 5–17.

Smith, B., and B. Amoaku-Adu. 1995. "Relative Prices of Dual-class Shares." *Journal of Financial and Quantitative Analysis*, 30 (2): 223–39.

Trigeorgis, Lenos. 1993. "Real Options and Interactions with Financial Flexibility." *Financial Management*, 22 (3, Autumn): 202–24.

Trigeorgis, L., and S. Mason. 1987. "Valuing Managerial Flexibility." *Midland Corporate Finance Journal*, (Spring): 14–21.

Weatherford, Larry, and S. Bodily. 1988. "Sprigg Lane (A)." Darden Case Collection (UVA-QA-302) and Associated Teaching Note (UVA-QA-302TN), University of Virginia.

Zingales, L. 1994. "The Value of the Voting Right: A Study of the Milan Stock Exchange Experience." *Review of Financial Studies*, 7 (1): 125–48.

REVIEW QUESTIONS

1. Given the following values, calculate the value of the call option. Use the option-pricing table from a standard corporate finance text like the one by Brealy and Myers.
   S = US$3 million
   X = US$3.5 million
   r = 5%
   T = 5 years
   Volatility = 35% p.a.
2. The cash flows from an acquisition are given.

						(in US$ million)	
Year	**0**	**1**	**2**	**3**	**4**	**5**	**6**
Cash flow	(125)	9.0	10.0	11.0	11.6	12.1	12.7
Terminal Value						191.0	

The acquisition is expected to lead to a second-generation project whose cash flows are given as:

							(in US$ million)
Year	**0**	**1**	**2**	**3**	**4**	**5**	**6**
Cash flow					(382)	23.1	25.4	28.0
Terminal Value								419.3

The cost of capital is 12%. Risk-free rate is 5%. Calculate the NPV of the acquisition. Is the acquisition worthwhile? Estimate the value of the second stage project as an option, assuming annual volatility of 40%. What is the true NPV of the acquisition?

3. A company is in the process of acquiring another company.[8] The forecast of free cash flows are prepared on the basis of the following assumptions:
   - Current sales are US$50 million.
   - Expected growth rate in sales is 6% for the next 10 years.
   - Cost of goods sold is 65% of sales.
   - Selling, general, and administrative expenses are 15% of sales.
   - Depreciation is 4% of sales.
   - Capital investment to support sales is 8% of sales
   - Tax rate is 35%.
   - WACC for the company is 9.5%.
   - The book value of the company's debt is US$10 million.

The target has an excellent distribution system that has value to the acquirer. The acquirer plans to set up a new plant if the acquisition goes through. The new plant requires an initial investment of US$6 million in year zero and US$8 million 1 year later. If plant construction is delayed, construction costs are expected to increase 10% p.a. Sales are expected to increase to 11% p.a. from 5% one year after the investment is made. Due to increased efficiency cost of goods sold will decrease from 65% to 60% of sales. Selling, general and administrative expenses (SG&A), depreciation, and capital investment remain the same. Capital expenditure required to maintain only the plant will equal depreciation expense of the plant. The new plant has the same risk complexion as the firm itself.

The managers of the company have decided to wait for 3 years before building the plant. In other words, the managers have a 3-year real option starting 3 years from now. The standard deviation of project returns and risk-free rate are 45% and 5% respectively.

- Estimate the value of the target company's equity without the new plant.
- Estimate the value of the real option assuming managers defer the construction of plant for 3, 4, and 5 years.

4. Discuss the different types of real options and a methodology for valuing timing and expansion options.

[8] This is based on Diane Lander (2000).

CHAPTER

6 Design of Consideration in Acquisitions: Cash and Stock Offers

Vishwanath S. R. and
Chandrasekhar Krishnamurti

Learning Objectives

- Highlight the importance of the choice of method of payment in acquisitions
- Provide a framework for choosing between cash and stock payment
- Highlight the impact of the method of payment on financial performance
- Suggest a methodology for estimation of exchange ratio

The acquirer can pay the target company in cash or exchange shares in consideration. Around 45.6% of 4,256 deals done in the USA between 1973 and 1998 were paid in cash (Heron and Lie 2002).

The analysis of acquisition for shares as opposed to acquisition for cash is slightly different. The steps involved in the analysis are:

- Estimate the value of acquirer's (self) equity.
- Estimate the value of target company's equity.
- Calculate the maximum number of shares that can be exchanged with the target company's shares.
- Conduct the analysis for pessimistic and optimistic scenarios.

Exchange ratio is the number of acquiring firm's shares exchanged for each share of the selling firm's stock. Suppose Company A is trying to acquire 100,000 shares of Company B at US$230. So the cost of acquisition is US$23 million. Company A has estimated its value at US$200 per share. To get 1 share of Company B, Company A has to exchange (230/200 =) 1.15 share or 115,000 shares for 100,000 shares of B.

Assume that the acquiring company (B) has 115 million shares, whereas the target company (A) has 175 million shares. The exchange ratio is 0.6. The relative ownership of the two firms after the merger is shown as:

	Shares Outstanding (Million)	Exchange Ratio	Shares in the Merged Company (Million)	%
A	175	0.6	105	47
B	115	1.0	115	53

The shareholders of the acquiring company, by design, get one share in the newly formed company for every share held in the original company. The shareholders of the target company exchange their shares for a specified number of the newly formed company's shares. This ratio is called exchange ratio. It is 0.6 in the previous example. Target company shareholders usually receive an acquisition premium, that is, their shares are purchased at a premium to the pre-announcement price. The acquiring firm can afford to pay a premium because the acquisition is expected to create synergistic benefits in terms of cost savings and revenue enhancements. The shareholders of the two companies share synergy in some proportion.

In the previous example, assume that the pre-announcement prices of the two companies (acquirer and target) are US$13 and US$23 respectively. The market capitalizations of the two companies are:

	No. of Shares	Price	Market Capitalization
A	175 million	US$13	US$2,275 million
B	115 million	US$23	US$2,645 million
			US$4,920 million

The market capitalization after the merger is more than the sum of stand-alone market values of the merging companies due to synergy. The market cap in the given example is US$4,920 million. The share price of the two companies after the merger can be estimated as follows:

Market cap without synergy	US$4,920 million
Synergy	US$500 million
Expected market cap	US$5,420 million

No of shares outstanding after the merger 220 million

Price of the acquiring company	5,420/220 = $24.36
Price of the target company	$24.36 × Exchange Ratio = US$14.78

The acquiring company controls 53% of the combined company. That is 0.53 × 5,420 million = US$2,764.2 million approximately. The target company's share is the balance.

The maximum premium that the acquiring company can pay is the amount of synergy expected. What if there are no synergies? The acquiring company's shareholders are worse off to the extent of the acquisition premium paid. The acquiring company's shareholders' loss is the target company shareholders' gain. The exchange ratio determines the percentage ownership of the two companies after the merger and, hence, the acquisition premium.

From the perspective of the shareholders of the target company, accepting shares rather than cash enables them to participate in the upside of the combined entity over and above the premium received. The downside is that they share losses if synergy does not materialize.

Stock offers can take any of the two forms: fixed shares or fixed value. In case of a fixed share offer, the number of shares to be issued is certain but the value of the offer can fluctuate due to changes in the acquiring company's stock price between the offer and the closing date. In other words, the acquired company shareholders suffer if the acquirer's stock price falls but the proportional ownership of the two companies remains unchanged.

In case of fixed value deals, the number of shares issued is not fixed until the closing date, and it depends on the prevailing price (on the closing date). By design, the proportional ownership of the two companies is not fixed in case of fixed value deals. Assume that the acquisition price and the stock price of the acquirer are US$2 billion and US$75 billion respectively on the offer date. The acquirer has to issue 2,000/75 = 26.6 million shares. Suppose the price declines to US$67 at the closing date. The acquirer has to issue 29.8 million shares. The increase in the number of shares issued to the target company reduces the acquirer's proportional ownership.

UNDER AND OVERVALUATION

So far we assumed that both the acquirer and the target company are fairly valued. Due to information asymmetry between managers and investors, it is possible for shares to be over or undervalued. Assume that the acquirer's stock price is US$75 whereas its "intrinsic value" is US$100. If the target company has 100 million shares priced at US$50, the purchase price is US$5 billion, ignoring the premium. To acquire the target, the acquirer has to issue 5,000/75 million shares if one were to consider the market price, whereas the acquirer has to issue 5,000/100 million shares if the "intrinsic value" is considered. In other words, the acquirer has to convince the target that its shares are undervalued: else it faces dilution. Likewise, if the target is undervalued, the acquirer can build the fact into the price determination by adding the amount of undervaluation to the market capitalization of the target to arrive at acquisition price. Obviously, acquiring company shareholders would want to give as little a premium, and the converse is true of target company shareholders. In sum, stock offer should be avoided if the acquirer is undervalued.

HOW DO MANAGERS CHOOSE A METHOD OF PAYMENT?

The asymmetric information theory hypothesizes that due to information asymmetry between managers and investors, shares could be over-or-undervalued. Managers, acting in the interest of existing shareholders, have an incentive to issue shares if they are overvalued. If this theory were right, we would expect managers to pay in stock rather than cash in the context of acquisitions.

The method of payment has tax consequences. Shareholders in the selling company will face a tax bill for capital gains if they accept cash. The tax treatment for stock-financed acquisitions favor the selling shareholders because they allow them to receive the acquirer's stock tax-free. In other words, the selling shareholders can defer taxes until they sell the acquirer's stock. Due to the existence of difference in tax treatments, the acquirer must pay a higher acquisition price in case of cash offer to offset the tax burden of the selling shareholders.

Managerial ownership refers to the percentage equity held by management and insiders in both the companies. The greater the managerial ownership, the more likely the cash financing is used in order to not dilute their holding.

THE IMPACT OF METHOD OF PAYMENT ON PERFORMANCE

The relative merits of acquisition for cash or shares should be analyzed after giving due consideration to the impact on earnings per share (EPS), capital structure, and so on. Consider two hypothetical situations, one in which the target is trading at a price-earnings (P/E) multiple of 20 and the other in which the target is trading at a P/E multiple of 15. The acquiring company's stock is trading at a P/E of 18. The summary statistics are given here.

	Before Acquisition		
		Target	
	Acquirer	A	B
EPS	2.50	5.0	5.0
MPS US$	45	100	75
P/E	18	20	15
Earnings	25	10	10

Situation 1: Acquirer Pays 22.5 Times Earnings

Suppose the target is acquired under the first situation at a P/E of 22.5. That is, the negotiated price is 225 million or 12.5% premium over current P/E. The acquirer issues 225 million/45 = 5 million shares.

Company B's EPS = 10 million/5 million = US$2/share

EPS of composite operations = Composite earnings/[acquirer's shares + new shares issued to A]
= [25 million + 10 million] ÷ [10 + 5] = US$2.33

Dilution of EPS for shareholders of Acquirer = 2.5 – 2.33 = 17 cents.

Situation 2: Acquirer Pays 15 Times Earnings (Current P/E)

The acquirer pays US$150 million or 15 times earnings. That is, the acquirer issues 150/45 (= 3.333) million shares.

EPS of target = 10 million/3.33 = $3/ share
Composite EPS = 35 million/13.333 million = $2.62
Gain to shareholders of acquirer = 12 cents
The summary statistics are given as:

	After Acquisition	
	A	B
Acquirer pays	22.50 times earnings	15 times earnings
Composite EPS	2.33	2.62
Gain/loss	(0.17)	0.12

The important point that emerges from the previous analysis is that dilution occurs if the increase in number of shares is proportionally greater than the annual increase in earnings. In the first case, the acquiring company's P/E multiple should increase to 19.3 to sustain its current market price. In the second case, the P/E multiple can come down to 17 without affecting the current price of acquirer. Here's a quick and dirty method to find out if dilution will occur: If the acquiring company's stock price is greater than or equal to the price attached to the target company, dilution will not occur.

The post-merger P/E multiple for the combined firm is the weighted average of the pre-merger ratios.

$$P/E_{(A+B)} = \frac{N_A P_A + N_B P_B + \Delta V}{N_A EPS_A + N_B EPS_B}$$

where $N_{A,B}$ = number of shares of acquiring and selling firms respectively.

$P_{A,B}$ = Stock price of acquiring and selling firms respectively.

EPS_A and EPS_B are their earnings per share.

ΔV is the increase in the value of firm's equity after the merger (synergy).

One approach for picking an exchange ratio is to recognize that the market value of the combined entity is equal to the sum of:

- The stand-alone value of acquirer
- The stand-alone value of target
- The value of the net merger benefits

In general, the exchange ratio is the product of negotiation between the merging companies. The healthier and better capitalized company, or the company that made the greater contribution to the merger contribution, would be negotiating from a position of greater strength. The exchange ratio determines how the shareholders of the merging companies share the net merger benefits. One response is that shareholders' entitlement to these benefits depends on how much of the merger benefits they have helped create. The exchange ratio, therefore, reflects a number of considerations such as size, asset quality, contribution to cost savings, and revenue enhancement. So it is logical to argue that the exchange ratio should be based on the relative size and profitability of the merging companies. One could calculate the exchange ratio on the basis of a number of financial parameters like the ones listed to calculate the exchange ratio.

	Acquirer	Target
Size		
Assets		
Equity (book)		
Equity (Market)		
Market Valuation		
Price/Earnings		
Price/Sales		
Price/Book value		

	Acquirer	Target
Profitability		
ROA%		
ROE %		
Capitalization		
Equity/Assets %		

Often the exchange ratio is set equal to the ratio of merging firms' stock prices. When the merger is consummated, the market value of all outstanding target company shares (which are extinguished under merger), by definition, must equal the market value of the new company shares given to target company shareholders in the exchange.

$$P_{target} \times N_{target} = P_{acquirer} \times \Delta N_{acquirer}$$

Rearranging,

$$\Delta N_{acq}/N_{target} = \text{Exchange ratio} = P_{target}/P_{acq}$$

The average of 3-month, 6-month, or 12-month stock prices might be used.

One can also estimate the merger synergies independently and assume an exchange ratio and estimate the premium over premerger value of the company. The exercise might be conducted for a range of exchange ratios.

MAXIMUM EXCHANGE RATIO FOR THE ACQUIRING FIRM

The post-merger price of the acquiring company's stock should be at least as high as the pre-merger price to maintain the wealth position, that us, $P_{A+B} \geq P_A$. But P_{A+B} is the total value of merged firm's equity divided by number of shares outstanding.

$$P_{(A+B)} = \frac{N_A P_A + N_B P_B + \Delta V}{N_A + r.N_B}$$

where r is the exchange ratio (B's shares for A's shares),

$$\frac{N_A P_A + N_B P_B + \Delta V}{N_A + r.N_B} \geq P_A$$

Solving for r,

$$r \leq \frac{N_B P_B + \Delta V}{N_B P_A}$$

This is the maximum exchange ratio that can preserve wealth. As is evident, r is a function of increase in the value of the firm's equity after the merger.

If $\Delta V = 0$,

$$r \leq \frac{N_B P_B}{N_B P_A}$$

That is,

$$r \leq P_B/P_A.$$

The exchange ratio can also be expressed as

$$r_{max} \leq \frac{P/E_{(A+B)}(N_A EPS_A + N_B EPS_B) - N_A P_A}{N_A P_A}$$

Maximum exchange ratio is a function of the P/M multiple expected to prevail soon after the merger.

MINIMUM EXCHANGE RATIO FOR THE SELLING FIRM

From the selling firms' shareholders perspective, the price of the shares sold should equal the price of the shares received for their wealth position to be maintained.

That is, r. $P_{(A+B)} \geq P_B$

Wealth after merger = wealth before merger

$$r_{min} \geq \frac{N_A P_A}{N_A P_A + \Delta V}$$

$$\geq \frac{N_A P_A}{P/E_{(A+B)}(N_A EPS_A + N_B EPS_B) - N_B P_B}$$

Value will decline for the selling firm's stockholders if an exchange ratio below this is accepted.

MARKET REACTION TO MERGER ANNOUNCEMENTS

To assess the profitability of M&A, academic studies have adopted two approaches (excluding clinical studies of one or a small group of companies). Event studies examine the abnormal returns to shareholders in the period surrounding the announcement of the transaction. The raw return for one day is simply the change in the share price and any dividends paid, divided by the closing share price the day before. The abnormal return is obtained by deducting a benchmark of what investors required that day (as estimated by the capital asset pricing model [CAPM] or any benchmark index return, say, S&P 500). Accounting studies examine the reported financial results of acquirers before and after acquisitions to see how financial performance changed. These studies match acquirers and nonacquirers in the same industry of similar size. The studies attempt to find out if acquirers outperformed the nonacquirers. The results of the event studies of returns to target and bidding firms for both stock and nonstock transactions are presented in Exhibit 6.1. The negative announcement period stock market reaction for acquiring firms is limited to those that finance the merger with stock. Acquiring firms that use stock to finance their acquisition experience an abnormal return of –1.5% while acquirers that do not use stock experience a small negative abnormal return (–0.4%), close to zero. How do we interpret this result? One explanation is based on the information asymmetry between investors and managers. Managers are more likely to issue equity when the firm's shares are overvalued. Equity investors realize it and greet equity issues negatively. But is the negative reaction to the announcement a response to the equity issue or the merger per se? In other words, to interpret the result, one needs to separate out the effect of equity issue from the effect of merger announcement.

Exhibit 6.1 *Announcement Period Abnormal Returns for Subsamples, 1973–98*

	Stock	No Stock
Combined		
[–1, +1]	0.6%	3.6%
[–20, Close]	–0.6%	5.3%
Target		
[–1, +1]	13.0%	20.1%
[–20, Close]	13.0%	20.1%
Acquirer		
[–1, +1]	–1.5%	0.4%
[–20, close]	–6.3%	–0.2%
No. Obs.	2,194	1,494

Source: Andrade et al. (2001).

Cash transactions are often funded with debt and, thus, tend to increase leverage. Conversely, stock transactions tend to decrease leverage. The increase in leverage generates tax shields (net of bankruptcy costs) due to which such transactions result in positive abnormal return while leverage decreasing transactions result in negative abnormal return.

Some studies have examined the long-run abnormal returns over the 3-to-5 years following a merger. Loughran and Vijh (1997) find that firms using stock financing have abnormal returns of –24.2% over the 5-year period after the merger, whereas the abnormal return is 18.5% for cash mergers.

TAKEOVER PAYMENT METHOD AND OPERATING PERFORMANCE

CFOs deciding whether to finance an acquisition with cash or stock might consider how the chosen form of currency will affect operating performance. Managers have incentive to manipulate earnings before a stock-financed acquisition by aggressively accumulating company stock, inflating its price and, thus, increasing its purchasing power. The question is whether manipulative accumulation actually occurs and, if it does, whether this kind of earnings management hurts the acquirer's operating performance after the deal closes.

This could explain why acquirer's stock often performs poorly after a stock-financed acquisition, compared to the stock of companies using cash.

Heron and Lie (2002) examined 859 acquisitions completed between 1985 and 1997 and found no difference in post-acquisition operating performance between cash and stock financiers. They find that acquirers perform better than the industry average both before and after the acquisition, regardless of payment method. Companies that showed the greatest improvements in operating performance included those that had acquired targets in the same industry and well-managed companies that had acquired poor performers.

If the operating performance has no relationship to payment method, why are both announcement returns and long-term acquisition returns lower for a stock acquisition? One explanation is that investors are overly optimistic about long-term growth prospects before an acquisition and revise their expectation later on. Changes in capital structure might also contribute. A dramatic increase in debt ratio after cash acquisitions may contribute to higher announcement and post-acquisition returns.

Stock acquisitions are exposed to the risk of stock price fluctuations. Stock acquisitions are generally structured as fixed value mergers and fixed exchange mergers. Under the second structure, the number of the acquirer's shares that each target stockholder will receive is calculated through a fixed ratio negotiated in the merger agreement. The target shareholders bear the risk of a decline in the acquirer's stock value. With a fixed value merger, the agreement first establishes the consideration per share that each shareholder will receive. It then calculates an exchanges ratio using the average price of the acquirer's stock over a certain period. Under this approach, target stockholders are not affected by declines in the acquirer's stock but they also may not benefit from increases.

In a fixed exchange ratio merger, the agreement may provide a floor value for the acquirer's stock, which protects the target shareholders, and a maximum value, which protects the acquirer from issuing shares at a high market value. The parties may provide for adjustment of the exchange ratio if the price of the acquirer's stock rises or falls too much. The agreement for a fixed value merger may also set a minimum and maximum fixed exchange ratio. Often the target will negotiate the right to terminate the deal if the acquirer's stock falls below an acceptable level.

Target stockholders sometimes desire long-term price protections. They may purchase over-the-counter derivatives to meet these needs. Financial institutions have developed costless collars through which a shareholder may buy a put and sell a call on the stock. If the price falls more than a certain percentage, the put is used, while the institution can call the stock if the price rises by the same percentage. Because the call and put are of equal value, no payment is required.

ILLUSTRATION: RELIANCE INDUSTRIES LTD AND RELIANCE PETROCHEMICALS LTD MERGER

On March 3, 2009, Reliance Industries Ltd (RIL) announced its merger with its subsidiary, Reliance Petrochemicals Ltd (RPL). RIL would issue 1 share for 16 shares of RPL (or 69.2 million new shares to shareholders of RPL). RIL's equity capital would rise to ₹16.43 billion and the founder's holdings would fall by 2% to 47%. RIL's absorption of RPL would be tax neutral for both the entities. The merger would give RIL the ability to undertake much larger projects as the merger simplified the group's corporate structure, giving RIL access to an additional 30% of cash flow generation from RPL. The merger would create an enterprise with a total refining capacity of 1.24 million barrels of crude a day, which was a quarter of the world's total refining capacity.

The company's CFO, Mr Agarwal, said that the merger would help source crude oil for the integrated refinery complex and aid the marketing of fuels such as gasoline and diesel globally at a time when demand was slumping. The merger would result in RIL emerging as the world's fifth-largest producer of polypropylene and becoming the world's largest producer of ultra clean fuels at a single location. The 1.24 million barrels per day refining capacity at Jamnagar in Gujarat was the single largest refining hub in the world, beating the Paraguana refinery in Venezuela.

Citigroup Global Markets India advised RPL on the deal, and Ernst & Young and Morgan Stanley India advised the RIL valuation.

Stock Market Reaction

Upon announcement, shares of RPL dropped as much as 8.3%, but recovered to close 2.3% lower at ₹74.60. RIL shares fell as much as 4.2% before closing 3.84% lower at ₹1,217.4 on the Bombay Stock Exchange (BSE). The market (BSE Sensitive Index) itself dropped 3.7% on that day. Market observers were of the opinion that the exchange ratio was unfavorable to RPL shareholders.

The pre-announcement stock prices of RIL and RPL were ₹1,266 and ₹74.6 respectively. Based on these prices, the exchange ratio works out to 1,225/95.6 = 13.24, that is, 13.24 shares of RPL equal one share of RIL. Of course, the assumption is that there is no synergy.

Analysts expected synergy to be equal to 1.66% of the total earnings of RIL and RPL in 2009 or ₹12.07 billion, assuming a perpetuity discounted at a blended cost of equity of 19.66%. This present value when divided by the total number of outstanding shares yields a per share value of just ₹6.5.

In other words, the proposed exchange ratio cannot be justified by the (ratio of) pre-announcement stock prices or synergies.

Oil and gas prices are highly volatile, which makes them eminently suited for real options analysis. Our analysis ignores the value of real options held by the combined entity.

CONCLUDING COMMENTS

As the deal description table presented at the beginning of the chapter suggests, roughly 8%–10% of all deals involve mixed payment, that is, these transactions are cash-and-stock transactions. The exchange ratio for the stock component determines the percentage ownership. The percentage ownership and the cash paid determine the premium. In case of all cash deals, target shareholders have no downside because they are not exposed to the price fluctuations of the acquirer's stock. In an all-stock deal, the shareholders are exposed to price fluctuations and there is no downside protection. Cash and stock deals fall in between.

Design of consideration is one of the most important aspects of the transaction. Acquirers should determine whether their own shares are over-or-undervalued and the probability that expected synergies do not materialize in designing the contents of the offer. Likewise, sellers should determine the value of their company as an independent entity and compare it with the price offered. The analysis for stock or cash-and-stock offers are similar to that performed by buyers.

REFERENCES AND SUGGESTED READINGS

Andrade, Gregor, Mark Mitchell, and Erik Stafford. 2001. "New Evidence and Perspectives on Mergers." *Journal of Economic Perspectives*, 15 (2, Spring): 103–20.

Auerbach, Alan, ed. 1998. *Corporate Takeovers: Causes and Consequences*. Chicago: University of Chicago Press.

Carleton, Willard T., David Guilkey, Robert Harris, and John Stewart. 1983. "An Empirical Analysis of the Role of the Medium of Exchange in Mergers." *Journal of Finance*, XXXVIII (3, June): 813–26.

Conn R. L., and J. F. Nielsen. 1977. "An Empirical Test of the Larson: Gonedes Exchange Ratio Determination Model." *Journal of Finance*, (June): 749–59.

Emery, Gary, and Jeanette Switzer. 1999. "Expected Market Reaction and the Choice of Method of Payment for Acquisitions." *Financial Management*, 28 (4, Winter): 126–39.
Hansen, Robert G. 1987. "A Theory for the Choice of Exchange Medium in Mergers and Acquisitions." *Journal of Business*, 60 (1): 75–95.
Heron, Randall, and Erik Lie. 2002. "Operating Performance and the Method of Payment in Takeovers." *Journal of Financial and Quantitative Analysis*, 37 (1, March): 137–55.
Jensen M. C., and Richard Ruback. 1983. "The Market for Corporate Control: The Scientific Evidence" *Journal of Financial Economics*, 11 (1–4): 5–50.
Larson, K. D., and N. J. Gonedes. 1969. "Business Combinations: An Exchange Ratio Determination Model." *Accounting Review*, (October): 720–28.
Loughran, Tim, and Anand Vijh. 1997. "Do Long-term Shareholders Benefit from Corporate Acquisitions." *Journal of Finance*, 52 (5): 1765–90.
Martin, K. 1996. "The Method of Payment in Corporate Acquisitions, Investment Opportunities, and Management Ownership." *Journal of Finance*, 51 (4): 1227–46.
Mitchell, Mark, and Erik Stafford. 2000. "Managerial Decisions and Long Term Stock Price Performance," *Journal of Business*, 73 (3): 287–329.
Rappaport, Alfred, and Mark L. Sirower. 1999. "Stock or Cash? The Trade offs for Buyers and Sellers in Mergers and Acquisitions." *Harvard Business Review*, (November–December): 147–58.
Stulz, Rene. 1988. "Managerial Control of Voting Rights: Financing Policies and the market for Corporate Control." *Journal of Financial Economics*, 20 (1–2): 25–54.
Sullivan, Michael J., Martin Jensen, et al. 1994. "The Role of Medium of Exchange in Merger Offers: Examination of Terminated Merger Proposals." *Financial Management*, 23 (3, Autumn): 51–62.
Zhang, Pinghshun. n.d. "What Really Determines the Payment Methods in M&A Deals." Working Paper No. 0103, Manchester School of Management.

REVIEW QUESTIONS

1. The following data is available for two firms contemplating on a merger.

	A	B
No. of outstanding shares (million)	50	70
Stock price before the announcement	120	45
Exchange ratio (from A's perspective)	0.45	

Assuming that the stock price is the best estimate of the value of two companies,

- What is the price premium for B?
- What is the value of the merged entity?
- What is the respective equity ownership of A & B in the merged entity?

2. Explain how fixed value deals are different from fixed price offers.
3. How does the method of payment affect post-merger performance?
4. Critically examine the results of event studies of stock market reaction to cash and stock offers.

CHAPTER

7 Accounting and Tax Issues in Mergers and Acquisitions

Vishwanath S. R.

Learning Objectives

- Describe the approaches for accounting for mergers
- Highlight M&A reporting practices
- Discuss taxation issues in M&A

Two important components of an M&A transaction are (a) the method of accounting imposed on the transaction by local regulators and (b) the tax implications created by the transaction. While the accounting treatment of M&A transactions is more uniform now, there is still considerable heterogeneity in accounting and tax treatments because these are often culturally dependent and country-specific. This chapter attempts to provide an overview of the accounting approaches to and tax consequences of M&A.

ACCOUNTING FOR MERGERS AND ACQUISITIONS

When a company obtains a majority ownership of the outstanding voting shares of another entity, it is usually the case that the acquirer will be required to reflect the financial results of the acquired entity on a consolidated basis with the parent company. The preparation of consolidated financial results is a standard requirement in many countries. In the absence of consolidation, investors would not have a clear picture of the financial position of the parent, or they would be forced to analyze several firm-level financial statements to get a true picture of the parent company. The preparation of consolidated financial statements also reduces the cost of financial reporting: companies will have to publish one consolidated financial statement rather than provide numerous, individual financial statements. The flip side of the coin is that consolidated financial statements provide an aggregated view of the business because of which it is often difficult to assess how individual business segments are performing.

All countries may not require that a majority-owned (or even wholly-owned) subsidiary be consolidated with the parent company (e.g., India and Indonesia in the 1990s). Instead, the controlled subsidiary may be accounted for using the *cost method* or the *equity method*. Under the cost method, the acquirer reports the ownership in the target in a single balance sheet account at the price that the company paid to acquire. This would appear as "Investment in Company ABC" in the balance sheet of the acquirer. Accounting Standard 23 of the Institute of Chartered Accountants of India relates to accounting for investments in associates. This standard requires that acquirers report a transaction using the equity method if the stake is more than 50%. Under the equity method, it would have initially reported the acquisition on its books in a single asset account (i.e., as "Investment in ABC"); but the value of this account would have been subsequently increased or decreased by any profits or losses earned by the target, and decreased for any dividends paid by target.

Where consolidated reporting of the parent and subsidiary is required, there are two approaches to the preparation of the consolidated financial data: purchase accounting and pooling-of-interests accounting. *Purchase accounting* is typically used in those restructuring transactions that are clearly an acquisition of one company by another. These transactions are usually executed by the exchange of cash for an acquiree's stock. Under purchase accounting, the acquiree is valued at the fair market value of the assets (both tangible and intangible) exchanged by the acquirer for the acquiree's stock. Such transactions frequently involve a step-up in the value of the acquiree's book value to its fair market value before the actual consolidation of data. These transactions are also typically characterized by the presence of goodwill (i.e., an amount paid in excess of the fair market value of an acquiree's net worth). Goodwill arises from an entity's ability to earn abnormal profits arising from name or brand recognition, location, customer loyalty, product quality, and management competence. In the USA, goodwill must be recorded as an asset and amortized over its useful life or a maximum of 40 years.

The acquirer recorsds liabilities assumed on a present value basis.

When an acquisition is executed by an exchange of voting stock (i.e., the stock of the acquirer is exchanged for the stock of the acquiree), it may be permissible to account for the transaction as a merger using the pooling-of-interests method, or what some call "merger accounting." Under pooling-of-interest method, the acquiree is valued at its current net worth, not the value of the shares exchanged. As a consequence, no goodwill is ever present under this accounting approach. Before considering these two approaches in greater detail, it is necessary to first explore the concept of full versus partial consolidation.

Full Versus Partial Consolidation

In most countries, when a company obtains a majority interest in the voting shares of another entity, accepted accounting practice dictates the use of consolidated reporting practice. Consolidated reporting, however, may involve either a full or partial combination of financial data. When a company acquires a 100% shareholding in another, the consolidated results under either full or partial consolidation are exactly equivalent. However, when an acquired shareholding is less than 100%, full and partial consolidation yield different consolidated financial results.

Partial consolidation assumes that the parent's consolidated balance sheet should reflect only its proportionate interest in the net assets (i.e., assets minus liabilities) of the acquired company. Full consolidation, however, assumes that since the parent company is the majority shareholder of the subsidiary, the parent effectively controls all of the subsidiary's net assets despite the fact that it might not own them all. Thus, under full consolidation, all of the subsidiary's net assets are consolidated with those of the parent. This practice, however, necessitates the creation of a new account—minority interest—to reflect the portion of the subsidiary's net assets not in fact owned by the parent company.

Goodwill

Another consideration in acquisition or purchase accounting involves goodwill. Goodwill arises when one entity acquires another and pays more than the fair market value of the acquiree. Not all acquisitions are executed in this manner. In some instances, the acquirer company may exchange its voting stock for the stock of the acquiree. When such stock exchanges occur, accounting standards sometimes permit the acquirer to utilize the pooling-of-interests method of accounting.

Under the pooling-of-interests method, the value assigned to the acquirer's shares exchanged in an acquisition is not their fair market value but is the book value of the investment as reflected on the acquiree's financial statements. The pooling method accounts for a combination of two firms as a union of the ownership interests of the two previously separated groups of stockholders. No sale or purchase is considered to have occurred. The assets and liabilities of the combining firms continue to be carried at their book values, that is, on the basis of their historical costs. Any goodwill carried on the target's books prior to the merger continues to be carried on the merged firm's books at its historical cost, but no new goodwill is recognized as a result of the pooling. The stockholders' equity of the merged firm is recorded at the sum of the book values of the two firms.

On September 7, 1999, the Financial Accounting Standards Board of the USA issued a draft with four significant changes to existing accounting practice:

1. Use of the pooling-of-interest method would be prohibited.
2. The prevailing 40-year maximum amortization period for goodwill would be reduced to 20 years.[1]
3. Companies would be required to present separate line items in the income statement for income before taxes and goodwill amortization, and for goodwill amortization net-of-tax basis.
4. The prevailing 40-year maximum amortization period for acquired intangible assets (other than goodwill) would be replaced with a presumption that their useful lives are 20 years or less.

In most countries, if goodwill is capitalized to the balance sheet under purchase accounting, it must be periodically amortized against earnings—although the amortization period varies greatly from country to country—or it is to be tested for impairment (in which case there would be no amortization). In Canada, for example, the typical amortization period was 40 years,[2] whereas in India, a 5-year amortization period is prevalent. In any case, the presence of goodwill on the consolidated balance sheet of the parent company represents a "drag" on the company's future earnings.

[1] It has been further reduced to 15 years since then.

[2] Canada too has reduced the amortization period to around 15 years.

In 2001, the FASB of the USA released Statement No. 141, accounting for business combinations, and Statement No. 142, accounting for goodwill and intangible assets that prohibit the pooling-of-interests method of accounting for business combinations and require a purchase accounting method that does not allow goodwill amortization. Instead, companies are required to conduct an annual goodwill impairment test based on the fair value of the asset.

Although goodwill is most commonly found as an asset account on the balance sheet, in some cases, an acquirer may find that its purchase price of an investment is less than the acquiree's recorded net book value. When this occurs, a negative goodwill is said to arise. The accounting for negative goodwill is also quite diverse. In some countries, negative goodwill is carried on the balance sheet as a credit balance and may be amortized to (i.e., added to) earnings over time. In other countries, negative goodwill may not be carried on a company's balance sheet and instead is usually written off against the remaining cost basis of an acquiree's long-term depreciable assets. Further, some countries permit the charge-to-equity method negative. Under this method, a negative goodwill may be added immediately to the acquirer's equity reserves. Each of these approaches produces a different effect on the acquirer's balance sheet and income statement. However, the cash flow effect depends on the tax regulations relating to the tax deductibility of goodwill.

Accounting Standard 14 of the Institute of Chartered Accountants of India deals with accounting for amalgamations. The salient features of the standard are given as:

- Purchase method is applied to acquisitions and pooling-of-interest for mergers.
- Assets and liabilities are recorded at carrying amounts on the balance sheet of the transferee company in case of pooling-of-interest.
- Uniform accounting method is to be adopted and any deviation must be disclosed.
- Carrying amount or fair value is to be used in case of purchase method.
- Goodwill is the difference between price paid and the book value.
- Goodwill can be written off over 5 years (or longer if it can be justified).

Illustration

Assume that a company acquired a target for ₹200 million in stock but used the purchase accounting. The acquirer would revalue the target's assets and liabilities to their fair values at the date of the acquisition and record any intangible assets that were not carried on the books of the target. Assume that the fair market and book values are as follows:

Fair Value	**Book Value**	
Fixed assets	50	35
Intangible assets (Patents and trademarks)	40	----
Current assets		
Cash	6	6
Accounts receivable	8	8
Inventory	9	10
Current liabilities		
Accounts payable	(14)	(14)
Notes payable	(12)	(15)
Fair value of net assets: 87		

Any difference between the purchase price and the fair value of net assets would be recorded as goodwill arising from the transaction. The goodwill would be ₹200 million – ₹87 million = ₹113 million.

The premerger balance sheet of the acquirer is given:

Equity	460	Fixed assets	250
Notes payable	170	Cash	185
Accounts payable	90	Accounts receivable	90
		Notes receivable	55
		Inventory	140
Total	720		720

The post-merger balance sheet would be:

Equity	660	Fixed assets	300
		Trademark and patents	40
		Goodwill	**113**
Notes payable	182	Cash	191
Accounts payable	104	Accounts receivable	98
		Notes receivable	55
		Inventory	149
Total	946		946

The goodwill would be amortized over 5, 15, 20, or 40 years, depending on the accounting regulation. If the acquirer were to use the pooling-of-interests method, the values of assets and liabilities for the newly merged firm would be the sum of the book values of the assets and the liabilities of the two firms. No goodwill would be recorded or amortized.

If the goodwill is to be amortized over a period of time (say 20 years), then net income would come down after adjusting for taxes. However, if the goodwill is subjected to an annual impairment test with no write-down, net income would not be affected. Consequently, the accounting treatment has a significant impact on income statement too.

TAXATION ISSUES IN MERGERS AND ACQUISITIONS

Companies often encounter complex taxation issues, especially in cross-border M&A. The goal of M&A is to minimize taxes—both at the time of transaction as well as ongoing income taxes of the surviving firms. In this section, we examine the major tax concepts and issues associated with M&A. The decision to purchase a target firm's assets as opposed to its shares will have a bearing on both types of taxes. As a rule of thumb, transaction taxes are lower for share purchases than for asset purchases. One advantage of an asset purchase is that an acquirer can selectively choose the assets to acquire without assuming responsibility for actual or contingent liabilities of the target company. However, this may not be allowed in all countries. In some countries, the acquirer assumes all liability for existing employment contracts, regardless of whether the acquisition is an asset or share purchase.

Another benefit of an asset purchase is the step-up in cost basis that may be associated with the acquired assets. The cost step-up may be used to reduce future capital gains taxes and/or increase-related depreciation deductions. The main disadvantage with an asset purchase is that the transaction is, generally, a taxable event for the target company and its shareholders. Under an asset purchase, there exists the potential for double taxation as the target company pays taxes on the capital gains of the assets sold and then again as the target's shareholders pay tax on the distributed proceeds if the target is subsequently liquidated.

In contrast, a share purchase can be structured as a "tax-free" exchange of shares. However, shareholders will have to pay taxes when they sell the newly acquired shares in future. Also an acquirer may be able to utilize any accumulated tax losses and net operating losses of the target company to lower current and/or future tax obligations of the consolidated entity.[3] These are again subject to local tax legislations.

Four conditions must be met to qualify a transaction for tax-free treatment under Internal Revenue Code Section 368 of the USA.

1. Continuity of ownership interest: At least 50% of the consideration is acquirer stock (sometimes transactions with 405 stock consideration have qualified for tax-free treatment).
2. Continuity of business enterprise: The acquirer must either continue the target's historical business or use a significant portion of the target's assets in an existing business for 2 years after the transaction.
3. Valid business purpose: The transaction must serve a valid business purpose beyond tax avoidance.
4. Step-transaction doctrine: The transaction cannot be part of a target plan that, taken in its entirely, would constitute a taxable acquisition.

TAXES INVOLVED IN MERGERS AND ACQUISITIONS

The taxes associated with an M&A transaction frequently include transfer taxes, capital gains, and value-added taxes (VAT). Transfer taxes, or stamp duty taxes, refer to taxes associated with the transfer of shares or assets from one entity to another. Companies may have to pay stamp duty tax on some assets, including land, buildings, and goodwill. In India, the stamp duty on transfer of shares is 0.25% of the value of shares transferred. Capital gains is defined as the difference between a seller's acquisition cost and the sale price. In many countries, the capital gains tax can be deferred on share purchases until the exchanged shares are disposed of. In India, if a capital asset is held by an assessee for not more than 3 years immediately prior to the

[3] Section 72A of the Income Tax Act in India provides that in case of amalgamation of a company owning an industrial undertaking with another company, the accumulated loss and the unabsorbed depreciation of the amalgamating company is deemed to be the loss/allowance for depreciation of the amalgamated company. The amalgamated company would then be entitled to carry forward such loss and depreciation, and set off such amounts against its future profits.

transfer, such capital asset would be a short-term capital asset. If the capital asset is held for more than 3 years, then it is a long-term capital asset. Any other capital asset would be a short-term capital asset. This distinction is important as the tax rates on short-term and long-term capital assets are usually different.

In an asset purchase where the object is to acquire the business of the seller, there may be a provision in the asset purchase agreement that the seller will recruit all employees of the target who accept offers of employment with the acquirer. Part of the consideration payable to the seller may be contingent on the number of employees who join the acquirer. It is possible that such a provision could amount to the provision of manpower recruitment services by the seller on which service tax at the rate of 15% (including surcharge and education cess) may be payable as per Finance Bill, 2016.

A final transactional tax is the VAT that may arise with an asset purchase. Generally speaking, the sale of an entire business as a going concern is outside the scope of VAT. The VAT or sales tax may be payable on a purchase of movable assets or goods of the target by the acquirer. Most Indian states have in the last few years replaced their state sales tax laws with laws levying VAT on the sale of goods. The law relating to VAT is state specific. Likewise, VAT may be applied in some countries on the sale of inventories in an acquisition.

Transaction-related costs are generally higher in the case of an asset purchase as compared to a share purchase. This is primarily because in a share purchase, there would usually be no incidence of sales tax/VAT/service tax, which may be levied on different aspects of an asset purchase. Further, the rate stamp duty is also usually higher in an asset purchase and, as discussed earlier, is dependent on the nature of the assets transferred.

REVIEW QUESTIONS

1. What is the difference between purchase method of accounting and pooling-of-interests method? When is the later adopted?
2. Outline the differences between asset and share purchase.
3. Discuss between cost and equity method of accounting for acquisitions.
4. Discuss the treatment of goodwill in different countries.
5. Write an essay on taxation issues in M&A.

CHAPTER 8 Cross-border Acquisitions

Vishwanath S. R. and
Chandrasekhar Krishnamurti

Learning Objectives

- Highlight the motivations for cross-border acquisitions
- Provide an overview of trends in cross-border acquisitions
- Highlight the empirical evidence on cross-border acquisitions
- Highlight issues in cross-border valuation
- Provide a summary of takeover code in select countries

A firm can expand into another country by way of a greenfield investment in a new facility or by merging/acquiring a local firm. Cross-border M&A, like their domestic counterparts, involve a change in the control of the target firm, whereas a greenfield investment creates new assets. In a cross-border merger, the assets and operations of the two companies are combined to establish a new entity, whereas in a cross-border acquisition, the control of assets is transferred from a local to the foreign company. The local firm then becomes an affiliate of the foreign parent. Depending on the percentage holding in the target firm, the acquisition creates a minority (10%–45% of voting shares) or a majority (50%–99% of voting shares) interest. Cross-border acquisitions can be classified as horizontal, vertical, and conglomerate. Horizontal mergers take place between competing firms in the same industry to achieve synergy, vertical mergers take place between firms in the different parts of the value chain (for example, buyer and supplier) to reduce transaction costs, and conglomerate mergers take place between companies in unrelated activities.

In the first three quarters of 2014, the value of global M&A hit US$2.66 trillion, according to Thompson Reuters—a 60% increase on the same period in 2013. Many deals announced during this time were mega deals. Exhibit 8.1 presents the statistics on cross-border deal volume during 2004–13. Exhibit 8.2 lists out the largest acquirer and target countries.

Exhibit 8.1 *World Cross-border M&A (US$billion)*

2004	475
2005	683
2006	936
2007	1,390
2008	629
2009	347
2010	627
2011	610
2012	599
2013	408

Source: Thomson Reuters M&A database.

Depending on the mood of the acquirer, acquisitions can be either friendly or hostile. In a friendly takeover, the target firm agrees to the transaction, whereas hostile takeovers are undertaken against the wish of the target company's board. A large number of transactions are friendly in nature, partly because of the acquirer's unfamiliarity of the culture and environment in the host country.

MOTIVATIONS FOR CROSS-BORDER ACQUISITIONS

Businesses now operate in a global economy where national borders mean little to multinational businesses employing worldwide personnel and financial strategies to suit their strategic objectives. M&A activity is driven by many factors such as strength of the currency and stock market, tax, regulatory and technological changes, and level of interest rates.

Exhibit 8.2 *Largest Acquirer and Target Countries, 2004–13 (US$billion)*

	Target		**Acquirer**	
	US$ billion	**% Value**	**US$ billion**	**% Value**
United States	1529	23	1322	20
United Kingdom	1038	15	935	14
Canada	398	6	370	6
Germany	391	6	331	5
Netherlands	361	5	336	5
Australia	264	4	206	3
France	214	3	508	8
Spain	177	3	233	3
Switzerland	113	2	253	4
China	86	1	183	3
Japan	74	1	269	4
Rest of World	2058	31	1758	26
Total Worldwide	6704	100	6704	100

Source: Thomson Reuters M&A database.

The following factors, among others, have contributed to the growth in cross-border acquisitions:

Globalization of markets: The European unification, for instance, has increased competition among acquirers. In a poll of corporate M&A officers conducted by *Mergers & Acquisitions*, nearly three-fifths of the respondents reported that the 1992 unification of the European common market into the European Community has prompted them to make or plan acquisitions overseas (Kissin and Herrera 1990). But an even greater number see globalization of industries as a far more pressing reason for going abroad. For example, 76% stated that their companies need to go abroad in response to globalization, and 65% said their companies were not sufficiently represented overseas. Only 8% contended their companies had enough overseas presence that allowed them to pass up acquisitions and joint ventures abroad.

Opportunity to add additional value: Many companies in many countries have already extracted a significant proportion of the available value from domestic opportunities. These companies have exhausted the opportunity to improve profitability through better cost management and efficiency gains by consolidation. Cross-border acquisitions provide additional opportunities to reap the benefits of economies of scale. Risk can be diversified across markets. The combination of large size and international scope can lower both overall costs and unit costs as activities are moved to the most advantageous locations.

Resurgence in economic activity: The lack of deal activity in the post-crisis years (after the global financial crisis of 2007–08) has contributed to a pent-up demand for transactions. Increased investor appetite for growth, the availability of cheap debt, and a lack of other obvious ways to cut costs also drive companies to seek out M&A opportunities. These conditions are likely to persist.

Other factors that contribute to the growth of cross-border M&A include international deregulation, which removes barriers; global perspective adopted by institutional investors who provide capital; and homogenization of customer profiles across markets.

TRENDS IN CROSS-BORDER MERGERS AND ACQUISITIONS

As pointed out in earlier chapters, the worldwide takeover activity has been averaging US$5 trillion in the recent years. Like initial public offerings (IPOs), mergers also come in waves in the USA; once in the late 1980s and again in the second half of the 1990s due to heightened industrial restructuring. The number of acquisitions with values in excess of US$1 billion has increased manifold over the last 25 years.

Companies from a number of other European States have also sought out deals across the Atlantic. Declining growth rates across the EU have forced European firms to rely on exports and globalization to achieve growth. Accordingly, European firms have been acquiring US targets at their fastest pace since 2008. In the third quarter of 2014 alone, European firms announced US$87 billion worth of deals in the USA, more than the whole of 2013 combined. The relative strength of the Euro has also helped to facilitate European activity abroad.

While European firms have turned to the USA, European targets have become increasingly popular among companies from emerging markets. For Asian acquirers in particular, Europe has become the "go-to destination" as they look for ready-made brands and market know-how that can be exported wholesale to domestic markets. The US$1.5 billion acquisition of the UK pizza chain Pizza Express by the Chinese private equity group Hony Capital is indicative of this trend.

THE EMPIRICAL EVIDENCE ON CROSS-BORDER ACQUISITIONS

The empirical studies of the impact of M&A on corporate performance can be classified into two categories. The first group is "event studies," which uses changes in share prices to gauge changes in firm value. The second group measures corporate performance mainly by comparing various measures of profitability before and after the transaction. The rate of success or failure is typically assessed by comparing the performance with a relevant control group of companies.

Event studies assume that stock markets are efficient in the sense that changes in share prices of the firms involved after controlling for market movements in general represent the value of the event. Corporate performance is measured by comparing the share prices from before and after the transaction relative to a relevant control group. Evidence on domestic (USA and UK) M&A indicates that a target firm's shareholders generally lose or break even (Jensen and Ruback 1983). Similar studies have been conducted on how cross-border acquisitions (from the perspective of a US acquirer) differ from domestic transactions, based on stock and operating performance measures. For a sample of 4,430 acquisitions between 1985 and 1995, Moeller and Schlingemann (2002) find that US acquirers experience significantly lower stock and operating performance for cross-border than for domestic transactions. They also find that bidder returns are negatively related to the target country's economic restrictiveness.

Based on an analysis of all public deals in Europe between 1996 and 2000, Boston Consulting Group found that, on average, cross-border deals created value (as measured by market value added [MVA])[1] for both the acquirer and the target, although acquiring companies experienced substantially lower returns (Boston Consulting Group 2000). The study finds that the average increase in value for the shareholders of the target companies was 30% and for the shareholders of the acquirer it was 1%.

CROSS-BORDER VALUATION

The discounted cash flow (DCF) methodology for evaluating a project or an acquisition involves estimation of cash flows and discount rate. If the net present value (NPV) is positive, the acquisition can be accepted; if NPV is negative, it should be rejected. Estimating cash flows for a foreign acquisition is just an extension of its domestic counterpart except that the cash might be more variable or volatile. More specifically, cross-border valuation involves

- Estimation of cash flows specific to the acquisition.
- Estimation of discount rate specific to the acquisition.

Managers evaluating an international acquisition need to address two questions: Should the acquisition be evaluated from the perspective of managers in the country in which the firm is located or that of parent company? Should the cash flows be adjusted downward or the discount rate be raised to account for differential political and economic risks?

[1] MVA is a short-term measure that looks at the difference between the market capitalization of an acquiring company five days before a deal is done and its market capitalization 5 days after.

An international acquisition can be evaluated in two stages. In the first stage, the firm is evaluated from the subsidiary's perspective. In the second stage, the amount and timing of profits repatriated (after paying taxes) to the parent company is estimated. It is common practice to make ad hoc adjustments to cash flows or discount rates. For instance, if a company were to use 15% discount rate for a domestic acquisition, it might raise it to 20% for foreign acquisition. Such adjustments, obviously, do not have a sound basis. Some academics suggest that it is better to adjust cash flows to account for risks (and not discount rate) because international risks are unsystematic in nature and, hence, diversifiable. Remember that only systematic risk matters in a capital asset pricing model (CAPM) universe. Whether or not the discount rate for foreign acquisitions should be revised depends on how managers view risks in international projects. If the risks are adequately reflected in the project beta, then it is inappropriate to add an additional risk premium to the discount rate. There are two alternative approaches for valuing overseas investments.

Approach 1

1. Forecast foreign currency cash flows using host country tax rate and inflation rate.
2. Estimate foreign currency discount rate using project (target firm)-specific capital structure and beta.
3. Calculate present value (PV) of the free-cash flows in foreign currency.
4. Convert to home currency using spot exchange rate.

Approach 2

1. Forecast foreign currency cash flows using host country tax rate and inflation rate.
2. Forecast future exchange rates using parity relationships and convert cash flows to home currency.
3. Estimate home currency discount rate using project-specific capital structure and beta.
4. Calculate PV in home currency.

The two approaches usually give the same answer.

Adjusting cash flows: The effect of international risk can be incorporated by charging a premium for political and economic risk against each year's cash flows, that is, incorporate the cost of buying an insurance to cover political risk from an agency such as Overseas Private Investment Corporation or the Lloyd's of London and the cost of covering economic risk by a forward cover in the currency market. Another approach is to estimate the probability of expropriation and the expected value (mean) of cash flows. Once the cash flow in the host country's currency is estimated, probabilities are attached to different exchange rates (between local currency and home currency) forecasted by the analyst to translate cash flows into home currency.

Adjusting discount rate: Whether or not the discount rate for a foreign project should be adjusted depends on how one views international risk. Modern finance theory suggests that only systematic risk of a project matters as unsystematic risk can be diversified away. A multinational, due to its global focus, can diversify country-specific risk as long as cash flows

Exhibit 8.3	Global Correlations
US/UK	0.508
UK/France	0.499
UK/Germany	0.429
US/France	0.414
US/Germany	0.378
France/Germany	0.620
Canada/Switzerland	0.59
Japan/Germany	0.34
Italy/France	0.69

Source: Author.

from these counties are not perfectly positively correlated. The standard measure of systematic risk is beta, which measures the sensitivity of asset returns to market returns. What is the appropriate proxy for the market portfolio in case of multinational investment? Is it the portfolio in country of operation or that in the home country or a *global* portfolio?

The cost of equity estimate depends on the company's beta, which could be estimated using the home country index or some global index. The choice depends on the investment opportunity set facing the company's investors. If investors are assumed to be internationally diversified, the returns on a global portfolio would be a better benchmark for assessing the cost of equity. As long as there are benefits from international diversification, a portion of what seems to be a systematic risk in a domestic context may be a diversifiable country risk at a global level. If markets are completely integrated, there would be no benefit from international diversification. Although the tendency of markets to move together has increased in the recent years, the correlation is still less than 1 (see Exhibit 8.3; Goetzmann, Li, and Rouwenhorst 2005). So there are still risk-reducing opportunities.

The impact of globalization of capital markets has important implications for cost of capital for international companies. An estimate of cost of capital based on local CAPM is based on the assumption that each market is segmented from the rest of the world. Using a global CAPM would give more realistic estimates of expected returns for international firms.

The global CAPM expressed in dollars states that (O'Brien 1999):

$$E(R_{\$}) = R_{f\$} + b_{g\$} \text{ [Global Risk premium in dollar]}$$

where $\beta_{g\$}$ = global beta in US dollars measured by regressing monthly data for the target firm against an international index such as MSCI Emerging Markets Data Processing & Reproduction Index (if the target is a software company).

$R_{f\$}$ = risk-free rate in dollars

Global risk premium = [return on the global portfolio in US dollar – dollar risk-free rate]

= 3 to 5.4% (say, 4%)[2]

The dollar rate might be used to discount dollar free-cash flows to estimate the value of equity.

[2] What cost of equity in Rupee is consistent with the dollar rate obtained from the global CAPM? How do you translate the weighted average cost of capital (WACC) in one currency into the WACC in another currency? The answer to these questions is beyond the scope of this book. Interested readers may refer to Tom O'Brien's (1999) article. Also see Schramm and Wang 1999).

THE CASE OF EMERGING MARKETS

In many emerging countries, the stock markets lack depth. More than half the market capitalization is accounted for by a handful of companies. So the stock market index would be a poor proxy for market portfolio, which is supposed to represent the portfolio of all risky assets held by the marginal investor in the company. The resulting beta estimate would be biased. The investor, in this case, is a multinational company. As there is no international index,[3] one could use the home country stock market index as market portfolio. If we assume that the systematic risk of a project, in say, Chile, is about the same as that elsewhere, the problem boils down to finding the beta in the home country.

The risk premium for a foreign project could be expressed as:

Risk premium = base premium for a mature market + country premium

Cost of equity = $R_f + \beta$ (base premium for mature market like the USA) + Country premium

where R_f = T-bond rate, a proxy for risk-free rate.

Base premium is the geometric average premium (i.e., $R_m - R_f$) earned by stocks over bonds over a long period of time—6.1% in case of the USA. The country premium is added on the assumption that country risk cannot be diversified due to cross-market correlation. Put differently, a major portion of the country risk is systematic. The equity risk premium of a country is a function of country default risk and the volatility of equity market relative to the country bond market.

$$\text{Country equity risk premium} = \text{Country default spread} \times [\sigma_{equity}/\sigma_{country\ bond}]$$

The country risk can be measured by the credit rating given by international credit rating agencies such as S&P and Moody's.[4] These agencies publish default spread over *T*-bond rate and spread over corporate bonds with similar rating in the USA. Exhibit 8.4 presents the Moody's country ratings and the default spread. Either the corporate spread or the country spread could be used as default risk premium. The default risk premium should be translated into equity risk premium.

Country equity risk premium = Country default spread $\times[\sigma_{equity}/\sigma_{country\ bond}]$

where σ_{equity} is the standard deviation of returns on the country's stock market index and $\sigma_{country\ bond}$ is the standard deviation of the country bond prices.

Assume the following data:

Rf = *T*-bond rate in US = 5.1%

Beta = 0.7

Base premium = 6.1%

Country default spread over US corporates with same rating = 1.75%

$\sigma_{equity}/\sigma_{country\ bond} = 3.2$

Country premium = 1.75 × 3.2 = 5.6%

Cost of equity for the project = 5.1 + 6.1 + 5.6%

= 16.8%.

[3] We can probably take the Morgan Stanley Capital Index as the best proxy.

[4] See www.moodys.com

Exhibit 8.4 *Country Ratings and Default Spread*

Country	Long-term Bond Rating*	Country Risk Premium
Argentina	Ba3	4%
Australia	Aa2	0.65%
Austria	Aaa	0.00
Belgium	Aaa	0.00
Brazil	B2	5.5%
Canada	Aa2	0.65%
Chile	Baa1	1.2%
China	A3	0.95%
India	Ba2	3%
Indonesia	B3	6.5%
Japan	Aa1	0.60%
Pakistan	Caa1	7.5%
Sweden	Aa2	0.65%
Switzerland	Aaa	0.00

Source: Damodaran.

***Spread between interest on foreign currency country bond and that on US corporate bonds with similar rating.**

The cost of equity can be used to discount free cash flow to equity investors to value the project.

GTE, an international telephone company, operates in many countries. To evaluate their investments in overseas markets like Venezuela, different discount rates need to be calculated. To come up with an overseas discount rate, they add a country risk premium to the domestic cost of capital that reflects various country risk ratings as well as the yields on stripped Brady bonds and sovereign debt (Bank of America Roundtable on Evaluating and Financing Foreign Direct Investment 1996). The company uses the second approach outlined earlier for estimating the NPV of the overseas investment.

Avon Products adds a 3% risk premium for investment projects with paybacks longer than 3 years. The company adds an additional risk premium related to project risk and to sovereign risk.

CONVERTING DISCOUNT RATES

Some academicians suggest that the discount rate be calculated in home currency and then translated to host currency. The conversion of home currency discount rate to host country discount rate involves application of interest rate parity condition. Interest rate parity stipulates that the expected rate of change in the spot exchange rate equals the ratio of the prevailing interest rates in the two currencies.

$$(1 + \Delta s) = \frac{(1 + R_1)}{(1 + R_2)}$$

where Δs = expected change in spot rate.

R_1 and R_2 are yields on comparable government bonds denominated in the currencies in question. The weighted average cost of capital in one currency can be converted into another by multiplying it by the expected annual change in the exchange rate. While changes in exchange rates may correspond with changes in the differential in national inflation rates in the long run, there are sharp deviations from this parity relationship for shorter intervals. The inflation rate in many emerging markets is much higher than that in stable economies. So discounting foreign cash flows with interest rate in that country would be inappropriate. Likewise, managers in low interest rate economies like Japan should not use the Yen rate. This will inflate the NPV of the investment.

Some executives calculate the discount rate as the sum of interest rate the home government would pay in the host country and a premium that reflects the spread over treasuries the company will have to pay when at home. The average of interest rates over a cycle might be used to discount cash flows. It is important to understand that the interest rate used to discount should be distinguished from the currency borrowed to finance the project to keep valuation and financing separate.

Thus, the discount rate for a Mexican company that pays 3% over treasuries when at home, for a project in the UK

= Rate at which the Mexican government borrows from UK + 3% premium.

CONCLUDING COMMENTS

Like domestic acquisitions, cross-border acquisitions usually fail to create value. But this should not discourage companies from expanding overseas. CEOs are usually overly concerned with the differences in national cultures while acquiring abroad. CEOs can enhance the value of cross-border deals by:

- Establishing a clear growth strategy and setting common goals for both the companies.
- Driving cultural change from the top.
- Appointing foreigners on the board.
- Taking all the usual steps one takes in a domestic acquisition.

Case Study

Bharti Airtel's Acquisition of Zain

On February 15, 2010, Bharti Airtel announced that it had entered into exclusive discussions with Mobile Telecommunications Company KSC (Zain) for the acquisition of Zain Africa International BV, and thereby the entire African operations of Zain, excluding the operations in Sudan and Morocco. The two rounds of arduous negotiations with MTN Group Limited, another African telecom company, was not successful. Bharti Airtel played it safe this time and made an offer to Zain that it just could not refuse. For an ailing company, Bharti Airtel's offer of US$10.7 billion was considered too high. Airtel hoped to turn Zain around by exporting its business model to Africa.

On March 30, 2010, Mr Sunil Bharti Mittal, chairman and managing director of Bharti Airtel, and Mr Asaad Al Banwan, chairman, Zain Group, executed the definitive agreements at Netherlands that transformed Bharti Airtel into an emerging-market multinational. The acquisition was the one of the largest by an Indian company, second only to the US$12 billion takeover of Corus group by Tata Steel in 2007. In the Indian telecom sector, the deal was the second largest after the US$11.2 billion Vodafone-Hutchison transaction in 2007.

The transaction was structured as an all-cash deal. Bharti Airtel agreed to pay:

1. US$8.3 billion within 3 months from the date of closing
2. US$700 million after 1 year from the date of closing; and
3. US$1.7 billion debt on the books of Zain

The acquisition was to be funded by borrowing US$7.5 billion from a consortium of banks led by Standard Chartered Bank and Barclays Bank and a Rupee loan amounting to US$1 billion from State Bank of India. To facilitate the acquisition, Airtel set up two subsidiaries in Singapore and Netherlands. The subsidiary in Netherlands would acquire the assets of Zain Africa International BV.

Company Backgrounds

Bharti Airtel Limited (Airtel) is an Indian telecommunications company that operated in 19 countries across South Asia and Africa. It operated a GSM network in all countries, providing 2G or 3G services depending upon the country of operation. It was the largest cellular service provider in India, with over 143 million subscribers. It had a 29% market share of the GSM mobile services in India. It also offered fixed line services and broadband services. It offered its telecom services under the Airtel brand and was headed by Sunil Bharti Mittal. The company also provided land-line telephone services and broadband Internet access (DSL) in over 96 cities in India. In January 2010, it acquired Warid Telecom, a 3-million-subscriber company based in Dhaka, Bangladesh, for US$300 million.

Zain was established in 1983 in Kuwait. It was a public company engaged in the provision of mobile telecommunication and data services in Kuwait and 21 other countries in the Middle East and North Africa. Zain Africa was a wholly owned subsidiary of Zain. It was incorporated in Netherlands and held the African operations of Zain. The company was originally named Celtel. It was acquired by Zain in 2005 and renamed as Zain International BV.

Deal Pricing

Bharti Airtel paid Zain an enterprise value of US$10.7 billion, which was 10 times the earnings before interest, taxes, depreciation, and amortization (EBIDTA). To put this valuation in perspective, Bharti Airtel itself traded at 7.2 times EBITDA. Even if significant EBITDA growth of 20%–22% for the next 2 years were factored in, an EV/EBITDA multiple of 6x–6.5x could have been justified. This made the transaction one of the most expensive emerging market telecom transactions.

The transaction exposed Bharti Airtel to important commercial, interest, and exchange rate risks. To acquire a financially sinking company, Bharti Airtel incurred an expensive loan of US$8.3 billion at an interest rate of 195 basis points over The London Interbank Offered Rate (LIBOR). The loan could be a drag on Bharti Airtel's earnings with no immediate returns from the loss-making target. The floating rate interest meant significant interest rate risk exposure. It also created foreign exchange exposure for Airtel as capital expenditure would have been in US dollars but revenue streams would be in local currencies.

However, it was common to link enterprise value to the number of subscribers rather than EBITDA in the telecom industry. The acquisition of 26% equity stake in Tata Tele by DoCoMo and 68% equity stake taken in Hutch Essar by Vodafone carried similar valuations on an EV/subscriber basis.

Financing

Bharti Airtel structured this acquisition as a leveraged buyout and the loan for financing the transaction was availed by two special purpose vehicles (SPV) created in Netherlands and Singapore for the purposes of the acquisition. The SPVs would borrow US$8.3 billion on their balance sheet. Bharti Airtel Netherlands BV would borrow US$5.5 billion and the Singapore SPV would borrow the rest of the amount.

The debt on the books of SPVs would not impact the parent's balance sheet in the near term as the parent was ring fenced from off-shore operations. Before the acquisition, Airtel's debt-equity ratio was 0.4. This would have shot up to 1.2 had Airtel assumed the loan on its books. It would have limited Airtel's ability to raise funds in the future for expansion into new third-generation technologies. However, creating SPVs did not absolve Airtel from overall responsibility of a borrower; it had to provide a guarantee to bankers for the loan on the SPVs books.

Rationale for the Acquisition

The Indian telecom market had almost reached its saturation point with very little scope for expansion left—only rural India offered some opportunities. Being a telecom company, it could not diversify its portfolio into other businesses. Geographic expansion into new markets was the only strategic alternative.

After the acquisition, Airtel would be the fifth-largest telecom services company in the world, with over 200 million subscribers. The acquisition would help Airtel diversify its asset base as well as provide a hedge to Indian operations. The company would have better bargaining power with equipment vendors. African countries had similar characteristics (e.g., low income and tariffs and substantial rural population) as India. The African market offered high growth potential as the region was currently underpenetrated. Only one in two Africans owned a mobile phone, and Zain had a strong presence in most countries. It had a 50%–75% market share in seven countries and a 25%–50% share in six, providing a strong platform for Bharti Airtel to build upon. Even though the company was running in losses, Airtel could utilize the infrastructure and facilities of Zain Africa to harness the potential of African markets. The average revenue per user (ARPU) of Zain Africa was high and that justified its current valuation.

Monthly ARPU in Africa averaged US$7.5, which was higher than India's ARPU of US$5. African customers consumed 100 minutes per month, whereas Indian consumers used 450 minutes per month. This suggests that Zain Africa's profitability was lower than Bharti Airtel's, despite a higher spending by its users.

Airtel's strategy was to make its customers talk more by reducing the call rates and concentrating on the rural population. Africa presented a good opportunity to experiment with the model that it had mastered in India. The demand for mobile services was growing at a rate of 25% across African countries. The strategy would be profitable if the demand for cellular services was price elastic.

On the flip side, Airtel faced significant challenges relating to infrastructure development, regulatory environment, language barriers, and political instability. The deal lacked commercial synergies too. Airtel had revenues of US$8 billion and net income of US$2 billion in the previous fiscal year. Zain Africa had made a marginal loss of US$112 million and the revenues were just US$100 million.

Stock Market Reaction

Upon announcement of the agreement, the stock price fell from ₹317 on February 11, 2010, to ₹289.80 on February 16, 2010. Over the next month, the stock rose gradually rose to pre-announcement levels of ₹317. Exhibit 8.5 presents the stock price evolution.

The Role of SPVs

Netherlands, with its efficient tax regime coupled with an investor-friendly business environment, had emerged as a preferred offshore jurisdiction for the setting up of holding companies. Netherlands also

Exhibit 8.5 *Stock Market Reaction to Announcement*

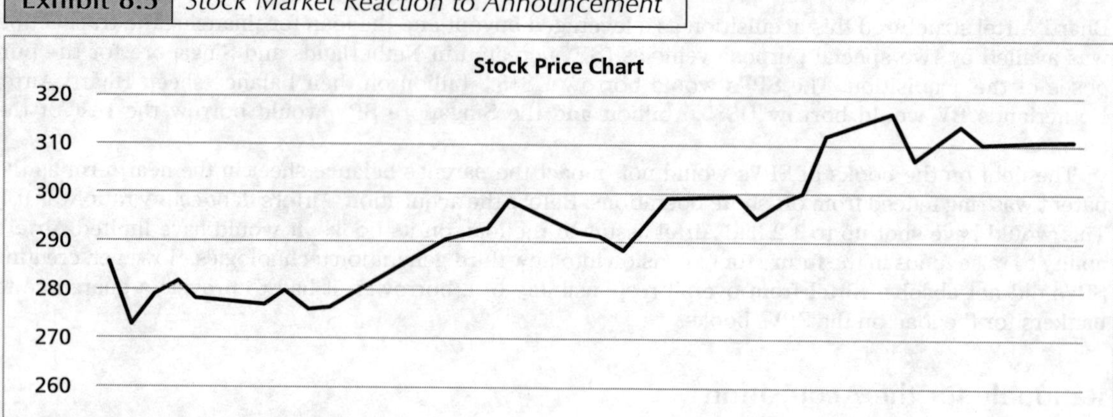

Source: Case writer.

provided various incentives under its tax regime including tax exemption on dividend payments and capital gains through the participation exemption regime. Netherlands had entered into double tax avoidance treaties with many African nations where Zain had business interests, and to that extent, it would provide for repatriation of profits.

Netherlands also had one of the widest networks of bilateral investment treaties, with close to 100 treaties. Bilateral investment treaties provided a safety net to a foreign investor with respect to its investments.

The structure adopted by Bharti Airtel for acquisition was efficient from a tax perspective, specifically with respect to repatriation of profits from Zain Africa to Bharti Airtel.

Under the domestic tax laws of Netherlands, no taxes are levied on dividends distributed between two companies resident in Netherlands, subject to compliance with the applicable participation exemption conditions. Thus, it should provide for a tax free transfer of profits from Zain Africa to Bharti Airtel Netherlands BV. Further, under the Netherlands-Singapore tax treaty, dividends paid by Bharti Airtel Netherlands BV to Singapore SPV would not be subject to any taxes in Netherlands since the Singapore SPV held 25% of the share capital of the company declaring the dividends.

Under the domestic tax laws of Singapore, foreign dividends are exempt from Singapore corporate taxes, provided the foreign dividends had been subjected to tax in the home country and the headline tax rate of the foreign jurisdiction is at least 15%. The headline tax rate in Netherlands was 25.5%. Dividends received by the Singapore SPV would be exempt from corporate taxes in Singapore because the home country had taxes although Airtel was exempted.

Singapore did not levy any withholding tax on distribution of dividends. Therefore, dividends distributed by the Singapore SPV to Bharti Airtel would only be taxable in India (when distributed) as per the provisions of the Income Tax Act, 1961.

Subsequent Events

The next five years were difficult for Airtel on account of the Zain acquisition. Zain missed the growth target because it had not invested adequately in assets and infrastructure. Airtel spent US$5 billion on network improvement. However, at the end of the March 2013 quarter, Airtel had 63.4 million subscribers from the 17 countries, with a net loss of US$345 million from a revenue of US$3.76 billion.[5] At the end of March 2015, Bharti Africa netted losses of US$585 million on a revenue of US$4.2 billion. The subscriber numbers stood at 76.2 million. Airtel had to absorb huge foreign currency losses because of currency volatility in Africa.

REFERENCES AND SUGGESTED READINGS

Bank of America Roundtable on Evaluating and Financing Foreign Direct Investment. 1996. *Journal of Applied Corporate Finance*, 9 (3, Fall): 64–79.

Blum, Stephen. 1995. "Combine & Conquer." *Journal of Business Strategy* (November–December): 26–28.

Boston Consulting. 2000. Crossing Borders: European Mergers and Acquisitions. (September). Boston Consulting Group Report.

Cakici, Nusrett, Chris Hessel, and Kishore Tandon. 1996. "Foreign Acquisitions in the United States: Effect on Shareholder Wealth of Foreign Acquiring Firms." *Journal of Banking and Finance*, 20 (2): 307–29.

Carter, Eugene, and Rita M. Rodriguez. 1979. *International Financial Management*. Englewood Cliffs, N.J.: Prentice Hall.

Collins, Simon. *Understanding Sector Trends*. KPMG Report. Available at http://www.ciionline.org/events/mergers_presentation/SIMON%20COLLINS.pdf (Accessed on January 2006).

Damodaran, Aswath. "Estimating Risk Premiums." Working Paper. Stern School of Business.

Dimson, Elroy, Paul Marsh and Mike Staunton. 2002. *Triumph of the Optimists: 101 Years of Global Investment Returns*. Princeton, NJ: Princeton University Press.

Divecha, A. B., J. Drach, and D. Stefek. 1992. "Emerging Markets: A Quantitative Perspective." *Journal of Portfolio Management*, 19 (1, Fall): 41–50.

Estrada, Javier. 2000. "The Cost of Equity in Emerging Markets: A Downside Risk Approach." *Emerging Markets Quarterly*, 4 (3, Fall): 19–30.

Eun, Cheol, Richard Kolodny, and Carl Sheraga. 1996. "Cross-border Acquisitions and Shareholder Wealth: Tests of the Synergy and Internationalization Hypotheses." *Journal of Banking and Finance*, 20 (9): 1559–82.

Evenett, Simon J. 2003, April. "The Cross Border Mergers and Acquisitions Wave of the Late 1990s." NBER Working Paper No. 9655. The National Bureau of Economic Research.

Goetzmann W., L. Li, and G. Rouwenhorst, 2005. "Long term Global Market Correlations." *Journal of Business*, 78 (1): 1–3.

Inkpen, Andrew, Anant K. Sundaram, and Kristin Rockwood. 2000. "Cross-Border Acquisitions of U.S. Technology Assets." *California Management Review*, 42 (3, Spring).

Jensen M. C., and R. Ruback. 1983. "The Market for Corporate Control: The Scientific Evidence." *Journal of Financial Economics*, 11 (1–4, April): 5–50.

Kissin, Warren D., and Julio Herrera. 1990. "International Mergers and Acquisitions." *Journal of Business Strategy*, 11 (4, July–August): 51–54.

Kedia, Simi. 2001, December. "Vodafone AirTouch's Bid for Mannesmann." HBS Case No. 9-201-096.

Lessard, Donald. 1981. "Evaluating International Projects: An Adjusted Present Value Approach." In *Capital Budgeting under Conditions of Uncertainty*, edited by Crum and Derkinderen. Martinus Nijhoff Publishing.

———. 1996. "Incorporating Country Risk in the Valuation of Offshore Projects." *Journal of Applied Corporate Finance*, 9 (3, Fall): 52–63.

Martynova, Martina, and Luc Renneboog 2006. "Mergers and Acquisitions in Europe." ECGI Finance Working Paper No. 114/2006, CentER Discussion Paper Series No. 2006-06. Available at SSRN: https://ssrn.com/abstract=880379 (Accessed on October 30, 2017).

[5] See http://www.livemint.com/Companies/5BNrEASu52s5lSKj7WWJMP/5-years-on-Airtels-Africa-business-still-off-target.html, accessed August 28, 2017.

Moeller, Sara, and Frederick P Schlingemann. 2002. "Are Cross Border Acquisitions Different from Domestic Acquisitions? Evidence on Stock and Operating Performance for U.S. Acquirers." Working Paper. Katz Graduate School of Business, University of Pittsburgh.

O'Brien, Thomas. 1999. "The Global CAPM and a Firm's Cost of Capital in Different Currencies." *Journal of Applied Corporate Finance*, 12 (3, Fall).

Shapiro, Alan. 1993. "International Capital Budgeting." *Midland Corporate Finance Journal*, 1 (1, Spring): 26–45.

Schramm, Ronald M., and Henry Wang. 1999. "Measuring the Cost of Capital in an International Framework." *Journal of Applied Corporate Finance*, 12 (3, Fall): 63–72.

Sirower, Mark. 1997. The Synergy Trap. New York, NY: Free Press.

United Nations World Investment Report: Cross-Border Mergers and Acquisitions and Development. 2000. New Delhi: Bookwell.

EXERCISE

In 2007, a US multinational requested a "bulge bracket" investment bank to value 2 of its divisions in Argentina and Brazil. Will Smith, an analyst with the bank, was asked to forecast free cash flow and estimate suitable discount rates for each of these divisions. Exhibit 8.6 presents the forecast of free cash flow for the 2 divisions.

Cash flows are expected to grow at 6% p.a. after 2012 in perpetuity. The cash flows from local currency were translated into USD using the estimated exchange rate for each period. The only task remaining is the estimation of discount rate. Smith discovered that the businesses in Latin America had no pure play proxies. Most of the competitors were subsidiaries of large, diversified companies. So the determination of beta for each country operation was difficult. In addition, the efficiency of the local stock markets was questionable and so was the estimate of risk premium.

The analyst obtained the dollar borrowing rate, tax rates, and target capital structure information from relevant sources. These are displayed in Exhibit 8.7.

To calculate the cost of equity, the analyst can choose between two approaches under the CAPM method. The first approach involves usage of local CAPM parameters. The second

Exhibit 8.6 *Forecast of Free Cash Flow (in US$'000)*

	2008	2009	2010	2011	2012
Argentina	6930	7117	7331	7617	7990
Brazil	10920	11215	11551	12002	12591

Source: Author.

Exhibit 8.7 *Borrowing Rates, Tax Rates, and Capital Structure*

Subsidiary	Borrowing Rate %	Tax Rate %	Target D/V %
Argentina	8	35	20
Brazil	12	35	20

Source: Author.

approach involves estimation of parameters (and cost of equity) for US, which would then be adjusted for individual country risk to yield estimates for these subsidiaries. Other relevant data are given as:

Foreign currency debt rating

	Moody's	S&P
Argentina	B1	BB-
Brazil	B1	B+

US Treasuries are yielding:

	YTM %
1 year T-Bill	5.92
10 year	6.80
30 year	7.0

Median beta and capital structure information for comparable US industries are given:

	1	2	3	4
Unlevered Median				
Beta[6]	0.86	0.79	0.74	0.76
Mean D/V ratio (Market values)	0.2	0.18	0.17	0.19

Refer to other data given in the chapter. Estimate an appropriate discount rate for and the value of each of the divisions.

REVIEW QUESTIONS

1. What factors are driving cross-border acquisitions?
2. Describe the two approaches for cross-border valuation.
3. Write a note on estimation of cost of equity in emerging markets.

[6] Beta when leverage is zero. The relationship between unlevered and levered beta is: $\beta_A = \beta_E$ [D/V].

CHAPTER 9

Empirical Evidence on Mergers

P. Raghavendra Rau

Learning Objectives

- Highlight the empirical findings on returns to acquiring as well as acquired firms
- Introduction to event studies, a type of empirical research methodology
- Summarize research on all aspects of mergers

Over the past four decades, mergers and takeovers have been the subjects of extensive research. Every decade, surveys of the literature have summarized the extent of our knowledge in the area. Examples of these surveys include Jensen and Ruback (1983), Jarrell, Brickley, and Netter (1988), Agrawal and Jaffe (1999), and Bruner (2002), among others. As the body of merger research becomes more and more extensive, the later surveys focus on specific areas. Agrawal and Jaffe (1999), for example, focus on the long-horizon post-merger stock performance of acquirers in mergers. Bruner (2002) focuses on whether M&A activities create value, especially for the bidding firm. Almost without exception, however, the surveys echo Jensen and Ruback (1983, 47) in concluding that the "knowledge of the sources of takeover gains still elude us." After 40 years of research, what do we know about mergers today? There are some well-known stylized facts that are often quoted in the financial press: mergers create value for target firms, mergers usually destroy value for acquiring firms, diversifying mergers destroy value more than others, mergers occur in waves, and so on. What evidence are these statements based on? In addition, this past decade has seen the largest merger wave in history as well as some of the largest merger failures. Do these stylized facts still hold true for recent mergers? This chapter will start by discussing the methodology that has been used in empirical research in mergers. Since the surveys cited in the first paragraph discuss empirical research in mergers till the beginning of the last decade, this chapter will focus mostly on research in the past decade and attempt to draw broad inferences as to where the field is heading. Unfortunately, in time-honored tradition, it will also conclude that we still do not have a clear idea of why mergers happen and why they create value.

MERGER STUDY METHODOLOGIES

There have been four major approaches to studying the causes and consequences of mergers. The simplest approach is a survey of executives. These are mostly practitioner studies, many of which were carried out by consulting firms such as McKinsey, PricewaterhouseCoopers, and so on. Bruner (2002) provides an overview and examples of such surveys. The problem with such surveys is that they are not run as controlled studies. Since the surveys are usually interviews with executives, their views as to the determinants of success and failure of acquisitions may not be related to the economic value created by the acquisition. Moreover, since no attempt is made to control for objective factors that have been shown to influence the success or failure of acquisitions, it is difficult to conclude anything from these studies. Take, for example, a (typical) survey by Coopers & Lybrand that examines 124 US companies in a variety of industries in 1996. Each of the companies, with average revenues of US$1.4 billion and 6,400 employees, had executed a merger or acquisition during the previous three years. The survey concludes that the speed of completing a deal has a direct bearing on its success. According to the report, "Accepted wisdom is that acquisitions differ so much by industry and participant that they defy any common analysis. But one variable is common to all deals—the speed at which integration of the acquirer and the target occurs," Coopers stated.

> The most compelling single finding of the survey was that, by a margin of nine to one, acquirers wish they could have conducted the transition period more quickly. Firms that followed a fast-track strategy reported achieving over 80% of their objectives. Firms following a more go-slow approach reported a failure rate approaching 50%. (*Success Goes to the Swift, Study Indicates* 1997)

In this study, none of the parameters being examined are objective. It is difficult to even determine the direction of causality. Perhaps slow-to-integrate firms were firms that had more difficulty with the integration and a priori might have been expected to have a greater probability of failure.

The second approach to studying mergers is the clinical case study. These studies explore particular mergers in depth, usually through extensive field interviews with the executives involved. Many of these studies often produce new insights. In 1996, for example, the National Bureau of Economic Research commissioned in-depth case studies of a small number of mergers (see Kaplan 2000). These studies revealed that the economic environment surrounding mergers is far too rich to be captured by large sample studies. However, clinical studies also suffer from the same defect that surveys do. While they are more objective than surveys, it is still difficult to get insights into the costs and benefits of the merger process in general.

The third and fourth approaches are related. The third approach, and by far, the most common approach, is the event study approach. An event study measures the effect of some company-specific information on the price of securities of the company or on its operating performance. Event studies have been used to study the stock price performance of acquiring and target firms in the immediate period around the merger announcement date up to 5 years after the completion of the merger. They have also been used to study the accounting/operating performance of the merged firms in the years surrounding the takeover. Since this method is so commonly used, it is worthwhile to spend some time considering its advantages and disadvantages. Perhaps the first published paper using the event study methodology was Dolley

(1933). This paper examines the price effects of stock splits in a sample of 95 splits between 1921 and 1931.

Over the next two decades, this methodology increased in sophistication until the first modern event studies were developed in papers such as Ball and Brown (1968) and Fama, Fisher, Jensen, and Roll (1969; FFJR). Ball and Brown investigated the information content of earnings, while FFJR studied the effects of stock splits after removing the effects of simultaneous dividend increases. Since then, the basic event study methodology has not changed.[1]

In a standard event study, a sample of firms is collected where all the sample firms have experienced a common event such as a merger. The event date is defined as the day or month of the announcement (or completion) of the event in a widely disseminated publication such as the *Wall Street Journal* (WSJ) or, more commonly, the Dow Jones News Retrieval index. The event firms are then lined up in event time and an event period is defined between $-t$ periods before to $+t$ periods after the event date. On each day or month of the event period, the return for each security is computed from time $-t$ to $+t$. A benchmark is used to compute what the returns to the event firms would have been if the event had not been announced. Then the abnormal returns (also called excess returns or residuals) are computed by subtracting these "normal" returns from the returns realized by the firm. These abnormal returns are then averaged across all firms in the sample and finally cumulated over the $-t$ to $+t$ period to obtain a cumulative abnormal return (CAR).

One of the primary assumptions made in the event study is the correct benchmark model of normal returns. The parameters of this model are usually estimated using data outside the event period $-t$ to $+t$. Hence, the two choices that have to be made are that of the correct model to use and the relevant estimation period to estimate the parameters of the model. The mean-adjusted return method, market-adjusted return method, market model residual method, capital asset pricing model (CAPM) residual method, empirical market line method, and comparison portfolio method have been among the most common methods in the literature to estimate the *ex ante* expected return.

The mean-adjusted return method assumes that the expected rate of return for security i is the average rate of return to the security in a hold-out period. This method assumes that the expected rate of return is constant over time and ignores contemporaneous market information. The market-adjusted return method assumes that the expected rate of return for the security is the expected return to the market, so the abnormal return e_{it}, conditional on observing the market return, R_{mt}, is equal to $R_{it} - R_{mt}$. This method ignores differences across securities but incorporates contemporaneous market movements. It also raises the additional issue of the choice of market index to use.

The market model residual method assumes that returns are generated by the market model

$$R_{it} = \alpha_i + \beta_i R_{mt} + e_{it}$$

where αi and βi are estimated in the estimation period so that

$$e_{it} = R_{it} - \alpha_i - \beta_i R_{mt}$$

This method recognizes differences between securities and incorporates contemporaneous market information. The CAPM residual method is very similar. It assumes that the conditional

[1] A detailed survey of the event study literature can be found in MacKinlay (1997).

expected rate of return is given by $R_{ft} + \beta_i(R_{mt} - R_{ft})$, where β_i is estimated in the estimation period so that

$$e_{it} = R_{it} - (R_{ft} + \beta_i(R_{mt} - R_{ft}))$$

It incorporates differences between securities, contemporaneous market information, and contemporaneous interest rate information. It assumes that the CAPM holds—an assumption that is being increasingly challenged in the literature.

The empirical market line model (also called the Fama-Macbeth residual method, after Fama and Macbeth [1973]) estimates beta of all securities in the market using 5 years of monthly data. These securities are then sorted in order of beta into 20 portfolios. The next 5 years are used to recompute the betas of the 20 portfolios. From year 11 onward, each month, a cross-sectional regression is run on the returns to each portfolio.

$$R_p = \alpha_{0t} + \alpha_{it}\,\beta_p + n_p$$

The abnormal return e_{it} is then equal to $R_{it} - \alpha_{0t} - \alpha_{it}\,\beta_{it}$, where the β_{it} are estimated using past data. The procedure is then repeated every year until the end of the sample period. Mandelker (1974), probably the first formal event study of mergers, uses this approach. Mandelker analyzed 241 mergers over the period 1941–62, where both the acquiring and target firms were listed on the New York Stock Exchange (NYSE) using the Fama-Macbeth residual method.

Finally, the comparison portfolio method ranks all stocks according to their beta and forms 20 portfolios. The excess return is then the difference between the return and the return to the portfolio with the same beta. A variant of this procedure ranks stocks according to size into five size-sorted portfolios and within each portfolio into five book-to-market (B/M)-based portfolios, so that we obtain 25 size-sorted B/M portfolios. Depending on the model of expected returns, other conditioning variables (such as industry) have also been used to form the comparison portfolios. In another variant of this procedure, an individual matching firm is picked instead of a matching portfolio. This matching firm approach brings its own attendant issues, such as how to deal with a delisting of the matching firm, and so on.

Note that all these methods assume that the parameters of the return-generating process are not influenced by the event. In many cases, we may have reason to believe that this is not a good assumption. For example, targets in takeover bids may become less risky after an announcement (beta falls) because after the announcement, the company's stock price is largely driven by speculation about the outcome of the takeover, which is largely unrelated to market events, especially in a cash offer.

The event-time methodology is conceptually simple, theoretically well-grounded, and easy to execute. It is no wonder that event studies have dominated the field since their inception. Using appropriate benchmarks, event studies have been used to measure both the stock price and operating performance, of acquirers, targets, and the combined entity, both in the short and long run.

The major weakness of the event study approach is that inferences drawn from it are always joint hypotheses—that the event earns abnormal returns and that the benchmark used provides the right measure of "normal" returns. Event studies require significant assumptions on market efficiency, rationality of market participants, and no limits on arbitrage. It is reasonable to argue that these assumptions are fulfilled for most stocks on average, especially in the short run. Long-run event studies—that measure abnormal performance over a period of years after the event—are more vulnerable to these criticisms. Brown and Warner (1980, 1985) discuss the issues involved in estimating short-horizon event studies using monthly and daily data respectively. Barber and Lyon (1997), Kothari and Warner (1997), and Lyon, Barber, and Tsai (1999) discuss the issues involved in estimating long-horizon event studies. Finally, Barber and Lyon (1996) discuss issues in estimating abnormal operating performance.

The final approach is a variant of the event-study approach. Here event firms are lined up in calendar time. An event portfolio is formed each period to include all companies that have completed the event in the prior n periods. Then the performance of this event portfolio is tracked over time relative to an explicit asset-pricing model or some other benchmark. This approach was first used by Jaffe (1974) and Mandelker (1974). The advantage of this method is that the cross-sectional correlations of the individual firm returns are accounted for in the portfolio variance at each point in calendar time.

To summarize the discussion so far, the typical approach to computing the economic effect of mergers is to compute abnormal returns (in the short- or long-term), form hypotheses about the factors that should explain these returns and regress the abnormal returns on these factors. In addition, some studies also examine subsequent company performance using earnings or managerial or earnings forecasts. Taking this methodology as given, therefore, the rest of the chapter will summarize the empirical results on mergers. As mentioned in the introduction, the focus will be on research over the last decade.

EMPIRICAL RESEARCH ON MERGERS

Over the past four decades, several major strands of merger research can be identified. In this section, I will touch upon recent research that examines the following questions:

1. Who wins and who loses in mergers?
2. In computing the gains to bidders and targets, what is the impact of
   a. Acquisition method: Merger or tender offer
   b. Means of payment: Stock or cash
   c. Attitude of the transaction: Hostile or friendly
   d. Regulation
   e. Ownership and governance structure: Managerial ownership, institutional holdings, bidder toeholds
   f. Nature of the industry
3. Why do acquirers acquire?
4. What are the characteristics of potential targets?

Note that this is by no means a comprehensive list. Other topics I will not touch upon include the role of financial intermediaries in mergers, the determinants of mergers waves, the effectiveness of takeover defenses, the value of corporate voting rights, and so on. Most empirical research in mergers has focused on the sources of gains to merger participants, so this section will start by examining the source of merger gains as well.

Who Wins and Who Loses in Mergers?

There are several parties who are affected by a merger. In addition to the bidder and the target shareholders, these include managers, bidder and target bondholders, preferred shareholders, and other firms in the same industry. Over the past three decades, empirical research on merger gains has tended to focus on bidder and target shareholders. The almost uniform conclusion is that target shareholders earn positive returns. In contrast, the results on bidder returns are more controversial. Some studies suggest that bidders earn zero or perhaps even negative returns. Other studies have documented that these results are sensitive to issues of methodology. Since the results on bidder and target gains from acquisitions are exhaustively reviewed in the surveys cited in the introduction, I will not discuss the individual studies here but focus more on the sources of the gains.

Returns to Targets

In a survey of the evidence till 1983, Jensen and Ruback (1983) document that target shareholders in successful acquisitions tend to earn abnormal returns of around 20% in mergers and 30% in tender offers. In unsuccessful acquisitions, on average, they do not lose. Bruner (2002) summarizes the evidence from 21 studies between 1978 and 2001 and documents gains of between 7% and 126.9% to target shareholders over periods ranging from 120 days before the acquisition announcement up to 5 years after the completion of the acquisition. Target shareholders, therefore, gain from acquisitions.

Returns to Acquirers

As mentioned earlier, the returns to acquirers are more controversial. These studies can typically be classified into short- and long-horizon studies. Short-horizon studies typically examine periods less than a year in length immediately around the announcement date, while long-horizon studies examine periods ranging up to 5 years after the completion of the acquisition.

Jensen and Ruback (1983) report returns to shareholders in acquiring firms of 4% in tender offers and 0% in bidders in the short-horizon around the announcement date. The conclusion that bidders tend to earn low returns has not changed greatly over next two decades. Bruner (2002) reports the results from 20 short-horizon studies over the period 1978–2001 that find negative returns to bidding firms, ranging from 1% to 3%. Thirteen of these are significantly negative. However, he also reports the results from 24 studies over the same period that find positive returns to bidding firms, with 17 of these being significantly positive. Overall, therefore, in the short-term, bidders do not seem to either gain or lose from acquisitions.

Agrawal and Jaffe (1999) review 22 studies that have examined bidder returns in the long-term up to 5 years after the completion of an acquisition. They document that acquirer shareholders in tender offers do not lose (and earn significantly positive abnormal returns in two studies), but acquirer shareholders in mergers earn significantly negative abnormal returns. This conclusion is robust to a wide variety of statistical techniques, and is documented over a long time period, in both the USA and the UK. There is not much recent research on post-merger performance following failed bids, but older research seems to suggest negative bidder returns following such bids.

As mentioned in the section "Merger Study Methodologies," these long-horizon results are sensitive to methodological issues and are more controversial than those from short-horizon studies. While it is tempting to argue that the long-term abnormal performance documented is simply an artifact of the methodology, similar results obtained from a wide variety of statistical tests, periods, and countries make it difficult to argue that there is nothing there.

One reason why these returns might persist is due to practical limits on arbitrage. Baker and Savasoglu (2002) construct risk arbitrage positions for 1,901 cash and stock M&A offers over the period 1981–96. Each position is designed to provide a fixed payoff if the deal is successfully completed according to its original terms. They argue that excess returns to these positions, around 0.6%–0.9% per month are due to practical limits on risk arbitrage. The risk-bearing capacity of arbitrageurs, who might be expected to drive the price to the correct value, is constrained by the deal completion risk and the size of the position they hold.

Returns to Bidders and Targets Combined

A third strand of research examines whether mergers create any economic value. Since the bidders are usually much larger than the targets, the large stock returns to targets documented here could be easily offset by a small loss to bidder shareholders, and the merger as a whole could destroy economic value. Bruner (2002) surveys 20 studies that examine this issue either by forming a value-weighted portfolio of the bidder and target firms or by examining the absolute dollar value of the returns. Almost all these studies report positive returns to bidder and target shareholders together. Over half of them report significantly positive returns.

Overall, therefore, M&A activity is economically valuable. Most of the gains, however, seem to go to target shareholders. Why are the gains to bidders so small? There are several explanations. Bradley, Desai, and Kim (1988) suggest that the bidder market is competitive, and this one-sided competition wipes out bidder gains. Bruner (2002) concludes that the zero abnormal returns earned by bidders mean that bidder shareholders do earn a normal risk-adjusted return. Other researchers (see, for example, Asquith, Bruner, and Mullins 1983) have suggested that this is simply an artifact of the relative size of the bidder and the target. There is also an asymmetric information effect—investors will rationally mark down the prices of firms that announce an acquisition if they interpret this as a lack of growth opportunities within the firm. Managers of bidding firms may be driven by nonvalue maximizing objectives such as the need to diversify. Morck, Shleifer, and Vishny (1990) find that returns to bidding shareholders are lower when their firm diversifies, when it buys a rapidly growing target, and when its managers performed poorly before the acquisition. Finally, market inefficiency may mean that we need to look at the long-horizon before the effect of the merger is fully incorporated into bidder stock returns. Some of these explanations are considered later in the section on motivations for acquisitions.

Returns to Rivals

A number of authors (see, for example, Eckbo 1983, or Mitchell and Mulherin 1996) find that rivals of acquisition targets earn significant positive abnormal returns. One explanation is that horizontal mergers increase the probability of successful collusion among rival producers. Under this collusion hypothesis, rivals of the merging firms benefit from the merger since successful collusion limits output, raises product prices, and/or lowers factor prices. However, this explanation has never found any empirical backing.

An alternative explanation, tested by Song and Walkling (2000) in a sample of acquisition bids in 1982–91, suggests that rival firms earn abnormal returns because of the increased probability that they will become targets themselves. They find that on average, rival firms earn positive abnormal returns regardless of the form and outcome of acquisition. These returns increase significantly with the magnitude of surprise about the initial acquisition. The cross-sectional variation of rival abnormal returns in the announcement period is systematically related to variables associated with the probability of acquisition.

Alternatively, the announcement of a merger might signal information regarding an innovative use of capital or a productivity increase that can be exploited by rival firms regardless of whether they are involved in a merger. Akhigbe, Borde, and Whyte (2000) distinguish this hypothesis from the Song-Walkling acquisition probability hypothesis by examining terminated bids. The acquisition probability hypothesis suggests that a terminated merger would lead to an increase in the probability for a rival receiving a bid, while the productivity increase hypothesis would suggest no additional post-termination abnormal returns for the bidders. Consistent with Song and Walkling, they find that termination results in significant negative returns for targets and significant positive returns for rivals, supporting the hypothesis that rival firms could become acquisition targets.

Returns to Bondholders and Preferred Shareholders

Suppose the assets of an acquirer are not perfectly correlated with the assets of the target firm. Kim and McConnell (1977) argue that when the two firms combine, the reduction in asset variance caused by the merger will result in an increase in the value of target debt (from the reduction in the probability of default). If this wealth transfer from target and acquirer bondholders is too large, the shareholders of the two firms may be reluctant to complete the acquisition.

However, Kim and McConnell and other authors (such as Dennis and McConnell 1986; Maquieira, Megginson, and Nail 1998; and Travlos 1987 among others) find that nonconvertible bondholders of bidding firms neither gain nor lose from mergers. Dennis and McConnell also analyze the rates of return and dollar value returns for various classes of merging firms' securities and find that target convertible and nonconvertible preferred stockholders, and convertible bondholders gain in the merger, as do the acquirers' convertible preferred stockholders. Similarly, Maquieira, Megginson, and Nail examine wealth changes for 1,283 publicly traded debt and equity securities of firms involved in 260 pure stock-for-stock mergers in the period 1963–96. They find no evidence that conglomerate stock-for-stock mergers create financial synergies or benefit bondholders at stockholders' expense. Conglomerate bidding-firm stockholders lose; all other security holders at least break even. Convertible security holders experience the largest gains, due mostly to their attached option values. Certain bond covenants are value-enhancing, while leverage increases are value-reducing.

Factors Affecting Gains in Acquisitions

Acquisition Method: Merger or Tender Offer

Research seems to document that returns to targets are smaller in mergers than in tender offers. One reason for this might be that mergers tend to be friendly. Since there is less scope for drastic restructuring and potential value creation after the merger, we might expect lower returns for targets in mergers. Van Hulle, Vermaelen, and de Wouters (1991) find that in a sample of Belgian mergers, target board members continue to own 33% of the board seats 1 year after the merger. In contrast, in tender offers, the figure is 13%.

An alternative explanation is that since mergers are predominantly paid for in shares, the merger or tender offer effect may simply be a proxy for the means of payment. One reason why tender offers are predominantly cash financed is because in the USA, a cash-financed tender offer is subject only to the Williams Act of 1968. Upon filing the appropriate documentation with the Securities and Exchange Commission (SEC) and after complying with the required waiting period, the offer may commence. Stock-financed offers must comply with the Securities Act of 1933, which can lead to a substantial delay. Franks and Harris (1989) examine over 1,800 UK takeovers in the period 1955–85. They find that target gains are higher in the UK after 1968, suggesting that increases in US target gains at the same time may not be attributable to the Williams Act.

Ultimately, though authors have postulated reasons why mergers are different from tender offers (means of payment, degree of hostility, and so on), the reason for the substantial difference between mergers and tender offers is still unclear. The final answer may be a combination of all these factors. As Agrawal and Jaffe (1999) document, authors increasingly treat the two forms of transactions as different and analyze them separately.

Method of Payment: Stock or Cash

There are several reasons why choice of stock or cash payments may influence the gains from a merger. The first reason is taxes. Payment with shares is tax-efficient relative to cash payments. Hence, stock bidders may have to compensate targets for the higher tax liability. Hayn (1989) finds that even after controlling for the degree of competition for the target, management opposition to the deal, the method of acquisition, and the relative size of bidder to target, the tax attributes of target firms are significant in explaining the abnormal returns to shareholders of both target and acquiring firms following acquisition announcements. The most prominent tax attribute in tax-free acquisitions is the amount of net operating loss carry forwards and tax credits due to expire. The most important tax attribute in taxable acquisitions is the step-up in the acquired assets' basis. Hayn also finds some evidence that tax considerations motivate acquisitions in that obtaining tax-free status for the proposed acquisition increases its likelihood of completion.

The second reason that stock-financed acquisitions perform worse than cash-financed acquisitions is an asymmetric information effect. In a Myers and Majluf (1984) type framework, rational investors will interpret a stock payment as evidence that the firm's shares are overvalued and will, hence, mark down the prices of firms that announce a stock-financed acquisition relative to a cash-financed acquisition. Alternatively, paying with cash might increase the bidder's leverage, signaling that the managers have lower available free cash flow. Travlos (1987) analyzes a sample of 167 successful mergers and tender offers in 1972–81 where payments were made either purely in stock, cash, or a mixture of the two. He finds that after controlling for the type of acquisition, bidder shareholders in pure stock-financed acquisitions earn significant negative abnormal returns on the announcement date, while bidder shareholders in cash-financed acquisitions do not lose.

A third reason for the differential performance between stock and cash-financed acquisitions focuses on the role of asymmetric information about the bidder's or target's value. Hansen (1987) derives a theoretical model where the bidder is uncertain about the target's value and uses stock to share the risk that the acquirer may have overpaid. Fishman (1989) adds bidder competition to this model and demonstrates that cash may not only signal a high value for the target but also preempt other firms from bidding. Choe, Masulis, and Nanda (1993) show that an increase in overall economic activity increases the likelihood of stock financing and argue that this is because firms face lower adverse selection costs, more promising investment opportunities, and less uncertainty about assets-in-place. Martin (1996) uses size and growth opportunities to proxy for the uncertainty in bidder and target value and finds that the bidder and target investment opportunities are important determinants of the method of payment, though bidder size is not related to payment method.

Attitude of the Transaction

In the academic literature, many researchers have distinguished between hostile and friendly takeovers in that the gains from hostile takeovers result from replacing incumbent managers and the gains from friendly takeovers result from strategic synergies. Schwert (2000) examines whether hostile takeovers can be distinguished from friendly takeovers, in a sample of 2,346 takeover contests in the 1975–96 period, based on accounting and stock performance data. Schwert uses several different definitions of hostility—if the deal was classified as hostile in the WSJ Index or in Securities Data Company (SDC), if the deal was an unnegotiated tender offer, if a 13D statement was filed in the year before the initial bid in which the buyer discloses an intent to seek control, or a combination of these. He finds that that most deals described as hostile in the press are not distinguishable from friendly deals in economic terms. Poor target management, proxied for by variables such as return on equity (ROE) and market-to-book (M/B) ratio, does not predict the likelihood of a hostile deal. There is some evidence that bidders identified as hostile, based on pre-bid events, earn lower stock returns, though other definitions of hostility do not show a relationship.

Regulation

In the USA, the major law governing the choice of acquisition form is the Williams Act of 1968. The Williams Act and its amendments mandate that bidding firms must file reports with the SEC describing their business plans relating to the target firm and method of financing the acquisition. The Act also contains provisions that increase target management's ability to block or delay tender offers by bringing suits in court. Several hypotheses have been advanced as to the effects of this Act on takeover activity. If the Act reduces takeover activity, then if there are close substitutes to tender offers, the Williams Act would not have any important effect on the acquisitions market. A second hypothesis deals with the increased disclosure requirements associated with the Williams Act. Public disclosure might serve to inform other public bidders about the profit opportunity and give them time to enter competitive bids. This competition places upward pressure on the offer premiums, and it transfers some returns from acquirer to target shareholders. However, if the regulations simply truncate the distribution of takeovers that actually occur by eliminating the less profitable takeovers, then this would reduce the returns to firms that do not become takeover targets and increase the measured average abnormal returns to targets of completed takeovers.

Malatesta and Thompson (1993) model the acquisition process and the effect of the Williams Act on both the expected gross present value of an acquisition attempt and the marginal cost of an attempt. They reject the substitution hypothesis since the parameters in their acquisition model change significantly around the time the Williams Act is passed. Though they cannot reject the truncation hypothesis using conventional tests, a Bayesian framework yields a higher posterior probability for the transfer hypothesis than the other two. Cash-financed acquisitions, under the Williams Act, involve fewer delays than acquisitions using stock as consideration. Consistent with this, Martin (1996) finds that bidders are more likely to use a cash-financed tender offer to preempt the competition when real or potential competition for the target exists.

Other papers examining the effect of regulation on takeover activity have focused on the effect of state anti-takeover laws, such as the 1990 Pennsylvania Senate Bill 1310, containing five provisions designed to make takeovers prohibitively expensive but allowing firms to opt out of some or all of the law's provisions. Some authors have examined the effect of disclosure requirements in different countries. Van Hulle, Vermaelen, and de Wouters (1991) for example, find that the lack of disclosure requirements in Belgium does not benefit bidders.

Ownership and Governance Structure: Managerial Ownership, Institutional Holdings, Bidder Toeholds, Board Structure

This is a complex issue. Managerial ownership can affect negotiation power and can align managerial and shareholder interests. Institutional ownership can affect the tax status of the marginal investor—pension funds with lower taxes on capital gains might be willing to sell at a lower cost. It can also affect the degree of monitoring of managers and the resulting concern for shareholder value. It can affect the outcome of offers—pension funds have to balance their fiduciary responsibilities against loyalty to management. Finally, institutional ownership can also help in overcoming free rider problems. Bidder toeholds can affect the negotiation power of the two parties, the degree of monitoring of target firm managers, and the extent of policy change and can also help in overcoming free rider problems.

Numerous studies have examined these issues in isolation and together. There is usually a positive relationship between managerial ownership and target/acquirer returns. For example, Amihud, Lev, and Travlos (1990) report significantly negative bidder returns for stock-financed acquisitions, but only for those bidders with low management ownership. Martin (1996) finds a nonlinear relationship between the use of stock payments and managerial ownership in the firm. The probability of stock financing is reduced in the presence of higher institutional blockholdings. Betton and Eckbo (2000) find that toeholds are largest in successful single-bid contests and smallest in multiple-bid contests. Bidders also pay smaller premiums when they already own a lot of shares. One interpretation of this is that it is easier for them to convince small shareholders that they have an incentive to overpay. *Ceteris paribus*, the probability of a successful offer is higher if the bidder has a large toehold. Target gains decrease with the size of the initial bidder's toehold, because the larger the toehold, the greater the probability of the low target payoff in the single-bid outcome. Interestingly, as Betton and Eckbo document, in spite of the benefits of bidder toeholds, a high proportion, around 47% of the initial bidders in their sample of 1,353 tender offers in the 1971–90 period, do not purchase a toehold.

Nature of the Industry

Several studies have examined bidder and target returns in specific industries. Acquisitions in regulated industries typically require regulatory approval. However, a priori, it is difficult to predict what this would imply for bidder or target returns. This requirement for regulatory approval raises the cost of a takeover, so that acquirers are likely to pursue only the more profitable acquisitions. Since managerial improvement is one motive for takeover, we might expect greater pre-acquisition underperformance for targets in regulated industries than in other industries. Alternatively, managerial discretion may be lower in regulated industries. This implies lower pre-takeover underperformance for targets in regulated industries.

As one example, the regulatory process for bank takeovers is very different from nonbank takeovers. Before a bank takeover can occur, prior approval is required from one of the three federal bank regulatory authorities (the Federal Reserve Board, Federal Deposit Insurance Corporation, and Comptroller of the Currency). In addition, approval at the state level is also required. Finally, after approval is granted, there is a 30-day waiting period so that the Justice Department can examine the takeover.

Houston and Ryngaert (1994) find that the overall gains (the weighted average of gains to the bidder and target firms) in a sample of bank mergers are slightly positive, but statistically indistinguishable from zero. In the longer term, Madura and Wiant (1994) measure the abnormal performance of banks subsequent to their acquisitions of other banks, and find a strong negative share price reaction following the acquisition, which tends to continue over a 36-month period. The long-run valuation effects across the acquiring banks are higher for banks that made acquisitions within their existing markets, experienced relatively poor pre-acquisition performance, and had relatively low pre-acquisition growth. DeLong (2001) classifies mergers of banking firms according to activity and geographic similarity (focus) or dissimilarity (diversification), and examines the abnormal returns to each group as a result of the merger announcement. She finds that mergers that focus both activity and geography enhance stockholder value by 3.0%, while the other types do not create value. Cornett, Hovakimian, Palia, and Tehranian (2003) extend DeLong's study by examining if the abnormal returns to focusing bank acquisitions can be related to corporate governance mechanisms (such as CEO share and option ownership, and a smaller board size). They find that these variables in the bidding bank are less effective in explaining abnormal returns in diversifying acquisitions than in focusing acquisitions. For example, the greater the equity stake (either through stock or options) of the CEO in the bidder bank, the greater the proportion of outsiders on the board; the older the CEO and the fewer the number of directors on the board, the greater the announcement period abnormal return. These results are generally consistent with the findings for industrial firms.

Why do Acquirers Acquire? Motives for Acquisitions

Acquirers choose to acquire targets for many reasons. From an economic efficiency perspective, bidders initiate mergers to create value. Value can be created in several ways. Good managers may acquire poorly performing firms and create value by firing target management and improving target operating performance. Financial synergies may be present between the bidding and target firms. If the market is inefficient and undervalues the target, then correctly valued bidders can acquire targets cheaply and create value. If the bidder is overvalued by the market, the bidder can pay for the acquisition using overvalued stock. Horizontal mergers may increase the market power of the combined firm and enable it to extract monopoly rents.

Alternatively, managers may be focused on their own self-interests. They may be interested in mergers to maximize firm size instead of shareholder value. Maximizing firm size increases job security because a hostile takeover is less likely in a large rapidly growing firm; increases bidder managers own power, status, and salaries; and creates more opportunities for lower and middle level managers at the bidding firm.

Finally, managers may make errors. Even if bidder management is focused on maximizing shareholder value for example, managers may overestimate their own ability to manage acquisitions, making bids out of hubris. Alternatively, they may be focused myopically on ratios such as earnings per share (EPS). Some of these reasons are discussed further.

Creating Value: Improving Managerial Efficiency

The popular press and academic literature cites the desire to improve poorly performing firms as a major factor motivating takeovers. A number of papers have examined the hypothesis that target firms are poor performers. They do this in several ways. Some authors have examined the *Q*-ratios of acquired firms prior to the takeover. A second approach is to estimate pre-takeover abnormal performance at either target or acquirer and compare it to post-takeover abnormal performance. A third approach is to predict the probability of takeover from the performance of the target firms, using past returns, financial ratios (such as price-earnings [P/E], Tobin's Q or M/B), or operating performance. Since the third approach is discussed in the section on target characteristics, I will not discuss it here. The final approach involves examining turnover at the target firms. If the managers at the target firms are poor, then we might expect to find increased turnover at these firms after the takeover. The results are ambiguous. While there is some evidence that mergers do result in an increase in performance, there is also evidence of the opposite conclusion.

Lang, Stulz, and Walkling (1989) and Servaes (1991) find that the shareholders of low *Q* targets benefit more from takeovers than the shareholders of high *Q* targets. Target *Q* ratios decline significantly over the 5 years before the tender offer. The target, bidder, and total returns are higher when the targets have low *Q*-ratios and the bidders have high *Q*-ratios, lending support to the inefficient target management hypothesis. Consistent with this, Mitchell and Lehn (1990) show that firms that make poor acquisitions that significantly reduce their equity value subsequently become takeover targets themselves. "Good" acquirers, on the other hand, make value-increasing acquisitions and are significantly less likely to become targets.

In contrast, however, Clark and Ofek (1994) examine a sample of distressed firms that were acquired. To find distressed firms, they examined all acquisitions listed on Mergerstat Review between 1981 and 1988 to find firms with market-adjusted returns of −15% or less in the year prior to the takeover or market-adjusted returns of −45% or less in the 3 years prior to the takeover. News releases about these firms were then examined to find indications of restructuring attempts (such as management turnover, reduction in dividends, layoffs, asset restructuring, debt downgrading, and so on.) They use different measures (such as earnings before interest, taxes, and depreciation [EBITD]/revenues, excess market returns, industry-adjusted returns, and so on) of the performance of the combined bidder and target firms, but are unable to find evidence that bidders are able to successfully restructure targets.

Linn and Switzer (2001) examine the relation between the change in operating performance of merging firms and whether the acquiring firm offered cash or stock as the method of payment. They find that the change in performance of the merged firms is significantly larger for cases in which the acquiring company offered cash as compared to stock offers. The results are not sensitive to whether the combination involved a tender offer or a negotiated merger, offer size, industry relatedness between the bidder's and the target's businesses, or bidder leverage.

Barber and Lyon (1996) advise that empirical tests of operating performance adjust for size, industry, and past performance. This may be important for mergers since acquiring firms undertake acquisitions following a period of superior performance, and they are generally larger than industry median firms. Using firms matched on performance and size as a benchmark, Ghosh (2001) finds no evidence that operating performance improves following acquisitions. Consistent with Linn and Switzer, he also finds that cash flows increase significantly following acquisitions that are made with cash, but decline for stock acquisitions.

Finally, in the most comprehensive study to date, Agrawal and Jaffe (2002) examine the operating and stock performance of over 2,083 target firms in the period 1926–96 to test the inefficient target management hypothesis. They find no evidence of pre-takeover underperformance for the target firms, using either operating or stock returns. This result also holds for subsamples of takeovers that are more likely to be disciplinary (such as tender offers, hostile takeovers, and multi-bidder contests).

Merger bids may, however, be able to create value simply because the bid acts as a wake-up call to poor target managers. Consistent with this, Safieddine and Titman (1999) find that targets that terminate takeover bids become better firms. They significantly increase their leverage ratios on average. Targets that increase their leverage ratios the most also reduce capital expenditures, sell assets, reduce employment, increase focus, and realize cash flows and share prices that outperform their benchmarks in the 5 years following the failed takeover. In other words, the increase in leverage acts as a signal that the target firm is committed to making the improvements that would be made by potential raiders.

Mergers may also create value if acquirer managers are superior managers. Heron and Lie (2000) investigate this issue in a large sample of firms that conducted acquisitions between 1985 and 1997. They examine the relation between the method of payment in acquisitions, earnings management, and operating performance for the acquirers in their sample. Prior to their acquisitions, acquirers exhibit levels of operating performance that exceed that of their respective industry peers. Subsequent to acquisitions, acquirers continue to exhibit superior performance relative to their industry and experience significantly higher levels of operating performance than control firms with similar pre-event operating performance. They find no evidence that the method of payment conveys information about the acquirer's future operating performance.

Martin and McConnell (1991) examine what happens to target management once a takeover happens. If corporate takeovers discipline the top managers of poorly performing target firms, the turnover rate should increase post-takeover. They find that the turnover rate for the top manager of target firms in tender offers significantly increases following the completion of the takeover, and that prior to the takeover, these firms were significantly underperforming compared to other firms in their industry as well as other target firms that had no post-takeover change in the top executive. In contrast, Franks and Mayer (1996), who examine board turnover in hostile takeovers in the UK. in 1985 and 1986, find evidence of high board turnover and significant levels of post-takeover restructuring. However, they find no evidence of poor performance prior to bids, suggesting that the high board turnover does not derive from past managerial failure. They conclude that hostile takeovers do not perform a disciplining function. Instead, rejection of bids appears to derive from opposition to post-takeover redeployment of assets, and renegotiation over the terms of bids.

Overall, we cannot unambiguously conclude that mergers create value by improving management or operating performance at target firms.

Creating Value: Financial Synergies

Synergies can be an important motive for a merger. Operating synergies between firms include the enhanced distribution of complementary product lines, lower operating overheads by consolidating personnel and accounting departments, or improved economies of scale and scope in product lines. Financial synergies arise when a high-growth and cash-poor firm is acquired by a cash-rich bidder. Using accounting data, Smith and Kim (1994) classify bidders as "high free cash flow" or "slack poor." Consistent with the financial synergy hypothesis, they find that the bidder, target, and total returns are highest for acquisitions that combine slack-poor and free cash-flow firms. They also find that negative returns of bidders are concentrated among combinations where bidders and targets are similarly classified. Bidder returns are more positive when associated with capital structure and liquid asset changes that mitigate bidder slack or free cash-flow problems.

Creating Value: Diversification

At first sight, diversification might not appear to create any value for shareholders since shareholders can diversify more cheaply on their own. However, diversification may still be beneficial because employees and managers cannot diversify their human capital. They may be willing to accept a lower salary or a larger commitment to the company if they take less risk. Ultimately, therefore, diversification may benefit shareholders.

Contrary to this hypothesis, Morck, Shleifer, and Vishny (1990), in a sample of 326 US acquisitions between 1975 and 1987, find that the returns to bidding shareholders are systematically lower when their firm diversifies. Servaes (1996) examines the diversification wave of the 1960s and the 1970s. If diversification benefits shareholders, diversified companies should be valued at a premium during this period when many corporations started to diversify. However, he finds no evidence that diversified companies were valued at a premium over single segment firms during the 1960s and the 1970s. On the contrary, there is a large diversification discount during the 1960s that declines to zero during the 1970s.

Looking at the other side of the coin, Comment and Jarrell (1994) document that greater corporate focus is consistent with shareholder wealth maximization in the 1980s, and large focused firms are less likely to be subject to hostile takeover attempts than other firms.

Creating Value: Timing

If managers act on behalf of their shareholders, then managers who perceive their firms' shares to be overvalued should issue shares, either as a seasoned equity offering or a stock-financed acquisition. Inefficient investors will underreact to the information in the stock-issue announcement and the overvalued firm managers may be able to create value for their shareholders. There is some evidence that managers time the market when issuing shares. Baker and Wurgler (2000) for example, find that firms issue relatively more equity than debt just before periods of low market returns.

Consistent with this, Loughran and Vijh (1997) examine 947 acquisitions during 1970–89, and report a relationship between the post-acquisition returns and the mode of acquisition and form of payment. During a 5-year period following the acquisition, on average, firms that complete stock mergers earn significantly negative excess returns of –25.0%, whereas firms that complete cash tender offers earn significantly positive excess returns of 61.7%. Over the combined pre- and post-acquisition period, target shareholders who hold on to the acquirer stock received as payment in stock mergers do not earn significantly positive excess returns. In the top quartile of the target to acquirer size ratio, they earn negative excess returns.

Dong, Hirshleifer, Richardson, and Teoh (2002; DHRT) examine the relation between irrational market valuation, the volume of takeovers and the behavior of participants in takeover contests. Since, as mentioned earlier, post-event abnormal returns are controversial, DHRT use the book/price (B/P) ratio and the ratio of residual income valuation to price (V/P) as contemporaneous measures of misvaluation for bidders and of targets. They find that the misevaluation of bidders, targets, and the aggregate stock market influences the aggregate volume of takeovers, the means of payment chosen, and the premiums paid. Overvalued acquirers are more likely to use stock as consideration, and are willing to pay more in such transactions.

In an interesting twist to this idea, Chang (1998) studies announcement period bidder returns when the target firm is privately held. Bidding firms offering stock in an acquisition may be faced with the asymmetric information problem of Myers and Majluf (1984). A stock payment in a merger will consequently result in negative abnormal returns. If the bidder is correctly valued (as opposed to being overvalued), it would like to signal this information to the target firm managers, a task that may be easier with private targets. Chang finds, in contrast to the negative abnormal return typically found for stock-financed bidders acquiring a publicly traded target, stock-financed bidders bidding for a private firm earn a positive abnormal return. In cash offers to private targets, bidders do not earn abnormal returns in cash offers.

Other Methods of Creating Value: Undervaluation and Market Power

These issues have been discussed elsewhere in this chapter, so I will only briefly discuss them here. In contrast to the timing hypothesis, the undervaluation hypothesis postulates that inefficient markets may undervalue the target, especially for small companies that are not followed by analysts or the popular press. In such cases, acquirers could create value by buying up undervalued companies and selling them when the market realizes their correct value. If this was the main explanation, however, the stock prices of target companies in unsuccessful bids would stay up. The empirical evidence is inconsistent with this.

Horizontal mergers may increase the probability of successful collusion among rival producers. This limits output and raises product prices and/or lowers factor prices, increasing monopoly-type rents to merging firms. As discussed in the section "Returns to Rivals," however, this explanation has never found any empirical backing.

Managerial Self-interested Behavior: Free Cash Flow

Jensen (1986) argues that the agency conflict between owners and managers is severest in the presence of free cash flows, cash flows above those needed to make payments to stakeholders, and fund positive net present value (NPV) projects. Managers, acting in their own self-interests, may choose to spend this cash rather than returning it to their shareholders. Acquisitions are one way they can spend their free cash flow.

One likely set of bidders with free cash flow are cash-rich firms. Harford (1999) examines whether the presence of excess cash in a firm leads managers to make value-decreasing acquisitions. He examines a sample of attempted M&A between 1950 and 1994, and documents that cash-rich firms are more likely than other firms to attempt acquisitions. Acquisitions by cash-rich firms are value decreasing—cash-rich bidders destroy seven cents in value for every excess dollar of cash reserves held. They are more likely to make diversifying acquisitions and their targets are less likely to attract other bidders. Mergers in which the bidder is cash-rich are also followed by abnormal declines in operating performance.

Managerial Errors: Hubris

Roll (1986) argues that successful bidders in acquisitions are subject to a winner's curse. The distribution of bidder valuations is truncated below by the target true value—we will not see acquisitions where the target believes itself to be worth more than the bid. Hence, on average, bidders will pay too much for their acquisitions.

Rau and Vermaelen (1997) argue that managers as well as other decision-makers, who have to approve an acquisition (such as large shareholders and the board of directors) indirectly receive feedback on the quality of the bidder's management from the market. In companies with low B/M ratios ("glamour" firms), managers are more likely to overestimate their own abilities to manage an acquisition, i.e., they will be infected by hubris. Such glamour firms are firms with high past stock returns and high past growth in cash flow and earnings, which should presumably strengthen the management's belief in its own actions. Moreover, in these firms, other stakeholders, such as the board of directors and large shareholders, are more likely to give the management the benefit of the doubt and approve its acquisition plans. On the other hand, in companies where the management has a poor track record, such as companies with high B/M ratios ("value" stocks), managers, directors, and large shareholders will be more prudent before approving a major transaction, which may well determine the survival of the company. Because these acquisitions are not motivated by hubris, they should create shareholder value rather than destroy it. According to this performance extrapolation hypothesis, the market only gradually reassesses the quality of the bidder as the results of the acquisition become clear. In other words, the market (as well as the management, board of directors, and large shareholders) extrapolates too much from the past performance of the bidder manager when it assesses the value of an acquisition. Hence, while in the short-run, that is, around the announcement of the acquisition, glamour bidders will experience higher abnormal returns than value bidders; in the long run, this performance will reverse.

Rau and Vermaelen find that value bidders far outperform glamour bidders in the 3 years after the completion of the merger or tender offer, with value acquirers earning statistically significant size and B/M-adjusted positive abnormal returns of 8% in mergers and 16% in tender offers. Glamour acquirers on the other hand, earn statistically significant size and B/M-adjusted negative abnormal returns of −17% in mergers and insignificant abnormal returns of 4% in tender offers. This finding that value bidders outperform glamour bidders is remarkably robust. The conclusions are unchanged when they exclude small acquisitions, when they exclude NASDAQ bidders, or when they exclude periods when events are clustered.

Hayward and Hambrick (1997) directly examine the role of a CEO's hubris in explaining the large size of some premiums paid for acquisitions. In a sample of 106 large acquisitions, they find that four indicators of CEO hubris are highly associated with the size of premiums paid: the acquiring company's recent performance, recent media praise for the CEO, a measure of the

CEO's self-importance, and a composite factor of these three variables. The relationship between CEO hubris and premiums is further strengthened when the board has a high proportion of inside directors and when the CEO is also the board chair.

Managerial Errors: EPS Myopia

Rau and Vermaelen (1997) postulate that bidding firm managers might be myopically focused on EPS. Merging with a company with a lower P/E ratio than the buyer's and paying for the acquisition by shares may inflate the buyer's EPS. Managers find it easier to justify an acquisition if it is accompanied by an EPS increase rather than a decrease. In fact, there is a widespread belief that companies should not acquire others with higher P/E ratios than their own (see Brealey and Myers 1996, 921–23). Consequently, managers might be willing to pay higher prices (and possibly overpay) for target firms if the acquisition results in an increase in EPS. For each merger in their sample, Rau and Vermaelen compute the difference between the actual growth in the bidder's EPS following the merger and the estimated growth if the merger had not taken place. They find no significant relationship between the impact of the merger on the EPS and the subsequent long-run performance of the bidder.

What Kinds of Targets Are Acquired? Target Characteristics

What kind of firms are potential targets in takeovers? The papers that attempt to answer this question usually employ a logistic probability model to examine the probability that a firm will be the target of an acquisition attempt. The regression model is of the type

$$Pit = 1/\left[1 + e^{-\beta x(i,t)}\right]$$

Where *Pit* is the probability that firm i is the target of a takeover bid in the period t, $x(i, t)$ is a vector of explanatory variables for firm i at time t, and β is the unknown parameter vector.

Target Size

Palepu (1986) hypothesizes that firms with poor performance are more likely to be acquisition targets, as potential bidders can acquire them and easily increase the value. He analyzes the probability that an acquisition is completed, using several financial performance ratios including the M/B ratio, the P/E ratio, return on equity, and sales growth. He also analyzes the effect of leverage and size. Firms with low leverage may have latent debt capacity that acquirers can use to finance the acquisition. Larger firms may be less likely to be taken over since the financing costs to acquire a large firm may be prohibitive. Moreover, the cost of integrating a large target into the acquirer increases with target size. Consistent with the hypotheses, Palepu finds that smaller firms and firms with low leverage are significantly more likely to be targets. Oddly, he also finds a negative relationship between industry takeover activity and the probability of the acquisition.

In contrast, Mikkelson and Partch (1989) find that while large firms are less likely to be acquisition targets, leverage has no effect on the likelihood of a takeover. Ambrose and Megginson (1992) extend the Palepu model by incorporating measures of insider and institutional shareholdings, and by considering the effect of varying proportions of fixed (tangible) assets in a firm's total asset structure, in a random sample of firms in nonregulated industries listed on the NYSE or Amex on January 1, 1981. Consistent with Palepu, they find that smaller firms are more likely to receive a takeover bid. However, the explanatory power of the Palepu model is reduced in their sample period. In addition, the probability of receiving a takeover bid is positively related to tangible assets and negatively related to the net change in institutional holdings.

Comment and Schwert (1995) examine a sample of exchange-listed target firms in the period 1975–91. They find that target firms have below-average sales growth, higher cash positions, lower M/B ratios, and lower debt-equity ratios, suggesting that target firms are poor performers making inefficient use of their financial capital. The lower M/B ratios may be evidence that targets have fewer growth options and more assets-in-place. Alternatively, they may simply be undervalued firms.

Overall, size seems to be the most successful predictor of takeover probability across all the studies. The other variables, sales growth, leverage, M/B ratio, and Q ratio, all have shown mixed results.

Target Leverage

The mixed results on the relationship between leverage and the probability of takeover may, in fact, partly be due to the co-insurance effect discussed earlier. Billett (1996) examines this coinsurance effect for a sample of 448 nonfinancial and nonregulated firms, listed on the Center for Research in Security Prices (CRSP) and Compustat with data on credit ratings. He finds that as the coinsurance potential of a firm's debt—measured as the amount of relatively risky debt outstanding—increases, its likelihood of being acquired decreases. This coinsurance deterrent is period-specific; however, it is strongest during the period 1985–90 and is strongest for firms with public debt outstanding.

Target Ownership Structure

Jensen and Ruback (1983) describe the takeover market as a market where alternative managerial teams compete for the right to manage corporate resources. According to this view, the shareholders of the firm do not actively control the company, hiring and firing managers depending on their performance. Instead, management teams are the active players with shareholders playing a relatively passive role. Investment banks, takeover specialists, and arbitrageurs facilitate the takeover market by acting as financial intermediaries.

Another important factor, therefore, that determines whether a firm is a potential takeover target may be managerial ownership. The effect of managerial ownership on takeover activity, however, is unclear. Increased managerial ownership aligns the incentives of managers with shareholders. Morck, Shleifer and Vishny (1988; MSV) and McConnell and Servaes (1990; MS) document that firms with a high level of managerial ownership also have higher levels of Tobin's Q. This may reduce the probability that these firms are taken over since there is less evidence that a new management team will add incremental value to the firm. However, MSV and MS also document that the relationship between Tobin's Q and managerial ownership is nonlinear. At high levels of managerial ownership, the relationship becomes negative as managers become increasingly entrenched. This degree of entrenchment may make poor managers better able to resist a takeover. Finally, increased managerial ownership may also result in higher takeover premiums as managers can bargain more effectively with potential acquirers.

Mikkelson and Partch (1989) examine managers' holdings in a random sample of 240 industrial firms, and test whether the degree of managerial ownership affects the probability of a takeover attempt being made for the firm. Though they find that the likelihood of successful acquisitions of firms is unrelated to target managerial holdings, this lack of a relation is caused by two opposing effects. Lower managerial ownership is associated with a higher probability that a firm will receive a takeover offer, but a lower probability that a takeover attempt will lead to a change in control. Song and Walking (1993) examine a sample of 153 target firms in acquisitions announced in the *WSJ* between 1977 and 1986. They contrast managerial ownership for this sample with two other samples of 153 industry-matched or randomly selected nontarget firms respectively. They find that managerial ownership is significantly lower in their target firms in comparison to the nontarget firms. Within the sample of target firms, managerial ownership is lower in contested compared to uncontested offers, and in unsuccessful compared to successful cases. Shivdasani (1993) finds that size, managerial stockholdings, and affiliate firm cross-shareholdings are negatively related to the likelihood of a hostile takeover.

Anti-takeover Defenses

In addition to managerial ownership, another way to keep control of the firm may be for target managers to use anti-takeover laws. Ambrose and Megginson (1992) also examine the deterrent effect of various takeover defenses, such as the presence of classified boards, fair charter provisions, dual-class capitalization, poison pills, or blank-check-preferred stock authorizations. They find that blank-check-preferred stock authorizations are the only common takeover defense significantly (negatively) correlated with acquisition likelihood.

The problem with drawing conclusions from a simple correlation between the presence of a takeover defense is that managers may choose to implement the takeover defense only when takeovers are likely. This will mask the relation between the effectiveness of the defense and the likelihood of takeover. In an extreme case, we may observe a positive relationship between the presence of a takeover defense and the likelihood that a company is acquired, suggesting that pills cause the takeover. Comment and Schwert (1995) use a two-stage approach to mitigate this problem. In the first stage, they estimate a model to predict poison pill coverage, using variables such as incorporation in a state with an anti-takeover law, size, sales growth, and liquidity. This gives them predictable and surprise elements of pill coverage. The surprise component is likely to be the pills adopted when managers have information about a pending takeover attempt. The second stage then uses these two components separately in a probit regression on a takeover dummy and a pill-adoption dummy. They find that poison pills and control share laws are positively associated with higher takeover premiums for selling shareholders, both unconditionally and conditional on a successful takeover. They conclude that anti-takeover measures increase the bargaining position of target firms, but they do not prevent many transactions. Consequently, poison pill rights issues, control share laws, and business combination laws do not systematically deter takeovers.

One unusual kind of anti-takeover defense may be observed in unionized firms. Firms with different unionization statuses may be reluctant to merge from fear that the nonunion partner in the merger might end up unionized. Wruck and Stephens (1992) note that when Safeway sold off its Dallas division, nonunion buyers did not want to hire Safeway employees because they were afraid of getting their operations unionized. This "contagion" effect, can be balanced against a "threat" hypothesis. The management of a unionized target firm can use the threat of merging with a nonunion firm to extract concessions from its unions. Fallick and Hassett (1996) explore whether unionization influences the decision of a firm to merge with another firm. They find that unionization increases the likelihood that a firm will enter the acquisition market and that firms with similar union statuses tend to merge with one another.

CONCLUSIONS

This chapter has attempted to provide a broad overview of the empirical research in mergers over the last three decades. It is by no means comprehensive. Some conclusions can be drawn—target firm shareholders seem to earn significantly positive returns, acquirers seem to earn zero or negative returns, bond holders do not seem to be hurt, and rivals may be benefited. Firms acquire other firms for a variety of reasons—to improve target management, out of hubris, to take advantage of their own overvaluation, to diversify, and so on. Many of these results are controversial; studies in different time periods, different countries, or different statistical methods yield contradictory results. There is still much to learn.

REFERENCES AND SUGGESTED READINGS

Agrawal, Anup, and Jeffrey F. Jaffe. 1999. "The Post-merger Performance Puzzle." In *Advances in Mergers and Acquisitions*, edited by Cary Cooper and Alan Gregory. Stamford, CT: JAI Press.

———. 2002. "Do Takeover Targets Under-perform? Evidence from Operating and Stock Returns." *Journal of Financial and Quantitative Analysis*, 38: 721–46.

Akhigbe, Aigbe, Stephen F. Borde, and Ann Marie Whyte. 2000. "The Source of Gains to Targets and Their Industry Rivals: Evidence Based on Terminated Merger Proposals." *Financial Management*, 29 (4): 101–18.

Ambrose, Brent W., and William L. Megginson. 1992. "The Role of Asset Structure, Ownership Structure, and Takeover Defenses in Determining Acquisition Likelihood." *Journal of Financial and Quantitative Analysis*, 27 (4): 575–89.

Amihud, Yakov, Baruch Lev, and Nickolaos G. Travlos. 1990. "Corporate Control and the Choice of Investment Financing: The Case of Corporate Acquisitions." *Journal of Finance*, 45 (2): 603–16.

Asquith, Paul, Robert F. Bruner, and David W. Mullins, Jr. 1983. "The Gains to Bidding Firms from Merger." *Journal of Financial Economics*, 11 (1): 121–39.

Baker, Malcolm, and Jeffrey Wurgler. 2000. "The Equity Share in New Issues and Aggregate Stock Returns." *Journal of Finance*, 55 (5): 2219–57.

Baker, Malcolm, and Serkan Savasoglu. 2002. "Limited Arbitrage in Mergers and Acquisitions." *Journal of Financial Economics*, 64 (1): 91–115.

Ball, Ray, and Philip Brown. 1968. "An Empirical Evaluation of Accounting Income Numbers." *Journal of Accounting Research*, 6 (2): 159–78.

Barber, Brad M., and John D. Lyon. 1996. "Detecting Abnormal Operating Performance: The Empirical Power and Specification of Test-statistics." *Journal of Financial Economics*, 41 (3): 359–99.

———. 1997. "Detecting Long-run Abnormal Stock Returns: The Empirical Power and Specification of Test Statistics." *Journal of Financial Economics*, 43 (3): 341–72.

Betton, Sandra, and B. Espen Eckbo. 2000. "Toeholds, Bid Jumps, and Expected Payoffs in Takeovers." *Review of Financial Studies*, 13 (4): 841–82.

Billett, Matthew T. 1996, "Targeting Capital Structure: The Relationship Between Risky Debt and the Firm's Likelihood of Being Acquired." *Journal of Business*, 69 (2): 173–92.

Bradley, Michael, Anand Desai, and E. Han Kim. 1988. "Synergistic Gains from Corporate Acquisitions and their Division Between Stockholders of Target and Acquiring Firms." *Journal of Financial Economics*, 21 (1): 3–40.

Brealey, Richard A., and Stewart C. Myers. 1996. *Principles of Corporate Finance*. New York, NY: McGraw-Hill, Inc.

Brown, Stephen J., and Jerold B. Warner, 1980. "Measuring Security Price Performance." *Journal of Financial Economics*, 8 (3): 205–58.

———. 1985. "Using Daily Stock Returns: The Case of Event Studies." *Journal of Financial Economics*, 14 (1): 3–31.

Bruner, Robert F. 2002. "Does M&A Pay? A Survey of Evidence for the Decision-maker." *Journal of Applied Finance*, 12 (1): 48–68.

Chang, Saeyoung. 1998. "Takeovers of Privately Held Targets, Methods of Payment, and Bidder Returns." *Journal of Finance*, 53 (2): 773–84.

Choe, Hyuk, Ronald W. Masulis, and Vikram Nanda, 1993. "Common Stock Offerings Across the Business Cycle: Theory and Evidence." *Journal of Empirical Finance*, 1 (1): 3–31.

Clark, Kent, and Eli Ofek. 1994. "Mergers as a Means of Restructuring Distressed Firms: An Empirical Investigation." *Journal of Financial and Quantitative Analysis*, 29 (4): 541–61.

Comment, Robert, and Gregg A. Jarrell. 1994. "Corporate Focus and Stock Returns." *Journal of Financial Economics*, 37 (1): 67–87.

Comment, Robert, and G. William Schwert. 1995. "Poison or Placebo? Evidence on the Deterrence and Wealth Effects of Modern Antitakeover Measures." *Journal of Financial Economics*, 39 (1): 3–43.

Cornett, Marcia Millon, Gayane Hovakimian, Darius Palia, and Hassan Tehranian. 2003. "The Impact of the Manager-Shareholder Conflict on Acquiring Bank Returns." *Journal of Banking & Finance*, 27 (1): 103–31.

DeLong, Gayle L. 2001. "Stockholder Gains from Focusing Versus Diversifying Bank Mergers." *Journal of Financial Economics*, 59 (2): 221–52.

Dennis, Debra K., and John J. McConnell. 1986. "Corporate Mergers and Security Returns." *Journal of Financial Economics*, 16 (2): 143–87.

Dolley, James C. 1933. "Characteristics and Procedure of Common Stock Split-ups." *Harvard Business Review*, 11 (3): 316–26.

Dong, Ming, David Hirshleifer, Scott Richardson, and Siew Hong Teoh. 2002, "Does Investor Misvaluation Drive the Takeover Market?" *The Journal of Finance*, LXI (2, April): 725–62.

Eckbo, B. Espen. 1983. "Horizontal Mergers, Collusion, and Stockholder Wealth." *Journal of Financial Economics*, 11 (1–4): 241–73.

Fallick, Bruce C., and Kevin A. Hassett. 1996. "Unionizations and Acquisitions." *Journal of Business*, 69 (1): 51–74.

Fama, Eugene F., and James D. MacBeth. 1973. "Risk, Return, and Equilibrium: Empirical Tests." *Journal of Political Economy*, 81 (3): 607–36.

Fama, Eugene F., Lawrence Fisher, Michael C. Jensen, and Richard Roll. 1969. "The Adjustment of Stock Prices to New Information." *International Economic Review*, 10 (1): 1–21.

Fishman, Michael J., 1989. "Preemptive Bidding and the Role of the Medium of Exchange in Acquisitions." *Journal of Finance*, 44 (1): 41–57.

Franks, Julian, and Colin Mayer. 1996. "Hostile Takeovers and the Correction of Managerial Failure." *Journal of Financial Economics*, 40 (1): 163–81.

Franks, Julian R., and Robert S. Harris. 1989. "Shareholder Wealth Effects of Corporate Takeovers: The U.K. Experience 1955–1985." *Journal of Financial Economics*, 23 (2): 225–49.

Ghosh, Aloke. 2001. "Does Operating Performance Really Improve Following Corporate Acquisitions?" *Journal of Corporate Finance*, 7 (2): 151–78.

Hansen, Robert G. 1987. "A Theory for the Choice of Exchange Medium in Mergers and Acquisitions." *Journal of Business*, 60 (1): 75–95.

Harford, Jarrad. 1999. "Corporate Cash Reserves and Acquisitions." *Journal of Finance*, 54 (6): 1969–97.

Hayn, Carla. 1989. "Tax Attributes as Determinants of Shareholder Gains in Corporate Acquisitions." *Journal of Financial Economics*, 23 (1): 121–53.

Hayward, Mathew L. A., and Donald C. Hambrick. 1997. "Explaining Premiums Paid for Large Acquisitions: Evidence of CEO Hubris." *Administrative Science Quarterly*, 42 (1): 103–27.

Heron, Randall A., and Erik Lie. 2002. "Operating Performance and the Method of Payment in Takeovers." *Journal of Financial and Quantitative Analysis*, 37 (1): 137–55.

Houston, Joel F., and Michael D. Ryngaert. 1994. "The Overall Gains from Large Bank Mergers." *Journal of Banking and Finance*, 18 (6): 1155–76.

Jaffe, Jeffrey F. 1974. "Special Information and Insider Trading." *Journal of Business*, 47 (3): 410–28.

Jarrell, Gregg A., James A. Brickley, and Jeffry M. Netter. 1988. "The Market for Corporate Control: The Empirical Evidence since 1980." *Journal of Economic Perspectives*, 2 (1): 49–68.

Jensen, Michael C. 1986. "Agency Costs of Free Cash Flow, Corporate Finance and Takeovers." *American Economic Review*, 76 (2): 323–29.

Jensen, Michael C., and Richard S. Ruback. 1983. "The Market for Corporate Control: The Scientific Evidence." *Journal of Financial Economics*, 11 (1–4): 5–50.

Kaplan, Steven N. 2000. *Mergers and Productivity*. Chicago, IL: University of Chicago Press/NBER.

Kim, E. Han, and John J. McConnell. 1977. "Corporate Mergers and the Co-insurance of Corporate Debt." *Journal of Finance*, 32 (2): 349–65.

Kothari, S. P., and Jerold B. Warner. 1997. "Measuring Long-horizon Security Price Performance." *Journal of Financial Economics*, 43 (3): 301–39.

Lang, Larry, Rene Stulz, and Ralph Walkling. 1989. "Managerial Performance, Tobin's Q and the Gains from Successful Tender Offers." *Journal of Financial Economics*, 24 (1): 137–54.

Linn, Scott C., and Jeannette A. Switzer. 2001. "Are Cash Acquisitions Associated with Better Post Combination Operating Performance than Stock Acquisitions?" *Journal of Banking and Finance*, 25 (6): 1113–38.

Loughran, Tim, and Anand M. Vijh. 1997. "Do Long-term Shareholders Benefit from Corporate Acquisitions?" *Journal of Finance* 52 (5): 1765–90.

Lyon, John D., Brad M. Barber, and Chih-Ling Tsai. 1999. "Improved Methods for Tests of Longrun Abnormal Stock Returns." *Journal of Finance*, 54 (1): 165–202.

MacKinlay, A. Craig, 1997. "Event Studies in Economics and Finance." *Journal of Economic Literature*, 35 (1): 13–39.

Madura, Jeff, and Kenneth J. Wiant. 1994. "Long-term Valuation Effects of Bank Acquisitions." *Journal of Banking and Finance*, 18 (6): 1135–54.

Malatesta, Paul H., and Rex Thompson. 1993. "Government Regulation and Structural Change in the Corporate Acquisitions Market: The Impact of the Williams Act." *Journal of Financial and Quantitative Analysis*, 28 (3): 363–79.

Mandelker, Gershon. 1974. "Risk and Return: The Case of Merging Firms." *Journal of Financial Economics*, 1 (4): 303–35.

Maquieira, Carlos P., William L. Megginson, and Lance Nail. 1998. "Wealth Creation Versus Wealth Redistribution in Pure Stock-for-stock Mergers." *Journal of Financial Economics*, 48 (1): 3–33.

Martin, Kenneth J., 1996. "The Method of Payment in Corporate Acquisitions, Investment Opportunities, and Management Ownership." *Journal of Finance*, 51 (4): 1227–46.

Martin, Kenneth J., and John J. McConnell. 1991. "Corporate Performance, Corporate Takeovers, and Top Management Turnover." *Journal of Finance*, 46: 671–87.

McConnell, John J., and Henri Servaes. 1990. "Additional Evidence on Equity Ownership and Corporate Value." *Journal of Financial Economics*, 27 (2): 595–612.

Mikkelson, Wayne H., and M. Megan Partch. 1989. "Managers' Voting Rights and Corporate Control." *Journal of Financial Economics*, 25 (2): 263–90.

Mitchell, Mark L., and J. Harold Mulherin. 1996. "The Impact of Industry Shocks on Takeover and Restructuring Activity." *Journal of Financial Economics*, 41: 193–230.

Mitchell, Mark L., and Kenneth Lehn. 1990. "Do Bad Bidders Become Good Targets?" *Journal of Political Economy*, 98 (2): 372–98.

Morck, Randall, Andrei Shleifer, and Robert W. Vishny. 1988. "Management Ownership and Market Valuation: An Empirical Analysis." *Journal of Financial Economics*, 20 (1–2): 293–315.

———. 1990. "Do Managerial Objectives Drive Bad Acquisitions?" *Journal of Finance*, 45 (1): 31–48.

Myers, Stewart C., and Nicholas S. Majluf. 1984. "Corporate Financing and Investment Decisions When Firms Have Information That Investors Do Not Have." *Journal of Financial Economics*, 13 (2): 187–221.

Palepu, Krishna G. 1986. "Predicting Takeover Targets: A Methodological and Empirical Analysis." *Journal of Accounting and Economics*, 8 (1): 3–35.

Rau, P. Raghavendra, and Theo Vermaelen. 1998. "Glamour, Value and the Post-acquisition Performance of Acquiring Firms." *Journal of Financial Economics*, 49 (2): 223–53.

Roll, Richard. 1986. "The Hubris Hypothesis of Corporate Takeovers." *Journal of Business*, 59 (2): 197–216.

Safieddine, Assem, and Sheridan Titman. 1999. "Leverage and Corporate Performance: Evidence from Unsuccessful Takeovers." *Journal of Finance*, 54 (2): 547–80.

Schwert, W. 2000. "Hostility in Takeovers: In the Eyes of the Beholder?" *Journal of Finance*, 55 (6, December): 2599–640.

Servaes, Henri. 1991. "Tobin's Q and the Gains from Takeovers." *Journal of Finance*, 46 (1): 409–19.

———. 1996. "The Value of Diversification During the Conglomerate Merger Wave." *Journal of Finance*, 51 (4): 1201–26.

Shivdasani, Anil. 1993. "Board Composition, Ownership Structure and Hostile Takeovers." *Journal of Accounting and Economics*, 16 (1–3): 167–98.

Smith, Richard L., and Joo-Hyun Kim. 1994. "The Combined Effects of Free Cash Flow and Financial Slack on Bidder and Target Stock Returns." *Journal of Business*, 67 (2): 281–310.

Song, Moon H., and Ralph A. Walkling. 1993. "The Impact of Managerial Ownership on Acquisition Attempts and Target Shareholder Wealth." *Journal of Financial and Quantitative Analysis*, 28 (4): 439–57.

———. 2000. "Abnormal Returns to Rivals of Acquisition Targets: A Test of the 'Acquisition Probability Hypothesis'." *Journal of Financial Economics*, 55 (2): 143–71.

Success Goes to the Swift, Study Indicates. 1997, July. Mergers & Acquisitions Report. Coopers & Lybrand.

Travlos, Nickolaos G. 1987. "Corporate Takeover Bids, Methods of Payment and Bidding Firms' Stock Returns." *Journal of Finance* 42 (4): 943–63.

Van Hulle, Cynthia, Theo Vermaelen, and Paul de Wouters. 1991. "Regulation, Taxes and the Market for Corporate Control in Belgium." *Journal of Banking & Finance*, 15, 1143–70.

Wruck, Karen H., and Steve-Anna Stephens. 1997. "Safeway, Inc.'s Leveraged Buyout Inc." Case Series. Harvard Business School Case No. 9-294-139 (Rev. 12/1/97), Harvard Business School.

REVIEW QUESTIONS

1. Write a brief note on event studies.
2. Review the empirical evidence on:
   a. Acquisition method: merger or tender offer
   b. Means of payment: stock or cash
   c. Attitude of the transaction: hostile or friendly
3. What is the hubris hypothesis of takeovers?

CHAPTER 10

Takeover Defenses

Sharon Hannes

Learning Objectives

- Highlight the different anti-takeover defenses
- Summarize the empirical findings on the impact of takeover defenses on shareholder value

INTRODUCTION

Unsolicited control transactions, otherwise known as hostile takeovers, became prevalent in the 1980s. The unique and defining feature of a hostile takeover is that the board of directors of the firm to be acquired opposes the proposed transaction. Thus, in order to overcome this opposition, the bidder must appeal to the shareholders of the corporate target. While the takeover wave of the 1980s was not the first wave of takeovers in the USA, and the "market for corporate control" was famously described much earlier in the seminal work of Henry Manne (1965), it was certainly the fiercest wave. During the 1980s, an unbelievable 30% of the Fortune 500 companies were subject to takeover bids (Davis and Stout 1992).

By law, directors are either elected or dismissed from office by the shareholders vote, which takes place at certain times or upon certain events, and in certain forms. However, if a bidder can successfully acquire a majority of shares of the target firm, it would only be a question of time before he or she would use the voting mechanism to replace the opposing directors. In practice, therefore, following a successful takeover, the incumbent directors tender their resignation without waiting for the inevitable vote (Coates 1999). For this reason, the voting mechanism was left virtually untouched by the hostile takeovers of the early 1980s.

Subsequently, however, innovative legal devices, which were eventually upheld by landmark judicial precedents, permanently altered the landscape on which hostile takeover battles were waged.[1] In order to impede hostile market transactions, corporate targets implemented a

[1] *See* the seminal case of Moran V. Household Int'l, Inc., 500 A.2d 1346 (Del. 1985).

garden variety of anti-takeover maneuvers. At the peak of such maneuvers, corporate attorneys crafted shareholder rights plans, which were notoriously referred to as "poison pills." Under the terms of such plans, the purchase of a significant portion of stock without the board of directors' approval triggers special rights for incumbent shareholders (Gilson and Black 1998). As a result, the value of a hostile purchase could be so severely diluted as to defeat any possible benefit of the takeover to the acquiror (Wachtell, Lipton, Rosen & Katz 1998). Moreover, because these plans to protect shareholder rights are, per the discretion of the board, distributed as in-kind dividends, shareholders' approval is not required in order to implement the harsh measures, which of course facilitate adoption thereof. The seminal Delaware court decision in *Moran* and subsequent litigation legitimized the use of these poison pills, despite their potential for conflict between shareholders and directors. This marked the end of pure market transactions as a possible means for achieving hostile takeovers.

Nevertheless, the development and judicial approval of the poison pills could not stop the lively market for unsolicited control transactions, since it did not temper the votes or proxy mechanisms of targeted firms. Thus, even if there is a poison pill, a bidder can solicit the votes of the shareholders in order to replace an incumbent board. The new directors can then move on to remove the poison pill since "poison pills can be removed by a board of directors as easily as they can be installed" (Coates 1999, 852), thereby allowing the bidder to proceed to purchase stock. The voting process may, therefore, circumvent the effects of a poison pill if it is not accompanied by any other defensive mechanism. Interestingly, the voting mechanism, which was initially designed to allow changes in corporate control, regained its leading role during the era of the poison pills.[2]

Although poison pills certainly made hostile takeovers much more expensive, the out-of-pocket costs of soliciting shareholder votes is not the primary deterrent to hostile takeovers. The power of the poison pill lies in the extremely costly delay it creates. Because market values fluctuate rapidly, deals that can be concluded without delay are of much greater value than those that cannot. Moreover, because takeover activity engages the bidder's management, significant opportunity costs are created. Finally, the longer it takes to conclude a deal, the greater the risk to the bidder of competition from other potential bidders. As a result, if the process of replacing the board of the targeted firm takes longer than the time necessary for a pure tender offer, the effect of the poison pill becomes far more salient.

Surprisingly, however, this need not be the case. If, for example, a majority of the shareholders can quickly dismiss an incumbent board without cause, and nominate a new board via written consent (without holding a meeting), then the process should not consume much more time than would have been spent had an offer been tendered in an ordinary takeover. Moreover, and rather surprisingly, this is precisely the default standard established, since proxy fights may be concluded within 45 days. Hence, a poison pill by itself does not allow managers of a defending target much time to rescue their sinking positions (Comment and Schwert 1995).

There are, nevertheless, delaying tactics that can be taken in order to strengthen the power of the poison pill. Unlike the poison pills, the adoption of which lies solely within a board's discretion, delaying the shareholders vote beyond the legal default must ordinarily be implemented

[2] The market mechanism to allow for such commitment is a contingent tender offer that is held in conjunction with the proxy fight for the board. In short, this is a simultaneous offer to replace the management of the company and buy its shares. See Mulherin and Poulsen (1998).

with shareholder approval. However, in the second half of the 1980s, as illustrated by the work of Karpoff and Danielson, managers easily obtained shareholder consent for various delaying mechanisms (Karpoff & Danielson 1998, table 2).

In our short survey of takeover tactics, we shall start with the various defenses that led to the invention and legitimization of the poison pill. We shall then move forward to discuss takeover defenses that impede the efficacy of the voting mechanism, since this mechanism is the most attractive alternative available to hostile bidders in the era of the poison pill. Thereafter, we shall discuss defenses that are deployed following a bid or when a bid is pending. The discussion shall also include the various legal standards that are used by the courts in their scrutiny of anti-takeover defenses. Finally, we shall wrap up the discussion with novel data about defenses, and suggest future avenues for research.

Defenses That Make the Purchase the Target's Shares Less Attractive

Defensive Transactions and Restructuring

While this chapter emphasizes legal tactics that are meant to avert a takeover, many defensive steps are actually business rather than legal maneuvers. Some of these maneuvers are highly beneficial for the shareholders, at least in the short run. The threat of a takeover may cause the management to cut costs, sell unneeded assets, and run the firm more efficiently. These measures may drive up the value of the enterprise and make the takeover attempt less attractive to the bidder. Even after a takeover attempt has been launched, the target's management may imitate the proposed agenda of the bidder, thus, proving the shareholders that value shall be created even without accepting the bid.

Another class of transactions or restructuring may prove harmful for the shareholders. For instance, the management may overload the balance sheet with debt, thus, reducing the potential of the firm to pay dividends in the future. Alternatively, management may sell major assets of the company, or even the company's "*crown jewel*," to a third party at less than the market price. The reduction in the value of the corporation and the loss of attractive assets may cause bidders to lose interest. A variant of the destruction-of-value tactic, which is even more effective, is value destruction that is keyed to the success of the takeover. For example, the incumbent management may persuade customers or suppliers to declare that they shall not cooperate with the bidder since they are loyal to the incumbent managers.

Another frequently used tactic is defensive acquisitions. The mere fact that the target acquires other entities or merges with them may make the corporation harder to acquire, but usually does not block the acquisitions. After all, following the takeover, the raider may divest the corporation from the acquired assets. However, some acquisitions may cause regulatory hurdles, such as antitrust concerns for the bidder, though a commitment to divest certain assets may overcome this barrier as well.

The "Pac-Man" Defense

This exotic defense that is infrequently used is a particular defensive acquisition. The acquisition that the target is contemplating is the acquisition of the bidder itself, and it must be accomplished before the bidder consummates the purchase of the target. The tactic is, therefore, possible only when the bidder itself is a widely held corporation. In a famous example, Martin Marietta countered Bendix's tender offer, by making its own bid for Bendix stock (DeMott 1983). And, since both bids were successful, it was hard to figure out which entity controls the other. The confusion was finally resolved in an agreement between the parties.

White Knights and Friendly Block-holders

Empirical evidence shows that only a minority of targeted firms is able to overcome a takeover bid and remain independent. However, not all the rest of the takeover attempts are successful from the point of view of the bidder. Often, the target's management is able to solicit a third party, a *white knight,* to counterbid and overcome the hostile bidder. The downside of this maneuver is that the company is sold to such a third party and forgoes the independence. The management preference for the white knight may be a matter of personal resentment to the hostile bidder, or the result of various benefits that the white knight offers them, whether in terms of employment or severance compensation.

Another possibility is to place a substantial portion of the company stock in the hands of a friendly party. Such party may help the management to avert a bid, while maintaining the target's independence. Finally, in some cases, in the face of a hostile bid, management issue shares to employee stock ownership trusts, knowing that the trustee will support the incumbent managers. When the issuance is made on the eve of a takeover attempt, or during a takeover battle, courts are highly suspicious with such practices.

Impediments to Second-step Transactions: Supermajority and Fair Price

In a majority of hostile takeovers, the bidder intends to conduct a second stage transaction in which the bidder merges with the target and freezes out the minority shareholders who did not tender their shares in the first stage. The merger between the bidder and the target combines the assets of the two entities, allowing the bidder to secure the loans it took to finance the takeover with the assets of the acquired firm.

Therefore, interference with the second-step transaction (whether it is a freeze-out merger or other similar transactions) may serve as a takeover impediment. Since all states require a shareholders vote to approve a merger, all that is needed to interfere with such a transaction is to add a charter provision, a *Shark Repellent* amendment, that requires a supermajority for the approving vote. Common supermajority approval rates run as high as 95% of the shareholders votes. And since the incumbent officers of the corporation usually hold some portion of the stock, such supermajority requirement may become a meaningful obstacle. The Shark Repellent amendment is usually accompanied by another charter provision that states that the Shark Repellent amendment may only be removed from the corporate charter by a supermajority vote. Otherwise, it would be easy for the bidder, following the first stage of the takeover, to nullify the Shark Repellent amendment. The downside of this tactic, as well as any other Shark Repellent charter amendment, is the fact that an amendment to the corporate charter requires the approvals of both the board of directors and the shareholders meeting.

Another familiar Shark Repellent charter provision that is aimed to impede second-step transactions is the fair price provision. Such provisions state a minimal price requirement (stated numerically or by a formula) for a second-step freeze-out transaction. In some cases, the fair price provision states a price, which is higher than the price in the first stage tender offer. In these circumstances, shareholders may hold out and refrain from tendering their shares in the front-end of the takeover, thus, preventing the takeover altogether.

Compulsory Redemption Charter Provisions

Another Shark Repellent charter provision, which is less common, is the compulsory redemption charter provision. The compulsory redemption charter provision is in a sense complimentary to the charter provisions that impede a second-step transaction. Sometimes the bidder is not interested in buying the entire target and aims merely to purchase control, while minimizing the cost of the acquisition. The compulsory redemption charter provision grants a put option to any minority shareholder, following a takeover, to sell its holdings to the company, and thus eliminates the privilege of the bidder to state the maximal portion of the target that it wishes to acquire. Moreover, the compulsory redemption charter provision states the redemption price. In the event that the redemption price is higher than the price offered in the tender offer, shareholders would once again hold out and refrain from tendering their shares to the bidder in the tender offer.

Dual-class Recapitalization

A highly potent takeover defense that is now prohibited by the exchanges regulation is the dual-class recapitalization. The idea is to alter the capital structure of the firm in a manner that would leave the public shareholders with shares that have inferior control rights. There are quite a few ways to manipulate the shareholders to achieve this goal. For instance, the management may declare a stock dividend of a new type of shares with multiple votes whose voting rights are suspended for a few years each time that the share is traded. Since public shareholders trade frequently, the managerial team that normally sticks to its holdings strengthens its control over the company. This effect is highlighted by the fact that trading frequency usually peeks once a takeover is launched since market professionals gather stock. Another tactic that aims to reach the same goal is a charter amendment that reduces the voting power of the corporation's common stock upon trading.

One way or the other, this type of defensive tactics is currently prohibited by exchanges regulation. It is still possible to prevent a takeover altogether by going public with a dual-class stock structure in the first place. However, studies show that firms that go public with duel class stock structures suffer from a sharp value discount and, therefore, only a few companies opt for this option.

Poison Debt and Control Clauses

Control clauses in contracts between the corporation and its suppliers, and first and foremost its suppliers of capital (poison deb), may serve as an anti-takeover impediment. For instance, the contracts provisions can state that the lender may accelerate the loan upon change of control, or raise the amount of interest charged. Similar provisions may appear in the agreements with other suppliers and major customers. Moreover, and even without such control clauses, an enterprise loaded with much debt may become takeover resistant, since the debt capacity of a corporation is limited and the bidder may need that capacity to serve the loans that are needed to finance the takeover.

Stock Repurchases to Strengthen the Managerial Holdings

When the target corporation has a significant block of insider shareholders who are loyal to the management, their stance can be enhanced by a buyback of the target stock. Such a maneuver would usually be achieved by a self-tender offer of the target to some percentage of its own stock, and at a higher price than the one offered by the pending or expected hostile bid. Ideally, the loyal shareholders would not tender their stock in the self-tender offer and, therefore, enhance their power. If their holdings were substantial in the first place they might be able, following the defensive stock repurchase, to block the hostile bid, or at least block some major corporate transactions by the bidder in the case where such transactions require a supermajority vote. The self-tender offer is much less effective when the management does not have a substantial loyal body of shareholders to start with. Nevertheless, even under these circumstances, the self-tender offer may cause the hostile bidder to raise its offer.

Golden Parachutes

Another practice that is commonly regarded as a takeover defense is the *Golden Parachutes* granted to the incumbent officers of the target. The Golden Parachute is simply a generous severance payment award that is granted upon an unsolicited change of control. The amount awarded usually does not run higher than three times the annual wages of the relevant officer. Beyond this limit, the internal revenue code does not allow the corporation to deduct the severance payment as an expense, while the office has to pay a 20% excise tax.

In any case, it is doubtful if the popular Golden Parachute is a takeover impediment at all. For one, only rarely would the total payments under the firm's Golden Parachutes top a couple of percentage of the market value of the firm (Lambert and Larker 1985). Second, Golden Parachutes are said to align the interests of managers and shareholders and may convince managers to approve a takeover, which they would otherwise oppose (Kroeber 1986).

The Flip-over (Nondiscriminatory) Poison Pill

The voice of institutional investors, which became loader and loader in the 1980's opposed some managerial defensive maneuvers. Managers of potential targets therefore looked for an effective takeover technique that did not require shareholders approval. Defensive transactions, which do not require shareholders approval, are costly for the firm, consume managerial time, and interrupt the day-to-day operations of the firm. The invention of the poison pill, crafted as a shareholders' right plan whose only operation is to deter bids, filled the need. It is especially designed to block a takeover without interfering with the operations of the firm and is entirely within the discretion of the board of directors.

The first generation of poison pills introduced the flip-over poison pills. Similar to charter provisions that are aimed to block a second-step transaction, the flip-over poison pill did not target the purchase of stock by the bidder but rather the bidders' ability to merge with the target in a second stage maneuver. As explained earlier, potential bidder that cannot merge with the target may lose interest in the target altogether. The flip-over shareholders right plan is triggered when the bidder, who already purchased a substantial portion of the target stock, merges with the target (or otherwise combines the operations of the two firms). The pill may be also triggered if the bidder sells a substantial portion of the firms' assets.

Once triggered, the shareholders right "flipover" and become rights to buy common shares of the bidder at a discount (usually half of the market price). The flip-over poison pill is a nondiscriminatory poison pill in the sense that the bidder itself enjoys the right to purchase its own stock, as the other shareholders of the target. However, the bidder suffers from a substantial dilution once the rest of the target shareholders exercise their rights.

While the flip-over poison pill has many advantages, it is still far from perfect as an anti-takeover mechanism. In some cases the bidder may do equally well without combining its business with the target, and therefore never trigger the pill. In other cases, such as the takeover of Crown Zellerbach by Sir James Goldsmith in 1985, the bidder may launce a tender offer and then negotiates with the management on the second-step transaction. The incumbent board of directors always preserves the power to redeem the pill since it wishes to allow friendly transactions.

The Flip In (Discriminatory) Poison Pill

The flaws of the flip-over poison pill brought lawyers to invent more lethal poison pills. In addition, the fact that the flip-over poison pill passed the courts scrutiny encouraged lawyers to try their luck with discriminatory pills. The discriminatory pill separates the treatment it gives to the bidder from that of the rest of the shareholders of the target. While the rights of the rest of the shareholders are triggered once the bidder acquires a substantial portion of the target stock (without awaiting a second-step transaction), the bidders rights are void.

Instead of receiving rights for common shares of the bidder, as in the flip-over case, the rights "flip in" and grants each holder to purchase the target's stock at a sharp discount. It is, therefore, important that the rights are discriminatory, or else the bidder's share of the target would not be diluted. It is also common to supplement the flip in poison pill with a flip-over component, for extra takeover protection. This second-generation pill is undoubtedly a fierce takeover defense. For one, it deters bidding, since success would lead to great dilution of the acquired share. And second, since every shareholder knows that his or her rights would become valuable if the bid is successful while he or she, personally, does not tender, no one would want to tender his or her shares to the bidder in the first place.

Finally, just like the flip-over poison pill, the board of directors of the target may redeem the flip in poison pill in order to entertain friendly transactions. As we have noted before, this feature of the pill, makes it susceptible for circumvention. If the bidder captures the corporate board by running a proxy contest, his newly elected directors will be able to redeem the poison pill. This possibility brought the corporate targets to try to interfere with the corporate vote mechanism, and also invent new types of pills. The courts, however, were reluctant, in most cases, to sanction the use of such pills. For instance, *a dead hand poison pill* preserves redemption power in the hands of the directors that launched the pill, whether or not they are in office. And a *no hand poison pill* does not permit redemption at all once the board is replaced. The courts usually rejected both novel versions of the pill on the grounds that the board of directors is not allowed to restrict its future discretion.[3] The other defensive tactics that impede the proxy mechanism are discussed further.

Common Proxy Contest Impediment Charter Provisions

While courts generally did not legitimize the dead hand poison pill they had to approve charter provisions that interfered with the ease of use of the voting mechanism. The reason is that the legislation in most of the states explicitly allows such provisions, even though they hurt the effectiveness and availability of the proxy process as a means to achieve unsolicited changes in corporate control. By and large, these charter (or bylaws) provisions that cause delay and impede the proxy mechanism of the firm may be divided into provisions that inhibit shareholders' opportunities to express their opinions and provisions that narrow shareholders' means to wrest control from the incumbent board of directors. Since each state has different relevant standards, the analysis concentrates on the Delaware case as the leading corporate domicile (Kaouris 1995; Romano 1985).

Provisions that Limit Shareholders Opportunities to Voice Their Opinion

Unlike the board of directors that can easily convene and sustain its will, the large body of shareholders is bounded to reach decisions in structured ways. To nominate or replace directors, shareholders can act through the shareholders' regular general meeting, a special shareholders meeting, or written consent in lieu of a meeting. Well-designed anti-takeover provisions (ATPs) may impede the effectiveness of each of these tools.

Written Consent In Lieu of a Meeting

The most rapid and easiest way for shareholders to voice their opinion and replace the board of directors is the written consent process. Consequently, even if the target firm is shielded by a poison pill, it may be captured within a minimal period of 45 days imposed by the federal proxy regulation (assuming that shareholders possess the right to remove directors without cause). The right to vote by written consent, in lieu of a vote in the shareholders' meetings, was legislated in a 1974 amendment to the Delaware Corporate Code.[4] As the market for corporate control was yet to be sparked, no one thought that this right would enhance the proxy mechanism potency as the major tool of the market for corporate control. In fact, the written consent option was presented to the Delaware Code as a mere cost-saving measure to replace expensive shareholders' meetings in cases of fairly concentrated ownership (Gordon 1549, 1564). However, the following decade, in the heyday of the market for corporate control, the shareholders' written consent procedure had an unexpected role in control contests.[5]

---

[3] Carmody v. Toll Bros., 723 A.2d 1180 (Del.Ch. 1998); Quickturn Systems, Inc. v. Shapiro 721 A.2d 1281 (Del. 1998).

[4] *See* Del. Code Ann., tit. 8, § 228 (1991).

[5] See generally Aguilar (1984, 27), and for an anecdote example see A. Sloan (1983, 146–47).

The important role of the written consent mechanism may be impeded by a simple takeover defense. Since the Delaware Code permits firms to opt out of the written-consent-right default by a charter amendment, firms can forbid shareholders' use of written consent in lieu of a meeting.[6] Managers of such firms are secured by this charter provision from being easily and rapidly expelled from office through a written consent maneuver. Moreover, using this takeover shield provides managers with another advantage, since the board of directors cannot closely regulate the consent process, while it may manipulate the agenda of the shareholders' meeting.

Special Shareholders Meetings

A special shareholders meeting is a meeting scheduled in addition to the annual shareholders meeting and can, thus, facilitate rapid replacement of the management even in the absence of a written consent procedure. The relevant default standard in the Delaware Code does not include a straightforward right for shareholders to summon a special meeting.[7] Interestingly enough, for the default states that unless otherwise provided in the charter, the bylaws can grant authority to summon a special shareholders meeting. Since the shareholders govern the bylaws, as a matter of law, they may amend the bylaws to include a right to summon a special shareholders' meeting (Brannigan 2001, A-4). However, equipped with the proper charter provision managers may still have the upper hand. Therefore, one can often find charter provisions that preclude or limit the right to call for a special shareholders meeting so that shareholders will not be able to circumvent the default by changing the bylaws. Once the charter explicitly impedes shareholders' right to summon a special meeting, the bylaws, and in turn the shareholders, lose control over the issue. Another technique is to install a supermajority bylaw requirement regarding special shareholders meetings within the bylaws so that shareholders would not be able to change it.

This sophisticated type of ATP that prevents special meetings postpones the opportunity of shareholders to express their opinion until the next annual meeting. With a right to summon a special meeting, proxy solicitation can be accomplished within 60–90 days, but without it shareholders have to wait for the regular annual meeting of the firm. The board is authorized to schedule annual meetings, and the period between two regular meetings could be stretched to as much as 360 to 540 days, depending on the state of incorporation.[8] This, undoubtedly, is a substantial delay.[9]

General Shareholder Meetings and the Staggered Board Provision

Evidently, unsolicited control transactions are frequently delayed even beyond the annual shareholders meeting. A most potent ATP, the charter provision that forms a staggered board, is to be blamed for such delays.[10] According to the Delaware Code, all members of the board

6 *See* Del. Code Ann., tit. 8, § 228 (1991).

7 *See* Del. Code Ann., tit. 8, § 211(d) (1991).

8 For the maximum days between annual meetings in the 50 different states see John C. Coates (2001, table B-5).

9 For an in-depth explanation on the period of delay *see* Coates (1999, 853).

10 See generally Background Report on Classified Boards (1994); Ambrose & Megginson (1992).

must stand for election annually.[11] However, a charter provision may form a staggered (classified) board, in which only a third of the board is replaced every year. Thus, to gain control over a company with a staggered board, one must win two consecutive proxy fights, and in some cases even three proxy fights if the company has a cumulative voting procedure.

A staggered board complicates the entire proxy mechanism. It makes control transfers lengthy and expensive. In some industries, waiting 2 years for a takeover bid to materialize is simply impractical. One can observe the detrimental effect of a staggered board from the anecdote of the infamous Moore-Walace's proxy battle. Moore Corp. had launched a US$60 per share tender offer for Wallace Computer Services Inc., which reflected more than a 50% premium on the market price. The bid was contingent upon the board's consent to redeem the firm's poison pill, but although 73.5% of the equity was tendered, the board refused to redeem the pill. Next, Moore won a proxy contest for the board, but since Wallace had a staggered board, Moore was only able to nominate a minority of three members out of an eight-member board.

Consequently, and even though it was overwhelmingly supported by Wallace shareholders, Moore decided to back out of the battle and not wait another year until the next annual meeting. In hindsight, a year after Moore's proposal, the stock price of Wallace did not reach the price offered by Moore, while the S&P 500 Index gained 20% in the same period (Abelson 1996; Greenberg 1995; Lipkin 1995; Miller 1995). This anecdote is a rare example of a bidder that won both a contingent hostile tender offer and a first annual meeting battle against a staggered board, but still had to decline. More often, the anticipation of the costs of delay created by staggered boards cause bidders not to engage targets with such takeover targets in the first place, unless there are extremely generous returns awaiting the winner.

The ability to delay takeovers for up to 2, and in some cases even 3 years (thanks to the addition of a cumulative voting mechanism), evidently became very attractive to some firms. In an upsurge from the early 1980s, today over 60% of all public companies have boards of directors that are not fully replaced every year (Monaco 1999). Undoubtedly, this is an extremely lethal and frequently used ATP.

Provisions that Limit Shareholders Means to Wrest Control

Assuming that shareholders have an opportunity to express their opinion, it does not automatically follow that they can easily alter the power structure in the boardroom. To complete a takeover, it is necessary for the bidder's proponents to occupy a majority of the board's seats. Such a majority could be achieved by replacing directors who have served their full term, removing and replacing directors while they serve in office, or expanding the board and packing it with a majority of new directors. Well-drafted ATPs can limit shareholders rights to dismiss directors or expand the board, leaving open only the opportunity to replace directors who have served their full term.

Provisions that Eliminate the Right to Dismiss Directors Without "Cause"

Assuming that shareholders can voice their opinion via written consent or a special shareholders meeting, they may dismiss directors and entertain a takeover without awaiting the shareholders

[11] *See* DEL. CODE ANN., tit. 8, § 141(d) (1991).

general meeting. This possibility should not, however, be taken for granted. Most default state laws indeed allow shareholders to dismiss directors from office without a cause, but firms can elect to opt out of this arrangement.[12] If a well-structured provision is added to the firm's charter, shareholders may not remove directors from office before their term is due.

Provisions That Foreclose Shareholders' Ability to Expand the Board

Even if shareholders may not dismiss directors from office without cause, they may still act prior to the regular shareholders meeting. When they can either act by written consent or a special shareholders' meeting, shareholders can expand the board of directors and occupy the new seats up to the point in which the incumbent directors become a minority. Thus, shareholders may shift control over the firm without dismissing any director from office.

The default law in Delaware requires that the number of directors be set in the charter or the bylaws. When the number is set in the bylaws, shareholders may use their power to amend the bylaws to enlarge the board and wrest control from the incumbent directors. To exemplify, in a recent takeover struggle, the bidder, Suntrust, tried to persuade the shareholders of the target, Wachovia to amend the bylaws in order to expand the board of directors so that pro-Suntrust directors could influence Wachovia. However, if the number of directors is set in the charter, shareholders cannot intervene and pack the board with new directors since the board has veto power over charter amendments. Such a charter provision is, therefore, an implicit ATP. Other techniques are to include a supermajority bylaws requirement or an explicit prohibition in the charter on shareholders' right to fill vacancies.

Post-bid Measures

Greenmail

Even after a bid is launched or after a hostile acquiror has accumulated a substantial block of the target stock, some defensive maneuvers are still available. One of those maneuvers, and perhaps the most notorious anti-takeover defense, is the *greenmail*. Greenmail is the term used for the repurchase by the target company of the shares held by a hostile aquirer. The hostile raider withdraws from the battle but enjoy the profits of the repurchase, which is negotiated with the target's management. While managements opt for greenmail after a bid is launched or when the bid is pending, the possibility of extracting a greenmail may attract a bid in the first place. Therefore, some firms adopt charter provisions that foreclose the ability of the firm to pay greenmail (Gilson 1988).

While the practice of paying greenmail started in the 1960s, and was sanctioned by the courts in the famous *Mathes* case, the humongous payments of the 1980s led to much criticism. This criticism eventually reduced greenmail events as it brought some state legislators, including

[12] In Delaware, unlike other states, only a charter provision that forms a staggered board may abolish shareholders' right to remove directors. *See* DEL. CODE ANN., tit. 8, § 141.

New York, to ban greenmail. The federal internal revenue code was also revised and a 50% nondeductible excise tax on greenmail profits was included.[13]

Litigation

Another highly popular, defensive post-bid tactic is defensive litigation. Defensive litigation is conducted even if the target has low chances of success. Management simply has nothing to loose, and for a target that was struck by a surprise bid, litigation is the first chance to fight back. In the litigation the target is usually asking for an injunction to block the bid, but even a preliminary court order that prolongs the bid period may help the target reorganize and search for an alternative to the hostile bid.

Often times, the grounds for litigation are shaky and the legal counsels of the target just try their luck with any possible claim. Antitrust claims are always raised, but are eventually rarely accepted. Other possible claims are based on securities disclosure, in which the target's counsel argues that the bidders omits material facts about the bid or makes some misrepresentations. These claims, however, usually do not buy the target much time since courts allow bidders to amend the bid documents, if necessary.

THE LEGAL STANDARDS FOR COURTS SCRUTINY OF DEFENSES

Before the takeover wave of the 1980s and management defensive response, American courts usually applied two standards of scrutiny to corporate acts. Most corporate decisions enjoy the broad protection of the *business judgment rule.* Once the board of directors show that it reached an informed decision, and has no conflicting self-interest in the decision, the courts do not give a second thought to the directors' conclusions. However, when the corporate act may be biased due to self-interest, such as the case of self-dealing with a controlling shareholder or director, the courts apply the *entire fairness* standard. Once the entire fairness standard is applied, the court considers all aspects of the decision to make sure that it has sound business justifications.

Corporate acts involving takeover defenses do not fit comfortably with any of these standards. On the one hand, the board of directors may be biased since it is most likely to be ousted if the takeover bid succeeds. But on the other hand, and unlike the regular self-dealing setting, a takeover event is a major transaction for the target's shareholders for which management judgment can be beneficial. Therefore, the Delaware Supreme Court in the seminal case of *Unocal* developed a novel standard, the *proportionality test,* to examine anti-takeover steps. The first prong of the proportionality test requires that the board of directors demonstrate "reasonable ground that a danger to corporate policy or effectiveness" exist by reason of the hostile takeover threat. And the second prong asks whether the defensive step is "reasonable in relation to the threat posed."

The first prong was never a real barrier for the adoption of takeover defenses. It was interpreted by the courts to require that the board of directors point to a corporate purpose in their acts, rather than a threat to the personal interest of the directors.[14] And since every takeover interferes with corporate policy, the first requirement of the proportionality test is easily fulfilled.

[13] Internal Revenue Code Sec. 5881.

[14] AC Acquisitions v. Anderson, Clayton & Co. Court of Chancery of Delaware, 1986 519 A.2d 103.

As for the second requirement of the proportionality test, things are more complicated. Initially, commentators debated whether boards' decisions to reject transactions, made under the shields of the poison pills or some other defensive maneuver, were about to be scrutinized in depth by the courts. On the one hand, Gilson and Kraakman, encouraged by early court decisions, advocated substantive scrutiny by the courts of any board decision regarding unsolicited offers to purchase the firm. Specifically, they highlighted an intermediate review standard that is not too harsh but nevertheless does not leave unconditional discretion to the board of directors (Gilson and Kraakman 1989). A few years later, Kahan explained that the Delaware court never intended and would never conduct such substantive scrutiny. The requirements that the board of directors is obliged to fulfill in a case of an offer to purchase the firm are mostly procedural and technical (Kahan 1994).

Eventually, the Delaware Supreme Court made it quite clear that only when the managerial defensive maneuver is coercive or preclusive, will it invoke the second prong of the *Unocal* proportionality test.[15] One exception to this lax approach to managerial defensive conduct exists when the board initiates a sale of the company to a third party. Under these circumstances, the court limits the board's ability to defend its sale plan against a hostile bid by another potential buyer.[16] It is also important to mention that the proportionality test is applicable only to unilateral defensive acts taken by the board of directors. Once the shareholders body approves a defensive measure, such as an approval of an anti-takeover charter amendment, the courts do not examine the defense with the enhanced proportionality test, and the takeover protection practically receives immunity.[17]

Finally, the courts' relatively lax response to most anti-takeover maneuvers evaporates once managers try to manipulate the corporate vote mechanism in a preclusive manner. Since the corporate vote mechanism is the only alternative for a hostile takeover in the era of the poison pill, such response from the courts is vital. Therefore, under the *Blasius* doctrine, any management proposed transaction or unilateral takeover defense that has the primary purpose of interfering with the corporate elections would not be sanctioned unless the board shows compelling justifications.[18] This standard of review is so demanding from the management that the court is very cautious in invoking it, but once it applies, it is almost impossible to overcome it.[19]

TRENDS IN DEFENSES ADOPTION AND FUTURE AVENUES OF RESEARCH

During the second half of the 1980s, many firms adopted anti-takeover charter provisions of the various types discussed earlier, but the phenomenon was not as widespread as the adoption of the poison pill. One should also remember that unlike the poison pill, which was literally unheard of until the mid-1980s, some anti-takeover charter provisions were present before the

[15] Unitrim, Inc. v. American General Corp. Delaware Supreme Court, 1995 651 A.2d 1361.

[16] *See* Revlon Inc. v. MacAndrews and Forbes Holdings, Inc., 506 A.2d 173, 181 (Del. 1986); Paramount Communications, Inc. v. QVC Network, Inc. Supreme Court of Delaware, 1994 637 A.2d 34.

[17] Williams v. Grier Supreme Court of Delaware, 1994 671 A.2d 1368.

[18] Blasius Industries, Inc. v. Atlas Corp. Court of Chancery of Delaware, 1988 564 A.2d 651.

[19] Chesapeake Corporation v. Shore Court of Chancery of Delaware, 2000 Del. Ch. Lexis 20.

wave of control contests. The invention of the poison pill magnified the vast impediment potential ingrained in these charter provisions. Out of a sample of approximately 400 large firms (primarily S&P 500), restrictions on the ability to act by written consent or to call a special shareholders meeting were present in 66 firms in 1984 and in 178 firms in 1989 (Karpoff and Danielson 1998, table 2). In the same sample, 143 firms had a classified board in 1984 and 253 had one in 1989. While this ratio remained more or less constant throughout the 1990s, it represents a striking uproar from the approximately 20% at the beginning of the 1980s.

To support the common agency theory understanding that these charter amendments are suboptimal, Jarrell and Poulsen, and Baghat and Jefferis illustrated that adoption of anti-takeover charter provisions was related to a small but statistically significant decline in the stock price (Bhaghat and Jefferis 1991; Jarrell et al. 1984). Moreover, there is direct evidence that such charter provision actually deter takeovers. Pound found that a combination of staggered boards and supermajority requirements for a merger in the firms' charter significantly decreased incidences of hostile bids (Pound 1987).[20] As mentioned before, all these harsh findings did not lead shareholders in the 1980s to withhold their approval and prevent managers from adopting ATPs (Danielson and Karpoff 1998; Mikkelson and Partch 1989).

By the 1990s, however, the ease of adopting ATPs had all but dissipated. The increased power and activity of institutional shareholders practically precluded managers from implementing ATPs in seasoned firms. Surprisingly, while institutional investors frequently block management proposals to adopt ATPs, they do not force firms that already have them to remove them, nor do they pressure initial public offering (IPO)-stage firms to defer implementation of anti-takeover defenses. Consequently, ATPs may be either adopted at the IPO stage or effectively abandoned forever. As phrased by one commentator: "After an IPO is complete and ownership dispersed, the takeover defenses of a public company in the U.S. in the 1990s have generally been fixed" (Coates 2001).

The recognition that after the IPO stage, anti-takeover defenses remain fixed led scholars to investigate the adoption trends of IPO-stage firms. Prior to the IPO, there is no divergence in incentives between shareholders and managers, and, thus, firms at such stage are assumed to reach an optimal governance structures. And, since such governance structure remains fixed in relation to takeover defenses, the outcomes of the study of IPO-stage firms was expected to finally reveal if anti-takeover defenses are inimical or beneficial. However, the results of the recent empirical studies regarding anti-takeover charter provisions in IPO-stage firms have puzzled corporate law scholars and have not satisfied any side of the debate (Coates 2001; Daines and Klausner 2001; Field and Karpoff forthcoming). While some companies adopt harsh and effective defenses, others have no such provisions whatsoever.[21] To understand the reason for this divergence in firm behavior, researchers investigated relevant dissimilarities between adopting and nonadopting firms. Surprisingly, the firms that had opted for defenses did not possess the special features identified by the classic literature as making defenses of particular value to a firm.

---

[20] For a summary of the empirical evidence of the harmful effects of ATPs, see Romano.

[21] One commentator recently presented the challenge to traditional corporate law as follows: "Standing alone, Lipton's position would suggest all companies should adopt defenses prior to an IPO, and Easterbrook & Fischel's position would suggest that no firm should adopt a defense; yet, in reality, about half do and half do not" (Coates 2001).

Consequently, researchers proposed a number of theories of market failure that provide alternative explanations to the classic literature for the adoption of anti-takeover shields. The feature common to all these theories is that they all reject the classic notion that the corporate governance structure of IPO firms maximizes the benefit of the entire shareholder body.[22] One study suggests that the market does not price the costs of an ATP and, therefore, IPO-stage firms can often get away with adopting detrimental defenses that protect managers from takeovers, at the expense of the public shareholders. A second study suggests that lawyers do not always give good advice to their clients with regard to ATPs and, therefore, firms fail to select the optimal tactic. Finally, a third study suggests that some pre-IPO firms have dominant managers who select takeover defenses at the expense of the nonmanagerial pre-IPO shareholders. The difference between this theory and the first one presented earlier is that this theory posits that the public markets price takeover defenses well and know that they are harmful for shareholders, while the former theory did not accept this classic proposition. Therefore, the public shareholders presumably pay less for firms with takeover defenses, making the nonmanagerial pre-IPO shareholders bear all the costs of adopting the defenses, while only the managerial pre-IPO team enjoys their benefits.

In reply to this line of arguments, I have argued elsewhere that all these explanations are excessive and that the seminal notion that IPO-stage firms select optimal governance terms may still stand. The reason that the classic literature failed to provide a full rationale for the firms' behavior is that it concentrated on what I call supply-side explanations. I view the decision to go public without defenses as a decision to produce an unshielded target and show that the classic literature focused on the costs of producing such a target. The literature explained that some firms have features that make defenses particularly valuable to them and, therefore, their costs of producing an unshielded target are high. Those firms, the argument goes, are the ones most likely to adopt defenses. However, I argue that the empirical studies failed to uncover such behavior because the classic literature never considered demand-side considerations.

The implied assumption of the classic literature is that the benefits of rejecting defenses do not fluctuate with the number of firms on the market that adopts defenses. I argue that the greater the number of firms that adopt defenses, the higher the benefits that accrue to the firms that reject them. The reason is that not only do takeover defenses prevent takeovers, they also divert takeover activity to unshielded targets. This argument may be formulated as a demand-side explanation. The more firms there are producing unshielded (and therefore the fewer the firms adopting defenses), the lower the price that the market is willing to pay for the unshielded product. Conversely, the fewer the number of firms producing unshielded targets, the higher the price the market will place on each unshielded target.

The reason that the adoption of defenses by a firm benefits its unshielded peers is that purchasers make comparative analyses in their decision-making processes (Akhigbe et al. 2000). This fact was readily shown by an empirical study that found that termination of a planned merger creates vast stock gains for industry rivals, suggesting that industry rivals are takeover-alternatives and may be purchased once the merger fails. In addition to looking at the functional characteristics of the different potential targets, bidders must also compare the degree of ease with which each target may be acquired. Therefore, in order to draw a complete picture of a company's takeover prospects, one must consider not only the company's defenses,

[22] This classic notion is attributed to the seminal work of Jensen and Meckling (1976).

but also those of its peers. In a sense, this externality argument is close to Shavell's diversion-of-crime argument. For example, placing bars on one's windows would result in a higher risk of burglary to one's neighbors (Shavell 1991).

Put differently, the takeover risk to an individual firm is not endogenous to its anti-takeover decisions. Each prospective bidder naturally confronts a limited pool of suitable targets from which to choose. Thus, every potential target must consider the defenses available to other prospective targets. The defensive decisions of one firm may divert takeover activity to another firm, which may, in turn, affect the average takeover premium that the latter may reasonably expect in a takeover event.

Taken together, the demand-side explanation that I suggested here and the supply-side explanations previously raised in the literature may help to solve the conundrum of the diversity of firm behavior at the IPO stage. Some firms may have features that cause them to derive greater benefit from adopting takeover defenses than do other firms. However, the greater the number of firms that adopt defenses, the higher the expected premium their unshielded peers can hope for. The market stabilizes at the point where the marginal firm is indifferent to the adoption of ATPs, since both tactics provide similar benefits.

The fact that the empirical studies could not find evidence that the adopting firms are those possessing the special features that make takeover defenses especially of value should not be taken as a discouraging sign. The supply effects may be mild or theoretically nonexistent, but nevertheless, only part of the firms would elect to remain unshielded. Put differently, even if all firms are similar in all relevant features, they may diverge in their anti-takeover decisions. The reason for this is that even if takeover defenses were to provide similar benefits to all firms, an adoption trend would raise the benefits accruing to unshielded firms. Eventually, at some ratio of defenses-adoption, the benefits of the two strategies would become equal for all firms, and the market would maintain this ratio. To sum up, the divergent behavior of IPO-stage firms regarding takeover shields does not necessarily point to any market failure.

Another promising avenue of research lies in the view that anti-takeover defenses are actually network products. In opposition to the dominant view in regards to the IPO stage, commentators have recently employed arguments from the network product theory in the corporate law products' arena (Klausner 1995). Network products, such as VCRs and computers, bear obvious extensive externalities on other users of similar products (Katz and Shapiro 1985). Although the empirical work of emphasizing the fact that this phenomenon can also be substantial in corporate law products (e.g., indentures or charters) is still in its incipiency, the argument has the necessary qualities to become a powerful argument for inefficiencies at the IPO stage (Katz and Shapiro 1985). If the analogy to network product markets is appropriate, it will not be surprising to find stagnation over the usage of inefficient standards (or inability to reach efficient standards).

As we have discussed earlier, empirical evidence of corporate charters reveals that while corporations usually adhere to the default arrangement offered by state corporate law, the opposite is true in regards to charter provisions that may impede hostile takeover attempts.[23] For seasoned firms, which were the first to adopt anti-takeover mechanisms, the adoption may be explained by managerial distorted incentives. However, if takeover defenses are network products, many IPO-stage firms may have opted for defenses in order to adhere to the standard

[23] *See* Karpoff and Danielson (1998, 354, table 2) for the data regarding seasoned firms.

that was adopted by the seasoned firms. For instance, when most of the market is shielded, the managers of an unshielded target may be taken over even if they perfectly perform. This may happen because such unshielded targets are simply easy to purchase. Hence, while some firms prefer not to be shielded, other things equal, they may opt for defenses when most of the market is shielded. If this is true, then the agency problem that led seasoned firms to adopt defenses has become contagious to some of the IPO-stage firms.

CONCLUDING COMMENTS

Takeover defenses can be classified into various categories such as corporate charter defenses, poison pill defenses, statutory defenses, and asset and capital structure defenses. Corporate charter defenses are provisions of corporation charters that impede takeovers. The super majority clause, for example, requires that a specified number of votes be cast in favor of a decision for it to be implemented. The company's management can control any decision by holding a certain number of shares that limits others from obtaining super majority. For instance, if the law requires that 60% of votes be cast in favor of a proposal, then the company's management can block a transaction by holding more than 40% of votes. Companies may block a takeover by making changes in the company's assets and liabilities. Leveraged recapitalizations, for example, make the target company unattractive due to its heavy debt load and the higher probability of going bankrupt. Finally anti-takeover legislations may prohibit companies from acquiring. Academic studies of takeover defenses suggest that most takeover defenses serve the company's management at the expense of shareholders. Many countries are removing anti-takeover legislation: a welcome move.

REFERENCES AND SUGGESTED READINGS

Abelson, Reed. 1996. "When Boards say 'No Deal' to Holders." *The NewYork Times* (June 10).

Aguilar, George C. 1984. "Firms Fear a New Tool in Takeover." *Wall Street Journal* (August 1): 27.

Akhigbe, Aigbe, Stephen F. Borde, and Ann Marie Whyte. 2000. "The Source of Gains to Targets and Their Industry Rivals: Evidence Based on Terminated Merger Proposals." *Financial Management*, 29 (4): 101.

Ambrose, Brent W., and William L. Megginson. 1992. "The Role of Asset Structure, Ownership Structure, and Takeover Defenses in Determining Acquisition Likelihood." *The Journal of Financial and Quantitative Analysis*, 27: 575–89.

Background Report on Classified Boards (1994). Investors Responsibility Research Center.

Bhaghat and Jefferis. 1991. "Voter Power in the Proxy Process: The Case of Antitakeover Charter Amendments." *Journal of Financial Economics*, 30 (1): 193, 200.

Brannigan, Martha. 2001. "SubTrust Seeks Wachovia Bylaw Change As Part of Attempt to Achieve Takeover." *Wall Street Journal* (June 5): A-4.

Coates, John C. 1999. "Measuring the Domain of Mediating Hierarchy: How Contestable are U.S. Public Corporations?" *Journal of Corporation Law*, 24: 837, 850.

———. 2001. "Explaining Variation in Takeover Defenses: Blame the Lawyers." *California Law Review*, 89: 1301, table B-5.

Comment, Robert, and William Schwert. 1995. "Poison or Placebo? Evidence on the Deterrence and Wealth Effects of Modern Antitakeover Measures." *Journal of Financial Economics*, 39 (1): 3.

Daines, Robert, and Michael Klausner. 2001. "Do IPO Charters Maximize Firm Value?" *The Journal of Law, Economics, and Organization*, 17: 83–120.

Danielson, Morris, and Jonathan Karpoff. 1998. "On the Uses of Corporate Governance Provisions." *Journal of Corporate Finance*, 4: 347–71.

Davis, Gerald, and Suzanne Stout. 1992. "Organization Theory and the Market for Corporate Control: A Dynamic Analysis of the Characteristics of Large Takeover Targets, 1980–90." *Administrative Science Quarterly*, 37: 605, 608.

DeMott, Deborah. 1983. "Pac-Man Tender Offers." *Duke Law Journal*, 32: 116.

Field, Laura C., and Jonathan M. Karpoff. 2002. "Takeover Defenses at IPO Firms." *The Journal of Finance*, 7 (5, October): 1857–89. Earlier draft available at http://papers.ssrn.com/sol3/papers.cfm?abstract_id=236043

Gilson, Ronald. 1988. "Drafting and Effective Greenmail Prohibition." *Columbia Law Review*, 88: 329.

Gilson, Ronald, and Reinier Kraakman. 1989. "Delaware Intermediate Standard for Defense Tactics: Is There Substance to Proportionality View?" *The Business Lawyer*, 44: 247, 256–60.

Gilson, Ronald J., and Bernard S. Black. 1998. *The Law and Finance of Corporate Acquisitions*, 2nd ed. p. 747. New York, NY: Foundation Press.

Gordon, Jeffrey N. 1989. "The Mandatory Structure of Corporate Law." *Columbia Law Review*, 89: 1549, 1564.

Greenberg, Larry M. 1995. "Moore Corp. Lets Deadline Pass On US$1.38 Billion Bid for Wallace." *Wall Street Journal*, (December 21).

Jarrell, Gregg, Michael Ryngaert, and Annette B. Poulsen. 1984. *Shark Repellants: The Role and Impact of Antitakeover Charter Amendments*. Office of the Chief Economist (SEC).

Jensen, Michael C., and William H. Meckling. 1976. "The Theory of the Firm: Managerial Behavior, Agency Costs and Ownership Structures." *Journal of Financial Economics*, 3 (4): 305–60.

Kahan, Marcel. 1994. "Paramount or Paradox: The Delaware Supreme Courts Takeover Jurisprudence." *The Journal of Corporation Law*, 19: 583.

Kaouris, Demetrios G. 1995. "Is Delaware Still a Haven for Incorporation?" *Delaware Journal of Corporate Law*, 20: 965, 1012.

Karpoff, J. M., and M. G. Danielson. 1998. "On the Uses of Corporate Governance Provisions." *Journal of Corporate Finance*, 4: 347, 354, table 2.

Katz, Michael L., and Carl Shapiro. 1985. "Network Externalities, Competition and Compatibility." *The American Economic Review*, 75 (3, June): 424.

Klausner, Michael. 1995. "Corporations, Corporate Law, and Networks of Contracts." *Virginia Law Review*, 81: 757.

Kroeber, Charles. 1986. "Golden Parachutes, Shark Repellents, and Hostile Tender Offers." *The American Economic Review*, 76 (1): 155.

Lambert, Richard, and David Larker. 1985. "Golden Parachutes, Executive Decision-Making, and Shareholder Wealth." *Journal of Accounting and Economics*, 7 (1–3): 179.

Lipkin, Steven. 1995. "Wallace Faces Test Today in Fighting Off Moore's Bid." *Wall Street Journal*, August 12.

Manne, Henry. 1965. "Mergers and the Market for Corporate Control." *The Journal of Political Economy*, 73 (2): 110.

Mikkelson, Wayne, and M. Megan Partch. 1989. "Managers Voting Rights and Corporate Control." *Journal of Financial Economics*, 25: 263, 267.

Miller, James P. 1995. "Wallace Computer Holders Elect Directors Backed by Moore Corp." *Wall Street Journal*, November 12.

Monaco, Alesandra. 1999. *Corporate Governance Service 1999 Background Report C: Classified Boards*. Investor Responsibility Research Center.

Mulherin, Harold, and Annette Poulsen. 1998. "Proxy Contests and Corporate Change: Implications for Shareholders Wealth." *Journal of Financial Economics*, 47 (3): 279, 286.

Pound John. 1987. "The Effects of Antitakeover Amendments on Takeover Activity: Some Direct Evidence." *The Journal of Law & Economics*, 30 (2): 353.

Romano, Roberta. 1993. *The Genious of American Corporate Law*. 60–75. Washington, DC: American Enterprise Institute.

Romano, Roberta. 1985. "Law as a Product: Some Pieces of the Incorporation Puzzle." *The Journal of Law, Economics, and Organization*, 1 (2): 224, 225.

Shavell, Steven. 1991. "Individual Precautions to Prevent Theft: Private Versus Socially Optimal Behavior." *International Review of Law and Economics*, 11: 123, 126.

Sloan, A. 1983. *Three Plus One Equals Billions: The Bendiz-Martin Maietta War*. p. 146–47. Arbor House Publishing Company.

Wachtell Lipton Rosen & Katz. 1998. "The Share Purchase Rights Plan." In *The Law and Finance Of Corporate Acquisitions*, 2nd ed., edited by R. J. Gilson and B. S. Black, (4–12). New York: Foundation Press.

REVIEW QUESTIONS

1. Write brief notes on:
   a. Pac-man defense
   b. White Knight
   c. Dual-class Capitalization
   d. Poison Pill
   e. Golden Parachutes
2. Review the empirical evidence on takeover defenses on shareholders wealth.
3. Are takeover defenses in the interest of shareholders? Why or why not?

CHAPTER 11

Post-merger Integration

Vishwanath S. R.

Learning Objectives

- Identify the core components of a post-merger integration
- Learn how to plan and implement a post-merger strategy

In recent years, the worldwide M&A volume has been averaging US$4 trillion. Deals running to several billion dollars are not uncommon. For example, in 2006, Mittal Steel of UK made a US$23 billion bid for Arcelor of France to create the biggest steel company in the world, accounting for 10% of world's production. The rise in volume and deal size has increased the need for sound practical frameworks for the analysis and structuring of transactions. There is overwhelming evidence that most acquisitions fail to produce desired results largely because of overpayment or poor integration. Consequently, there is a need for a coherent framework to think about post-merger issues. For instance, Hewlett Packard's CEO, Carleton "Carly" Fiorina, proposed to acquire rival computing company Compaq in September 2001 (Burgelman and McKinney 2005). Following the consummation of the merger in May 2002, the organizational integration of HP and Compaq was initially considered a success as the company was initially exceeding its goals. By the end of 2004, however, it had become clear that HP was missing the merger's long-term revenue and profit goals. It was unclear whether this was due to the details of the organizational and cultural integration taking much longer to be worked out than initially expected, the original strategic assumptions being wrong, or some combination of both.

THE PATH TO INTEGRATION

As M&A activity becomes the norm in large companies, senior executives are struggling to maintain control over acquisition activity that is increasingly different in kind and decentralized. Companies have to balance the need to centrally monitor and manage a growing portfolio of acquisitions with the need to decentralize and tailor due diligence, and deal structure and integration to reflect the strategic driver and size of each deal. Seeking to improve acquisition success rates, chief financial officers (CFOs) have focused more attention on selecting the right acquisition target and devising an optimal deal structure. However, research indicates that the areas where CFOs focus most of their attention—deal structure and purchase price—have very little impact on long-term deal success.

This chapter focuses on the integration of resources, processes, and corporate responsibilities following a merger. Post-merger integration (PMI) is the complex process of combining and reorganizing the two business entities to realize synergies that motivated the merger or acquisition. The process of combining the merging organizations has critical implications for assets, resources, people, and roles. Hence, integration planning is one of the most important areas of a merger or an acquisition that needs to be addressed before the transaction.

Surveys of industry executives suggest that leading acquisition integrators tend to have higher total shareholder returns (TSR; i.e., dividend yield + capital gains) than their peers, while lagging integrators underperform their peers (*Integration Insights* 2007). Leading acquirers produced a 3-year average TSR of 50% relative to the peer group, whereas lagging acquirers produced –26%. They also find that the integration of customers has a greater impact on TSR performance than the integration of operations or employees.

The organizations most successful in achieving the anticipated benefits of the merger or acquisition place a high value on project management and performance measurement (Bourke, Laidlaw, and Woods 2000, 10–13). Strong performers understand that speed is critical in post-merger integration and recognize the danger of being internally focused for too long. Large, complex integration requires substantial analysis and planning. Therefore, it is necessary to have a project management approach.

Similarly, smooth integrators have a detailed understanding of desired outcomes such as organizational structure, distribution channels, product range, and the associated milestones. This target setting must be accompanied by a performance measurement system that monitors progress. A typical timeline of events is presented in Exhibit 11.1.

Identifying the Key Issues in the Merger

We need to recognize the fact that not all mergers serve similar goals. Hence, it is necessary to approach each merger differently (Bower 2001). Managers of companies that merge to addresses overcapacity in the industry must decide how to rationalize resources, including human capital, in order to become more efficient. A merger that is supposed to provide geographic expansion would need to have several local units, with executives managing each unit. Here, retention of key executives would be the key issue. Likewise, product or market extensions and industry convergence would have different integration issues. Having a one-size-fits-all approach would be disastrous.

Role of the Integration Manager

Most companies appoint an integration manager to oversee the PMI process. This is a vice-president-level position responsible for the executive management of the Merger Integration Project Management Office (PMO) as it relates to the company's values and business goals. The PMO reports to the business executive who owns the respective acquisition and is fully responsible for the successful integration process and business continuity of the newly acquired

Exhibit 11.1 *Post-merger Integration Timeline*

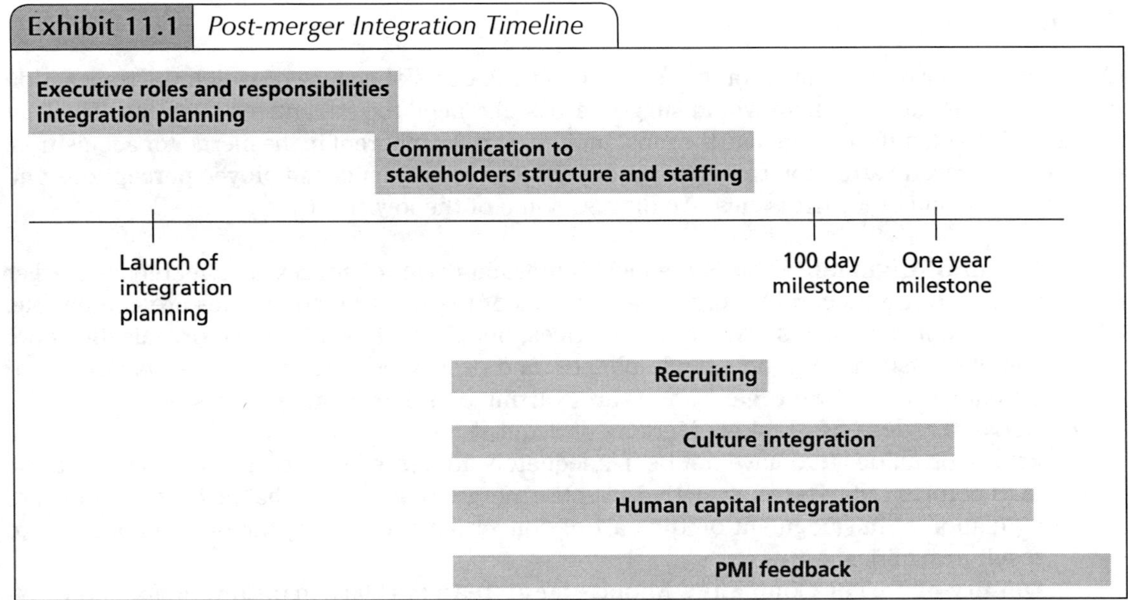

Source: Author.

company and integrated business unit. Basic principles of this position include enterprise-level program strategy and coordination. The integration manager is responsible for the planning and integration of multiple projects comprising large and complex enterprise-level programs inclusive of developing company-wide resource requirements and dashboard reporting at the executive level. The integration manager works closely with senior management, steering committees, audit committees, project and program management offices, business and technology function managers, and individual project managers to steer projects toward achieving the intended business results. The integration leader is a member of a cross functional due diligence team. Potential integration risks are identified during due diligence and the integration plan is drafted *prior* to the deal announcement.

The executive is responsible for overseeing and delivering on the development, implementation, and execution of the program and project infrastructure necessary for completing program definition; creating baseline program and project plans; establishing program budgets; and tracking, monitoring, and reporting program and project progress to plan and budget. The position assures that processes are established and executed for requirements and scope management; issues identification and resolution; continuous risk management and mitigation; and quality and audit assurance.

DuPont, a chemical manufacturer, for example, begins planning acquisition integration during the due diligence phase, during which it selects and assigns integration managers to the due diligence team to begin assessing and planning for integration hurdles (*After the Acquisition* 2001). Devoting integration resources this early in the deal process helps quickly capitalize on information gathered during due diligence and diffuse potential integration landmines prior to deal completion.

Deal Risks

A typical merger or an acquisition has several sources of risk because of which the transaction may fail. Understanding them would suggest areas that need top executives attention. The best organizations identify and manage the most important risks inherent in the merger or acquisition.

They pay careful attention to key areas of business performance, employee perceptions and expectations, and other HR issues. We discuss some of the key risks:

- **Cultural Alignment:** This is the most important driver of success in a merger. A merger is likely to be successful only if the cultures of the merging companies are compatible. Every company has its own set of practices, beliefs, and values. Since organizations are complex systems of people, technologies, and processes, no real progress is possible if executives of the two organizations are warring on systems and processes.
- **Attractiveness of Market:** Mergers or acquisitions are often aimed at addressing market opportunities that have not been adequately addressed by either of companies. If the market turns out to be unattractive after the merger (e.g., due to changes in governmental regulation or misjudgment on the part of concerned executives) the deal is not likely to result in significant synergy.
- **Quality of Target Company's Management Team:** In 2002, in the aftermath of the dot-com bubble, Jamie Dimon, CEO of JPMorgan Chase, opined, "I'd rather have a first-rate execution and second-rate strategy any time than a brilliant idea and mediocre management." It is now well documented that strategies more often fail because they are not well executed (Bossify, Charan, and Burck 2002).
- **Talent Retention:** Much of forecasted synergy can be realized only if the organization is able to retain the most talented employees.
- **Customer Retention:** It is far easier to retain existing customers than find new ones. An integration plan must address how the new organization would serve its customers.
- **Revenue Synergy Assumptions:** In the chapter on value drivers and target valuation, we demonstrated how synergy estimates are built into the discounted cash flow (DCF) valuation. All estimates are based on assumptions, and assumptions can go wrong. For this reason, it is necessary that executives from all functional areas are involved in the estimation process. More importantly, everyone must know the assumptions made. Downside surprises can be costly.
- **Supply Chain Management:** A sound PMI plan must address supply chain issues before the merger. For instance, the acquisition of Corus group by Tata Steel was aimed at manufacturing in UK and Netherlands and selling throughout the world. Obviously this opened up several supply chain issues for Tata Steel. Tata Steel addressed this by setting up shipping companies.

RETAINING AND INTEGRATING HUMAN RESOURCES

Often acquirers focus almost entirely on financial and operational data with scant attention given to people issues in the deal. Not performing human resource due diligence could lead to loss of executives soon after the deal announcement (Harding and Rouse 2007). Research shows that companies continue to lose disproportionate numbers of executives years after their merger has closed (Krug 2003). By making human due diligence a part of the exercise, acquirers can identify the differences in decision-making processes and culture, address the issues, and avoid attrition.

Executive sponsors of the acquisition should identify key managerial talent prior to the deal closure and lock them in with monetary incentives immediately after the deal closure. Prior to closing the deal, functional integration teams (finance, marketing, R&D, and so on) work to identify key talent; human resources works with the integration teams to identify and recreate financial and nonfinancial drivers of key talent retention.

Nortel, a telecommunications equipment manufacturer with US$30.3 billion in revenue, devised an integration approach that identifies and retains key talent and business practices at the acquired company to catalyze substantial change at Nortel. This approach combines early and consistent communications to employees with a proactive effort to identify and replicate the financial and nonfinancial drivers of key talent retention.

Pfizer, a pharmaceutical company, charges its integration team with conducting detailed line of business reviews before a deal closes to determine the relative strengths and weaknesses of its own internal operations and staff. Armed with these detailed self-assessments, Pfizer can conduct a rapid competency assessment of the target company's operations and determine the optimal mix of staff and organizational structures (*After the Acquisition* 2001).

INTEGRATING FINANCIAL AND TANGIBLE RESOURCES

One of the key steps in PMI is the integration of financial and tangible resources. During the due diligence phase, executives would have spent time in understanding the target's asset and liability structure. These have to be integrated with that of the acquirer soon after the acquisition. This would entail physically integrating facilities, factories, warehouses, and distribution facilities as well as integrating banking relationships. There is a popular belief that merged entities can borrow more and at better rates. Lenders would want to reduce their exposure to larger entities because of which banks may lend less to the merged company.

INTEGRATING REPUTATIONAL AND INTANGIBLE RESOURCES

The rise in acquisitions has placed considerable stress on all corporate functions to smoothly integrate operations; in particular, the value of the corporate brand often declines due to poor integration preparation. After deal closure, companies often struggle to determine the branding outcome of the acquisition. Instead, companies must articulate the strategic goals for the acquired brand and work toward those objectives. Specifically, consumer products companies often base their acquisition strategies on the value of the targeted brand. They may purchase undermarketed brands with strong name recognition and provide the resources to develop the product image. This strategy values brand as the primary driver of the acquisition decision, requiring early preparation to facilitate brand integration.

In integrating brands the following observations would be helpful (Managing Brand Integration after an Acquisition 1999):

Make brand planning a part of due diligence: Lack of agreement or inadequacies in brand valuation methods dissuades executives from a formal brand evaluation exercise.

Nevertheless, making brand planning a part of due diligence helps companies in positioning themselves for integration.

Conduct a formal analysis of the brand: Conducting a formal analysis helps in developing positioning strategies for the brand.

Set up a brand oversight committee: Often there is a gap between the intended positioning of the brand as conceptualized during the merger and tactical revisions of the brand because these are the responsibilities of different groups of executives within an organization. To bridge the gap, it is necessary to set up an oversight committee to ensure alignment. This committee could comprise of executives from different functional areas.

Prepare and disseminate internal and external communications during and soon after the merger.

INTEGRATING IT SYSTEMS

It is important to understand that often the IT systems cannot be simply added (i.e., scaled) after a merger. It is more than that. It is likely that the companies operate with disparate systems, making it difficult to put together a unified architecture. Managers should address this before the merger. Seventy-five percent of an integration effort during a merger or acquisition is determining which systems to keep, what data is important, and how much integration is actually needed before the companies are technically joined. Once that kind of planning is complete, the actual hands-on work would be like any other IT project (Worthen 2002).

INTEGRATING COMPENSATION PLANS

Just as IT systems need to be stitched together, the merging companies must decide how compensation strategies of the two entities would be integrated. Compensation plans vary, often dramatically, across companies and industries. Some companies may have stock option or economic value added (EVA) compensation plans, whereas others may have a fixed salary with an annual bonus paid according to a preset formula. Sometimes companies may start from scratch and design a uniform compensation structure. Once a common structure is put in place, it must be communicated to employees.

ADDRESSING STAKEHOLDER EXPECTATIONS

Brand equity and goodwill often account for a large fraction of a company's market capitalization. Acquirers usually pay a premium over the prevailing stock price, which is classified as goodwill. Often the goodwill is substantial. Adverse news can result in a decline in stock prices. For example, in May 2015, Indian food safety authorities banned the production and sale of Maggi, a popular instant noodles brand, amid claims that the product contained high levels of lead. Nestlé had to destroy 400 million packets of Maggi products and stop production in the wake of the tests. The product recall cost the company US$67 million.

Consequently, companies should proactively manage stakeholder relationships and reputation risks (Eccles 2007). Such a proactive management involves assessment of the company's current reputation among key stakeholders in various categories such as product quality, sensitivity to environmental concerns, and financial performance and bridging the gap between expected performance and actual performance.

Nestlé was also criticized for what was seen as a slow reaction to the crisis. A new CEO was brought in to handle the crisis from Nestlé's unit in the Philippines. Fresh tests mandated by an Indian court found that the lead content in Maggi noodles was at a safe level. As the Nestlé experience suggests, companies should keep track of societal expectations, governmental regulations, and shareholders and bondholders expectations and engage the stakeholders to ensure that the damage is minimized in times of adverse conditions. This is particularly true at the time of mergers and acquisitions when stakeholders are apprehensive of the evolution of the combined entity.

CONCLUDING COMMENTS

Integration failure is often set-up during the due diligence process. Companies frequently rely on insular due diligence teams that lack operations expertise or integration accountability to assess and value acquisitions, resulting in overlooked integration landmines and unrealistic valuations and value-realization timelines. Furthermore, the transfer of information from the due diligence team to the integration team is far from seamless, slowing the integration process.

A well laid out integration plan includes the following:

- A dedicated integration manager
- Comprehensive integration plan
- Experienced executives in charge of integration
- Commitment from senior executives, including the CEO
- Consensus on key value drivers
- Mechanism for tracking progress and milestones
- Adequate financial budget for integration activities
- Incentives for personnel to exceed performance targets

REFERENCES AND SUGGESTED READINGS

After the Acquisition: Best Practices in Post-merger Integration. 2001. Washington, DC: Corporate Executive Board Research Brief.

Bossify, L., R Charan, and C. Burck. 2001. *Execution: The Discipline of Getting Things Done.* New York, NY: Penguin Random House.

Bourke, Evelyn Gillian Laidlaw, and Ian Woods. 2000. "Achieving Post Merger Integration." *EMPHASIS,* (1): 10–13.

Bower, J. L. 2001. "Not All M&As are Alike—And that Matters." *Harvard Business Review,* 79 (3, March): 92–101.

Burgelman, Robert A., and Webb McKinney. 2005. "Managing the Strategic Dynamics of Acquisition Integration: Lessons from HP and Compaq." *California Management Review,* 48 (3): 6–27.

Eccles, Robert, Scott Newquist, and Roland Schatz. 2007. "Reputation and its Risks." *Harvard Business Review,* 85 (2, February): 104–14.

Harding, David, and Ted Rouse. 2007. "Human Due Diligence." *Harvard Business Review* (April): 124–31.

Integration Insights: Findings from the 2006 Corporate Strategy Board M&A Pulse Survey. 2007. Washington, DC: Corporate Executive Board.

Krug, Jeffrey. 2003. "Why Do They Keep Leaving?" *Harvard Business Review*, 81 (2, February): 14–15.

Managing Brand Integration after an Acquisition. 1999, December. Washington, DC: Corporate Strategy Board Report.

Worthen, Ben. 2002. "Success Factors for Integrating IT Systems after a Merger." *CIO* (August).

REVIEW QUESTIONS

1. Why is post-merger integration important?
2. Explain the role of top management in post-merger integration.
3. Draw up a timeline diagram of a typical post-merger integration.
4. Prepare a checklist of items for post-merger integration.

CHAPTER 12

Spin-offs, Carve-outs, and Targeted Stock Offerings

Vishwanath S. R. and Chandrasekhar Krishnamurti

Chapter Objectives

- Highlight the forces driving corporate restructuring initiatives around the world
- Explain the different types of restructuring
- Provide a summary of empirical findings on the different types of restructuring
- Introduce targeted stocks, an innovative type of restructuring
- Describe a landmark restructuring in an emerging market

In recent years, we have witnessed a large number of divestitures, spin-offs, split-ups, and such other corporate restructuring activities that change the asset and liability composition of firms. A few decades ago, the "diversified conglomerate" was the in thing. It is no longer fashionable to be in unrelated businesses. The companies that once manufactured everything from hairpin to aircrafts have divested many businesses in which they do not have a competitive advantage. General Mills, for example, in its mission to become an "all-weather-growth company," diversified into household appliances, military electronics, chemicals, and consumer foods in a span of three decades, and ended up with an inefficient organizational structure, inappropriate capital allocation system, and dissension among operating managers (Donaldson 1990, 1991).

Diversification as a strategy is based on the premise that a downturn in one company's fortune will be offset by an upturn in another company's earnings. Modern finance theory hypothesizes that unsystematic risk is not priced in markets, and, hence, is irrelevant. So a diversifying company can create value only by providing a better risk-return trade-off which is unavailable through simple portfolio diversification. There are six ways in which diversification can create value (Salter and Weinhold 1978, 1979).

- Applying one company's knowledge of the industry and skills to the competitive problems and opportunities of the other.
- Investing in related businesses to reduce long-run average cost.
- Achieving a critical mass in an area of competence.
- Reducing systematic risk by diversifying into related product markets.

- Profitable allocation of cash among units to maximize efficiency.
- Lowering cost of debt and weighted average cost of capital due to risk pooling. The debt capacity of the combined entity may increase due to "coinsurance."

One of the disadvantages of a diversified firm is that when the more profitable units subsidize, the less profitable ones lead to heart burns and managerial defection.

The general conclusion of some financial economists is that unrelated diversification does not increase returns, although related diversification may help to some extent. A recent study suggests that the average value loss due to diversification is about 13%–15%, largely a product of overinvestment and cross-subsidization (Berger and Ofek 1995). Why do so many diversifications go bad? What is the secret of successful diversification (e.g., 3M)? Companies would do well to ask some commonsensical questions (such as the following) before they diversify:

- What can our company do better than our competitors?
- Can we catch up to or leap frog our competitors?
- What can our company learn by diversifying, and are we sufficiently organized to learn it?

FORCES DRIVING RESTRUCTURING INITIATIVES

When a firm's condition deteriorates to the extent where it cannot meet its financial obligations, the firm is said to be in a financial distress. Usually, the first signals of distress are violation of debt covenants, suspension of dividends, and so on. Bankruptcy includes financial reorganization and liquidation. Financial reorganization involves rearranging a firm's cash flow (e.g., converting debt into equity), whereas liquidation ends the firm's operations. It involves selling off tangible assets and paying off claimants to the extent possible. Recent examples of distressed firms are LA Gear, Enron, Iridium, Chrysler, Massey Ferguson, and Marvel Entertainment. Some of these companies, once considered the darling of the investment community, have left millions of investors with worthless paper. Why do some apparently well-run companies get into financial distress? The causes and consequences of distress can be inferred from the ex ante characteristics of the companies that became distressed and from the ex post consequences on the company's stakeholders. Some generic reasons for restructuring are:

Shareholder Activism

The Anglo-Saxon model recognizes shareholder wealth maximization as the primary objective of a corporation. Companies making value-destroying investments are often disciplined by active shareholders. This trend is spreading to other parts of the world as well. In Netherlands, for instance, a group of leading pension funds has begun to increase their influence in company boardrooms, pressing companies to change strategy and create value.

Till recently, the primary focus of Japanese companies was on growth in sales, assets, and market share with no attention given to cost of capital. Competitive challenges are forcing them to acknowledge the fact that capital is not a free resource. The seniority system which existed in most Japanese companies for many years is now being replaced by pay-for-performance incentive plans. In India, the Unit Trust of India, a large government owned mutual fund, is communicating to all its nominees on company boards about what they should seek from companies in which they are directors. UTI's list on corporate governance initiatives being sought include setting up board-level committees, having a majority of nonexecutive directors on the board, appointment of quality outside directors, and proper disclosure norms and succession planning at the top, including quality selection process for chief executives (*Business Standard* 1999).

Failure of Internal Control Systems

Changes in ownership through mergers and acquisitions generally lead to an increase in shareholder value. Many academic studies in America report increases in shareholder returns of target companies. Mergers and acquisitions enable transfer of assets to owners who value them most. In well-planned acquisitions, the gain is primarily due to better governance and improved efficiency. In a market-oriented economy like the USA, companies making value-destroying investments are disciplined by capital markets. The takeover wave of the 1980s in the USA was largely due to de-conglomeration. That is, companies sold off unrelated businesses and acquired related businesses. In many countries, the market for corporate control is either weak or nonexistent. In some Asian and European countries, the market is restricted because of complex cross-holdings, pyramid structures, and anti-takeover laws. In the absence of an effective market for corporate control, companies are not subject to the discipline of the stock market. Even when the market for corporate control is active, companies may still escape any disciplinary mechanism. By nature, organizations resist control systems and ineffective governance, which is a major part of the problem with many distressed firms. General Motors (GM), for example, one of the world's high-cost producers in a market with substantial excess capacity, avoided making major changes in its strategy for over a decade (Jensen 1993). Yet the board acted to remove the CEO Robert Stempel only in 1992, after the company had reported losses of US$6.5 billion in 1990 and 1991 and an opportunity loss of over US$100 billion in its R&D and capital expenditure program from 1980 to 1990. GM is not the only example. IBM, Eastman Kodak, and Iridium have all changed strategy or CEO, or filed for bankruptcy (as the case may be) only after experiencing severe losses.

Capital Structure

According to modern finance theory, companies with lots of investment opportunities can be expected to issue short-term debt to preserve financial flexibility and to protect lenders against greater uncertainty in the company's future.[1] Further, growth firms ought to use relatively less debt to prevent the underinvestment problem. Conversely, for mature companies whose value comes mostly from assets-in-place, the costs of bankruptcy are likely to be low. Such firms can afford to have high leverage ratios to prevent wastage of free cash flow by managers.

Conventional wisdom suggests that companies should avoid combining high operating leverage (which leads to high business risk) and high financial leverage (which leads to high

[1] The cost of long-term debt would be unacceptably high for growth firms because of uncertainty in their future.

financial risk). Earnings are boosted in good times because of the presence of fixed costs and debt, but (earnings) get depressed in bad times for the same reason, namely, presence of interest payments on debt and other fixed costs. Massey Ferguson, a multinational producer of farm machinery, industrial machinery, and diesel engines, sought to increase its market share by turning to the Third World for growth. Massey manufactured its products in the UK and Canada and sold the output to LDCs (less developed countries) in the late 1970s. This strategy worked quite well in the initial years. Compared with competitors, Massey had an aggressive debt policy *and* an aggressive product market strategy. It was unwise to couple a risky strategy in a cyclical industry with high (short-term) debt.[2] When short-term interest rates shot up and the demand (and, hence, revenue) dried up for its products for various reasons, Massey was thrown into distress. John Deere, its major competitor, however, had moderate debt ratio because of which it had the financial flexibility to make capital investments. When Massey and another competitor International Harvester were busy resolving distress, Deere pursued aggressive tactics to lock up the market share.

In the 1980s, a large number of American firms undertook leveraged recapitalizations and leveraged buyouts to improve shareholder value and operating efficiency. Many firms that undertook management buyouts in the late 1980s encountered distress due to poor structure of the deals (in terms of price) and adverse regulatory and economic developments. Academic studies in the USA find that the firms encountering distress were more highly leveraged than other firms and exhibit poor post-recap operating performance due to industry wide problems (Denis, J. and Denis, K. 1995).

Managerial Myopia

Modern finance theory hypothesizes that the objective of a corporation is to maximize shareholder value. Due to agency conflicts, managers may enrich themselves at the expense of shareholders. One way to control such conflicts is to award stock-based compensation plans because the equity ownership induces managers to think and act like shareholders. This is based on the premise that other costs like behavioral costs can also be addressed through incentive compatibility. When managers are overconfident of their strategy, or have biased estimates of payoffs from a project, or have a distorted view of what is in their own interest, incentives alone will not help (Shefrin 1999, 2001). For instance, Sony Corporation spent substantial time and money on the development of color television receiver in the 1960s at the behest of Ibuka, one of Sony's founders.[3] Although the company had not achieved a commercially viable manufacturing process, Ibuka insisted on selling the product at a negative profit margin. It was only when the managers announced that Sony was close to ruin that Ibuka abandoned the project. In this case, for example, there was no agency conflict in the sense that Ibuka was a major shareholder himself. Yet he would not abandon a loss-making project until it almost ruined the company because of loss aversion. In other words, overconfidence and loss aversion can lead to distress even in the presence of high powered incentives.

---

[2] Customers in LDCs are more risky compared to customers in developed countries.

[3] Akio Morita, the other founder was, apparently, not in favor of the project.

Currency and Interest Rate Shocks

Many steel companies in Asia are highly leveraged and depend on high tonnages to survive. When the Asian economies shrank, these companies were badly affected. This trend is not specific to the steel sector. A survey of the five countries most affected by the East Asian financial crisis—Indonesia, the Republic of Korea, Malaysia, the Philippines, and Thailand—found that 63% of firms are illiquid (with earnings less than debt service) and 31% technically insolvent (with financial obligations exceeding their equity; Classens, Djankov, and Ferri 1999). For the entire period 1988–96, the average debt ratios in Korea and Thailand were much higher than that in Germany and the USA. East Asian firms had not only too much debt but also the wrong type of debt, namely, short-term. The average share of short-term debt in total debt was about 66% in Malaysia and Thailand in contrast with 25% in the USA and 45% in Germany. Although the share of short-term debt increases gradually, this was one of the causes of distress. In addition, Korean and Malaysian firms had substantial share of foreign currency short-term debt. When the domestic currency is devalued, the value of foreign currency debt (denominated in, say, US dollars) increases. Sovereign governments may increase interest rates to stabilize their currencies. But this has a negative impact on corporate profitability. This is another reason for the poor performance by East Asian firms.

Undervaluation and Underperformance

For many companies, restructuring is a response to deterioration in financial and competitive position. The need for restructuring often arises when the company's market value falls below its intrinsic value due to mistakes in the company's strategy or the inability of the capital market to correctly value the company's stock. The "value gap" (the difference between current stock price and the potential price that would result from various improvements) can be sometimes as high as 60% (Fruhan 1988). Companies can reduce the value gap by improving operations, using leverage, and selling divisional units to the best owner, thereby unlocking value.

Over the last 10 years, the global steel industry, for instance, has earned about 4% return on assets due to intense competition from new entrants with superior plants and lowering of entry barriers due to technological changes. The operating rates have been 70%–80% of capacity, which exerts pressure on returns. Managers respond to such situations by merging with competitors to create scale economies, slashing overheads, retrenching employees, promoting early retirement, negotiating salary reductions, and reducing purchasing costs. At some point, most companies will have to consider layoffs, if the law permits.[4] Between 1987 and 1991, over 85% of Fortune 1000 firms downsized their white-collar workforce; over five million jobs were affected. Approximately 25 million people—one out of every five US workers—were unemployed for some portion of 1991. Nearly one million US managers with salaries of US$40,000 or more were laid off in 1991 (Heckscher and Applegate 1994).

Retrenchments are often challenged in courts and on the streets. Hyundai's plan to lay off 1,600 workers, FAG's plan to shed 15,000 employees, and Scott Paper's decision to lay off 23,000 employees, all set off riots. But does downsizing itself pay? In its 1994 study, the American Management Association found that while corporate downsizing was common, less than 35%

---

[4] For example, Layoffs are not permitted in Japan.

of downsized firms reported significant improvements in productivity and only 44% reported significant improvements in operating profits (Lewin and Johnston 2000). In contrast, the same study found that nearly 1/3 of downsized firms actually experienced productivity decreases during the same period. Additionally, firms that had downsized two or more times between 1989 and 1994 reported average gains of about 58% in operating profits and 44% in productivity.

Two academic studies examined the impact of layoff announcements on shareholder value. A study by Worrel, Davidson, and Sharma found a small negative reaction—down by 1% during a 10-day interval and 3% over 90 days—in response to 194 layoff announcements in 1979–87 (Worrell, Davidson, and Sharma 1991, as quoted in Bowman Singh, Useem, and Bhadury 1999). Another study by the Institute for Policy Studies found that the stock prices of 17 of the 22 sample firms rose or stayed the same the day of the announcement of the layoffs (Anderson and Cavanagh).[5] A company can scrutinize its cost structure and benchmark competitors. Some generic strategies for reducing cost of goods sold are:

- Improving relationship with suppliers
- Reducing product complexity and range
- Making purchasing a strategic issue
- Improving manufacturing efficiency.

RESTRUCTURING IN EMERGING MARKETS

Emerging markets such as India and Korea are dominated by business conglomerates, some of whom control as many as 90 (group) companies. The big businesses in Korea, the *chaebol*, typically own 30–50 companies in all key business areas and the big five—Daewoo, Samsung, Hyundai, LG, and SK—account for 20% of all borrowing and contribute to almost 50% of the GDP. Debt ratios at the top 30 chaebol commonly range between 500 and 800. Would the mantra of scaling down of operations developed in the West be equally applicable to these companies?[6] In these countries, it appears, there are certain important benefits from being a part of a business house not available to other stand-alone companies (Khanna and Palepu 1997, 1999). Emerging markets are characterized by illiquid capital markets, scarce managerial talent, and poor judicial system. These business groups often perform several useful institutional roles not available in the country. For instance, they act as venture capitalists to start up ventures within the group, solve information problems to customers by attaching their group brand name to products manufactured by the group companies (i.e., assure a certain level of quality), act as business schools by providing high quality management education to managers, and so on. In other words, business groups that act as proxy market institutions create greater value for shareholders than do more focused, unaffiliated companies. Given this benefit, it appears, it is probably not prudent to dismantle them. Despite this benefit, several business groups create little or no value. The total shareholder returns (dividends + capital gains) of some big business groups in India is shown in Exhibit 12.1. The total shareholder returns are based on average of the compounded annual rate of return of major companies in the group. The returns are

[5] See www.corpowatch.org

[6] The chaebol in Korea have since been forced to scale down operations, improve performance, and create sustainable businesses.

Exhibit 12.1 *Total Shareholder Return of Some Big Business Groups*

	TSR (%)			
Business Group	**1994–98**	**1995–98**	**1996–98**	**1997–98**
Tata	(2.6)	0.4	0.8	21.8
TVS	(1.9)	(7.7)	(18.1)	(10.6)
Reliance	(8.1)	(10.5)	9.0	(7.4)
Aditya Birla	(18.5)	(21.8)	(18.4)	(13.1)
R. P. Goenka	(21.7)	(28.2)	(30)	(5.5)
Modi	(23.4)	(24)	(11.4)	(9.8)
Essar	(31.7)	(30.1)	(13.5)	(3.4)
B. K. Birla	(30.7)	(31.7)	(33)	(23.2)
L. M. Thapar	(24.4)	(33.3)	(30.9)	16.80
C. K. Birla	(21.7)	(34.90)	(37.5)	(16.0)
UB	(11.9)	(10.6)	(2.90)	13.0

adjusted for index (Bombay Stock Exchange 30-Stock index) returns. As can be seen, many of them have not performed due to family squabbles, business recession, and reliance on government-controlled businesses where profitability is low, and so on. Contrast this with the total shareholder returns of stocks of some multinational companies shown in Exhibit 12.2. Many stocks have performed well despite bearish market conditions. When the market declined by 31%, the MNC stocks, on an average, appreciated by 22%.

A recent study of 1,000 firms from seven emerging markets (Hong Kong, India, Indonesia, Malaysia, Singapore, South Korea, and Thailand) in 1995 finds that diversified firms' trade at a discount of 7% compared to single-segment firms (Lins and Servaes 2002). Further, they find that diversified firms are also less profitable than single-segment firms and that the discount exists only for those firms that are part of industrial groups and for diversified firms with management ownership concentration between 10% and 30%.

Types of Restructuring

A firm is a collection of contracting relationships among claimants. These contracts represent claims on the cash flows generated by the firm's assets. Restructuring is a process by which a firm changes the terms of its contracts. So restructuring is about reconstructing.[7] In this chapter, I intend to address the following questions:

- How do managers figure out what kind of restructuring is most appropriate for addressing the particular problems facing the firm?
- How do stock markets react to different types of restructuring?
- How can one estimate the value creating potential of a particular type of restructuring?
- How do ownership, compensation and responsibilities of management change after restructuring?

[7] This was noted by Gilson (1998).

Exhibit 12.2 *TSR of Some MNC Stocks*

Company	TSR (%) 1994–98	1995–98	1996–98	1997–98
HLL	34.2	43.5	45.8	42.1
Bata	(2.5)	40.8	69.2	77.0
P&G	19.9	38.3	47.7	62.8
ITC	17.8	34.7	45.6	32.8
Pfizer	16.4	33.9	34.8	112.0
Nestle	23.2	31.3	31.8	85.9
Glaxo	23.1	30.7	32.2	17.4
Cadbury	23.9	30.2	22.7	36.8
SmithKline Beecham	10.6	23.7	14.6	9.3

Source: Business Line, August 13, 1998 (Prices in August considered for all the years).

ASSET SALES

A sell off or a divestiture involves the sale of a subsidiary, a division or a product line in exchange for cash or securities or some combination thereof. The buyer can be another company, the firm's management (in which case it is called management buyout), or another management team (in which case it is called a leveraged buyout). The cash realized from the sale might be used to retire debt or pay a dividend to shareholders.

Often, the divested divisions would have been acquired under another acquisition program. If companies were acquired to create value, then how can acquisitions and subsequent divestitures both be rational? The shareholders of the selling company win only if the selling price is greater than the present value of expected cash flows from the division/company, that is, the asset should be worth more to the buyer than to the seller. This is possible if the asset can provide synergies to the buyer not available to the seller. If the buyer can generate higher cash flows from the business or lower the cost of capital, the value of the division increases. Another plausible reason for divestitures is that they enable the selling company to correct past mistakes. Those assets that no longer fit the company's portfolio may be divested, thereby unlocking shareholder value.

It is logical to divest those divisions that do not earn the cost of capital. To decide whether the firm should continue with an existing division, liquidate, or sell it to someone else, a manager should estimate the value of the division not only to the firm but also to other potential acquirers. There are three measures of value. The first is the continuing value, which is the present value of the expected cash flows from continuing with the investment through the end of the asset's life. The second is the liquidation value, which is the cash flow a firm will receive if it terminated the division today. The third is the divestiture value, which is the price paid by the highest bidder. The decision to continue, liquidate, or sell depends on which of the three values is the highest. If the continuing value is the highest, the firm should continue with the division even if the division is not earning the cost of capital. If the divestiture value is the highest, then there is a potential for value creation by selling the division to the highest bidder.

The decision to sell a company/division is as important as buying one. But selling generally lacks the kind of planning that goes into buying. Quite often, the decision and the choice of the buyer is arbitrary, resulting in a raw deal for the selling company's shareholders. It is important to understand that selling needs the same set of skills required for buying. At some point in time, the executives of a company may have to take the decision to divest a division. There is nothing wrong in selling a division if it is worth more to someone else. The decision to sell may be prompted by poor growth prospects for a division or consolidation in the industry, that is, divisions with low productivity are more likely to be sold. Given the fact that the need to sell may arise any time, it makes sense for executives to be prepared. More specifically, managers need to know their company's worth. Consideration may be given to strengths and weaknesses in production, marketing, value of synergy to potential buyers, value of brand equity, and so on.

Brand equity is created by combination of brand loyalty, consumer awareness, perceived quality, and brand associations. Although companies have long realized the value of brands, the interest in valuing them is recent. Brand valuation quantifies the benefits of brand equity to the owner of the brand. Appendix 12A describes a methodology for valuing brands.

As pointed out earlier, divestitures should become a part of a company's strategy. To implement a proactive program:

1. Prepare the organization by explaining to employees the rationale for the divestiture and why it is necessary to divest. Analyze specifics of business and business needs. Assess likely demand for the business under various configurations. Implement any organizational restructuring necessary prior to sale to make the business more attractive to buyers.
2. Establish objective criteria for identifying potential candidates for a divestiture. The criteria may be purely financial or otherwise. While identifying candidates, consideration may be given to its legal, tax, and other implications. Set a floor price for sale.
3. Communicate the decision to employees once the sale is through.
4. Evaluate alternate offers and sell to the most suitable acquirer.[8]
5. Without wasting much time, invest the sale proceeds in attractive business opportunities and create a new combination of businesses.

EMPIRICAL EVIDENCE ON SELL-OFFS

Academic studies of divestitures have found that, on average, stock markets react positively to divestitures and shareholders experience abnormal returns. Linn and Rozeff (1984) examined the price reaction to announcements of divestitures by firms and reported an average excess return of 1.45% for 77 divestitures between 1977 and 1982.[9] Exhibit 12.3 presents the results of other studies on sell-offs. Studies that have looked at the operating performance of parent firms after divestitures report improvements in operating margins and return on capital and stock prices of divesting firms tend to outperform the market. When companies dispose of assets, they convey information not only about the value of the asset but also about the intended use

[8] The most suitable acquirer is usually the highest bidder.

[9] More recent studies have documented conflicting results.

Exhibit 12.3 *Empirical Evidence on Sell-offs*

Authors	Period Studied	Sample Size	Stock Price Impact on Announcement Day	Stock Price Impact on Announcement Through Completion of Sale
Hite, Owers, and Rogers	1963–78	55	1.50%	2.30%
Klein	1970–79	202	1.10%	2.40%

of the asset and the financial health of the seller. So it is not clear what one can conclude from these studies.

An Illustration

Sears diversified into financial services by acquiring Dean Witter and Coldwell Banker Real Estate group in 1981. Although these subsidiaries were doing well, the capital intensive nature of these businesses and debt burden was pressurizing the company to restructure. Throughout the 1980s, the company's return on equity (ROE) never touched the 15% mark, the catalog business was losing US$160 million a year, its chain of department stores was being outclassed by Wal-Mart and Kmart and the stock price did not reflect the value of the financial services subsidiaries. In addition, shareholder activist Robert Monks had chosen Sears as one of the targets of his agitation campaign to improve performance.

Most companies would probably sell the unprofitable divisions and invest the proceeds in the more profitable ones. Sears did the opposite. In 1993, Sears sold 20% of Dean Witter and spun the rest of to shareholders, sold 20% of Allstate Insurance in the largest initial public offering (IPO) in US history as well as its Coldwell Banker residential real estate business and its own mortgage company, and it streamlined its merchandizing operation by dropping the 97-year-old catalog and closing down unprofitable stores. The company raised US$4 billion and cut its debt from US$37 billion to US$17 billion. By the end of the year, Sears's share price had climbed by more than 80% from a 1990 low of around 25 to almost 60. The company's total share value rose from US$12 billion to US$28 billion.

SPIN-OFFS

Recent years have witnessed a large number of spin-offs. In the USA alone US$257 billion of spin-offs have been done in 2015.[10] For example, AbbVie was spun-off as Abbott Laboratories in a US$55 billion transaction. In a spin-off, one or more divisions of a listed company are detached from the parent, and the parent company distributes shares in a controlled subsidiary to its shareholders, pro rata, as dividend. These entities continue to be owned by the original shareholders of the parent company. The spun-off company, thereby, becomes a stand-alone company and gets listed on a stock exchange. The announcement of spin-offs is usually accompanied by an increase in the

[10] See https://corpgov.law.harvard.edu/2016/03/26/2016-spin-off-guide/ (accessed August 30, 2017).

value of the original business, suggesting that investors view the components as worth more than the whole. A number of explanations have been suggested for such positive reaction.

Conglomerate Discount

Large, diversified groups tend to lose focus and find it difficult to assess the performance of divisions or set realistic financial targets, and spin-offs correct the situation. There is a popular belief that conglomerates trade at a discount to their intrinsic value because investors and analysts find it difficult to understand a complicated combination of businesses and assign a lower price-earnings (P/E) multiple than what the company deserves. For instance, Du Pont's P/E fluctuates around 18, a valuation more in line with basic chemical activities than with life sciences activities, which the market values at 30–50 times the earnings. Spin-offs are based on the premise that investors can better understand and evaluate a pure play (single line of business). The quality of information conveyed to managers regarding product market strategy, business, and management also improves after the shares of the detached subsidiary gets listed on a stock exchange. Due to separate financial reporting of the erstwhile division, the quality of information disclosure improves after a spin-off and the discount disappears. The prime reason why Westinghouse Electric, a multi-industry company, did not outperform the market is that it had a capital structure and capital need that did not fit either of the businesses—a very high cash flow, low capital-investment media business with high margins and high earnings multiples, and a much slower growth power business that requires lot of working capital. The power business was a drag on the media business because of which the stock market was assigning a P/E multiple less than the sum of the theoretical multiples for the two businesses. The spin-off of CBS was intended to provide the valuation of a pure media company (*CFO Magazine* 1997).

Improved Analyst Coverage

The stock market performance of a company is influenced, at least partly, by security analyst recommendations. Typically, security analysts are required to track 25–30 companies. This leaves little time to get to know the complexities of a small division of a large company because of which the growth prospects of the division might not be fully reflected in the price of the company's stock. That is, analysts are less likely to cover conglomerates. When companies spin-off their divisions, the new company may attract new coverage that may correct the discount on the stock price. A recent study reports that there is indeed an increase in analyst coverage after a spin-off (Gilson, Healy, Noe, and Palepu 1998). In the two fiscal years after the breakup, mean analyst coverage at the sample firms increases from approximately 17 to 24 analysts. Gilson et al. (1998) also document significant decreases in analyst earnings forecast errors. Their findings suggest that companies experience improvements in the quality of analyst coverage around spin-offs, carve-outs, and targeted stock offerings.

ATTRACTING NEW INVESTORS

Investors have their investment preferences regarding the companies and industry groups they wish to invest in. Assume that a company has two divisions: pharmaceuticals and software. This company appeals to investors who want to invest in *both* pharmaceuticals and software. There is no reason why all potential investors should be interested in both. A multidivisional company may not attract as many investors it would attract as two separate pure plays because of this drawback. Spin-offs correct the situation by creating pure plays. Spin-offs indeed attract new investors (Subramaniam, Anslinger, and Klepper 1999).

Some of the commonly cited rationale for spin-offs include:

- Creating pure plays to cure undervaluation
- Separating out divisions which do not have synergy
- Reduction in risk

As pointed out earlier, spin-offs create pure plays that investors can understand better. Consequently, the sum of the (equity) values of the separated entities is usually more than the value of the erstwhile conglomerate.

At times, a company would have been acquired due to synergy in operations. Over time, due to changes in the company's strategy or business environment, it might no longer be attractive to operate both the units under one roof, especially if one of them is not doing well. A spin-off is desirable in such circumstances.

Assume that one of the divisions of a company has incurred substantial environmental liability due to the nature of the business (e.g., chemicals). It might be better to isolate the subsidiary so that the entire company is not affected. In the 1990s, American Cyanamid came under pressure to focus on its core business and improve performance (Wruck and Roper 1997). The chemicals operation was not doing well and was not in line with the company's mission of becoming a life sciences company. The chemicals operation was spun off into a separate entity named Cytec Industries. The newly formed company was forced to carry substantial environmental and retiree liabilities. Contingent liabilities must be taken into account at the time of spin-off. Otherwise, the shareholders of either the parent or the subsidiary may file suit against the other at a later stage citing damages due to the spin-off.

Two Examples

Thermo Electron Corporation is a global leader in providing technology based instruments, components, and systems that offer total solutions for markets ranging from life sciences to telecommunications and to drug and beverage production. In October 2001, Thermo Electron Corporation announced that its board of directors had approved the spin-off of its wholly owned Viasys Healthcare subsidiary as a dividend to Thermo Electron shareholders on record. After the distribution, Thermo Electron no longer owns shares of Viasys Healthcare. Viasys Healthcare designs, manufactures, and markets a variety of medical devices, instruments, and specialty products for use in healthcare services. According to the spin-off plan, Thermo Electron would distribute 1,428 shares of Viasys Healthcare common stock for each share of Thermo Electron.

Vendex, a conglomerate in Netherlands, spun-off its recruitment and retail interests into two new companies: Vendior and Laurus. Vendex itself was left as a department store business.[11] The transaction is shown below.

[11] Euromoney, January 2000.

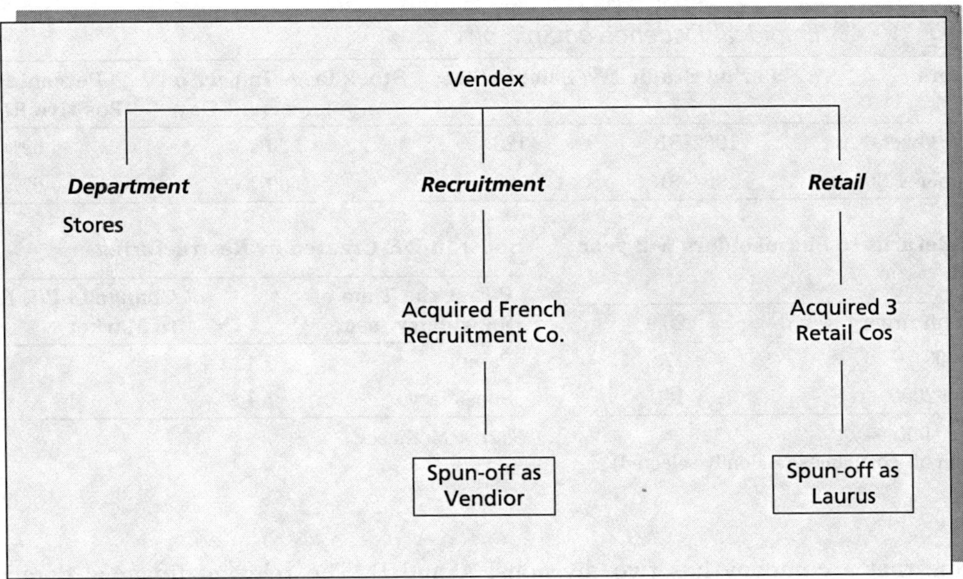

To reiterate, in a spin-off,

- The parent relinquishes ownership and control
- Current shareholders retain share in the parent
- No cash payment is involved
- The current managers of the division are usually asked to run the new company and often managers are given substantial equity interest in the new company.

Often subsidiaries will not have the financial or strategic planning skills, although they may have experience in manufacturing and sales. The independence through a spin-off brings in additional responsibilities. So retaining talented managers in the initial years is crucial for a spun-off entity. One way to achieve this is to award carefully designed incentive schemes. Thermo Electron, for instance, provides stock options to business unit managers that allow them to share about 1%–7 % of the upside value in the unit.

EMPIRICAL EVIDENCE ON SPIN-OFFS

One set of academic studies have documented the impact of spin-off on the parent company's stock. Schipper and Smith (1983) examined 93 firms that announced spin-offs between 1963 and 1981, and reported an average excess return of 2.84% in the two days surrounding the announcement. These studies also find that large spin-offs generate excess returns than small spin-offs, and those with the expressed aim of specialization realize significantly larger returns than those done for other reasons. Exhibit 12.4 presents the empirical evidence on spin-offs. At the time of spin-off, the company's management must decide on the allocation of assets and liabilities to the parent and the subsidiary.

Exhibit 12.4 *Empirical Evidence on Spin-offs*

Authors	Period Studied	Sample Size	Stock Price Impact on Announcement Day	Percentage of Positive Reaction
Hite & Owers	1962–81	123	3.30%	69%
Schipper & Smith	1963–81	93	2.80%	67%

Total Returns to Shareholders % 2 year, CAGR

Spun-off firms	26.9
S&P 500	17.2
Russel 2000	14.1

Source: McKinsey.
(34 spun off companies randomly selected)

Boost in P/E Created by Restructuring

P/E at the Time of Subsidiary Issue		Change in P/E Relative to Market %
Parent	12.2	7
Subsidiary	14	15

Source: McKinsey.

Assume that a company has two divisions: A and B. The relevant financial details of the company are given in Exhibit 12.5. The company's officials believe that the market is undervaluing the company because the less profitable division (A) is a drag on division B. They decide to do spin-off. The spin-off plan is presented in Exhibit 12.6.

Exhibit 12.5 *Before the Spin-off*

Liabilities and Equity		**(US$ million)**
Bank loans @ 7%	300	
Bonds @ 10%	700	
Equity	1200	2200
Earnings		
EBIT:		
Division A	87	191
Division B	104	
Interest		
On bank loans	21	
On bonds	70	91
PBT	100	
Taxes @ 34%	34	
PAT	**66**	
No. of shares (million)	120	
P/E multiple	23.60X	
Market Cap. US$ million	1560	
EBIT/Interest	2.09X	

Exhibit 12.6 *The Spin-off Plan*

Liabilities and Equity	Company A	Company B (US$ million)
Bonds @ 10%	800	
Equity	600	600
Bank Loan @ 7%		300
	1400	**800**
Earnings		
EBIT:		
Division A	87	
Division B		104
Interest		
On Bonds	80	21
PBT	7	83
Taxes @ 34%	2.38	28.22
PAT	**4.62**	**54.78**
P/E multiple	15X	30X
Market cap. US$ millions	222.2	1769
EBIT/Interest	1.08X	4.95X

The market assigns a higher multiple to Company B than was prevailing before the plan and a lower multiple to Company A. The value created by the spin-off = Post spin-off market capitalization – Pre-spin-off market capitalization = \$(222.2 + 1769) – 1560 million = \$ 431.20 million.

The (ex ante) theoretical market value of the divisions may be estimated by multiplying the average P/E multiple of comparable companies in the respective industry groups and the theoretical earnings per share (EPA) of the two divisions. That is,

$$\text{Market Value of Division A} = EPS_A \times P/E_{\text{(industry average)}}$$
$$\text{Market Value of Division B} = EPS_B \times P/E_{\text{(industry average)}}$$

To estimate EPS for the divisions, debt (interest) and overhead expenses have to be allocated to the two divisions. The amount of overhead expenses allocated to a particular division obviously affects its earnings. This is one of the contentious issues in a spin-off. Note that the interest coverage ratio of Company A is only 1.08 as opposed to 4.95 of Company B. What does it suggest? One of the potential sources of gain in a spin-off (approximately 431 million in this case) is the transfer of wealth from bondholders to shareholders, assuming that debt is not assigned to the spun-off entities in a fair manner (in which case a bondholder is neither better off nor worse off). The allocation of liabilities to the spun-off entities should take into consideration the earnings potential of the division. A division that does not have adequate growth prospects when saddled with debt, will, for obvious reasons, go down. The bondholders suffer losses because the collateral base has shrunk and the division's ability to service debt is limited. The possibility of wealth transfer can pit bondholders against shareholders leading to lawsuits.

Bond covenants prohibit certain events such as M&As and sale of assets because these actions alter the asset (collateral) base which leads to wealth loss.

In 1992, due to recession in the industry and worsening financial condition, Marriott Corporation announced its decision to spin-off its lodging management and food service and distribution businesses into a new entity called Marriott International. Its other business, ownership of hotel and other properties, would be called Host Marriott. In other words, Marriott Corp would become two companies. According to the spin-off plan Marriott International would manage the properties of Host Marriott on a contract basis, and much of the debt would be concentrated in Host. The pro forma balance sheets of Marriott International and Host Marriott are given in Exhibit 12.7. The stock market reacted positively to the spin-off, but bond price fell because of deterioration in interest coverage and downgrading of the company's bonds by the bond-rating agencies. Unfortunately, the covenants did not cover an "event risk" like spin-off, and a company, normally has no responsibility to safeguard the interests of bondholders other than by observing indenture provisions. This is a clear case of wealth transfer from bondholders to shareholders.

Within a month, several law suits were filed against Marriott, and bondholders formed committees to block the transaction. Negotiations with the bondholders committee resulted in major changes in the plan. Marriott, among other things, agreed to:

- Transfer US$450 million additional debt and assets from Host Marriott to Marriott International.

Exhibit 12.7 *The Initial Spin-off Plan of Marriott Corporation*

(US$ million, except ratios)

	Marriott Corp.	Marriott Intl. (proforma)	Host Marriott (proforma)
Assets			
Current Assets	1230	1130	250
Property	3672	360	3310
Other assets	1431	870	1060
Total	6333	2360	4620
Liabilities and Equity			
Current liabilities	1189	1130	210
Long-term debt	2891	20	2870
Other liabilities	1500	690	1310
Shareholders' equity	753	520	230
Total	6333	2360	4620
Income Statements			
Revenue	8331	7426	1656
Operating profits	478	314	148
Net income	82	145	–66
EBITDA/Interest	2.6	20.3	1.3

Source: Parrino (1997).

Exhibit 12.8 *The Final Spin-off Plan of Marriott Corporation*

			(US$ million, except ratios)
	Marriott Corp.	**Marriott Intl. (proforma)**	**Host Marriott (proforma)**
Assets			
Current assets	1496	1250	301
Property	3461	772	2689
Other assets	1453	995	898
Total	6410	3017	3888
Liabilities and Equity			
Current liabilities	1496	1280	394
Long-term debt	2732	899	2313
Other liabilities	1397	400	794
Shareholders' equity	785	438	387
Total	6410	3017	3888
Income Statements			
Revenue	8722	7787	1691
Operating profits	483	331	152
Net income	85	136	–44
EBITDA/Interest	2.8	6.5	1.8

Source: Parrino (1997).

- Exchange existing bonds for new ones paying higher interest rate and with extended maturities.
- Pay for the legal expenses incurred by the bondholders group.

Exhibit 12.8 presents the final spin-off plan.

LONG-RUN PERFORMANCE OF SPUN-OFF FIRMS

Some argue that the increase in value of a company in a spin-off is primarily due to the information problem a spin-off solves and not due to real operating improvements in the spun-off entity. Since stock markets react positively to spin-offs, if stock markets are efficient, we would expect the spun off entities to do well in the long run. Empirical studies of spin-offs have found that spin-offs are indeed accompanied by substantial improvements in operating performance and profitability. These studies have recorded the growth rate in accounting variables such as net sales, operating income, total assets and capital expenditure from 3 years before the spin-off to 3 years after the spin-off (Cusatis, Miles, and Woolridge 1994). The results are shown here.

[12] Growth rate for the company—Median growth rate for 12,000 companies listed on Compustat.

Accounting Measure	Growth Rate	Adjusted Growth Rate[12]
Net sales	55 %	15 %
Operating income	72 %	24 %
Capital expenditure	61 %	39 %
Total assets	53 %	20 %

Changes in Variables—Raw and Industry Adjusted for the Period, 1965–91

Variable	–3 to –1	–2 to –1	–1 to +1	–1 to +2	–1 to +3
Net Sales					
Median % Change	21.88	7.36	23.03	37.08	54.89
Median Industry-adjusted	5.31	–0.14	5.70	2.37	15.25
Operating Income Before Depreciation					
Median % Change	22.36	17.00	35.16	42.80	72.09
Median Industry Adjusted %	0.86	8.11	8.71	15.47	23.70

Another study by McKinsey suggests that there is a substantial increase in return on invested capital and revenue growth in the 2 years after the spun-off units begin trading (Subramaniam, Anslinger, and Klepper 1999). The improvement in operating performance is probably due to the fact that spin-offs enable the corporate office to separate out winners and losers and provide better incentives to winning managers. Another benefit of spin-offs is that they facilitate transfer of assets to those who value them most. Related studies have also found that the shareholders of both the parent and the spun-off units experience positive abnormal returns after the spin-off. Given below is the common stock returns for 199 spin-offs for the 1965–96 period (Miles and Rosenfeld 1983. Also see Schipper and Smith 1983; Hite and Owers 1983). Returns are reported from 1 month after the initial day of trade to 6, 12, 18, 24, and 36 months.

Holding Period

	1–6	1–12	1–18	1–24	1–36
Mean return	9.2%	19.6%	31.4%	53.8%	73.7%
Matched firm-adjusted returns	2.8	6.8	14.6	24.7	29.5

THE CHOICE BETWEEN SELL-OFFS AND SPIN-OFFS

A comparison between sell-offs and spins-offs is in order:

- Sell-off is the desirable alternative if another party is willing to pay more than what the entity is worth on a stand alone basis. Spin-off is the only alternative if there are no buyers.

- Spin-offs are tax favored in the USA, the UK, and many other countries. A company can avoid taxation if it satisfies the following requirements of the Internal Revenue Code in the USA:
  - The parent must have owned at least 80% of the outstanding shares of the subsidiary for at least 5 years.
  - The parent must distribute at least 80% of its stock in the subsidiary.
  - The transaction must have a valid business purpose.
  - Both the parent and the subsidiary must carry on with their business for at least 5 years.

In the case of an asset sale, the parent company recognizes gain or loss equal to the difference between sale proceeds and tax basis in a subsidiary. Parent firm shareholders recognize no income or loss unless proceeds are distributed as dividend. In America, any company that has used the proceeds of the sale of a portion of its business that results in 2% reduction in net assets, gross revenues, and employees to buy back stock or make a special pro rata distribution can designate proceeds of the sales of businesses as "partial liquidations." With this designation, shareholders are not only taxed at the capital gains rate rather than the dividend rate but also can treat distributions as if they result from a stock sale even though no stock is exchanged (Corman 1997).

- Spin-off is the desirable alternative when there is no synergy between a company's different businesses.
- An asset sale generates cash, whereas spin-offs do not. So a company in need of cash may prefer a sell-off.

As far as financial accounting is concerned, a parent accounts for a spin-off transaction as a stock dividend but recognizes gain or loss equal to difference between sales proceeds and book value in case of an asset sale. The Securities Exchange Act of 1934 requires that the parent file Form 10 with the Securities and Exchange Commission (SEC). The company must provide historic financial statements showing the impact of the spin-off on the parent and the subsidiary. Companies often seek legal counsel on the tax status of the spin-off. Just as in an IPO, the parent must file an application for listing the subsidiary on a stock exchange.

EQUITY CARVE-OUTS

In an equity carve-put, a public company sells a portion of its stake in a subsidiary to the general public in an IPO. The carved-out subsidiary becomes an independent company with its own board and management. The parent continues to provide administrative support. A carve-out differs from a spin-off in at least two ways. First, a spin-off results in the distribution of subsidiary shares to existing shareholders, whereas a carve-out is a sale of subsidiary shares to general investing public which brings in new capital. Second, in a spin-off, the parent relinquishes control over the subsidiary, whereas a carve-out creates a public minority interest. Typically, the parent continues to hold a substantial portion of the subsidiary's shares. Maintaining a majority ownership over the subsidiary helps retain control. Indeed, the accounting and tax consolidation of the carved-out subsidiary with the parent depend on the extent of retention of ownership. Given here is the schedule of ownership stake and the associated treatment.

Ownership Stake	Consolidate
>= 80%	For tax and accounting purposes Deduct 100% of dividends received for tax
50% – 80%	For accounting purposes Deduct 80% of dividends received

Since a carve-out involves selling of securities to the general investing public, the company must file a registration statement with the concerned authority (the SEC in case of the USA). The proceeds can be retained by either the parent or the subsidiary.

In short a carve-out creates a public market for the subsidiary stock. Thermo Electron, Enron, Genzyme, and The Limited have carved-out in the recent years. In 1998, Du Pont carved out roughly 30% of its oil subsidiary Conoco Inc. in a public offering raising US$4.4 billion. It is one of the biggest carve-outs of all times in the USA.

RATIONALE FOR CARVE-OUTS

There are several benefits from a carve-out. First, a carve-out brings new capital to the parent or the subsidiary. So an equity carve-out is the preferred alternative when the subsidiary has high growth opportunities and investment needs Second, a carve-out, like a spin-off, creates a public market for the subsidiary's stock and, hence, provides for public scrutiny, that is, the subsidiary is answerable to investors. This, usually, improves the performance of companies. Equity carve-outs are also usually associated with pay-for-performance incentive plans in which the managers of the carved-out units are awarded equity interest in their own company rather than the parent. This helps in retaining managerial talent. This is probably the reason for superior performance of carve-outs. Indeed, there is evidence to prove that those companies that do not change their compensation system do not do well. Like spin-offs, carve-outs also attract new investors.

EMPIRICAL EVIDENCE ON CARVE-OUTS

Unlike seasoned equity offerings, carve-outs elicit positive response from stock markets. A study by Schipper and Smith (1986) suggests that, on average, the stock price of the parent company increases by 2% on the announcement of the carve-out. They also report that, in their sample of 76 firms, 26 of the carved units were reacquired by their parents, 7 were spun–off, and 15 were divested. Recently, McKinsey examined the performance of carve-out subsidiaries (between 1985 and 1995). Over a 3-year period, the subsidiaries in their sample showed average compound annual returns of 20.3%. They also found that those companies that repeatedly sold stakes do even better. Three years after the carve-out, the subsidiaries showed annual returns of 36.8%, while the parents themselves experienced annual returns of 31.1%. Exhibit 12.9 presents the results of empirical studies on carve-outs. Academic studies have also documented the growth rate for median accounting variables for all available carve-outs on a raw and on an industry adjusted basis. The results are presented as follows:

	Years Relative to Carve-out's First Trade		
	−2 to −1	**−1 to +1**	**−1 to +3**
Net Sales (US$million)			
Median raw growth rate	11.63%	41.30%	59.39%
Industry-adjusted rate	3.18%	20.66%	29.79%
Operating Income Before Depreciation			
Median raw growth rate	15.57%	52.72%	67.99%
Industry-adjusted rate	−2.11%	27.84%	35.58%

Exhibit 12.9 *Empirical Evidence on Equity Carve-outs*

Author	Period Studied	Sample Size	Stock Price Impact on Announcement Day
Schipper & Smith	1963–83	76	1.80%

Average Shareholder Return %

	1 year	2 year	3 year
Subsidiary carve-out sample	34.2	25.2	20.3
Russel 2000 Index	11.2	11.4	10.7
Difference	23	13.8	9.6
Sample size	119	105	76

The Choice Between Spin-offs and Carve-outs

A comparison between spin-offs and carve-outs is in order:

- Both spin-offs and carve-outs cure undervaluation. But (we would expect) those firms that are confident of their quality would do a carve-out since a public offering of shares as in a carve-out involves scrutiny by financial intermediaries and entails a higher cost. In other words, low quality firms are more likely to resort to a spin-off.
- A carve-out, as mentioned earlier, involves public sale of shares, which results in an inflow of capital. The cost of doing a carve-out, for this reason, is substantially more than that of a spin-off.
- Academic studies find that carve-out subsidiaries perform better than spun-off firms.

TARGETED STOCKS

Targeted stocks, also called tracking stocks, are a class of parent company stock that track the performance of a particular division, line of business, geographic segment, or product line. The control of the division in question remains in the hands of the company's management, unlike in spin-offs and carve-outs in which a new board and management team is created. Further, the assets of the division are not separated from those of the parent company as in a spin-off. The revenues and earnings of the divisions are reported separately, and dividends are computed on the basis of earnings of the targeted division. As with spin-offs, assets and liabilities are allocated to divisions. But the allocation in case of targeted stocks is for financial reporting. The legal titles to the assets and responsibility for the liabilities will not be affected by allocation. It is important to understand that although the tracking stock tracks the performance of a division, the stock is a legal claim on the company and not on the division. To sum up, in a spin-off, there are two (or more) stocks and two (or more) companies, whereas in a targeted stock, there are two (or more) stocks and one company. Exhibit 12.10 presents the difference between a conglomerate and a targeted stock structure. Targeted stocks are usually distributed pro rata to existing shareholders as special dividend, although companies may issue tracking stocks to outside investors.

Exhibit 12.10 *Conglomerate Structure Versus Targeted Stock Structure*

Common Stock Structure	Targeted Stock Structure
• Valuation on the basis of performance of all divisions	Valuation on the basis of the unit being tracked
• Common voting rights	Differential voting rights
• Fixed dividend rights	Differential dividend rights

The objective of the targeted stock structure is to realize some of the benefits of "pure plays," while at the same time preserve some of the advantages of integration. In other words, a targeted stock structure is a compromise between the conglomerate structure and a spin-off. After the issue, the company continues to provide consolidated financial statements in addition to separate statements for each class of stock created. USX Corp, Genzyme, Kmart, Ralston Purina, and Fletcher Challenge, among other companies, have issued tracking stocks.

USX Corp., which started of as a steel manufacturer, diversified into energy business by acquiring Marathon Oil. During the 1980s and 1990s, the company acquired and sold both steel and energy properties. In 1991, the company decided to issue two new class of common stock: USX-US Steel, which was intended to reflect the performance of the corporation's steel business, and USX–Marathon group stock to reflect the performance of the company's energy business. In 1992, the company created a third class of common stock, USX–Delhi group which was intended to reflect the performance of Delhi Gas Pipeline Corporation and certain related companies. The Delhi stock was redeemed in 1998 as a result of the sale of this business to Koch Industries in 1997. The company explained that the tracking stock structure would enable the company to retain the benefits of integration, namely, coinsurance, and create pure plays at the same time.

SETTING VOTING RIGHTS, DIVIDENDS, AND LIQUIDATION RIGHTS

Because the targeted stock structure creates different classes of shares, the dividend, voting and liquidation rights of different classes of shareholders vary. The issuer must design these features at the time of issue. A typical design is discussed below:

The voting rights of a class of stock depend on the relative market value of the group. For instance, if the market value of Division A is twice that of Division B, then the shareholders of A will receive twice as many votes as shareholders of B.

In the event of liquidation of the business, the proceeds are shared by shareholders in proportion to the relative market value of the stock.

Dividends are set on the basis of long-term earning prospects and cash flow needs of the division and dividend policy of other comparable companies. Dividends are either set at a fixed level and then allowed to float with income or set as fixed percentage of net income. Appendix 12B presents the key features of targeted stocks.

ADVANTAGES AND DISADVANTAGES OF TARGETED STOCKS

Since targeted stocks create pure plays like spin-offs, investors find it easy to value the businesses. This should eliminate the discount on the company's stock. As dividends on a class of stock are set on the basis of the performance of that division, the structure allows for differential dividend policy among shareholders that would not be possible under a conglomerate structure. Further, managers can be awarded incentives tied to the performance of the division. Tracking stocks also enable companies to acquire through relevant divisions.[13] Since the units are physically tied, the losses from one business can be set off against profits from other divisions, thereby saving taxes. A tracking stock structure preserves the coinsurance effect of diversification that could reduce the cost of debt because the assets of the entire company (not just the division) continue to back the liability. If everything about targeted stocks is great, why do not we see more of targeted stock offerings?[14] Unlike a spin-off, which creates two boards, a targeted stock has a single board responsible for all the units. Since the board has discretion over allocation of common costs among the units, the management can, at least in theory, favor one division to the detriment of other divisions. The allocated costs reduce the earnings and, hence, dividends of a division. This could give rise to costly conflicts among managers (and shareholders). Likewise, management has the discretion over appropriation of profits. If the profit is invested in the more profitable unit, the shareholders of that division get higher dividends in future (because dividends are a function of future higher profits) and the shareholders of other units do not get a penny. Similarly, if the profit from the profitable unit is used to grow the unprofitable units, the shareholders of the former suffer. Tracking stocks can pit classes of shareholders against one another leading to lawsuits. GM had issued a letter stock to the shareholders of Hughes Electronics division (class H share). If GM were to sell its Hughes Electronics subsidiary, its shareholders were to receive GM common shares with a market value equaling 1.2 times the prior market value of their class H stock. Further, the shareholders of class H stock would not be entitled to any price appreciation due to the announcement of the transaction. When GM sold parts of Hughes, holders of H shares sued GM's board complaining of unfair treatment (*Business Week* 1999).

A number of companies adopting tracking stock structure subsequently eliminate them. Tracking stocks may be eliminated through an asset sale, spin-off or retirement. In October 2001, USX reversed its earlier decision of creating tracking stocks and announced a tax-free

[13] For instance, Bell South was considering a tracking stock for its wireless unit which could be used as a currency to buy more wireless companies like Voice Stream Wireless Corp.

[14] About 18 companies had proposed 24 issues up till 1997.

spin-off of the steel business into a publicly traded company to be known as United States Steel Corporation. The company's chairman explained that separating the two businesses would give each company more flexibility in expanding its business through stock based acquisitions and enable the new companies to focus on their core business, precisely the same reason given for creating tracking stocks!

Long-term Performance of Tracking Stocks

If targeted stocks retain the benefits of a conglomerate while at the same time enhancing transparency, we would expect stocks of firms issuing targeted stocks to display higher returns in the long run. Billett and Vijh (2001), in contrast, find that tracking stocks earn significantly negative buy-and-hold excess returns during a 3-year period following the issue date. They also find significantly negative returns surrounding the earnings announcements during this period. This evidence contrasts with the post-issue returns of spin-offs, which are known to be positive, and of carve-outs, which are known to be insignificant. Second, contrary to a common justification given to adopt tracking stocks, they find that tracking stocks do not increase the transparency of firm earnings.

CONCLUDING COMMENTS

It is usually believed that the pressure to restructure arises from competitive forces and that the process is largely involuntary. As pointed out by Gordon Donaldson in his study of General Mills, restructuring could be voluntary as well, although the process may take several years or even decades to consummate. Indeed, a voluntary restructuring is more effective than involuntary restructuring arising out of hostile takeovers in which the value of the company may get destroyed due to the target company's defense tactics. Restructuring is a lengthy process. A company, on an average, takes 1 year to complete restructuring. The initial announcement may be followed by a variety of other actions (such as declaring bankruptcy or sell-offs). So the share price reaction to initial announcement does not capture the full wealth effects of the restructuring (Boone and Mulherin 2001).

A summary of the different types of restructuring is given here:

	Spin-off	Carve-out	Tracking Stock
Change of ownership	Yes	No	Usually No
Raise capital	No	Yes	usually No
Stock market reaction	+ve	+ve	+ve
Preserve synergy	No	Yes	Yes
Cure undervaluation	Yes	Yes	Yes
Attract new investors	Yes	Yes	Yes/No
Improved analyst coverage	Yes	Yes	Yes

Case Study

Downsizing at Steel Authority of India

Creating Value through Corporate Restructuring

In February 2000, Arvind Pande, the chairman of Steel Authority of India (SAIL), was given the government approval to go ahead with the proposed restructuring of SAIL. Under the plan, SAIL would bring down its debt/equity (D/E) ratio as well as reduce its stake in noncore businesses and focus on the core area of its operations. A restructuring package to the tune of ₹84.54 billion was offered by the Government of India (GoI) to assist SAIL back to profitability. SAIL was the largest producer of steel in India as well as one of the "navaratnas" (nine gems) among PSUs (public sector units) identified by the government on the basis of size, performance, nature of activity, future prospects, and potential for becoming a global player.[15]

SAIL was once a model PSU. However, over the years, its profitability eroded and it went on to become one of the highest loss-making units. Steel being a cyclical industry, its fortunes largely depended on the economic conditions prevailing in India and the world. The late 1990s saw a severe recession, which caused profits and demand to plummet. Competition from Japan and Korea further depressed profits of Indian steel companies, particularly SAIL, which was not a low-cost producer. Furthermore, the fact that there was overcapacity in the industry caused prices to hit a new low. The government was left with little option but to go ahead and restructure SAIL to be more competitive. SAIL appointed international consultants Mckinsey and Co. to advice.

Steel Authority of India

After Independence in 1947, the GoI assumed responsibility of developing the core sectors such as steel. The government set-up three plants in the 1950s and one in the 1960s. SAIL was a government-owned public sector company formed in January 1973 as a holding company for other companies manufacturing steel and related products. The shares held by the GOI in various steel companies such as Hindustan Steel, Bokaro Steel, Hindustan Steelworks Construction, Salem Steel, and National Mineral Development Corporation were transferred to SAIL. In October 1976, the Durgapur, Rourkela, and Bhilai steel plants were transferred from Hindustan Steel to become fully owned subsidiaries of SAIL. SAIL operated four integrated steel plants (at Bhilai, Rourkela, Bokaro, and Durgapur), one alloy steel plant (at Durgapur) and one stainless steel plant (at Salem). At that time SAIL was the 11th-largest steel company in the world. Exhibits 12.11 and 12.12 present the financial details and stock price history of SAIL.

During the early 1980s, the company faced several problems and incurred losses. V. Krishnamurthy, the then chairman of SAIL, turned the company around between 1985 and 1990 with a massive modernization program. The modernization was aimed to enhance the proportion of steel made by the more efficient basic oxygen furnace method instead of the older open-hearth method. SAIL incurred a cost of ₹98.50 billion between 1988 and 1992 on modernization. During the initial years of liberalization, the company performed very well and was often cited as an example of aPSU that did well after liberalization.

[15] The other Navaratnas are IOC, MTNL, VSNL, GAIL, NTPC, IPCL, BHEL, BPCL, and HPCL. The government also granted "mini ratna" status to 39 profit-making PSUs. Subject to certain guidelines, these companies enjoy the freedom to make capital expenditure, enter into joint ventures, effect organization restructuring, create and wind up posts below the board level, and raise capital from domestic and international markets. To retain the status, these companies should have earned profits for 3 years continuously, have positive net worth, do not seek budgetary support, have not sought guarantees from the government, and have not defaulted on repayment of loans or interest to the government. The deteriorating financial performance of SAIL prompted the Department of Public Enterprises to recommend constitution of an interministerial committee of secretaries under the cabinet secretary to review the navaratna status in December 2000.

Exhibit 12.11 *Financials of SAIL (in ₹'0 million except ratios)*

	1996	1997	1998	1999	2000
Sales	15,784	15,362	15,694	16,000	17,178
Contribution	3,683	3,178	3,275	2,334	2,014
Break even sales	11,212	11,869	12,767	20,475	2,800
Operating Leverage	1.77	1.83	2.11	5.84	25.77
Cost per rupee of sales					
Raw materials	49.86	56.56	55.05	51.24	45.78
Wages & salaries	10.56	11.05	11.19	11.85	12.59
EBDIT	2,711	2,461	2,607	1,547	1,201
PAT	1,318	515	133	–1,574	–1,720
Current ratio			1.18	1.07	0.96
D/E			2.34	3.03	3.16
Gross working Capital cycle (days)		313	298	237	
Net worth	8,109	8,469	8,557	6,988	5,264

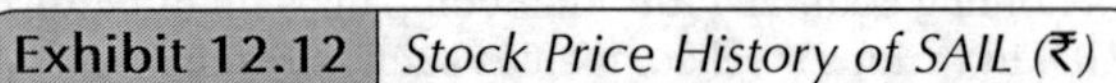

Exhibit 12.12 *Stock Price History of SAIL (₹)*

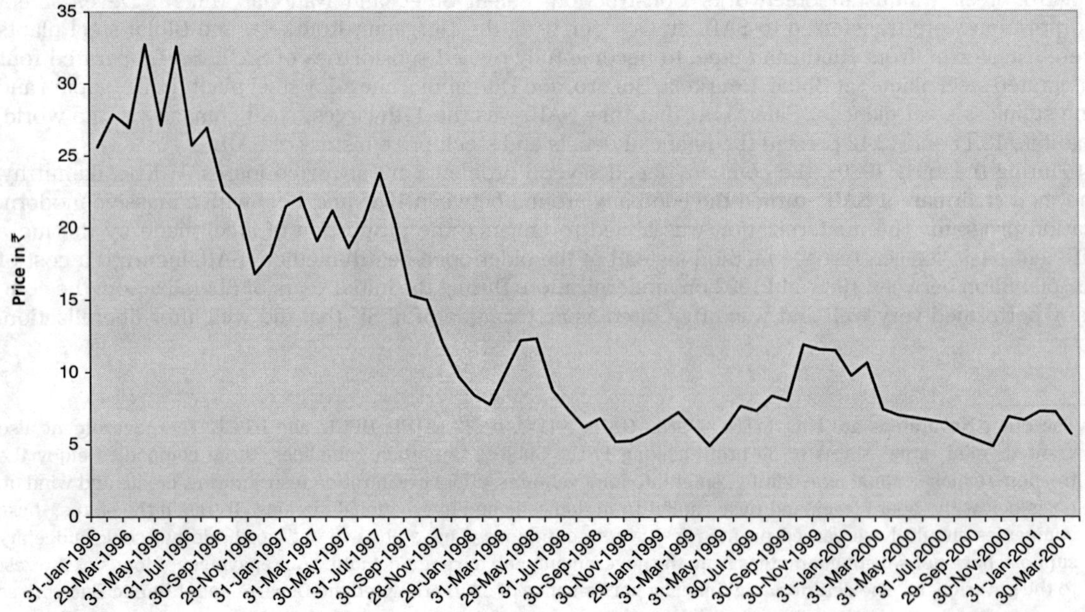

Exhibit 12.13 *Performance of Public Sector Undertakings*

Company	Incremental MVA (₹'0 million)	Return on Capital %
ONGC	–214.09	7.53
Indian Oil	–2948.53	8.34
MTNL	–1547.48	8.95
GAIL	–1261.37	18.12
HPCL	559.5	12.39
BHEL	–40.84	11.97
Bharat Petroleum	–592.47	14.30
VSNL	–3176.56	20.27
Container Corp.	–132.1	17.34
IPCL	–2134.46	6.02
NLC	–4905.98	5.69
SAIL	–4835.93	2.97

Source: Business Today, February 2000.

However, this did not last long, and by 1997–98 the company was back into the red and was one of the worst performers of all PSUs. Exhibit 12.13 presents the return on capital and incremental market value added (MVA) (between 1997 and 1998) for all the major public sector undertakings.

Ironically, the modernization programs at two of its plants became a drain on SAIL. The most important was the implementation delays of between 4 and 6 years that led to huge cost overruns and resulted in high interest and depreciation costs. For instance, the expenditure at both Durgapur and Rourkela plants shot up by over 100% to approximately US$1 billion each. That forced SAIL to raise resources through market borrowings. Consequently, its debt burden catapulted from US$1 billion in 1989–90, when the two programs were finalized, to US$4 billion a decade later and interest costs rose seven times to more than half a billion dollars. The second reason for the modernization programs to become a drain on SAIL was that they were based on wrong assumptions. One report revealed that the requirement of hot metal in the post-modernization period would be 2 million tonnes per annum (mtpa), but no attempt to increase the annual capacity of the blast furnaces was made, which was assessed at 1.35 mtpa. So the entire down-stream investment proved to be futile.

In order to enhance the level of service to the customers and improve the overall organizational performance, the company followed the Tata Business Excellence Model since 1995. The Tata Quality Management Services (TQMS), a division of Tata Sons Ltd,[16] conducted the assessment of all companies in the Tata group on the basis of this model. There was a steady improvement in the company's performance as a result of this practice.

SAIL made a successful GDR (global depositary receipt) issue in 1996. The GDR issue came as a shot in the arm for the company, which was in desperate need of funds for the second phase of its ongoing modernization program. This issue came at a time when the government stopped funding SAIL, and it had to subsequently meet its requirement through internal sources and by issuing bonds with interest rates as high as 16%–18%.

In the first round of PSUs' disinvestment, the government divested a small portion of the company's equity. As of March 31, 1998, the GOI held 85.82% of the company's equity and the financial institutions

[16] The Tata group is one of the largest business groups in India.

held 8.86%. GDR holders controlled 3.10% of the equity; individuals 0.75%, mutual funds and banks 0.41%; foreign institutional investors 0.98% and the balance was held by a few domestic companies. The government had expressed its intention of reducing its stake further to 26% in the due course of time.

The State of the Global Steel Industry[17]

India was among the largest steel manufacturers in the world. The top three steel producers namely SAIL, Tata Iron & Steel Company (TISCO, now Tata Steel), and Rashtriya Ispat Nigam Ltd (RINL) accounted for about 50% of steel production in the country. The steel industry can be broadly classified on the basis of the process of manufacture into primary producers or the integrated steel plants and the secondary steel producers which includes the mini steel plants and induction furnace units.

Steel can be manufactured by either of two processes: the blast furnace process or the electric arc furnace (EAF) process. The integrated plants use the former method. In this process, iron ore is reduced in the presence of coke to get hot metal that is further refined to get liquid steel. Liquid steel is cast directly into blooms, slabs, and billets using continuous casting method. The mini steel plants employ the EAF to manufacture liquid steel. In the EAF process, a mixture of scrap and sponge iron is melted in an electric furnace and then refined to produce molten steel. Molten steel is further case using the continuous casting or ingot casting route. Semi-finished steel is later processed in different rolling mills to manufacture flat or long steel products. In the 1990s, the blast furnace method dominated steel production worldwide. The EAF method was expected to gain importance in future due to lower capital costs and flexibility in product mix. In Exhibit 12.14, we present the details of a small list of prominent steel companies.

The creation of fresh steel capacities is highly capital intensive, and this poses a constraint on small- and medium-size companies. While an economic capacity of 1 mtpa in the blast furnace plant was likely to cost ₹30 billion, an EAF based-capacity of 0.2 mtpa was expected to cost about ₹5 billion. The problem was exacerbated by long gestation periods. The industry depended on the government for major inputs such as coal and power besides infrastructure support like Railways for transport.

The location of a steel plant assumed significance in determining its competitiveness. Integrated steel plants required large volumes of iron ore and coking coal, whereas EAF-based facilities needed steel scrap and sponge iron for producing liquid steel. The transport of large volumes of raw materials to the plant site resulted in high inward freight costs, and plants had to be situated close to their input sources. Further, they had to be situated near their end users to minimize transportation costs.

In India, a major part of the steel was consumed in engineering applications, followed by automobiles and construction. As industrial investments tapered off after the boom of the late 1990s and auto industry entered recession, the steel industry suffered. The industry had been hit by stagnating demand and also by domestic oversupply and falling prices of steel in the international market. The domestic oversupply situation was due to the enthusiasm with which industrial groups went about setting up very large projects with scant attention to expected returns. Most projects were conceived/implemented (primarily for hot rolled coils) at a D/E ratio of 200% or more with rupee debt borrowed at 18%–20% p.a. and price assumptions for HRC of US$ 350/t or more. Most producers expected demand growth to average 10%–13%, whereas in reality the growth rate never touched 10%. The oversupply scenario was expected to continue for quite a few years. With low prices and stagnating demand, most of the fresh investments in steel turned unviable. Promoters who mismanaged project implementation siphoned off funds and started other ambitious projects, compounded the problem. The net result was large time and cost overrun. Most of these projects can only turnaround if long-term lenders wrote off a large portion of the debt.

A high debt equity ratio, low operating margins, and the oversupply scenario in the domestic market continued to plague the share prices of steel companies. The growth of steel sector was dependent on the growth of the economy in general and the growth of industrial production and infrastructure sectors in particular. The major reasons for the slow growth in the previous years included:

[17] See www.nic.com

Exhibit 12.14 *Competition in the Steel industry*

Panel A: Technology Adopted by Competitors

Name	Technology	Raw Materials	Capital Cost (₹/MT)	Players
Integrated Steel Plants	Open hearth	Iron ore & coke	25,000	SAIL RINL TISCO
Mini Steel	MBF-EAF	Iron ore & coke	20,000	Essar Steel Ispat Industries Lloyds

Source: CRISIL.

Panel B: Comparison of SAIL with Major Competitors

	SAIL	TISCO	RINL
Plant locations	Bhilai, Bokaro Rourkela, Durgapur	Jamshedpur	Vishakapatnam
Manufacturing Process	Blast furnace	Blast furnace	Blast furnace
Raw material sourcing	Captive iron ore coal partly imported	Captive iron ore and coal mines	Iron ore sourced coal is imported
Technology	Some are relatively old Plants	Old facilities undergoing Modernization	Latest
Marketing	Established network	Established network	Mainly exports
Workforce	Overstaffed	Overstaffed	Automated
Productivity	Low	Low	Low

Source: CRISIL.

- Sluggish demand in the steel-consuming sectors
- Overall economic slow down in the country
- Lack of investment by government/private sector in major infrastructure projects
- Cost escalation in the input materials for iron and steel
- Continuous reduction in import duty on iron and steel
- Continuous increase in excise duty on iron and steel
- Greater competition from imports
- Dumping of finished steel in the country
- Adverse conditions in export markets for iron and steel

Globally, the steel industry was plagued by excess capacity. From 1991 and 2001 the world steel demand grew by just 2.1 % p.a. (see Exhibit 12.15). Asia's share in the world steel consumption increased from less than 20% in 1985 to about 35% in 1995 and is expected to reach 45% by 2010 (see Exhibit 12.16 for world steel consumption). The growth rate in steel consumption was low, although most industries such as automotive, construction, and appliances relied on steel because steel was being replaced by other materials and improvements in mechanical properties of steel itself reduced the consumption. As growth was strong, large investments were made. As the Asian economies GDP shrank, their steel consumption declined. A large part of the Asian capacity had been set up in the 1990s. These were highly leveraged companies that depended on high tonnages to survive. Once installed, it was hard to eliminate capacity because of high exit costs. Often, it was cheaper for integrated plants to avoid temporary shutdowns because of high cost of first idling and then bringing on stream a series of integrated facilities such as blast furnaces, steel shops, and strip mills. By 1998, the steel industry in most countries were bleeding. Most countries restricted trade by placing quota restrictions or raising import tariffs, and many companies merged to consolidate. Thyssen and Krupp, British Steel and Hoogovens, for example, merged to create

Exhibit 12.15 *Global Demand for Steel*

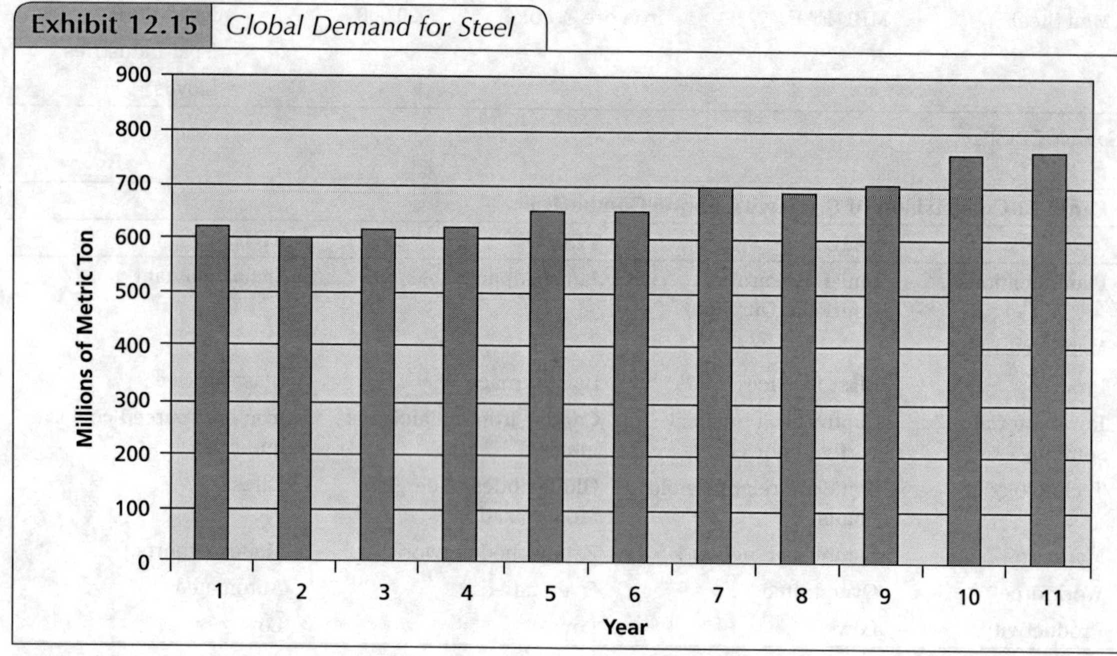

Exhibit 12.16 *World Steel Consumption (million tons)*

	1990	1996	1997	1998	1999	2004
Americas						
U.S	86.5	107.1	113.0	119.5	111.4	108.0
Canada	10.2	12.9	15.5	16.1	15.9	15.8
Mexico						
Brazil						
Latin Am ex-Brazil						
Asia						
P.R. China	53.0	92.0	94.0	100.0	105.0	122.0
India	16.9	22.8	22.1	22.9	23.0	23.0
Japan	99.0	83.60	86.0	74.0	69.0	73.0
Korea						
Taiwan						
Pacific Rim						

	1990	1996	1997	1998	1999	2004
Europe						
EU 15	119.5	112.9	127.9	136.1	130.2	152.0
Other Europe						
Former USSR						
Other Regions						
Australia & NZ	5.5	6.3	6.6	6.8	7.0	6.8
Africa	12.9	11.2	12.6	13.0	13.5	15.0
Middle East	10.1	12.3	13.9	10.3	11.2	17.5
World Total	**657.4**	**651.4**	**691.6**	**687.6**	**684.7**	**772.6**

Source: Merrill Lynch Equity Research.

scale economies. Although worldwide the steel industry is fragmented, consolidation is taking place in several parts of the world, most notably Western Europe. The top five steel companies in Europe were expected to attain a market share of 80%. A merger itself does not create value unless the combined entity is more profitable as a whole.

Consolidation was expected to increase in the future for several reasons:

- The economics of buying companies are better than building new plants.
- Consolidation improves the bargaining power vis-à-vis its main customers.
- Smaller number of companies results in greater control over capacity and price.

Apart from consolidation, many countries were planning reduction in manpower. For instance, China's steel industry was planning to cut down employee strength from more than 1 million to 800,000 by 2002 in a bid to improve efficiency.

China's joining the WTO was one of the reasons why the Chinese government had to speed up the restructuring the steel industry. The steel sector in China began restructuring in 1996. Among 69 of the largest steel producers in the country, the number of employees has already declined to 890,000 in 2000 from more than 1.13 million in 1996. The companies now have a per capita output of 122.8 tons against 40 tons in 1996. The growth in the Chinese economy has led to increased imports of steel into the country.

Performance Comparison

As pointed out earlier, the steel industry in India was dominated by three companies: SAIL, TISCO, and RINL. TISCO was incorporated in 1907. TISCO manufactured steel and steel-related products. It had an installed capacity of 2.7 million tonnes of saleable steel and manufactured a wide range of products which included bars and rods, sheets, hot rolled strips, hot rolled coils, structural, and other semifinished products. In 1999 the capacity was upgraded to 3.2 million tonnes to move toward more value-added products such as flats which are deployed in high end uses such as making bodies for automobiles and refineries. The company operates mines, collieries, and quarries to source raw materials for its plants.

RINL was incorporated in 1982 as a public sector company to take over Vizag steel plant project from SAIL. The project faced many hurdles since inception and ran into delays and cost escalation. It took more than 20 years for the project to become operational. Abnormal delays, the mushrooming of rebellious trade unions at the site, wild cat strikes by the contract labor, and inadequate resource mobilization blocked the project at various stages. The project was commissioned in 1992. The plant became fully operational in 1994–95. During the period, the cost of the project went up from ₹25 billion to ₹85 billion. Much of the increased costs were met through loans from financial institutions and the government. As a result of the huge debt burden, the good performance of the company did not get reflected in its financial results. The company's interest expenses were almost 15% of revenues. It resulted in huge losses despite making a operating profit. The company almost filed for bankruptcy in 1997. To allow the company to sail through, the government allowed RINL to convert almost ₹14 billion of debt to preference capital. This arrested the interest outgo and the company made its first profit in 1998. Exhibit 12.17 compares key financials of the three companies.

The D/E ratio of SAIL was 3.34 in 2001, whereas for TISCO it was 1.18. Bringing down the debt ratio would result in interest savings. The employee cost for SAIL is ₹31,348 million compared to ₹9,224 million for TISCO. If SAIL brought down employee cost to those of its competitors' levels, it would be able to save ₹20 billion per annum. If we assume that the savings are perpetual, the present value of savings can be estimated by applying a suitable discount rate. Further, SAIL had relatively high proportion of short-term debt (25%), which made it vulnerable to interest rate swings. To complete the analysis, one might estimate the sales/employee ratio for the competitors and benchmark the best by either bringing down the number of employees or increasing sales or both.

Predicting Distress

Lenders lend money in exchange for interest and principal payments over a specified period of time. Credit risk refers to the chance that the expectation will not be met. One approach to estimating default risk is to compute a composite risk measure based on a firm's financial ratios advocated by Altman (1968). His *Z*-score model combines select financial ratios to come up with a score as follows:

$$\begin{aligned} Z = {} & 0.012 \times \text{Net working capital/Total assets} \\ & + 0.014 \times \text{Retained earnings/Total assets} \\ & + 0.033 \times \text{EBIT/Total assets} \\ & + 0.006 \times \text{Market value of equity/Book value of liabilities} \\ & + 0.999 \times \text{Sales/Total assets} \end{aligned}$$

A high *Z*-score represents a low probability of default and a low *Z*-score represents a high probability of default. The model's classification accuracy was 95% one year before bankruptcy and 72% two years before. Accuracy of the model decreases as the time period is extended (it may also be unreliable in its predictive ability). Based on the study, it was concluded that firms with a *Z*-scores less than 1.81 are all bankrupt, while those with *Z*-scores greater than 2.99 fall into the nonbankrupt group. Those falling into the area between 1.81 and 2.99 require more analysis to determine their solvency status. The nonliquid asset ratios such as total debt to total assets and cash flow to total debt are, in general, better predictors of bankruptcy than the liquid assets ratios such as quick ratio or net working capital to total assets.

Managers may use distress prediction models as a first step to understand the solvency status of their firms. A low *Z*-score (below 1.81) itself does not suggest that bankruptcy will occur. A firm may avoid bankruptcy by cash infusion and/or waiving of loan covenants by lenders.

Managing Contingencies

The Altman *Z*-score model could be used as a warning signal. The next step in the process is to plan for contingencies. Companies resort to one of the following generic strategies to deal with distress:

- Restructure their bank and private debt through negotiations
- Exchange public debt with securities and cash
- Get new capital
- Sell major assets
- Reduce capital expenditure
- Tighten controls and reduce costs

To test the company's viability, one may prepare pro forma financial statements based on historical balance sheet and income statement relationships. For the company to remain viable, the company's executives must strive to get sales back to where it was during good times and bring costs down to normal levels. One may use a "normal" year or a "good" year to estimate profit margins, sales growth, and so on to input into the pro forma statements. The purpose of this analysis is to understand the company's future. The end result of this analysis is a course of action regarding inventory levels, employment, capital expenditure, administrative overhead, marketing expenditure, product mix, pricing, changes in volume of sales, and so on. The funds flow/cash flow statements are retrospective in nature. To plan for the future, what one needs is a cash budget, a planning tool. Financial officers typically try to balance cash inflows and outflows. Contingencies affect inflows. To develop a suitable course of action, one has to identify an inventory of resources available to the firm to meet unforeseen shrinkage in inflow and suitable strategies for reducing outflow. A typical pro forma for a specified time period (say, 1–3 years) may look like the one given here:

A. Uncommitted Reserves	
Cash US$	XX
Unused lines of credit US$	XX
Additional Bank Loans US$	XX
Additional long-term debt US$	XX
Issue of New Equity US$	XX
B. Reduction of Planned Outflows	
Change in production schedule US$	XX
R&D budget US$	XX
Administrative overhead US$	XX
Capital expenditure US$	XX
Dividend payments US$	XX
C. Liquidation of Assets	
Sale of unit US$	XX
Shutdown US$	XX
Total US$	XX

The Restructuring Plan

In September 1999, SAIL, which posted the biggest ever loss by any PSU for the first time in 1998–99 during the last 15 years, appointed international consultants Mckinsey and Company to make recommendations on restructuring. However, when the recommendations were made, the Steel Executive Federation of India (SEFI) refused to acknowledge them. SEFI criticized Mckinsey for not having come up with any far-reaching recommendations (*Business World* 1999). SEFI refused to let any of Mckinsey's proposals such as closing down the loss-making alloy steel plant at Durgapur to be effected. After negotiations, it agreed to revamp the central marketing organization. It also expressed doubts over Mckinsey's ability to suggest a turnaround for the company. Mckinsey was criticized for failing to predict SAIL's losses accurately. Mckinsey had predicted a loss of ₹12,600 million in November 1998, but the actual figure was ₹15,730 million, almost ₹3000 million off the mark. According to SEFI, at this rate, predictions for a 4-year period could go totally wrong. SEFI also alleged that if Mckinsey gained access to the sensitive and classified information, it would be best equipped to advise a prospective buyer of the steel major (Vans.com 1999f).

Further, Mckinsey had proposed the closing down of SAIL's Alloy Steel Plant (ASP) at Durgapur due to its continued loss-making operations. The SAIL management was undecided whether to revive the ASP or to accept Mckinsey's proposal in view of SEFI's displeasure. Nevertheless, many tenders were received from the L. N. Mittal's Ispat group and many international steel companies for buying the ASP (Vans.com 1999d).

The long-awaited wage agreement finalization was delayed because of the Mckinsey controversy. SAIL had agreed to pay its 168,000 employees an interim relief in the form of ad hoc adjustable advance on a monthly basis with effect from June 1999. The total outgo was expected to be ₹1,400 million. However, industrial relations took a turn for the worse when the management announced that it would not pay the advance given the current financial situation. In spite of this decision, the Bhilai plant, the only profitable center, paid its employees the ex gratia amount. The other plants found themselves in a position wherein they had to make ex gratia payments, despite being in the red.[18]

By September 1999, there had been no clear signal about the government coming out with any bailout package for SAIL. The proposed restructuring plan had been awaiting approval for 10 months. The company incurred a huge loss of ₹15.730 billion in 1998–99. The company's chairman announced that the company may have to be referred to the Board for Industrial and Financial Reconstruction if drastic steps are not taken. Following this announcement, CRISIL (Credit Rating & Information Services of India Limited) downgraded SAIL debt to risky. ICRA (Investment information & Credit Rating Agency of India) downgraded SAIL's debt to LBBB+ (long-term), Ma (medium-term), and A3+ (short-term) to project moderate safety (Vans.com 1999b).

After a long wait, the GOI finally approved the restructuring plan of SAIL. The salient features of the plan include a conversion of a portion of the debt into equity to bring down the D/E ratio from 3:1 to 1.5:1. The government offered a restructuring package worth ₹84.54 billion, consisting of a host of concessions to bring SAIL back into profitability. It also included a waiver of 75% of the loan provided by the Steel Development Fund (SDF). The SDF loan stood at ₹52.8 billion as on March 31, 1999. A 75% waiver would bring down the debt by ₹39.6 billion, expecting to reduce SAIL's interest burden by ₹3.8–4 billion per annum. Initially, the government had intended to convert the SDF loans into equity. However, a high court order filed by the some of SAIL's competitors prevented this (Vans.com 1999a). It was claimed that the government was favoring SAIL simply on account of being the majority stakeholder in SAIL.

Of the various turnaround measures planned by the company, the most significant one is its plan to reduce its workforce from 175,000 to 105,000 in phases through a voluntary retirement scheme (VRS). In 1999, when SAIL offered VRS to its employees, the response was higher than the projection of 8,000 to 10,000. So SAIL revised the target to 15,000 employees (Vans.com 1999e). With a huge workforce of around 170,000 SAIL finds itself in a disadvantageous position. The manpower costs constitute about 15% of turnover. Reducing workforce to around 100,000 would ease the burden on the company.

Also under the plan, SAIL would reduce its stake in noncore businesses and concentrate on core areas of operations. Global tenders were invited for the oxygen plant in Bhilai which was to be set up as a joint venture company. SAIL would also divest three units of the Rourkela plant, namely, the captive power plant, fertilizer plants, and central power training institute. The three captive power units were expected to fetch ₹9 billion; Indian Iron & Steel Company, a subsidiary, was expected to be sold for ₹5 billion; and the steel unit at Salem was expected to fetch another ₹5 billion. Mannesman Demag of Germany and Evesta Sheffield of England showed interest in purchasing the Salem steel unit. Furthermore, the government guaranteed additional market borrowings of ₹25 billion, out of which, ₹15 billion would be used for VRS.

Whether or not SAIL would emerge a viable company depended on political will, maturity of labor union, and the speed with which the company implemented the restructuring package. Often, restructuring involves substantial infusion of capital. A challenge for most companies in distress is to raise capital at an acceptable cost. SAIL had the challenge of raising ₹8 billion by 2004 to implement the restructuring package. A large part of the fund requirement was expected to be raised from asset sales. If other public sector steel companies in distress were any indication, there is a cause for concern. RINL, another loss-making public sector steel company, had appointed A. T. Kearney to advice. RINL was in loss for several years despite the assistance of an international consultant.

[18] Its managing director, V. Gujral, was a serious contender for the chairman's post; he was pipped to the post by the then vice chairman Arvind Pande (Vans.com 1999c).

Exhibit 12.17 *Performance Comparison (for 1999, 2000, and 2001 in ₹' 0 million except ratios)*

Company	SAIL			TISCO			RINL		
Year	**1998–99**	**1999–2000**	**2000–01**	**1998–99**	**1999–2000**	**2000–01**	**1998–99**	**1999–2000**	**2000–01**
Sales	16002.3	17257.1	17320.4	6885.1	7015.2	7845.2	2627.5	2714.0	3596.2
Cost of production	11564.7	11821.7	12368.3	4733.1	4179.8	4375.1	2647.3	2595.5	2716.2
Gross fixed assets	30771.5	28307.9	28129.6	10032.2	10668.3	11258.2	8615.5	8635.3	8649.1
Current ratio	1.07	0.83	0.79	1.05	0.94	0.92	0.11	0.77	0.89
Total interest bearing debt as a % of total assets	61.1%	57.2%	54.9%	50.6%	43.8%	40.2%	26.8%	29.9%	34.4%
Total short-term interest bearing debt as a % of total interest bearing debt	20.4%	24.2%	25.5%	6.3%	8.4%	8.9%	34.6%	31.4%	28.4%
Net working capital cycle (days)	257	200	162	113	117	95	172	132	136
Avg. days of debtors (days)	46	42	39	74	70	62	15	17	17
Avg. days of creditors (days)	42	36	43	91	100	104	73	77	76
Inventories (closing)	6832	4606	4519	1017	945	922	1009	1111	1207
Raw materials	689	720	650	173	160	179	189	176	192
WIP	0	0	0	25	28	29	398	0	0
Finished goods	4782	2819	2939	564	527	474	0	494	597
Inventory turnover ratio (times)									
Raw materials turnover	6.43	7.21	7.93	7.04	6.62	6.65	5.96	7.7	8.08
Stores turnover	1.41	1.59	1.73	1.44	1.34	1.55	0.66	0.69	0.66
Semi-finished goods turnover				207.59	155.84	151.99	13.29	13.03	
Finished goods turnover	2.56	3.81	4.53	9.95	9	10.18	7.95	11.11	5.32
D/E ratio	3.03	3.12	3.34	1.81	1.33	1.18	0.78	0.63	0.78
Quick ratio	0.18	0.19	0.19	0.44	0.38	0.37	–0.52	0.14	0.16
Interest coverage ratio	0.18	0.04	0.56	1.29	1.64	2.11	–0.25	–0.44	0.18
Debtors turnover	7.9	8.77	9.34	4.94	5.22	5.85	24.29	22.02	21.15
Creditors turnover	8.61	10.13	8.57	4.02	3.66	3.5	5.01	4.74	4.78
Employee cost (wages)	2393.9	2772.4	3134.8	1065.4	957.1	922.4	255.2	272.5	407.7
Number of employees	NA	NA	NA	NA	NA	NA	NA	NA	NA

In 1991, General Dynamics was in a similar situation as SAIL—an industry plagued by excess capacity (Dial and Murphy 1994). When other defense contractors diversified into nondefense areas, GD adopted an objective of creating shareholder value by downsizing, restructuring, and partially liquidating. To achieve this, the company installed a new management team and an incentive compensation plan that tied executive pay to stock price performance. As part of the turn around strategy, William Anders, the CEO and chairman of the company, implemented

- A gain sharing bonus plan for the top 25 executives.
- An accelerated stock option and restricted stock grants to 150 upper-level managers and executives.
- An option exchange program for 1,150 managers in which managers would get new options (in place of old ones) at a lower price.

Between 1991 and 1993, General Dynamics sold the data system unit to Computer Sciences Corp, the Cessna Aircraft Subsidiary to Textron, its missile business to GM's Hughes Electronics Subsidiary, its electronics division to Carlyle group, and its space systems to Martin Marietta. During the same period, the company reduced its workforce from 98,150 to 26,800. The company's stock price rose from US$55 to over US$92 between 1992 and 1993, and shareholders gained a return of 426%.

REFERENCES AND SUGGESTED READINGS

Alexander, Gordon J., George Benson, and Joan Kampmeyer. 1984. "Investigating the Wealth Effects of Announcements of Voluntary Corporate Sell Offs." *Journal of Finance*, 39 (2): 503–17.

Altman, Edward. 1968. "Financial Ratios, Discriminant Analysis and the Prediction of Corporate Bankruptcy." *Journal of Finance*, 23 (4): 589–609.

———. 1993. *Corporate Financial Distress and Bankruptcy*, 2nd ed. Somerset, NJ: John Wiley.

Anderson, Sarah, and John Cavanagh. 1996. *CEOs Win, Workers Lose: How Wall Street Rewards Job Destroyers*. Washington, DC: The Institute for Policy Studies.

Asquith, Paul, Robert Gertner, and David Scharfstein. 1991, December. "Anatomy of Financial Distress: An Examination of Junk-Bond Issuers." NBER Working Paper No. 3942.

Anslinger, Patricia, Dennis Carey, Kristin Fink, and Chris Gagnon. 1997. "Equity Carve–Outs: A New Spin in the Corporate Structure." *The McKinsey Quarterly*, 1.

Baldwin, Carliss Y., and Scott P. Mason. 1990. *Massey-Ferguson Ltd, 1980*. Harvard Business School Case No. 9-282-043.

Barclay, Michael J., and Clifford Smith, Jr. 1995. "The Maturity Structure of Corporate Debt." *Journal of Finance*, L (2, June): 609–31.

Berger, Philip, and Eli Ofek. 1995. "Diversification's Effect on Firm Value." *Journal of Financial Economics*, 37 (1): 39–65.

Bhide, Amar. 1999. "Reversing Corporate Diversification." In *The New Corporate Finance: Where Theory Meets Practice*, edited by Donald Chew. Boston, MA: McGraw Hill.

Billett, Mathew T., and David Mauer. 1998, October. "Diversification and the Value of Internal Capital Markets: The Case of Tracking Stock." Working Paper. University of Iowa.

Billett, Mathew T., and Anand Vijh. 2001, February. "The Market Performance of Tracking Stocks." Working Paper. University of Iowa.

Birkin, Michael. 1994. "Assessing Brand Value." In *Brand Power*, edited by Paul Stobart, 209–23. New York University Press.

Boone, Audra L., and Harold Mulherin. 2001, May. "Valuing the Process of Corporate Restructuring." Working Paper, Smeal College of Business, Pennsylvania State University.

Bowman, Edward H., Harbir Singh, Michael Useem, and Raja Bhadury. 1999. "When Does Restructuring Improve Economic Performance." *California Management Review*, 41 (2, Winter): 33–54.

Business Standard. 1999. *Business Standard*, March, 20.

Business Week. 1999. "Is AT&T Ready for Lift Off?" *Business Week* (December 13).

Business World. 1999. "SAIL in Storm." *Business World* (September 27).

CFO Magazine. 1997, April. "Split Decision." *CFO Magazine*.

Chemmanur, Thomas, and Imants Paeglis. 2000, June. "Why Issue Tracking Stock? Insights from a Comparison with Spin Offs and Carve Outs." Working Paper. Boston College.

Classens, Stijin, Simeon Djankov, and Giovanni Ferri. 1999, January. "Corporate Distress in East Asia: The Effect of Currency and Interest Rate Shocks." Public Policy for Private Sector, World Bank.

Corman, Linda. 1997, April. "A Dirty Word? Partial Liquidation Does Not Sound So Bad to Shareholders Who Have Enjoyed the Tax Benefits." *CFO Magazine*. Available at http://ww2.cfo.com/accounting-tax/1997/07/a-dirty-word-liquidation/ (Accessed on October 13, 2017).

Cusatis, Patrick, James Miles, and Randall Woolridge. 1993. "Restructuring through Spin Offs: The Stock Market Evidence." *Journal of Financial Economics*, 33: 293–311.

———. 1994. "Some New Evidence That Spin Offs Create Value." *Journal of Applied Corporate Finance*, 7 (2, Summer).

DeAngelo, Harry, Linda DeAngelo, and Karen H Wruck. 2002. "Asset Liquidity, Debt Covenants and Managerial Discretion in Financial Distress: The Collapse of L.A Gear." *Journal of Financial Economics*, 64 (1, April): 3–34.

Denis, David J., and Diane K Denis. 1995. "Causes of Financial Distress Following Leveraged Recapitalizations." *Journal of Financial Economics*, 37 (2): 129–57.

Dial, Jay, and Kevin Murphy. 1994. "Incentives, Downsizing and Value Creation at General Dynamics." *Journal of Financial Economics*, 37 (3): 261–314.

Donaldson, Gordon. 1969. "Strategy for Financial Emergencies." *Harvard Business Review*, 47 (November–December): 67–79.

———. 1990. "Voluntary Restructuring: The Case of General Mills." *Journal of Financial Economics*, 27 (1): 117–41.

———. 1991. "The Voluntary Restructuring of General Mills." *Journal of Applied Corporate Finance*, 27 (1, Fall): 117–41.

———. 1994. "Corporate Restructuring in the 1980s–and Its Import for the 1990s." *Journal of Applied Corporate Finance*, 6 (4, Winter): 60–71.

Dranikoff, Lee, Tim Koller, and Antoon Schneider. 2002. "Divestiture: Strategy's Missing Link." *Harvard Business Review* (May).

D'Souza, J., and Jacob J. 2000. "Why Firms Issue Targeted Stock." *Journal of Financial Economics*, 56 (3): 459–83.

Fridson, Martin, and Jon Jonsson. 1997. "Contingent Claims Analysis." *Journal of Portfolio Management*, 23 (2, Winter): 30–43.

Fruhan, William. 1998. "Corporate Raiders: Head 'em Off at Value Gap." *Harvard Business Review*, 68 (July–August): S. 63–68.

Garvin, David A. 1983. "Spin-Offs and the New Firm Formation Process." *California Management Review*, XXV (2, January): 3–20.

Gillan, Stuart, John Kensinger, and John Martin. 2000. "Value Creation and Corporate Diversification: The Case of Sears, Roebuck & Co." *Journal of Financial Economics*, 55 (1, January): 103–37.

Gilson, S. C. 1998. "Course Overview: Creating Value Through Corporate Restructuring." Working Paper. Harvard Business School.

Gilson, Stuart. 2001, July. *Creating Value through Corporate Restructuring: Case Studies in Bankruptcies, Buyouts and Breakups*. Hoboken, NJ: John Wiley & Sons.

Gilson, S., and Jeremy Cott. 1994. "Humana Inc." Case No. 9-294-062, Harvard Business School.

———. 1996. "USX Corporation" Case No. 9-296-050, Harvard Business School.

Gilson, Stuart, Paul Healy, Christopher Noe, and Krishna Palepu. 1998, June. "Information Effects of Spin offs, Equity Carve Outs and Targeted Stock Offerings." Working Paper No. Harvard Business School.

Habib, M. A., D. B. Johnsen, and N. Y. Naik. "Spin Offs and Information." *Journal of Financial Intermediation*, 6 (2).

Healy, Paul, and Krishna Palepu. 1995. "The Challenges of Investor Communication: The Case of CUC International Inc." *Journal of Financial Economics*, 38 (2): 111–40.

Heckscher, Charles, and Lynda M. Applegate. 1994. "Introduction." In *The Post-Bureaucratic Organization: New Perspectives on Organizational Change*, edited by Charles Heckscher and Anne Donnellon, 14–62. SAGE Publications.

Hite, G .and J. Owers. 1983. "Security Price Reactions Around Corporate Spin Off Announcements." *Journal of Financial Economics*, 12 (4): 409–36.

Hite, Gailen, James Owers, and Ronald Rogers. 1987. "The Market for Interfirm Asset Sales: Partial Sell Offs and Total Liquidations." *Journal of Financial Economics*, 18 (2): 229–52.

Jain, Prem C. 1985. "The Effect of Voluntary Sell off Announcements on Shareholders Wealth." *Journal of Finance*, 40 (March): 2019–24.

Jensen, Michael, 1989. "Active Investors, LBOs and the Privatization of Bankruptcy." *Journal of Applied Corporate Finance*, 2 (1, Summer): 35–44.

Jensen M. C. 1993. "The Modern Industrial Revolution, Exit and the Failure of Internal Control Systems." *Journal of Finance*, 48 (3, July): 831–80.

Khanna, Tarun, and Krishna Palepu. 1997. "Why Focused Strategies May Be Wrong for Emerging Markets." *Harvard Business Review*, 75 (4, July–August): 41–51.

———. 1999. "The Right Way to Restructure in Emerging Markets." *Harvard Business Review*, 77 (4, July–August): 125–34.

Klein, A. 1986. "Timing and Substance of Divestiture Announcements: Individual, Simultaneous and Cumulative Effects." *Journal of Finance*, 41 (3): 685–96.

Lang, Larry, Annette Poulsen, and Rene Stulz. 1995. "Asset Sales, Firm Performance, and the Agency Costs of Managerial Discretion." *Journal of Financial Economics*, 37 (1): 3–37.

Lewin, Jeffrey, and Wesley Johnston. 2000. "The Impact of Downsizing and Restructuring on Organisational Competitiveness." *Competitiveness Review*, 10, (1): 45–55.

Linn, Scott C., and Michael Rozeff. 1984. "The Corporate Sell Off." *Midland Corporate Finance Journal*, 2 (Summer): 17–26.

Lins, Karl V., and Henri Servaes. 2002. "Is Corporate Diversification Beneficial in Emerging Markets?" *Financial Management*, 31 (2, Summer): 5–31.

Logue, Dennis, James Seward, and James Walsh. 1996. "Rearranging Residual Claims: A Case for Targeted Stock." *Financial Management*, 25 (1, Spring): 43–61.

Maksimovic, Vojislav, and Gordon Phillips. 2001. "The Market for Corporate Assets: Who Engages in Mergers and Asset Sales and Are there Efficiency Gains." *The Journal of Finance*, LVI (6, December): 2019–65.

Markides, Constantinos C. 1997. "To Diversify or Not to Diversify." *Harvard Business Review*, 75 (6, November–December): 93–99.

Michaely, Roni, and Wayne H. Shaw. 1995. "The Choice of Going Public: Spin-offs vs. Carve-outs." *Financial Management*, 24 (3, Autumn): 5–21.

Monroe, Ann. 1994. "Sale of the Century." *CFO Magazine*, (January 1994).

Nichols III, Charles, and Lynn Sharp Pyne. 1997, June 26. "Marriott Corporation." Case Study No. 9-394-085. Harvard Business School.

Parrino, Robert. 1997. "Spin-offs and Wealth Transfers: The Marriott Case." *Journal of Financial Economics*, 43: 241–74.

Salter, Malcolm, and Wolf Weinhold. 1978. "Creating Value via Diversification." *Harvard Business Review*, (July): 166–76.

———. 1979. *Diversification Through Acquisition*. New York, NY: The Free Press.

Schipper K., and A. Smith. 1983. "Effects of Recontracting on Shareholder Wealth: The Case of Voluntary Spin Offs." *Journal of Financial Economics*, 12 (4, December): 437–67.

———. 1984. "The Corporate Spin Off Phenomenon." *Midland Corporate Finance Journal*, 2 (Summer): 22–26.

———. 1986. "A Comparison of Equity Carve Outs and Seasoned Equity Offerings: Share Price Effects and Corporate Restructuring." *Journal of Financial Economics*, 15 (1–2): 153–86.

Shefrin, Hersh. 2001. "Behavioral Corporate Finance." *Journal of Applied Corporate Finance*, 14 (3, Fall): 113–26.

———. 1999. *Beyond Fear and Greed: Understanding Behavioral Finance and the Psychology of Investing*. Boston: Harvard Business School Press.

Slovin, Myron, Marie Sushka, and Steven Ferraro. 1995. "A Comparison of the Information Conveyed by Equity Carve-outs, Spin Offs and Asset Sell Offs." *Journal of Financial Economics*, 37 (1): 89–104.

Stein, Jeremy. *USX: Targeted Stock Restructuring*. Boston: Casenet, Southwestern College Publishing. ISBN 0-538-56940-2.

Stern, Joel, Bennett Stewart, and Donald Chew, ed. 1989. *Corporate Restructuring and Executive Compensation*. The Institutional Investor Series in Finance. Harper and Row.

Subramaniam, Somu, Patricia Anslinger, and Steve Klepper. 1999. "Breaking Up is Good to Do." *The McKinsey Quarterly*, (1): 16–27.
Vans.com. 1999a. "HC Restraint Govt., JPC from Converting SAIL Loan to Equity." Vans.com, August 28, 1999.
———. 1999b. "ICRA Decides to Reaffirm SAIL Ratings." Vans.com, (September 29).
———. 1999c. "SAIL Not to Make Ex-gratia Payments." Vans.com, (August 27).
———. 1999d. "SAIL Rejects Mckinsey Suggestion to Close ASP." Vans.com, (September 4).
———. 1999e. "SAIL Revises Target for VRS." Vans.com, (August 27).
———. 1999f. "SEFI Up In Arms Against Mckinsey & SAIL." Vans.com, (August 30).
Vijh, A. 1999. "Long Term Returns from Equity Carve Outs." *Journal of Financial Economics*, 51 (2): 273–308.
Weston, Fred. 1992. "Divestitures: Mistakes or Learning." In *The Revolution in Corporate Finance*, edited by Joel Stern and Donald Chew. Basil Blackwell.
Worrell, Dan L., Wallace N. Davidson III, and Varinder M. Sharma. 1991. "Layoff Announcements and Stockholder Wealth." *Academy of Management Journal*, 34 (3): 662–78.
Wruck, Karen, and Sherry Pelkey Roper. 1997. "Sink or Swim? Cytec Industries' Spin-Off." Case No. 5-897-053. Harvard Business School.
Zuta, S. 2000. "Diversification Discount and Targeted Stock: Theory and Empirical Evidence." Working Paper. University of Maryland.

REVIEW QUESTIONS

1. What factors are driving corporate restructuring initiatives?
2. Should business groups in emerging markets be dismantled? Why or Why not?
3. Compare and contrast spin offs, carve outs and targeted stocks.
4. What are the advantages and disadvantages of spin offs and targeted stocks?
5. Review the empirical evidence on spin offs, carve outs and targeted stocks.

APPENDIX 12A: VALUATION OF BRANDS

Brands are valued by a variety of methods. Under the cost based method, the value of a brand is the money spent on it in creating it. The replacement cost method suggests that the value of a brand is the amount necessary to create a brand with similar turnover, profitability; distribution reach etc. The Interbrand approach is the most popular methodology for estimating the value of brands (Birkin 1994).

A brand's value is the product of:

- Average annual after-tax profits of the brand adjusted for earnings of an equivalent unbranded product and
- A multiple reflecting the brand's strength.

Interbrand takes 7 factors into account to arrive at a "brand strength multiple." They are:

Leadership: A brand which has the ability to influence the market in setting price points and commanding distribution gets a higher score (Max: 25)

Stability: Those brands which enjoy a strong consumer franchise are considered stable and awarded a higher score (Max: 15)

Market: Brands in markets such as foods and soft drinks are less vulnerable to shifts in fashion and technology (Max: 15)

Geographic spread: Brands which have an international appeal are stronger then regional brands (Max: 25)

Trend: The long-term appeal to consumers (Max: 10)

Support: Consistency in investment and strength of communication (Max: 10)

Protection: Legal protection available to the brand owner

To assess the brand strength, Interbrand conducts a detailed audit of trade and retail outlets among other things. The final multiple assigned to the brand depends on the brand strength score. To illustrate, if the brand score is 56, Interbrand may apply a multiple of 8.42. Brand valuation involves the following steps.

- Collect most recent profit data (3 years).
- Restate the prior period (year – 2, year – 1) profits to present day values by inflating at a suitable rate.
- Attach a weighting factor to the restated profit figures. Usually, a simple weighting of three times the current year, twice the previous year, and once before is used. These aggregate earnings are divided by the sum of the weighting factors (3 + 2 + 1 = 6).
- Deduct operating income of an equivalent unbranded product.
- Deduct taxes at the medium-term effective tax rate.
- Apply a suitable multiple depending on the brand strength.

APPENDIX 12B: FEATURES OF TARGETED STOCKS

Company	Voting Rights	Liquidation Rights in Proportion to	Dividend Policy Tied to Tracked Businesses?	Managerial Compensation Tied to Tracked Businesses?
GM (EDS)[19]	Fixed	Voting Rights	Yes	Yes
GM (Hughes)	Fixed	Voting rights	Yes	Yes
USX Corp 1	Variable	relative value	Yes	Yes
USX Corp 2	Variable	–do–	Yes	Yes
Ralston Purina	–do–	–do–	Yes	Yes
Kmart	–do–	–do–	–do–	–do–
Genzyme 1	–do–	Relative shares[20]	–do–	–do–
Genzyme 2	NA	NA	NA	NA

Source: Billett and Mauer (1998).

[19] The E class and H class shares are called letter stocks. The subtle difference between letter stocks and targeted stocks lies in the rights of shareholders.

[20] Based on fixed number of liquidation units per share.

CHAPTER

13

Bankruptcy and Reorganization

Vishwanath S. R. and Chandrasekhar Krishnamurti

Learning Objectives

- Highlight the causes of financial distress
- Survey the bankruptcy code in the USA, the UK, India, and several other countries
- Suggest a methodology for valuation of bankrupt firms
- Summarize the results of academic studies on various aspects of bankruptcy

We thank Professor P. V. Viswanath, Lubin School of Business, Pace University, New York, for his helpful comments.

When a firm's condition deteriorates to the extent where it cannot meet its financial obligations, the firm is said to be in a financial distress. Usually the first signals of distress are the violation of debt covenants and suspension of dividends. Bankruptcy includes financial reorganization and liquidation. Financial reorganization involves rearranging a firm's cash flow (for example, converting debt into equity), whereas liquidation ends the firm's operations. It involves selling off tangible assets and paying off claimants to the extent possible. Recent examples of distressed firms are LA Gear, Enron, Iridium, Chrysler, Massey Ferguson, and Marvel Entertainment. Some of these companies, once considered the darling of the investment community, have left millions of investors with worthless paper. Why do some apparently well-run companies get into financial distress? The causes of distress can be inferred from the ex ante characteristics of the companies that became distressed. We attack the issue of distress by using ex ante and ex post information on the characteristics of some high profile distressed firms and try to make some generalizations.

CAUSES OF DISTRESS

Although companies may go bankrupt due to numerous reasons, there are some generic reasons such as failure of control systems, loss aversion and overconfidence, changes in the macroeconomic environment, and high levels of debt.

Managerial myopia: Modern finance theory suggests that the objective of a corporation is to maximize shareholder value. Due to agency conflicts, managers may enrich themselves at the expense of shareholders. One way to control such conflicts is to award stock-based compensation plans because the equity ownership induces managers to think and act like shareholders. This is based on the premise that other costs, like behavioral costs, can also be addressed through incentive compatibility. When managers are overconfident of their strategy, when they have biased estimates of payoffs from a project, or when they have a distorted view of what is in their own interest, incentives alone will not help (Shefrin 1999, 2001). Behavioral finance theorists argue that some financial phenomena can be understood using models in which some agents are not fully rational. The field draws from psychology, which catalogues the deviations from rationality. Either managers or investors could be irrational. For instance, Sony Corporation spent substantial time and money on the development of the color television receiver in the 1960s at the behest of Ibuka, one of Sony's founders.[1] Although the company had not achieved a commercially viable manufacturing process, Ibuka insisted on selling the product at a negative profit margin. It was only when the managers announced that Sony was close to ruin that Ibuka abandoned the project. In this case, for example, there was no agency conflict in the sense that Ibuka was a major shareholder himself. Yet, he would not abandon a loss-making project until it almost ruined the company because of loss aversion. In other words, overconfidence and loss aversion can lead to distress even in the presence of high-powered incentives. The case of Sony can be interpreted as irrationality on the part of managers themselves rather than that of investors. Sony's managers were under the impression that they were maximizing firm value, when in reality they were not.

Failure of internal control systems: Changes in ownership through mergers and acquisitions generally lead to an increase in shareholder value. Many academic studies in America report increases in shareholder returns of target companies. Mergers and acquisitions enable transfer of assets to owners who value them most. In well-planned acquisitions, the gain is primarily due to better governance and improved efficiency. In a market-oriented economy like the USA, companies making value-destroying investments are disciplined by capital markets. The takeover wave of the 1980s in the USA was largely due to deconglomeration, that is, companies sold off unrelated businesses and acquired related businesses. In many countries, the market for corporate control is either weak or nonexistent. In some Asian and European countries, the market is restricted because of complex cross holdings, pyramid structures, and anti-takeover laws. In the absence of an effective market for corporate control companies are not subject to the discipline of the stock market.

Even when the market for corporate control is active, companies may still escape any disciplinary mechanism. By nature organizations resist control systems and ineffective governance is a major part of the problem with many distressed firms. General Motors (GM), for example, one of the world's high-cost producers in a market with substantial excess capacity, avoided making major changes in its strategy for over a decade (Jensen 1993). Yet the board acted to remove the CEO, Robert Stempel, only in 1992, after the company had reported losses of US$6.5 billion in 1990 and 1991 and an opportunity loss of over US$100 billion in its R&D and capital expenditure program from 1980 to 1990. GM is not the only

[1] Akio Morita, the other founder, was apparently not in favor of the project.

example. IBM, Eastman Kodak, and Iridium have all changed strategy or CEO or filed for bankruptcy (as the case may be) only after experiencing severe losses.

Derivatives are financial instruments whose value depends on one or more underlying variables such as the price of stock or commodity. Derivatives are traded in both organized and over-the-counter (OTC) markets. The OTC market is several times bigger than the organized market. Enron started off as an energy company in 1985. As a part of its corporate strategy, it decided to differentiate itself from its competitors by offering derivative solutions to its customers. Because gas prices are highly volatile, Enron's customers attach value to stability of prices. Enron would supply gas under long-term contracts at constant prices and hedge the risk of price fluctuation in the derivatives market. Slowly, its exposure to and revenues from derivatives trading grew. The OTC derivative market is largely unregulated, and so was Enron's trading. The question of why Enron failed relates to derivative deals between Enron and its off-balance sheet subsidiaries.[2] Enron used derivatives to hide losses on its speculative investments in technology firms and debt incurred by unprofitable businesses, and to inflate the value of unprofitable businesses.

Capital structure: According to modern finance theory, companies with lots of investment opportunities can be expected to issue short-term debt to preserve financial flexibility and to protect lenders against greater uncertainty in the company's future.[3] Further, growth firms ought to use relatively less debt to prevent the underinvestment problem. Conversely, for mature companies whose value comes mostly from assets-in-place, the costs of bankruptcy are likely to be low. Such firms can afford to have high leverage ratios to prevent wastage of free cash flow by managers.

Conventional wisdom suggests that companies should avoid combining high operating leverage (which leads to high business risk) and high financial leverage (which leads to high financial risk). Earnings are boosted in good times because of the presence of fixed costs and debt, but (earnings) get depressed in bad times for the same reason, namely, the presence of interest payments on debt and other fixed costs. Massey Ferguson, a multinational producer of farm machinery, industrial machinery, and diesel engines, sought to increase its market share by turning to the Third World for growth. Massey manufactured its products in the UK and Canada and sold the output to LDCs (less developed countries) in the late 1970s. This strategy worked quite well in the initial years. Massey had an aggressive debt policy *and* an aggressive product market strategy when compared with competitors. It was unwise to couple a risky strategy in a cyclical industry with high (short-term) debt.[4] When short-term interest rates shot up and the demand dried up for its products for various reasons, Massey was thrown into distress. John Deere, its major competitor, however, had a moderate debt ratio because of which it had the financial flexibility to make capital investments. When Massey and another competitor International Harvester were busy resolving distress, Deere pursued aggressive tactics to lock up the market share.

---

[2] The June—July 2002 issue of *Financial Engineering News* carries two excellent articles on Enron. They are available at www.fenews.com

[3] The cost of long-term debt will be unacceptably high for growth firms because of uncertainty in their future.

[4] Customers in LDCs are more risky compared to customers in developed countries.

In the 1980s, a large number of American firms undertook leveraged recapitalizations and leveraged buyouts to improve firm value and operating efficiency (see the previous chapter). Many firms that undertook management buyouts in the late 1980s encountered distress due to poor structure of the deals (in terms of price) and adverse regulatory and economic developments. Academic studies in the USA find that the firms encountering distress were more highly leveraged than other firms and exhibit poor post-recap operating performance due to industrywide problems (Denis, David J. and Denis, Diane K. 1995).

Currency and interest rate shocks: The steel companies in Asia were highly leveraged and depended on high tonnages to survive before they went bust. When the Asian economies shrank, these companies were badly affected. This trend is not specific to the steel sector. A survey of the five countries most affected by the East Asian financial crisis—Indonesia, the Republic of Korea, Malaysia, the Philippines, and Thailand—found that 63% of the firms are illiquid (with earnings less than debt service) and 31% technically insolvent (with financial obligations exceeding their equity; Classens, Djankov, and Ferri 1999). For the entire period 1988–96, the average debt ratios in Korea and Thailand were much higher than that in Germany and the USA. East Asian firms had not only too much debt but also the wrong type of debt, namely, short-term. The average share of short-term debt in total debt was about 66% in Malaysia and Thailand in contrast with 25% in the USA and 45% in Germany. Although the share of short-term debt increased gradually, it was one of the causes of distress. In addition, Korean and Malaysian firms had substantial share of foreign currency short-term debt. When the domestic currency is devalued, the value of foreign currency debt (denominated in, say, US dollars) increases. Sovereign governments may increase interest rates to stabilize their currencies. But this has a negative impact on corporate profitability. This is at least one of the reasons for the poor performance by East Asian firms.

HOW COSTLY IS BANKRUPTCY?

The costs of bankruptcy are of two kinds: direct and indirect. Direct costs include lawyers' and accountants' fees, other professional fees, and the value of managerial time spent on administering bankruptcy. Indirect costs include lost sales (and, hence, lost profits), the possibility that the firm may not be able to obtain additional credit or to issue securities except under strict terms. A firm may lose sales rapidly if the firm is a manufacturer of long lived products that require continuous servicing or replacement parts as customers may use their *perception* of the financial condition of the company to make their purchase decisions. For instance, the value of a computer is not only determined by its hardware but also by the manufacturer's continued provision of hardware and software support. An obsolete software or hardware is worthless. So a customer may settle for an inferior alternative with a lower probability of bankruptcy based on the perception that this firm is risky. Software firms may refuse to support computer firms that have high probability of bankruptcy because these companies are unlikely to be around for long, thereby accelerating distress. Likewise, airlines depend on frequent-flier plans to attract business travelers. No amount of advertising may bring credibility to the claim made by those companies. Similarly, retailing companies may not obtain goods or credit from wholesalers. Since these firms do not get credit, their competitiveness will be lost. The indirect cost of bankruptcy can arise from the bankruptcy process itself. The bankruptcy trustee, as an agent of the court, may not run the firm in a value maximizing way as he or she has no incentive to do so. The firm incurs an opportunity loss due to the suboptimal decision-making of the agent. Another possible indirect cost of bankruptcy is the higher compensation that the managers of a highly levered firm will receive because of the higher probability of unemployment they may face. Because the indirect costs are mainly lost opportunities, it is difficult to measure them.

Based on the foregoing discussion, we would expect firms with large intangible assets to keep their leverage low to reduce the probability of future bankruptcy. Thus, Microsoft, which derives much of its value from growth opportunities, should keep the debt level low.

From the perspective of a firm choosing a capital structure, it is the expected cost of bankruptcy at the time of decision-making that matters.

Expected cost of bankruptcy = Probability of bankruptcy × bankruptcy cost in rupees. To illustrate, if the probability is 0.3 and the bankruptcy cost is 20% of current market value of the company (which is, say, US$100 million),

$$E\ (\text{bankruptcy}) = 0.3 \times 0.2 \times 100$$
$$E = \text{US\$3 million.}$$

As pointed out earlier, bankruptcy cost includes direct, deadweight costs such as administrative and legal expenses, and indirect costs such as lost sales, lost investment opportunities, interest paid on emergency loan (if any), higher salary for chief executive (due to increased riskiness of leverage), and so on. There is no surefire formula to estimate bankruptcy cost. The proportion of companies that have gone bankrupt in the company's rating class can be taken as proxy for probability. Generally, expected bankruptcy cost is taken as 20%–30% of firm value. A practical way of adjusting for risk of disruption, impact on capital rationing, impact on morale, efficiency, and effectiveness of spending programs would be to:

- Take the cost of bank credit agreement as proxy for cost of disruption.
- Take the net present value (NPV) of projects cancelled as proxy for capital rationing.
- Assume a subjective sum for lost efficiency, say, US$5 million a year.
- Subjectively set a value for loss in sales.

A recent study in the USA examined the industry adjusted change in sales, operating income, and market value of highly levered firms in industries experiencing downturn (Opler and Titman 1994).[5] Industry downturns were defined as drops in sales and market values of 30% or greater. The study found that highly levered firms lost an additional 14%, 12%, and 7% of sales, operating income, and market value relative to the average firm in the industry, and 26%, 27% and 15% more than the least levered firm in the industry after controlling for industry performance. This study provides a pointer to the magnitude of distress costs.

[5] Another study of high-leverage transactions suggests that the costs of financial distress are 10% of the firm value. See Andrade, Gregor and Steven Kaplan (1998). Also see Kaplan's (1994) study of Federated.

THE US BANKRUPTCY CODE

Bankruptcy is the legal process of settling claims between debtors and creditors. There are two types of bankruptcy procedures in the USA—Chapter 7 and Chapter 11—and the laws are enforced through bankruptcy courts, which are divisions of district courts. The bankruptcy judges are appointed to preside over bankruptcy cases. Chapter 7 provides for liquidation of the company. Either the debtor (the company) or the creditor may initiate the bankruptcy process. Once the bankruptcy petition is filed, an automatic stay comes into effect that prevents pre-petition creditors from collecting debt, and it remains in effect till the end of the bankruptcy case. Soon after the petition is filed, the bankruptcy judge appoints a trustee (an attorney or accountant or a business person) to oversee the bankruptcy process. The creditors then hold a meeting to assess the problem, and determine the types of debt and the location (and perhaps quality) of debtor's assets. The trustee may seek outside expertise (legal/tax/accounting) to work on the case. The trustee then gathers debtors' assets and liquidates them by auction or private sale. The proceeds of the liquidation are disbursed on the basis of priority: secured claims, administrative claims, employee compensation, customer claims, tax, general unsecured claims, and equity claims, in that order.

Chapter 11, in contrast, allows a firm to remain in operation while a plan of reorganization is being worked out. Unlike Chapter 7, the company's management remains in charge (called debtor-in-possession). Although the company's management remains in charge, they are required to seek approval from the court as far as certain actions such as asset sales or new credit are concerned. During the 120 days after filing for Chapter 11, the debtor is given the exclusive right to formulate a plan of reorganization and during the same period the debtor may invite creditors for a meeting to negotiate a plan. The plan is put into action when a certain fraction of shareholders and creditors (2/3rd the dollar amount of claims and a majority of the class) vote in favor of the plan. The court accepts the plan only if all classes vote in favor or if the plan is considered fair and equitable to those who did not vote in its favor.

US Chapter 11 provisions provide the most protection for bankrupt firms' assets and result in a greater likelihood of successful reorganization than is found in other countries where liquidation and sale of the assets for the benefit of creditors is more likely the result. But, the US Code's process is usually lengthy (averaging close to 2 years, except in case of a "pre-packaged" Chapter 11) and expensive; furthermore, the reorganized firm often ends up re-filing under Chapter 11 (Altman 1998). A Chapter 11 case may also get converted into Chapter 7. Pan American World Airways and Eastern Airlines had initially filed for Chapter 11. However, significant operating losses during bankruptcy and the inability to attract new funding forced the companies to liquidate (Fenster 1993).

INTERNATIONAL COMPARISONS

Some argue that the US bankruptcy code is biased toward the debtor in the sense that it allows managers to run the firm when negotiations are under way and gives them the exclusive right to propose a reorganization plan. Seeking protection from creditors itself does not suggest that the law is pro-debtor because preserving the going concern value will benefit other claimants.

Another important question that some pose is whether the bankruptcy code is needed in the first place because the code limits the contracts that can be written between creditors and debtors and the redrawing of contracts itself does not require a bankruptcy law. A problem arises when there are multiple claimants. The contract itself may not specify the pecking order of claimants (that is, the order in which claims will be settled) in the event of bankruptcy, and a claimant may withhold an agreement that is collectively in the interest of all parties concerned in an effort to garner disproportionate benefits. A bankruptcy law eliminates such problems.

Many countries in the world do not have a bankruptcy law in place. Authorities in such countries would be interested in selecting an efficient code. A bankruptcy code would be considered efficient if:

- It preserves promising companies while liquidating uneconomic ones.
- It allows reorganization or liquidation at minimal cost.
- It facilitates information production to all concerned parties.[6]
- It should facilitate the discovery of the best option for the firm, including preserving the value of assets.
- It should preserve the absolute priority of claims, that is, senior creditors should be paid before junior creditors are paid.

Shareholders provide equity in exchange for dividend and voting rights. Likewise, creditors lend money in exchange for interest and principal payments, and the right to possess collateral when the company defaults on its payments. The differences in governance in different parts of the world are partly due to the differences in the rights of shareholders and creditors (La Porta, Lopez-de-Silanes, and Shleifer 1997, 1998; Shleifer and Vishny 1997).

There are two broad law systems: civil law and common law. According to Duhaime's Law Dictionary, the main features of common and civil law are as follows:[7]

- Law inspired by old Roman law, the primary feature of which was that laws were written into a collection, codified, and not determined, as is *common law*, by judges. The principle of civil law is to provide all citizens with an accessible and written collection of the laws which apply to them and which judges must follow.
- Judge-made law is law that exists and applies to a group on the basis of historical legal precedents developed over hundreds of years. Because it is by judges rather than politicians, it is also referred to as "unwritten" law. Judges seek these principles out when trying a case and apply the precedents to the facts to come up with a judgment.
- Common law is often contrasted with *civil law* systems that require all laws to be written in a code or written collection. Common law has been referred to as the "common sense

[6] Perfect information production typically leads to efficient solutions. Otherwise, one creditor may, for instance, use privately available information to his or her advantage.

[7] See http://lawinfo.com/lawdictionary/

of the community, crystallized and formulated by our ancestors." *Equity* law was developed after the common laws to offset the rigid interpretations that medieval English judges were giving the common law. For hundreds of years, there were separate courts in England and its dependents—one for common law and one for equity—and the decisions of the latter, where they conflicted, prevailed. It is a matter of legal debate whether or not common law and equity are now "fused." It is certainly common to speak of the "common law" to refer to the entire body of English law, including common law and *equity*.

According to La Porta et al. (1998, 2000), there are a few major legal families—among them are the English (common law), which is to be found in England and its former colonies, including the USA, Canada, Australia, and New Zealand; the French, which is found in France and her former colonies, as well as in the former Dutch, Belgian, and Spanish colonies, including Latin America; the German, which is found in Germany and the Germanic countries of Europe; and the Scandinavian.

A shareholder, as a residual claimant, has the right to attend annual general meetings and vote on various corporate matters such as asset sales, mergers and acquisitions, elections of directors, and so on. Often, widely dispersed shareholders do not actively take part in the governance process. In those countries where voting by mail is not allowed, the company's management can get away uncontested. In some countries such as Italy and Belgium whose legal systems are based on the French Civil law, shareholders are not allowed to vote by mail. In general, countries following the common law tradition (the USA, the UK, Australia, Canada, and so on) provide the best investor protection. Likewise, creditor rights vary from country to country. Some countries allow possession of collateral, whereas some do not. Again, the common law tradition provides the best, and the French civil law countries the weakest protection to creditors. German civil law and Scandinavian countries fall in between. Creditors of defaulting firms can resort to one of two strategies: liquidate or reorganize. Since liquidation of a firm has undesirable social consequences, reorganization is usually preferred. La Porta et al. (1998) have documented the status of creditor rights around the world. The same for select countries is shown in Exhibit 13.1.

Further, in many countries, companies can issue shares with different voting rights. The one-share, one-vote rule is followed in the US, the UK, and many other countries. But it is common in countries such as Brazil and Chile to issue shares with different voting rights. Some companies restrict the voting rights of foreign investors. For example, some companies from Latin America and Europe have issued (depository) shares with differential voting rights (Pinegar and Ravichandran 2001). The shareholders of B class shares of Saga Petroleum, a Norwegian company, have no voting rights but holders of A class shares have full voting rights. Mexican companies have issued L shares that provide limited rights to elect the number of directors and such other matters. Two Swedish firms—Astra and Scania—have issued two classes of shares: A and B. The A class shares have one vote each, and the B shares carry 1/10 vote each.

ABB has 24,345,619 shares with 0.1 vote per share and a par value of 5 SEK, as well as 66,819,757 shares with one vote per share and a par value of 5 SEK. Investors, in general, are better protected in countries where the one-share, one-vote rule is enforced. In the absence of such a law, the insiders of the company can have disproportionate control on the company in relation to their investment.

Exhibit 13.1 *Creditor Rights Around the World*

Country	No Automatic Stay on Assets	Secured Creditors First Paid	Restrictions for Going into Reorganization	Management Does not Stay in Reorganization	Creditor Rights
Creditor Rights (1 = creditor protection is the law)					
Australia	0	1	0	0	1
Canada	0	1	0	0	1
India	1	1	1	1	4
UK	1	1	1	1	4
US	0	1	0	0	1
Argentina	0	1	0	0	1
Brazil	0	0	1	0	1
Chile	0	1	1	0	2
Indonesia	1	1	1	1	4
Austria	1	1	1	0	3
Germany	1	1	1	0	3
Japan	0	1	0	1	2
Switzerland	0	1	0	0	1
Denmark	1	1	1	0	3
Finland	0	1	0	0	1
Norway	0	1	1	0	2

Source: La Porta et al. (1998).

BANKRUPTCY CODE IN THE UNITED KINGDOM

There are three possible routes to reorganization in the UK:

- Liquidation
- Receivership
- Voluntary arrangements

The Insolvency Act of 1986 is different from the Chapter 11 procedures in several ways:

- Creditors run the show, by and large (Hill 1994).
- Tax claims are first, in many cases (argued that this reduces the incentive for creditors to agree to reorganization plans).
- Floating charge agreements that allow banks to act as bankruptcy administrators (unique to the UK).
- Liquidation is encouraged, as opposed to reorganization.
- Preserving employment is not a policy objective. (But this might be changing.)
- More attention is paid to directors' actions before the bankruptcy to see whether they made sound business judgments.

Liquidation involves the sale of the company's assets to repay creditors. Receivership involves appointment of a receiver by a creditor who has a specific lien on the firm's assets and is not subordinate to other creditors. He has full powers to run the firm on behalf of the creditor. This would not be permitted under Chapter 11 because of automatic stay. Voluntary arrangement involves a formal arrangement between the company and its creditors with a minimum of court involvement, similar to Chapter 11.

A comparison of insolvency codes in select countries is given in Appendix 13A.

CORPORATE DEBT RESTRUCTURING IN INDIA[8]

In order to protect the interests of lenders to firms in distress. the Reserve Bank of India (the central bank) issued guidelines relating to corporate debt restructuring (CDR) on August 23, 2001, for implementation by financial institutions and banks. The CDR mechanism was a voluntary, nonstatutory system based on debtor-creditor agreement (DCA) and inter-creditor agreement (ICA). An approval by a super-majority of 75% of creditors (by value) made it binding on the remaining 25% to comply with the majority decision. The mechanism covered only multiple banking accounts, syndication or consortium accounts, where all banks and institutions together had an outstanding aggregate exposure of ₹100 million or more.

Reference to CDR mechanism could be triggered by:

- Any of the creditors having a minimum of 20% share in either working capital or term finance, or
- The concerned company, if supported by a bank/financial institution having a minimum of 20% share as above.

Debtors were required to execute the DCA, either at the time of reference to CDR cell or at the time of original loan documentation (for future cases). The DCA had a legally binding "stand still" agreement whereby both the debtor and creditor(s) agreed to "stand still" and commit themselves not to take recourse to any legal action during the period. It was necessary to enable the CDR system to undertake the necessary debt-restructuring exercise without any outside intervention, judicial or otherwise. However, the agreement was applicable only to any civil action, either by the borrower or any lender against the other party, and did not cover any criminal action.

The CDR system in India had a three-tier system comprising of a standing forum, an empowered group (EG), and a CDR cell. The CDR standing forum, the top tier of the system, was a representative general body comprising of chief executives of scheduled commercial banks and financial institutions. It laid down policies and guidelines to be followed by the EG and CDR cell for debt restructuring. The individual cases of CDR were decided by the CDR-EG, which was the second tier of the CDR mechanism. The EG considered the preliminary report of all cases of requests of restructuring submitted to it by the CDR cell. After the EG decided that restructuring of a company's debt was prima facie feasible and the concerned enterprise was potentially viable in terms of the policies and guidelines evolved by the standing forum, a

[8] See http://www.cdrindia.org/

detailed restructuring package was worked out by the referring institution in conjunction with the CDR cell. The EG was mandated to look into each case of debt restructuring, examine the viability and rehabilitation potential of the company, and approve the restructuring package within a specified time frame of 90 days, or at best within 180 days of reference to the EG.

Borrowers were classified into four categories for the purpose of stipulation of conditions. Class–A borrowers comprised of companies affected by external factors pertaining to the economy and industry. Class –B borrowers were such borrowers who, besides being affected by external factors, also had weak resources and inadequate vision, and did not have the support of professional management. Class-C borrowers were those who had diversified into related or unrelated fields with or without lenders' permission, and those classified as Class-D were financially undisciplined borrowers.

Once the final restructuring plan was approved and confirmed by the EG, the CDR cell issued a letter of approval (LOA) for the restructuring package to all the concerned lenders. The individual lenders were required to sanction the restructuring package within 45 days from the date of issue of LOA and, thereafter, fully implement it in the next 45 days.

The status of sanction and implementation of restructuring packages was reviewed frequently at EG meetings. However, in order to place greater emphasis on the implementation of approved packages, the standing committee of core group member banks took-up monitoring to ensure that the packages were implemented expeditiously.

PREDICTING DISTRESS

Lenders lend money in exchange for interest and principal payments over a specified period of time. Credit risk refers to the chance that the expectation will not be met. One approach to estimating default risk is to compute a composite risk measure based on a firm's financial ratios advocated by Altman (1968, 2000). His model is based on multiple discriminant analysis (MDA), which is a statistical technique used to classify an observation into one of several a priori groupings dependent upon the observation's individual characteristics. It is used to classify and make predictions in problems where the dependent variable appears in qualitative form (bankrupt or nonbankrupt). After groups are established, data are gathered for the objects in the group. MDA attempts to derive a linear combination of these characteristics which best discriminates between the groups. The final discriminant function as follows:

$$
\begin{aligned}
Z = {} & 0.012 \times \text{Net working capital/Total assets} \\
& + 0.014 \times \text{Retained earnings/Total assets} \\
& + 0.033 \times \text{EBIT/Total assets} \\
& + 0.006 \times \text{Market value of equity/Book value of liabilities} \\
& + 0.999 \times \text{Sales/Total assets}
\end{aligned}
$$

The *Z*-score model is dependent on five variables. The working capital to total assets ratio is a measure of net liquid assets of the firm relative to the total capitalization. A firm experiencing consistent losses will have shrinking current assets. The retained earnings to total assets ratio measures the leverage of the firm. Those firms with high retained earnings relative to total assets have financed their operations with retained earnings rather than debt. The third ratio, earnings before interest but after taxes (EBIT) to total assets, is a measure of productivity of the firm's assets. The fourth ratio, market value (MV) of equity to total liabilities, measures how much the firm's assets can decline in value before the liabilities exceed the assets and the firm becomes insolvent. The fifth ratio, sales to total assets, measures the sales-generating ability of the firm's assets.

A high *Z*-score represents a low probability of default, and a low *Z*-score represents a high probability of default. The model's classification accuracy was 95% one year before bankruptcy and 72% two years before. Accuracy of the model decreases as the time period is extended (it may also be unreliable in its predictive ability). Based on the study, it was concluded that firms with a *Z*-scores less than 1.81 are all bankrupt, while those with *Z*-scores greater than 2.99 fall into the nonbankrupt group. Those falling into the area between 1.81 and 2.99 require more analysis to determine their solvency status. The nonliquid asset ratios such as total debt to total assets, and cash flow to total debt are, in general, better predictors of bankruptcy than the liquid assets ratios such as quick ratio or net working capital to total assets.

Managers may use distress prediction models as a first step to understand the solvency status of their firms. A low *Z*-score (below 1.81) itself does not suggest that bankruptcy will occur. A firm may avoid bankruptcy by cash infusion and/r waiving of loan covenants by lenders.

ACQUISITION OF DISTRESSED FIRMS

Because of agency conflicts associated with operating a firm in distress, some suggest that the bankruptcy law should encourage a sale of the company through auction. Distressed firms are often acquired under competitive bidding. Acquirers are typically competing firms, and targets are purchased at a discount to prices paid for nonbankrupt firms.

A sell-off of assets can take place either through Section 363 of the US Bankruptcy code or as part of a plan of reorganization (Hotchkiss and Mooradian 1998; McBride 1996). Under a 363 sale, the company must first obtain an offer and then notify the court. The court in turn informs the shareholders and creditors. Creditors may engage advisers to seek other buyers. The judge at a court hearing must approve any sale.

A sale can also take place through a plan of reorganization. Creditors and shareholders are asked to vote on the plan and indicate their bid preference.

The company's management would be interested in evaluating competing bids in order to choose the best bid. A bid could be considered fair if the proposed investment by each bidder equals or exceeds the expected market value of the new securities that each is to receive under the proposed plan of reorganization. Typically, bidders may receive a combination of new debt, equity, preferred stock, and warrants in exchange for their investment. One may estimate the value of equity stake after the reorganization and compare it with the proposed purchase price. The difference between the two implies the value of the remaining securities being offered.[9]

VALUATION OF BANKRUPT FIRMS

In free cash flow valuation, the weighted average cost of capital (WACC) is used to discount cash flows. An algebraically equivalent, yet superior method is the CCF valuation (Ruback 2000).

[9] It is often difficult to estimate the value of other securities such as warrants and new debt.

Free cash flow valuation excludes interest tax shields because the discount rate, WACC, incorporates the tax advantage of debt. In CCF valuation, free cash flows plus interest tax shields are discounted at *pre-tax* WACC (expected asset return). Since the asset return does not change when capital structure changes, it is easier to implement CCF valuation.

Capital cash flow = Net Income + Depreciation – Capital expenditure – Δ Working capital + Cash interest

Or

= EBIT (1-T) + Depreciation – Capital expenditure – D Working capital + Interest tax shields

It is easier to implement the former approach because it incorporates corporate estimates of taxes that reflect the special circumstances facing the firm rather than mechanically finding the product of tax rate and taxable income.[10]

The appropriate discount rate is a before tax rate because the tax benefits of debt are already included in the capital cash flows (CCFs). The correct discount rate is the pre-tax WACC.

Pre-tax WACC = Weighted average costs of debt and equity = (D/V) K_D + (E/V) K_E

D/V and E/V are debt-to-value and equity-to-value ratio respectively; K_D and K_E are costs of debt and equity.

Cost of debt = $K_D = R_f + \beta_D$ (risk premium)

Cost of equity = $K_E = R_f + \beta_E$ (risk premium)

$$\text{pre-tax WACC} = \frac{D}{V}(R_f + \beta_D \times R_P) + \frac{E}{V}(R_f + \beta_E \times R_P)$$
$$= R_f + (D/V\ \beta_D + E/V\ \beta_E)\ R_P$$
$$= R_f + \beta_A\ (R_P)$$

$$\text{Since } \beta_A V = \beta_D D + \beta_E E$$
$$\text{Or } \beta_A = \beta_D D/V + \beta_E E/V$$

Note that the discount rate depends on R_f, β_A, and risk premium and does not incorporate D/V or E/V, that is, the pre-tax WACC is independent of capital structure and, hence, can be applied to all cash flows regardless of the capital structure in existence. In other words, pre-tax WACC, which is a function of asset beta, is constant. Both free cash flow valuation and CCF valuation provide the same answer. CCF valuation, however, is easier to implement.

The CCF valuation methodology is especially appropriate when the company being restructured has high leverage and complicated tax status resulting from net operating losses (NOLs), which is usually true of bankrupt firms. In a restructuring situation, all concerned parties would be interested in estimating the value of their claim after the transaction. Typically, creditors get equity in exchange for debt; promoters (majority shareholders) invest equity to keep the company alive. So they would be interested in estimating the value of equity after the transaction. To get an estimate, one should forecast CCF and discount it using pre-tax WACC. The terminal value is calculated assuming that CCFs grow at a constant rate in perpetuity, starting with the last year of the projections. Many bankrupt firms will have unused NOL carry forwards at the end of the projection period. These NOLs are not forecasted to continue in perpetuity (Gilson et al. 2000). Therefore the terminal value is estimated in two parts. The first

---

[10] In other words, in many instances it does not reflect the actual tax paid.

part extends the financial projections and simulates a firm's use of NOLs until the NOLs are used up or expire. During this extended projection period, CCFs are calculated as:

$$([\text{EBIT} - \text{interest}) \times \text{tax rate}] + \text{Cash flow adjustments} + \text{Tax shield due to NOLs} = \text{Capital cash flows}$$

In the second part of the terminal value calculation, the value of the firm is estimated as a growing perpetuity of CCF in the year following the extended forecast period. This cash flow does not include any NOL benefits. The present value of this portion of the terminal value is added to the present value of the CCFs during the extended forecast period to estimate the total terminal value.

The result of this exercise is the value of the *firm*. Subtracting the value of post-transaction debt yields the value of equity.[11]

THE ROLE OF VULTURE INVESTORS

Any large corporation is dependent on a large number of small investors for capital, as it is not possible for any single investor or a small group of investors to provide the necessary capital because, by definition, large companies have large requirements. Further, the law in some countries prevents financial institutions (e.g., banks) from holding equity or cross a certain threshold (e.g., mutual funds are prevented from holding more than a certain percentage of shares in any one company). Due to the wide dispersion of shareholding, no single investor will have an incentive to monitor a company. Since diversification can be achieved by holding a dozen stocks, it is possible for institutional investors to hold a small number of stocks and actively monitor the portfolio companies.

Shareholder activism comes from two sources: institutional shareholders and wealthy individuals. Activism may take on two approaches:

- Presenting a proposal at a shareholders' meeting
- Prodding the company's management to change the strategy and/or CEO.

Agency costs are more severe for distressed firms in the sense that they can resort to Chapter 11 as a means of entrenchment. An active market for trading of financial claims of distressed firms has emerged in the last two decades. Vulture investors purchase a significant share of the firm's debt with the objective of influencing the terms of the restructuring. For instance, Marvel Entertainment was the target of Carl Icahn when it filed for bankruptcy. While some vulture investors buy undervalued financial claims (debt) with the objective of making a profit, others join the board of directors and become the CEO or chairman. The post-restructuring performance of firms in which vultures have active participation tend to be somewhat better than anticipated (Hotchkiss and Mooradian 1997). Both stock and bond markets react positively to vulture purchases. One plausible explanation for the positive reaction is that

[11] One may also use the adjusted present value methodology to value the firm.

vultures expedite the resolution of distress, resulting in higher firm value that benefits everyone.

THE SENSITIVITY OF CEO PAY TO PERFORMANCE IN DISTRESSED FIRMS

The rise in the usage of stock options and management compensation has attracted lot of attention in the media. The critics complain that executive compensation is excessive and that stock-based compensation does not motivate employees to outperform competitors. Academic studies of the link between pay and performance in solvent firms have sought to address the following issues:

- What elements of compensation lead to superior corporate performance? For example, do those executives who get fixed salaries do as well or better than those who get a variable pay?
- How should CEO pay be correlated with performance?
- How has direct stock ownership of CEOs changed over time?
- How sensitive is pay for performance?

Most CEO pay packets contain salary, bonus, stock options, and long-term incentive plans. To test the association between pay and performance, it is necessary to define pay and performance correctly. Academic studies have broadly tested for correlation between pay (as measured by salary and bonus) and changes in the market value of the firm. One of the most widely quoted studies on executive compensation is by Jensen and Murphy (1990a, 1990b). They use a least squares regression to calculate the relation between the dollar change in salary and bonus, and in the shareholder wealth for all companies with at least 7 years of pay-change data from 1975 to 1988. They use the previous year's performance (shareholder wealth) in addition to the current year's performance. The regression result for one CEO is given below:

(Change in Salary and Bonus) = $32,300 + 0.000986 (Change in this year's shareholder wealth) – 0.000219 (Change in last year's shareholder wealth).

The total expected change in salary and bonus is the sum of the two coefficients +98.6 cents and –21.9 cents (= 77 cents) per US$1,000 change in value. They estimate regressions for all CEOs and find that for the median CEO in the 250 largest companies, a US$1,000 change in corporate value corresponds to just 6.7 cents in salary and bonus over 3 years. CEOs also hold stock options. Jensen and Murphy also estimate the changes in market value and the value of stock option holding. If we account for all monetary benefits—cash, bonus, stock options, and shares owned—a US$1,000 change in corporate value corresponds to a change in CEO compensation of US$2.59.

The sensitivity of CEO wealth to firms' stock price performance after financial distress is, however, much higher (Gilson and Vetsuypens 1993). They find that almost one-third CEOs are replaced in the year of default; those who retain their job experience large declines in salary and bonus; CEOs who come from outside the organization are often compensated with stock options. They also find that when shareholder wealth increases by US$1,000 in years after bankruptcy or restructuring, outside replacement CEOs realize an average US$49.10 increase in their personal wealth.

POST-BANKRUPTCY CAPITAL STRUCTURE AND PERFORMANCE

Care must be taken in designing the company's capital structure when it emerges from bankruptcy, especially when the industry is volatile. As a thumb rule, one may benchmark nonbankrupt firms or the industry average. If the company emerges with a high level of debt, it may have to issue equity to bring down the leverage in future. This is especially important when the company is making large capital investments that require financial flexibility; a company with heavy debt load may have to pass up valuable investment opportunities. The post-bankruptcy capital structure depends on the securities issued to the bidder.

Some studies have documented the equity performance of firms emerging from bankruptcy. These studies find that the stocks of such companies produce positive abnormal long-run (200 days after emergence) returns (about 25%). Further, long-term returns are higher when institutional investors accept only equity in a reorganized firm. Other studies of post-bankruptcy performance find that over 40% of firms (in the sample) that emerge from Chapter 11 continue to experience operating losses in the 3 years following bankruptcy; 32% reenter bankruptcy or privately restructure their debt.

CONCLUDING COMMENTS

Most bankruptcy systems have two prime objectives, namely, allocating risk among participants in the economy in a way that is equitable and transparent, and maximizing the value of the insolvent firm for the benefit of all concerned parties. Disputes usually center on whether to liquidate or reorganize the firm, whether to allow the exiting management to continue or not, and who gets paid, how much, and when. Where to strike the balance between the rights of debtors and creditors is a political decision.

REFERENCES AND SUGGESTED READINGS

Altman, Edward. 1968. "Financial Ratios, Discriminant Analysis and the Prediction of Corporate Bankruptcy." *Journal of Finance*, 23 (4): 589–609.

———. 1993. *Corporate Financial Distress and Bankruptcy*, 2nd ed. Somerset, NJ: John Wiley.

———. 2000, July. "Predicting Financial Distress of Companies: Revisiting the Z-score and Zeta Models." Stern School of Business (working paper, available at http://pages.stern.nyu.edu/~ealtman/Zscores.pdf [Accessed on October 13, 2017]).

Altman, Edward, Haldeman R., and P. Narayanan. 1997. "Zeta Analysis: A New Model to Identify Bankruptcy Risk of Corporations." *Journal of Banking and Finance*, 1 (1, June): 29–54.

Altman, Edward, J. Caouette and P. Narayanan. 1998. "Credit Risk Measurement and Management: The Ironic Challenge in the Next Decade," *Financial Analysts Journal*, (January–February): 7–11.

Andrade, Gregor, and Steven Kaplan. 1998. "How Costly is Financial (Not Economic) Distress? Evidence from Highly Leveraged Transactions that Became Distressed." *Journal of Finance*, 53 (5, October): 1443–93.

Asquith, Paul, Robert Gertner, and David Scharfstein. 1991, November. "Anatomy of Financial Distress: An Examination of Junk-Bond Issuers." *Quarterly Journal of Economics*, 109 (3): 625–58.

Baldwin, Carliss Y., and Scott P. Mason. 1990. *Massey-Ferguson Ltd, 1980*. Harvard Business School Case No. 9-282-043, Harvard Business School.

Barclay, Michael J., and Clifford Smith, Jr. 1995. "The Maturity Structure of Corporate Debt." *Journal of Finance*, L (2, June): 609–31.

Claessens, Stijn, Simeon Djankov, and Daniela Klingebiel. 1999, November. How to Accelerate Corporate and Financial Sector Restructuring in East Asia. Note No. 200, Public Policy for the Private Sector, World Bank.

Claessens, Stijn, Simeon Djankov, and Giovanni Ferri. 1999, January. "Corporate Distress in East Asia: The Effect of Currency and Interest Rate Shocks." Note No. 172, Public Policy for the Private Sector, World Bank.

DeAngelo, Harry, Linda DeAngelo, and Karen. H Wruck. 2002. "Asset Liquidity, Debt Covenants and Managerial Discretion in Financial Distress: The Collapse of L.A Gear." *Journal of Financial Economics*, 64 (1, April): 3–34.

Denis, David J., and Diane K. Denis. 1995. "Causes of Financial Distress Following Leveraged Recapitalizations." *Journal of Financial Economics*, 37 (2): 129–57.

Donaldson, Gordon. 1969. "Strategy for Financial Emergencies." *Harvard Business Review*, 47 (November–December): 67–79.

Eberhart, Allan C., Edward Altman, and Reena Aggarwal. 1999. "The Equity Performance of Firms Emerging from Bankruptcy." *Journal of Finance*, 54 (5, October): 1855–68.

Fenster, Steven R. 1993, November. "Note on International Comparisons Concerning Troubled Companies." Harvard Business School Case No. 9-293-090, Harvard Business School.

Fialski, Heiko. 1994. "Insolvency Law in the Federal Republic of Germany." in *Corporate Bankruptcy and Reorganization Procedures in OECD and Central and Eastern European Countries*. Organization for Economic Co-operation and Development.

Franks, Julian R., Kjell Nyborg, and Walter N. Torous. 1996. "A Comparison of US, UK and German Insolvency Codes." *Financial Management*, 25 (3, Autumn): 86–101.

Franks, Julian R., and Walter Tourous. 1994. "A Comparison of Financial Recontracting in Distressed Exchanges and Chapter 11 Reorganizations." *Journal of Financial Economics*, 35: 349–70.

Gilson, S. C. 1989. "Management Turnover and Financial Distress." *Journal of Financial Economics*, 25 (2): 241–62.

———. 1992. "Continental Airlines-1992." HBS Case No. 9-293-132, Harvard Business School.

———. 1995. "Investing in Distressed Situations: A Market Survey." *Financial Analysts Journal*, 51 (6, November–December): 8–27.

Gilson, S. C., Edith Hotchkiss, and Richard Ruback. 2000. "Valuation of Bankrupt Firms." *Review of Financial Studies*, 13 (1): 43–74.

Gilson S. C., and Michael Vetsuypens. 1993. "CEO Compensation in Financially Distressed Firms: An Empirical Analysis." *Journal of Finance*, XLVIII (2, June).

Hausch, Donald, and Ramachandran. 1999, November. "Corporate Debt Restructuring: A Proposal for East Asia." Note No. 201, Public Policy for the Private Sector, World Bank.

Hegedus, Eva. 1994. "The Hungarian Framework for Bankruptcy and Reorganization and its Effect on the National Economy." In *Corporate Bankruptcy and Reorganization Procedures in OECD and Central and Eastern European Countries*. Organization for Economic Co-operation and Development.

Hill, Steve. 1994. "Corporate Workouts: Options under UK Legislation." In *Corporate Bankruptcy and Reorganization Procedures in OECD and Central and Eastern European Countries*. Organization for Economic Co-operation and Development.

Hotchkiss, Edith. 1995, March. "Post-bankruptcy Performance and Management Turnover." *Journal of Finance*, L (1): 401–32.

Hotchkiss, Edith S, and Robert Mooradian. 1997. "Vulture Investors and the Market for Control of Distressed Firms." *Journal of Financial Economics*, 43 (3): 401–32.

———. 1998. "Acquisition as a Means of Restructuring Firms in Chapter 11." *Journal of Financial Intermediation*, 7 (3, July): 240–62.

Jensen M. C. 1991. "Corporate Control and the Politics of Finance." *Journal of Applied Corporate Finance*, 4 (2): 13–33.

———. 1993. "The Modern Industrial Revolution, Exit and the Failure of Internal Control Systems." *Journal of Finance*, 48 (3, July) 831–80.

Jensen M. C., and Kevin Murphy. 1990a. "CEO Incentives: It's Not How Much You Pay, But How." *Harvard Business Review*, 68 (3, May–June): 138–53.

Jensen M. C., and Kevin Murphy. 1990b. "Performance Pay and Management Incentives." *Journal of Political Economy*, 98 (2, April): 225–64.

Jensen, Michael. 1989. "Active Investors, LBOs and the Privatization of Bankruptcy." *Journal of Applied Corporate Finance*, 2 (1, Spring): 35–44.

Kaplan, Steven. 1994. "Campeau's Acquisition of Federated: Post-bankruptcy Results." *Journal of Financial Economics*, 35 (1): 123–36.

La Porta, Rafael, Florencio Lopez-de-Silanes, and Andrei Shleifer. 1998. "Law and Finance." *Journal of Political Economy*, 106 (6): 1113–55.

La Porta, Rafael, Florencio Lopez-de-Silanes, Andrei Shleifer, and Robert Vishny. 1997. "Legal Determinants of External Finance," *Journal of Finance*, 52 (3, July): 1131–50.

———. 2000. "Investor Protection and Corporate Governance." *Journal of Financial Economics*, 58 (1–2): 3–27.

Lafont, Hubert. 1994. "The French Bankruptcy System." In *Corporate Bankruptcy and Reorganization Procedures in OECD and Central and Eastern European Countries*. Organization for Economic Co-operation and Development.

Leechor, Chad. 1999, September. "Innovations in Bankruptcy-Pricing the Priority of Insolvency Claims." Note No. 198, Public Policy for the Private Sector, World Bank.

Luehrman, Timothy, and William A. Teichner. 1992, January. "Note on Bankruptcy in the United States." Harvard Business School Case No. 9-292-062, Harvard Business School Case.

McBride, J. Michael. 1996. *Purchase and Sale of Assets in Bankruptcy*. New York, NY: John Wiley & Sons.

Opler, Tim, and Sheridan Titman. 1994. "Financial Distress and Corporate Performance." *Journal of Finance*, 49 (3): 1015–40.

Organization for Economic Co-operation and Development. 1994. *Corporate Bankruptcy and Reorganization Procedures in OECD and Central and Eastern European Countries*. Paris, France: OECD.

Pinegar, Michael, and R. Ravichandran. 2001, May. "The Idiosyncratic Nature of Sibling ADRs Issued by Mexican Firms: A Clinical Study." Unpublished Working Paper, Northern Arizona University.

Ramachandran, S. 1995, March. "Bankruptcy's Role in Enterprise Restructuring: A Hammer to Turn a Screw. Note No. 38, Public Policy for the Private Sector, World Bank.

Rowat, Malcolm. 1999, June. "Reforming Insolvency Systems in Latin America." Note No. 187, Public Policy for the Private Sector, World Bank.

Ruback, Richard S. 2000, March. "Capital Cash Flows: A Simple Approach to Valuing Risky Cash Flows." *Financial Management*, (Summer): 85–103.

Shefrin, Hersh. 1999. *Beyond Fear and Greed: Understanding Behavioral Finance and the Psychology of Investing*. Boston: Harvard Business School Press.

———. 2001. "Behavioral Corporate Finance." *Journal of Applied Corporate Finance*, 14 (3, Fall): 113–26.

Shleifer, A., and R. W. Vishny. 1997. "A Survey of Corporate Governance," *The Journal of Finance*, LII (2, June): 737–83.

Swaim, C. Hall. 1994. "United States Bankruptcy: Reorganization Laws." In *Corporate Bankruptcy and Reorganization Procedures in OECD and Central and Eastern European Countries*. Organization for Economic Co-operation and Development.

Szlezak, Andrzej. 1994. "Polish Bankruptcy and Reorganization Law." In *Corporate Bankruptcy and Reorganization Procedures in OECD and Central and Eastern European Countries*. Organization for Economic Co-operation and Development.

Tichy, Lubos. 1994. "The Bankruptcy Code of the Czech Republic." In *Corporate Bankruptcy and Reorganization Procedures in OECD and Central and Eastern European Countries*. Organization for Economic Co-operation and Development.

White and Case, LLP. 2000. "Amendment to Czech Bankruptcy Act." Available at http://www.whitecase.com/memo_czech_bankruptcy_act.html (Accessed on January, 2006).

Yakovlev, V. F. 1994. "The Legislation of the Russian Federation Concerning Bankruptcy." In *Corporate Bankruptcy and Reorganization Procedures in OECD and Central and Eastern European Countries*. Organization for Economic Co-operation and Development.

REVIEW QUESTIONS

1. What are the causes of financial distress?
2. Write a note on valuation in distressed settings.
3. Compare and contrast the insolvency code in US and UK.
4. Explain the debt restructuring mechanism in India.
5. Describe Altman's distress prediction model.

APPENDIX 13A: A COMPARISON OF INSOLVENCY CODES

Characteristics	UK	US	Germany	France
Direct costs	Lower	Higher	Medium	NA
Automatic stay of secured debt	Yes	Yes	No	Yes
Control rights	Creditors in control	Debtor in control	Creditors committee in control	NA
New financing in reorganization	Constrained	Easily accommodated	Can be arranged	NA

Source: Franks, Julian R. et al. (1996), Fialski, Heiko (1994), Hill, Steve (1994).

CHAPTER

14 Employee Share Ownership Plans

Corey Rosen

Learning Objectives

- Highlight the legislative models of employee ownership in an international context
- Highlight the nonlegislated models of employee ownership
- Highlight the US experience with employee share ownership plans (ESOP)
- Highlight the empirical evidence on the link between employee ownership and corporate performance

EMPLOYEE OWNERSHIP IN A GLOBAL CONTEXT

Employee ownership is growing rapidly in many countries around the world, largely as a result of explicit government policies, changes in the organization of work, and, in some cases, tightening labor markets. The USA has been the leader in the development of employee ownership, through employee stock ownership plans (ESOPs), employee stock purchase plans (ESPPs), and stock option plans that provide options to most or all of a company's employees. There are about 11,500 ESOPs in the USA, covering an estimated 8.5 million employees, and 7 to 10 million employees now receive stock options through broad-based stock option plans. ESOPs are found primarily in closely held companies (companies whose stock is not traded on a stock exchange); options are more common in public companies and rapidly growing knowledge-intensive companies. It is estimated that approximately 20% of all public companies in the USA now offer options to all or most employees, at least five times what the number was at the beginning of the decade. In addition, millions of employees buy stock in their companies through ESPPs (ESOPs and stock options are paid for by the company). While there is no firm estimate of just how many people buy stock, it certainly exceeds 10 million.

However, employee ownership is not just growing in the USA. Several countries have passed laws to encourage broad-based ownership, while companies in many other countries are using existing laws on stock ownership to craft more broadly granted ownership plans. A few hundred multinational companies also now offer ownership to employees across multiple boundaries. This chapter looks at the forms or broad-based ownership. The second section of this chapter looks at the US experience in detail, because that is where the idea has most firmly taken root. The first section looks at specific models for employee ownership legislation in other countries, along with a brief description of employee ownership alternatives where there is no specific legislation.

Britain and Ireland have legislation similar to the USA. Both have ESOPs, stock options plans that are increasingly being offered to rank-and-file employees, and savings plans that encourage investment in employer stock. The Blair government has established a goal of making employee ownership commonplace in the next several years. At least 500 companies with several million employees have plans in those two countries combined. On the European continent, France requires larger companies to provide profit sharing for employees, with one of the options being to invest in company stock. A number of Canadian provinces also now have plans to encourage employee purchases of shares in their companies.

In addition, many former communist countries, as well as China, are using employee ownership as a major part of their privatization programs. Generally, these programs provide employees with opportunities to purchase shares on very favorable terms. In Poland, employee ownership has been responsible for more privatizations than any other method, while Hungary has specific legislation similar to the US and British ESOP model. About 150 Hungarian companies have used this model to privatize. Slovenia has used employee ownership very successfully to privatize a number of its industries. Employee ownership has played a more nominal role in many privatizations in Western countries as well. In addition, there are large worker cooperative sectors in Spain and Italy. Employee ownership is less common, however, in developing countries, where only a few countries, most notably Egypt, Jamaica, and Zimbabwe, have made an explicit effort to encourage this development. Egypt has progressed the farthest, with legislation requiring all privatizations to include broad employee ownership through a trust-like arrangement. Employees must own at least 10% of all privatized companies. Jamaica has the most comprehensive statute of any country, offering multiple modes for employees to become owners, but serious economic problems in that country have impeded the development of employee ownership.

LEGISLATIVE MODELS FOR EMPLOYEE OWNERSHIP

The USA, Britain, Ireland, and Canada have the most comprehensive employee ownership legislation among the developed countries; Poland, Hungary, Slovenia, and Russia the most developed frameworks in former communist countries; and Egypt and Jamaica the strongest government role in developing countries. Employee ownership may actually proceed fastest in China. Although it lacks any legislative model, local governments appear to be using employee ownership widely as a means to privatize businesses they own, especially in the booming southwest part of the country.

The US/UK model has three basic components. First, ESOPs provide that companies can establish nontaxable employee benefit trusts to hold shares for employees. Companies fund these trusts by (a) contributing new issues of shares directly to them, (b) contributing cash to buy shares, or (c) having the trust borrow money to buy shares, with the company repaying the loan. Within very broad parameters, company contributions in each case are tax deductible. Employees do not purchase shares, directly or indirectly, under these arrangements. Sellers of shares to these plans in nonlisted companies can also qualify for special tax treatment of their capital gains, and employees do not pay tax on the benefit they receive until they actually take the shares out of the trust. In return for tax benefits, companies must run the plans in defined ways that do not discriminate in favor of higher paid employees. Companies have the right to determine who the trustees of the plan will be, but the trustees must comply with legal standards to act "for the exclusive benefit of plan participants." Employees do not get their shares until they leave the company, at which time they can shelter taxation of the shares by putting them into a retirement account. ESOPs are found in both listed and nonlisted companies.

A second legislative component encourages employee share purchases. In the USA, this is done through two approaches. One approach allows companies to provide employees the opportunity to use after-tax payroll deductions to purchase shares at up to a 15% discount off either the current price or a price defined at the time they committed to make the purchase (most plans provide for this "look-back" feature over a 6- or 12-month period). For instance, an employee might join the plan on June 1, pledging to put US$50 per week into the plan for the next 26 weeks. At the end of that 6-month period, the employee can take the US$1,300 that has accumulated and purchase shares at either 15% off the price of the stock on June 1 or 15% off the price of the shares on December 1. Some companies provide a longer offering period, while others provide shorter periods or less generous discounts. There are no special tax incentives for these plans for companies or employees.

A second approach allows employees to purchase shares out of pre-tax earnings in a special kind of savings plan; companies often put their own shares into these plans as a company contribution as well. For instance, an employee might agree to defer US$50 per week, before taxes are paid on that amount, into a company-sponsored savings plan. He or she could invest part or all of that in company stock, and the company might match some of that investment with company stock as well. While the investments are in the plan, they are not taxed.

In the UK, the plans are very similar. The Save-as-You-Earn plan allows employees to put pre-tax money aside into an account where it earns interest, with an option during a defined period to purchase company shares at the price they were offered at the start of the savings period. If the employee chooses not to purchase shares, he or she gets the money put aside back, plus interest.

Under a newly enacted plan, the so-called share investment plan (SIP, formerly called the AESOP, or all-employee share ownership plan), companies are given a menu of choices:

1. Employees can buy up to 3,000 pounds of stock per year from pre-tax salary.
2. Employers can match employee deferrals with tax-deductible free shares on up to a two-for-one basis.
3. Employers can contribute tax-deductible free shares on a nonmatching basis for up to 3,000 pounds per employee per year.
4. Dividends on shares can be reinvested in dividend shares.

Shares left in the AESOP trust for 5 years are not subject to payroll or social insurance taxes. Matching or free shares are held 3 to 5 years; employees pay income tax on the market value of the shares at the lower of the current market price or the price on grant. If these shares are held under fewer than 3 years, taxes are due on the market value of their shares as of the date they are withdrawn. Shares employees purchase are subject to income and social insurance taxes based on the gain made on the shares.

Finally, companies in both countries, as well as a growing number of other countries, are offering stock options not just to executives but to most or all employees. Options allow employees to purchase shares at a price fixed for a defined number of years into the future. If the shares do not go up in value, the option is not exercised; if they do, they can be exercised, and the employee realizes an often substantial gain. The specific tax and accounting treatment of these plans vary, but generally, the employee does not pay any tax until the option is exercised and an actual gain is received. Generally, if the shares are held for a minimum period, the gains are taxed as a capital gain (which is usually a lower rate); otherwise, they are taxed as wages. Companies can usually deduct the cost of providing the option when it is taxed as ordinary income; treatment varies for the company when it is taxed to the employee as a capital gain.

Companies are granting broad options mostly to attract and retain good people, not because of any specific legislative strategy, although the potentially favorable tax treatment of options to employees relative to other forms of income makes them an attractive compensation vehicle. However, the tax treatment of options is not always favorable. Some countries, such as France, provide punitive taxes on options; others, such as some Northern European counties, tax options on grant, meaning that the employee must pay tax on the acquisition of the right to buy shares. An employee might never actually use this right, however, if the share price goes down.

Increasingly, multinational companies, especially those based in the USA and the UK, are offering variations of their options or share purchase plans to all their employees worldwide. This is occurring despite the manifold difficulties of implementing and administering these plans in multiple countries with widely varying laws.

A few provinces in Canada have created a somewhat different approach to employee ownership. British Columbia has the most advanced of these systems. There the government provides a tax credit of up to 40% of the cost of purchase for employees who buy shares in British Columbia-based companies. The legislation requires that the share purchase program must be available to all employees in the company. Employees can also purchase the shares through their holdings in private, tax-deductible savings plans called Royal Savings Plans, further increasing the tax benefit. In addition, the government funded a provincial organization to promote the concept. Thanks to these efforts, the program has had considerable success in the province.

In former communist countries, as well as in China, employee ownership plays a role of varying significance as a means to privatize state-owned enterprises. In Russia, for instance, most large (over 200 employee) enterprises were privatized by allowing employees to buy a majority of the shares at heavily discounted prices. Employees would end up with a majority of the shares in these companies but were free to sell them at any time. As a result, employee ownership is gradually diminishing in Russia, although some companies will remain significantly owned by their workers for many years. In Poland, majority employee ownership through direct employee purchases also has been the most popular way to privatize enterprises, although most of the largest companies were sold in other ways. Unlike Russia, however, employees are holding on to their shares for much longer periods of time. Hungary created laws somewhat similar to the US ESOP, and about 150 companies were sold to employees this way. Most of these companies will remain employee-owned for some time because the shares are held in trust, not individually. Other Eastern European and former Soviet republics have used employee ownership as well, to varying degrees. Only in Poland, Slovenia, and Hungary, however, does employee ownership appear to have a chance to have any long-term presence in the economy.

In Egypt, the law requires that employees own at least 10% of privatized companies. Most large enterprises in Egypt were at one time owned by the government. They are now gradually being sold off, usually to the highest bidder. Employees, however, also acquire a stake in these companies through what is called an "employee shareholder association (ESA)." The ESA is given the shares at what is usually a less than market value, and they must pay for them over time out of dividends the shares earn. Employees can acquire larger stakes in the companies as well, and several companies have been sold entirely to employees. The employees receive an allocation of shares through the association and receive the shares when they leave the company, when they must be sold back to the association to allocate to new employees. Some of the ownership arrangements have been very successful, and employees have bought a majority stake in a number of companies. The difficulty with the Egyptian law is that it does not allow for share acquisitions through means other than dividends, so when companies do not make profits, the loans for the shares have to be renegotiated. Egyptian officials are currently reexamining the law to look for ways to make it work more effective.

The Slovenian law provides that 20% of the shares of a company are transferred to special pension and social funds for the benefit of the general populace, 20% are transferred to a special investment fund for future distribution to all Slovenian citizens, 20% are made available to free distribution to employees, and 40% are sold either to insiders on preferential terms or to commercial interests on market terms. If the 40% stake is sold to insiders, employees can buy shares at a 25% discount, with a cash down payment for at least 20% of these costs. The remaining shares are bought at a fixed price indexed for inflation over 4 years at an interest rate of 2%. In some cases, however, the entire company can be sold to employees via something like the Hungarian ESOP.

China presents one of the most intriguing, but difficult to document, cases. The central government has decreed that employee ownership is an important part of "socialism with Chinese characteristics." In the last few years, it has become the preferred method of privatization. Generally, employees can buy shares in privatized companies, and then can sell them only to other employees. Some provinces and/or companies provide for financing for the purchases. Unfortunately, good information on just how this is occurring, or how often, is very difficult to obtain. The National Center for Employee Ownership (NCEO) has held two conferences in China and received delegations from the State Committee of Economic Restructuring, officials from which have indicated that hundreds or thousands of businesses are being transformed this way. However, they do not know just how this is occurring or how often, but the number of enterprises sold this way is probably in the thousands.

The design of the Jamaican ESOP law is perhaps one of the most progressive in the world. The alternative forms of employee share ownership encompass employee share purchase arrangements, employer share granting schemes, and share option plans. The provision of the law that allows entities that have a "significant economic relationship" with an employer to receive ESOP shares is the only one of its kind in the world. The acquisition of shares can be accomplished through the following mechanisms:

- Employee purchases: Salary deferral, purchases made from loans by the company, or purchases made by savings or loaned funds from other sources than the employer.
- Employer grants: Either straight share grants or grants made to payoff a loan from a bank.

- Option awards: Where the appreciation of share value is captured by employees through the exercise of an option to purchase shares at a fixed price over a certain period of time.

However, a number of factors have hindered ESOP acceptance and implementation in Jamaica, including:

1. A prolonged economic decline that has resulted in drastically depressed share prices, high interest rates, sliding exchange rates, financial sector crisis, a halt to government divestments, and weakened investor confidence;
2. Antagonistic labor/management relations that result in mistrust, hostile negotiations, and high levels of employee terminations;
3. Structural concerns with the ESOP law itself, including restrictive provisions on participation requirements, ratios on the amount of shares that top and bottom level employees can purchase, and valuation issues;
4. Historical conceptions of ownership resulting in current owners forgoing provisions of the law that would allow employee grants of shares and insisting that any transformation of ownership be accomplished by employees purchasing shares; and
5. High costs of designing and administering an ESOP based on historical standards of what is the "normal" cost of implementing an employee benefit plan.

The use of employee ownership in privatizations has been primarily to win political support for the process by giving workers some of its benefits. That same idea informed a number of privatizations in Western countries, particularly England and to some extent in France. Employees could buy shares, usually up to 10% of the offering, at a reduced price, but they could (and usually did) sell them soon after when the share value went up.

Outside of Egypt, Zimbabwe is the only developing countries to look seriously at employee ownership so far on a countrywide basis. It is now in the stage of evaluating how to proceed.

EVALUATING EMPLOYEE OWNERSHIP MODELS

In evaluating the success of legislative approaches to employee ownership, one of the most notable features is that even with the best-developed legislation, the use and acceptance of plans is slow, taking place gradually over years or decades. The original legislation is almost invariably amended, sometimes frequently, as legislators learn about barriers that were previously not anticipated. In the USA, for instance, there have been about 400–800 new ESOPs set up every year since the law became effective, out of about 250,000 companies that would be candidates for ESOPs. The ESOPs now cover about 7% of the private sector workforce. In England, ESOP legislation has actually not been used very much; instead, plans similar to what the law envisions, but not completely within its bounds, have been submitted case by case to the government for approval. The new Labor government now appears likely to take these experiences and incorporate them into the basic statute.

Similarly, some of the most dramatic developments in employee ownership occur outside of the legislative models specifically designed to encourage it. This is most notable in the case of stock options. Originally, these were conceived simply as a means to reward executives. There were no special rules to encourage companies to grant them more widely. But starting in the late 1980s, many companies in the USA, and now in Britain as well, started giving them to most or all employees. This can raise some regulatory and legislative issues about how to rethink the laws for these plans so that they fit the emerging practice.

It is also notable that in every country where employee ownership has become a permanent and successful part of the economy, there are private organizations whose sole function is to promote a better understanding and awareness of the concept, such as the NCEO and the ESOP Association (and several local organizations) in the USA, the ESOP Centre in London, the Employee Share Ownership and Investment Association in Canada, and the ESOP Center in Hungary. These organizations provide information through meetings and publications, conduct training, maintain lists of qualified professional advisors, perform research, and help companies learn about "best practices" in the management of employee ownership, both legally and in terms of employee relations. They also help publicize successful models so that businesses and unions have a sense of how employee ownership can succeed. These organizations take time to develop and, once developed, more time to have an impact. Sharing ownership is a major change for most companies and employees; it is not realistic to expect that any law, no matter how well crafted, will result in a dramatic growth in employee ownership over the short term. It thus seems imperative that any country considering employee ownership assure that such an infrastructure is created along with it.

EMPLOYEE LEGISLATION APPROACHES

In terms of models for employee ownership legislation, there are three principal approaches. The most common is for employees to be allowed to purchase shares on some kind of subsidized and/or tax-favored basis. This has intuitive appeal. It is relatively simple. In privatization scenarios, it helps provide support for the sale of government enterprises to private interests. In reassures shareholders that they are not giving away ownership to employees, although there may be some company support to help employees buy stock. Perhaps most important, it complies with what seems to be a commonly held, if unproven, assumption that employees will really only value ownership if they have to pay for it themselves.

This approach raises many difficult issues, however. In many countries, employees cannot realistically be expected to buy much stock. Unless the plans require universal involvement, or have terms so appealing that hardly anyone will say no, it means that participation in the offering may be limited in terms of the percentage of employees buying shares. There will also usually be large disparities in shareholdings between employees. In many privatization cases, the subsidies are only offered at the time of privatization, meaning future employees will have little incentive to become owners. In nonprivatization cases, these plans rarely result in employees owning more than a small percentage of the company. Finally, and perhaps most seriously, the ability of employees to sell when they want (usually a feature of these plans) means that few will hold on to the shares very long. Often this means that not only will the total number of shares held by employees decline, but the number of employees owning stock will decline as well, especially where the subsidies are offered primarily at the program's start.

The second common approach is to offer broad-based stock options. While this does require employees to actually purchase shares at some point, it would be foolish for people not to buy the shares when the options are "in the money" (you can buy stock for less than its market price), unless of course the employee does not have the cash to make the purchase or there is an extended holding period subsequent to the purchase before employees can sell the stock (in which case there is at least a risk that the share price will decline below the purchase price). Companies usually solve this problem by providing mechanisms to make the money available to employees, or to provide a "cashless" exercise in which the company buys the shares for the employees and gives them the difference between the grant and exercise price, either in cash or in shares.

Option plans can be designed so that everyone participates, and by granting options on a regular basis, employees always have a future equity stake in the company even if they do periodically exercise some of their options and sell their shares.

On the other hand, shareholders sometimes object that options are granted too widely and too generously, diluting shareholder value. They may also complain that employees can get rewarded simply for the stock market in general going up, although option plan design can address this. Absent government rules about how options are distributed, there is a tendency to provide disproportionate amounts to top management, or provide only token amounts to employees. Employees also cannot use options to buy control of a company, and employees rarely hold a substantial collective ownership interest because they tend to sell shares quickly after they exercise the options. Options are, as a result, not a means for employees to exercise influence or control in a company.

Finally, there is the trust-based model, most notably the ESOP, but also the Jamaican and Egyptian versions. Unlike share purchase and option models, ESOPs do aggregate ownership and can be used to acquire large and ongoing stakes in the company for employees. New employees are automatically included in the pan under rules designed to assure equitable participation. Tax benefits can make the plans attractive to companies and employees.

On the other hand, ESOPs typically require the largest government subsidies. They are more complicated than other plans to design, regulate, and administer. They generally do not require direct employee investment. That is a plus in that it assures greater employee ownership, but to many shareholders and managers, it is a negative. They believe employees should have to purchase shares, not just be given them. This has been a particular issue in public companies, where shareholders want these plans to be "shareholder neutral," meaning employees either have to pay for the shares directly or through concessions.

There is, however, no perfect model for employee ownership. Each country's culture, tax and legal framework, economic situation, labor relations situation, corporate structure, and other issues must be addressed. In drafting legislation, however, several key issues need to at least be considered:

1. Is the goal to make employee ownership an ongoing and significant part of the economy, or is it just a transition vehicle? If it is the former, then means have to be created to assure that employees will have an ongoing equity stake in the company, not just shares they can quickly sell. Provisions also have to exist for new employees to become owners.
2. Is the goal to have employees own significant collective interest in companies that can be used as a substantial part of their personal wealth? If so, there will have to be incentives for the company and/or the employee to provide or acquire shares. It will be the rare case that employees will end of with large equity stakes primarily out of their own investment decisions, perhaps with small subsidies.
3. Is employee ownership seen as a way to transform corporate culture? If so, it is critical that the plan provide for significant amounts of ownership to all employees on an ongoing

basis. Having some employees own stock, but not others, makes it impossible for companies to ask employees to think and act like owners.

4. Is employee ownership seen as a mechanism for employees to exert control? If so, employees need to have specified voting rights, rights for board representation, and mechanisms for ongoing significant ownership.
5. Are there mechanisms in place to assure equitable treatment of participants? Most laws are at least aimed at equitable treatment for employees. Issues such as how shares are allocated, who can participate, when the share values can be realized, and so on need to be thought through carefully.
6. Are there procedures to assure stock is bought and sold at fair prices and that if employees are purchasing shares, they have appropriate information to make the choice?
7. Is there a way to make sure that companies and employees know about the program and the best practices for operating it? Absent such a central source of information, no employee ownership program is likely to succeed.

The creation of employee ownership legislation is obviously a complex process. The results that employee ownership has achieved, however, make it appear to be one that is well worthwhile.

NONLEGISLATED APPROACHES

In many countries, most notably India (in the technology sector) and Finland (in all sectors), it is very common for companies to provide options to a broad range of employees, and often to all employees. Tax laws for options vary considerably from country to country, but there is an emerging direction of change such that options are not taxed when they are granted, but rather either when they are exercised or the stock is sold (or both).

Stock options are just one form of an individual equity arrangement, so-called because stock is allocated to individuals, not to a trust or other collective ownership interest. There are four common kinds of individual equity plans, each of which can be found to varying degrees in different countries: stock options, restricted stock, equity equivalent plans—primarily stock appreciation rights (SARs) and phantom stock—and stock purchase plans. With limited exceptions, they can be given to anyone on any basis the company and the employee contractually agree to.

The most common form of individual equity compensation plans is the *stock option.* A stock option gives its holder the right to buy shares at a price fixed on grant for a defined number of years into the future. There are two principal kinds of stock options: nonqualified options and incentive stock options (ISOs). These will be described in more detail further.

The second-most common form of individual equity compensation is *restricted stock.* Restricted stock can entail an outright grant of stock or the sale of shares, either for full price or at a discount. The holder of the restricted stock, however, cannot take possession of the shares until specified conditions have been met, usually a certain number of years of service or some form of performance requirement (such as the company meeting profit targets or the individual's department meeting sales targets).

SARs and *phantom stock* are not actual awards of stock or the right to buy stock. Instead, they give the holder a cash bonus based on either the increase in the value of shares over a period of time (*SAR*) or the value of the stock itself (*phantom stock*). In theory, this award could be made in the form of an equivalent value in shares, but this is not common practice.

Restricted stock, phantom stock, and SARs are discussed in the next chapter in more detail.

STOCK OPTIONS DEFINITIONS

A few key concepts help define how stock options work:

Exercise: The purchase of stock with an option.

Exercise price: The price at which the stock can be purchased. This is also called the *strike price*. In most plans, the exercise price is the current fair market value of the stock at the time the exercise is made.

Grant price: How much the option holder must pay to exercise the option.

Spread: The difference between the grant price and exercise price at the time of exercise.

Option term: The amount of time the employee can hold the option prior to its expiring.

Vesting: The requirement, usually in years of service, which must be met for an option holder to be able to exercise an option.

In a typical option cycle, a company grants an employee options to buy a stated number of shares at a defined grant price. The options vest over a period of time. Once vested, the employee can exercise the option at the grant price at any time over the option term up to the expiration date. For instance, an employee might be granted the right to buy 1,000 shares at US$10 per share. The options vest 25% per year over 4 years and have a term of 10 years. If the stock goes up, the employee will pay US$10 per share to buy the stock. The difference between the US$10 grant price and the exercise price is the spread. If the stock goes to US$25 after 7 years, and the employee exercises all options, the spread would be US$15 per share.

Restricted Stock

Restricted stock provides the employee with the right to purchase shares at fair market value or a discount, or simply grants shares to employees outright. However, the shares employees acquire are not really theirs yet—they cannot take possession of the shares until specified restrictions lapse. Most commonly, the restriction is that the employee work for the company for a certain number of years, often three to five. The time-based restrictions may pass all at once or gradually. However, any restrictions could be imposed. The company could, for instance, restrict the shares until certain corporate, departmental, or individual performance goals are achieved. While the shares are subject to restrictions, companies can choose whether to pay dividends, provide voting rights, or give the employee other benefits of being a shareholder.

Phantom Stock and Stock Appreciation Rights

SARs and phantom stock are very similar plans. Both essentially are cash bonus plans, although some plans pay out the benefits in the form of shares. SARs typically provide the employee with a cash payment based on the increase in the value of a stated number of shares over a specific period of time. Phantom stock provides a cash or stock bonus, based on the value of a stated number of shares, to be paid out at the end of a specified period of time. SARs may not have a specific settlement date; like options, the employees may have flexibility in when to choose to exercise the SAR. Phantom stock may dividends; SARs would not. When the payout is made, it is taxed as ordinary income to the employee and is deductible to the employer. Some phantom plans condition the receipt of the award on meeting certain objectives, such as sales, profits, or other targets. These plans often call their phantom stock performance units. Phantom stock and SARs can be given to anyone, but if they are given out broadly to employees, there is a possibility that they will be considered retirement plans and will be subject to federal retirement plan rules. Careful plan structuring can avoid this problem.

Because SARs and phantom plans are essentially cash bonuses or are delivered in the form of stock that holders will want to cash in, companies need to figure out how to pay for them. Does the company just make a promise to pay or does it really put aside the funds? If the award is paid in stock, is there a market for the stock? If it is only a promise, will employees believe the benefit is as phantom as the stock? If it is in real funds set aside for this purpose, the company will be putting after-tax dollars aside and not into the business. Many small, growth-oriented companies cannot afford to do this. The fund can also be subject to excess accumulated earnings tax. On the other hand, if employees are given shares, the shares can be paid for by capital markets if the company goes public or by acquirers if the company is sold.

If phantom stock or SARs are irrevocably promised to employees, it is possible the benefit become will taxable before employees actually receive the funds. A "rabbi trust," a segregated account to fund deferred payments to employees, may help solve the accumulated earnings problem, but if the company is unable to pay creditors with existing funds, the money in these trusts goes to them. Telling employees their right to the benefit is not irrevocable, or is dependent on some condition (working another 5 years, for instance), may prevent the money from being currently taxable, but it may also weaken employee belief that the benefit is real.

EMPLOYEE STOCK PURCHASE PLANS

Broad-based Plans

Millions of employees become owners in their companies through ESPPs. These plans generally allow employees to have deductions taken out of their pay on an after-tax basis. These deductions accumulate over an "offering period." At a specified time or times, employees can choose to use these accumulated deductions to purchase shares or they can get the money back. Some plans can offer discounts on the price of the stock. Some plans allow this discount to be taken based on *either* the price at the beginning or end of the offering period (the so-called look-back feature). Other plans offer employees free matching shares for buying stock and/or holding on to stock after purchase.

ESPPs are found almost exclusively in public companies because the offering of stock to employees usually requires compliance with costly and complex securities laws. However, closely held companies can, and sometimes do, have these plans.

THE US EXPERIENCE

There are now over 25 million US employees who own stock in their companies through ESOPs, broadly granted stock options, or 401(k) plans with heavy concentrations of employer stock (a 401(k) plan is a kind of employee savings plan).

There are a number of reasons for this. ESOPs provide attractive tax benefits. They allow companies to borrow money and repay it in pre-tax dollars. They provide a way for owners of closely held businesses to sell all or part of their interests and defer taxation on the gain. And they make it possible for companies to provide an employee benefit simply by contributing tax-deductible shares of their own stock, among other benefits. Broad stock options do not provide special tax benefits, but give growing companies a way to compensate employees with equity rather than more cash. Putting company stock in 401(k) plans provides a less expensive way for companies to match employee deferrals than matching in cash. ESPPs (often called Section 423 plans, although not all such plans fall under this part of the tax code from which the name derives) allow employees to put aside part of their paychecks to buy stock, usually at a significant discount.

Just as important, however, are potential productivity gains. Studies consistently show that when broad employee ownership is combined with a highly participative management style, companies perform much better than they otherwise would be expected to do. Neither ownership nor participation accomplishes these significant gains on its own. Companies want employees to "think and act like owners." What better way to do that than to make them owners?

Finally, employees are beginning to expect equity, at least in some sectors. In technology firms, for instance, it is increasingly the norm to offer all employee stock options because companies do not have a hard time attracting good people.

As a result of all this, during the last decade, the number of companies sharing ownership broadly with employees has grown substantially. While precise numbers are not available, we estimate that employees own, or have options to own, stock worth about US$800 billion, or about 8% of all the stock in the USA.

As of January 2001, there were about 11,500 ESOPs in the USA covering over 8.5 million participants and controlling about US$500 billion in assets. Of these, about 5% are in publicly traded companies and 95% in closely held firms. The median percentage ownership for ESOPs in public firms is about 10%–15%. Most public firms maintain an ESOP along with other benefit plans. The median percentage ownership for private firms is about 30%–40%, with about 3,000 companies now majority employee-owned. While the typical firm has 20 to 500 employees, employees own a majority of the stock of such companies as Lifetouch (15,000 employees), TTC, Inc. (30,000 employees), Publix Supermarkets (109,000 employees), and Science Applications (39,000 employees). About half the ESOPs in private firms are used to buy out an owner; the rest are typically used as a primary employee benefit plan, sometimes in conjunction with borrowing money for capital acquisition.

While ESOPs are the main vehicle for employee ownership, 401(k) plans are not far behind. By 2000, these plans owned about US$250 billion in company stock, primarily in public companies. Based on various recent surveys, it appears about 60% of the corporate matching funds in public company 401(k) plans is in company stock, with a much smaller percentage in private firms. Employees can usually also choose to buy shares in their own company in public company 401(k) plans as well. Overall, in 2000, about 18% of all 401(k) assets were in the form of employer stock. While these plans own a great deal of company stock, they rarely own more than 10% of any one company, and few companies with employer stock in 401(k) plans really think of themselves as "employee ownership" companies.

In addition, a growing number of companies are providing stock options to most or all employees. PepsiCo, Starbucks, and Microsoft are among the better known examples. An estimated 15% to 20% of all public companies now do this, as well as perhaps thousands of private firms (no precise estimates are available). In one survey of electronics firms, just over half the responding companies said they provide options to most or all employees, with companies under 100 employees being the most likely to do so. A 2000 study by the NCEO concluded that at least 7 to 10 million employees now receive stock options through plans that offer stock to most or all employees. No reliable data are available on the value of all the outstanding employee options, but various surveys put it in the neighborhood of US$500 billion as of early 2001 (although a majority of that is in the hands of senior management). Stock option companies are not motivated by tax incentives, but rather by the conviction that sharing ownership builds a stronger company.

Finally, as many as 15 million employees participate in ESPPs, almost entirely in public companies. Typically, these plans allow employees to put aside payroll deductions for 6 to 12 months. Accumulated deductions can (but do not have to be) then used to buy stock, typically at 15% off the lowest of either the price at the end of the deduction period or the beginning. These plans have no special tax benefits for companies, but offer employees the potential to treat gains as capital gains. Unfortunately, there are no good data on the exact number of participants or the size of their holdings, but it would clearly be much less than the 401(k) plan assets in company stock.

Because ESOPs are the most complicated and most powerful employee ownership tool, we will start this overview with an explanation of how they work, followed by a discussion of stock options and 401(k) plans.

WHAT IS AN ESOP?

An ESOP is a kind of employee benefit plan. Governed by ERISA (the Employee Retirement Income Security Act), ESOPs were given a specific statutory framework in 1974. In the ensuing 12 years, they were given a number of other tax benefits. Like other qualified deferred compensation plans, they must not discriminate in their operations in favor of highly compensated employees, officers, or owners. To assure that these rules are met, ESOPs must appoint a trustee to act as the plan fiduciary. This can be anyone, although larger companies tend to appoint an outside trust institution, while smaller companies typically appoint a manager or create an ESOP trust committee.

The most sophisticated use of an ESOP is to borrow money (a "leveraged" ESOP). In this approach, the company sets up a trust. The trust then borrows money from a lender. The company repays the loan by making tax-deductible contributions to the trust, which the trust gives to the lender. The loan must be used by the trust to acquire stock in the company. Proceeds from the loan can be used by the company for any legitimate business purpose. The stock is put into a "suspense account," where it is released to employee accounts as the loan is repaid. However, for purposes of calculating the various contribution limits described further, the employee is considered to have received only his or her share of the principal paid that year, not the value of the shares released. After employees leave the company or retire, the company distributes to them the stock purchased on their behalf, or its cash value. In practice, banks often require a second step in the loan transaction of making the loan to the company instead of the trust, with the company reloaning the proceeds to the ESOP.

In return for agreeing to fund the loan through the ESOP, the company gets a number of tax benefits, provided it follows the rules to assure that employees are treated fairly. First, the company can deduct the entire loan contribution it makes to the ESOP, within certain payroll-based limits described further. That means that the company, in effect, can deduct interest and principal on the loan, not just interest. Second, the company can deduct dividends paid on the shares acquired with the proceeds of the loan that are used to repay the loan itself (in other words, the earnings of the stock being acquired help pay for the stock itself). Again, there are limits, as described in sections on the rules of the loan and contribution limits.

The ESOP can also be funded directly by discretionary corporate contributions of cash to buy existing shares or simply by the contribution of shares. These contributions are tax-deductible, generally up to 25%% of the pay of the total payroll of plan participants.

ESOP APPLICATIONS

The ESOP can buy both new and existing shares, for a variety of purposes.

- The most common application for an ESOP is *to buy the shares of a departing owner of a closely held company*. Owners can defer tax on the gain they have made from the sale to an ESOP if the ESOP holds more than 30% of the company's stock (and certain other requirements are met). Moreover, the purchase can be made in pre-tax corporate dollars.
- ESOPs are also used *to divest or acquire subsidiaries, buy back shares from the market (including public companies seeking a takeover defense), or restructure existing benefit plans* by replacing current benefit contributions with a leveraged ESOP.
- The use of ESOPs first envisioned by ESOP creator Louis Kelso was *to buy newly issued shares in the company, with the borrowed funds being used to buy new productive capital.* The company can, in effect, finance growth or acquisitions in pre-tax dollars while these same dollars create an employee benefit plan.
- These uses generally involve borrowing money through the ESOP (a leveraged ESOP), but a company can simply contribute new shares of stock to an ESOP, or cash to buy existing shares, *as a means to create an employee benefit plan.* As more and more companies want to find ways to tie employee and corporate interests, this is becoming a more popular application. In public companies especially, an ESOP contribution is often used as part or all of a match to employee deferrals to a 401(k) plan.

RULES FOR ESOP LOANS

ESOPs are unique among benefit plans in that they can borrow money. Typically, a lender will loan to the company, with the company reloaning the money to the ESOP. The ESOP then uses the loan proceeds to buy new or treasury shares of stock (when the ESOP is used to finance growth) or existing shares (when the ESOP is used to buy shares of current owners). Of course, the ESOP itself does not have any money to repay the loan, so the company makes tax-deductible contributions to the plan, which the plan then uses to repay the lender. This means, in effect, the company can deduct principal and interest on the loan, provided the requirements are met.

The ESOP can borrow money from anyone, including commercial lenders, sellers of stock, or even the company itself. However, any loan to an ESOP must meet several requirements. The loan must have reasonable rates and terms, and must be repaid only from employer contributions, dividends on shares in the plan, and earnings from other investments in the trust contributed by the employer. There is no limit on the term of an ESOP loan other than what lenders will accept (normally 5 to 10 years), and the proceeds from the sale of shares to the ESOP can be used for any business purpose.

Shares in the plan are held in a suspense account. As the loan is repaid, these shares are released to the accounts of plan participants. The release must follow one of two formulas. The simplest is that the percentage of shares released equals the percentage of principal paid, either that year or during whatever shorter repayment period is used. In such cases, however, the release may not be slower than what normal amortization schedules would provide for a 10-year loan with level payments of principal and interest. The principal-only method usually has the effect of releasing fewer shares to participants in the early years. Alternatively, the company can base its release on the total amount of principal and interest it pays each year. This method can be used for any loan, but must be used for loans of over 10 years.

In either case, it is important to remember that the value of the shares released each year is rarely the same as the amount contributed to repay the principal on the loan. If the price of the shares goes up, the amount released will be higher, in dollar terms, than the amount contributed; if the price goes down, the dollar value of the amount released will be lower. The amount *contributed* to repay the principal on the loan is what counts for determining if the company is within the limits for contributions allowed each year and for the purpose of calculating the tax deduction. The value of the shares released, however, is the amount used on the income statement, where it counts as a compensation cost.

LIMITATIONS ON CONTRIBUTIONS

In 2001, Congress made significant changes to contribution limits in all employee retirement plans. The discussion given describes how plans will operate when these rules become effective on January 1, 2002. At the end of this section, the major differences under law prior to this are described.

First, it is important to understand that in a leveraged ESOP, the amount the company is considered to have contributed to the ESOP, or that is defined as an "annual addition" to an employee's account, is based on the amount of principal paid off each year attributable to each employee's account. The actual addition to an employee's account, however, is the value of the shares released, but this value is not the one used for contribution and annual addition testing.

Congress was generous in providing tax benefits for leveraged ESOPs, but there are limits. Generally, companies can deduct up to 25% of the total eligible payroll of plan participants to cover the principal portion of the loan, and they can deduct all of the interest they pay. Eligible pay is essentially all the pay, including employee deferrals into benefit plans, of people actually in the plan, of US$200,000 per participant or less (in 2002 dollars). However, company contributions to other defined contribution plans, such as stock bonus, 401(k), or profit-sharing plans, must be counted in this 25% of pay calculation. On the other hand, "reasonable" dividends paid on shares acquired by the ESOP can be used to repay the loan, and these are not included in the 25% of pay calculations. If employees leave the company before they have a fully vested right to their shares, their forfeitures, which are allocated to everyone else, are not counted in the percentage limitations. If the ESOP does not borrow money, the annual contribution limit is now also 25% of covered pay (it had been 15%). Again, contributions to other plans reduce this amount.

However, there are a number of limitations to these provisions. First, no one ESOP participant can get a contribution of more than 100% of pay in any year from the principal payments on the loan that year that are attributable to that employee or more than US$40,000 (a number that will be increased for inflation in US$1,000 increments), whichever is less. In figuring payroll, pay over US$200,000 per year (in 2002 dollars) does not count toward total contribution limits. Second, if there are other qualified benefit plans, these must be taken into account when assessing this limit. This means that employee deferrals into 401(k) plans, as well as other employer contributions to 401(k) plans, stock bonus, or profit-sharing plans, are added to the ESOP contribution and cannot exceed 100% of pay in any year.

Third, the interest is only excludable from the 25% of pay individual limit if not more than one-third of the benefits are allocated to highly compensated employees, as defined by the Internal Revenue Code (Section 414 (q)). If the one-third rule is not met, forfeitures are also counted in determining how much an employee is getting each year. If the company sponsoring the ESOP is an S corporation, interest is also not deductible.

The rules that have been described apply for plan years after December 31, 2001. For plan years prior to that, rules were much more restrictive with respect to contribution limitations. The major differences are as follows:

- The limit on employer contributions in nonleveraged plans is only 15% of pay. "Pay" is defined to exclude employee deferrals into 401(k) plans (after 2001, it is included).
- The limitation on how much can be added to an employee account each year from employer contributions and employee deferrals is 25% of pay.
- Pay over US$170,000 is not defined as "eligible pay" for contribution limits.

USING DIVIDENDS TO REPAY THE LOAN

The Tax Reforms Act of 1986 allowed companies to take a tax deduction when using "reasonable" dividend payments to repay the ESOP loan. These payments do not count against the contribution limits described earlier. While the term "reasonable" has never been defined, most consultants believe it is a percentage of share value consistent with what other companies in the industry would pay, given similar levels of profits. Many companies are using preferred stock in their ESOPs to allow for higher dividend payments. Whatever kind of stock is used, the amount of the dividends must be allocated to employee accounts. Companies normally allocate these amounts in the form of shares released from the suspense account.

Companies can also "pass through" dividends directly to employees. Typically, companies would pay dividends on allocated shares (whether in a leveraged or nonleveraged plan). These dividends are also tax-deductible to the company. Finally, dividends that are voluntarily reinvested by the employee back into company stock in the ESOP are also tax-deductible to the company. It is possible to combine this arrangement with a 401(k) plan in such a way that the employee can do this on a pre-tax basis, something that is done mostly in publicly traded companies.

HOW SHARES GET TO EMPLOYEES

The rules for ESOPs are similar to the rules for other tax-qualified plans in terms of participation, allocation, vesting, and distribution, but several special considerations apply. All employees over age 21 who work for more than 1,000 hours in a plan year must be included in the plan, unless they are covered by a collective bargaining unit, are in a separate line of business with at least 50 employees not covered by the ESOP, or fall into one of several anti-discrimination exemptions not commonly used by leveraged ESOPs. If there is a union, the company must bargain in good faith with it over inclusion in the plan.

Shares are allocated to individual employee accounts based on relative compensation (generally, all W-2 compensation is counted), on a more level formula (such as per capita or seniority), or some combination. The allocated shares are subject to vesting. Employees must be 100% vested after 5 years of service, or the company can use a graduated vesting schedule not slower than 20% after 3 years and 20% per year more until 100% is reached after 7 years. A faster vesting schedule applies where the ESOP contribution is used as a match to employee 401(k) deferrals. The "cliff" vesting must be complete in 3 years and graduated vesting must start after 2 years and be completed no later than after 6 years.

When employees reach age 55, and have 10 years of participation in the plan, the company must either give them the option of diversifying 25% of their account balances among at least three other investment alternatives, or simply pay the amount out to the employees. At age 60, employees can have 50% diversified or distributed to them.

When employees retire, die, or are disabled, the company must distribute their vested shares to them not later than the last day of the plan year following the year of their departure. For employees leaving before reaching retirement age, distribution must begin not later than the last day of the sixth plan year following their year of separation from service. Payments can be in substantially equal installments out of the trust over 5 years, or in a lump sum. In the installment method, a company normally pays out a portion of the stock from the trust each year. The value of that stock may go up or down over that time, of course. In a lump sum distribution, the company buys the shares at their current value, but can make the purchase in installments over 5 years, as long as it provides adequate security and reasonable interest. ESOP shares must be valued at least annually by an independent outside appraiser unless the shares are publicly traded.

Closely held companies and some thinly traded public companies must repurchase the shares from departing employees at their fair market value, as determined by an independent appraiser. This so-called put-option can be exercised by the employee in one of two 60-day periods: one starting when the employee receives the distribution and the second period 1 year after that. The employee can choose which one to use. This obligation should be considered at the outset of the ESOP and factored into the company's ability to repay the loan.

VOTING RULES

Voting is one of the most controversial and least understood of ESOP issues. The trustee of the ESOP actually votes the ESOP shares. The question is, "who directs the trustee?" The trustee can make the decision independently, although that is very rare. Alternatively, management or the ESOP administrative committee can direct the trustee, or the trustee can follow employee directions.

In private companies, employees must be able to direct the trustee as to the voting of shares *allocated* to their accounts on several key issues, including closing, sale, liquidation, recapitalization, and other issues having to do with the basic structure of the company. They do not, however, have to be able to vote for the board of directors or other typical corporate governance issues, although companies can voluntarily provide these rights. Instead, the plan trustee votes the shares, usually at the direction of management. In listed corporations, employees must be able to vote on all issues.

Voting rights are more complicated than they seem. First, voting is not the same as tendering shares. So while employees may be required to vote on all issues, they may have no say about whether shares are tendered. In public companies, this is a major issue. Almost all public companies now write their plans to give employees the right to direct the tendering, as well as voting, of their shares, for reasons to be explained later.

Second, employees are not required to be able to vote on unallocated shares. In a leveraged ESOP, this means that for the first several years of the loan, the trustee can vote the majority of the shares, if that is what the company wants to do. The company could provide that unallocated shares, as well as any allocated shares for which the trustee has not received instructions, should be voted or tendered in proportion to the allocated shares for which directions were received.

What this all means is that for almost all ESOP companies, governance is not really an issue unless they want it to be. If companies want employees to have only the most limited role in corporate governance, they can; if they want to go beyond this, they can do that as well. In practice, companies that do provide employees with a substantial governance role find that it does not result in dramatic changes in the way the company is run.

VALUATION

In closely held companies and some thinly traded listed companies, all ESOP transactions must be based on a current appraisal by an independent, outside valuation expert. The valuation process assesses how much a willing buyer would pay a willing seller for the business. This calculation is performed by looking at various ratios, such as price-to-earnings, at discounted future cash flow and earnings, at asset value, and at comparable companies, among other things. It is then adjusted to reflect whether the sale is for control (owning a controlling interest in a business is worth more than owning a minority interest, even on a per share basis) and marketability (shares of public companies are worth more than closely held firms because they are easier to buy and sell). ESOP company shares have better marketability than nonESOP firms, however, because the ESOP provides a market, albeit not as active as a stock exchange.

TAX BENEFITS TO THE SELLING SHAREHOLDER

One of the major benefits of an ESOP for closely held firms is Section 1042 of the Internal Revenue Code. Under it, a seller to an ESOP may be able to qualify for a deferral of taxation of the gain made from the sale. Several requirements apply, the most significant of which are:

1. The seller must have held the stock for 3 years prior to the sale.
2. The stock must not have been acquired through options or other employee benefit plans.
3. The ESOP must own 30% or more of the value of the shares in the company and must continue to hold this amount for 3 years unless the company is sold. Shares repurchased

by the company from departing employees do not count. Stock sold in a transaction that brings the ESOP to 30% of the total shares qualifies for the deferral treatment.
4. Shares qualifying for the deferral can neither be allocated to accounts of children, brothers or sisters, spouses, or parents of the selling shareholder(s), nor to other 25% shareholders.
5. The company must be a "C" corporation.

If these rules are met, the seller (or sellers) can take the proceeds from the sale and reinvest them in "qualified replacement securities" within 12 months after the sale or 3 months before and defer any capital gains tax until these new investments are sold. Qualifying replacement securities are defined essentially as stocks, bonds, warrants, or debentures of domestic corporations receiving not more than 25% of their income from passive investment. Mutual funds and real estate trusts do not qualify. If the replacement securities are held until death, they are subject to a step-up in basis, so capital gains taxes would never be paid.

Increasingly, lenders are asking for replacement securities as part or all of the collateral for an ESOP loan. This strategy may be beneficial to sellers selling only part of their holdings because it frees the corporation to use its assets for other borrowing and could enhance the future value of the company.

It is also important to note that people taking advantage of the "1042" treatment cannot have stock reallocated to their accounts from these sales if they remain employees. Other 25% shareholders and close relatives of the seller also cannot receive allocations from these sales.

FINANCIAL ISSUES FOR EMPLOYEES

When an employee receives a distribution from the plan, it is taxable unless rolled over into an IRA or other qualified plan. Otherwise, the amounts contributed by the employer are taxable as ordinary income, while any appreciation on the shares is taxable as capital gains. In addition, if the employee receives the distribution before normal retirement age and does not roll over the funds, a 10% excise tax is added.

While the stock is in the plan, however, it is not taxable to employees. It is rare, moreover, for employees to give up wages to participate in an ESOP or to purchase stock directly through a plan (this raises difficult securities law issues for closely held firms). Most ESOPs either are in addition to existing benefit plans or replace other defined contribution plans, usually at a higher level of pay.

DETERMINING ESOP FEASIBILITY

Several factors are involved in determining if a company is a good ESOP candidate:

- *Is the Cost Reasonable?* ESOPs typically cost US$20,000 and up, depending on complexity and the size of the transaction. This is usually much cheaper than other ways to sell a business, but more expensive than other benefit plans.
- *Is the Payroll Large Enough?* Limitations on how much can be contributed to a plan may make it impractical to use to buy out a major owner or finance a large transaction. For

instance, a US$5 million purchase would not be feasible if the company has US$500,000 of eligible payroll because annual contributions could be no larger than US$125,000 (25%) per year, not enough to repay a loan for that amount.

It may be possible to go over this amount somewhat, however, through the use of deductible dividends. Companies can also set up the loan so that the bank loans to the company on one term (say 7 years) and the company reloans the money to the ESOP on another (say 12 years), meaning that the principal payments are stretched out longer and the percentage of pay required each year is smaller.

- *Can the Company Afford the Contributions?* Many ESOPs are used to buy existing shares, a nonproductive expense. Companies need to assess whether they have the available earnings for this.
- *Is Management Comfortable with the Idea of Employees as Owners*? While employees do not have to run the company, they will want more information and more say. Unless they are treated this way, research shows, they are likely to be demotivated by ownership.

REPURCHASE CONSIDERATIONS

One of the major issues ESOPs must face is the obligation that companies sponsoring them provide for the repurchase of the shares of departing employees. The legal obligation rests with the company, although it can fund this by making tax-deductible contributions to the ESOP, which the ESOP uses to repurchase the shares. Most companies either do this or buy the shares back themselves and then recontribute them to the ESOP (and take a tax deduction for that). Either way, shares continue to circulate in the plan, providing stock for new employees. Some companies, however, buy back the shares and retire them or have other people buy them (for instance, a manager).

The repurchase obligation may seem like a reason not to do an ESOP ("You mean we have to buy back the shares continually?," people often ask). In fact, all closely held companies have a 100% repurchase obligation at all times. An ESOP simply puts it on a schedule and allows the company to do it in pre-tax dollars. Nonetheless, repurchase can be a major problem if companies do not anticipate and plan for it. A careful repurchase study should be done periodically to help manage this process.

ESOPS IN SUBCHAPTER S COMPANIES

ESOPs can now own stock in Subchapter S corporations. While these ESOPs operate under most of the same rules as in a C corporation, there are important differences.

First, interest payments on ESOP loans count toward the contribution limits (they normally do not in C companies). Dividends paid on ESOP shares are also not deductible.

Second, and most importantly, sellers to an ESOP in an S corporation do not qualify for the tax-deferred rollover treatment.

Third, for plan years prior to January 1, 2002, the annual limit on contributions is 15% of pay per year, although the ESOP could be combined with a money purchase plan to get to the 25% limit.

On the other hand, the ESOP is unique among S corporation owners in that it does not have to pay federal income tax on any profits attributable to it (state rules will vary). This can make an ESOP very attractive in some cases. It also makes converting to an S corporation very appealing when a C corporation ESOP owns a high percentage of the company's stock.

For owners who want to use an ESOP to provide a market for their shares, generally it will make sense to convert to C status before setting up an ESOP. Where selling shares is not a priority, or where the seller either does not have substantial capital gains taxes due on the sale or has other reasons to prefer staying an S corporation, an S ESOP can provide significant tax benefits. However, owners must keep in mind that any distributions paid to owners must be paid pro rata to the ESOP. The ESOP can use these distributions to purchase additional shares, build up cash for future repurchases of employee shares, or just add to employee accounts.

While the S corporation rules make an ESOP very attractive, legislation passed in 2001 makes it clear that these rules are not meant to be abused by companies seeking to create the ESOP primarily to benefit a few people. For instance, some accountants were promoting plans in which a company would set up an S corporation management company owned by just a few people that would manage a large C corporation. The profits would flow through the S corporation, which would then not be taxed.

The rules Congress enacted are complicated, but boil down to two essential points. First, people who own more than 10% of the allocated shares in the ESOP or who own 20%, counting their family members, are considered "disqualified" persons. The ESOP ownership is defined to include synthetic equity as well, such as options. Second, if these disqualified people together own more than 50% of the company's shares (counting their synthetic equity), then they cannot get allocations in the ESOP without extraordinary tax penalties. Congress also directed the Internal Revenue Service (IRS to apply this onerous tax treatment to any plan it deems to be substantially for the purpose of evading taxes rather than providing employee benefits.

STEPS IN SETTING UP AN ESOP

If you have decided an ESOP is worth investigating, there are several steps to implement a plan. At each point, you may decide you have gone far enough, and that an ESOP is not right for you.

1. ***Determine if other owners are amenable***. This may seem like an obvious issue, but sometimes people take several of the steps listed here before finding out if the existing owners are willing to sell. Employees should not start organizing a buyout unless they have some reason to think that the parent firm is willing to sell (it may not be, for instance, if its goal is to reduce total output of a product it makes at other locations). Or there may be other owners of a private firm who will never agree to an ESOP, even if it seems appealing to the principal owners. They could cause a good deal of trouble down the road.
2. ***Conduct a feasibility study***. This may be a full-blown analysis by an outside consultant, replete with market surveys, management interviews, and detailed financial projections, or it may simply be a careful business plan performed in-house. Generally, full-scale feasibility studies are only needed where there is some doubt about the ESOP's ability to repay the loan. Any analysis, however, must look at several items. First, it must assess just how much extra cash flow the company has available to devote to the ESOP

and whether this is adequate for the purposes for which the ESOP is intended. Second, it must determine if the company has adequate payroll for ESOP participants to make the ESOP contributions deductible. Remember to include the effect of other benefit plans that will be maintained in these calculations. Third, estimates must be made of what the repurchase liability will be and how the company will handle it.

3. ***Conduct a valuation***. The feasibility study will rely on rough estimates of the value of the stock for the purpose of calculating the adequacy of cash and payroll. In public companies, of course, these estimates will be fairly accurate because they can be based on past price performance. In private companies, they will be more speculative. The next step for private firms (and some public companies as well) is a valuation. A company may want to have a preliminary valuation done first to see if the range of values produced is acceptable. A full valuation would follow if it is.
   Doing a valuation before implementing a plan is a critical step. If the value is too low, sellers may not be willing to sell. Or, the price of the shares may be too high for the company to afford. The valuation consultant will look at a variety of factors, including cash flow, profits, market conditions, assets, comparable company values, goodwill, and overall economic factors. A discount on value may be taken if the ESOP is buying less than 5% of the shares. The process is described in more detail later in this book.
4. ***Hire an ESOP attorney***. If these first three steps prove positive, the plan can now be drafted and submitted to the IRS. You should carefully evaluate your options and tell your attorney just how you want the ESOP to be set up. This could save you a considerable amount of money in consultation time. The IRS may take many months to issue you a "letter of determination" on your plan, but you can go ahead and start making contributions before then. If the IRS rules unfavorably, which rarely happens, normally you just need to amend your plan.
5. ***Obtain funding for the plan***. There are several potential sources of funding. Obviously, the ESOP can borrow money. Banks are generally receptive to ESOP loans, but, as with any loan, it makes sense to shop around. Sellers or other private parties can also make loans, but do not qualify for the interest income exclusion. Larger ESOP transactions can also tap the bond market or borrow from insurance companies. Another source of funding is ongoing company contributions, outside of loan repayments. While ESOPs must, by law, invest primarily in employer securities, most ESOP experts believe they can temporarily invest primarily in other assets while building up a fund to buy out an owner. A third source is existing benefit plans. Pension plans are not a practical source of funding, but profit-sharing plans are sometimes used. Profit-sharing assets are simply transferred in part, or entirely, into an ESOP. Many ESOP companies do this, but it must be done cautiously. If employees are given no choice in the switch, trustees of the plan must be able to demonstrate that the investment in company stock was prudent; if they are given a choice, there could be a securities law issue. Finally, employees can contribute to the plan, most commonly by wage or benefit concessions. Most ESOPs do not require these, but they are necessary in some cases. Clearly, this is an issue that must be handled very carefully.
6. ***Establish a process to operate the plan***. A trustee must be chosen to oversee the plan. In most private companies, this will be someone from inside the firm, but some private and most public companies hire an outside trustee. A separate article later in this publication addresses the pros and cons on this issue. An ESOP committee will direct the

trustee. In most companies, this is made up of management people, but many ESOP firms allow at least some nonmanagement representation. Finally, and most importantly, a process must be established to communicate how the plan works to employees and to get them more involved as owners. These issues are also addressed in more detail later in this publication.

BROAD-BASED STOCK OPTIONS

ESOPs each are "qualified" plans, meaning they must meet federal rules to assure that participation in them does not excessively favor more highly compensated people. Not every company wants to abide by these rules, nor does every company want the additional tax benefits they can offer. Moreover, some companies believe ownership means more if employees have to put something up to get it. Some growing companies find that contributing or purchasing existing stock is too much of a strain on either their capital structure or their finances, or both. They would prefer to give employees a right to future ownership. Many growing private companies do not pay taxes, so the tax benefits of an ESOP may not be attractive, making the greater flexibility of options more appealing. Finally, options have very favorable accounting treatment, something of particular significance to public companies.

For companies persuaded by one or more of these arguments, broad stock options make an attractive choice. The concept of granting stock options to most or all employees was almost unheard of as late as the end of the 1980's, with the exception of some start-up high growth firms. Microsoft, for instance, has created over 10,000 millionaires by giving stock options broadly to employees. Now, an estimated 15% to 20% of all public companies, such as PepsiCo, Starbucks, Bank of America/Nations Bank, Walgreens, Whole Foods, and Whirlpool, are providing options to most or all employees. As these examples indicate, these firms are not confined to high-tech fields; the trend cuts across all kinds of businesses. At the same time, a growing percentage of high-tech firms are giving stock options broadly. In a 1992 survey of electronics firms by ShareData, a San Jose stock options plan administrator, 30% of the respondents said they gave stock options to most or all full-time employees; the percentage grew to 54% by the time the survey was repeated 2 years later. The survey indicated that the smaller the company, the more likely it was to include most employees. A study by Joseph Blasi at Rutgers in 2000 found that 97 of the top 100 e-commerce companies granted options to most or all employees.

STOCK OPTION PROCEDURES IN THE USA

A stock option gives an employee the right to buy shares at a price fixed today (usually the market price, but sometimes lower) for a defined number of years into the future. The options might be granted on a percentage of pay basis, a merit formula, an equal basis, or any other formula the company chooses. Most broad-based plans provide grants regularly (every 1 to 3 years), either on the basis of the passage of time (for instance, every year) or an event (for instance, a promotion, meeting certain corporate or group targets, or a performance appraisal). The options are typically subject to a 3 to 5-year vesting, meaning that if someone is 20% vested, he or she can only exercise 20% of the options. An employee can usually exercise vested options at any time. Most options have a 10-year life, meaning the employee can choose to buy the shares at the grant price at any time they are vested for up to 10 years. The difference between the grant price and the exercise price is called the "spread."

Most public companies offer a "cashless exercise" alternative in which the employee exercises the option and the company gives the employee an amount of cash equal to the difference between the grant price and the exercise price, minus any taxes that are due.

Options can also be exercised with cash, although employees must have enough to pay for the shares and taxes (if any) by exchanging existing shares employee own, or by selling just enough of the shares acquired through the options to pay the costs and taxes, then keeping the remaining shares.

In closely held firms, employees usually have to wait until the company is sold or goes public to sell their shares, although some companies have arrangements to purchase the shares themselves or help facilitate buying and selling between employees. When an employee exercises an option, however, this constitutes an investment decision subject to securities laws. At a minimum, these require "anti-fraud financial disclosure statements" and, in some cases, will require securities registration as well. For this reason, broad stock options are used primarily in closely held firms when the intention is to sell or go public.

For public companies, broad options can impose a substantial dilution for other shareholders as new shares are issued to satisfy option holders. Alternatively, if the company buys shares to satisfy option exercises, there is a significant cash cost. Companies sponsoring these programs, however, contend that shareholders should be satisfied because the costs will only exist if their share price has increased. Management of these companies believe that the broad options more than pay for themselves in terms of increased corporate value.

Nonqualified Options

Most broad-based plans provide employees with nonqualified stock options, options that do not qualify for any special tax consideration. Anyone, employees or nonemployees, can be given a nonqualified option on any basis that the company chooses. When a nonqualified option is exercised, the employee must pay ordinary income tax on the "spread" between the grant and exercise price; the company can deduct that amount.

For example, say that Chip Salter, a mechanic at PepsiCo's Frito-Lay division, makes US$20,000 per year. Under PepsiCo's plan, Chip gets options worth 10% of pay each year, which vest at 20% per year over 5 years. So Chip gets to buy US$2,000 worth of PepsiCo stock at current market prices for 10 years. We'll assume that they were trading at US$40 when granted, so Chip has options on 50 shares ($40 x 50 = $2,000). Assume he holds onto these options for the full 10 years. At the end of 10 years, assume PepsiCo shares are now worth US$100. Chip can buy 50 shares worth US$100 each for just US$40, making a profit of US$60 per share, or US$3,000, on paper. To buy the shares at US$40 each, he can borrow the money or use cash. If he has existing shares, he can exchange those for the new shares he is purchasing (US$200 in shares would buy five shares at US$40 each, for instance). However he acquires the shares, he must pay ordinary income tax on US$3,000 in gain. PepsiCo gets a corresponding tax deduction.

Alternatively, and most commonly, he can have PepsiCo buy the shares for him, pay his tax, and give him what is left, probably about US$2,000.

INCENTIVE STOCK OPTIONS

With an ISO, a company grants the employee an option to purchase stock at some time in the future at a specified price. With an ISO, there are restrictions on how the option is to be structured and when the option stock can be transferred. The employee does not recognize ordinary income at option grant or exercise (although the spread between the option price and the option stock's fair market value may be taxed under the alternative minimum tax purposes), and the company cannot deduct the related compensation expense. The employee is taxed only upon the *disposition* of the option stock. The gain is all capital gain for a qualifying disposition. For a disqualifying disposition (i.e., one not meeting the rules specified for a qualifying disposition), the employee will recognize ordinary income.

For a stock option to qualify as an ISO (and, thus, receive special tax treatment under Code Section 421(a), it must meet the requirements of Section 422 of the code when granted and at all times beginning from the grant until its exercise. The requirements include:

- The option may be granted only to an employee (grants to nonemployee directors or independent contractors are not permitted) who must exercise the option while still an employee or no later than 3 months after termination of employment (unless the option is disabled, in which case this 3-month period is extended to 1 year).
- The option must be granted under a written plan document specifying the total number of shares that may be issued and the employees who are eligible to receive the options. The plan must be approved by the stockholders within 12 months before or after plan adoption.
- Each option must be granted under an ISO agreement, which must be written and must list the restrictions placed on exercising the ISO. Each option must set forth an offer to sell the stock at the option price and the period of time during which the option will remain open.
- The option must be granted within 10 years of the earlier of adoption or shareholder approval, and the option must be exercisable only within 10 years of grant.
- The option exercise price must equal or exceed the fair market value of the underlying stock at the time of grant.
- The employee must not, at the time of the grant, own stock representing more than 10% of the voting power of all-stock outstanding, unless the option exercise price is at least 110% of the fair market value and the option is not exercisable more than 5 years from the time of the grant.
- The ISO agreement must specifically state that the ISO cannot be transferred by the option holder other than by will or by the laws of descent and that the option cannot be exercised by anyone other than the option holder.
- The aggregate fair market value (determined as of the grant date) of stock bought by exercising ISOs that are exercisable for the first time cannot exceed US$100,000 in a calendar year. To the extent it does, Code Section 422(d) provides that such options are treated as nonqualified options.

TAX IMPLICATIONS OF ISOS FOR EMPLOYEES

An employee receiving an ISO realizes no income upon its receipt or exercise. Instead, the employee is taxed upon disposition of the stock acquired pursuant to the ISO. A disposition of ISO stock generally refers to any sale, exchange, gift, or transfer of legal title of stock. The tax treatment of the disposition of option exercise stock depends upon whether the stock was disposed of in a qualifying disposition within the statutory holding period for ISO stock. The ISO statutory holding period is the later of 2 years from the date of the granting of the ISO to the employee or 1 year from the date that the shares were transferred to the employee upon exercise. If the ISO is exercised more than 3 months after the employee has left the employ of the company granting the option, however, favorable tax treatment is not available. Upon a qualifying disposition, the employee recognizes capital gain, measured by the difference between the option exercise price and the sale proceeds. However, the gains on an incentive option are subject to alternative minimum tax treatment.

If the disposition occurs within 2 years of the employee's receipt of the option or within 1 year of receipt of the stock, the employee recognizes at the time of the disposition the ordinary income measured by the difference between the option exercise price and the fair market value of the stock at the time of option exercise (the "bargain purchase element"), or the exercise price and the sale price, if the difference is lower. If shares are held after a disqualifying disposition (as could be the case if they were transferred), then any additional gain or loss would be treated as a capital gain or loss.

An employer granting an ISO is not entitled to a deduction with respect to the issuance of the option or its exercise. If the employee causes the option to be disqualified (by disposing of his or her stock prematurely prior to the end of the requisite holding period), however, the employer usually may take a deduction for that amount recognized by the employee as ordinary income in the same year as the employee recognizes the income.

In addition, the employer that granted the ISO does not have any withholding obligation with regard to the ordinary income an employee recognizes upon a disqualifying disposition (the IRS may change this position).

401(K) PLANS

401(k) plans allow employees to defer part of their pay on a pre-tax basis into an investment fund set up by the company. The company usually offers at least four alternative investment vehicles. Because the law requires that participation in the plans not be too heavily skewed toward more highly paid people, companies generally offer a partial match to encourage broad participation in these voluntary plans. This match can be in any investment vehicle the company chooses, including company stock. There is a limit of 25% of taxable pay that the company can contribute to the plan.

While ESOPs have received the lion's share of attention as the vehicle of choice for employee ownership, 401(k) plans actually now hold almost as much company stock as ESOPs do. Most of the "own-company stock" investments in 401(k) plans are in larger companies. In companies with fewer than 200 employees, only 2% is in company stock; it is 8% in companies under 1,000 employees. This increases to 17% for companies with 1,000 to 5,000 people and 32.4% for companies with over 5,000. These data also reveal how much of 401(k) assets are in larger companies in general. In companies with over 1,000 employees, a Hewitt Associates study found that 25% of employee contributions to 401(k) plans are in company stock, while about 70% of employer matches are in the form of company stock. Collectively, about 18% of 401(k) assets are in company stock, which, as of 2001, would be worth about US$250 billion.

While these numbers add up to impressive absolute amounts, employees rarely own more than 10% of a company through a 401(k) plan. Moreover, research at the NCEO has found that few companies that provide stock in this way think of themselves as "employee ownership companies." Instead, companies simply see this as a convenient or financially favorable investment option.

The continued growth of 401(k) plans suggests, however, that they must be taken seriously as employee ownership vehicles. Over the next decade, if current trends continue, employees could often own 20% or more of many large, public companies. While it is only speculation, we think that at some percentage of ownership, corporate management may start realizing that it would be to its advantage to start thinking of itself as a substantially employee-owned company, just as employees will start realizing how much their retirement benefits depend on company performance.

There are several factors that favor the use of a 401(k) plan as a vehicle for employee ownership in public firms. From the company's perspective, its own stock may be one of the most cost-effective means of matching employee contributions. If there are existing treasury shares or if the company prints new shares, contributing them to the 401(k) plan may impose no immediate cash cost on the company; in fact, it would provide a tax deduction. Other shareholders would suffer a dilution, of course. If the company has to buy shares to fund the match, at least the dollars being used are used to invest in itself rather than other investments. From the employee standpoint, company stock is the investment the employee knows best and so may be attractive to people who either do not want to spend the time to learn about alternatives or have a strong belief in their own company. Balanced against these advantages, of course, must be an appreciation on both the part of the employee and the company that a failure to diversify a retirement portfolio is very risky.

For closely held companies, 401(k) plans are less appealing, although very appropriate in some cases. If employees are given an option to buy company stock, this can often trigger securities law issues that most private firms want to avoid. Employer matches make more sense, but require the company to either dilute ownership or reacquire shares from selling shareholders. In many closely held businesses, the first may not be desirable for control reasons and the second because there may not be sellers. Moreover, the 401(k) approach does not provide the "rollover" tax benefit that selling to an ESOP does, and the maximum amount that can be contributed is a function of how much employees put into savings. That will limit how much an employer can actually buy from a seller through a 401(k) plan to a fraction of what the ESOP can buy.

401(k) contributions cannot be leveraged either, so a sale of company stock would have to proceed slowly in annual increments. For example, if a company can get 60% of its workforce to participate in a 401(k) plan, and they put up 5% of pay (a reasonable but fairly high amount in practice), the company might match this on a dollar-for-dollar basis, but this would still only come to perhaps 4% of the payroll (assuming 401(k) participants tend to be higher paid than nonparticipants).

Despite these limitations, 401(k) plans and their new, simpler cousins SIMPLE plans (plans for employers under 100 employees that are much like 401(k) plans but with stricter rules and easier administration) are attractive as ownership vehicles in cases where a company simply wants employees to become owners, but has no need to buy out owners or use the borrowing features of an ESOP. A company can simply match employee deferrals with company stock or make a straight percentage of pay contribution to all employees eligible to be in the plan in the form of company stock.

401(k) plans and ESOPs can also be combined, with the ESOP contribution being used as the 401(k) match. This can work on either a nonleveraged or leveraged basis. In the nonleveraged case, the company simply characterizes its match as an ESOP. That adds some set-up and administrative costs, but allows the company to reap the additional tax benefits of an ESOP, such as the 1042 rollover. In a leveraged case, the company estimates how much it will need to match employee contributions each year, then borrows an amount of money such that the loan repayment will be close to that amount. If it is not as much as the promised matching amount, the company can either just define that as its match anyway, make up the difference with additional shares or cash (if the loan payment is lower), or pay the loan faster. If the amount is larger, the employees get a windfall. Combination plans must meet complex rules for testing to determine if they discriminate too heavily in favor of more highly paid people.

EMPLOYEE STOCK PURCHASE PLANS

Finally, millions of employees become owners in their companies through ESPPs. Many of these plans are organized under Section 423 of the tax code and, thus, are often called "423" plans. Other ESPPs are "nonqualified" plans, meaning they do not have to meet the special rules of Section 423 and do not get any of the special tax treatment. Most of these plans, however, are very similar in structure.

Under Section 423, companies must allow all employees to participate, but can exclude those with less than 2 years' tenure, part-time employees, and highly compensated employees. All employees must have the same rights and privileges under the plan, although companies can allow purchase limits to vary with relative compensation (most do not do this, however). Plans can limit how much employees can buy, and the law limits it to US$25,000 per year.

Section 423 plans, like all ESPPs, operate by allowing employees to have deductions taken out of their pay on an after-tax basis. These deductions accumulate over an "offering period." At a specified time or times, employees can choose to use these accumulated deductions to purchase shares, or they can get the money back. Plans can offer discounts of up to 15% on the price of the stock. Most plans allow this discount to be taken based on *either* the price at the beginning or end of the offering period (the so-called look-back feature). The offering period can last up to 5 years if the price employees pay for their stock is based on the share price at the end of the period, or 27 months if it can be determined at an earlier point.

Plan design can vary in a number of ways. For instance, a company might allow employees a 15% discount on the price at the end of the offering period, but no discount if they buy shares based on the price at the beginning of the period. Some companies offer employees interim opportunities to buy shares during the offering period. Others provide smaller discounts. Offering periods also vary in length. NCEO studies, however, show that the large majority of plans have a look-back feature and provide 15% discounts off the share price at the beginning or end of the offering period. Most of the plans have a 12-month offering period, with 6 months the next most common.

In a typical plan, our friend Chip Salter might start participating in an ESPP plan when the shares are worth US$40. He puts aside US$20 per week for 52 pay periods, accumulating US$1,040. The offering period ends on the 52nd week and Chip decides to buy shares. The current price is US$45. Chip will obviously choose to buy shares at 15% off the price at the beginning of the offering period, meaning he can purchase shares at US$34. For his US$34, he gets shares now worth US$45. If the share price had dropped to US$38 at the end of the offering period, Chip could buy shares instead at 15% off US$38.

The tax treatment of a 423 plan is similar to that of an ISO. If Chip holds the shares for 2 years after grant and 1 year after exercise, he pays capital gains taxes when he actually sells the stock on all of the gain he has made except the 15% discount (US$6 per share in our example). If he sells the shares after meeting the holding rules at a price less than US$40, he would pay ordinary income tax just on the difference between the purchase and sale price. The company gets no tax deduction, even on the 15% discount.

If Chip does not meet these rules because he sells earlier, then he pays ordinary income tax on the entire difference between the purchase price (US$34) and the exercise price (US$45), plus long-term or short-term capital gains taxes on any increase in value over US$45. The company gets a tax deduction for the spread between the purchase price and the exercise price (US$11 per share in this case).

Nonqualified ESPPs usually work much the same way, but there are no rules for how they must be structured and no special tax benefits. The employee would pay tax on the discount as ordinary income *at the time the stock is purchased* and would pay capital gains on any subsequent gain. In our example, Chip would pay tax on US$11 per share at the time the shares were purchased. The company would receive a corresponding deduction.

ESPPs are found almost exclusively in public companies because the offering of stock to employees requires compliance with costly and complex securities laws. However, closely held companies can, and sometimes do have these plans. Offerings of stock only to employees can qualify for an exemption from securities registration requirements at the federal level, although they will have to comply with anti-fraud disclosure rules and, possibly, state securities laws as well. If they do offer stock in a stock purchase plan, it is highly advisable they obtain at least an annual appraisal.

ESPPs are very popular in public companies as they offer a benefit to employees and additional capital to companies. Any dilution resulting from the issuance of new shares to satisfy the purchase requests, or from the company repurchasing outstanding shares and reselling them at a discount, is usually so small that shareholders do not object. Rates of participation vary widely, with the median levels around 30% to 40% of eligible employees. Because most employees do not commit large amounts to these plans, and many do not participate at all, ESPPs should generally be seen as an adjunct to other employee ownership plans, not a means in themselves to create an ownership culture.

EMPLOYEE OWNERSHIP AND EMPLOYEE MOTIVATION

During the early 1980s, the NCEO conducted an exhaustive investigation of how employees react to being owners. We surveyed over 3,500 employee owners in 45 companies. We looked at hundreds of factors in an effort to determine whether it mattered to employees that they had stock in their company and, if so, when.

The results were very clear. Employees did like being owners. The more shares they owned, the more committed they were to their company, the more satisfied they were with their jobs, and the less likely they were to leave. Naturally, some employees in some companies liked being owners more than others. Individual employee response to ownership was primarily a response to how much stock they got each year. After that, employees responded more favorably if they had ample opportunities to participate in decisions affecting their jobs, worked in companies whose management really believed in the concept of ownership and not just the tax breaks, and were provided regular information about how the ownership plan operated.

By contrast, the size of the company, the line of business, demographic characteristics of the employees, seniority, job classification, presence or absence of voting rights or board membership, percentage of the company owned by employees (as opposed to the size of the annual contribution), and many other factors did not have any impact. Employees looked at the employee ownership plan and asked "How much money will I get from this?" and "Am I really treated like an owner?" If they liked the answers to these questions, they liked being an owner.

EMPLOYEE OWNERSHIP AND CORPORATE PERFORMANCE

In 2000, Douglas Kruse and Joseph Blasi of Rutgers University analyzed all the ESOPs set up between 1988 and 1994 for which data were available. They then matched these companies to comparable nonESOP companies and looked at the sales and employment data for the paired companies for 3 years prior to a company setting up an ESOP to the period 3 years after. They found that when they indexed out for the performance of the competitor companies, the ESOP companies grew 2.3% to 2.4% faster after setting up their plan than would have been expected otherwise. That seemed to give strong evidence that ESOPs do make a significant and positive contribution to corporate performance.

Impressive as these findings were, however, they did not indicate what it was about employee ownership that caused the improved performance or whether the improved performance was accounted for by just a subset of ESOP companies with particular characteristics. Other research, however, suggests that it is the combination of employee ownership and employee involvement that really makes the difference.

Knowing the answer to whether employee ownership motivates employees seems to provide the answer to whether ownership improves corporate performance. Not so. In most companies, labor costs are under 30%–40% of total costs. Motivation on its own, presumably, makes employees work harder. We often ask managers just how much more work they think they could hope to get from more motivated employees, based on an 8-hour day. Fifteen minutes is a typical response. That comes to just 3% more time. Three percent times even a high estimate of 40% for labor costs results in just a 1.2% savings, assuming everyone will be more motivated, which is, of course, far from true.

While a 1% improvement can be a lot of money, it is not what distinguishes the really successful companies from the mediocre ones. The star performers are those that react to their environment in creative, innovative ways, providing better value to their customers than competitors. How is that achieved? Through processing information and acting on it intelligently. In most companies, information gathering is limited to a group of managers. The generation of ideas is similarly limited. So is decision-making. The assumption is that only these people have the talent, and perhaps motivation, to carry out these tasks.

In fact, no one has more daily contact with customers than employees, at least in most companies. No one is closer to the day-to-day process of making the product or providing the service than the employees. And, employees often do have useful ideas they could share with management.

Thus, for a company to use employee ownership effectively, it needs to do more than just motivate people to work harder at what, after all, may not be the most efficient or effective thing to do. Instead, it must enlist employee ideas and information to find the best ways to do the most important things. To do that, companies need to get employees involved. Managers should seek their opinions. Employee task forces, ad hoc and permanent, should be established to solve problems. Quality circles and employee involvement teams can be set up. Individual jobs can be enhanced and supervision limited. Suggestion systems can be implemented. This all may seem like common sense, and it is. It is not very common practice in most companies, however.

Data indicate that it *is* becoming common in employee-ownership companies. In a 1987 General Accounting Office (GAO) report, about one-third of all ESOP firms had some degree of employee participation. By 1993, a study of Ohio firms by the Northeast Ohio Employee Ownership Center and Kent State University found that about 60% of the companies now had active employee-involvement programs, such as autonomous work teams, total quality management, or similar programs. The incidence of participation roughly doubled after the initiation of an ownership plan. These participative firms, the GAO reported, showed a strong improvement in productivity when they combined their ESOPs with participative management practices.

In a study by the NCEO published in the September/October 1987 *Harvard Business Review*, we found that participative ESOP firms grew 8% to 11% faster with their plans than they would have without them. In both the NCEO and GAO studies, no other factors had any influence on the relationship between ownership and performance. Three other recent studies confirmed both the direction and magnitude of these findings. Only participation can translate the motivation of ownership into the reality of a fatter bottom line. Participation is not enough on its own either, as hundreds of studies have shown. One reason is that few participation programs last more than 5 years in conventional companies. By contrast, over the last decade we have not found a single ESOP company that has dropped its program.

The structure of participation varies from company to company, but basically boils down to employees forming groups to share information, generate ideas, and make recommendations.

At United Airlines, for instance, employee task teams were formed soon after the employees purchased the company. Over the ensuing 2 years, the teams took apart every aspect of the business, making recommendations for often substantial changes. The teams were appointed to include a broad cross section of employees, but anyone could volunteer to join one. The ideas helped generate hundreds of millions of dollars in cost savings and new revenues. Ironically, when the teams completed their work, management backed away from the idea of participation, causing the airline some well-reported difficulties in the years that followed. The ESOP is now frozen and both managers and employees feel that it was not a success; United recently declared bankruptcy and is trying to reorganize. United shows clearly that just setting up an ESOP, and even starting off in the right direction, is not enough. Companies must commit to a long-term ownership culture program.

Stone Construction Equipment Company in Honoeye, NY, is a good example. Its ESOP set-up in the late 1970s was having little impact. Then the company hired a new president, Bob Fien, who started a participative management program. Eventually, all employees were trained in "just-in-time" management and organized into work cells that schedule and control their own work flow and have considerable input into the design and organization of their jobs. Stone had been limping along and had developed a reputation for poor quality; by 1991, the company had made so much progress, *Industry Week* named it one of America's top 10 manufacturers.

At Springfield ReManufacturing in Springfield, Missouri, employee owners are taught to read detailed financial and production data. Meeting in work groups, they go over the numbers then figure out ways to improve them. Employees are sometimes given 90-page financial statements to digest. Springfield's stock went from 10 cents a share when it started its ESOP in 1983 to US$21.00 in 1994. Employment increased over 500%.

Other approaches include employee advisory committees to management, eliminating levels of supervision while giving nonmanagement employees more authority, meetings between management and randomly selected groups of employees, suggestion boxes, and anything else companies can imagine to get people involved.

This "high-involvement" management style has, of course, become conventional wisdom, if still unconventional practice, at many companies. Is ownership really essential to make it work? There is no conclusive data on this, but there is good reason to believe that ownership, if not essential, is at least highly desirable. First, ownership is a cumulative benefit. Each additional year, an employee has more and more at stake in how well the company performs. It is not unusual in mature plans for the appreciation in share value and employer contributions to add up to 30% to 50% or more of pay in a year. In profit sharing or gainsharing, both of which are paid periodically and almost always amount to a small portion of total compensation, the benefit always remains relatively minor. Second, ownership has a stronger emotive appeal. People may be very proud to say they are an owner; few would brag to friends they are a profit-sharer. Finally, only ownership encourages people to think about all aspects of a business, not just short-term profits or some efficiency measure. This is especially important in companies moving toward open-book management systems.

CONCLUSION

The continued growth of employee ownership reflects, above all, a changing view of the role of employees in the workplace. To be sure, for some time companies have been saying that "people are our most important resource." This was little more than rhetoric, however, for all but a handful of companies. Investors, capital, technology, and, above all, top management were really seen as the keys to the company's future. Employees would be laid off or have their compensation limited before these other assets were harmed. Increasingly, however, companies are coming to the view that attracting and retaining good people at all levels and then giving them the authority to make more decisions about more things, is essential to being an effective competitor. In large part, this is a function of technology. The vast amounts of information, and the speed with which it can be processed, leaves companies with little choice but to get more people involved in more things. As people are asked to take more responsibility for the company, it simply makes sense for them to be rewarded accordingly.

REVIEW QUESTIONS

1. Write a note on ESOP plans in the USA.
2. Compare and contrast stock options, restricted stocks, stock appreciation rights, and phantom stocks.
3. How do employee share ownership plans affect corporate performance?
4. Compare and contrast defined benefit plans and defined contribution plans.

Teaching Cases

CASE 1

Corporate Governance Scandal at Satyam Computer Services Ltd[1]

Description: The case highlights a US$1.4 billion fraud committed by the founder of a New York Stock Exchange (NYSE)-listed information technology (IT) firm in India. In response to the crisis, the Indian government appointed an interim board to find a strategic investor in the company. The case traces the events leading to the fall of the company. Students are asked to analyze the governance and intermediation failures, assess the financial position of the company, and estimate the intrinsic value of the company from an acquirer's perspective.

Learning Objective: To introduce various aspects of corporate governance and to study the reasons for governance failure at major corporations, introduce corporate governance code in an emerging market context, and build skill in acquisition and financial and valuation analyses.

Subjects Covered: Corporate governance, takeovers, financial management, valuation

> The Phoenix hope, can wing her way through the desert skies, and still defying fortune's spite; revive from ashes and rise.
>
> —Miguel de Cervantes Saavedra Spanish writer, author of the masterwork *Don Quixote* (1547–1616)

"Oh, God, I think it's a shocker," exclaimed Jayesh Shah, an analyst at a major mutual fund after reading an open letter from the founder of Satyam.[2] On January 7, 2009, Ramalinga Raju, the founder and chairman of Satyam Computer Services Ltd, an NYSE-listed, Indian IT services firm, revealed one of the biggest frauds in Indian corporate history (*The Economic Times* 2009c). SEBI (Securities Exchange Board of India, the capital market regulator) Chairman Chandrashekhar Bhave had received this letter from Raju that was addressed to the directors on the board of his company saying he wanted to "ease the burden on his conscience" by disclosing how the company's books had been manipulated for years.

---

[1] Professors Vishwanath S. R. and Vijaya Narapareddy prepared this case as the basis for class discussion rather than forthrightly illustrating either effective or ineffective handling of an administrative situation.

[2] In many Indian languages, *Satyam* means "Truth"!

In his letter to the entire financial market community (see Exhibit E1.1),[3] the chairman stated that the company's profits had been manipulated over the last 7 years, with the balance sheet as on September 30, 2008, carrying an inflated (nonexistent) cash and bank balance of ₹50.4 billion[4] (as against ₹53.6 billion reflected in the books), a nonexistent accrued interest of ₹3.76 billion, an understated liability of ₹12.3 billion on account of funds arranged by the promoters, and an overstated debtor position of ₹4.9 billion (as against ₹26.51 billion reflected in the books).[5] The revelations were particularly shocking in light of the board's constitution. Satyam's board consisted of Krishna Palepu, a Harvard Business School accounting professor; Vinod Dham, the creator of the Pentium chip; Tata Ramachandra Prasad, a former cabinet secretary in the Government of India; Ram Mohan Rao, dean of the Indian School of Business; Mangalam Srinivasan, advisor to the JFK School of Government, Harvard; and V. S. Raju, a former director of the Indian Institute of Technology, New Delhi; and the involvement of PricewaterhouseCoopers (PwC) as auditor for 9 years.

These revelations came a few weeks after the company's aborted bid to buy Maytas[6] Infrastructure and Maytas Properties. The Maytas episode was the last effort by the management of Satyam to fill the gaping hole in the company's balance sheet. Raju said that in the second quarter (July–September) of 2008, Satyam showed an operating margin of ₹6.49 billion (24% of revenue) when it was actually only ₹610 million (3% of revenue).[7] This, he indicated, was part of an exercise over years to inflate profits to keep the stock price up and to meet investor expectations. Exhibit E1.1 presents the excerpts from Raju's letter to the board.

This announcement sent Indian equity markets crashing, with the Bombay Stock Exchange Sensitive Index (Sensex) falling 7.3%. Satyam's stock price crashed to ₹30.70, a fall of 83% from the opening price of ₹179.10.[8] Investors, analysts, and industry observers wondered what the reasons for governance and intermediation failures were, what the fate of Satyam Computers would be, and what it implied for the Indian IT industry since the Satyam episode could have a rub-off effect on other IT firms that relied heavily on export revenues.

COMPANY BACKGROUND[9]

Satyam was incorporated as a private limited company in 1987 in Hyderabad, India. It went public in 1991 with its initial public offering being oversubscribed 17 times. It was assessed at

[3] The letter was made available to the public soon after it was received by stock exchanges and SEBI.

[4] This amounts to C$ 1.26 billion and USD 1.03 billion at the prevailing exchange rates of ₹39.74/C$ and ₹48.50/USD respectively.

[5] The letter also stated that the employee strength was not 53,000 as claimed by the company. On January 22, 2009, the Criminal Investigation Department said in court that the actual number of employees was only 40,000, not 53,000 as reported earlier, and that Raju had been allegedly withdrawing ₹200 million every month as salaries of nonexistent employees.

[6] Satyam spelled backwards.

[7] Infosys Technologies, the industry leader earned 33% in the same quarter. See *Times of India* (2009).

[8] It fell to ₹11.50 on January 10, 2009, its lowest level since March 1998, compared to a high of ₹544 in 2008.

[9] Details of the company are from the company's website.

Software Engineering Institute (SEI) Capability Maturity Model (CMM) Level 5[10] in 1999. Its Internet subsidiary (Satyam Infoway) became the first Indian company to be listed on NASDAQ in 1999. Satyam operated in 30 countries around the world and employed 10,000 associates in 2000. Throughout its history, Satyam had earned many laurels. It received the National HRD award from the Indian government; it became the world's first ISO 9001:2000 company to be certified by Bureau Veritas Quality International (BVQI),[11] and was one of the earliest Indian companies to be listed on the NYSE. By 2008, Satyam's revenues had surpassed ₹80 billion, making it the fourth-largest IT services company in India. Exhibits E1.2 through E1.8 present the company's financial statements, valuation metrics, shareholding pattern, stock price history, composition of board committees, and historical time line.

As of 2008, at least four well-known Indian brokerages—Edelweiss Research, Religare Research, Reliance Money, and Karvy Stock Broking—had issued "buy" or "hold" recommendations with price targets ranging from ₹435 to ₹570 when the stock was trading at 19 times earnings and four times book value (George et al 2008; George and Sangoi 2009; Hota 2008; Purohit and Punjabi 2008; Ravi et al. 2008). However, all brokerages were not as optimistic. CLSA, one of the most highly rated financial services groups in Asia, pointed out in a report in September 2008 that it was abnormal for a company with ₹52 billion cash to have a ₹350 million debt.

THE INDIAN INFORMATION TECHNOLOGY INDUSTRY IN EARLY 2009

The Indian IT industry accounted for about 5% of India's GDP and export earnings in 2009. It provided employment to almost 2.5 million professionals. Many large companies in the West preferred to outsource IT services to companies in India due to cost advantages of Indian IT firms. Further, they also found it difficult to keep pace with technological developments in the field since their core business was not IT. India's outsourcing industry was expected to touch US$225 billion by 2020. The industry was dominated by homegrown multinationals such as Tata Consultancy Services, Infosys Technologies, Wipro and global corporations such as HP, IBM, and Accenture. The global financial crisis in 2008 affected most Indian as well as global IT service providers. The IT Index declined by 28% during the third quarter of 2008–09, reflecting the recession.

EVENTS LEADING TO THE CONFESSION

In 1998, Raju and his family members founded two real estate companies named Maytas Properties and Maytas Infrastructure Ltd. These companies were headed by Raju's sons. Using Raju's political connections, the group secured government projects in irrigation, power, transportation, and also the Hyderabad Metro Rail project. Raju inflated cash and bank balances

[10] CMM was developed by the Software Engineering Institute of Carnegie Mellon University, USA. See http://www.sei.cmu.edu/cmmi/

[11] The world's leading quality certification body.

in the books of Satyam and pledged promoters' shareholding in Satyam to acquire 6,800 acres of land. These investments put enormous pressure on the group. In 2008, the Indian stock market crashed and so did the real estate sector. The lenders started selling Raju's pledged shares due to falling stock and real estate prices.[12]

In December 2008, the company, in a strange move, announced the acquisition of two of its group companies, Maytas Properties (an unlisted company) and Maytas Infrastructure (a listed company), which the chairman in his letter acknowledged as a last attempt to fill the fictitious assets with real ones. The deal was called off within 24 hours due to strong opposition from the other stakeholders although the board did not resist the acquisition.[13]

This was followed by a suit filed by a client, Upaid, a UK-based online and mobile payments enabler, claiming damages of US$1 billion. In another blow to the company, the World Bank, one of the biggest clients of the company, imposed an 8-year ban on the company from doing any offshore work with it based on reports of data theft. These raised serious corporate governance issues for Satyam, and also raised concerns about the corporate governance ethos of Indian companies.

As the discussions of a potential merger with Maytas progressed, the team of investment bankers at Merrill Lynch discovered blatant violations of accounting principles. When the implications of these discoveries became clear, Merrill Lynch communicated its inability to continue as Satyam's advisor. It then sounded out SEBI, the market regulator. The banker also sent a letter to SEBI briefly explaining that it had found serious accounting irregularities. After this, Raju had little choice but to inform the company's board about the mess the company was in.

CORPORATE GOVERNANCE REFORMS IN INDIA

The need for corporate governance reforms came to the fore following several high-profile, stock market-related scandals that occurred after the financial liberalization in 1991. The capital market regulator was established in 1992. SEBI set out on its governance reforms agenda by constituting four high-powered committees from 1996 to 2003 under the leadership of well-known industrialists such as Rahul Bajaj (chairman of the Bajaj group), Kumar Mangalam Birla (chairman of the Birla group), Naresh Chandra (founder of Zee TV Network), and Narayana Murthy (the founder of Infosys Technologies, another well-known IT multinational from India). SEBI implemented Birla Committee recommendations through Clause 49 of the stock exchange listing agreements. The salient features of the clause were:

1. Fifty percent of the directors must be nonexecutives if there was a full-time chairman.
2. The audit committee must contain three independent directors and a chairman with a sound financial background. The finance director and internal audit head were to be

[12] Raju and his family decreased their shareholding from 15.67% in 2006 to 8.6% in 2008. Raju transferred these shares to another family company SRSR Holdings from which he took out loans using the shares as collateral. In early 2009, promoter's holdings had come down to 2.3%. See *The Economic Times* (2009a).

[13] Apparently, Raju convinced the board members that IBM was contemplating on a hostile takeover bid for Satyam and it was necessary to merge the two companies to fend off the takeover threat.

special invitees. A minimum of three meetings were to be convened each year. The committee was responsible for review of financial performance on a semiannual/annual basis, appointment/removal/remuneration of auditors, and review of internal control systems and their adequacy.

3. At least four board meetings were to be held each year. A director could not be a member of more than 10 committees, and a chairman could not serve on more than five committees across all companies where he held appointments.
4. The management discussion and analysis report (in the annual report) had to include a discussion of industry trends, opportunities, risks, future outlook, and segment performance.
5. Shareholders were entitled to quarterly results, analyst presentations, half-yearly financials, and significant event reports.

The Narayana Murthy committee set up in 2003 proposed additional features. Exhibit E1.9 presents the excerpts from the committee's recommendations.

And yet, despite such corporate governance reforms and precautions, Raju had managed to fraudulently declare excess cash and revenues of US$1 billion and US$121 million respectively.

THE AFTERMATH

Top SEBI officials then met to decide on the next course of action. The letter from Raju came in at the right time to launch a probe and an inspection of the company's books, which was announced later during the day.

Not satisfied with the response of some of the independent directors on the board of Satyam, SEBI sought more details on what exactly transpired at the last board meeting of the company and what prompted these independent directors to approve the proposal to invest in two firms linked to the founder. The probe would examine whether insiders benefited in any transaction prior to the events of the last few days. In addition to SEBI, the Securities Exchange Commission (the US capital market regulator) was also bound to act against the company because Satyam's American depository receipts (ADRs) were traded in the USA.

The company was stripped of the Golden Peacock Award for Excellence in Corporate Governance given by the World Council for Corporate Governance, London, in 2008 (*Live Mint* 2009). Most brokerages suspended coverage of Satyam. In a swift move, the Ministry of Corporate Affairs of the Government of India decided that while there would be no financial bailout for the company, it would provide interim governance in order to preempt an implosion of the company. The ministry petitioned to the Company Law Board to suspend the company's board, which was implemented on January 9, 2009. Two days later, the ministry installed a three-member caretaker board comprised of veterans from the Indian industry.[14] The board size

[14] They were Kiran Karnik, former president of the National Association of Software and Service Companies (NASSCOM), Deepak Parekh, chairman of Housing Development Finance Corporation, and C. Achutan, former member of SEBI. Deepak served on the boards of some 19 prominent companies and Karnik served on the boards of six other companies.

was later expanded to six.[15] However, these new members were not compensated. On February 5, 2009, the six-member board appointed by the government named A. S. Murthy as the new CEO of the firm with immediate effect. Murthy had been with Satyam since January 1994 and was heading the global delivery section. The board also appointed Homi Khusrokhan (CEO of Tata Chemicals belonging to the US$70 billion Tata group) and Partha Datta, a chartered accountant, as special advisors, and Deloitte and KPMG as the new auditors.

The Institute of Chartered Accountants of India (ICAI), the top accounting body in India, issued show-cause notice to Satyam's auditor, PwC, on its role in the scam. That same day, the crime investigations department interrogated V. Srinivas, Satyam's then chief financial officer. He was then arrested and kept in judicial custody.

Trading in Satyam ADRs was suspended after it plunged by over 90% to 85 cents in pre-market trade in the USA following Raju's confession. In separate lawsuits filed in US courts by law firms Vianale & Vianale LLP and Izard Nobel LLP, Satyam Computer was charged with cheating American investors of billions of dollars by artificially inflating the share price (*The Economic Times* 2009b).

Interestingly, Merrill Lynch, besides being a banker to Satyam, had also provided funding to the firm along with four other institutions. In July 2008, the broking arm of Merrill Lynch, which was acquired by Bank of America, had given a "buy" recommendation to Satyam with a target price of ₹530. In November 2008, it assigned a "neutral" rating and on December 16, 2008, downgraded it to "underperform" with a target price of ₹130; on the same day the stock closed at ₹226 (*The Economic Times* 2009c).

THE SITUATION IN MARCH 2009

After interacting with bankers, customers, and company managers, the new board appointed by the government concluded that Satyam's business model was fundamentally sound. It decided in favor of finding a strategic investor who would bring the company back on track. At this point in time, the company seemed to be a lucrative acquisition target with low insider shareholding, reduced investor confidence, and vulnerable financial position.

At its meeting in the second week of March, Satyam's board of directors said that it had taken steps to release the request for proposals to all registered bidders. Further, the board requested Sam Bharucha, former chief justice of India, to oversee the selection process. The board met with Bharucha on March 11, 2009, in Mumbai and discussed the proposed process for the induction of a strategic investor. Under the procedure finalized by the board, interested bidders had to submit the expression of interest (EOI) along with proof of funds of ₹1.5 billion (US$290 million based on an exchange rate of ₹51.635/US$1) by March 20, 2009. Bidders who submitted compliant EOIs and executed certain pre-transaction documents would have access to data and information regarding the company to enable them to submit technical and financial bids.

[15] The new members included Tarun Das, chief mentor, Confederation of Indian Industry; T. N. Manoharan, former president of Institute of Chartered Accountants of India; and S. B. Mainak, executive director, Life Insurance Corporation of India.

On March 13, 2009, Tech Mahindra officially announced its interest in Satyam Computer Services. The other bids came from Larsen & Toubro (L&T), an engineering and construction giant; WL Ross & Co.; and Cognizant Technology Solutions.[16]

L&T had recently hiked its stake in Satyam from 4% to 12%t, becoming the largest shareholder in Satyam (Rediff.com 2009). L&T perceived synergy between the core strengths of Satyam and that of L&T Infotech, its unlisted IT subsidiary. Satyam focused on enterprise applications and the engineering segment. These two complemented L&T Infotech since a large fraction of its work also came from ERP (enterprise resource planning) practice. Satyam's ERP business accounted for 45% of revenues, whereas engineering solutions contributed about 6.5%. Satyam would also bring in horizontal solutions capability such as business intelligence to L&T. The company would get access to new verticals and service offerings as well as entry into new geographical areas. Analysts felt that the transition would be smoother and faster if L&T took over Satyam.

Based on data available, interactions with some bidders, and Satyam's current clients, Forrester, a market research firm, believed that L&T was the front-runner to acquire the troubled company. L&T had the most service overlap and relevant IT industry experience. Its corporate reputation, ability to manage acquisitions, reputation in the Indian industry, and relationships with government agencies made it the most likely winner. However, a report by Kotak Institutional Equities, a leading brokerage, stated that while L&T had the resources to acquire, it would be better if the group used it to address the challenges the core business was facing.

L&T had outstanding mutual fund investments of ₹4 billion at the end of financial year 2008 in addition to cash of ₹10 billion and a gross debt-equity of 0.4X at the end of the same period.

Tech Mahindra was formed as a joint venture between Mahindra & Mahindra, a prominent Indian business group,[17] and British Telecommunications (BT). It operated in only the telecom sector with one client (BT) providing 65% of revenues. For the year ending 2009, Tech Mahindra had revenues of US$935 million and employed around 25,000 professionals. Exhibit E1.10 presents the income statement of Tech Mahindra if it acquired Satyam with internal accruals and ₹20 billion debt.[18]

For Tech Mahindra, this would be a good diversification strategy. It was heavily dependent on one sector. Raising capital for the acquisition was, however, a concern. As of December 31, 2009, Tech Mahindra had cash and cash equivalents of ₹5.2 billion. Fitch Ratings had downgraded the company's rating in light of its race for Satyam. This could hamper its prospects of raising capital abroad. Moreover, Deepak Parekh, a member of the Satyam board, had also been on the board of Mahindra and Mahindra since 1990. If Tech Mahindra decided to bid, it would raise concerns of conflict of interest.

WL Ross & Co., a private equity firm run by US billionaire investor Wilbur Ross, was known to be joining hands with Cognizant Technology Solutions to bid for Satyam. Ross was known for restructuring failed companies in a wide range of industries such as steel, coal, telecommunications, and textiles.[19] He specialized in leveraged buyouts. He ran a private equity

[16] B. K. Modi's Spice group withdrew its offer due to lack of clarity and transparency; other contenders like IBM dropped out too.

[17] Anand Mahindra, chairman of Mahindra & Mahindra, is a well-respected businessman with strong connections in business and government.

[18] On account of lack of financial data on other acquirers (and for the sake of brevity), the case considers only Tech Mahindra's financial position.

[19] The details of the company are available at www.wlross.com

fund with Rothschild Investments. Ross entered India with the acquisition of OCM India for US$37 million in cash. The acquisition was developed by WL Ross's US$300 million India Asset Recovery Fund LP, with co-investment from WLR Recovery Fund III LP and the Housing Development Finance Corporation.[20]

Cognizant Technology Solutions was started by Satyam and Dun & Bradstreet (D&B) Corporation in 1994.[21] D&B had a 76% stake in that venture, called Dun & Bradstreet Satyam Software (DBSS), while Satyam held a 24% stake. D&B bought out the stake from Satyam after the second year of operations and Cognizant was formed. Cognizant was heavily tilted toward banking, financial services, and insurance and healthcare segments. Acquiring Satyam would automatically give them entry into enterprise applications such as systems, applications and products (SAP) and manufacturing. Besides, Satyam had a much better geographical spread.

While the acquisition made sense to all bidders, investors wondered who would be the most suitable acquirer.

REFERENCES AND SUGGESTED READINGS

The Economic Times. 2009a. "Raju's Stake Dips 3.14% as Lenders Sell Pledged Satyam Shares." *The Economic Times*, January 2. Available at http://articles.economictimes.indiatimes.com/2009-01-02/news/27640665_1_satyam-shares-promoters-share-sale (Accessed on September 7, 2017).

———. 2009b. "Satyam Charged with Duping U S Investors of Billions of Dollars." *The Economic Times*, Jan 8. Available at http://articles.economictimes.indiatimes.com/2009-01-08/news/27663420_1_izard-nobel-llp-thousands-of-american-investors-satyam-adss (Accessed on September 7, 2017).

———. 2009c. "The Truth Behind Raju's Confessions." *The Economic Times*, January 8, 2009. Available at http://articles.economictimes.indiatimes.com/2009-01-08/news/27658989_1_investment-bank-satyam-computer-services-raju (Accessed on September 7, 2017).

George, Viju, et al. (2008, May 15). *Satyam Computer Services*. Mumbai: Edelweiss Research.

George, Viju., and Kunal Sangoi. (2009, January 28). *Satyam Computer Services*. Edelweiss Research.

Healy, P., and K. Palepu. (2003). "The Fall of Enron." *Journal of Economic Perspectives*, 17 (2): 3–26.

Hota, Sanjeev. (2008, April 24). *Satyam Computer Services*. Mumbai: Reliance Money.

Live Mint. 2009. "Satyam to be Stripped of Golden Peacock Award," *Live Mint*, January 7. Available at http://www.livemint.com/Companies/m8UzpSkhzmP5wT2ai6Ma2O/Satyam-to-be-stripped-off-Golden-Peacock-Award.html (Accessed on September 7, 2017).

Mahindra Satyam. 2008–09. *Annual Reports*.

———. 2009–10. *Annual Reports*.

Murthy, R. 2009. "Satyam Fraud Check Switches to PwC." *Asia Times Online*. Available at http://www.atimes.com/atimes/South_Asia/KA10Df02.html (Accessed on September 7, 2017).

Purohit, Anurag, and Hitesh Punjabi. (2008, April 22). *Satyam Computers*. Mumbai: Religare Research.

Ravi, R., et al. (2008, May 20). *Satyam Computer Services*. Mumbai: Karvy Broking.

Rediff.com. 2009. "The Bidders for Satyam," Rediff.com, April 13.

Shah, H. (2009, April 15). *Tech Mahindra*. Mumbai: Angel Broking.

Times of India. 2009. "Did Raju Own Up Only Lesser of the Two Crimes?" *The Times of India*, January 2. Available at http://articles.timesofindia.indiatimes.com/2009-01-09/india-business/28024635_1_ramalinga-raju-satyam-staffer-ceo-ram-mynampati (Accessed on September 7, 2017).

[20] Deepak Parekh was also the chairman of HDFC.

[21] The details of the company are available at www.cognizant.com

REVIEW QUESTIONS

1. Identify the governance and intermediation failures in the context of Satyam and debate why they occur. In doing so, analyze the role of top management and their compensation, independent directors, audit committee, external auditors, institutional investors, and security analysts.
2. What are the pressures that lead executives and managers to manipulate the books and what type of fraudulent accounting schemes are typically used?
3. Comment on the government's action in light of the fall of Satyam, especially with regard to the appointment of the new board and the incentives of new board members in governance.
4. Does the acquisition make sense to Tech Mahindra? Why or why not?[22]
5. Examine the impact of the acquisition on Tech Mahindra's financial performance. Use the following assumptions for your analysis

   Revenues of Satyam = US$1.3 billion
   EBITDA Margin = 3%
   Debt Assumed for the merger = ₹20 billion; balance is financed through internal accruals
   Interest on debt = 10%
   ₹/US$ Exchange Rate = ₹48.50; ₹/C$ Exchange Rate = ₹39.74
6. What is the intrinsic value of Satyam stock? Perform a multiples valuation. Assume that a comparable IT services company has an earnings before interest and taxes of US$14,000 per employee.

Exhibit E1.1 *Excerpts from Raju's Letter to the Board*[23]

It is with deep regret and tremendous burden that I am carrying on my conscience that I would like to bring the following facts to your notice:

1. The balance sheet carries as of September 30, 2008, (a) inflated (nonexistent) cash and bank balances of ₹50,400 million (as against ₹53,610 million reflected in the books); (b) An accrued interest of ₹3,760 million, which is nonexistent; (c) understated liability of ₹12,300 million on account of funds arranged by me; and (d) overstated debtors' position of ₹4,900 million (as against ₹26,510 million reflected in the books).
2. For the September quarter (Q2) we reported a revenue of ₹27,000 million and an operating margin of ₹6,490 million (24% of revenue) as against the actual revenues of ₹21,120 million and an actual operating margin of ₹610 million (3% of revenues). This has resulted in artificial cash and bank balances going up by ₹5,880 million in Q2 alone.

The gap in the balance sheet has arisen purely on account of inflated profits over several years (limited only to Satyam standalone, books of subsidiaries reflecting true performance). What started as a marginal gap between actual operating profit and the one reflected in the books of accounts continued to grow over the years. It has attained unmanageable proportions as the size of the company operations grew significantly (annualized revenue run rate of ₹112,760 million in the September quarter, 2008, and official reserves of ₹83,920 million).

[22] While an analysis can be made for all three bidders, instructors may concentrate on only one bidder.

[23] Raju's letter reached market intermediaries and the general investing public within a few hours of releasing it to the stock exchanges and SEBI.

The differential in the real profits and the one reflected in the books was further accentuated by the fact that the company had to carry additional resources and assets to justify a higher level of operations thereby significantly increasing the costs. Every attempt made to eliminate the gap failed. As the promoters held a small percentage of equity, the concern was that poor performance would result in the takeover, thereby exposing the gap. It was like riding a tiger, not knowing how to get off without being eaten.

The aborted Maytas acquisition deal was the last attempt to fill the fictitious assets with real ones. Maytas' investors were convinced that this is a good divestment opportunity and a strategic fit. Once Satyam's problem was solved, it was hoped that Maytas' payments can be delayed. But that was not to be. What followed in the last several days is common knowledge.

I would like the board to know:

1. That neither myself, nor the managing director (including our spouses) sold any shares in the last 8 years—excepting for a small proportion declared and sold for philanthropic purposes.
2. That in the last two years a net amount of ₹12,300 million was arranged to Satyam (not reflected in the books of Satyam) to keep the operations going by resorting to pledging all the promoter shares and raising funds from known sources by giving all kinds of assurances (statement enclosed only to the members of the board).
3. Significant dividend payments, acquisitions, capital expenditure to provide for growth did not help matters. Every attempt was made to keep the wheel moving and to ensure prompt payment of salaries to the associates. The last straw was the selling of most of the pledged shares by the lenders on account of margin triggers.
4. That neither me nor the managing director took even one rupee/dollar from the company and have not benefited in financial terms on account of the inflated results.

None of the board members, past or present, had any knowledge of the situation in which the company is placed.

Under the circumstances, I am tendering the resignation as the chairman of Satyam and shall continue in this position only till such time the current board is expanded. My continuance is just to ensure enhancement of the board over the next several days or as early as possible.

I am now prepared to subject myself to the laws of the land and face the consequences thereof.

(B. Ramalinga Raju)

Exhibit E1.2 *Income Statement (₹m)*

	2006	2007	2008
Revenues	47,926	64,851	84,735
Employee cost	28,044	38,579	52,595
SG & A expenses	8,220	5,130	0
EBITDA	11,662	15,377	18,348
Depreciation	1,373	1,484	1,636
EBIT	10,289	13,893	16,712
Net interest	55	159	201
Adjusted PAT	11,490	14,046	16,879
Dividend pay-out (%)	45.8	32.7	15.7
Growth Metrics (%)			
Net sales	36.1	35.3	30.7
EBITDA	34.3	31.9	19.3
Reported Net Profit	60.4	23.0	20.2

Source: Edelweiss Research, Company Annual Reports.

Note: ₹/US$ Exchange Rate = ₹48.50/US$.

Exhibit E1.3 *Balance Sheet (figures given in ₹million)*

Share capital	1,577	1,868	1,797
Reserves and surplus	41,596	55,658	71,049
Borrowings	1,027	1,479	350
Minority interest	42	0	0
Sources of funds	**44,241**	**59,005**	**73,196**
Goodwill and intangible assets	938	938	938
Property and equipment	3,832	4,269	6,860
Capital work in progress	803	3,017	425
Total fixed assets	5,573	8,223	8,223
Deferred tax	46	437	175
Investments	2	0	520
Cash and marketable securities	31,117	39,914	52,532
Accounts receivable	11,684	17,432	19,036
Other current assets	2,949	2,945	4,255
Total current assets	45,750	60,291	75,823
Accounts payable	4,370	5,745	6,695
Provisions	2,760	4,201	4,850
Total current liabilities & provisions 7,130	9,947	11,545	
Working capital	38,621	50,345	64,278
Application of funds	**44,241**	**59,005**	**73,196**

Source: Edelweiss Research, Company Annual Reports.

Note: ₹/US$ Exchange Rate = ₹48.50/US$.

Exhibit E1.4 *Cash Flow Statement (₹m)*

	2006	**2007**	**2008**
Cash flow from operations	10,133	14,133	18,978
Cash for working capital	(2,605)	(4,078)	(1,316)
Net operating cash flow (A)	7,529	10,056	17,662
Net purchase of fixed assets	(2,446)	(3,827)	(1,636)
Net purchase of investments	0	(15,129)	(520)
Others	301	2,130	0
Cash flow from investments (B)	(451)	(17,088)	(2,156)
Dividends	(1,838)	(2,611)	(2,989)
Proceeds from issue of equity	1,399	3,016	1,431
Proceeds from LTB/STB	838	452	(1,129)
Interest paid & other items	(55)	(155)	(201)
Cash flow from financing (C)	343	702	(2,889)
Exchange rate differences (d)	12	92	0
Change in cash (A + B + C) + (D)	7,433	(6,238)	12,617

Source: Edelweiss Research, Company Annual Reports.

Note: ₹/US$ Exchange Rate = ₹48.50/US$.

Exhibit E1.5 *Valuation Metrics and Shareholding Pattern*

Valuation Metrics			
	2006	**2007**	**2008**
Price/Earnings (x)	31.7	23.0	19.2
P/CF (x)	25.2	20.8	17.4
P/BV (x)	7.5	5.6	4.4
EV/EBITDA (x)	25.1	18.5	14.7
EV/Revenues (x)	6.1	4.4	3.2
Market cap/revenues (x)	6.7	5.0	3.8
Shareholding in 2008			
Promoters	8.7%		
Mutual funds, financial institutions and banks[24]	13%		
Foreign institutional investors	48.2%		
Others	30.1%		

Source: Edelweiss Research, Company Annual Reports.

Exhibit E1.6 *Satyam Share Price History (Jan 1, 2005 to Jan 7, 2009, ₹)*

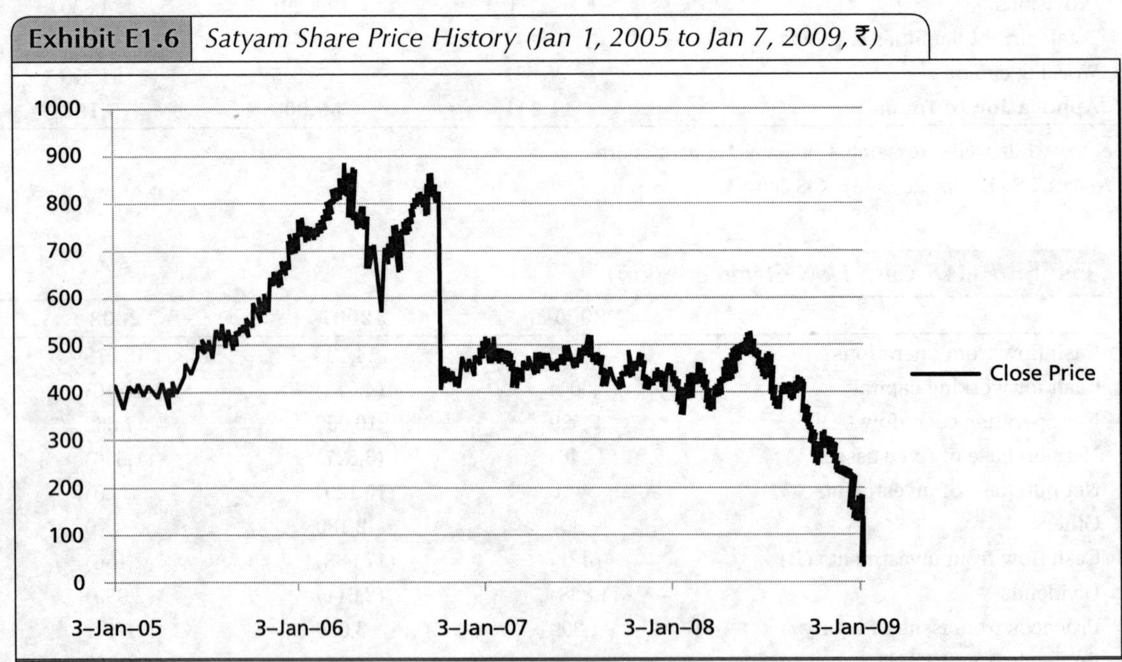

Source: Bombay Stock Exchange.

[24] The institutional investors included Fidelity, Life Insurance Corporation of India, L&T, Land Capital and Religare Securities.

Exhibit E1.7 *Composition of Satyam Board Committees*

Audit Committee

The audit committee comprised of only independent directors.

The functions of the audit committee included:

1. Oversight of the company's financial reporting process and disclosure of financial information to ensure that the financial statements are correct, sufficient, and credible.
2. Recommending to the board the appointment, re-appointment and, if required, the replacement or removal of the statutory auditor and the fixation of audit fees.
3. Approval of engagement and payment to statutory auditors for any other nonaudit services rendered by the statutory auditors.
4. Reviewing with the management, the quarterly financial statements before submission to the board for approval.
5. Reviewing with the management, performance of statutory and internal auditors, and adequacy of the internal control systems.
6. Reviewing the adequacy of internal audit function including the structure of the internal audit department, staffing and seniority of the official heading the department, and reporting structure, coverage, and frequency of internal audit.

Committee Composition and Number of Meetings

Name	Held	Attended
M. R. Rao	5	4
Mangalam Srinivasan	5	3
T. R. Prasad	5	5
V. S. Raju	5	5

Compensation Committee Composition and Number of Meetings

The compensation committee evaluated compensation and benefits for executive directors and framed policies and systems for associate stock option plans.

Name	Held	Attended
M. R. Rao	2	1
Mangalam Srinivasan	2	2
Vinod Dham	2	1
V. S. Raju	2	2

Compensation of Independent Directors (₹)

S.no.	Name of Director	Commission	Sitting Fees	Other
1	Dr Mangalam Srinivasan	1,200,000	90,000	Nil
2	Professor Krishna G. Palepu	1,200,000	20,000	6,527,000*
3	Mr Vinod K. Dham	1,200,000	30,000	Nil
4	Professor M. Rammohan Rao	1,200,000	80,000	Nil
5	Mr T. R. Prasad	1,200,000	100,000	Nil
6	Professor V. S. Raju	1,200,000	120,000	Nil
Sub-Total		7,200,000	440,000	6,527,000*

* Represents management consultancy fee paid.

(continued)

Exhibit E1.7 *(continued)*

Compensation of Executive Directors	
Ramalinga Raju	₹4,549,412[25]
B. Rama Raju	₹4,341,519
Ram Mynampati (whole time director)	₹21,531,310[26]

Employees were also granted stock options. The details of Associate Stock Option Plans (ASOP) are given as:

Particulars	**ASOP– A**	**ASOP – B**	**ASOP – ADS ASOP–RSUs**	**ASOP – RSUs (ADS)**
Total number of options in force	10,815	12,062,094 1,195,642	2,767,973	495,175

Source: Mahindra Satyam Annual Report 2008–09 and 2009–2010.
Note: ₹/US$ Exchange Rate = ₹48.50/US$.

Exhibit E1.8 *Time Line of Company History*

1987 to 2008	
1987	Incorporated as a private limited company
1991	Goes Public; IPO is oversubscribed 17 times
1993	Awarded ISO 9001 certification
1999	Assessed at SEI CMM Level 5
	Satyam Infoway becomes the first Indian Internet company listed on NASDAQ
	Presence established in 30 countries
	Forms JV with TRW Inc.
2000	Associate count reaches 10,000
	Receives National HRD award from Indian government
2001	Becomes world's first ISO 9001: 2000 company to be certified by BVQI
	Listed on New York Stock Exchange
	Asia Pacific headquarters established in Singapore
2002	Satyam BPO launched
2005	Largest global development center outside India (in Melbourne) begins operation
	Citisoft and Knowledge Dynamics acquired
2006	Sets up the first "Global Innovation Hub" in Singapore
	Sets up operations in Guangzhou, China
2007	Satyam becomes the official IT service provider for the FIFA world cups, 2010 (South Africa) and 2014 (Brazil)
	Acquires UK-based Nitor Global Solutions
	Opens development center in Malaysia
	Becomes the first Asian company to feature in the *Training Magazine*'s list of top 125 companies for learning
2008	Enters agreement to acquire S&V Management Consultants, a Belgium-based, supply chain management consulting firm
	Becomes the first company to launch a secondary listing on Euronext Amsterdam under NYSE Euronext's new "Fast Path" process for cross listings in New York and Europe
	Becomes the first company to be invited by the National Stock Exchange (NSE) to ring the opening bell
	Enters into a definitive agreement to acquire Chicago-based Bridge Strategy Group

Source: Company website, 2009.

[25] About US$100,000.

[26] Ram Mynampati was also granted 514,860 stock options from 2001–07.

Exhibit E1.9 *Excerpts from Narayana Murthy Committee Recommendations on Corporate Governance*

Audit Committees
Audit committees of publicly listed companies should be required to review the following information mandatorily:

- Financial statements and draft audit report, including quarterly/half-yearly financial information
- Management discussion and analysis of financial condition and results of operations
- Reports relating to compliance with laws and to risk management
- Management letters/letters of internal control weaknesses issued by statutory/internal auditors, and
- Records of related party transactions

Financial Literacy
All audit committee members should be "financially literate" and at least one member should have accounting or related financial management expertise.

Explanation 1: The term "financially literate" means the ability to read and understand basic financial statements, that is, balance sheet, profit and loss account, and statement of cash flows.

Explanation 2: A member will be considered to have accounting or related financial management expertise if he or she possesses experience in finance or accounting, or requisite professional certification in accounting, or any other comparable experience or background that results in the individual's financial sophistication, including being or having been a chief executive officer, chief financial officer, or other senior officer with financial oversight responsibilities.

Audit Reports and Audit Qualifications

In case a company has followed a treatment different from that prescribed in an accounting standard, management should justify why they believe such alternative treatment is more representative of the underlying business transaction. Management should also clearly explain the alternative accounting treatment in the footnotes to the financial statements.

Related Party Transactions

A statement of *all* transactions with related parties including their bases should be placed before the independent audit committee for formal approval/ratification. If any transaction is not on an arm's length basis, management should provide an explanation to the audit committee justifying the same.

Nonexecutive Director Compensation

All compensation paid to nonexecutive directors may be fixed by the Board of Directors and should be approved by shareholders in general meeting. Limits should be set for the maximum number of stock options that can be granted to nonexecutive directors in any financial year and in aggregate. The stock options granted to the nonexecutive directors shall vest after a period of at least 1 year from the date such nonexecutive directors have retired from the Board of the Company.

Companies should publish their compensation philosophy and statement of entitled compensation in respect of nonexecutive directors in their annual report. Alternatively, this may be put up on the company's website and reference drawn thereto in the annual report.

Companies should disclose on an annual basis, details of shares held by nonexecutive directors, including on an "if-converted" basis. Nonexecutive directors should be required to disclose their stock holding (both own or held by/for other persons on a beneficial basis) in the listed company in which they are proposed to be appointed as directors, prior to their appointment. These details should accompany their notice of appointment.

Independent Directors
The term "independent director" is defined as a nonexecutive director of the company who:

- Apart from receiving director remuneration, does not have any material pecuniary relationships or transactions with the company, its promoters, its senior management or its holding company, its subsidiaries and associated companies

(continued)

Exhibit E1.9 *(continued)*

- Is not related to promoters or management at the board level or at one level below the board.
- Has not been an executive of the company in the immediately preceding three financial years.
- Is not a partner or an executive of the statutory audit firm or the internal audit firm that is associated with the company, and has not been a partner or an executive of any such firm for the last three years. This will also apply to legal firm(s) and consulting firm(s) that have a material association with the entity.
- Is not a supplier, service provider or customer of the company. This should include lessor-lessee type relationships also, and
- Is not a substantial shareholder of the company, that is, owning 2% or more of the block of voting shares.
- The considerations as regards remuneration paid to an independent director shall be the same as those applied to a nonexecutive director.

Analyst Reports

- Disclosure in the report issued by a security analyst whether the company that is being written about is a client of the analyst's employer or an associate of the analyst's employer, and the nature of services rendered to such company, if any, and
- Disclosure in the report issued by a security analyst whether the analyst or the analyst's employer or an associate of the analyst's employer hold or held (in the 12 months immediately preceding the date of the report) or intend to hold any debt or equity instrument in the issuer company that is the subject matter of the report of the analyst.

Source: Committee Report.

Exhibit E1.10 *Income Statement of Tech Mahindra (₹'0 million)*

Revenues	4,350
EBITDA	1,000
EBITDA margin %	23
Debt assumed	2,000
Existing interest	5.3
Additional interest	200
PBT	920
PBT margin %	21.2
PAT before minority interest	782
Minority interest	
PAT after minority interest	783
PAT margin %	18
Number of shares (million)	131
EPS (₹)	59.8

Source: Angel Broking.

CASE

2

Financing Strategy at Tata Steel[1]

Description: The case documents the issue of equity by a world-scale steel company in India. Students are asked to evaluate the attractiveness of the offer and its timing, apart from undertaking an analysis of the historical choice of securities.

Learning Objective: To teach students capital structure theories, the thought process behind security issuance, the dynamic nature of finance, and the role of a CFO and to build skill in valuation analysis.

Subjects Covered: Financial management, financing, takeovers.

In January 2011, Anuj Gupta, an analyst at a major brokerage was reviewing the red herring prospectus of Tata Steel Ltd (TSL) to issue shares to the investing public.[2] On January 17, 2011, TSL, a world-size steel company in India, announced the issue of 57 million equity shares of ₹10 face value amounting to ₹34.77 billion. The company gave a formal notice to the Securities Exchange Board of India, the stock market regulator, that it would launch a follow-on public offer (FPO) on January 19. The issue comprised a net issue to the public of 55 million shares and a reservation of 15 million equity shares for subscription by eligible employees. It would constitute 5.94% of the post-issue paid-up equity share capital of the company. The proceeds of the issue would be used (a) to part-finance the company's share of capital expenditure for expansion of existing works at Jamshedpur,[3] (b) to redeem certain redeemable

[1] This case was prepared by Rajesh Haldipur, Independent, Kulbir Singh of Institute of Management Technology, Nagpur, India, and S. R. Vishwanath of Shiv Nadar University, Uttar Pradesh, India, as a basis for class discussion rather than to illustrate either the effective or ineffective handling of an administrative or business situation.

[2] See http://www.moneycontrol.com/news/ipo-tip/tata-steel-fpo-opens-should-you-subscribe_514217.html

[3] The expansion work at the Jamshedpur plant scheduled for completion by March 2011 would augment the steel production capacity of the plant to 10 million tons per annum.

nonconvertible debentures issued by the company on a private placement basis,[4] and (c) for general corporate purposes. The issue would open on January 19, 2011, and close on January 21, 2011. The issue would be 100% book built. The issue price would be set in the band of ₹594–₹610 per share at a price discovered through book building. Upon subscription, the shares would be listed on the Bombay Stock Exchange and the National Stock Exchange of India. The company appointed Kotak Mahindra, Citigroup, Deutsche Equities, HSBC Securities, RBS Equities, SBI Capital, and Standard Chartered Securities as book running lead managers.

Anuj had noticed that TSL had issued at least half a dozen securities during 2007–11. He wondered what led to TSL's ever-growing financing needs. In light of the company's analysis he had to give an investment recommendation to subscribe or avoid the issue.

On the Bombay Stock Exchange, Tata Steel shares were trading at ₹621 per share on January 17, down 2.47% from the previous close.

COMPANY BACKGROUND

Incorporated in 1907, TSL was India's largest steel company with a steel production capacity of approximately 25.2 million tons per annum (mtpa; see Table E2.1 for the breakup of capacity). The company had a presence across the entire value chain of steel manufacturing, including production and distribution of finished products as well as mining and processing iron ore and coal for its steel production. According to WSA (World Steel Association), the company was the seventh-largest steel company in the world in terms of crude steel production volume in 2009. Tata Steel's operations were primarily focused in India, Europe, and other countries in the Asia Pacific. In 2010, the company's operations in Europe and India represented 62.9% and 28.8% of its total steel production respectively.

TSL offered a broad range of steel products including a portfolio of high value-added downstream products such as hot rolled coils, sections, plates, and wires. Tata Steel was also a large producer of ferrochrome in India. The company's customers primarily comprised the construction, automotive, aerospace, consumer goods, material handling, and general engineering industries. Its main facilities were located at Jamshedpur, India, where it operated a 6.8 mtpa crude steel production plant and a variety of finishing plants close to the iron ore and coal reserves.

Exhibits E2.1 through E2.6 present TSL's financial statements, key ratios, steel industry peer group ratio comparison, and stock price history.

COMPETITIVE STRENGTHS AND STRATEGY

Tata Steel had a number of competitive strengths:

Global scale: With operations in India, Europe, and the Asia Pacific, it could attract multinational customers who increasingly rely on maintaining relationships with a few global suppliers.

[4] Tata Steel had a net debt of US$10.7 billion. It was expected to use ₹10,900 million from the FPO proceeds to pay the redemption amount of some of the maturing redeemable nonconvertible debentures.

Table E2.1 *Steel Production Capacity*

	Steel Production Capacity (in mtpa)
Europe	
IJmuiden steelworks, Netherlands	7.7
Port Talbot steelworks, West Glamorgan, Wales	4.9
Scunthorpe steelworks, South Humberside, England	4.5
Rotherham steelworks, South Yorkshire, England	1.3
India	
Jamshedpur Steelworks, Jharkhand	6.8
Total	**25.2**

Source: Tata Steel RHP.

Cost competitiveness: In India, TSL had captive iron ore and coal mines because of which it was insulated from the volatility of raw material prices. Further, its labor cost was much lower when compared to other multinational steel companies. Because of these reasons, TSL had a strong cost advantage. Consequently, it had the highest earnings before interest, tax, depreciation and amortization (EBITDA)/ton when compared to domestic peer companies.

Strong market position: TSL had a strong position in flat and long products in India and served customers in a variety of industries. While the customer industries were growing rapidly, competition from other Indian companies was limited because of high entry barriers

Through the acquisition of the Corus group of UK, TSL had established a strong position in Europe. Europe accounted for 46% of TSL's sales in 2010.

Economies of scale: The Corus acquisition helped TSL achieve greater economies of scale and cost efficiencies. The acquisition allowed TSL to manage its supply chain better by reducing logistics and procurement costs, and providing bargaining power with suppliers.

Tata Steel's strategy had four key elements:

- It had grown significantly in recent years with its steel production capacity increasing from approximately 5.0 mtpa in 2006 to 27.2 mtpa in 2011. The company intended to increase its size further as demand for steel grew. The increase in size was expected to provide scale economies and cost advantage.
- Tata Steel sought proprietary access to raw materials in order to avoid cyclical fluctuations and reduce volatility in production cost.[5]

[5] The top three mining companies, BHP Billiton, CVRD, and Rio Tinto, control the supply of processed iron ore to steel mills and therefore have significant bargaining power. Substantial increases in iron ore prices by these mining companies had forced steel producers to raise prices to maintain margins in recent years. Many leading steel companies were also looking to pursue investments in mines as a safeguarding measure against rising raw material costs. In addition, steelmakers were adjusting to a recent shift in the pricing of iron ore and coking coal after Vale, BHP Billiton and other raw material suppliers abandoned the 40-year tradition of annual prices in favor of the quarterly, index-linked, contracts system. This change to quarterly pricing exposed steel producers to additional volatility and price risk.

- It planned to increase its access to ports and shipping lines in order to gain control over its distribution channels, improve supply chain processing, and reduce freight and logistics costs.
- The company planned to expand its operations through strategic alliances with joint venture (JV) partners throughout its chain of operations, including for raw material procurement (primarily for mining), steel production, and port and shipping. Its strategic partners included New Millennium Capital, JFE Steel, Nippon Steel, and POSCO for mining; Vietnam Steel Corp, Vietnam Cement Industries Corp, BlueScope Steel for steel production; and Larsen & Toubro and NYK Line for ports and shipping.

INDUSTRY BACKGROUND[6]

The global steel industry is cyclical, with its growth linked to the economic cycles of countries. In particular, industrial production, infrastructure development, trade policies of countries, regional demand-supply imbalances, all affected the industry. Manufacturers of steel attempted to reduce the impact of cyclicality by diversifying manufacturing operations, customer base, and product mix and focusing on value added products.

According to the WSA, global crude steel production in 2009 was approximately 1,224 mt, while global steel consumption was 1,127 mt.

Global Steel Production

Growth in steel production had been volatile. According to the WSA, global steel production grew on average by negative 0.5% per year from 1990 to 1995, 2.4% per year from 1995 to 2000, and 6.1% per year from 2000 to 2005.

During 2005–09, global steel production increased by approximately 1.7% per year. Individual rates for these years ranged from 9.0% in 2006 to –7.9% in 2009.The overall global crude steel production in 2009 was 1,224 mt, a 7.9% decrease in production over the previous year.

For the 10 months ending on October 31, 2010, the WSA estimated that total crude steel production in 66 countries (which accounted for more than 98% of the total global crude steel production in 2009) was 1,165.1 mt—a growth of approximately 17.5% over the same period in 2009. China recorded a 10.7% increase in production for the 10 months ending October 31, 2010, as compared to the same period in 2009, and production in the USA and EU27 grew by approximately 44.7% and 29.1% respectively, over the same period. This was preceded by declines in the USA and Europe of 43.6% and 36% respectively for the 10 months ending October 31, 2009, as compared to the same period in 2008. Over the past decade, steel production had continued

[6] This section is reproduced from Tata Steel's Red Herring Prospectus.

to shift, from its traditional base in heavily industrialized countries to fast-growing developing markets such as China and India.

Global Steel Consumption

The USA and Europe have historically been the major consumers of steel. In 2000, the USA and EU27 accounted for 37.8% of consumption of steel globally, while Japan accounted for 10% and India and China accounted for 3.6% and 16.3% respectively. By 2005, the USA and EU27 accounted for 26.4%, Japan accounted for 7.3%, and China and India accounted for 33.2% and 3.8% of global steel consumption.

In 2009, the contribution of the USA and EU27 in aggregate was just 15.8% and that of Japan was 4.7%. However, China accounted for 48.1% and India accounted for 4.9% of the global steel consumption in 2009.

Overall steel consumption in 2009 was 1,127.3 mt, a 6.7% decrease over the previous year. Over this period, steel consumption decreased in all regions except China and India. The EU 27 consumption was 118.7 mt, a 34.9% decrease over the previous year. The EU 27 decrease represented 78.2% of the total global decrease in consumption. The progression of the US financial crisis into a global economic crisis brought about a massive and regionally synchronized global decline in demand for steel in late 2008. For most of the world, this trend continued into the first quarter of 2009. According to the WSA, in 2009, China was the largest single steel consumer of finished steel products in the world, consuming approximately 542.4 mt of finished steel products, which represents a 24.8% increase over 2008. In 2009, India was the fourth-largest steel consumer, consuming approximately 55.3 mt of crude steel.

Global Steel Prices

Steel prices are volatile and fluctuate in response to changes in global supply and demand, raw material costs, and general economic conditions. After a downturn in demand beginning in 1998, global steel prices reached a historic low in the third quarter of 2001. Since then, global steel prices have increased, reflecting stronger global demand, notably led by China. In the third quarter of 2008, global steel prices declined sharply due to weak global economic conditions, which led to a fall in global demand. The steel industry also fluctuates in response to a combination of factors, including the availability and cost of raw materials global production capacity the existence of, and changes in, steel imports, exchange rates, transportation, and labor costs; and protective trade measures. In recent years, global steel prices have also been increasingly volatile due to increased communications across global markets and levels of steel trading as a percentage of total steel production.

Global Steel Outlook

According to the WSA, in 2009, steel consumption in the USA declined by 39.8% compared to 2008, but was expected to increase by 32.9% in 2010 and 9.4% in 2011, bringing it back to 80% of its 2007 level. Europe had been the most affected outside the NAFTA region. The EU27, the other Europe, and the Commonwealth of Independent States had shown declines of 35.7%,

17.3% and 28.3% respectively in their steel consumption in 2009. Japan had also been affected by a sharp decline in the exports of its steel-using industries, especially the automotive and machinery industries. Steel consumption in Japan declined by 32.3% in 2009 but was expected to increase by 19% in 2010. Steel consumption in EU27 was expected to increase by 18.9% in 2010 and 5.7% in 2011. Other Europe was also expected to witness growth in steel consumption by 20.1% in 2010 and 9.5% in 2011. Steel consumption in the NAFTA region was likely to grow by 31.3% in 2010 and 8.7% in 2011. Steel consumption in EU is expected to increase by 18.9% in 2010 due to inventory rebuilding and strength in the export sector. In 2011, an increase in real usage was expected to drive the steel demand to 147.4 mt, bringing it to 75% of the 2007 peak.

Emerging economies were affected by the economic crisis as well, but to a lesser degree. India was projected to have a positive growth of 13.9% in steel consumption in 2010 and 13.7% in 2011 after growing 7.7% in 2009. The economies of the BRIC countries (Brazil, Russia, India, and China) as a whole were forecasted to grow by 8.6% in 2010 and 4.9% in 2011 after growing 17.5% in 2009. The BRIC economies were expected to contribute 37.4% and 50.5% of the incremental demand in 2010 and 2011.

China was expected to witness a growth of 6.7% in steel consumption in 2010 and 3.5% in 2011 after growing 24.8% in 2009. Steel consumption for the world, excluding China, was expected to increase by 19.0% in 2010 and 6.8% in 2011.

THE CORUS ACQUISITION

Tata Steel had recently included in its fold NatSteel, Singapore, and Millennium Steel, Thailand, creating a manufacturing network in eight markets in South East Asian and Pacific Rim countries.

Commenting on the acquisitions, Koushik Chatterjee, Group CFO of Tata Steel said:

> meeting our growth goals through organic means in India, unfortunately, is not the fastest approach, especially for large capital projects, due to significant delays on various fronts. Nor are there many opportunities for growth through acquisitions in India, particularly in sectors like steel, where the value to be captured is limited—for example, in terms of technology, product profiles, the product mix, and good management. India actually needs a faster pace of increased organic capacity in steel in the near future to meet its growing demand.
>
> So to pursue our overall growth strategy, we needed to go beyond India. And as the first step, we looked at the ASEAN rim for our initial acquisitions, due to the nearness of the markets. When we acquired NatSteel Asia, headquartered out of Singapore, in 2004, it gave us immediate access to six markets in the region, including Vietnam, the Philippines, and Malaysia. They may not be very big now, but these countries have meaningful populations and are on a trajectory for growth over the longer term, making them very attractive for the future. And by the way, these first regional acquisitions also let us test the waters of M&A and taught us how to run a transnational business, to understand the cultural issues, and to integrate larger organizations. (*McKinsey Quarterly* 2009)

On October 20, 2006, the board of directors of Anglo-Dutch steelmaker Corus accepted a US$7.6 billion takeover bid from Tata Steel, the Indian steel company. The following months saw a lot of negotiations from both sides of the deal. Tata Steel's bid to acquire Corus Group was challenged by Companhia Siderúrgica Nacional (CSN), the Brazilian steel maker. Finally, on January 30, 2007, Tata Steel purchased a 100% stake in the Corus Group at 608 pence per share in an all cash deal, cumulatively valued at US$12.04 billion. The deal was the largest Indian takeover of a foreign company and made Tata Steel the world's fifth-largest steel group.

To finance the acquisition, Tata Steel put together a package consisting of many securities, including a new security entitled Convertible Alternative Reference Security. After examining several alternatives of coming together, Corus and Tata Steel finally decided that a leveraged buyout (LBO) would be the best way to go. For that, they needed a scheme of arrangement wherein they could acquire 100% of the shareholding of Corus. The management felt that anything less would mean leakage of funds, because the cash flows generated by the acquired entity was expected to flow to the acquirer or its bankers through dividends declared at short intervals. If the holding (in the acquired company) was less than 100%, the minority shareholders whose shares were not acquired would also be entitled to the dividends declared. The dividends paid to these minority shareholders would then represent a leakage of funds.

The board of Corus recommended Tata Steel's bid to its shareholders. However, there was another bidder—CSN, a Brazilian company—which also had a business relationship with Corus. Like TSL, CSN too could assure raw material security for Corus as it had substantial iron ore and coal mining interests. Lack of raw material security was a major reason why Corus had a post-tax profit of 5%, whereas Tata Steel was four times as profitable, though TSL was one-fourth the size of Corus. Therefore, an auction was conducted by the UK government to ensure the best deal for Corus shareholders. This turned out to be a bruising auction that went into eight rounds, with at least US$750 million being added to the bid with every round.

The eventual price paid was 608 pence per share, when the price of a Corus share was less than 50 pence just 4 years earlier. This was funded in a large measure by nonrecourse borrowing by Tata Steel through three special purpose vehicles (SPVs) incorporated in Netherlands. The Dutch law did not permit a lender to go beyond the immediate borrower and "pierce the corporate veil" to recover money from the parent company. This was a costlier form of borrowing but suited the Tata group very much because it would insulate Tata Steel from a possible failure of Corus and the consequent debt default. Thus, Tata Steel was able to structure the deal such that the predominant portion of funding came from debt that would be repaid from the cash flows of Corus after the acquisition, while at the same time ensuring that the parent company's leverage ratio remained low enough for it to continue to raise money.

The compelling reasons for acquiring Corus (from the perspective of the Tatas) were two-fold:

1. In a single stroke it would catapult TSL from the 60th position to the 6th position among steel producers of the world.
2. It would be possible for Tata Steel to make Corus more competitive over a period by:
    a. Aggressively addressing the vulnerability of Corus to vagaries of raw material prices through acquisition of strategic stakes and ownership of key raw material sources from all over the world.
    b. Shifting the business model gradually over 5–10 years so that the expensive, inefficient primary steel manufacturing (billets/ingots) could be shifted to India or other countries rich in iron ore and coal/gas, while the creation of value-added saleable steel products (flats and longs) could take place in UK/Europe (i.e., near the markets). This made sense because primary steel could be cheaply transported by sea, and raw material (as well as labor) was much cheaper in India. This had enabled Tata Steel to

become the lowest cost producer of steel in the world, despite not enjoying the benefits of scale.

The acquisition was financed as follows:

- Tata Steel's subsidiary in Singapore became the vehicle for raising the equity portion of the money. This way, India's case-by-case approval and foreign direct investment (FDI) limits could be circumvented, because the acquisition and investment was by a wholly owned subsidiary outside India, thanks to a "loophole" in the FDI provisions.
- Tata Sons and Tata Steel together contributed around ₹40 billion to the equity of this wholly owned subsidiary. Tata Sons raised its stake largely by selling about 0.8% of shares in Tata Consultancy Services, another Tata group company, at about ₹.9 billion, which hardly made any difference because it held nearly 80% of the shares in this software and IT services giant. Tata Steel, till the Corus acquisition, was a cash-rich company, with about ₹30 billion in liquid investments, adding about ₹50 million every day to this kitty. The acquisition transformed Tata Steel from a cash-rich, low debt company to a cash-hungry giant that would be in constant fund-raising mode over the next several years. Almost all its liquid investments disappeared to fund the Corus acquisition.
- The equity contribution from Tata Sons and Tata Steel were not enough, so a significant amount of "bridge loans" were taken to finance the "equity" portion of the funding requirement (about ₹120 billion). The bridge loans for equity used in the acquisition were repaid by June, 2008, after which the complete loan acquisition funding pattern became clear. The compositions of acquisition funding structures before and after paying off the bridge financing are shown in Figures E2.1a and E2.1 billion.
- Together with the contributions of Tata Steel and Tata Sons, the entire "equity" portion was transferred to the three SPVs in the Netherlands (as equity contribution).[7] These SPVs then raised debt in the ratio of (approximately) 3:1, leading to total fund collection of around ₹650 billion, the acquisition price of 100% of Corus.
- Between the time that Tata Steel won the right to buy out Corus in the auction and the time the company's shareholder and creditor approvals were put in place, the Tata group managed to renegotiate the lending terms for financing the leveraged nonrecourse debt. Two of the original three bankers were changed, and it is believed that over the lifetime of the loans, probably US$1 billion was saved in interest costs due to the renegotiation. In addition, key concessions were negotiated in the matter of pre-payment penalties, and so on. These would have an uncertain beneficial impact on the company.

LIFE AFTER THE CORUS ACQUISITION

In November 2007, Tata Steel purchased a 35% stake in a coal venture owned by Riversdale Mining Limited in the Tete province of Mozambique (Benga Project) for AU$100 million. The company had 40% off-take rights of the total output. In addition, Tata Steel also increased its

[7] The SPVs were created to ring-fence and collect repayments of three bankers who funded the acquisition.

stake in the parent, Riversdale Mining, to 24%, increasing its economic interest in the Benga project to 50.6%.

Later on, Rio Tinto, another mining giant, made an all-cash offer for Riversdale at AU$16/ share, valuing the company at AU$3.9 billion. The bid was recommended by all directors of Riversdale except Tata Steel's representative. Rio Tinto's bid for Riversdale implied a value of US$920 million (₹46 per share) for Tata Steel's stake in Riversdale. Industry observers believed that Tata Steel would maintain its status quo stand because counter bidding would stretch its balance sheet, and selling its stake would lead to lower integration.[8]

All of the above happened in spite of a world-wide recession leading to price and demand crashes in 2008.

In September 2010, Tata Steel acquired an 80% interest in a Canadian iron ore project New Millennium Capital Corporation (NML), along with 100% off-take rights for the project. In addition, the company acquired approximately 27% of the common shares of NML.

Also, in 2010, raw material suppliers got together and switched from annual to quarterly rate contracts, thus, making raw material prices, and, hence, steel prices more volatile.

In January 2011, TSL and Nippon Steel, entered into a JV agreement to construct a continuous annealing and processing line, which would produce automotive cold-rolled flat products. TSL would have a 51% stake in the JV. The expected capacity of the plant was 0.6 mtpa and it would be situated in Jamshedpur, India. It was scheduled to be completed by 2013.

The company was constructing a multipurpose industrial park at Gopalpur in the Ganjam district of Orissa. The park would primarily consist of office and industrial space and cater to companies in the ores and minerals, gems and jewelry, engineering, auto ancillary, chemicals and drugs, textiles, and marine processing sectors as tenants.

The company, in an effort to secure more coking coal for Indian operations, purchased a 5% interest in the Carborough Downs Coal Project located in Queensland, Australia. It also entered into an agreement that entitled it to purchase up to 20% of the project's annual coal production (with a minimum off-take of 5%), with 12 months notice and at market prices, over the life of the project. This JV had Vale, JFE Steel, Nippon Steel, and Posco as partners.

It entered into a:

1. 50-50 JV with Steel Authority of India Limited (SAIL) to acquire and develop coal mines in India. It had been working toward acquiring several coal blocks in India.
2. JV with Vicem and VN Steel to construct an integrated steel plant in Vietnam. TSL, VNSteel, and Vicem, would have equity stakes of 65%, 30%, and 5% respectively in the JV. The initial capacity of the plant was expected to be 4.5 mtpa.
3. 50-50 JV with L&T Ltd to develop a deep seaport at Dhamra, Odisha, in order to enhance the company's import and export logistics capabilities from India. The port was expected to be capable of handling 13 mtpa of coal and 6 mtpa of iron ore. It could accommodate vessels with a capacity of 180,000 dead weighttons. The port commenced its trial operations in September 2010.

TSL was also trying to sell its noncore assets and improve its liquidity situation. In August 2010, Tata Steel signed a memorandum of understanding with Sahaviriya Steel Industries Public

8 Analysts expected the net market value (i.e., market value-cost of investment) to be about US$540 million.

Company Limited (SSI), Thailand's largest steel producer, whereby SSI would acquire from Corus the Teesside Cast Products (TCP) business in a transaction valued at US$500 million. Along with this, TSL also sold of 27.03% in Southern Steel Berhad, Malaysia, under its subsidiary NatSteel Holdings Pt Ltd for a total consideration of US$72 million.

Apart from the earlier rationalization of assets, the company also raised ₹10.7 billion in financial year 2011 through the issue of stock and warrants to promoters and would further receive ₹5.3 billion on conversion of warrants by the promoters in financial year 2012. Tata Steel planned to further reduce its leverage by the issue of equity shares through its FPO. The issue would lead to a dilution of 6.3% and reduce promoter's stake by 2.4%. It planned to (a) utilize ₹18 billion of the issue proceeds for the expansion of Jamshedpur plant, (b) repay debt to the tune of ₹10 billion, and (c) invest in international raw material projects in Mozambique and Canada.

Analysts expected the three mtpa capacity expansion in India to generate US$700 million of incremental EBITDA.

RECENT HISTORICAL FINANCING

Although, over the years, the net debt position of Tata Steel reduced considerably, it was still quite high.

After the Corus acquisition, Tata Steel had been proactively seizing opportunities to either re-negotiate terms or exchange securities, or raise money at lower costs and/or longer tenors well before the commitments fell due. It had also raised equity whenever it could. It explored several novel fund-raising options, including a trademarked security with the acronym of CARS (cumulative alternative reference securities; see further).

Commenting on TSL's challenges after the Corus acquisition (due to the financial crisis in Europe), Koushik Chatterjee, the company's CFO, said:

> Since the Corus acquisition, we have become a large, diverse organization in a very short time, adding significant complexity to the business, which means I spend a lot of time focusing on performance management, capital allocation, and liquidity management. But we'd been building a liquidity cushion and buffers long before the crisis. I think the best time to raise capital is when you don't need it immediately but have a long-term deployment strategy in place. That gives you the leeway to get the best out of negotiations with the providers of capital, because you're not under duress. These last 6 months have reaffirmed my view on that point, and our buffers are in long-term capital—3, 5, or 7 years—that won't need refinancing in the short term. We have also raised equity recently, which will be deployed in some very attractive capital projects, especially the growth projects in India. Given the volatility and uncertainty of the global environment, it is important to keep an adequate liquidity buffer. (*McKinsey Quarterly* 2009)

As of September 30, 2010, the company had a net debt of about US$10.7 billion (₹487,900 million), out of which US$5.32 billion was in lieu of loans taken by the company for expansion of its Indian operations. The outstanding debt also included a part of the US$4.58 billion loan taken by the company to acquire Corus in 2007.

In November, the Tata Steel board had approved a proposal to raise up to ₹70 billion (US$1.5 billion) through various instruments. Subsequently, on December 24, the company secured shareholders' approval to raise a maximum of ₹50 billion. The company's financing history for the period 2006–11 has been described:

2010–11

In July 2010, the company issued GDRs (global depository receipts) worth US$500 million at US$7.644/ share (each GDR equals one share). This was one of the largest GDR offerings by an Indian Company on the London Stock Exchange.

In addition, in July 2010, it issued warrants amounting to US$158.23 million and ordinary shares amounting to US$198 million to Tata Sons, the parent holding company.

In December 2010 and January 2011, it raised ₹30 billion via issuance of 20-year nonconvertible debentures, where the company will have no cash outgo on account of interest for the first 3 years.

2009–10

In November 2009, the company made an offer to exchange CARS it had issued in 2007[9] into foreign currency convertible bonds (FCCB) with the objective of lengthening its debt maturity profile, reducing cost, and potentially reducing future repayment obligations.[10] CARS worth US$493 million were tendered for exchange into FCCBs worth US$546.935 million.

The Company also prepaid ₹20 billion of its term debt in December 2009 and January 2010. It prepaid US$300 million of foreign currency term loans in February and March 2010. In addition, Tata Steel Europe prepaid £100 Million of its term debt in June 2009.

The company achieved financial closure for its expansion of 2.9 mtpa in Jamshedpur, for which it contracted long-term rupee borrowing aggregating to ₹93.39 billion in TSL and its subsidiary to be drawn over the next 3 years and to be repaid over a period of 7 years.

The company also tied up Export Credit Agency (ECA)-backed long-term buyer's credit (import financing) of €264 million to be drawn over the next two-and-half years and repaid over the next 10 years. The company was also in the process of obtaining an additional €70 million by way of further ECA-backed long-term buyer's credit.

In the second half of financial year 2009 and the first quarter of financial year 2010, the company had focused on raising additional debt in order to maintain a liquidity buffer given the uncertain nature of the steel markets. As a result, in April 2009, the company raised ₹20 billion from a term loan, and in May 2009, it privately placed ₹21.5 billion of nonconvertible debentures repayable after 10 years. It also contracted a term loan of ₹6.5 billion for 10 years and one of ₹1.99 billion for 7 years.

2007–08 and 2008–09

The company issued a series of 3-, 7-, 8-, and 10-year nonconvertible debentures of various amounts during 2007–09.

[9] The CARS amounting to US$875 million issued in September 2007 had a coupon of 5.15% and a tenor of 5 years. They would get converted into ordinary shares at ₹733.13 per share.

[10] The FCCBs carried a coupon of 4.5% and a tenor of 5 years. They would get converted into shares at ₹605.53 per share.

In May 2008, it raised ₹20 billion, including a green shoe option, through a private placement of redeemable nonconvertible Rupee debentures in three series:

- ₹6.2 billion worth of nonconvertible debentures Series 1 (NCDs-Series 1). They mature in May 2015 and carry a coupon rate of 10.2% payable annually. They are listed on the wholesale debt segment of the NSE.
- ₹10.9 billion worth of nonconvertible debentures Series 2 (NCDs-Series 2) with a 3-year maturity and floating rates.
- ₹2.9 billion worth of nonconvertible debentures Series 3 (NCDs-Series 3) with a 3-year maturity and fixed rate.

In November 2008, ₹12.5 billion worth of 12.5% nonconvertible debentures were issued by the company. They mature in November 2016 and carry a coupon rate of 12.5% payable annually. They are listed on the wholesale debt segment of the NSE.

2006–07

The company made a preferential issue of 27,000,000 ordinary shares with face value of ₹10 each, at a premium of ₹506 and 2,85,00,000 warrants to Tata Sons Ltd, where each warrant entitled Tata Sons to subscribe to one ordinary share of the company against payment in cash. The option to convert the warrants into ordinary shares was exercisable on or after April 1, 2007.

In addition, a share issue aggregating to ₹13.932 billion was made.

On April 16, 2007, Tata Sons exercised its option to convert 28.5 million warrants into ordinary shares at a price of ₹484.27 per share. Accordingly, ordinary shares were allotted to TSL on April 17, 2007, at a premium of ₹474.27 per share aggregating to ₹13,801.7 million.

The company raised US$100 million A loan (equivalent to ₹4,353.5 million) and US$300 million B loan from International Finance Corporation, Washington (equivalent to ₹13,060.5 million) by way of secured loans.

The company also incurred several unsecured loans the details of which are given as:

- Japanese Yen syndicated loan of US$495 million (equivalent ₹21,626.6 million).
- External commercial borrowing loan of US$5 million (equivalent ₹217.7 million) from Canara Bank, London.
- Euro Hermes Loan equivalent ₹104.7 million from Deutsche Bank, Frankfurt.
- Japanese Yen syndicated loan of US$750 million (equivalent ₹32,988.8 million) from Standard Chartered Bank.

In addition, the company also took a short-term loan of ₹2.5 billion from IDBI Bank. Exhibits E2.7a, E2.7b, and E2.7c provide a snapshot of Tata Steel's financing during 2007–11.

TSL was able to embark on this policy of opportunistically raising money, and reducing leverage and financial costs mainly because of the advantage it gained in the re-negotiation of its LBO funding package. The result was a package unlike most other LBOs in that the terms, as finally negotiated, allowed pre-payments. A standard LBO funding package consists of no more than 20% amortizable (i.e., debt that can be reduced by repayments, like term loans) loans, and the remainder is repayable at the end of years 7–10. These bullet-repayment loans are the most expensive component, and usually prepayment of these loans is prohibited. The banks agreed to relax these terms, probably because a group as large as the Tatas had enough clout and credibility to hold out the prospect of participation in possible large future deals.

CONCLUSION

In pricing the FPO, investment bankers commonly used the peer comparison approach to justify the issue price. Under the peer comparison approach, the company's implied price-earnings[11] and other multiples were compared with peer companies. Exhibits E2.8a and E2.8b present TSL's stand-alone and consolidated earnings per share and return on net worth. Exhibits E2.9a and E3.9b present the data on peer company financials and multiples.

Anuj reviewed all the documents and sat down to write his investment thesis. He also noticed that at least five brokerages, namely, Anand Rathi, Emkay Global Financial Services, ICICI Securities, India Infoline, and Networth Direct, had issued a "buy" recommendation (Bhanushali 2011; Burde 2011; Chakraborty 2011; Pandey et al. 2011; Tata Steel 2011).

REFERENCES AND SUGGESTED READINGS

Bhanushali, Tarang. 2011, January 18. *Tata Steel.* India Infoline.
Burde, Pawan. 2011, Jan 11. *Tata Steel.* Anand Rathi.
Capital Market. 2010, December 13–26. XXV (21). Available at www.capitalmarket.com (Accessed on October 16, 2017).
———. 2010/2011, December 27–January 9. XXV (22). Available at www.capitalmarket.com (Accessed on October 16, 2017).
Chakraborty, Goutam. 2011, January 19. *Tata Steel.* Emkay Global.
McKinsey Quarterly. 2009. "An Indian Approach to Global M&A: An Interview with the CFO of Tata Steel." *McKinsey Quarterly,* (October). McKinsey & Co.
Pandey, Pankaj. 2011, January 19. *Tata Steel.* ICICI Securities.
Tata Steel. 2011, January 18. Networth Direct.
Tata Steel Analyst Meet Presentation, May 25, 2011.
Tata Steel Annual Reports 2007–08, 2008–09, 2009–10, 2010–11.
Tata Steel Investor Presentation, December 2010.
Tata Steel Investor Presentation, January 2011.
Tata Steel Red Herring Prospectus.

REVIEW QUESTIONS

1. Why does TSL need to raise capital? Explain.
2. What securities make sense for TSL in early 2011? Why?
3. How has TSL performed in the recent past?
4. How would you explain the company's choice of securities in the recent years?

[11] P/E implied by the issue price assuming lower or higher of the prices within the price band used for book building.

5. In light of the facts presented in the case, would you invest in the company? Why or Why not?
6. As Anuj what recommendation would you give? Why?
7. Undertake a multiples valuation of the company's shares using the data in the case. What does your analysis suggest?
8. Value the company's equity by the sum-of-the-parts valuation methodology. Assume the following for your analysis:

EBITDA (Tata Steel)	₹125,626 million
EBITDA (Corus)	₹41,231 million
EBITDA (Asian subsidiaries)	₹3,842 million
Net Debt	₹416,029 million
No. of shares outstanding	914.85 million
Exchange rate	US$1 = ₹45

Optional Question

9. Value the company by the free cash flow valuation methodology. Assume the following:

Risk Free Rate = 7%
Market Risk Premium = 9%
Beta = 1.12
Cost of Debt = 11%
Tax Rate = 30%

Figure E2.1a *Composition of Corus Acquisition Funding Structure before the Repayment of Bridge Loans*

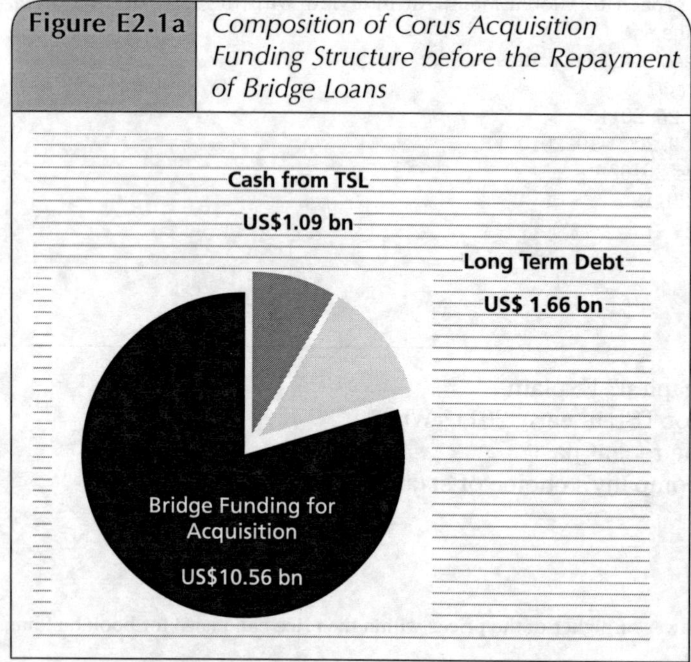

Source: Tata Steel.

Figure E2.1b *Composition of Corus Acquisition Funding Structure after the Repayment of Bridge Loans*

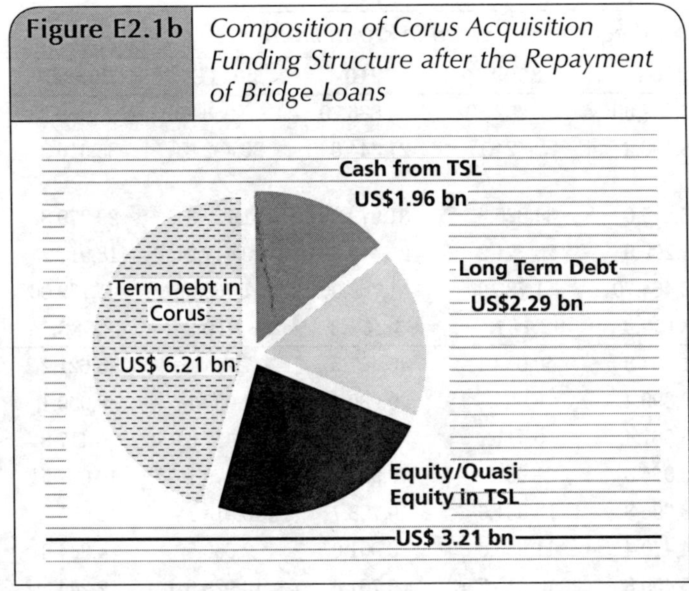

Source: Company.

Exhibit E2.1 *Consolidated Income Statements (figures given in ₹ '0 million)*

	2007	2008	2009	2010	2011E	2012E
Net sales	25,212.4	131,535.9	145,686.3	101,757.8	109,286.1	122,442.4
Other income	438.10	574.2 0	265.70	1,185.90	500.00	500.00
Raw materials	3,489.0	33,324.6	41,531.7	31,004.5	33,227.7	36,685.4
Power	1,315.0	44,929.3	5,957.40	4,051.7	4,462.00	4,940.10
Employee expenses	1,885.0	16,673.2	17,975.1	16,463.0	15,256.7	16,857.3
Freight	1,508.4	6,005.20	6,024.90	5,549.1	5,941.90	6,481.6
Total expenses	17,762.2	113,542.8	129,201.6	94,350.5	95,814.0	105,400.2
EBITDA	7,888.20	18,567.3	18,127.7	8,042.7	13,972.1	17,542.2
Depreciation	1,011.00	4,137.00	4,265.4	4,491.7	4,673.2	5,173.1
Interest	411.20	4,183.80	3,290.2	3,022.1	3,148.3	2,992.3
PBT	6,313.00	16,371.1	6,743.2	31.00	6,650.5	9,876.8
Tax	2,147.40	4,049.30	1,894.0	2,151.8	2,535.9	3,487.6
Net profit	4,177.30	12,350.0	4,950.9	–2,009.2	4,204.6	6,479.2
Dividend %	22.6	9.70	26.3	–33.4	21.9	14.1
EPS-Basic ₹	64.6	177.0	67.80	–22.7	47.4	73.1
EPS-Diluted ₹	64.60	163.10	60.40	–22.6	44.6	68.7

Source: Capitaline Database and ICICI Securities.

Exhibit E2.2 *Consolidated Balance Sheet (figures given in ₹'0 million)*

	2007	2008	2009	2010	2011E	2012E
Share capital	580.00	6,202.60	6,202.80	886.70	958.70	958.70
Reserves and surplus	14,235.8	28,198.2	22,324.1	27,344.0	30,492.8	35,916.2
Secured loans	4,961.2	35,415.0	34,329.3	31,979.3	31,129.3	29,279.3
Unsecured loans	19,964.3	18,209.8	25,571.2	21,417.2	20,417.2	18,917.2
Net deferred tax	785.90	2,464.70	1,785.60	1,769.00	1,769.00	1,769.00
Total liabilities	**42,408.5**	**92,420.4**	**92,167.7**	**85,261.3**	**86,810.3**	**88,883.7**
Net block	14,220.5	41,966.3	40,959.4	45,467.6	47,794.4	45,621.2
Capital WIP	3,326.40	8,899.4	8,930.1	9,930.1	11,930.1	9,930.1
Investments	16,497.5	3,367.4	6,411.1	5,417.8	5,417.8	5,417.8
Inventories	3,888.10	23,064.3	21,668.7	16,987.1	17,279.1	19,087.5
Sundry debtors	1,686.50	18,696.3	13,031.6	10,728.7	10,913.1	12,055.3
Cash and bank	11,228.6	4,470.4	11,383.3	6,901.0	2,650.5	4,344.0
Loans and advances	1,980.30	15,459.8	13,015.7	6,761.5	10,928.61	2,244.2
Current assets	16,804.4	46,240.1	46,090.5	34,623.7	30,849.4	35,493.6
CL and provisions	7,523.80	32,818.8	30,251.0	21,656.6	22,827.2	24,541.5
Net current assets	11,261.00	28,881.1	28,855.2	19,728.5	18,950.8	23,196.4
Total assets	**42,408.5**	**92,420.4**	**92,167.7**	**85,261.3**	**86,810.3**	**88,883.7**

Source: Capitaline Database and ICICI Securities.

Exhibit E2.3 *Cash Flow Statement (figures given in ₹million)*

	2009	2010	2011E	2012E	2013E
Operating cash flow	95,011	71,290	120,092	111,978	126,789
– Capex	83,611	69,472	91,450	78,500	58,000
Free cash flow	11,400	1,819	28,642	33,478	68,789
– Dividend	12,266	13,209	14,686	16,396	17,936
+ Equity raised	4	24,215	2,059	13,999	–
+ Debt raised	20,514	(26,866)	15,184	20,000	(20,000)
– Investments	28,712	(17,530)	–	–	–
– Misc Items	(30,253)	(2,908)	0	0	0
Net cash flow	21,192	6,396	31,198	51,081	30,852
+ Opening cash	40,291	61,482	67,878	99,077	150,158
Closing cash	61,484	67,878	99,076	150,158	181,010

Source: Anand Rathi Research.

Exhibit E2.4 *Key Ratios*

	2007	2008	2009	2010	2011E	2012E
EPS (₹)	64.6	177.0	67.8	–22.7	47.4	73.1
Cash EPS (₹)	80.2	236.3	126.2	28.0	100.1	144.6
Book value (₹)	229.1	493.1	390.7	318.4	354.7	457.5
Adj. book value (₹)	229.9	234.4	180.3	154.4	192.7	279.3
EBITDA margin (%)	31.3	14.1	12.4	7.9	12.8	14.3
Net profit margin (%)	16.6	9.4	3.4	–2.0	3.8	5.3
RONW (%)	28.2	35.9	17.4	–7.1	13.4	17.6
ROCE (%)	16.2	15.6	15.0	4.2	10.7	13.9
EV/EBITDA	4.7	4.8	4.8	11.9	7.0	5.4
Price-to-book value	2.7	1.2	1.6	1.9	1.7	1.4
P/BV Adj.	2.7	2.6	3.4	4.0	3.2	2.3

Source: Capitaline Database and ICICI Securities.

Exhibit E2.5 *Peer Group Ratio Comparison*

Interest Coverage Ratio

Company/Year	03/31/10	03/31/09	03/31/08	03/31/07	03/31/06	03/31/05	03/31/04	03/31/03
Tata Steel Ltd[12]	4.42	5.91	8.61	25.92	31.03	24.15	12.74	5.28
JSW Steel ltd	4.13	2.76	6.02	5.71	3.53	4.1	1.73	0.66
Essar Steel Ltd	0.99	1.59	2	1.92	2.06	2.65	1.13	0.99
Ispat Industries Ltd	0.75	0.71	1.1	1.02	–0.19	1.77	1.17	0.74
SAIL	26.2	37.23	46.7	29.37	13.2	15.36	3.75	0.67
JSL Stainless ltd	1.76	0.19	2.61	4.54	3.86	7.24	4.5	2.49

Debt/Equity Ratio

Company/Year	03/31/10	03/31/09	03/31/08	03/31/07	03/31/06	03/31/05	03/31/04	03/31/03
Tata Steel Ltd	0.78	0.78	0.67	0.51	0.31	0.53	0.99	1.35
JSW Steel Ltd	1.29	1.2	0.88	0.83	1.06	1.85	4.9	7.74
Essar Steel Ltd	1.85	1.46	1.47	1.69	2.1	4.41	10.8	49.56
Ispat Industries Ltd	9.19	5.37	4.5	4.84	3.91	4.35	6.62	6.84
SAIL	0.39	0.21	0.18	0.28	0.44	0.94	2.86	5.02
JSL Stainless Ltd	4.12	3.18	2.14	2.01	1.98	1.59	1.62	1.9

Net Assets/Net Worth

Company/Year	03/31/10	03/31/09	03/31/08	03/31/07	03/31/06	03/31/05	03/31/04	03/31/03
Tata Steel Ltd	1.68	2.31	2.07	1.67	1.23	1.36	1.71	2.33
JSW Steel ltd	2.26	2.51	2.06	1.8	2	2.31	4.82	8.91
Essar Steel Ltd	3.41	2.59	2.37	2.74	6.17	5.43	9.9	14.23
Ispat Industries Ltd	–22.55	–111.13	14.95	17.83	15.84	5.64	11.2	11.36
SAIL	1.5	1.27	1.13	1.23	1.32	1.53	2.65	5.91
JSL Stainless Ltd	4.93	5.36	3.33	2.88	3.19	2.72	2.4	3.14

Source: Capitaline Database.

[12] The ratios of TSL reflect consolidated results.

Exhibit E2.6 *Tata Steel Stock Price Chart (₹)*

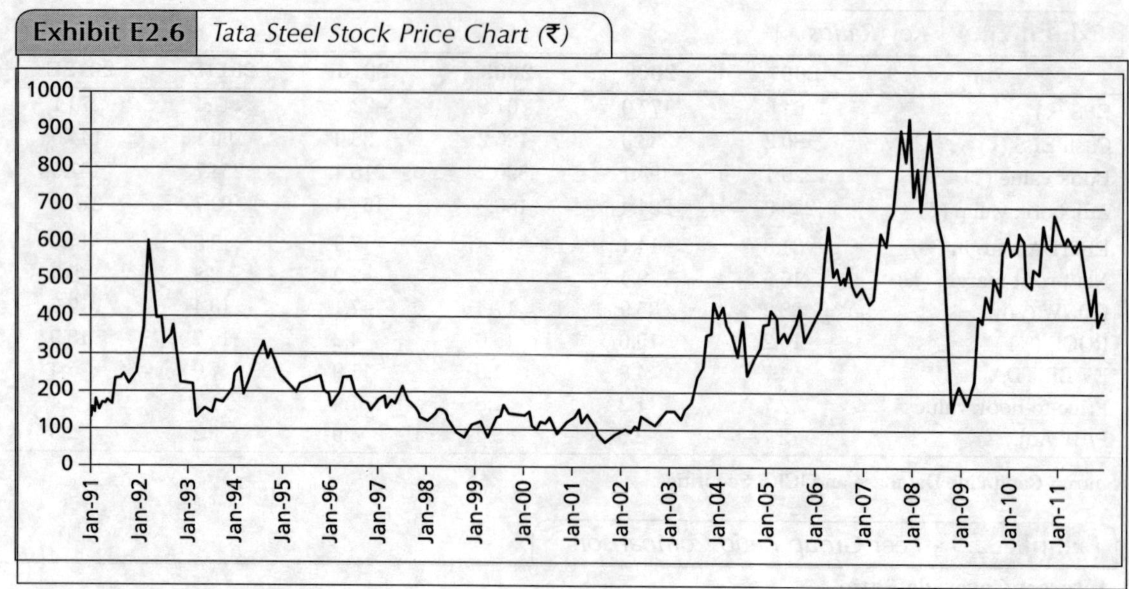

Source: Bombay Stock Exchange.

Exhibit E2.7a *Historical Financing 2009–11*

Year	Instrument	Amount
2010–11	NCD	₹30 billion No cash interest outgo for 3 years; 20 year
2010–11	GDR	US$500 million
2009–10	FCCB	CARS worth US$493 million were exchanged into FCCBs, 5 year Tenor
2009–10	Rupee term loan	₹93,390 million; 7 year tenor
2009–10	Buyer's credit	€264 million
2009–10	Term loan	₹20 billion
2009–10	NCD	₹21.50 billion (privately placed)
2009–10	Term loan	₹6.50 billion (10 years)
2009–10	Term loan	₹1.99 billion (7 years)

Source: Company website, analyst reports.

Exhibit E2.7b *Historical Security Issuance 2007–09*

Year	2009–10	2009–10	2008–09	2008–09	2008–09	2008–09
Security	NCD[13]	NCD	NCD	NCD Series 1	NCD Series 2	NCD Series 3
Amount (₹million)	15,000	6,510	12,500	6,200	10,900	2,900
Issue date	May-09	May-09	Nov-08	May-08	May-08	May-08

Year	2009–10	2009–10	2008–09	2008–09	2008–09	2008–09
Maturity date	May-19	May-19	Nov-16	May-15	May-11	May-11
Coupon %	11	10.4	12.5	10.2	Mibor + 250bp	9.8
Coupon payment	Annual					
Listing	NSE India	NSE India	NSE India	NSE India	NSE India	NSE India
Rating	AA (Fitch) AA+ (CARE)	AA (Fitch) AA+ (CARE)	AAA (Fitch)	AAA (Fitch)	AAA (Fitch)	AAA (Fitch)
Year	**2007–08**					
Security	CARS					
Amount (US$ million)	382					
Issue date	Sep-07					
Maturity date	Sep-12					
Coupon %	1					
Coupon payment	Semi annual					
Listing	SGX, Singapore					

Source: Capitaline Database, company website.

Exhibit E2.7c *Summary of Capital Raised/Repaid*

₹'0 m	Raised/ (Repaid)		
3,938	CARS	Sep 07	Used to retire bridge financing
2,000	NCDs	May 08	Used to retire bridge financing
1,250	12.5% NCDs	Nov 08	Used to retire bridge financing
5,473	Cum. Conv. Preference shares issued	Dec 08	
1,500	11.5% NCDs	May 09	
651	10.4% NCDs	May 09	
–900	Prepayment	Jun 09	
1,800	Injection as per re-negotiation	Jun 09	
2,250	GDRs Issued	Jul 09	
1,800	Injection as per re-negotiation	Sep 09	
–2,465	CARS Exchanged	Nov 09	
2,730	FCCBs issued	Nov 09	
500	10.25% NCDs	Dec 10	
–2,000	Prepaid rupee debt	Dec 10	Q4
–1,350	Prepaid foreign currency debt	Dec 10	
2,500	10.25% NCDs	Jan 11	
3,477	FPO	Jan 11	

Source: Casewriter estimates.

[13] Nonconvertible debenture.

Exhibit E2.8a *Stand Alone and Consolidated EPS of TSL*

Standalone Earning Per Share (Face Value ₹10 per Equity Share)

	Basic (₹)	Diluted (₹)	Weight
FY 2008	66.8	62.1	1
FY 2009	69.4	62.9	2
FY 2010	60.3	57.3	3
Weighted Average	**64.4**	**60.0**	
Six months ended September 30, 2010	40.8	38.7	

Consolidated Earnings Per Share (Face Value ₹10 per Equity Share)

	Basic (₹)	Diluted (₹)	Weight (₹)
FY 2008	107.4	106.4	1
FY 2009	48.0	44.9	2
FY 2010	(24.3)	(24.3)	3
Weighted Average	**21.8**	**20.6**	
Six months ended September 30, 2010	42.6	40.4	

Source: Tata Steel RHP.

Exhibit E2.8b *Stand Alone and Consolidated Return on Net Worth of TSL*

Stand Alone RONW

	RONW %	Weight
FY 2008	17.2	1
FY 2009	17.1	2
FY 2010	13.4	3
Weighted Average		**15.3**
Six months ended September 30, 2010	8.7	

Consolidated RONW

	RONW %	Weight
FY 2008	22.0	1
FY 2009	12.9	2
FY 2010	(8.7)	3
Weighted Average	**3.6**	
Six months ended September 30, 2010	13.7	

Net Asset Value per Equity Share

Net Asset Value per Equity Share as of September 30, 2010 is ₹463.6 on a standalone basis and ₹307.7 on a consolidated basis

Source: Tata Steel RHP.

Exhibit E2.9a *Domestic Peer Comparison FY 2009–10*

Name of the Company	Consolidated/ unconsolidated	EPS ₹	P/E	NAV ₹	RoNW %
Tata Steel	Unconsolidated	57.3	–	418.9	13.4
Tata Steel	Consolidated	(24.3)	–	259.7	(8.7)
JSW Steel	Unconsolidated	10	13.5	662.3	23.3
SAIL	Unconsolidated	10	12.2	80.7	22.0
Bhushan Steel	Unconsolidated	2	11.4	186.2	28.2

Source: Capital Market (2010; Industry-Steel Large).

Industry P/E	
Highest	16.3
Lowest	1.8
Industry Composite	10.9

Source: Capital Market (2010/2011; Industry-Steel Large) P/E Ratios based on TTM EPS and price as of December 20, 2010.

Exhibit E2.9b *Forecasted Multiples for Domestic and Global Steel Companies*

	P/E		EV/EBITDA		ROE		ROA	
	2011E	**2012E**	**2011E**	**2012E**	**2011E**	**2012E**	**2011E**	**2012E**
Domestic								
Tata Steel	13.0	8.6	7.0	5.4	10.7	13.9	6.8	7.4
SAIL	11.2	9.5	6.7	5.3	16.0	17.0	9.6	9.8
JSPL	15.1	12.0	10.4	8.3	33.4	30.9	14.2	14.1
JSW Steel	12.9	8.4	9.0	6.3	12.8	15.6	5.3	7.4
Global								
Arcelor Mittal	15.3	13.1	9.3	7.5	5.9	6.5	3.4	3.2
POSCO	8.9	8.3	5.9	5.4	12.5	12.1	9.3	9.1
Nippon Steel	13.2	10.7	7.1	6.5	7.4	9.4	4.4	5.1
KOBE Steel	12.9	12.0	5.7	5.4	9.2	9.9	3.7	6.1

Source: ICICI Securities.

CASE

3

IVEY | Publishing

Kingfisher Airlines Ltd: Debt Restructuring[1,2]

Description: A large Indian airline company experiences severe financial difficulties brought on by poor management practices, an ill-conceived capital expenditure plan, and an industry recession. The company is in the process of restructuring its assets, liabilities, and manpower. Students are required to assess the debt restructuring plan, determine if the company is viable, and decide whether they would invest in the company. The case teaches how to restructure a troubled firm in an emerging market like India where significant constraints on companies' ability to restructure debt (or lay off employees) exist.

Learning Objective: This case analyzes a corporate restructuring program undertaken by a large Indian company and assesses the impediments to restructuring in countries like India. It highlights the interaction between financing policy and corporate strategy, and introduces students to issues surrounding a typical restructuring. It can be used to teach a four-part framework to analyze companies.

Subjects Covered: Corporate governance, corporate restructuring, financial reporting.

In September 2011, Vijay Mallya, the chairman and managing director of Kingfisher Airlines, a leading airline company in India, stated:[3]

> The company has incurred substantial losses and its net worth has been eroded. However, having regard to improvement in the economic sentiment, rationalization measures adopted by the company, fleet recovery and the implementation of the debt recast package with the lenders and promoters (founders), including conversion of debt into share capital, these interim financial statements have been prepared on the basis that the company is a going concern and that no adjustments are required to the carrying value of assets and liabilities.

---

[1] This case has been written on the basis of published sources only. Consequently, the interpretation and perspectives presented in this case are not necessarily those of Kingfisher Airlines Ltd or any of its employees.

[2] Durga Prasad, Kulbir Singh, and S. R. Vishwanath wrote this case solely to provide material for class discussion. The authors do not intend to illustrate either effective or ineffective handling of a managerial situation. The authors may have disguised certain names and other identifying information to protect confidentiality.

[3] Chairman's letter to shareholders, Company Press Release, September 28, 2011.

This news was widely covered by Indian and international press. Analysts and media were of the opinion that Kingfisher needed equity infusion to steer it through the distress. Because of its financial difficulties, the company's stock was trading at near historic lows. Two analysts at a Canadian investment firm startled the world investment community by pointing out that Kingfisher's equity value was, in fact, negative (Monga and Raj 2011). Mallya himself was emphatic that the company was on the road to recovery, although he was negotiating a second debt restructuring with banks. In light of all these developments, the stock price had slid from a high of ₹276 in March 2007 to ₹25 in 2011.

COMPANY BACKGROUND[4]

Kingfisher Airlines was established in 2003. It was owned by the United Breweries (UB) group, which belonged to Mallya and his family. The airline started commercial operations with a fleet of four new Airbus A320 aircrafts in 2005, and started its international operations 2 years later. Its principal activity was to provide commercial airline services in India. Kingfisher operated a low-cost carrier (LCC) through Air Deccan (*Times of India* 2001), a company that was incorporated in 1995. Air Deccan went public in an initial public offering during May 2006. The company had incurred cash losses during 2006 and 2007, with accumulated losses totaling more than 50% of its net worth.[5] In order to infuse equity into the business, Air Deccan entered into an agreement with the UB group, wherein a preferential allotment of 26% of the equity shares of the company would be made at a price of ₹155 per share, helping Air Deccan raise ₹5.46 billion.[6] In 2006–07 the company issued 35 million equity shares of ₹10 each at a premium of ₹145 per share to Kingfisher Radio Ltd, who, along with UB (Holdings) Limited and UB Overseas Limited, had to make an open offer to the shareholders of the company to comply with the Securities Exchange Board of India's takeover regulations. It acquired 27 million equity shares, representing 20% of shares at a price of ₹155.[7] This resulted in an increase in the voting shares held by Kingfisher Radio Ltd and associated companies to 46%. Kingfisher Airlines merged with Air Deccan in April 2008, and the name of the company was changed to Kingfisher Airlines Ltd (see Exhibits E3.1 through E3.5).

THE UNITED BREWERIES GROUP[8]

The UB group was a conglomerate with businesses in industries that included beverages, aviation, engineering, and chemicals. The company marketed its beer under the brand name of Kingfisher and owned many other alcoholic beverage brands. Mallya served as the chairman

[4] This is based on the information contained on the company's website, www.flykingfisher.com (accessed April 2014), and Kingfisher Airlines, *Data Monitor Research Report*, January 12, 2011.

[5] *Air Deccan Annual Report*, 2007.

[6] *Kingfisher Annual Report*, 2007; *Air Deccan Annual Report*, 2007.

[7] *Kingfisher Annual Report*, 2007.

[8] This section is based on the information contained in the UB group website, www.unitedbreweries.com, http://theubgroup.com/business_landing.aspx (accessed September 12, 2017).

of the group. He also served as a member of the Indian parliament. With a personal wealth of US$800 million,[9] Mallya was listed among *Forbes'* richest 100 people in 2014 (*The Economic Times* 2014).

The UB group operated its alcoholic beverages business through two subsidiaries: United Breweries Ltd (UBL) and United Spirits Ltd. (USL). The group had more than 60% of the market share in alcoholic beverages and had 79 distilleries and bottling units around the world. In March 2005, McDowell &Company (the parent of USL) acquired Shaw Wallace from Jumbo World Holdings Limited in Dubai. The US$220 million acquisition gave the UB Group a 54.5% equity stake in Shaw Wallace. In 2006, several group companies were merged to form USL. The combined entity became the third-largest manufacturer of spirits in the world after Diageo and Pernod Ricard.[10] Several brands belonging to the group were among the fastest growing in the world. In a bid to become the top spirits company in the world ahead of Diageo, USL purchased Whyte and Mackay, a Scottish distiller, in 2007.[11]

THE AIRLINE INDUSTRY IN INDIA

The Indian airline industry had total revenue of US$7 billion in 2009, representing a compound annual growth rate (CAGR) of 19.6% from 2005 to 2009. Industry volumes increased at a CAGR of 20.6% between 2005 and 2009. The industry was expected to grow at a CAGR of 20.8% during the period from 2009 to 2014, driving the industry value to US$17.9 billion by the end of 2014.[12]

The aviation industry was a monopoly of the state until 1986, when private companies were allowed to operate as air taxi operators. In 1994, private companies were permitted to operate scheduled services. Jet Airways, Sahara, Modiluft, Damania and East West Airlines were granted scheduled carrier status in 1995. By 1997, four out of the six operators had shut down (Jet Airways and Sahara continued to operate). Air Deccan was the first to start operations as an LCC. Kingfisher, SpiceJet, Indigo, Go Air, and Paramount started operations in 2005 (Ghosh, Ray, Dewan and Shah 2012; Sabarad and Mhatre 2007).

Demand for air travel was growing in India as a result of economic development, globalization, liberalization of the industry, and declining airfares. In 2007, the industry had five full-service companies (Jet Airways, Air India, Indian Airlines, Kingfisher, and Paramount) and five low-cost airline companies (Sahara, Air Deccan, SpiceJet, Go Air, and Indigo Airlines). Jet Airways acquired Sahara in 2007, rebranding it as Jet Lite to indicate its low-cost status. Kingfisher merged with Air Deccan, and Air India merged with Indian Airlines and rebranded it as Air India Express (Sabarad and Mhatre 2007; Ghosh, Ray, Dewan and Shah 2012). Air India,[13] the state-owned carrier, was generally perceived as slow and inefficient in adapting to changing conditions. The company was being considered for privatization but bureaucratic hurdles had

---

[9] All currencies are in US$ unless otherwise stated. Exchange rates are available on the Reserve Bank of India website, https://rbi.org.in/scripts/ReferenceRateArchive.aspx.

[10] United Breweries annual reports, 2005, 2006, and 2007.

[11] Ibid.

[12] "India Airlines Market Overview," Datamonitor, 0102 – 0756 – 2009; Kingfisher Airlines Investor presentations dated January 2011, October 2011, March 2011 and June 2011.

[13] Air India handled international travel whereas Indian Airlines handled domestic travel.

stalled Air India's privatization program since 2000. Jet Airways, the oldest private carrier in the industry, had a fleet size of 71 aircrafts and commanded a market share of 22.5%. The top three companies—Jet, Air India, and Kingfisher—commanded a total market share of 88.5% after the consolidation.[14]

Due to their low-cost structures, LCCs were able to attract price-sensitive customers. Their market share increased from 1% (in 2004) to 17% (in 2007; Sabarad and Mhatre 2007). Buoyed by this success, LCCs started adding capacity at a frantic pace. Indigo alone had ordered 100 aircrafts from Airbus. Collectively, the industry had ordered 138 airplanes from Boeing and 334 airplanes from Airbus.[15]

While India provided many avenues for growth, there were several concerns as well. The director general of civil aviation, the regulatory authority, in an order on route disbursal guidelines, had stated that a scheduled airline service provider operating category I routes was required to deploy at least 10% of available seat kilometres on category II routes and at least 50% of available seat kilometers on category III routes.[16] Category II routes to less attractive destinations were not remunerative and constituted 6% of the capacity of an airline. This could easily wipe out 1.5% of an airline's margin. Lack of infrastructure at airports, leading to congestion and soaring air turbine fuel (ATF) prices, was also a cause for concern.

Crude oil prices escalated rapidly in 2008, from US$100 per barrel in January to a new record high of US$140 per barrel in June. Due to these spiraling oil prices, Oasis Hong Kong Airlines slipped into bankruptcy after just 17 months of operations (Cranky Flier 2008). In India, fuel accounted for 47% of airline revenues (compared to the global average of 30%), leading to a compression of 13% in margins—primarily because Indian companies faced additional fuel taxes. Consequently, domestic ATF prices were higher than international prices by 60% to 70% (Goel and Singhania 2008). Airline companies in India and Asia responded to high fuel prices by scaling back expansion plans, raising airfares, adopting more efficient aircraft technologies and shedding wastages. Domestic airfares went up by 30%. The increase in airfares affected the LCCs adversely. Domestic passenger traffic declined. Carriers were also forced to reduce capacity. The top five carriers reduced capacity by 12% to 20% by grounding aircrafts (Goel and Singhania 2008).

By November 2008, ATF prices fell by almost 40% from their peak (August 2008), providing relief to airline companies. The massive capacity reduction undertaken by the top five carriers resulted in supply falling below demand, which led to better passenger load factors. The business environment improved in 2011, due to improved passenger traffic and stable fuel prices (see Exhibits E3.6, E3.7, and E3.8).

In the short run, airlines had to deal with challenges arising out of high indebtedness and illiquidity. Most needed to bring down indebtedness by issuing equity. In the long run, they needed to reduce costs and rationalization of aircrafts and routes. In order to facilitate industry viability, the government initiated measures to allow foreign airline companies to make equity investments up to 49% of equity in Indian companies, allow airlines to directly import ATF, and to lift the freeze on international expansion of private airlines (Ghosh, Ray, Dewan and Shah 2012).

[14] "India Airlines Market Overview," Datamonitor, 0102 – 0756 – 2009.

[15] Ibid.

[16] Ibid.

OPERATING AND FINANCING HISTORY

After the termination of the state monopoly over scheduled air transport, three full-service carriers and six LCCs emerged. In 2010, the total fleet size of the industry was approximately 380 aircrafts, out of which, 38% was owned by the National Aviation Company of India Ltd, 28% by Jet Airways (along with Jet Lite), and 22% by Kingfisher. The remaining 12% was distributed among the other LCCs. In terms of market share, Jet Airways was the market leader (with a 26% market share) followed by Kingfisher (with a 22% market share). Indigo and SpiceJet controlled 15% and 13% respectively.[17]

Throughout its history, Kingfisher had won many awards, including three global awards at the Skytrax World Airline Awards and the Best New Domestic Airline for Excellent Services and Cuisine by the Pacific Area Travel Writers Association. It was listed as the top airline in customer satisfaction by *Business World* and was among the top 100 most trusted brands in *The Brand Trust Report*.[18]

Kingfisher embarked on a massive capital expenditure program in an attempt to dominate the airline industry. In 2005, it ordered five A380s (these were cancelled subsequently), five A350-800s and five A330-200s, totaling more than US$3 billion. (Skytrax 2008) From 2008 to 2010, the company accumulated 67 Airbus aircrafts, financing the purchase largely through dry leases.[19] Kingfisher also heavily used bank loans to finance capital expenditure and working capital (see Exhibit E3.9). As collateral to these loans, Kingfisher had pledged all its movable assets, trademarks, goodwill of the company, and receivables and hypothecated Kingfisher House, the company headquarters. Grant Thornton undertook a valuation of the Kingfisher brand and the company pledged its brand as collateral with its lenders for ₹41 billion (US$660 million). The loans raised amounted to three times the company's market value.[20]

Yet Kingfisher had been reporting losses ever since it commenced operations. After acquiring Air Deccan, Kingfisher suffered losses of more than ₹10 billion for 3 consecutive years. It reported a net loss of ₹4.19 billion during the second quarter of 2009. Its income from operations also declined by 13.6% during the quarter compared to the same period the previous year.[21] In view of these huge losses and capacity reduction, Kingfisher decided to lay off nearly 100 pilots (*The Hindu* 2009b). As the business was consuming cash rapidly, Kingfisher's board approved a resolution to raise US$100 million by various instruments, including global depository receipts (*The Hindu* 2009a). This was in addition to a rights issue of equity shares amounting to ₹5 billion.

The airline accumulated losses of approximately US$1 billion by 2011, with half of its fleet grounded and several members of its staff going on strike. Kingfisher's market share fell dramatically to 14%, with the year-on-year growth turning negative. LCCs such as Indigo and SpiceJet benefited from Kingfisher's financial woes and locked up higher market shares.

---

[17] Parkar, Aviation Sector Note, Dolat Capital India Research, March 2, 2010.

[18] See www.flykingfisher.com

[19] The airline industry uses two types of leases: a wet lease is normally used for short-term purposes and a dry lease is used for long-term purposes.

[20] Kingfisher annual reports, 2007–11.

[21] Ibid.

In the height of the crisis, Kingfisher hired Sanjay Aggarwal as its new chief executive officer (CEO) to turn around the ailing company. Aggarwal had served as CEO of SpiceJet Ltd. and was credited with steering SpiceJet toward profit. He had quit the airline after media baron Kalanithi Maran bought a 37.7% equity interest in SpiceJet, following Wilbur Ross' decision to sell off his equity interest. Aggarwal had also served as the chief operating officer and strategy officer of Flight Options LLC, and as the senior director in charge of information technology and strategic and operations planning at Marriott International.[22]

SIGNS OF TROUBLE

There were numerous court cases against Kingfisher for dishonoring contracts with vendors and lessors. Since 2008, the company had been unable to pay aircraft lease rentals on time (Natarajan 2014) and had grounded several of its aircraft as it was unable to meet the expenses. As a result, GE Commercial Aviation Services, a lessor, threatened to repossess leased planes on account of default (Kumar 2008). Kingfisher defaulted in repayment of loans and interest to banks and financial institutions in 2009. The auditors to the company noticed delays ranging up to 61 days (in payment of overdue installment) and up to 84 days (in payment of overdue interest) in several months. The unpaid overdue installments and interest to banks totaled ₹2.7 billion and ₹2.19 billion respectively.[23]

In addition, Kingfisher had trouble paying its fuel bills. In 2009, Bharat Petroleum Corporation Ltd filed a case against Kingfisher for nonpayment of dues (Chatterjee 2009). The High Court of Karnataka State ordered that the entire amount of ₹2.45 billion (US$50 million) be paid by November 2010, and the airline paid it in installments. In 2011, DVB Aviation Finance Asia Ltd, a lessor from Singapore, sued Kingfisher Airlines for lease rental default in a case filed in the UK (*The Economic Times* 2010a). Soon thereafter, Hindustan Petroleum Corporation Ltd, another petroleum company owned by the Indian government, stopped ATF supplies to Kingfisher Airlines due to nonpayment of dues (although the situation was later resolved; *The Economic Times* 2010b). Similarly, as of September 2011, several vendors had petitions against Kingfisher pending before the Karnataka High Court.

The company incurred substantial losses, and its net worth was eroded in 2009. However, financial statements were prepared on the basis that the company was a going concern and that no adjustments were required to the carrying values of assets and liabilities due to the recently launched international operations, loans granted by banks, group support, and capital-raising plans (*Business Standard* 2014). The auditors pointed out that the appropriateness of the policy was dependent on the company's ability to infuse requisite funds for meeting its obligations. They also noted that:[24]

> [T]he scheduled air operator's permit issued by the Director General of Civil Aviation has lapsed, the Karnataka State High Court has admitted petitions by the consortium of bankers and one unsecured

[22] See www.flykingfisher.com (accessed February 2013).

[23] These amounts were paid after March 31, 2009.

[24] *Kingfisher Airlines Annual Report*, 2011.

creditor for winding up of the company.... These events cast significant doubt on the ability of the company to continue as a going concern.

In the past, the auditors had observed that several accounting policies of the company were not in conformity with Indian accounting standards (see Exhibit E3.10).

THE 2010 RESTRUCTURING

Kingfisher accumulated losses amounting to ₹42 billion between April 2005 and March 2010 (see Exhibit E3.1). In November 2010, to prevent an implosion, the company's board of directors approved a debt recast package with lending banks, following a one-time relaxation in restructuring guidelines sanctioned by the Reserve Bank of India. The salient features of the recast included:

- Conversion of debt of ₹13.55 billion provided by lenders into equity.
- Conversion of debt of ₹6.48 billion provided by promoters into equity.
- Re-scheduling of repayment of the balance debt to lenders over 9 years with a moratorium of 2 years.
- Reduction in interest rates.
- Sanction of additional fund- and non-fund-based facilities by the lenders.[25]

The promoter (founder) group of Kingfisher had supported the airline through direct investment, advances from the holding company, and guarantees from the holding company.[26] The group also helped Kingfisher secure third-party investments to meet exigencies, and had invested ₹21.18 billion as equity. This included a sum of ₹50 billion, which was converted into preferences shares and thereafter into ordinary equity shares at the time of the debt recast. Besides this, UB Holdings had also procured third-party finances from associates by way of convertible bonds amounting to ₹7.1 billion.[27] In these ways, UB Holdings had provided Kingfisher with corporate guarantees totaling ₹91.35 billion (Live Mint 2013). In addition, Mallya himself had given personal guarantees amounting to ₹61.56 billion, for which the lenders had given him a commission of ₹5.60 billion (Kazmin and Lucas).

Kingfisher Airlines completed the restructuring of ₹80 billion of debt, with all 18 lenders agreeing to cut interest rates and convert a portion of the loans to equity.[28] Lenders converted ₹6.5 billion of debt into preference shares. These preference shares would be converted into equity when the airline listed on the Luxembourg Stock Exchange by selling global depository receipts. The preference shares would be converted into ordinary equity at the price at which the global depository receipts would be sold to investors. In addition, another ₹8 billion debt was converted into redeemable preference shares for 12 years. Due to the restructuring, the airline's average interest rate would come down to 11%, helping the airline save ₹5 billion

[25] *Kingfisher Airlines Investor Presentation*, 2011.

[26] UB Holdings had investments in marketable securities amounting to ₹50,033 million, from company balance sheets.

[27] Chairman's Letter to Shareholders, Company Press Release, September 28, 2011.

[28] *Kingfisher Airlines Investor Presentation*, October 2011.

(US$80 million) every year in interest payments. The recast plan involved the issuing of several types of instruments. The convertible preferred stocks would be compulsorily converted into shares, and the cumulative preferred stock would be redeemable. In addition to these issues, 9,700,000 six percent redeemable preference shares of ₹100 face value issued to UB Holdings were converted to 97,000,000 units of 6% mandatory convertible preference shares of ₹10 each (see Exhibits E3.11, E3.12, and E3.13).[29] The debt recast package required Kingfisher Airlines and its founder companies, UB Holdings and Kingfisher Finvest Ltd, to pledge their equity stake in the airline.[30]

Following the debt restructuring, the airline undertook several steps to cut costs and face the challenges ahead. These steps included changes to the business model, reduction in interest and lease rentals by converting some loans into foreign currency loans, streamlining of fleet orders with Airbus, and reconfiguration of aircrafts to add more seats. The conversion of loans into foreign currency loans was expected to decrease interest expenses by ₹650 million. Other improvements were expected to add ₹17.96 billion in savings.

The restructuring quickly resulted in improvements in performance. In 2011, Kingfisher had an earnings before interest, taxes, depreciation and amortization (EBITDA) margin of 20%, whereas Jet Airways had a margin of 17%. Its earnings before interest, tax, depreciation, amortization and rentals (EBITDAR) were –0.8%, whereas competitors such as Jet and SpiceJet had margins of –9.2% and –11.7% respectively.

THE VERITAS REPORT

At the time of Mallya's disclosure to the Bombay Stock Exchange, two analysts at Veritas, a Canadian investment research firm, pointed out that both Kingfisher Airlines and its parent, UB Holdings, were on the verge of bankruptcy when the stocks of these two companies were trading at ₹25 and ₹114, respectively (Monga and Raj 2011). This led many to question the company's accounting practices, its future prospects, and the debt recast plan; however, other analysts at ICICI Direct, a prominent brokerage in India, had given a "buy" recommendation on the stock (Shah 2011).

REFERENCES AND SUGGESTED READINGS

Business Standard. 2014. "Kingfisher Results Defy Accepted Accounting Standards: Auditors." *Business Standard*, (February 12).

Chatterjee, Dev. 2009. "BPCL Sues Kingfisher Airlines." *The Economic Times*, June 25. Available at http://articles.economictimes.indiatimes.com/2009-06-25/news/28385851_1_kingfisher-airlines-indian-oil-kfa (Accessed on May 7, 2015).

Cranky Flier. 2008, December 31. "Airlines We Lost in 2008." Cranky Flier. Available at http://crankyflier.com/2008/12/31/airlines-we-lost-in-2008/ (Accessed on January 2014).

Ghosh, Ray, Dewan, and Shah. 2012, March. "Indian Aviation Industry." ICRA Research Report. Mumbai.

[29] *Kingfisher Airlines Investor Update*, October 2011.

[30] "4.1 Customer Based Brand Equity (CBBE) Pyramid," http://ir.inflibnet.ac.in:8080/jspui/bitstream/10603/33920/5/chapter4.pdf (accessed September 12, 2017).

Goel, Ashutosh, and Anirudh Singhania. 2008, September 25. "Aviation Sector Update." Mumbai: Edelweiss Research.

Kazmin and Lucas. "Mallya May Sell Whisky Stake to Diageo." *Financial Times*, www.ft.com/cms/s/0/e55c5c30-0723-11e2-b148-00144feabdc0.html#axzz3Qlfjpiqa (Accessed on February 2014).

Kumar, Nirbhay. 2008. "Indian Airline Defaults on Payments to GE." *Bloomberg Business*, November 5. Available at www.bloomberg.com/bw/stories/2008-11-05/indian-airline-defaults-on-payments-to-gebusinessweek-business-news-stock-market-and-financial-advice (Accessed on May 7, 2015).

Live Mint. 2013. "Kingfisher Airlines: The Beginning of the End-game?" *Live Mint*, January 14. Available at www.livemint.com/Opinion/RvAmZQhi7Q6jra34xtQJwO/Kingfisher-Airlines-the-beginning-of-the-endgame.html (Accessed on September 12, 2017).

Sabarad, Mahantesh, and Aniket Mhatre. 2007, December. "Aviation." Prabhudas Liladhar Research. Mumbai.

Monga, Neeraj, and Varun Raj. 2011. September, 12. *UB Holdings & Kingfisher Airlines Ltd.* Toronto, Ontario: Veritas Investment Research.

Natarajan, N. 2014. "Good Times Bad Times." *The Shopping Express*, August 15. Available at www.theshoppingexpress.in/articles/issue-125-good-times-bad-times (Accessed on September 12, 2017).

Shah, Rashesh. 2011, February 16. "Kingfisher Airlines." ICICI Securities. Mumbai.

Skytrax. 2008. "Kingfisher Airlines Unveil New Airbus A330-200 Which is Designed to Take the Customer Experience to the Highest Quality Level." Skytrax, July 2008. Available at www.airlinequality.com/news/140708_KINGFISHER.htm (Accessed on February 2014).

The Economic Times. 2010a. "DVB Aviation Sues Kingfisher Airlines for Default on Aircraft Rentals." *The Economic Times*, July 21. Available at http://articles.economictimes.indiatimes.com/2010-07-21/news/27572533_1_oil-dues-kingfisher-airlines-clear-dues (Accessed on May 7, 2015).

———. 2010b "HPCL Does Not Encash ₹500 Million Cheque from Kingfisher Airlines." *The Economic Times*, May 21.

———. 2014. "Mallya Drops Out of India's Richest 100 Club." *The Economic Times*, September 25. Available at www.celebritynetworth.com/richest-businessmen/richest-billionaires/vijay-mallya-net-worth/ (Accessed on September 12, 2017).

The Hindu. 2009a. "Kingfisher Airlines to Raise US$100 million." *The Hindu*, August 31. Available at www.thehindu.com/business/companies/kingfisher-airlines-to-raise-100-mn/article12478.ece (Accessed on May 7, 2015).

———. 2009b. "Kingfisher to Lay Off Nearly 100 Pilots." *The Hindu*, November 4. Available at www.thehindu.com/business/kingfisher-to-lay-off-nearly-100-pilots/article43156.ece (Accessed on September 12, 2017).

Times of India. 2001. "Kingfisher Buys Control of Air Deccan." *Times of India*, June 1. Available at http://timesofindia.indiatimes.com/business/india-business/Kingfisher-buys-control-of-Air-Deccan/articleshow/2090124.cms (Accessed May 7, 2015).

REVIEW QUESTIONS

1. Why was Kingfisher restructured in 2010?
2. Why is the leverage high in the airline industry?
3. Why is the airline industry's profitability low? Using Porter's five forces model assess the attractiveness of the airline industry in India.
4. Identify the key accounting policy changes that Kingfisher has made so far. Is the company justified in assuming that it is a going concern despite erosion of net worth? Do you agree with the company's management or the auditors? Why?
5. What are the motives of Kingfisher's management in adopting its financial reporting policies? Will investors "see through" these in pricing the company's stock?
6. Assess the financial performance of Kingfisher. Compare and contrast it with that of competition.

7. Assess the company's future prospects given your insights from the previous questions and the information in the case on the company's turnaround strategy. As an investor would you invest in Kingfisher Airlines? As a lender, would you have approved the debt recast?

For the purpose of your analysis assume that:

EBITDAR for Kingfisher in 2011 = ₹10,015 million
EBITDAR multiple for domestic companies = 8.0
EBITDAR multiple for international companies = 6.0
Number of shares outstanding = 498 million

Exhibit E3.1 *Income Statement (figures given in ₹millions)*

	2006	2007	2008	2009	2010	2011
Sales turnover	12,364	16,221.30	14,413.90	52,389.80	50,679.20	63,596
Excise duty	0	0	0	0	706.9	380.3
Net sales	12,364	16,221.30	14,413.90	52,389.80	49,972.30	63,216
Other income	1,154.1	3,818.5	1,285.1	8,406.9	2,031.2	1,359
Total income	13,518.10	20,039.80	15,699	60,796.70	52,003.50	64,575
Power and fuel cost	6,254.5	9,795	8,908.4	26,092.10	18,105.50	22,806
Employee cost	1,693.3	2,507.5	2,451.3	8,254.2	6,887.6	6,760
Other manufacturing expenses	4,720.7	5,129.4	4,470.2	12,356.50	11,793.20	12,720
Selling and administration expenses	3,475.1	5,652.9	5,445.4	23,050.50	21,844.70	20,397
Miscellaneous expenses	289.5	316.1	288	3,478	4,897.7	1,558.9
Total expenditure	16,433.10	23,400.90	21,563.30	73,231.30	63,528.70	64,243
Operating profit	–2,915	–3,361.1	–5,864.3	–12,434.60	–1,525.20	331.9
Interest	319.6	624	778.8	7,785.5	11,025.90	13,129.40
Gross profit	–3,234.6	–3,985.1	–6,643.1	–20,220.10	–22,551.10	–12,797.50
Depreciation	133.4	176.7	182.8	1,332	1,628	2,410.4
Profit before tax	–3,368	–4,161.8	–6,825.9	–21,552.10	–24,179.10	15,207.90
Tax	0	0	0	0	0	0
Fringe benefit tax	37.5	34	35.5	125	–60.6	0.03
Deferred tax	0	0	–4,980	–5,588.8	–7,646.3	–4,943.2
Reported net profit	–3,405.5	–4,195.8	–1,881.4	–16,088.3	–16,472.2	–10,274
Extraordinary Items	504.3	2,884.6	494.3	–6.6	–3,551.5	–918
Adjusted net profit	–3,909.8	–7,080.4	–2,375.7	–16,081.70	–12,920.70	–9,356

Source: Capitaline Database.

Exhibit E3.2 *Balance Sheet (figures given in ₹millions)*

	2006	2007	2008	2009	2010	2011
Sources of Funds						
Share capital	98.18	135.47	135.8	362.91	362.91	1,050.88
Reserves	118.37	238.21	52.98	–2,496.37	–4,240.86	–4,002.07
Total shareholders' funds	216.55	373.68	188.78	–2,125.35	–3,870.47	–2,951.19
Secured loans	448.16	716.71	592.38	2,622.52	4,842.43	5,039.91
Unsecured loans	3.5	200	342	3,043.04	3,080.17	1,986.31
Total debt	451.66	916.71	934.38	5,665.56	7,922.6	7,026.22
Other liabilities	0	0	0	0	0	33.19
Total liabilities	668.21	1,290.39	1,123.16	3,540.21	4,052.13	4,108.22
Gross block	247.33	340.77	322.33	1,891.8	2,048.13	2,254.26
Less: Accumulated depreciation	16.4	33.74	43.55	316.28	493.62	682.37
Net block	230.93	307.03	278.78	1,575.52	1,554.51	1,571.89
Capital work in progress	286.53	357.62	346.25	1,630.94	980.61	0
Investments	0.41	0.41	0	0.05	0.05	0.05
Current assets, loans and advances						
Inventories	57.26	61.62	48.64	147.25	171.32	193.08
Sundry debtors	12.87	35.24	27.16	274.23	322.48	440.53
Cash and bank	256.48	817.05	280.12	171.87	206.47	252.36
Loans and advances	167.57	176.15	303.67	1,606.34	1,936.9	871.57
Total current assets	494.18	1,090.06	659.59	2,199.69	2,637.17	1,757.54
Less: Current liabilities and provisions						
Current liabilities	376.99	486.55	667.08	3,494.68	3,501.37	4,108.82
Provisions	5.93	6.94	9.52	45.55	53.2	41.61
Total current liabilities	382.92	493.49	676.6	3,540.23	3,554.57	4,150.43
Net current assets	111.26	596.57	–17.01	–1,340.54	–917.4	–2,392.89
Miscellaneous expenses not written off	39.08	28.76	16.64	4.51	0	0
Deferred tax assets	0	17.47	528.81	2,034.08	2,841.03	3,286.9
Deferred tax liability	0	17.47	30.31	364.35	406.67	359.12
Net deferred tax	0	0	498.5	1,669.73	2,434.36	2,927.78
Other assets	0	0	0	0	0	2,001.39
Total assets	668.21	1,290.39	1,123.16	3,540.21	4,052.13	4,108.22

Source: Capitaline Database.

Exhibit E3.3 *Cash Flow Statement (figures given in ₹millions)*

	2007	2008	2009	2010	2011
Cash flow summary					
Cash and cash equivalents at beginning of the year	817.05	320.91	171.87	206.47	252.36
Net cash from operating activities	**–519.55**	**–645.78**	**–1,665.09**	**2.22**	**–885.54**
Cash flow from operating activities					
Net profit before tax and extraordinary items	–416.18	–682.59	–2,155.21	–2,417.92	–1,520.78
Adjustment for					
Depreciation	17.67	18.28	133.2	162.8	241.04
Interest (Net)	16.88	31.4	688.63	998.48	1,110.19
P/L on sales of assets	–288.91	–24.98	7.82	–2.5	0.55
Prov. and W/O (Net)	27.17	20.58	49.41	63.33	34.71
P/L in Forex	0	0	–217.67	–38.74	27.98
Fin. lease and rental charges	0	0	0	0	0
Others	4.07	–23.31	–1.57	–0.63	–4.95
Total adjustments (PBT and extraordinary Items)	–223.12	21.97	659.82	1,182.74	1,409.52
Op. profit before working capital changes	–639.3	–660.62	–1,495.39	–1,235.18	–111.26
Adjustment for					
Trade and other receivables	–23.28	8.83	–80.48	–48.25	–130.2
Inventories	–4.36	12.98	–55.34	–17.63	–22.77
Trade payables	89.39	204.86	1,838.76	34.37	601.86
Loans and advances	31.63	–75.64	–850.3	–393.7	–325.19
Others	–0.83	0	0	0	0
Total (OP before working capital changes)	92.55	151.03	852.64	–425.21	123.7
Cash Generated from/(used in) operations	–546.75	–509.59	–642.75	–1,660.39	12.44
Direct taxes paid	–5.83	–9.96	–3.03	–4.7	–10.22
Total-others	–5.83	–9.96	–3.03	–4.7	–10.22
Cash flow before extraordinary items	–552.58	–519.55	–645.78	–1,665.09	2.22
Extraordinary Items					
Net cash used in investing activities	**13.82**	**206.63**	**235.13**	**–38.05**	**–387.57**
Cash flow from investing activities					
Purchased of fixed assets	–182.98	–27.89	–5.13	0	0
Sale of fixed assets	296.88	24.98	399.28	349.62	86.31
Interest received	5.35	16.73	20.23	10.78	8.88
Others	0.23	0	–207.7	–125.27	–133.24
Net cash used in financing activities	**–31.2**	**290.11**	**1,464.56**	**81.72**	**1,203.02**

(continued)

Exhibit E3.3 *(continued)*

	2007	2008	2009	2010	2011
Cash flow from financing activities					
Proceeds from issue of shares	576.04	2.06	0.5	0	0
Proceed from issue of debentures	0	0	0	0	0
Proceed from other long term borrowings	114.41	20.61	1,030.62	2,412.84	2,334.68
Proceed from bank borrowings	259.72	0	0	0	0
Payment of the long-term borrowings	–125.14	0	0	0	–1,411.53
Payment of the short-term borrowings	–46.25	0	0	0	0
Payment of financial liabilities	–1.68	0	0	0	0
Interest paid	–26.17	–53.87	–741.01	–948.28	–841.43
Others	0	0	0	0	0
Net cash used in financing activities	993.68	–31.2	290.11	1,464.56	81.72
Net Inc/(dec) in cash and cash equivalent	–536.93	–149.04	34.6	45.89	–70.09
Cash and cash equivalents at end of the year	280.12	171.87	206.47	252.36	182.27

Source: Capitaline Database.

Exhibit E3.4 *Financial Summary, Ratios, and Margins*

	2006	2007	2008	2009	2010	2011
Book Value (₹)	22.06	27.58	13.9	–83.88	–149.48	–70.4
Market Capitalization (₹millions)	8,428.8	13,798	16,574.4	8,881.4	12,431.3	19,861.4
Stock Price – High (₹)	148	162	335	158	73	91
Stock Price – Low (₹)	81	64	100	22	31	36
Fixed Assets Turnover Ratio	6.54	5.52	5.8	4.73	2.57	2.96
Inventory Turnover Ratio	21.12	27.29	34.86	53.49	31.82	34.9
Debtors Turnover Ratio	93.58	67.43	61.6	34.77	16.99	16.67
Interest Cover Ratio	–11.12	–10.29	–7.76	–1.77	–0.87	–0.16
EBITDA Margin (%)	–27.66	–38.5	–40.69	–23.73	–15.73	0.52
EBIT Margin (%)	–28.73	–39.59	–41.95	–26.28	–18.95	–3.27
Net Profit Margin (%)	–31.62	–43.65	–13.05	–30.71	–25.5	–16.16
Return on Capital Employed (%)	0	0	0	0	0	0
Return on Net Worth (%)	0	0	0	0	0	0
Price Earning (P/E)	0	0	0	0	0	0
Price to Book Value (P/BV)	3.89	4.99	8.78	–0.4	–0.31	–0.57
Price/Cash EPS (P/CEPS)	–2.58	–4.64	–9.76	–0.6	–0.84	–2.53
EV/EBITDA	0	0	0	0	0	263.93
Market Cap/Sales	0.68	1.15	1.15	0.17	0.25	0.31

Source: Capitaline Database.

Exhibit E3.5 *Details of Kingfisher Board (as of March 2011)*

Director Name	Designation	Designation Category	Board Meetings Attended	Total Remuneration (₹)	No. of Committee Post Held	No. of Board Positions
Vijay Mallya	Chairman and Managing Director	Executive	6	0		19
S. R. Gupte	Vice Chairperson	Non-Executive-Non Independent	7	190,000	10	10
A. K. Ravi Nedungadi	Director	Non-Executive-Non Independent	7	220,000	5	9
Vijay Amritraj	Director	Non-Executive-Independent	1	20,000	6	3
Anil Kumar Ganguly	Director	Non-Executive-Independent	6	200,000		2
Piyush Mankad	Director	Non-Executive-Independent	4	80,000	12	12
Naresh Trehan	Director	Non-Executive-Independent		0		
Diwan Arun Nanda	Director	Non-Executive-Independent	4	110,000	5	11
Ghyanendra Nath Bajpai	Director	Non-Executive-Independent	5	110,000	14	20
Bharath Raghavan	Company Secretary	Non-Executive		0		N.A.

Source: CMIE Prowess Database.

Exhibit E3.6 *ATF Prices*

Year	Domestic ATF Delhi ₹/Kiloliter	Domestic ATF Mumbai ₹/Kiloliter
2004/05	25,872.00	26,454.60
2005/06	33,385.90	34,270.00
2006/07	38,616.60	39,915.70
2007/08	40,935.80	42,318.10
2008/09	49,684.50	51,706.00
2009/10	37,105.10	38,262.10
2010/11	44,531.10	45,477.70

Source: Centre for Monitoring Indian Economy (CMIE).

Exhibit E3.7 *Key Ratios and Margins of Air Transport Companies*

Year	2007	2008	2009	2010	2011
No. of Companies	**14**	**17**	**26**	**24**	**28**
Debt-Equity Ratio	1.79	2.25	2.85	4.55	1,339.36
Long Term Debt-Equity Ratio	1.59	2.07	2.62	3.88	1,078.89
Debt/Assets Ratio	0.769	0.681	0.705	0.783	0.967
Current Ratio	1.18	1.13	0.99	0.84	0.72
Fixed Assets Turnover Ratios	0.98	1.02	0.64	0.68	0.6
Inventory Turnover Ratios	13.11	19.53	18.39	26.14	25.84
Debtors Turnover Ratios	6.92	8.11	6.65	9.5	9.31
Interest Coverage Ratio	0.17	−2.16	−0.89	0.37	−0.04
EBDIT Margin (%)	6.8	−2.4	−2.33	12.98	8.28
EBIT Margin (%)	0.48	−9.35	−6.55	3.87	−0.58
EBDT Margin (%)	4.02	−6.73	−9.7	2.64	−5.15
Fuel/Total Expenditure	0.34	0.35	0.37	0.29	0.2
Fuel Expenses/Sales	0.37	0.39	0.43	0.29	0.19
Employee Cost/Total Expenditure	0.15	0.17	0.17	0.18	0.17

	Jet Airways			SpiceJet		
	2009	**2010**	**2011**	**2009**	**2010**	**2011**
Debt-Equity Ratio	9.01	14.24	16.49	0	0	0
Interest Coverage	−1.46	0.46	0.87	0	0	0
EBDIT Margin (%)	−9.45	13.53	13.64	−19.29	3.98	4.61
Net Profit Margin (%)	−15.11	−5.15	−0.97	−20.87	2.82	3.14
ROCE (%)	0	0	6.52	0	16.23	11.96
ROE (%)	0	0	−10.58	0	251.6	11.88
Price Earning (P/E)	0	0	399.24	0	22.95	15.32
Price to Book Value (P/BV)	1.13	5.01	4.61	−0.75	−3.91	4.84
Enterprise Value/EBITDA	65	11.61	8.6	0	16.1	11.11

Source: Capitaline Database.

Note: This list includes all domestic air transport companies, including chartered flight operators.

Exhibit E3.8 *Key Operating Indicators and Valuations for the Global Airline Industry*

Company Name	M cap	EV	Sales	Net profits	EBIT-DAR	RoE	ASKMs	RPKMs	PLF	Yield	FC/ ASKM	P/E Ratio		EV/ EBITDA		P/BV	P/CF
	Current (US$ billion)	Current (US$ billion)	2011 (US$ billion)	2011 (US$ billion)	2011 (%)	2011 (%)	2011 in billion	2011 in billion	2011 (%)	2011 US$	2011 US$	2012e x	2013e x	2012e x	2013e x	2012e x	2012e x
FSC Carriers																	
Delta Airlines	7.9	18.0	8.4	0.4	18.8	–	235	193	82.1	16	3.7	4.2	3.5	3.9	3.9	7.4	2.4
Air China Ltd	12.2	23.6	6.7	1.1	40.3	37	132	106	80.0	10	2.8	6.8	7.7	7.5	7.2	1.1	3.4
Singapore Airlines	10.2	7.1	2.8	0.1	31.6	8	108	85	78.5	9	3.1	27.2	19.5	4.2	3.8	1.0	6.9
All Nippon Airways	7.7	15.8	8.2	0.1	22.5	5	87	58	67.5	0	3.6	30.4	17.2	5.9	5.3	1.2	4.4
China Southern Airlines	7.0	14.7	6.3	0.6	32.2	31	140	111	79.2	10	2.6	5.8	6.9	6.4	6.1	0.9	2.1
China Eastern Airlines	6.3	15.2	6.1	0.5	31.4	60	119	93	78.0	10	2.7	5.3	6.1	7.4	6.8	1.2	1.9
Qantas Airways	4.1	7.6	6.7	0.0	19.8	4	133	107	80.1	11	3.0	13.1	8.6	3.9	3.2	0.6	2.4
Korean Airlines	3.6	14.6	10.7	(0.3)	–	–11	–	–	–	–	–	8.8	8.4	8.3	7.4	1.2	2.2
Garuda Indonesia	1.5	1.9	2.2	0.1	21.8	15	26	18	71.7	8	2.7	14.8	8.6	7.9	6.0	1.8	–
Asiana Airlines	1.3	–	4.8	0.0	–	–	37	28	76.4	–	–	6.9	5.5	6.7	5.7	1.2	2.9
Air New Zealand	0.8	1.3	1.5	0.0	12.8	5	32	27	83.4	11	2.8	15.0	8.0	3.4	2.8	0.6	2.6
Jet Airways	0.6	3.1	3.2	0.0	27.0	–5.00	40	31	78.6	9	2.9	–	–	88.2	10.2	4.0	–
Kingfisher Airlines	0.2	1.7	1.4	(0.2)	13.0	–	16	13	81.0	9	3.1	–	–	–	–	–	–
LCC Carriers																	
Ryan Air	8.1	8.8	1.1	0.0	41.4	17	63	53	84.1	6	2.7	13.1	12.8	7.3	7.1	1.9	7.1

(continued)

Exhibit E3.8 *(continued)*

Company Name	M cap	EV	Sales	Net profits	EBIT-DAR	RoE	ASKMs	RPKMs	PLF	Yield	FC/ ASKM	P/E Ratio		EV/ EBITDA		P/BV	P/CF
	Current (US$ billion)	Current (US$ billion)	2011 (US$ billion)	2011 (US$ billion)	2011 (%)	2011 (%)	2011 in billion	2011 in billion	2011 (%)	2011 US$	2011 US$	2012e x	2013e x	2012e x	2013e x	2012e x	2012e x
Southwest Airlines	6.3	6.9	4.1	0.2	17.6	3	121	98	80.9	15	4.8	11.4	8.3	3.7	3.3	0.9	5.0
Air Asia	3.3	5.1	–	–	–	–	26	21	80	–	–	11.1	902.0	8.2	7.2	1.9	6.2
Cebu Air	0.9	1.1	–	–	–	–	10	9	85	–	–	9.6	8.0	6.2	5.0	1.7	5.3
Tiger Airways	0.5	0.8	0.5	0.0	30.3	23	10	8	85.8	6	1.8	–	78.0	–	16.3	2.4	–
SpiceJet	0.2	0.2	0.6	0.0	18.5	–	10	9	82.5	7	2.6	–	–	–	–	–	–

Source: S. Dewan Ray and S. Shah, Indian Aviation Industry, ICRA Rating Feature, March 2012.

Note: FC = full capacity; MV = market value; EV = enterprise value; ASKM = available seat kilometers; PLF = passenger load factor = revenue passenger mile/ available seat KM; yield = passenger revenue/revenue passenger mile; RPKM = revenue passenger kilometer; P/BV = price/book value; P/E = price/earnings per share; FSC = full-service carriers.

Exhibit E3.9 *Financing Snapshot—Secured Loans (in ₹millions)*

	2007	2008	2009	2010	2011
Term loans from banks (₹loans)	1,797	1,546	8,068	30,288	42,230
Cash credit[31] facility from banks	1,869	172	3,479	5,073	2,825
Short-term loans from banks	1,526	2,485	4,270	4,784	NA
Vehicle loans from banks/financial institutions	16	10	4.8	NA	NA
Finance lease obligations[32]	22	12	9,405	7,253	6,104
Term loans from financial institutions and others	742	629	996	1,023	6,848
Hire purchase	1,142	1,045	NA	NA	NA
Total	7,114	5,899	26,222.8	48,421	58,007

Source: Company Annual Reports 2007–11.

Exhibit E3.10 *Excerpts from Auditors' Report, 2008–11*[33]

The working results for the nine months ended March 31, 2008 are after charging off ₹28,270,478 and ₹2,628,571 toward amortization of training and pre-operative expenses, respectively, based on the company's accounting policy of amortizing the expenditure over three years. The corresponding amounts for the year ended June 30, 2007 were ₹86,443,502 and ₹16,358,477, respectively. We are of the opinion that such accounting treatment is not in accordance with Accounting Standard 26 on "Intangible Assets" issued by the Institute of Chartered Accountants of India and such expenses were required to be written off to the profit and loss account as and when incurred.[34]

Other income for the 15 months ended June 30, 2006 included a sum of ₹267,220,000 toward certain subsidy provided to the company by one of its suppliers in conjunction with lease of aircrafts on operating lease basis. The previous auditors had reported that they were of the opinion that such accounting treatment was not in accordance with Accounting Standard (AS) 19 on "Leases" and the subsidy should be recorded on a straight-line basis over the period of the lease. Their audit report on the financial statements for the 15 months ended June 30, 2006 was modified in this matter. We concur with the views of the said auditors in principle that such subsidy should be recognized on a systematic basis in the profit and loss account over the periods necessary to match them with the related costs, which they are intended to compensate although the matter does not appear to be covered explicitly by the said AS 19.

We further report that, except for the effect, if any, of the matters stated in paragraph 11(a) below and paragraph 4 of the annexure, whose effect are not ascertainable, had the observations made in paragraphs 4 and 5 above been considered, the loss after tax for the period ended March 31, 2008 would have been ₹1,814,834,524 (June 30, 2007—₹4,045,462,520) as against the reported loss of ₹1,881,361,073 (June 30, 2007—₹4,195,761,015), the debit balance in profit and loss account as at March 31, 2008 would have been ₹9,845,694,445 (June 30,

---

31 This is a type of working capital facility in which the security is inventory. The cash credit permits the borrower to borrow up to a specified limit. The interest is charged only on the utilized portion but a service charge is levied on the unutilized portion.

32 The company also had operating leases amounting to ₹46.175 billion in 2011, from company balance sheets.

33 *Kingfisher Annual Reports*, 2008–11.

34 The accounting policy was reversed in 2008, *Company 2008 Annual Report.*

2007—₹8,021,206,713) as against a reported figure of ₹9,677,557,223 (June 30, 2007—₹7,786,542,942), deferred revenue expenses as at June 30, 2007 would have been ₹256,624,965 as against the reported figure of ₹287,524,014, and other liabilities would have been ₹680,362,049 (June 30, 2007—₹982,925,507) as against the reported figure of ₹512,224,827 (June 30, 2007—₹779,160,785).

Attention of the members is invited to note 19 of schedule 19 regarding recognition of deferred tax credit during the year aggregating to ₹5,588,761,517 (period ended March 31, 2008—₹4,984,997,384; total amount recognized up to March 31, 2009—₹16,697,320,245) by virtue of which its loss for the year and debit balance in profit and loss account each stand reduced by ₹5,588,761,517 (period ended March 31, 2008—₹4,984,997,384) and ₹16,697,320,245 (as at March 31, 2008—₹4,984,997,384), respectively. We cannot express any independent opinion in the matter.

Attention is invited to the change in the method of accounting of costs incurred on major repairs and maintenance of engines of aircrafts taken on operating lease during the year aggregating to ₹2,070 million, which have been included under fixed assets and amortized over the estimated useful life of the repairs. In our opinion, the revised accounting treatment is not in accordance with current accounting standards.

Source: Company Annual Reports 2008–11.

Exhibit E3.11 *Debt Recast Plan*

Particulars	Debt Before Recast	Conversion of Debt				Additional Loan		Debt Post Recast	Debt as of March 31, 2011
		to CCPS	to CRPS	to OCDS	to WCTL	FITL	RTL		
Working capital	5,905.0				(2,974.0)			**2,931.0**	**2,931.0**
Term loan	42,634.9	(7,501.0)	(5,531.0)		2,974.0	2,484.2	7,683.0	**42,744.1**	**44,892.3**
PDP loan	1,664.4							**1,664.4**	**1,692.7**
Founder loan	6,563.0	(6,480.0)						**83.0**	**380.0**
Inter corporate deposit (ICD)	11,373.2			(7,093.2)				**4,280.0**	**3,104.1**
Sub-total	**68,140.5**	**(13,981.0)**	**(5,531.0)**	**(7,093.2)**		**2,484.2**	**7,683.0**	**51,702.5**	**53,000.1**
Other short-term loan	752.0							**752.0**	**3,016.5**
Hire purchase	861.5							**861.5**	**715.4**
Finance lease	6,757.3							**6,757.3**	**6,740.4**
Grand total	**76,511.3**	**(13,981.0)**	**(5,531.0)**	**(7,093.2)**		**2,484.2**	**7,683.0**	**60,073.3**	**63,472.4**

Source: Company Investor Update, October 2011.

Exhibit E3.12 *Proposals to Reduce Debt (in ₹millions)*

Debt before recast	76,510
Recast benefit	16,430
Fuel impact	5,130
Debt (June 30, 2011)	65,210
Group debt-to-equity	6,750
Other conversion	10,000
Other debt reduction	4,500
Finance to operating lease	6,740
Potential debt	37,220

Source: Company Investor Update, October 2011.

Notes: Additionally substituting ₹12,000 million of term loans with foreign currency loans was expected to lower the interest cost by 6%.

Finance to operating lease conversion on 10 ATRs, two A320s and one ACJ to reduce debt by another 6.74 billion.

Exhibit E3.13 *Instruments to Be Issued as Part of Restructuring*

Instrument	Dividend/ Interest %	Number	Price ₹	Recipient
Cumulative preferred stock	8	575,000,000	10	Lenders
Convertible preferred stock	7.5	780,000,000	10	Lenders
Convertible preferred stock	7.5	648,000,000	10	Lenders
Convertible bonds	8	20,000,000	100	Star investments
Convertible bonds	8	30,000,000	100	Margosa consultancy
Convertible bonds	8	30,000,000	100	Redect consultancy

Source: Company Investor Update, October 2011.

CASE

4 Reliance Communications Ltd: A House of Cards?[1]

Description: Reliance Communications Ltd, a large Indian telecom company, has experienced severe financial difficulties brought on by poor management practices, an ill-conceived capital expenditure of more than US$6 billion, a debt load of ₹350 billion (US$5.8 billion),[2] and changing industry dynamics. Interestingly, two analysts at a Canadian Investment Research firm gave a "sell" recommendation on the stock with a target price of ₹15 when the stock was trading at ₹93. The analysts also pointed out a possible rip-off of minority shareholders by the firm's founders. The company's stock price fell from a high of ₹844 in 2008 to ₹46 in 2012. The company is in the process of restructuring its assets and liabilities. The case considers the economics of the business from the perspective of shareholders. Students are required to assess the company's performance and decide whether they would invest in the company's shares.

Learning Objective: The first half of the case describes the company's constituent businesses and the strategy followed by the wireless division. This gives students an opportunity to critique RCL's marketing strategy and pricing of its services. The second half of the case describes the company's financial strategy, the instruments it issued, and its restructuring initiatives. The case allows students to examine problems associated with high leverage and the challenges to restructuring in emerging markets.

Subjects Covered: Financial management, financing, restructuring.

---

[1] Professors Vishwanath S. R. and Vijaya Narapareddy prepared this case as the basis for class discussion rather than to illustrate either effective or ineffective handling of an administrative situation.

[2] At an exchange rate of ₹60/US$.

On September 4, 2012, Reliance Communications' chairman, Mr Anil Ambani, vowed to bring down the high debt on the company's books over the next 3 years.[3] The second-largest company in the Indian telecom industry was fighting a fiercely competitive battle with well-entrenched companies such as Airtel and Idea Cellular. A sharp fall in call prices and high license fees for 3G spectrum had exerted pressure on profit margins. To make matters worse, the company was saddled with a staggering debt of ₹[4] 350 billion as of June 2012 and had been unsuccessful[5] in its efforts to raise capital through the partial sale of its equity stake in its business units.

Ambani proposed a four-pronged strategy to bring down Reliance Communication's debt: (a) improve capital productivity, (b) monetize assets to increase revenue growth (c) enhance profitability and unlock value in Reliance Infratel either by a (partial) equity stake sale or an initial public offering, and (d) list Reliance Globalcom on the Singapore Stock Exchange and use the proceeds to pay down debt. Following the announcement of the new strategy, the company's shares gained 1.7% from an all-time low of ₹46 per share that prevailed in August 2012. In June 2012, two Canadian analysts had given a "sell" recommendation on the company's stock with a price target of a mere ₹15 when the stock was trading at ₹93. Industry observers wondered how the company got into a financial bind, why its earlier restructuring attempts had failed, whether the current plan would succeed, and whether there were governance problems at the company.

RELIANCE GROUP BACKGROUND

Reliance Communications was part of the Reliance group, a conglomerate, founded by Dhirubhai Ambani in 1996. Reliance group was India's largest industrial group with a total of over 100 million customers worldwide. With over 12 million shareholders, it was one of the largest companies in the world. One out of every four investors in India was a Reliance shareholder. In 2012, the group's revenues were over US$15.4 billion and it had an equity of over US$40 billion. The group's revenue was equivalent to about 3.5% of India's GDP and contributed nearly 10% of the country's indirect tax revenues and over 6% of India's exports. The group's businesses included exploration and production of oil and gas, petrochemicals, textiles, financial services, power, and telecom.

After Dhirubhai Ambani's demise, the group was allotted to his sons—Anil Ambani and Mukesh Ambani. The part of the Reliance group belonging to Anil Ambani was renamed as Anil Dhirubhai Ambani Group.[6] Anil Ambani, a prominent business leader in India, served as a member of the Wharton School[7] Board among others. In June 2004, he was elected for a -year term as an independent member of the Rajya Sabha, the upper house of India's Parliament—a position he held till March 2006. He received the first Wharton Indian Alumni Award by the

---

[3] See http://profit.ndtv.com/news/corporates/article-how-anil-ambani-plans-to-trim-reliance-communications-rs-35-000-crore-debt-310294, accessed on September 13, 2017.

[4] The rupee is the Indian currency.

[5] As of September 2013, Reliance Communications had not succeeded in raising additional capital needed to bring down its debt obligations.

[6] Reliance Communications was one of the companies in the group.

[7] Anil Ambani is an alumnus of the Wharton Business School.

Wharton India Economic Forum in December 2001 and was selected by *Asia Week* magazine for its list of "Leaders of the Millennium in Business and Finance" in 1999, among others.

RELIANCE COMMUNICATIONS BACKGROUND

Reliance Communications Limited (RCL) was originally incorporated on July 15, 2004, as Reliance Infrastructure Developers Private Limited. On August 3, 2005, the name of the company changed to Reliance Communication Ventures Limited. In less than a year, that is, on June 7, 2006, the company's name was changed again to its present name, that is, RCL. The company went public with an initial public offering in March 2006 and was listed on the Bombay Stock Exchange and the National Stock Exchange of India.

RCL was a late entrant in the Indian telecom market. Other companies began their operations in the mid-1990s when the Indian market opened up for private competition. RCL made a foray into the market with the launch of its CDMA (code division multiple access)-based mobile services.[8] The company set up a pan-India state-of-the-art network with the objective of transforming the industry through "disruptive competitive pressure." Between 2004 and 2006, RCL was the market leader with a presence in 22 telecom circles (i.e., zones). RCL had a presence across the telecom value chain—from distribution of mobile handsets to after-sales service. The company's handset distribution network covered a total of 5,000 towns across the country, serviced by around 1,500 distributors. At the end of February 2007, RCL was India's second-largest integrated telecom solutions provider with 32.4 million mobile subscribers. Of these, 28.3 million subscribers were users of CDMA technology, while the balance 4.1 million subscribers were users of GSM (**g**lobal **s**ystem for **m**obile communication) technology. The company offered a full portfolio of telecom and telephony solutions including mobile services, wire-line services, national and international long-distance services, enterprise broadband, global voice and data services, provision of bandwidth to global corporates, infrastructure, and managed services. Exhibits E4.1 through E4.5 present the company's financial statements, key ratios, and stock price history.

RCL divided its operations into three strategic business units:[9] wireless, global, and broadband.

Wireless

This business accounted for the largest share of RCL's revenues (62% of gross revenues in 2012). The company provided cellular services through this business unit and was the second-largest company in the Indian telecom market. At the end of 2006, RCL's total mobile subscriber base stood at 20.2 million, of which 18.3 million subscribers were CDMA subscribers, while the balance, 1.9 million subscribers, were GSM users. The company's all-India market share stood

---

[8] Telecom service providers throughout the world used either the CDMA or the GSM technology.

[9] RCL also had several associate/subsidiary companies such as Reliance Petroleum Limited, Reliance Telecom Limited, Reliance Leasures Private Limited, Reliance World Traders Private Limited, Reliance Strategic Investment Private Limited, Reliance Agrotech Private Limited, Reliance Entertainment Private Limited, Reliance Energy and Project Development Private Limited, Reliance Hydrocarbon and Investment Private Limited, Reliance Consolidated Enterprises Private Limited, Reliance Paging Private Limited, Reliance Global Management Services Private Limited, and Reliance Detective and Security Consultancy Services Private Limited. By 2011 the company had 116 associate/subsidiary companies around the world.

at 21% in 2006. At the end of February 2007, RCL's subscriber base had grown to 32.4 million and the company's all-India market share stood at 20.4%. RCL's mobile subscriber base had grown at a compound annual growth rate (CAGR) of 61.3% from 2004 to 2006. The all-India mobile subscriber base had grown at a CAGR of 95.3% from 2002 to 2006.

The CDMA technology was considered more efficient then GSM for several reasons:

- CDMA enabled multiple users to occupy the same frequency at the same time, that is, CDMA enabled sharing of spectrum. Since availability of spectrum was a major entry barrier, CDMA provided a clear advantage over GSM.
- The number of subscribers (i.e., traffic) handled by GSM towers was 15% to 30 % lower than CDMA networks.
- Capability and data transfer speed of CDMA was 40% better than GSM network. Thus, the capital expenditure required for CDMA technology to support more traffic was lower than GSM.
- CDMA was the preferred technology for third-generation (3G) services.

The CDMA technology enabled RCL to be much more aggressive in setting tariffs. Efficient technology coupled with cheaper handsets helped RCL to become the second-largest telecom company in India. One of the key features of CDMA technology was that handsets were not compatible with other service providers, leading to high switching costs for consumers. Consequently, RCL's monthly churn rate at 1.8% was significantly lower than that of its peers. Despite these advantages, GSM was the preferred technology worldwide for two reasons: increased demand for international roaming services and choice of a wider range of handsets. Consequently, RCL planned to completely shift to GSM technology by 2009. Reliance handsets were expected to have a "dual SIM" facility, that is, its SIM cards could accommodate CDMA and GSM technologies. CDMA subscribers could simply switch between GSM and CDMA when the company activated such a facility.

In the third quarter of 2008, the company received 2G spectrum to commence all-India GSM-based cellular mobile services. Till then, the company was operating GSM-based services in only eight circles across the country. With the receipt of spectrum in the remaining 14 circles, the company could commence operations in these circles to become a pan-India GSM player in due course. The company paid ₹16.51 billion for the license. In the same year, in an analyst meet, Ambani reiterated his ambitions to develop RCL into an integrated telecommunications company comparable to AT&T and Verizon (Shah 2008).

Reliance Telecom Infrastructure Ltd (RTIL), a 100% subsidiary of RCL, was a telecom infrastructure provider set up in April 2007. The company had an infrastructure of 13,000 towers in 2007 and had planned to increase it to 50,000 by March 2010. This would enhance the coverage from 10,000 towns and 300,000 villages to 25,000 towns and 600,000 villages in 2008. This would be supported by RCL's national fiber network. RCL would be the anchor tenant for RTIL and would have a 10-year master service agreement with RTIL. Both its CDMA and GSM business would be separate tenants for the tower business.

Global

RCL offered national and international long-distance calling services through this business unit. This business offered wholesale carriage and termination to other carriers as well as to other business units of RCL. RCL entered the long-distance market in India in mid-2003, and had become the largest carrier, with a market share of over 40%. In January 2004. Reliance Communications acquired Flag Telecom for US$211 million for a control of 100% equity of the company. Flag Telecom started in 1990 as a provider of international wholesale network transport and communication services, with 50,000 km of undersea cables. In 2001, Flag filed for bankruptcy under Chapter 11. In 2002, it emerged from bankruptcy. It was acquired by RCL later on. After the merger, Flag was renamed Reliance Globalcom. Through Flag, RCL owned and operated the largest private submarine cable system in the world connecting 28 countries from the East coast of the USA to Europe, the Middle East, India, South and East Asia, and Japan. Through its global submarine cable systems Flag and Falcon RCL was the largest provider of international bandwidth in Asia and the Middle East.

The acquisition of Vanco, a global virtual network operator, in May 2008, added US$365 million (₹15.5 billion) to the annual revenue of Reliance Globalcom, and increased Reliance Globalcom's tally of enterprise customers to over 1,400. Vanco's customer base included Siemens and British Airways. Through this acquisition RCL added nine network management centers.

Reliance Communications acquired Yipes, a company based in San Francisco, for US$300 million in July 2007. Yipes provided RCL with high-speed data network access to 1,000 customers in 14 US cities. Yipes operated an optic fiber network of more than 22,000 km. Yipes would operate as a strategic business unit of Reliance Globalcom. RCL would spend ₹10 billion to roll out Yipes services in India, Asia, Africa, the Middle East, and Europe over the next 1 year. The company expected synergies between Yipes' and Flag's operations given their complementary products, services, and networks.

Broadband

Through this business unit, RCL offered a range of enterprise voice, data, video, Internet, and IT infrastructure services, including national and international private leased circuits, broadband Internet access, audio and video conferencing, MPLS-VPN, Centrex, and managed Internet data center (IDC) services. The company's enterprise customer base included 750 of the top 1,000 Indian enterprises and multinationals. In the consumer segment, RCL offered fixed line phone services and broadband Internet access services.

On April 24, 2008, Reliance Infocom BV, a division of Reliance Globalcom and wholly owned subsidiary of Reliance Communications, announced the acquisition of a controlling equity interest in eWave World, a UK headquartered telecom company.[10] eWave focused on the rapidly developing market for wireless telephony services using the WiMAX (a wireless communications standard designed to provide 30–40 megabit per second data rates) technology standard. Over the next 2–3 years, Reliance Globalcom, through eWave World, would invest around US$500 million (₹20 billion) to build and acquire WiMAX networks in emerging markets in Asia, Europe, Latin America, and Africa. Recently eWave World had entered into a joint venture in China to invest in nationwide broadband operations. The company held WiMAX licenses and had received spectrum to commence WiMAX services in several countries.

[10] See http://www.relianceglobalcom.com/pdf/2008/RGCOMacquiresGlobalWIMAX.pdf (accessed on September 13, 2017).

Other Businesses

Apart from these businesses, RCL launched its direct-to-home service—Reliance Big TV Ltd—on August 19, 2008. "Big TV" had the advanced MPEG4 technology that would ensure better quality sound and superior clarity of pictures. It targeted a 40% market share within one year. Besides Big TV, RCL was also planning to launch Internet Protocol Television (IPTV) in association with Microsoft. The venture would require an investment of US$500 million for software licenses and infrastructure. Through the IPTV technology, RCL would serve metros in the initial phase and gradually spread to 30 other cities. The IPTV features for RCL were to be developed by Redmond, a reputed Washington-based company. RCOM enlisted leading content providers for its IPTV with an objective of providing 400 channels to customers.

INDUSTRY BACKGROUND

The Indian telecom industry is an excellent example to highlight the success of the Indian government's reforms program kick started in 1991. The sector grew rapidly over several years on the back of heightened competition, resulting in lower of telecom tariffs, higher disposable income (due to strong GDP growth rate), and greater coverage by mobile service operators. Before the reforms, the telecom sector was a government-controlled monopoly with three companies—MTNL, VSNL, and BSNL—providing landline services. MTNL was licensed to provide fixed-basic telecom services in the Indian cities of Mumbai and New Delhi, while BSNL was licensed to provide services to the rest of the country. BSNL was also licensed to provide national long-distance (NLD) services. VSNL, on the other hand, provided international long-distance (ILD) services. However, in 1994, the sector was opened up to private competition and cellular licenses were issued. Initially, the cost of telecom services was high due to the prohibitively high cost of licenses resulting in very few additions to the mobile subscriber base. In fact, at the end of 1998, there were a mere 880,000 cellular subscribers in the country. The National Telecom Policy introduced in 1999 changed the mode of license fee payment from a fixed price to a revenue-sharing regime. Other initiatives such as unified access licensing, implementation of the "calling party pays" regime (that makes incoming calls free), and lower regulatory costs to telecom operators resulted in a quantum jump in the cellular subscriber base.

With 159.1 million subscribers in early 2007, India had a low mobile teledensity of 15%, suggesting huge opportunities for growth. The Indian telecom industry was divided into 23 circles (or service areas). These services areas were further divided into metropolitan cities, and Circles A, B, and C. This division had been done on the basis of the revenue potential of the circle. Metros had the highest revenue potential followed by circles A, B, and then C. New Delhi, Mumbai, Kolkata, and Chennai were metros. The Indian states of Karnataka and Maharashtra we part of Circle A, whereas smaller states such as Jammu & Kashmir and Assam were part of Circle C.

The Indian telecom sector continued to demonstrate strong growth in spite of sluggishness in the global economic environment. The total base of landline and wireless subscribers in India grew to 621.28 million and the teledensity to 52.74% as on March 31, 2010. The annual growth of 44.58% was primarily driven by rural expansion and the proliferation of affordable devices. Wireless subscribers reached 584.32 million and wireless teledensity stood at 49.60%. The share of private sector in wireless connections touched 87.24% as on March 31, 2010. The year witnessed a dramatic drop in telecom tariffs. With the launch of services by several new operators, the total number of telecom operators stood at 15. The competition caused a further shift, with operators focusing on increased value-added and data services to subscribers in the saturated urban markets. The bulk of the subscriber growth in the industry was to come from lowvalue customers, which would place restrictions on revenue growth. The entry of new competitors into an already highly competitive market brought down tariffs, putting pressure on revenue growth. On the regulatory side, the industry was regulated by the Telecom Regulatory Authority of India (TRAI) established in 1997 by an act of parliament. TRAI was responsible for orders and directions on various subjects such as tariffs, direct-to-home services, and mobile number portability. In 2007, for example, the authority prescribed a ceiling of ₹1.40/minute for regional or national roaming calls.[11]

OPERATING AND FINANCING HISTORY

In the first quarter of 2008, Reliance Communications posted exemplary results. Net profit grew by 138% to ₹12.21 billion, and revenues were at ₹43.04 billion, showing an increase of 32% on account of huge subscriber additions. EBITDA (earnings before interest, tax, depreciation, and amortization) margins stood at 42.7%, which was the best amongst all the telecom companies in India. Buoyed by its performance, the company announced an ambitious expansion plan.

In January 2006, Reliance launched the "One Nation, One Tariff" scheme that permitted prepaid users to call anywhere in India at one rupee per minute. Later, in the same month, it launched the "Hello Capital Plan" to enable its subscribers in 19 state capitals to call each other at the local call rate of 40 paise[12] per minute. These actions resulted in acquiring 1.4 million subscribers in December 2006. Around the same time, it slashed ILD rates by up to 66%. In April 2008, it announced unlimited free STD (subscriber trunk dialling) calls. In December 2009, the company initiated a radical move in the Indian telecom industry by launching 1,000 free minutes of usage for GSM subscribers for calls made within the Reliance network within the New Delhi region. Later on, it waived tariffs on local and intra-circle calls to all fixed lines of any network and to Reliance CDMA and GSM mobiles.

The total number of subscribers, average revenue per user, revenue/minute, and total number of minutes are the key drivers of success in the telecom business. Exhibit E4.6 shows these metrics for the wireless business of RCL. On account of free calls and free minutes, the average revenue per user plunged from ₹364 to ₹122 from the second quarter of 2008 to the second quarter of 2011. To arrest the declining average revenue per user (ARPU), the company started reducing free minutes on the network. Likewise, due to seasonality and such other factors, minutes of usage/month (MoU) fell from 490 to 276 during the same period.

In 2010, the 3G[13] and 4G telecom spectrum were auctioned in a highly competitive bidding. The winners were awarded spectrum in September. The private companies which participated in the auction were Airtel, Aircel, Idea, Reliance, Tata Teleservices, S Tel, and Vodafone India. Reliance won 3G spectrum in 13 telecom circles for a total payout of ₹85.9 billion. The company

[11] See http://www.trai.gov.in/WriteReadData/UserFiles/mpci/torder24jan07.pdf (accessed on September 13, 2017).

[12] 100 paise = 1 Indian Rupee just as 100 cents = US$1.

[13] Short for *third generation* of mobile telecommunications technology.

was unable to win broadband wireless access (BWA) spectrum in even a single circle and dropped out of the bidding process citing irrational bid prices.

The industry landscape changed with the government issuing over 120 licenses to new operators and the number of companies going up from 5–6 per circle to 9–10 in most circles. These new operators had been allotted spectrum in about 18 to 20 circles, and some of them had joint ventures with large, global companies. The industry had about 300,000 towers in 2010, with ample opportunities for existing infrastructure providers to offer tower tenancies to new domestic and multinational operators.

By the end of 2010, RCL launched 3G services in Mumbai, Delhi, Kolkata, and Chandigarh, becoming the second private operator after Tata DoCoMo and the fourth overall after BSNL, MTNL, and Tata Teleservices to do so. The company started offering a variety of plans including bundled voice and data, only data, USB data cards, and mobile TV services. Earlier that year, in a game-changing move, Reliance broke through the clutter of myriad tariffs, with one single rate for all local and STD calls to any mobile or landline network, anytime, anywhere in India, without any condition or restriction. Reliance Communications set a new industry standard, offering unbelievable, never-before prices in a simple and transparent manner. The "Simply Reliance Plan" offered three variants to meet the needs of customers with different calling patterns, namely, 50 paise per minute, 1 paise per second, and ₹1 per call for duration of 3 minutes across India available to all customers.

It formed an alliance with Polycom Inc., a global leader in tele-presence, video, and voice solutions, to introduce the world's first wireless, high-resolution video and CD-quality audio conferencing service along with simple-to-use content sharing capabilities. Using this, service events such as live meetings, online education, medical procedures, family events, weddings, parties, and ceremonies could be webcasted live on a pay-per-use basis.

With the emergence of smart phones and the increased use of mobile Internet, usage of phones was expected to be driven by mobile applications and mobile versions of popular Internet services. RCL entered into strategic tie-ups and alliances with more than 350 technology and content partners, various leading M-commerce solutions providers.

Its Enterprise Business Unit partnered with Microsoft to combine the power of virtualization technology and cloud computing and launched "Reliance Cloud Computing Services." This is a hosted infrastructure service for its customers in India to access a variety of enterprise scale IT solutions, business applications, and services such as server hosting, data storage and archival, enterprise resource planning (ERP), and document management. There is a full suite of applications and services based on the cloud computing model. Microsoft's virtualization and management technologies helped them in reducing the input costs involved in providing these services, thereby enabling Reliance to pass on the cost benefits to the customers.

Capital Expenditure

As of 2007, the company had planned a capital expenditure of US$2.5 billion for its domestic network expansion and a capital expenditure of US$1.5 billion spread over 3 years for overseas expansion (to increase the capacity of its submarine cables). In 2008, the company scaled up its Capex guidance to US$5.2 billion (from US$4.5 billion announced earlier) for getting a universal access service license for its GSM-based services, further expansion of its CDMA services, and the acquisition of Yipes Holdings. Simultaneously, the company gave a preliminary guidance of US$6 billion (₹240 billion) Capex in 2009, which included US$2 billion toward the cost of the passive infrastructure component of the cellular network, US$1.3b toward the cost of the active component and the balance as Capex for the company's newer business initiatives such as DTH and IPTV, apart from existing businesses such as long distance, enterprise broadband, and Flag. The company made a total capital expenditure of ₹264.3 billion (about US$6 billion) during 2007–12.

Financing

In February 2007, to finance its ambitious expansion plans, RCL completed its US$1 billion foreign currency convertible bond (FCCB) offering in international markets, slated to be India's largest zero-coupon FCCB offering. The instrument had a tenor of 5 years and a conversion price of ₹661 per share. This represented a premium of 30% over the prevailing market price. The offering was oversubscribed. However, on account of the Rupee depreciation in the first quarter of 2009, the company's total realized and unrealized losses stood at ₹10.63 billion. Rather than charging this off to the profit and loss account as mandated by Accounting Standard 11 (AS-11) issued by the Institute of Chartered Accountants of India (ICAI), the company adjusted this in the carrying cost of fixed assets. The company clarified that this was done on the basis of legal advice received by it and is in compliance with Schedule VI of the Companies Act, 1956. Had the company followed AS-11, the bottom-line for the quarter would have been just ₹4.49 billion, lower by as much as 63.2% over the previous year.[14] Again in the first quarter of financial year 2011, RCL and some of its subsidiaries incurred forex losses on account of exchange rate differences relating to loans/liabilities amounting to ₹8.2 billion. Out of this, the company did not debit ₹7.8 billion to the profit and loss account (Shah 2010).[15] By December 2010, RCL's gross debt ballooned to ₹378 billion, of which ₹149 billion was domestic debt raised primarily to pay 3G license fees, and the rest was foreign currency debt.[16] Exhibit E4.7 provides a snapshot of financing during 2008–12.

RESTRUCTURING INITIATIVES

In order to monetize the tower assets, RCL entered into a deal to sell off 5% stake in its tower company to a group of investors for ₹14 billion (US$337.5 million) in 2007. The placement was made to leading international financial investors from the USA, Europe, and Asia, such as Fortress Capital, HSBC Principal Investments, Galleon Group, New Silk Route, GLG Partners, Quantum Fund (George Soros), and DA Capital. The deal valued the tower company at ₹270 billion (US$6.75 billion) or ₹135 per share.

In February 2008, the tower division planned an initial public offering of shares, but the offer had to be withdrawn due to poor market conditions. Again in September 2009, RCL outlined

[14] The company reversed this policy later on.

[15] Likewise, the company used to write off telecom electronic equipment over 10 years in financial year 2009 but increased it to 18 years from financial year 2010.

[16] These foreign currency borrowings were unhedged. The exchange rate between Indian Rupee and USD had approximately averaged ₹49/US$, ₹45/US$, ₹49/US$, and ₹52/US$ during 2009–12.

plans for flotation of 10% of equity pegging the value of company at US$1 billion,[17] but the offer did not materialize. Market observers speculated that the company might first sell a partial equity stake to a strategic investor before doing an IPO or a sell-off.[18]

In India, five companies—Reliance Infratel (RTIL), GTL, Tata Quippo, Bharti Infratel Ltd and Indus Towers Ltd—operated telecom towers. GTL, Quippo and Bharti Infratel, operated around 120,000 towers. Indus Towers, owned by Bharti Airtel and Vodafone Essar had at least 100,000 towers.[19] Reliance Infratel had tower sharing agreements with at least five telecom operators. These firms included Etisalat of United Arab Emirates, Aircel, and Tata Indicom. Reliance Infratel, which also housed RCL's optical fiber cable network, would be especially attractive for companies that had won broadband wireless spectrum in the 3G auction.

On June 6, 2010, the company's board approved a stake sale in the tower business. Reliance Infratel started negotiating a deal with GTL Infrastructure to merge its 50,000-tower portfolio with GTL Infrastructure in a cash and stock deal, making it the largest independent tower company in the world with 82,500 towers and 125,000 tenancies from 10 operators. Anil Ambani would retain a 25% equity stake in the new entity, but entirely in his personal capacity as a strategic financial investor. The combined enterprise value of Reliance Infratel and GTL Infra, including debt and equity of the two, would be about US$11 billion (₹500 billion). This included Reliance Infratel's debt of an estimated ₹180 billion (about US$3 billion). This debt would be transferred to GTL, drastically reducing RCL's debt burden. The talks with GTL fell through in September 2010 on account of valuation concerns.[20] GTL was trading at ₹42.65 on the National Stock Exchange, down 5.6% from the previous day's close, but Reliance Communications share was up 0.3% at ₹163. In early 2011, Tata-Quippo (now called Viom Networks), another tower company, pulled out of talks to buy Reliance Infratel after the two companies could not agree on a price. Reliance was seeking US$5 billion for the company, which Viom described as "unrealistic." In November 2011, RCL entered into negotiations with two private equity groups—Blackstone and Carlyle—in an attempt to sell a equity interest in its tower company.[21] Exhibit E4.8 presents analyst forecast of financials for the tower business.

Flag IPO

In 2012, Global Telecommunications Infrastructure Trust, a wholly owned trust of RCL, was looking to raise US$700 million–US$1 billion by way of an IPO of Globalcom in Singapore, implying a total enterprise value of US$1.5 billion.

---

[17] See http://www.cellular-news.com/story/39788.php (accessed on September 13, 2017).

[18] It was believed the RCL was in talks with international telecom firms such as the Abu Dhabi-based Emirates Telecommunications Corp., known as Etisalat, South Africa's MTN Group Ltd and AT&T Inc. of the USA for a possible stake sale.

[19] See Âhttp://www.livemint.com/Home-Page/beXDVra6TmXS8ULawpnHPI/Reliance-Infratel-may-sell-stake-first.html (accessed on September 13, 2017).

[20] See http://articles.economictimes.indiatimes.com/2010-09-07/news/27610867_1_rcom-gtl-infrastructure-tower-business (accessed on September 13, 2017); India's telecom tower market had witnessed two transactions in the last 5 months. GTL Infrastructure Ltd bought Aircel Ltd's 17,500 towers for ₹4.8 million/tower and Quippo Infrastructure Ltd purchased Tata Teleservices (Maharashtra) Ltd's 2,500 towers for ₹5.2 million/tower.

[21] See http://www.cellular-news.com/story/51765.php (accessed on September 13, 2017).

2G SPECTRUM SCAM

The 2G spectrum scandal involved politicians such as A. Raja, the then telecom minister, and government officials that included the then telecom secretary who allegedly undercharged telecom companies for frequency allocation licenses. The shortfall between the actual money collected and what could have been collected was pegged at US$27 billion[22] by the comptroller and auditor general of India. In January 2008, the Department of Telecommunications (DoT) decided to issue licenses on a first-come-first-serve basis, advancing the cut-off date to September 25 from October 1, 2007. Apparently, later the same day, the DoT posted an announcement on its website that those who apply between 3.30 pm and 4.30 pm would be issued licenses, which the Delhi High Court held as illegal. The CAG observed that there were large-scale irregularities in the spectrum allocation. The Central Vigilance Commission directed the Central Bureau of Investigations to investigate the irregularities. The scam led to several court cases and investigations against those involved. Raja resigned as the telecom minister in November 2010. Raja and the telecom secretary were arrested in February 2011 and remanded in judicial custody. The chargesheet named Reliance Communications as one of the accused. Gautam Doshi, the group managing director, and Hari Nair and Surendra Pipara, two senior executives at Reliance, were arrested and later released on bail. On September 29, 2011, the CBI said that the role of Anil Ambani was being probed. In February 2012, the Supreme Court of India cancelled all 122 licenses allotted by A. Raja and imposed fines on several telecom companies.

In 2009, the DoT appointed Parekh & Co as special auditors to conduct an audit of the accounts of the company and its subsidiaries for the financial years 2006–07 and 2007–08. The telecom department had appointed the special auditor after the Cellular Operators' Association of India had alleged underreporting of revenues by RCL.[23] The special auditors appointed by DoT had alleged that RCL inflated revenues by over ₹29 billion, while at the same time, underreporting revenues to the Telecom Regulatory Authority of India with the intention of evading licensing fee of over ₹3 billion. However, the company denied any wrongdoing.

THE VERITAS REPORT

In June 2012, two analysts at Veritas, a Canadian investment research firm, startled the world investment community by downgrading the price target of RCL stock to a mere ₹.15 when the stock was trading at ₹93 (Reliance Communications Ltd: A House of Cards 2012). They questioned RCL's accounting policies and corporate governance standards. The company's stock was badly hammered, dropping to a 52-week low of ₹60 after the report was released.[24] The two analysts valued the core business at ₹15 per share by applying a 50% "governance discount" to their approximate equity valuation of ₹30 per share. Veritas had earlier released

---

[22] There are differences of opinion on the losses incurred by the government.

[23] See http://articles.economictimes.indiatimes.com/2009-10-26/news/28398825_1_government-appointed-auditor-special-auditors-rcom-inflated-revenues (accessed on September 13, 2017).

[24] See http://www.livemint.com/Companies/TUkJANKsZnE0L13I58JsZO/RCom-falls-to-record-low-on-Veritas-report.html, accessed on September 13, 2017; http://articles.economictimes.indiatimes.com/2011-07-22/news/29803314_1_rcom-scrip-report-telecom-tower-business, (accessed on September 13, 2017).

another report in July 2011in which the analysts wrote (Reliance Industries Ltd and Reliance Communications Ltd 2011):

> Reliance Communications Ltd is the poster child of everything that is wrong with corporate India, and irrespective of management's assertions about "values" and "integrity" in various annual reports, we find no credible evidence of either in its financial statements or those of its former parent, Reliance Industries Ltd. Doubts about management's integrity and the short shrift to shareholders arise right at inception, when the demerger from RIL was undertaken on August 31, 2005, and the company was listed on Indian bourses on March 6, 2006.

Veritas estimated that during the formation of Reliance Communications, RIL (Reliance Industries Ltd) shareholders invested ₹136.75 billion into the business, compared to a paltry ₹1.86 billion by the management, but after listing on the Bombay Stock Exchange, the shareholding of minority RIL shareholders declined from 61.73% to 37%. According to Veritas analysts, on the 821.48 million shares issued to management at the formation of RCL, RIL shareholders suffered a loss of ₹252.04 billion based on RCL's March 6, 2006, closing price of approximately ₹307. The company, of course, dismissed the report as baseless and malicious.

CONCLUSION

As of 2012, there were wide differences of opinion among security analysts about RCL's valuation. Analysts had given hold, neutral, or sell recommendations. It was unclear if RCL would be able to deleverage and improve the performance of its businesses. Exhibit E4.9 presents an analyst forecast of RCL's financials as of 2012.

REFERENCES AND SUGGESTED READINGS

Aggarwal, A. and D. Sabharwal. 2010, September 6. *Reliance Communications Ltd.* Mumbai: Tata Securities.

Chauhan, D. 2007, September 10. *Reliance Communications Ltd.* Mumbai: Asit Mehta Research.

Chawla S., and Y. K. Khare. 2008, October 31. *Reliance Communications Ltd.* Mumbai: Anand Rathi.

———. 2009, January 24. *Reliance Communications Ltd.* Mumbai: Anand Rathi.

Duvvuri, G. 2012, August 13. *Reliance Communications Ltd.* Mumbai: Edelweiss.

Esty, B., and Iridium LLC. 2003, April 11. *Iridium LLC.* Harvard Business School Case Study No. 9-200-039. Harvard Business School.

Javeri, D., and A. Chaudhury. 2007, December 10. *Reliance Communications Ltd.* Mumbai: Edelweiss.

Javeri, D., and S. Anand. 2008, December 12. *Reliance Communications Ltd.* Mumbai: Edelweiss.

Khare, S. 2007, November 1. *Reliance Communications Ltd.* Mumbai: MF Global.

Modi, S. 2009, January 28. *Reliance Communications Ltd.* Mumbai: Emkay Research.

Moghe, A. 2011, February 15. *Reliance Communications Ltd.* Mumbai: Avendus Research.

Monga, Neeraj, and Varun Raj. 2012, June 8. Reliance Communications Ltd: A House of Cards. Ontario, Canada: Veritas Investment Research.

Reliance Communications. *Annual Reports*, 2007–2012.

Reliance Industries Ltd. and Reliance Communications Ltd. 2011, July 18. *Brothers in Arms: Misappropriating a Fortune.* Veritas Investment Research.

Seth, N. 2012, July 11. *Reliance Communications Ltd.* Mumbai: Emkay Research.

Shah, H. 2007, November 1. *Reliance Communications Ltd.* Mumbai: Angel Broking.

Shah H. 2010, August 16. Reliance Communications, Karvy Stock Broking Report. Mumbai.
———. 2008, April 1. Reliance Communications. Angel Broking Research Report. Mumbai.
———. 2008, October 31. *Reliance Communications Ltd.* Mumbai: Angel Broking.
———. 2010, September 6. *Reliance Communications Ltd.* Mumbai: Karvy Stock Broking.
Shah, H., and A. Gupta 2012, August 13. *Reliance Communications Ltd.* Mumbai: Karvy Stock Broking.

REVIEW QUESTIONS

1. As of 2012 would you invest in RCL? In answering this question analyze the company's strategy, Strengths/Weaknesses/Opportunities/Threats, quality of accounting, and financial performance.
2. What is the intrinsic value of the company? Do you agree with the valuation done by Veritas analysts? Why or why not?
3. Why did RCL get into financial trouble? Is it bad strategy or bad luck?
4. With regard to its capital structure did the company have the wrong capital structure, issue wrong kinds of capital or issue capital in the wrong sequence?
5. Critically evaluate the restructuring initiatives taken by the company. Why did they fail?
6. What lessons do you draw from this case study?

Assume the following market related data wherever required:

10-Year Treasury bond rate in 2010 = 8%
10-Year Treasury bond rate in 2012 = 8.2%
Market Risk Premium = 8%
Beta of RCL in 2010 = 1.5 (from Capitaline database)
Debt/Value ratio for Tower business = 0.5
WACC for tower business = 11.1%

Exhibit E4.1 *Income Statement (figures given in ₹million)*

	2012	2011	2010	2009	2008	2007
Sales turnover	221,330	248,980	239,021.5	247,360	206,055	186,842
Net sales	196,770	224,310	214,963	222,505	188,273	171,903
Other income	7,050	7,430	33,740	24,671.8	31,231	10,496
Total income	**203,820**	**231,740**	**248,704**	**247,177**	**219,505**	**182,400**
EXPENDITURE:						
Power and fuel cost	16,620	15,790	15,094	8,418.5	5,443.3	3,960
Employee cost	12,830	14,690	14,993	16,758	11,669.9	10,843
Other manufacturing expenses	72,280	72,460	72,821	69,039	56,527	63,420
Selling and Administration expenses	36,480	35,920	40,166	38,387	28,736	23,896
Miscellaneous expenses	710	1,340	417	2,680	7,631	6,448
Total expenditure	**138,920**	**140,200**	**143,492**	**135,283**	**110,008**	**108,567**
Operating profit	64,900	91,540	105,211	111,893	109,496	73,832

	2012	2011	2010	2009	2008	2007
Interest	16,300	11,330	15,518	13,849	10,681	8644
Gross profit	48,600	80,210	89,693	98,044	98,815	65,188
Depreciation	39,780	65,040	37,4651	36,077	28,052	29,192
Profit before tax	8,820	15,170	52,228	61,967	70,762	35,995
Tax	–1,060	–2,800	3,725	327.6	1,644.9	529.1
Fringe benefit tax	0	0	0	162.3	189.7	191.6
Deferred tax	0	2,920	728.9	–1,007.8	1,001.6	10.3
Net profit	9,880	15,050	47,774	62,485	67,926	35,264
Minority interest (after tax)	610	1,500	1,192.5	2,051.7	13,900	–49.2
Profit/Loss of associate company	1	–100	–31.9	15.9	–14.7	0
Net profit after minority interest & p/l associate company	9,280	13,450	46,550	60,449.3	54,011	35,313
Extraordinary items	786	3,173	1,569	3,187	13,766	8.3
Adjusted net income	9,201.4	10,276.5	449,80.9	57,261.4	40,245.4	35,305.2
Equity dividend (%)	5	10	17	16	15	10
Dividend per share (₹)	0.25	0.5	0.85	0.8	0.75	0.5

Source: Capitaline Database.

Exhibit E4.2 *Balance Sheet (figures given in ₹million)*

	2012	2011	2010	2009	2008	2007
Share capital	10,320	10,320	10,320	10,320	10,320	10,223
Reserves	356,890	394,670	423,286	412,483	279,943	219,083
Total shareholders' funds	367,210	404,990	433,606	422,803	290,263	229,306
Minority interest	8,600	8,240	6,583.9	6,549.2	24,309.3	56.1
Secured loans	359,640	216,930	30,000	30,000	9500	51,135.7
Unsecured loans	23,390	173,780	267,154.2	361,622.5	248,717	123,247.6
Total debt	383,030	390,710	297,154.2	391,622.5	258,217	174,383.3
Other liabilities	20,410	14,180	0	0	0	0
Total liabilities	**779,250**	**818,120**	**737,344.5**	**820,974.9**	**572,789.6**	**403,745.9**
Gross block	1,045,710	868,380	836,629	807,316.4	499,041.8	376,029.1
Less: Accumulated depreciation	331,100	273,400	190,671	141,144.2	89,561	55,192.1
Less: Impairment of assets	0	0	0	0	0	733.9
Net block	714,610	594,980	645,958	666,172.2	409,480	320,103
Capital work in progress	50,260	166,000	116,556.5	113,096	149,299.3	36,906.8
Investments	6,520	5,700	41,598.9	95,657	109,996.3	77,114

(continued)

Exhibit E4.2 *(continued)*

	2012	2011	2010	2009	2008	2007
Current assets, loans and advances						
Inventories	5,660	5,170	54,46.3	5,427.2	4,058.8	4,821.2
Sundry debtors	35,840	37,530	33,116.7	39,617.7	27,223.7	18,316.1
Cash and bank	5,500	48,660	8,185.4	16,829	8,781.8	72,006.4
Loans and advances	73,260	68,600	74,824.5	85,270	65,752	35,986
Total current assets	120,260	159,960	121,572.9	147,144.7	105,817.2	131,130.4
Less: Current liabilities and provisions						
Current liabilities	110,810	94,320	147,084.6	159,718.3	156,212.5	114,333.6
Provisions	26,660	31,120	40,266.7	41,095.7	44,563.7	47,148.8
Total current liabilities	137,470	125,440	187,351.3	200,814	200,776.2	161,482.4
Net current assets	**–17,210**	**34,520**	**–65,778.4**	**–53,669.3**	**–94,959**	**–30,352**
Deferred tax assets	6,450	6,800	7,553.0	121	1,298	178.8
Deferred tax liability	16,630	10,470	8,543.8	402	2,325.6	204.8
Net deferred tax	–10,180	–3,670	–990.5	–281	–1,027.6	–26
Other assets	35,250	20,590	0	0	0	0
Total ASSETS	**779,250**	**818,120**	**737,344.5**	**820,974.9**	**572,789.6**	**403,745.9**

Source: Capitaline Database.

Exhibit E4.3 *Cash Flow Statements, 2007–12 (figures given in ₹million)*

	2012	2011	2010	2009	2008	2007
Cash and cash equivalents at beginning of the year	38,130	820	5,351.5	1,926.6	66,872.2	0.5
Net cash from operating activities	**33,390**	**7,260**	**10,754.3**	**18,877.8**	**29,813.9**	**105,087.9**
Cash flow from operating activities						
Net profit before tax and extraordinary items	1,550	–8,600	6,194.7	48,150.7	26,040.9	24,208.5
Adjustment for						
Depreciation	17,410	15,940	15,112.4	19,335.1	18,436.6	18,361.2
Interest (Net)	6,690	700	5,360.2	3,914.7	8,247.3	2,949.2
P/L on sales of assets	–70	–4,260	0	–30,634.3	–0.7	50.3

	2012	2011	2010	2009	2008	2007
P/L on sales of invest	−230	−190	−2.4	0	38.4	−217.8
Prov. and W/O (Net)	450	1,310	−817.4	1,050.4	1,465.8	1,385.8
P/L in Forex	−1,300	−2,410	−20,449.8	−2,469.9	−3,838.5	−1,011.7
Fin. lease and rental charges	−30	−30	−29.2	0	0	0
Others	−50	−70	−311.4	−4,790.9	130.9	131.5
Total adjustments (PBT and extraordinary items)	22,870	10,990	−1,137.6	−13,594.9	24,479.8	21,648.5
Op. profit before working capital changes	24,420	2,390	5,057.1	34,555.8	50,520.7	45,857
Adjustment for						
Trade and other receivables	1,330	−6,350	−6,486.3	−16,410.7	−4,253.6	32,309.9
Inventories	−230	−80	−452	−519.2	−1,027.1	−325.4
Trade payables	7,210	10,980	12,978.2	3,336.6	−14,893	27,764.5
Total (OP before working capital changes)	8,310	4,550	6,039.9	−13,593.3	−20,173.7	59,749
Cash generated from/(used in) operations	32,730	6,940	11,097	20,962.5	30,347	105,606
Direct taxes paid	650	320	−2390	−2,113.8	−533.1	−518.1
Others	0	0	2047.3	29.1	0	0
Total-others	650	320	−342.7	−2084.7	−533.1	−518.1
Cash flow before extraordinary items	33,380	7,260	10,754.3	18,877.8	29,813.9	105,087.9
Gain on Forex exch. tran	10	0	0	0	0	0
Net cash used in investing activities	**−21,150**	**−28,020**	**43,402.6**	**−79,505.4**	**−157,007**	**−150,466**
Cash flow from investing activities						
Investment in assets:						
Purchased of fixed assets	−24,680	−87,460	−8,433.6	−43,826.2	−73,198.4	−27,278.3
Sale of fixed assets	2,160	2,080	0	100	2.6	5.9
Financial/Capital investment:						
Purchase of investments	−269,370	−175,730	−38,142.8	−1,748.3	−112,007	−84,174
Sale of investments	272,140	198,910	28,420.5	230.5	72,749.4	91,604.9
Interest received	4,230	4,820	5,818.6	102.5	777.6	1,013.5
Loans to subsidiaries	−158,960	−285,130	−423,850	−38,0301	−36,962.8	−31,000
Others	153,330	314,490	479,589.9	345,936.6	−8,368.9	−10,0638
Net cash used in financing activities	**−48,590**	**58,070**	**−58,686.6**	**64,052.5**	**62,347.5**	**46,062.4**
Cash flow from financing activities						
Proceeds:						
Proceed from issue of debentures	20,000	0	0	30,000	0	0

(continued)

Exhibit E4.3 *(continued)*

	2012	2011	2010	2009	2008	2007
Proceed from other long-term borrowings	78,920	51,860	24,280.7	0	58,912.2	1,116.6
Proceed from short-term borrowings	0	40,160	0	68,351.1	75,509.1	75,190.6
Payments:		0	0	0	0	0
On redemption of debenture	−65,070	0	0	0	0	0
Of the long-term borrowings	−14,840	−21,290	0	−9,500	−40,385.2	−5,671
Of the short-term borrowings	−50,600	0	−69,502.3	−905.9	−22,343.1	−19,879.5
Dividend paid	−1,190	−2,020	−1,911.2	−1,792.3	−1,182.8	0
Shelter assistance reserve	0	0	0	0	0	0
Interest paid	−13,540	−10,640	−11,553.8	−10,911.5	−8,163.3	−4,694.3
Others	−2270	0	0	−11,188.9	0.6	0
Net cash used in financing activities	−48,590	58,070	−58,686.6	64,052.5	62,347.5	46,062.4
Net Inc/(Dec) in cash and cash equivalent	−36,350	37,310	−4,529.7	3,424.9	−64,845.6	684
Cash and cash equivalents at end of the year	1,780	38,130	821.8	5,351.5	2,026.6	684.5

Source: Capitaline Database.

Exhibit E4.4 *Key Ratios of Reliance Communications and Telecom Industry Peer Companies*

							Domestic Industry Average	Global Industry Average
	2012	2011	2010	2009	2008	2007	2012	2012
Debt-equity ratio	0.98	0.81	0.79	0.87	0.8	0.76	0.63	0.42
Long-term debt-equity ratio	0.62	0.46	0.54	0.54	0.52	0.61	0.43	
Current ratio	0.51	0.47	0.45	0.39	0.46	0.67	0.76	
Turnover Ratios								
Fixed Assets	0.23	0.29	0.29	0.38	0.47	0.4	0.1	
Inventory	40.87	46.91	43.96	52.15	46.41	31	9.53	
Debtors	6.03	7.05	6.57	7.4	9.05	8.16	2.46	
Total asset turnover ratio	0.28	0.32	0.31	0.35	0.42	0.37	0.12	
Interest cover ratio	1.54	1.99	4.37	5.47	6.28	5.16	2.01	91.35
PBIDT margin (%)	29.32	35.19	44.02	45.23	46.16	39.52	23.42	
PBIT margin (%)	11.35	9.06	28.34	30.65	32.55	23.89	9.43	
PBDT margin (%)	21.96	30.64	37.53	39.64	40.98	34.89	18.73	

	2012	2011	2010	2009	2008	2007	2012	2012
Cash Profit margin (%)	22.44	30.89	35.66	39.85	39.9	34.5	17.19	
PAT margin (%)	4.46	4.77	19.99	25.26	26.28	18.87	3.2	10.52
ROCE (%)	3.15	2.9	8.69	10.88	13.74	8.85	1.13	
ROE (%)	2.5	2.78	10.99	16.8	19.91	12.3	0.64	13.68
Price earning (P/E)	18.85	16.75	7.62	5.99	19.52	30.55	37.91	12.01
Price-to-Book value (P/BV)	0.47	0.55	0.81	0.85	3.61	3.74	2.52	
Price/Cash EPS (P/CEPS)	3.5	2.78	4.15	3.67	10.96	13.36	4.67	
EV/EBIDTA	8.49	6.17	6.1	6.57	11.86	13.02	1.90	5.28
Market cap/Sales	0.88	0.99	1.64	1.62	5.57	5	1.41	

Source: Capitaline Database, Avendus Research, Case Writer Estimates.

Note: The global peer group consists of China Mobile, AT&T, Vodafone, Verizon, NTT, Deutsche Telekom, MTN, Bharti Airtel, Telenor Asia, Telecom Italia, Telecomunicacoes De Sao Paulo, and Idea cellular. The domestic peer group consists of Bharti Airtel, Idea, MTNL, and Tata Teleservices.

Exhibit E4.5 *Stock Price History (₹)*[25]

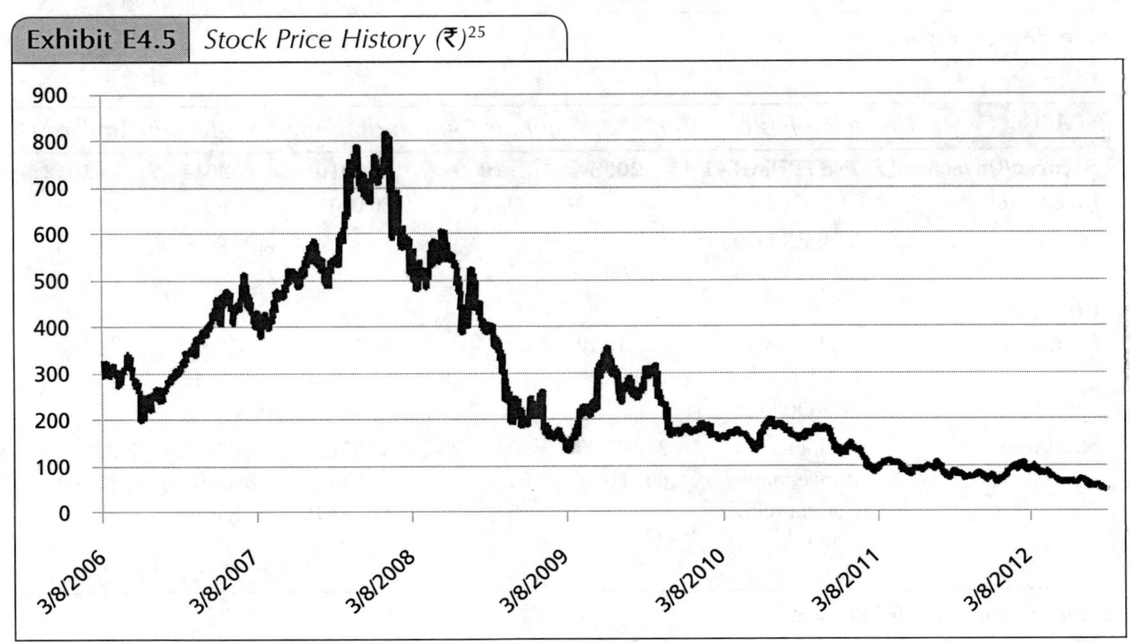

Source: Bombay Stock Exchange.

[25] RCL Stock had an equity beta of 1.8 in 2012.

Exhibit E4.6 *Performance of Wireless Business*

Particulars	2QFY08	1QFY09	2QFY09	3QFY09	2QFY11	3QFY11	4QFY11	1QFY12
Gross revenues (₹million)	37,230	41,190	43,360	44,120	511,830	40,640	419,780	432,670
Mobile subscriber base (million)	36.3	50.8	56.0	61.3	117	125.7	135.7	143.3
Mobile ARPUs (₹/user/month)	364	284	271	251	122	**112**	**107**	**103**
Total minutes of usage (million)	50,700	62,000	67,800	72,100	94,600	91,500	94,400	97,300
Revenues per minute (₹)	0.73	0.66	0.64	0.61	0.44	0.44	0.44	0.44
MoUs per user per month	490	424	423	410	276	251	241	233
EBITDA (₹million)	14,870	16,620	16,860	16,620	165,950	117,920	114,900	117,270
EBITDA margins (%)	39.9	40.4	38.9	37.7	32.4	29.0	27.4	27.1
EBIT (₹million)	10,240	10,490	10,320	9660	–23,480	63,430	67,100	63,070
EBIT margins (%)	27.5	25.5	23.8	21.9	–59	0.0	0.0	0.0

Source: Analyst Reports.

Exhibit E4.7 *Financing History 2007–12, Amounts Outstanding (figures given in ₹million)*

Secured/Unsecured	INSTRUMENT	2008	2009	2010	2011	2012
(a) Secured	11.2% NCD[26]		30,000	30,000	30,000	30,000
	5.5% FX Loan				105,960	183,550
	Term loan	9,500				
(b) Unsecured						
Long-term	FX Loans	56,019.70	89,674.30	95,582.60	16,200	6,620
	FCCB[27]	54,932.30	70,835.10	64,595.50	66,964.90	
	Term loans		36,000			
Short-term	FX loans	21,662.30	23,629.20	23,351.60	8340	22,200
	Rupee loans	60,750	53,000	18,000	85,500	26,000
	Commercial paper		5,897.5	12,953.10	1,463.6	9,440
	Cash credit[28]					3,000

Source: Company Annual Reports.

Note: During 2007 and 2012 the company also had operating leases worth ₹56,110 m of which ₹25,430 m had tenors more than 5 years and the remaining had tenors less than 5 years.

26 Non-convertible debentures.

27 Foreign currency convertible bonds.

28 Working capital facility from banks.

Exhibit E4.8 *Financial Forecast for Tower Business (figures given in ₹million)*

	2010	2011	2012	2013	2014	2015	2016	2017	2018	2019	2020
Total towers	55,995	62,514	68,256	73,686	78,582	82,795	86,306	89,388	92,549	95,793	99,120
Tenants/tower	0.8	0.8	0.8	0.8	0.8	0.8	0.8	0.8	0.8	0.8	0.8
Total tenants	44,796	50,011.2	54,604.8	58,948.8	62,865.6	66,236	69,044.8	71,510.4	74,039.2	76,634.4	79,296
Annual rental/ tower	0.32	0.33	0.34	0.35	0.36	0.37	0.38	0.39	0.4	0.42	0.43
Revenue	14,334.72	16,503.7	18,565.63	20,632.08	22,631.62	24,507.32	26,237.02	27,889.06	29,615.68	32,186.45	34,097.28
Incremental EBITDA margin	0.8	0.85	0.85	0.85	0.85	0.85	0.85	0.85	0.85	0.85	0.85
Incremental EBITDA	11,467.78	14,028.14	15,780.79	17,537.27	19,236.87	20,831.22	22,301.47	23,705.7	25,173.33	27,358.48	28,982.69
Incremental free cash flow	8492	10375	11668	12974	14251	15465	16605	17714	18890	20139	21464

Source: MF Global Research.

Exhibit E4.9 *Financial Forecast for RCL (figures given in ₹million)*

	2010	2011	2012	2013E	2014E
EBIT	40,739	25,777	24,722	33,529	36,820
Interest expenses	(11,863)	10,724	15,901	22,521	20,903
Net profit	48,149	14,936	9,882	11,047	15,122
Minority interest	1,224	1,605	609	593	593
Profit after minority interest	46,550	13,458	9,260	10,454	14,529
Depreciation	37,465	65,039	39,783	34,069	37,103
Other noncash charges	8,164	(13,317)	609	593	593
Changes in working capital	(3,466)	50,340	(8,266)	20,759	9,600
Capex	74,959	99,604	43,055	14,954	20,000
Debt	297,154	390,714	369,178	357,504	339,248
Total assets or liabilities	737,346	803,950	694,904	694,199	690,435
Shares outstanding	2,133	2,133	2,133	2,133	2,133
Debt/Total Assets%	40.3	48.5	53.1	51.4	49.1

Source: Agarwal and Hadkar (2012).

CASE 5

Wipro Ltd: The Demerger Decision[1]

Description: In November 2012, Wipro Ltd, a New York Stock Exchange (NYSE)-listed IT services company, announced its plan to demerge the non-IT businesses into an unlisted entity: Wipro Enterprises. The case highlights the governance, valuation, and ethical issues surrounding the demerger. Shareholders were given three options to choose from. One of them was that they could exchange Wipro Enterprises shares that they would receive after the demerger with Wipro Ltd shares because Wipro Enterprises would remain unlisted. The case asks the student to analyze the restructuring from an investor's perspective. The case is especially interesting in that it provides a platform to discuss governance issues in the context of a family-owned public firm.

Learning Objectives:

1. Evaluate the advantages and disadvantages of corporate demergers
2. Undertake valuation in the context of demergers or spinoffs
3. Highlight the ethical and legal issues surrounding demergers
4. Conceptualize the fiduciary responsibilities of corporate boards as they relate to protecting the interests of minority shareholders

Subjects Covered: Demergers, valuation, ethics, corporate governance

In 2012, Wipro Ltd, a NYSE-listed, IT services company announced its plan to demerge its nonIT businesses into an unlisted entity—Wipro Enterprises Limited (WEL). Wipro Consumer Care & Lighting, Wipro Infrastructure Engineering (Hydraulics & Water businesses), and Medical Diagnostic Product & Services Business would be held under a separate company, WEL. Under the plan, Wipro Limited (WL) would remain a publicly listed company and focus

[1] Professors Vishwanath S. R. and Vijaya Narapareddy prepared this case as the basis for class discussion rather than to illustrate either effective or ineffective handling of an administrative situation.

exclusively on information technology (IT), whereas WEL would be an unlisted company.[2] Mr Azim Premji, chairman of WL, was convinced about the merits of the plan. He strongly believed that the demerger was in the best interest of shareholders.

Mr Azim Premji said:[3]

> I am confident that the demerger will enhance value for our shareholders, and provide fresh momentum for growth. Each of our distinct businesses is best of breed in its respective industry, and we are committed to both the businesses.

The agenda for the board meeting to be held on November 1, 2012, included a final vote on the demerger plan. On December 28, 2012, shareholders were expected to vote on the proposed demerger, as required by the Indian Court. Chairman Premji hoped that he would receive support for his demerger plan from his board and Wipro shareholders.

AZIM PREMJI

Premji, a Stanford graduate in electrical engineering, was a prominent Indian business leader, well known for his wealth as well as philanthropy. He was the recipient of numerous accolades in the USA, Europe, Asia, and India. In March 2003, *Forbes* named him as one of 10 people globally with most "power to effect change." In August 2003, *Fortune* honored him as one of the 25 most powerful business leaders outside the USA. In October 2003, he was featured on the cover of *Business Week* as "India's Tech King." Two years later, (in October 2005) *Financial Times* included him in the global list of 25 people who contributed to "dramatically reshaping the way people live, work or think." The *Journal of Foreign Policy* listed him in November 2011 among the top global thinkers. Premji became the first Indian recipient of the coveted Faraday Medal and was conferred honorary doctorates by Wesleyan University, USA, and the Indian Institutes of Technology in Bombay and Roorkee, among others. In January 2011, the Government of India presented him the Padma Vibhushan, one of India's highest civilian awards, and the Republic of France presented him the "Legion of Honor." In November 2012, Forbes India honored him as the "Outstanding Philanthropist of the Year." In 2012, at a personal wealth of US$12.2 billion, he was ranked by *Forbes* as the third-richest man in India and 41st in the world. He served as a nonexecutive director on the board of the Reserve Bank of India, India's central bank, as a member of the prime minister's Councils for National Integration and for Trade & Industry in India, and as a member of the Indo-UK and the Indo-France CEOs' forum.

In 2001, Premji established the Azim Premji Foundation, a not-for-profit organization dedicated to building a better society and improving the quality and equity in education in India. He was among *TIME* magazine's top 100 most influential people in 2004 and 2011. Recognizing his contributions, Bill Gates, founder of Microsoft, wrote in 2011:

---

[2] Wipro press release, http://www.wipro.com/documents/investors/Wipro_Charts_a_New_Course.pdf (accessed on September 13, 2017).

[3] Wipro press release, November 1, 2012, http://www.wipro.com/newsroom/press-releases/Wipro-Ltd-Announces-Demerger-of-its-Consumer-Care-&-Lighting-incl-Furniture-Business-Infrastructure-Engineering-Hydraulics-&-Water-Business-and-Medical-Diagnostic-Product-&-Services-Business-into-a-Se/ (accessed on September 13, 2017).

If anyone personifies India's economic transformation, it is Azim Premji, chairman of the information-technology powerhouse Wipro Ltd. But it may be his pioneering leadership in India's nascent field of philanthropy that will be Premji's lasting legacy. His recent US$2 billion donation to his foundation was the largest charitable contribution in the history of modern India.[4]

COMPANY BACKGROUND

Established in 1945 as Western India Vegetable Products Limited, the company went public through an initial public offering in February 1946. It ventured into the fledgling IT industry in 1981 and established a software products and exports subsidiary, Wipro[5] Systems Ltd, in 1983. Wipro was a pioneer in marketing indigenous personal computers. The company entered IT services in the 1990s by pioneering the offshore development concept. Around the same time, it established a joint venture with General Electric (GE) in 1989 to manufacture medical equipment. It entered the business process outsourcing (BPO) business in the early 2000s and the eco-energy business in 2008. In 2013, Wipro was recognized by the Ethisphere Institute, a leading business ethics think-tank, as one of the world's most ethical companies for the second year in a row.

Wipro was listed on the NYSE:WIT in 2000 to reflect its global nature of business. It was the first People Capability Maturity Model (PCMM) Level 5 and Software Engineering Institute Capability Maturity Model (SEI CMM) Level 5 certified IT services company globally. As of 2012, Wipro had over 142,905 employees. It was a leading Indian company with a diversified portfolio of businesses in IT and BPO services, domestic hardware, consumer lighting, and consumer care. It also had a wide range of services, including systems integration, IT-enabled services, package implementation, software application development and maintenance, and R&D services. Additionally, it had a strong presence in niche market segments of infrastructure engineering and consumer products and lighting.

IT Business

The IT products division sold a range of Wipro personal desktop computers, Wipro servers, and Wipro notebooks. It was also a value-added reseller of desktops, servers, notebooks, storage products, networking solutions, and packaged software for international brands. Wipro entered the technology business in 1981 and had over 130,000 employees and customers in 54 countries. IT revenues stood at US$5.9 billion for the year ended March 31, 201, with a repeat business ratio of over 95%.

Consumer Care and Lighting

Wipro Consumer Care and Lighting, a business unit of WL operated in the fast-moving consumer goods (FMGG) segment offering a wide range of consumable commodities. The division was

[4] See http://content.time.com/time/specials/packages/article/0,28804,2066367_2066369_2066101,00.html (accessed on September 13, 2017).

[5] Wipro is the acronym for Western India Products.

established in 1945.The first product introduced by the division was vegetable oil, later popularized under the brand name Sunflower Vanaspati. It offered personal care products such as Wipro Baby Soft and Wipro Safewash, toilet soaps such as Santoor and Chandrika, and international brands such as Yardley. Its portfolio of lighting solutions included products such as Smartlite CFL, LED, and emergency lamps. The consumer division contributed just about 9% of the total revenues of the company and 6% of earnings before interest and taxes. The division had grown at a compound annual growth rate of 38% for the past few years. It was present in 40 countries with over 6,500 employees. It had eight plants in India and five overseas.

In the domestic market, Wipro's Santoor (brand name) soap ranked third with a market share of 8.8%, while the market leader, Hindustan Unilever, had a total market share of 45%. Godrej Consumer Products commanded a 11% share. In deodorants, Wipro was again ranked third. In Malaysia, in the toiletries category, the division had a market share of 48% and in fragrances it led the industry with a 24% share. In facial cleansers and hand and body lotion categories it had market shares of 27% and 17% respectively.

Through its popular products and acquisitions, Wipro Consumer Care and Lighting had become a fast-growing company in the FMCG segment. It acquired UNZA, a personal care company based in Singapore, in 2007 and Yardley's operations in Asia, the Middle East, and Africa in 2009. The division had made eight acquisitions in 9 years for a total price of US$500 million. Exhibit E5.1 lists the details of acquisitions made by the consumer care division.

Infrastructure Engineering

This division housed the hydraulics business of WL. It manufactured hydraulic cylinders, truck cylinders, and their components and solutions to international original equipment manufacturers and represented Kawasaki, Sun Hydraulics, and Teijin Seiki in India. It had entered into partnerships with Kawasaki and EADS, an aerospace giant. Wipro Infrastructure Engineering was the second-largest independent manufacturer of cylinders in the world. The company had recently ventured into water treatment systems and solutions to cater to the needs of various industries.

Medical Systems

Wipro GE Medical Systems Limited is Wipro's joint venture with GE Healthcare South Asia. It was engaged in the research and development of advanced solutions to cater to patient and customer needs in healthcare. This partnership, which began in 1990, offered equipment for diagnostics, healthcare IT solutions, and services to help healthcare professionals combat cancer, heart disease, and other ailments.

Exhibit E5.2 presents the financial performance of Wipro's businesses.

INDUSTRY BACKGROUND

The Indian IT could be categorized into four main categories: software products and engineering services, IT services, IT-enabled services, and hardware. The industry's total revenues were US$100.9b in 2012. The industry provided employment to almost 2.5 million professionals in

India. Many large companies in the West outsourced IT services to companies in India due to cost advantages of Indian IT firms. India's outsourcing industry was expected to touch US$225 billion by 2020. The industry was dominated by homegrown multinationals such as Tata Consultancy Services (TCS), Infosys Technologies, Wipro, and global corporations such as HP, IBM, and Accenture. The Indian IT/ITES industry was expected to generate aggregate revenues of US$428.8b in 2010–11 (Mandal, Dasgupta, and Srinivasan 2012). Revenues of the top three companies (TCS, Infosys, and Wipro) grew by 19.8% in 2011 to ₹958.4 billion. The top five Indian companies were consistently ranked among the top global service providers. Exhibits E5.3, E5.4, and E5.5 present financial data for Wipro and its key competition. Exhibit E5. 6 presents stock price and stock market index related data.

THE RESTRUCTURING

In 2011, Wipro, which had been performing somewhat poorly compared to peers such as TCS and Cognizant Technology Solutions, announced a number of changes in its top management as well as a new structure aimed at making it more agile and focused. Wipro began a restructuring exercise with the appointment of T K Kurien as the new CEO (Agarwal and Hadkar 2013). Wipro's board of directors and executive leadership are presented in Exhibits E5.7 through E5.9.

The company split its IT services business into six strategic business units (SBUs) based on industry domains. Each SBU was expected to operate as an independent profit center. This exercise was expected to make the company more customer-centric and improve its large-deal market share. The exercise yielded results quickly. The company increased the number of US$100 million clients from three to seven within a year.

The demerger was another step in restructuring. Under the plan, the board would remain unchanged and the demerger would have no impact on the management structure of WL. The Wipro brand would be jointly owned by both the companies. The demerger would not result in a change in the leadership of any of Wipro Enterprises businesses. Azim Premji would remain executive chairman of the board of WL and assume the position of nonexecutive Chairman of WEL.

Commenting on the demerger, Suresh Senapaty, chief financial officer and executive director of Wipro Ltd, noted:[6]

> The businesses of Wipro Enterprises Limited are diverse, and this demerger gives them an opportunity to pursue their independent growth plans. I believe the demerger scheme reflects a high standard of governance, transparency and fairness for all stakeholders.

T. K. Kurien, chief executive officer-IT business, and executive director, Wipro Ltd, added:

> Creating a technology-focused company will allow us to better serve the needs of our customers, and accelerate investments necessary to capitalize on market growth opportunities.

The business models were distinct, as displayed in Exhibit E5.10.

---

[6] Wipro press release, http://www.wipro.com/documents/investors/Wipro_Charts_a_New_Course.pdf (accessed on September 13, 2010).

According to the proposed restructuring scheme, resident Indian shareholders of WL could choose from multiple options as per their investment objectives. They could opt to:

1. Receive one equity share with face value of ₹10 in WEL for every five equity shares with face value of ₹2 each in WL that they held; or
2. Receive one 7% redeemable preference share with a face value of ₹50 in WEL for every five equity shares of WL that they held; or
3. Exchange the equity shares of WEL and receive as consideration equity shares of WL held by the founder. The exchange ratio would be 1:1.65 (i.e., 1 equity share in WL for every 1.65 equity shares in WEL).

Each redeemable preference share would have a maturity of 12 months and be redeemed at a value of ₹235.20.

Nonresident shareholders and ADR (American depository receipts) holders would be entitled to receive equity shares of WEL in the ratio mentioned earlier. Nonresident shareholders had the option to exchange WEL equity shares with equity shares of WL held by the founder. According to the proposed restructuring scheme, the WEL equity shares that the ADR holders were entitled to receive would be compulsorily exchanged for equity shares of WL held by the founder in the above ratio. Subject to receipt of all Indian and US Securities and Exchange Commission approvals, the ADR holders would be issued additional ADRs representing WL equity shares. If such approvals were not forthcoming or were not received prior to the record date of the demerger, the company's management expected the depository to sell the equity shares of WL, and distribute the proceeds to ADR holders.

RATIONALE FOR THE DEMERGER

In the USA, it is common for companies to restructure through spinoffs. In 2011, spinoffs amounting to US$115.8 billion had been announced in the USA.[7] In a spinoff, one or more divisions of a listed company are separated from the parent. The parent company distributes shares in a controlled subsidiary to its shareholders on a pro-rated basis as dividend. These entities continue to be owned by the original shareholders of the parent company. The spun-off company, thereby, becomes a standalone company and gets listed on a stock exchange. Netflix, Abbott Labs, Tyco, and McGraw-Hill had recently restructured themselves through spinoffs.

Like their US counterparts, Indian companies were restructuring themselves through demergers. A spinoff is a type of demerger. In the case of Wipro, the demerger of nonIT businesses would facilitate the creation of a simple structure with two separate entities:

1. A pure-play IT services company similar to its peers and
2. An unlisted independent company, Wipro Enterprise Ltd, comprising of diversified businesses.

[7] See http://www.efinancialnews.com/story/2011-08-12/eagle-spin-off-amr (accessed on September 13, 2017).

An analyst at Angel Broking said: "The hiving[8] off of non-IT business would result in an increase in ROCE (Return on Capital Employed) and ROE (Return on Equity) of the listed entity, as non-IT businesses have lower return ratios. We remain positive on the stock."[9] In their note, two analysts from J. P. Morgan suggested: "The focus on IT services will sharpen, and financial metrics such as margins will be relatively cleaner; hence, (there will be) easier comparisons with peers". The proposed demerger along with the contributions by segment is shown in Exhibit E5.11.

However, some analysts were not positive. They wondered how the valuation had been worked out and what the demerger would accomplish. An analyst at Edelweiss Capital, said:

> Wipro should, in fact, list the consumer care division. Indian FMCG companies get the highest P/E multiples among all countries and it would turn out to be a good move if Wipro does list it.[10]

In the fiscal year 2011–12, Wipro's IT business contributed to 86% of its revenue and 94% of operating profit. The demerger was anticipated to provide fresh impetus for both WL and WEL to pursue their individual growth strategies. The demerger was also expected to improve the competitiveness in their respective markets.

According to Clause 40A of the listing agreement promulgated by the Securities Exchange Board of India (SEBI), the stock market regulator in India, publicly listed and traded companies needed to have at least 25% public shareholding before June 2013. In case of Wipro Ltd, the founder group led by Azim Premji owned or controlled 78.3% of the company's total shareholding (see Exhibit E5.12 for shareholding pattern). This meant that Wipro would have to issue more stock to the public to meet the 25% minimum public shareholding requirement.

Wipro constituted a special committee of its board of directors to oversee the planning and execution of the demerger plan. The special committee was comprised of independent directors Bill Owens, N. Vaghul, and M. K. Sharma (shown in Exhibit E5.7). The appointed date for the demerger was the opening of business hours on April 1, 2012, and the demerger was expected to be completed by the following fiscal year. The demerger was subject to approvals by regulatory bodies and the High Court in the state of Karnataka where Wipro was headquartered. A trust was proposed to be set-up to oversee the share exchange and settlement of all claims.

Demerger Time Line

Under the Indian law, demerger is a scheme of arrangement under section 391–94 of Companies Act 1956 that required approval by a majority of shareholders (three-fourth value) in a meeting convened for the purpose and by the High Court. Shareholders were expected to vote on December 28, 2012. As the restructuring required several meetings with stakeholders and approvals from regulatory authorities, the whole process was expected to take anywhere up to 6 months from the demerger date. Exhibit E5.12 presents the time line of restructuring and Exhibit E5.13 presents a process-flow diagram.

---

8 Analysts and market participants in India use the term "hive off" to mean "demerger or spin off."

9 New Moves for Indian IT Firms, Knowledge @ Wharton, November 8, 2012.

10 Wipro Consumer going places with overseas buys, Business Line, March 3, 2013.

Valuation

The valuation process was jointly undertaken by Deloitte Touche Tohmatsu India Private Limited and N. M. Raiji & Co, while fairness opinions were provided by JM Financial Institutional Securities Private Limited and Citigroup Global Markets India Private Limited. JM Financial also acted as the sole financial advisor to WL. These companies, in their fairness opinion, agreed to the valuation and scheme of arrangement proposed by the earlier mentioned valuers.[11]

In its fairness opinion, Citigroup Global Markets, while agreeing to the swap ratio, pointed out that in arriving at their opinion on the consideration, the valuers (Deloitte and Raiji) did *not* perform a fundamental valuation analysis of Wipro and the transferred businesses and that they recommended the consideration based on accounting, income tax, and statutory principles and based on discussions with the management and special committee of independent directors of Wipro.

Incremental Costs

While the demerger provided some benefits, there were some costs too. In an information statement provided to investors, the company pointed out that there would be duplication of some corporate costs in operating the diversified businesses, which might result in increased operating costs. Also, the demerger would result in loss of any synergistic benefits, if any, between the IT and non-IT businesses. These incremental costs could not be quantified with any accuracy.

THE SITUATION IN LATE 2012

On December 10, 2012, the consumer care division of Wipro, which was in the process of being demerged, announced that it had reached a definitive agreement to acquire Singapore's LD Waxsons Group, an FMCG company, for US$144 million.[12] The acquisition was expected to be completed in two months. L. D. Waxson Group had leading skin care brands such as Bio-Essence and Ginvera, and a health care brand, Ebene. The company had manufacturing facilities in China and Malaysia and a strong footprint in Singapore, Malaysia, China, Taiwan, Hong Kong, and Thailand. The acquisition was expected to get the consumer care division an entry into the facial skincare business. It would also increase the division's market share in Malaysia from 16% to 26%.

THE FINAL VOTE

In November 2012, Wipro's board was slated to vote on the demerger plan. And in December during the same year, shareholders were expected to vote on the proposed demerger at a court convened meeting. Security analysts were divided on the benefits of the demerger and whether the proposal was fair to shareholders.

---

[11] Information Statement, Wipro Ltd, December 6, 2012.

[12] Wipro gains nearly 3% on Singapore acquisition, US$200 million order win report; see www.economictimes.com, (accessed on December 10, 2012).

Exhibit E5.1 *Acquisitions by Wipro's Consumer Care Business*

Acquisition	Category	Year of Acquisition	Consideration Value (₹milion)
Glucovita	Energy drink	2003	—
Chandrika	Ayurvedic soap	2003	—
North West	Light switches	2006	1,020
UNZA Singapore	Personal care	2007	13,250
Yardley Asia, Africa Middle East	Personal care	2009	2,450
Aramusk	Personal care	2011	—
Clean Ray	LED lighting	2011	—
Yardley UK	Personal care	2012	—
LD Waxson Singapore	Personal care	2012	7,780

Source: Business Line.

Exhibit E5.2 *Wipro's Financial Performance by Segment*

Division	2009	2010	2011	2012
IT Services Business				
Revenue (₹million)	191,661	202,469	234,850	284,313
EBIT (₹million)	40,323	47,749	53,407	59,265
Operating margin	21.0%	23.6%	22.7%	20.8%
Capital employed (₹million)	114,447	133,489	147,654	139,843
ROCE %[13]	36.5	37.08	37.2	43.65
IT Products Business				
Revenue (₹million)	34,552	38,322	36,910	38,436
EBIT (₹million)	1481	1752	1609	1787
Operating margin	4.3%	4.6%	4.35	4.6%
Consumer Care and Lighting Business				
Revenue (₹million)	20,830	23,774	27,258	33,401
EBIT (₹million)	2,548	3,100	3450	3956
Operating margin	12.2%	13.0%	12.6%	11.84%
Capital employed (₹million)	18,689	20,003	21,161	21,798
ROCE	14%	16%	16.3%	18.1%

Source: Wipro annual reports.

Note: ₹ = Indian Rupee; ROCE = Return on Capital Employed.

[13] EBIT of IT services and products divided by capital employed in IT products and services.

Exhibit E5.3 *Select Financial Data for Wipro and its Key Competitors (₹million unless otherwise mentioned)*

	WIPRO				TCS				INFOSYS			
Year	**2009**	**2010**	**2011**	**2012**	**2009**	**2010**	**2011**	**2012**	**2009**	**2010**	**2011**	**2012**
Net worth	125,149	176,922	213,202	243,525	133,463	150,166.5	194,795.2	247,566.3	178,090	220,360	245,010	297,570
Capital employed	175,288	232,224	266,039	299,342	134,873.4	151,523.9	198,267.2	253,132	178,090	220,360	245,260	297,780
Gross block of fixed assets	57,433	67,613	77,793	88,078	43,592.4	48,712.1	60,301.6	72,820.2	59,860	63,570	69,340	71,730
Sales	216,128	230,063	264,012	318,034	22,4060.8	230,448.4	292,756.8	38,8587.9	202,640	211,400	253,850	31,2540
EBDIT	42,783	63,682	64,416	72,704	55,645.9	68,492.7	92,582.6	140,709	74,100	83,290	95,620	123,760
PAT	29,738	48,980	48,437	46,851	46,962.1	56,185.1	75,699.9	109,759.8	58,190	58,030	64,430	84,700
Book value ₹	85.42	120.51	86.88	99.05	136.38	76.73	99.53	126.49	311.35	3839	426.85	518.41
Market capitalization	359,498.7	1,037,724	1,173,940	1,079,391	528,444	1528,182	2,314,389	2,285,716	758471	1,500,597	1,858,348	1,645,169
CEPS ₹	23.26	36.44	21.29	21.12	49.79	27.66	39.07	55.41	109.88	110.98	115.24	153.76
Earnings per share ₹	19.62	32.49	18.84	18.08	45.53	25.26	36.32	51.89	97.74	96.92	102.35	139.93
Dividend (annualized %)	200	300	300	300	1400	2000	1400	2500	470	500	1200	940
Payout (%)	20.39	18.47	31.85	33.18	30.75	79.18	38.55	48.18	24.06	25.78	58.64	33.6
Cash flow from operating activities	44,105	44,774	37112	29,979	493,169	62,789.2	57,198.8	31746.3	52,250	57,870	42750	60,150
Cash flow from investing Activities	–36,627	–31,261	–14,389	–2446	–318,534	–45,566.4	–8303.7	4643.8	–1950	–32,980	32,350	6750
Cash flow from financing activities	–707	–962	–27,333	–17,238	–160,449	–19,696.5	–46,056.1	–38,972.2	–24,300	–14,810	–36,420	–22,980
Human resource												
Total (Nos.)	97,810	108,071	122,385	n.a	126,150	140,619	198,614	n.a	104,850	113,796	130,820	n.a

Revenue per employee (₹million)	2.9	2.7	2.8	2.3	2.3	2.2	n.a	2.21	2.08	2.25	n.a	n.a
Cost per employee (₹million)	1.9	1.7	1.8	1.8	1.6	1.5	n.a	1.20	1.10	1.21	n.a	n.a
					Key Ratios and Margins of Wipro, TCS, and INFOSYS							
Debt-equity ratio	0.37	0.35	0.26	0.22	0	0	0	0	0	0	0	0
Long-term debt-equity ratio	0.37	0.22	0.1	0.09	0	0	0	0	0	0	0	0
Current ratio	2.11	1.66	1.58	1.73	1.91	1.63	1.56	1.74	3.97	4.47	4.62	4.69
Fixed assets ratio	5.39	3.68	3.63	3.83	5.9	4.99	5.37	5.84	3.86	3.43	3.82	4.43
Inventory ratio	47.62	43.14	39.65	42.12	1312.6	1942.25	4819.04	8172.2	0	0	0	0
Debtors Ratio	5.34	4.86	4.89	4.63	5.99	6.52	7.19	5.59	6.25	6.37	6.81	6.5
Interest cover ratio	19.03	58	42.95	10.77	691.82	668.75	435.8	816.02	3358	3761	8822	5791
PBIDT Margin (%)	19.8	27.68	24.4	22.86	24.84	29.72	31.62	36.21	36.57	39.4	37.67	39.6
PBIT Margin (%)	17.33	25.16	22.13	20.51	22.97	27.68	29.79	34.44	33.14	35.58	34.75	37.06
PBDT Margin (%)	18.88	27.25	23.88	20.96	24.8	29.68	31.56	36.17	36.56	39.39	37.66	39.59
CP Margin (%)	16.23	23.81	20.62	17.08	22.82	26.42	27.69	30.02	32.14	31.27	28.3	29.64
ROCE (%)	22.72	28.41	23.45	23.08	42	44.55	49.86	59.29	42.92	37.76	37.89	42.66
RONW (%)	24.71	32.43	24.83	20.52	38.67	39.5	43.83	49.53	37.18	29.13	27.69	31.22

Source: Capitaline Database.

Note: ROCE = Return on capital employed, RONW = Return on net worth.

Exhibit E5.4 *Industry Averages*

Panel A: IT Company Ratios

Year	2012	2011	2010	2009	2008	2007	2006
No. of Companies	**13**	**13**	**14**	**17**	**15**	**13**	**13**
Current ratio	2.26	2.04	2.22	2.5	2.4	2.3	2.18
Fixed assets	3.73	3.52	4.55	4.9	4.83	4.37	4.44
Inventory	145.04	147.55	181.81	226.02	303.36	301.64	293.2
Debtors	5.41	5.08	5.38	4.95	5.23	5.19	5.93
Interest coverage ratio	90.46	53.21	57.66	120.8	229.31	198.11	295.08
EBDIT margin (%)	27.04	27.6	24.62	27.06	28.7	28.76	29.33
EBIT margin (%)	24.17	24.27	21.39	23.95	25.53	25.3	26.08
PBDT margin (%)	26.78	27.15	24.25	26.86	28.59	28.64	29.24
PAT margin (%)	19.96	20.15	18.43	21	22.85	21.93	22.5
ROCE (%)	30.99	32.08	34.91	35.51	40.6	38.74	40.23
RONW (%)	28.09	29.83	32.99	32.46	36.59	33.82	35.44

Source: Capitaline Database.

Panel B: Personal-Care Industry Ratios

Year	2012	2011	2010	2009
No. of Companies	**1**	**4**	**4**	**8**
Key Ratios				
EBIDT margin (%)	17.6	20.8	16.7	14.5
EBIT margin (%)	15.9	19.7	15.6	13.4
EBDT margin (%)	17.3	20.1	15.3	13.3
PAT margin (%)	12.3	15.5	12.3	10.4
ROCE (%)	15.5	39.9	34.2	49.2
RONW (%)	16.4	40.7	38.7	52.3

Source: Capitaline Database.

Exhibit E5.5 *Financial Ratios, Valuation Multiples, and Growth Rates of Wipro and Its Competition*

Panel A: Valuation Multiples for Wipro and Major Competition, 2009–12

	Price/Earning (P/E)					Price to Book Value (P/BV)			
	2009	2010	2011	2012		2009	2010	2011	2012
WIPRO	12.51	21.75	25.39	24.28	**WIPRO**	2.87	5.87	5.51	4.43
TCS	11.86	30.91	32.56	22.51	**TCS**	3.96	10.18	11.88	9.23
INFOSYS	13.55	26.98	31.62	20.47	**INFY**	4.25	6.81	7.58	5.53

(continued)

Exhibit E5.5 *(continued)*

Price/Cash EPS (P/CEPS)					EV/EBIDTA				
WIPRO	10.55	19.4	22.47	20.79	WIPRO	8.54	16.27	18.15	14.72
TCS	10.85	28.23	30.27	21.08	TCS	9.22	21.82	24.67	16.02
INFY	12.05	23.56	28.09	18.63	INFOSYS	9.02	16.84	17.85	11.71
Market Cap/Sales									
WIPRO	1.66	4.51	4.45	3.39					
TCS	2.36	6.63	7.91	5.88					
INFOSYS	3.74	7.1	7.32	5.26					

Source: Capitaline Database.

Panel B: Valuation Multiples and Profitability Measures of IT Services Companies at the End of 2012

Company	Market Capitalization (₹million)	P/E x	P/BV x	EV/EBITDA x	ROE %	ROCE %
Tata Consultancy Services	2,618,342.20	21.3	10.58	16.02	49.5	59.3
Infosys Technologies	1,616,284.60	17.93	5.43	11.71	31.2	42.7
Wipro	1,003,981.60	17.58	4.12	14.72	20.5	23.1
HCL Technologies	472,432.90	19.02	7.15	11.74	31.3	32.3
Mahindra Satyam	142,005.10	11.15	4.28	4.78	35.7	26.6
Tech Mahindra	128,654.60	22.56	3.74	12.21	14.9	14.5
MphasiS	77,688.80	14.09	2.14	9.36	17.4	20.2
Patni Computers	70,064.60	14.73	2.08	8.41	15.8	18.7

Source: Analyst Reports, Case Writer Estimates.

Panel C: Growth Rates for Wipro and Key Competitors in the IT Industry

	WIPRO			
	2009	2010	2011	2012
Net worth (%)	8.29	41.37	20.51	14.22
Capital employed (%)	13.58	32.48	14.56	12.52
Gross block (%)	151.66	17.73	15.06	13.22
Sales (%)	22.4	6.45	14.76	20.46
PBIDT (%)	5.83	48.85	1.15	12.87
PBDT (%)	3.97	53.58	0.59	5.69
PBIT (%)	4.41	54.58	0.91	11.69
PBT (%)	2.25	60.34	0.29	3.73
PAT (%)	–2.92	64.71	–1.11	–3.27

(continued)

Exhibit E5.5 *(continued)*

	TCS			
	2009	**2010**	**2011**	**2012**
Net worth (%)	22.39	12.52	29.72	27.09
Capital employed (%)	22.36	12.35	30.85	27.67
Gross block (%)	34.52	11.74	23.79	20.76
Sales (%)	22.49	2.85	27.04	32.73
PBIDT (%)	1.8	23.09	35.17	51.98
PBDT (%)	1.73	23.08	35.07	52.13
PBIT (%)	2.79	23.95	36.69	53.46
PBT (%)	2.71	23.94	36.58	53.63
PAT (%)	4.16	19.64	34.73	44.99

	INFOSYS			
	2009	**2010**	**2011**	**2012**
Net Worth (%)	32.02	23.74	11.19	21.45
Capital Employed (%)	32.02	23.74	11.3	21.41
Gross Block (%)	32.79	6.2	9.08	3.45
Sales (%)	29.5	4.32	20.08	23.12
PBIDT (%)	30.83	12.4	14.8	29.43
PBDT (%)	30.81	12.41	14.82	29.42
PBIT (%)	31.22	12	17.28	31.29
PBT (%)	31.21	12	17.3	31.28
PAT (%)	30.18	–0.27	11.03	31.46

Source: Capitaline Database.

Panel D: Valuation Multiples of Consumer Care Companies in 2012

	Price/Earnings	**Market Cap/Sales**
Godrej Consumer Products	28.2	5.26
Marico	32.56	3.61
Nirma	54.98	1.21
P&G Hygiene	42.01	5.46
Colgate	38.79	5.41
Dabur	43.43	4.90

Source: Capitaline Database.

Exhibit E5.6 *Stock Price Information*

Panel A: Stock Price Chart

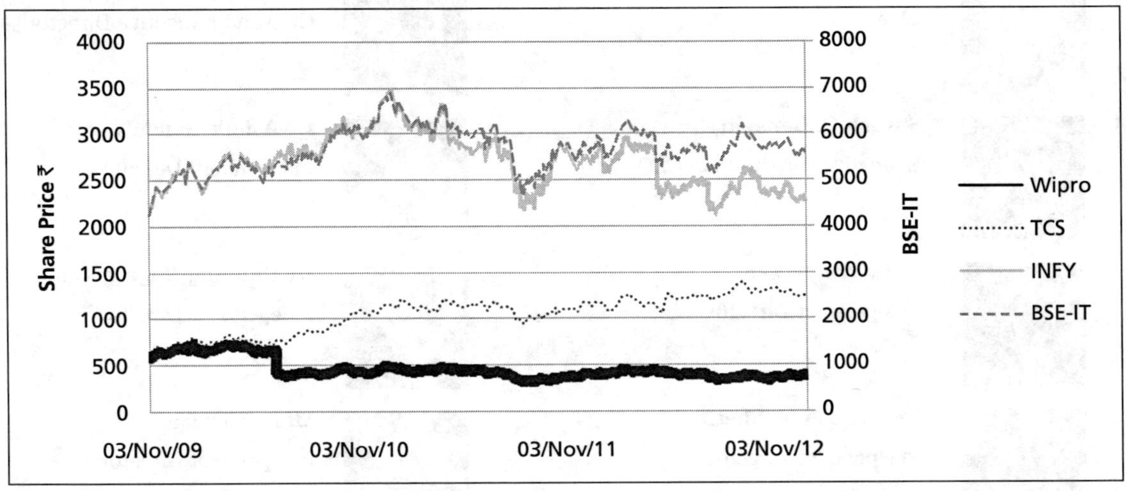

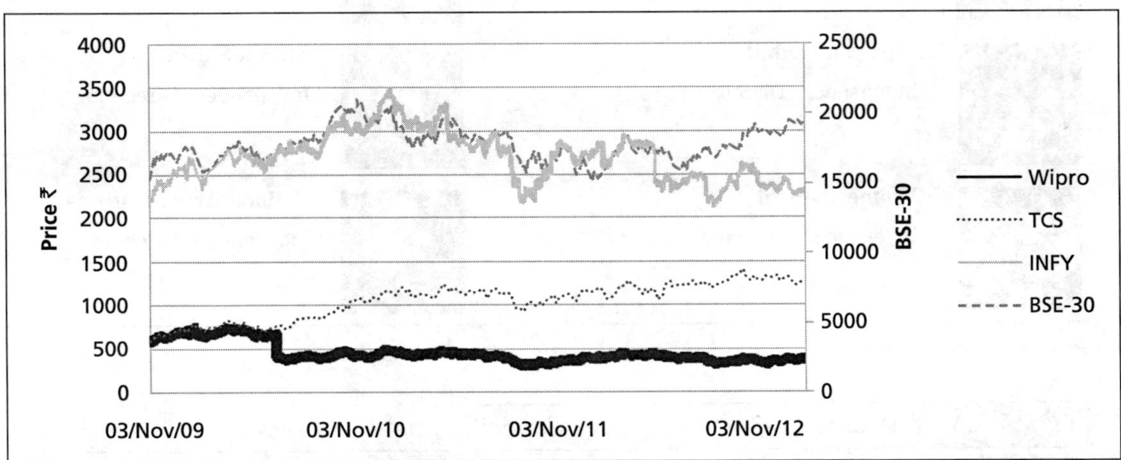

Panel B: Historical Stock Price of Wipro and Index Values

Year	Open	High	Low	Close	Close	Close
		WIPRO			BSE SENSEX	S&P BSE IT
2008	522	537	181	233	9647	2227
2009	236	699	195	679	17464	5186
2010	697	753	327	490	20509	6824
2011	492	494	310	398	15454	5751
2012	399	452	325	394	19426	5684

Source: Bombay Stock Exchange.

Exhibit E5.7 *Wipro's Board of Directors*

Azim H. Premji

Chairman

T. K. Kurien

CEO and Executive Director

Suresh C. Senapaty

Executive Director and CFO

Dr Ashok Ganguly

Independent Director

B. C. Prabhakar

Independent Director

Dr Henning Kagermann

Independent Director

Dr Jagdish N. Sheth

Independent Director

M. K. Sharma

Independent Director

Narayan Vaghul

Independent Director

Shyam Saran

Independent Director

Vyomesh Joshi

Independent Director

William Arthur Owens

Independent Director

Source: www.wipro.com

Exhibit E5.8 *Wipro's Corporate Executive Council*

Azim H. Premji, Chairman

Wipro Ltd.

T. K. Kurien

CEO and Executive Director, Wipro Ltd.

Suresh C. Senapaty

Executive Director and CFO, Wipro Ltd.

Pratik Kumar

Executive Vice President, Human Resources, Wipro Ltd.

Vineet Agrawal

President, Wipro Consumer Care and Lighting

Anurag Behar

Chief Sustainability Officer, Wipro Ltd.

Source: www. wipro.com

Exhibit E5.9 *Profiles of Wipro's Independent Directors*

Dr Ashok S. Ganguly, Independent Director. Dr Ganguly had served as a director on the Board since 1999. He was the Chairman of Wipro's Board Governance & Nomination Committee and Compensation Committee. He was the Chairman of ABP Pvt. Ltd (Ananda Bazar Patrika Group). Dr Ganguly also served as a nonexecutive director of Mahindra & Mahindra Limited and Dr Reddy Laboratories Limited. And was on the advisory board of Diageo India Private Limited He was a member of the Prime Minister's Council on Trade and Industry and the India-USA CEO Council, established by the Prime Minister of India and the President of the USA. Dr Ganguly was a member of the upper house of Indian parliament (Rajya Sabha). He was a former member of the Board of British Airways Plc (1996–2005) and Unilever PlC/NV (1990–97) and a Chairman of Hindustan Unilever Limited (1980–90). Dr Ganguly was on the Central Board of Directors of the Reserve Bank of India (2000–09). In 2006, Dr Ganguly was awarded the CBE (Hon) by the United Kingdom. In 2008, Dr Ganguly received the Economic Times Lifetime Achievement Award. He received the Padma Bhushan award by the Government of India in January 1987 and the Padma Vibhushan award in January 2009.

Mr B. C. Prabhakar, Independent Director. Mr Prabhakar served as a director on the Board since February 1997. He had been a practicing lawyer since 1970. He served as a nonexecutive director of 3M India Limited. He was also a member of the Audit, Risk and Compliance Committee and Chairman of the Administrative and Shareholder Investor Grievances Committee of Wipro Limited.

Dr Henning Kagermann, Independent Director. Dr Kagermann became a director of the Company on October 27, 2009. He served as Chief Executive officer of SAP AG until 2009. He had been a member of the SAP Executive Board since 1991. He was also President of Acatech (German Academy of Science and Technology) and a member of supervisory boards of Deutsche Bank AG, Munich Re, Deutsche Post, BMW Group in Germany and Nokia. Dr Kagermann was a professor of Theoretical Physics at the Technical University, Braunschweig, Germany and received an honorary doctorate from the University of Magdeburg, Germany.

Dr Jagdish N. Sheth, Independent Director. Dr Sheth served as a director on the Board since January 1999. Dr Sheth had been a professor at Emory University since July 1991. Previously, Dr Sheth served on the faculty of Columbia University, Massachusetts Institute of Technology, the University of Illinois, and the University of Southern California.

M. K. Sharma, Independent Director. Mr Sharma became a director of the Company on July 1, 2011. He was a member of the Audit, Risk and Compliance Committee. He served as Vice Chairman of Hindustan Unilever Limited from 2000 to 2007. He served as a whole-time director of Hindustan Unilever Limited from 1995 to 2000. He served on the boards of ICICI Lombard General Insurance Co. Limited, Fulford India Limited (Indian affiliate of MSD), Thomas Cook (India) Limited, Birla Corporation Limited, KEC International Limited and The Andhra Pradesh Paper Mills Limited.

Shyam Saran, Independent Director. Mr Saran became a director of Wipro on July 1, 2010. He had been a director of Indian Oil Corporation Limited since March 2012. He was a career diplomat who served in significant positions in the Indian government for over three decades. He joined Indian Foreign Service in 1970. He last served as the Special Envoy of the Prime Minister of India (October 2006 to March 2010) specializing in nuclear issues, and also was the Indian envoy on climate change. Prior to this he was the Foreign Secretary of the Government of India from 2004 to 2006. He also served as the Ambassador of India to Nepal, Indonesia, Myanmar and Mauritius. His diplomatic stints had taken him to Indian missions in Geneva, Beijing and Tokyo. He had been a Fellow of the United Nations Disarmament Program in Geneva, Vienna and New York, USA. He received the Padma Bhushan award by the Government of India for his contribution in civil services.

Narayanan Vaghul, Independent Director. Mr Vaghul has served as a director on the Board since June 1997. He was the Chairman of Audit, Risk and Compliance Committee, a member of the Board Governance & Nomination Committee and a member of the Compensation Committee. He was the Chairman of the Board of ICICI Bank Limited from September 1985 to April 2009. Mr Vaghul was also on the Boards of Mahindra and Mahindra Ltd, Mahindra World City Developers Limited, Piramal Healthcare Limited, and Apollo Hospitals Enterprise Limited. Mr Vaghul isa recipient of the Padma Bhushan award by the Government of India in 2010. Mr Vaghul also received the Economic Times Lifetime Achievement Award.

Vyomesh Joshi, Independent Director. Mr Vyomesh Joshi joined the Wipro Board of Directors in October 2012. Hewas a member of Dean's Advisory Council at The Rady School of Management, University of California, San Diego. Prior to joining Wipro, Mr Joshi served as the Executive Vice President of Hewlett-Packard's Imaging and Printing Group. He joined Hewlett-Packard as a Research & Development engineer and held various management positions in his 32-year career with the group. Mr Joshi was also on the Board of Yahoo! for 7 years until 2012. Mr Joshi had featured in Fortune's diversity list of most influential people in 2005.

William Arthur Owens, Independent Director. Mr Owens had served as a director on the Board since July 1, 2006. He was a member of the Board Governance and Nomination Committee. He had held a number of senior leadership positions at large multinational corporations. From April 2004 to November 2005, Mr Owens served as Chief Executive Officer and Vice Chairman of the Board of Directors of Nortel Networks Corporation, a networking communications company. From August 1998 to April 2004, Mr Owens served as Chairman of the Board of Directors and Chief Executive Officer of Teledesic LLC, a satellite communications company. From June 1996 to August 1998, Mr Owens served as President, Chief Operating Officer and Vice Chairman of the Board of Directors of Science Applications International Corporation (SAIC), a research and engineering firm. Presently, Mr Owens serves as a member of the Board of Directors of Polycom Inc., Intelius, Flow Mobile, Prometheus, and Chairman of Century Link Inc., a communications company.

Source: www.wipro.com

Exhibit E5.10 *Distinct Business Models*

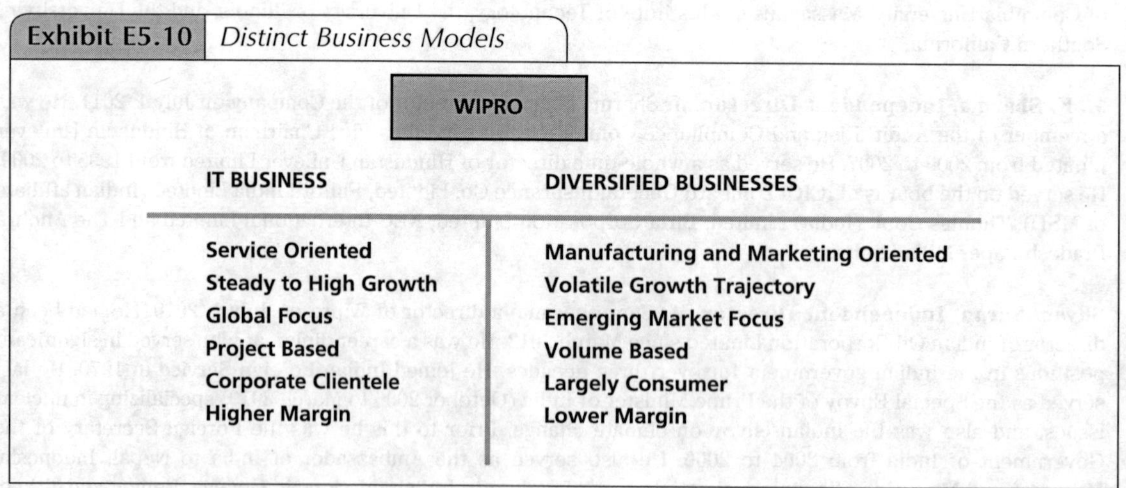

Source: Wipro and casewriter.

Exhibit E5.11 *Proposed Demerger and Contribution by Segments (for FY 12)*

	IT Business	Diversified Businesses
Revenue	86%	14%
EBIT	94%	6%
EBIT margin	19%	8%
Employees	140,000	7500

Source: Wipro.

Exhibit E5.12 *Shareholding Pattern, 2012*

Category of Shareholder	Total Shareholding as a % of Total No. of Shares
Promoter and promoter group	78.30
Public shareholding	
Institutions	10.05
Noninstitutions	9.93
Shares held by custodians against which Depository receipts have been issued	1.73
Total	100

Source: Company documents.

REFERENCES AND SUGGESTED READINGS

Agarwal, A. 2012, November 1. *Wipro Demerges Non-IT Businesses*. Mumbai: Tata Securities Institutional Research.

———. 2012, November 1. *Wipro, Event Update*. Mumbai: SPA Financial Advisors.

Agarwal, S. and O. Hadkar. 2012, November 1. *Wipro: Fair Demerger, India Equity Research*. Mumbai: Edelweiss Capital.

———. 2013, January 18. "Wipro: At an Inflection Point." Mumbai: Edelweiss Research Report.

Bhushan, S. and P. Shah. 2012, November 1. *Wipro: Demerger of Consumer Business*. Mumbai: Prabhudas Liladhar.

Mandal, A. K., Jayashri Dasgupta, and Ajay Srinivasan. 2012, February. *IT Services Annual Review*. Mumbai: CRISIL Research.

Shah, H. and A. Gupta. 2012, November 1. *Wipro: Demerger of Non-IT Business*. Mumbai: India Research, IDFC.

———. 2012, September 24. *Wipro: Re-organization Strategy Needs a Macro Boost*. Mumbai: India Research, IDFC.

Shindadkar, A. and Aishwarya. 2012, November 1. "Wipro Ltd: What's Changed...." Equity Research Report.ICICI Direct.

Wipro Annual Reports, 2008–09, 2009–2010, 2010–2011, 2011–2012.

Wipro Analyst Day Presentation, 2012.

Wipro Media Presentation, Nov. 2, 2012.

Wipro Presentation to Investors, October-December 2012.

Wipro Information Statement Provided to the shareholders and American Depositary Share holders, December 6, 2012.

REVIEW QUESTIONS

1. What are the responsibilities of the board of directors in setting the strategic direction of a publicly-held company? What is their role in governing the organization?
2. What are the various alternatives available for restructuring firms? Does restructuring improve a company's performance and enhance shareholder wealth?
3. What risks do minority shareholders encounter in family-owned companies? What are the duties and responsibilities of the Board as they pertain to protecting the interest of minority shareholders? Do the country culture and reputation of the leader affect the corporate governance dynamics in the boardroom?
4. What reasons do you find for Wipro's leadership's desire to demerge the company and separate its IT business from the other businesses?
5. Should Wipro demerge? Why or Why not?
6. Analyze the financial and stock market performance of Wipro. Is Wipro underperforming?
7. Undertake a valuation of Wipro using multiples. Is Wipro undervalued?
8. What does the WEL demerger accomplish?
9. Identify the risks faced by investors in the demerger.
10. Are there potential ethical concerns in the demerger? What are they?
11. As a shareholder, would you vote in favor of the demerger?
12. What did you learn from this case?

CASE

6

Suzlon Energy Ltd: Debt Restructuring[1]

Description: The case highlights the ambitious growth strategy of Suzlon, an Indian company specializing in nonconventional (wind) energy. In 2007, Suzlon announced the acquisition of REpower of Germany, one of the top wind power companies in the world. It issued zero-coupon and coupon-bearing foreign currency (US dollar) convertible bonds (FCCB) amounting to US$760 million to finance the acquisition. These bonds were listed in Singapore. Due to deteriorating business conditions, the company experienced a sharp decline in profitability and stock price, resulting in a debt overhang. At the same time the Indian Rupee depreciated from ₹44 to ₹55, leading to losses on largely unhedged, foreign currency coupon payments. The company had to restructure its capital structure to escape bankruptcy. Since FCCB holders did not agree to restructure the terms of the instrument, the company had to turn to senior lenders to restructure debt.

Learning Objectives: The case can be used to teach parity conditions in international finance, design of capital structure, and dangers of financing high technology ventures with foreign currency denominated convertible debt.

The case enables students to:

- Critically analyze a debt restructuring.
- Develop an appreciation of the interaction between financing strategy and business strategy.
- Undertake an analysis of parity conditions in international finance with the objective of exploiting arbitrage opportunities to source cheaper capital.
- Critically evaluate the rationale for foreign currency convertibles.

Subjects covered: Takeovers, corporate restructuring, financing strategy, international finance, risk management

[1] Professors Vishwanath S. R., Jaskiran Arora, Durga Prasad, and Kulbir Singh prepared this case as the basis for class discussion rather than to illustrate either effective or ineffective handling of an administrative situation.

On October 29, 2012, Suzlon Energy Ltd, one of the top five wind energy companies in the world, announced that its senior secured lenders had agreed to restructure its debt. The plan was to get amoratorium on the payment of interest and principal. Upon announcement, Suzlon shares closed 10.7% higher at ₹17.10.[2]

Kirti Vagadia, the chief financial officer (CFO) of Suzlon Group said:[3]

> Our senior secured lenders are supportive of our long-term business plan, and our efforts to consolidate our overall debt to achieve a sustainable capital structure. This is an important step towards stabilizing our business. Considering our overall business outlook, we recognize that despite strong business fundamentals and a US$7.2 billion order book, the timeline of the corporate debt restructuring process will continue to impact performance.

Under the debt restructuring plan, lenders agreed to enhance working capital facilities by ₹18 billion (US$350 million) and convert interest of ₹15 billion (US$270 million) during the moratorium period into equity over 2 years. From the perspective of the CFO and the bankers at SBI Capital Markets (Suzlon's advisor), the task was to choose a plan of action from the available alternatives, such as asset sales and raising equity, to restore the financial health of the company.

COMPANY BACKGROUND[4]

Suzlon Energy was set up in 1995 by Tulsi Tanti and his three brothers. The company had its headquarters at Pune, India. The company had the vision of being one of the top three companies in wind energy. In 2011, it was the fifth-largest wind turbine manufacturer with an installed capacity of 20,000 MW across 30 countries and a workforce of more than 13,000 employees. The company had operations in Asia, Australia, Europe, Africa, and North America. The company offered a product portfolio that ranged from 600 KW onshore turbines to 6.15 MW offshore turbines. The company had a vertically integrated manufacturing base. It had developed one of the largest wind farms in the western Indian states of Gujarat and Rajasthan with a cumulative capacity of over 1,000 MW.

During 2009–11, the company's sales fell from ₹74,164.60 million to ₹47,183.60 million but climbed back to ₹72,190.50 million in 2012, reflecting its product market difficulties soon after the global financial crisis of 2007–08. During the same period, the company accumulated losses of more than ₹25 billion (See Exhibit E6.1). Its cash flow from operations dwindled from ₹21 billion to ₹5.4 billion during 2010–12 (see Exhibit E6.2).

---

[2] The ₹to USD exchange rate at that time way ₹55.7877/USD.

[3] Suzlon Group announces formal approval of corporate debt restructuring proposal, Suzlon press release, January 24, 2013.

[4] This is based on the information available in the company's website http://www.suzlon.com/about_suzlon/l2.aspx?l1=1&l2=1, accessed on September 11, 2017.

INDUSTRY BACKGROUND

The Indian power sector has grown considerably over the past decade. The installed generation capacity of the power sector had increased to 181,500 MW at the end of August 2011 (GOI 2012). The Indian power sector was largely coal-based, with the total installed capacity comprising of 99,503 MW (55 %) coal-based and 20,162 MW (11%) renewable energy power plants. The capacity addition requirement during the 12th five-year plan during 2012–17 was expected to be 75,715 MW. Of this, 42,131 MW was to be generated by the private sector. Renewable sources of energy were becoming increasingly important in bridging the demand-supply gap.

Wind energy was the fastest growing sector in India and had an installed capacity of more than 19GW.[5] It accounted for more than 70% of the total installed capacity in renewable energy. India was an energy deficient nation because of which all power companies, including wind energy companies, had significant growth potential.[6] The demand-supply gap persisted due to delay in implementation of power projects. The wind energy industry in India was expected to add another 15,000 MW during 2012–17. The industry had grown rapidly in the past few years due to various incentives such as accelerated depreciation offered by the government of India. However, some of the incentives were rolled back by the government in 2011.This limited the growth prospects and aggravated the situation for Suzlon, which had already been struggling due to a slowdown in overseas markets (Vithlani and Singh 2012).

The Indian states of Tamil Nadu, Gujarat, Maharashtra, Karnataka, and Rajasthan were among the leading states in terms of installed wind energy capacity. The quantum of energy generated from wind stood at 23.4BU in 2011–12, registering a growth rate of 19.7% since 2008,[7] Apart from generation, India was also a key player in the global wind energy equipment manufacturing. The wind power equipment production capacity stood at 8,000 MW in 2012. There were 19 wind turbine manufacturers in India, and new companies were expected to enter the market. Vestas Wind Systems of Denmark was the industry leader. General Electric of the USA, Enercon of Germany, and Gamesa Technologies of Spain occupied the next three positions. The top conventional power producers in India included NTPC, PGCIL, NHPC, Neyveli Lignite, Torrent Power, and CESC. Power producers using coal and other fossil fuels such as oil and gas were exposed to fluctuations in not only the price of input but also the availability of input.[8] Wind energy, on the other hand, was more sustainable.

Exhibits E6.3 and E6.4 present key ratios for Suzlon and other power generation and equipment manufacturing companies.

---

[5] Netscribes Report, *Wind Energy Sector Update*, 2012.

[6] The power deficit was estimated at 9.1% in July 2012.

[7] Renewable Energy Sector in India report, e-Research and Publications India Private Limited.

[8] The coalgate scandal in India concerned the allocation of coal deposits to public and private enterprises. The comptroller and auditor general of India accused the government of inefficient allocation. In response to the report, the Supreme Court of India cancelled the mining rights given to several companies. As a result, coal-based power plants faced huge raw material supplies. Several of them had to temporarily shut down.

OPERATING AND FINANCING HISTORY[9]

Suzlon was known for its operational excellence and had received a number of awards such as the best manufacturer, best service provider, and the best company in corporate social responsibility at the Wind India Conference held annually in India. In 2006, the company expanded its geographical spread by signing a contract with Australia Gas & Light (AGL) to manufacture the largest wind farm in Australia. It signed another contract with Technogias Energeticas (TECHNERIA) to build a high capacity turbine in Portugal. In December 2006, the company signed a turnkey contract with British Petroleum for setting up a 40 MW wind power plant in the Indian state of Maharashtra. In March 2007, it constructed a 2.1 MW turbine in Australia and a 150 MW plant for DLF Limited in India. To establish Suzlon as a key global player, Tulsi Tanti began acquiring key competitors worldwide. In 2006, Tanti acquired Hansen Transmissions of Belgium for US$565 million. The next year it made a bid for Germany's Repower AG.

Repower Acquisition

Repower was Germany's leading wind energy firm with forecasted revenues of €450 million in 2006. The company had established a strong presence in Europe and was seeking a position in China, India, and the USA.

In January 2007, Areva S. A., the largest single shareholder of REpower Systems AG, declared its intention to acquire REpower and made an offer of €105 per share to its shareholders. The offer price was at a premium of 44% to the 3-month average stock price of REpower. However, soon after Areva's offer, Suzlon Windenergie GmbH, an affiliate of Suzlon, made a counter offer at €126 per share (which corresponded to apremium of 72% to the 3-month average stock price of REpower) and exceeded Areva's offer by 20%. Suzlon Windenergie further revised its offer to €150 in response to the revised offerof €140 by Areva and completed the acquisition (Reuters 2007). By May 2007, Suzlon had received 25.46% of REpower's shares. Suzlon wanted to control 75% of REpower and be the fourth-largest wind-turbine maker after Eneron, ReGen Gamesa, and Vestas. Suzlon ended up controlling 87.1% of votes due to voting-pool arrangements with Martifer and Areva. Upon announcement, Suzlon's stock price remained flat while the market rose marginally.

Suzlon hoped that the partnership with REpower would bolster Suzlon's R&D efforts. The combination was expected to not only bring together R&D and technology teams but also provide geographical expansion into European markets. In addition, the combined entity would be better positioned to make capital investments. The partnership would create products that were the most reliable with the best lifecycle costs. Exhibit E6.5 presents a forecast of free cash flow to equity shareholders of Repower.

The investment bankers for the transaction were ABN AMRO, State Bank of India, and ICICI Bank. In February 2007, Suzlon and its associates entered into a credit arrangement with ABN AMRO Bank, wherein several tranches of debt were to be provided for funding the acquisition. The credit line was provided to cover the acquisition of 6,057,209 shares (amounting to €793,208,334) and transaction costs. This would increase the debt servicing burden from €669 million to €1,736 million.

[9] The information contained in the section is based on the company annual reports http://www.suzlon.com/investors/annual_result.aspx?l1=6&l2=23&l3=42 (accessed on September 14, 2013) and its website www.suzlon.com

After the REpower acquisition, Suzlon continued to consolidate its position by setting up subsidiaries and winning new orders throughout the world. In the ensuing years, Suzlon incurred capital expenditure amounting to ₹88.87 billion to fund the expansion.

Financing

Suzlon funded its acquisition by a combination of term loans from banks, nonconvertible debentures, and coupon-bearing and zero-coupon FCCBs. During 2007–12, the company issued FCCBs amounting to approximately US$760 million. Exhibit E6.6 provides a snapshot of the company's financing program.

Foreign Currency Convertible Bonds

An FCCB is a hybrid instrument that provides investors the option of converting the bond into equity shares on a specified date or after an initial lock-in period. The conversion price is usually set at a premium to the market price of the issuing company's stock at the time of issue.

Convertible bonds were popular among issuers because they carried lower coupon rate as compared to straight bonds and provided the possibility of accretion to share capital in the event of conversion of bonds into equity shares. FCCBs did not involve front-end equity dilution as is the case with equity shares. Investors found convertible bonds attractive because these instruments allowed investors to benefit from the upside potential of the company while retaining the safety of debt. These instruments carried attractive yields to maturity. As far as taxation was concerned, interest payments on bonds (until the conversion option was exercised) were subject to a withholding tax of 10%. Dividends on the converted portion of the bond were subject to deduction of tax at source at the rate of 10%. Investors were not liable to capital gains tax in India when FCCBs were converted into shares.

During 2004–06, Indian companies mobilized US$10.6 billion by issuing FCCBs. Indian companies were able to issue FCCBs at low coupon rates. Out of the 78 issues made during 2004–06, 41 were zero-coupon bonds and another 26 carried coupon rates of less than 2% (Hajra and Swant 2006). The YTM (yield to maturity) on FCCBs, however, ranged between 4% and 8.5% with an average of 6.1%.[10] Most FCCBs were priced to yield 5%–7%. YTMs on FCCBs were favorable compared to straight debt issues. The coupon on FCCBs was 30%–40% less compared to straight bonds, foreign currency loans, and external commercial borrowings. This translated into cost savings of 2%–3% p.a. One-third of the issuers could raise funds at yields lower than the sovereign yield. FCCBs carried fewer covenants than syndicated loans and debentures. Hence, these were more convenient to issuers (Banka 2005).

In most cases, the conversion price embedded in the bond involved a substantial premium to the market price at the time of issue. On average, FCCB issues commanded a premium of 44%. FCCB bondholders who chose not to convert would receive the principal at an exchange rate fixed at the time of the issue.

---

[10] In most cases a redemption premium is payable at maturity if the bond is not converted. Redemption premiums ranged from 5% to 60%.

As interest rate on foreign debt was considerably lower than the benchmark prime lending rate in India, it made sense for Indian firms to borrow in a foreign currency when the domestic currency strengthened relative to the foreign currency. This resulted in lower cash outflows due to interest and principal payments. Most FCCBs were denominated in US Dollars. The bonds were mainly listed in Singapore, Luxembourg, London, and Hong-Kong.

During 2003–07, the Indian stock market was experiencing a cyclical bull run. Indian FCCBs provided an attractive investment opportunity to international investors who were looking for international diversification opportunities without being exposed to emerging market equity risks.

FCCBs denominated in US Dollars appealed to Suzlon because its revenues were also mostly denominated in US Dollars. In 2009, Suzlon had foreign exchange earnings of ₹41.115 billion and foreign currency expenses of ₹37.541 billion. Suzlon's coupon-bearing bonds carried a semi-annual interest rate of 7.5% and a redemption premium ranging up to 150% of the principal amount. These bonds were listed in Singapore. Top global corporations such as Tata Motors, Tata Steel, Reliance Communications, and Larsen & Toubro were among the biggest issuers of foreign currency (FX) converts (Nathwani and Sridhar. n.d.). Exhibit E6.7 presents the details of FCCBs issued by Suzlon and the stock market reaction to securities issued by it.

Indian companies treated FCCBs as pure debt instruments. The income statements of companies did not account for debt service when they issued zero-coupon convertibles. In case of coupon-bearing bonds, debt service was generally charged directly to reserves rather than to the income statement, thereby overstating profits and earnings per share (EPS). This was an anomaly in the accounting treatment.

Apart from FCCBs and term loans, Suzlon had issued 207,565,299 shares at a price of ₹61 on a rights basis to its existing shareholders to raise ₹3528.60 million in June 2010. In the previous year, it had issued global depository receipts (GDRs) at a price of US$7.40 per GDR to raise US$108.04 million.

Suzlon had a dedicated treasury team monitoring the foreign exchange fluctuations with the objective of minimizing the impact of adverse currency fluctuations. Exposures were managed and hedged on contractual basis. It used forward and option contracts to hedge its foreign exchange risk. However, the zero-coupon convertible bonds issued in 2007 were *unhedged*. So were the debtors, creditors, loans given and received, and bank balances. These amounted to ₹24 billion in 2008 and ₹80 billion in 2009.[11] Exhibit E6.8 presents historical interest rates, inflation rates in Indian Rupee and US Dollar, and exchange rates between the two currencies.

Operating and Financial Performance

In 2008, Suzlon's turbine blades developed cracks in the USA. This adversely affected orders from the USA and, hence, sales (Stromsta 2009). The global financial crisis of 2008 led to a tight credit situation. This hurt Suzlon more, particularly because it purchased REpower at stretched valuations. Due to competition from Enercon, ReGen, Gamesa, and Vestas, Suzlon's market share fell from 58% in 2008 to 35% in 2012.[12] At its peak in 2007–08, Suzlon had a net income of

[11] In 2009 Suzlon had foreign exchange earnings of ₹41.115 billion and foreign currency expenses of ₹37.541 billion.

[12] "₹110 billion debt: Can Suzlon Energy weather the big storm?" PANCHABUTA renewable Energy and Cleantech in India, http://panchabuta.com/2012/07/08/rs-110-billion-debt-can-suzlon-energy-weather-the-big-storm/ (accessed on September 11, 2017).

₹10,170 million. In financial years 2010 and 2011, it incurred losses of ₹9,820 million and ₹10.96 billion. However, in 2012 the company managed to reduce its losses to ₹4,780 million. The company's long-term debt had been downgraded from AA- in 2009 to BBB- in 2012 in line with the company's deteriorating financial position.

On February 15, 2010, due to poor financial performance, Suzlon announced its intention to reduce conversion prices of its US$300 million zero-coupon bonds issued in June 2007 and US$200 million zero-coupon convertible bonds issued in October 2007. On May 18, 2010, convertible bond holders agreed to:[13]

1. Remove financial covenants.
2. Effect a reduction in
   a. the conversion price of the US$300 million zero-coupon convertible bonds from ₹359.68 per equity share to ₹97.26 per equity share and
   b. the conversion price of the US$200 million zero-coupon convertible bonds from ₹371.55 per equity share to ₹97.26 per equity share.
3. Set the fixed exchange rate at US$1 = ₹44.60, and replace the respective fixed exchange rates in the terms and conditions of the US$300 million zero-coupon convertible bonds due in June 2012 and US$200 million zero-coupon convertible bonds due in October 2012.

In 2012, Suzlon had debt amounting to more than ₹110 billion (US$2 billion). It needed US$360 million in June and US$206 million in October to redeem the FCCBs. Its high leverage, high financing costs, and repeated business losses left very little cash to redeem the bonds. It had to urgently raise US$360 million before the FCCBs matured in June 2012. The bondholders approved the proposal for a 45-day extension. The company had to arrange funds to pay the bondholders by July 27. In 2012 alone, the company was obligated to repay debt amounting to ₹39.2 billion (US$700 million) and had to pay another US$250 million in the next financial year. To infuse equity capital, Suzlon had to either get the banks to restructure debt, sell its equity interest in REpower or merge REpower with itself,[14] or sell its noncritical assets such as the wind farm in India or China. The sale of noncritical assets, however, was expected to fetch only US$100 million. The company's stock price fell from a high of ₹446 in January 2008 to ₹19.75 in July 2012 to reflect these concerns. At that valuation, the company's debt was three times its market capitalization of ₹35 billion. Exhibit E6.9 presents historical stock prices and Exhibit E6.10 presents a timeline of events from 2007 to 2012.

CORPORATE DEBT RESTRUCTURING IN INDIA[15]

Under the Chapter 11 bankruptcy procedure in the USA, the debtor retains the possession of assets and operates the business under the supervision of a bankruptcy court. The debtor has a fiduciary responsibility toward the creditors. A trustee is appointed to oversee the business

---

[13] Suzlon Press Release, May 18, 2010, http://www.suzlon.com/media_center/press_release.aspx?l1=7&l2=31 (accessed on September 11, 2017).

[14] REpower was debt free and had cash balances of approximately ₹15,000 million.

[15] See http://www.cdrindia.org/

when the debtor is ineffective. This type of insolvency code was absent in India. The government was yet to bring out a legislation to deal with bankruptcies. The corporate restructuring mechanism in India left the responsibility of debt restructuring to banks themselves. In 2011, in order to protect the interests of lenders to firms in distress, the Reserve Bank of India (India's central bank) issued guidelines relating to corporate debt restructuring to be implemented by banks. Corporate debt restructuring (CDR) was a voluntary nonstatutory system which was based on the debtor-creditor agreement (DCA) and inter-creditor agreement (ICA). The arrangement provided for multibanking accounts, and syndication or consortium accounts, wherein all banks and institutions together could have an outstanding exposure of ₹100 million or more.

DCA had a legal binding on both the debtor and the creditor(s) to not take a recourse to any legal action during the period of the contract and take a "stand still" position.

CDR in India had a three-tier structure comprising of a standing forum, an empowered group (EG), and a CDR cell.

- On the top of this three-tier system was the CDR forum, which was a representative general body comprising of chief executives of commercial banks and financial institutions. It laid down policies and guidelines to be followed by the other two tiers in debt restructuring.
- The second tier was the EG, which screened the preliminary reports of all cases reported by the CDR cell and deliberated on the individual cases of corporate structuring. After it concluded the feasibility of the project, it, along with the CDR cell, prepared a detailed restructuring package. This task was to be completed within 90 days or a maximum of 180 days of reference to EG.
- The third tier—the CDR cell—issued the letter of approval (LOA), once the restructuring plan was approved and confirmed by the empowered group. The lenders were required to approve the restructuring plan within 45 days from the issue of the LOA and execute the restructuring within next 45 days.

THE 2012 RESTRUCTURING

Suzlon defaulted on payment to FX convertible bondholders as bondholders did not agree to further extend the maturity dates. On October 28, 2012, the company commenced its discussions on corporate debt restructuring with its senior lenders. Suzlon requested an extended maturity period of up to 10 years, and a moratorium on the interest and principal payments for the next 2 years. The consortium of 19 domestic banks went through the CDR mechanism outlined earlier and approved the company's debt restructuring package of ₹95 billion (US$1.8 billion). The package included (a) a 2 year moratorium on interest and principal payments, (b) a 3% reduction in interest rates, and (c) a 6-month moratorium on working capital interest. Further, to bring financial stability, US$270 million of 2 years' interest payments during moratorium was to be converted into equity over the next 2 years. The package included a 10-year end-to-end back-ended repayment plan. It also included increased working capital facilities of ₹18 billion (US$350 million), which would allow the company to accelerate the execution of its order book. The founders were required to bring in an additional equity of ₹2,500 million (US$50 million). As a consequence, Suzlon was to consolidate by selling few of its overseas subsidiaries.

It was required to open an escrow account with State Bank of India (SBI). Suzlon appointed SBI Capital Markets (the investment banking unit of SBI) to advise the company on the debt recast. In order to deal with distress, Suzlon could sell noncore assets that would fetch US$100 million, sell equity shares to the public, or sell off its shareholding in REpower. It was not clear if any of these was a viable alternative.

REFERENCES AND SUGGESTED READINGS

Banka S. 2005, November. "Foreign Currency Convertible Bonds." The Chartered Accountant. New Delhi: Institute of Chartered Accountants of India.

Dimson, Elroy, Paul Marsh, and Mike Staunton. 2006, April 7. *The Worldwide Equity Premium: A Smaller Puzzle.* Available at http://papers.ssrn.com/sol3/papers.cfm?abstract_id=891620 (Accessed on September 13, 2017).

GOI (Government of India), Ministry of Power. 2012, January. Report of the Working Group on Power for Twelfth Plan. Available at http://planningcommission.gov.in/aboutus/committee/wrkgrp12/wg_power1904.pdf (Accessed on July 2015).

Hajra, S., and P. Swant 2006, November. *FCCBs and Financial Position of Indian Companies.* Anand Rathi Research Report.

Nathwani A., and C. Sridhar. n.d. "Impact of Global Economic Meltdown on FCCBs Issued by Indian Companies." Mumbai: CRISIL Research.

Reuters. 2007. "India's Suzlon Energy Completes REpower Acquisition". *Reuters*, June 2.Vithlani, B., and C. Singh. 2012, May 29. *ENAM Securities India Research Report.* Mumbai: Suzlon Energy.

Stromsta, Karl-Erik. 2009. "Cracked Turbine Blades Drag SUZLON to Q3 Losses." *Recharge*, February 2009. Available at http://www.rechargenews.com/wind/article1277834.ece (Accessed on September 11, 2017).

REVIEW QUESTIONS

1. Is restructuring necessary?
2. Why is Suzlon in distress?
3. Was the purchase price paid to REpower high? You may answer this question by undertaking multiples and DCF valuation of REpower.
   [ques1]In your valuation of REpower assume the following:
   R_f = German 10 year Eurobond Rate = 3.81%
   Beta = 0.88
   Germany's Risk Premium = 5.28% (Dimson, Marsh, and Staunton, 2006)
   Number of outstanding shares = 8,993,576
   Profit after Tax in 2007 = €7,053,555
   Equity in 2007 = €187,829,789
4. Why did Suzlon choose to issue FX Convertibles? In which currency has it been cheaper to borrow during 2007–12?
5. What were the options for Suzlon in dealing with financial distress?
6. As a lender would you approve the restructuring? Why or Why not?

Exhibit E6.1 *Financial Summary of Suzlon Energy (₹million)*

	2009	2010	2011	2012
Total income	74,164.60	40,123.20	47,183.60	72,190.50
Revenue	72,544.70	35,057.20	43,586.60	68,719.90
Income from financial services	1,550.10	2,557.00	3,316.70	3,470.60
Change in stock	683.7	–2,549.70	2,237.00	962.3
Total expenses	79,530.50	51,714.40	51,277.20	78,206.60
Raw materials, stores, and spares	46,148.90	22,400.10	29,778.90	45,273.10
Power, fuel, and water charges	44.6	39.3	50.5	88.5
Compensation to employees	1,990.70	1,810.10	2,152.30	3,374.30
Indirect taxes	97.8	168.8	17.9	40.5
Selling and distribution expenses	9,727.10	2,976.80	2,174.90	3,925.40
Interest paid	3,801.20	6,535.90	5,780.40	7,843.20
Depreciation	1,013.00	1,275.10	1,568.90	1,826.80
Profit				
EBDITA	6,251.60	5,294.80	9,015.40	13,993.80
Profit after tax (PAT)	–4,682.20	–14,140.90	–1,856.60	–5,053.80
Total liabilities	179,140.60	172,920.20	174,930.80	206,630.30
Net worth	65,803.20	56,043.10	67,019.20	54,197.60
Paid up equity capital	2,996.60	3,113.50	3,554.70	3,554.70
Reserves and surplus	61,856.60	52,929.20	64,390.10	51,424.40
Borrowings	73,294.80	76,012.20	66,773.30	87,332.40
Current liabilities and provisions	40,042.60	40,864.90	40,212.70	64,318.80
Total assets	179,140.60	172,920.20	174,930.80	206,630.30
Net fixed assets	5,515.00	9,171.60	8,631.70	9,672.80
Investments	71,278.00	75,926.00	78,450.60	88,156.20
Current assets	67,622.20	45,356.50	35,178.40	57,663.90
Loans & advances	30,101.70	42,362.30	50,817.70	50,225.60

Source: Centre for Monitoring Indian Economy's PROWESS database.

Exhibit E6.2 *Cash Flow Statement of Suzlon Energy (₹million)*

	2009	2010	2011	2012
Net cash flow from operating activities	–3,703.80	21,070.60	7,248.50	5,443.60
Net profit before tax and extraordinary income	4,330.00	–7,996.50	–2,232.30	–1,498.40
Add: Adjustments for noncash and nonoperating expenses	10,751.60	11,058.30	10,575.80	12,657.00
Depreciation	991.6	1,262.70	1,568.90	1,826.80
Amortisation	70.4	84.6	22.9	19.8
Unrealised foreign exchange losses	6.3	415.5		922.3
Other provisions	5,882.10	2,745.50	3,126.20	1,992.00
Interest paid	3,801.20	6,535.90	5,780.40	7,843.20
Loss on sale of assets		14.1	29.3	48.8
Other noncash and nonoperating expenses			48	4.1
Less: Adjustments for noncash and nonoperating income	1,527.90	2,229.00	3,357.80	3,470.60

	2009	2010	2011	2012
Unrealised foreign exchange gain			41.1	
Interest income	1,224.30	2,227.90	2,927.40	3,466.70
Dividend income	112.9	1.1	389.3	3.9
Profit on sale of investments	189.1			
Profit or loss on sale of assets	1.6			
Operating cash flow before working capital changes	13,553.70	832.8	4,985.70	7,688.00
Add: Cash inflow due to:	5,489.00	24,021.50	5,899.70	8,009.70
Decrease in trade and other receivables		18,163.30	5,899.70	
Decrease in inventories	996	5,858.20		
Increase in trade and other payables	4,493.00			8,009.70
Less: Cash outflow due to:	16,641.80	656.1	3,947.10	10,172.10
Increase in trade and other receivables	16,641.80			8,011.60
Increase in inventories			2,171.50	2,160.50
Decrease in trade and other payables		656.1	1,775.60	
Cash flow generated from operations	2,400.90	24,198.20	6,938.30	5,525.60
Cash outflow due to direct taxes paid	644.1	77.5		82
Cash outflow due to dividend tax paid	243.9			
Cash flow before extraordinary items	1,512.90	24,120.70	6,938.30	5,443.60
Cash outflow due to extraordinary items	5,216.70	3,050.10		
Cash inflow due to extraordinary items			310.2	
Net cash inflow from investing activities	–35,831.80	–25,965.30	–7,515.20	–11,512.60
Less: Cash outflow due to investing activities	41,026.00	28,645.80	11,679.00	16,351.50
Add: Cash inflow due to investing activities	5,194.20	2,680.50	4,163.80	4,838.90
Net cash inflow or (outflow) from financing activities	32,904.60	8,762.90	–3,136.30	7,399.10
Less: Cash outflow due to financing activities	5,627.30	28,809.00	13,082.00	8,585.10
Issue expenses	50.5	163.8	93	130.9
Interest paid	3,658.90	6,460.20	5,780.20	7,271.30
Dividend paid	1,498.30			
Repayment of borrowings	419.6	21,229.30	7,208.80	1,182.90
Repayment of long-term liabilities	419.6	993.6	128.8	1,182.90
Repayment of short-term liabilities		20,235.70	7,080.00	
Add: Cash inflow from financing activities	38,531.90	37,571.90	9,945.70	15,984.20
Proceeds from share issue	1,019.40	5,231.30	10.1	
Proceeds from borrowings	37,510.20	32,340.60	9,935.60	15,984.20
Proceeds from long-term borrowings	8,900.00	32,340.60	9,935.60	9,562.70
Proceeds from short-term borrowings	28,610.20			6,421.50
Net increase or (decrease) in cash and cash equivalents	–6,631.00	3,868.20	–3,403.00	1,330.10

Exhibit E6.3 *Key Ratios of Suzlon and Domestic Competitors*

	Suzlon Energy Ltd						Bharat Heavy Electricals Ltd					
YEAR	**2012**	**2011**	**2010**	**2009**	**2008**	**2007**	**2012**	**2011**	**2010**	**2009**	**2008**	**2007**
Debt-equity ratio	1.23	1.14	1.23	0.77	0.4	0.23	0.01	0.01	0.01	0.01	0.01	0.04
Long-term debt-equity ratio	0.8	0.89	0.75	0.4	0.2	0.05	0	0.01	0.01	0.01	0.01	0.04
Current ratio	0.84	1.23	1.36	1.49	1.93	2.12	1.78	1.56	1.37	1.4	1.45	1.47
Fixed asset turnover	4.27	3.12	3.07	8.54	10.29	11.12	5.66	6.02	5.86	5.89	5.07	4.78
Inventory turnover	5.53	4.81	3.2	5.05	4.85	4.34	4.11	4.37	4.03	4.17	4.35	4.78
Debtors turnover	2.4	1.65	0.9	1.8	2.62	3.03	2.16	2.16	1.89	2.04	2.01	2.27
Interest cover ratio	0.84	0.67	−0.09	1.98	12.52	12.03	201.9	165.54	197.73	158.89	126.08	87.22
EBDITA margin (%)	13.45	13.65	1.72	13.22	26.48	24.06	22.19	21.82	20.47	18.3	21.92	21.31
EBIT margin (%)	10.78	10.05	−1.9	11.85	25.23	22.69	20.6	20.58	19.14	17.13	20.55	19.87
EBDT margin (%)	0.55	−1.45	−19.25	7.22	24.46	22.17	22.09	21.69	20.37	18.19	21.76	21.08
PAT margin (%)	−2.21	−3.34	−29.69	6.83	21.95	19.72	14.01	13.66	12.46	11.01	13.16	12.7
ROCE (%)	0	3.28	−0.49	7.16	23.5	30.58	28.56	35.94	45.47	40.73	45.23	45.16
ROE (%)	0	−2.35	−17.01	7.31	28.55	32.61	30.93	33.33	29.88	26.47	29.23	30.02
Price earning (P/E)	0	0	0	0	31.8	27.7	9.27	17.51	28.35	24.57	36.84	23.83
Price-to-book value (P/BV)	0.8	1.17	2	0.98	5.68	7.79	2.48	5.01	7.34	5.69	9.34	6.3
EV/EBIDTA	22.79	25.85	0	0	26.96	22.88	5.06	9.52	15.12	12.17	19.4	12.24
Market cap/sales	0.66	1.82	3.21	0.88	5.7	5.36	1.25	2.29	3.37	2.58	4.63	2.91

	Triveni Turbines Ltd						CESC Ltd					
	2012	**2011**	**2010**	**2009**	**2008**	**2007**	**2012**	**2011**	**2010**	**2009**	**2008**	**2007**
Debt-equity ratio	1.74	0	0	0	0	0	0.67	0.83	0.96	0.91	1.03	1.38
Long-term debt-equity ratio	1.13	0	0	0	0	0	0.51	0.73	0.9	0.85	0.93	1.29
Current ratio	0.74	0.73	4.26	0.36	0.7	0.98	1.83	1.47	1.25	1.35	1.29	1.37
Fixed asset turnover	3.89	3.85	35.47	6.81	11.79	6.51	0.43	0.41	0.37	0.41	0.41	0.39
Inventory turnover	7.59	6.55	25.13	8.25	8.08	6.51	16.16	15.93	14.9	15.91	16.47	14.94
Debtors turnover	7.76	5.91	40.2	63.86	112.98	8.5	6.2	7.92	7.33	8.6	7.75	5.4
Interest cover ratio	13.12	12.42	0	−19.38	−8.41	23	3.04	2.83	3.22	3.41	3.22	2.64
EBITDA margin (%)	23.74	22.95	−127.36	−21.92	−7.47	5.61	27.8	28.67	28.71	26.96	26.63	27.9
EBIT margin (%)	22	21.08	−134	−23.21	−7.99	5.16	21.72	22.37	22.58	21.29	20.67	21.66
EBDT margin (%)	22.07	21.25	−127.36	−23.12	−8.42	5.38	20.65	20.77	21.69	20.72	20.2	19.71
PAT margin (%)	13.72	11.51	−125.87	−24.84	−8.72	2.02	11.65	11.51	12.92	13.27	12.56	11.88
ROCE (%)	138.36	0	0	0	0	76.67	10.33	11.1	10.71	10.82	11.62	12.68
ROE (%)	424.68	0	0	0	0	30	12.1	12.02	12.01	12.87	14.31	16.5
Price earning (P/E)	18.02	0	0	0	0	0	6.28	8.13	11.3	6.58	14.91	10.86
Price-to-book value (P/BV)	23.88	0	0	0	0	0	0.72	0.93	1.28	0.79	1.75	1.62
EV/EBIDTA	10.15	0	0	0	0	0	4.25	4.98	7.65	5.52	8.93	7.09
Market cap/sales	2.37	0	0	0	0	0	0.72	0.92	1.43	0.85	1.83	1.27

Source: Centre for Monitoring Indian Economy's PROWESS Database.

Exhibit E6.4 *Comparison with Broad Industry Peer Companies (Domestic and Global)*

Panel A: Domestic Peer Group

Year	2012	2011	2010	2009	2008	2007
No. of companies	**12**	**14**	**15**	**11**	**8**	**9**
Debt-equity ratio	1.04	1.03	1.06	0.71	0.45	0.35
Long-term debt-equity ratio	1.01	0.86	0.67	0.38	0.22	0.12
Current ratio	2.22	1.94	1.51	1.55	1.72	1.67
Fixed assets turnover	3.85	3.28	3.64	6.83	6.41	7.34
Inventory turnover	4.83	4.69	4.37	5.6	4.55	5.08
Debtors turnover	1.91	1.6	1.42	2.19	2.63	3.69
Interest coverage ratio	1.18	1.13	0.54	2.42	11.67	7.25
EBITDA margin (%)	14.28	14.07	8.63	12.98	23.27	18.16
EBIT margin (%)	12.05	11.54	6.23	11.7	22.08	16.85
EBDT margin (%)	4.05	3.84	–2.97	8.15	21.37	15.83
PAT margin (%)	0.84	1.38	–9.34	6.91	18.68	13.09
ROA (%)	6.72	5.45	2.85	8.62	21.69	28.43
ROE (%)	1	1.4	–9.25	8.88	26.61	29.85

Source: Centre for Monitoring Indian Economy's PROWESS Database.

Panel B: Valuation Ratios of Global Peer Companies

	Gamesa Corp Tecnologica SA				
	2008	**2009**	**2010**	**2011**	**2012**
Price-to-book ratio	2.04	1.82	0.86	0.46	0.40
Price earnings ratio (P/E)	17.39	24.71	27.44	11.71	–
Market cap to revenue	0.802	0.8997	0.5125	0.2606	0.1562
	Vestas Wind Systems A/S				
	2008	**2009**	**2010**	**2011**	**2012**
Price-to-book ratio	4.73	3.40	1.74	0.65	0.53
Price earnings ratio (P/E)	14.69	67.38	30.84	–	–
Market cap to revenue	1.24	1.70	0.69	0.28	0.11

	Peer Group Averages (International)		
	2008	**2009**	**2010**
Price/Earnings	34.52	27.43	19.72
Price/Book Value	1.58	2.52	1.61
Market Cap/Sales	18.7	33.22	12.41

Source: Bloomberg.

Exhibit E6.5 *Forecast of Free Cash Flow to Equity of Repower (figures given in Euro €)*

	2008	2009	2010	2011	2012	Terminal Year
Sales	782,183,944.8	899,511,536.5	1,034,438,267	1,189,604,007	1,368,044,608	1,436,446,839
NOPAT/Sales	20%	20%	20%	20%	20%	20%
Depreciation/ Sales	1%	1%	1%	1%	1%	1%
Capex/Sales	1.5%	1.5%	1.5%	1.5%	1.5%	1.5%
ΔWorking capital/Sales	15%	15%	15%	15%	15%	15%
Net debt/Sales	−0.20%	15%	−0.20%	−0.20%	−0.20%	−0.20%
Free cash flow to equity	33,633,910	175,404,750	44,480,845	51,152,972	58,825,918	61,767,214

Source: Case Writer.

Exhibit E6.6 *Financing History 2006–12, Amounts Outstanding in ₹Million*

Secured/ Unsecured	INSTRUMENT	2006	2007	2008	2009	2010	2011	2012
(a) Secured	12.5% Secured redeemable nonconvertible debentures			0.0	3,000.0			
	Term loan							
	Banks	252.8	161.0	70.0	5,651.0	17,733.7	17,875.9	16,321.4
	Financial institutions	1,373.1	1,061.8	150.6	148.4			14,020.6
	Others					6094.1	14,36.4	
	Foreign currency							
	Working capital facilities							
	Rupee loans	1,140.2	4,015.8	983.5	20,556.7	12,616.3	8,815.1	
	Foreign currency loans	0.0	2,479.2	5,518.5	10,706.2	2,467.5	2,940.0	
(b) Unsecured								
Long-term	Zero-coupon convertible bonds			20,055.0	25,355.0			
	Foreign currency convertible Bonds					21,508.9	21,362.7	13,481.9
	Term loans							
	Banks					1,453.2	11,840.3	
	Financial institutions	293.4	203.2	111.2	69.3			
	Loans and advances							1,450
Short-term	Banks	0.0	3,445.4	3,958.6	7,245.7	1.4	0.0	18,887.6
	Financial institutions	294.2	0.0	0.0	562.5	3,750.0	0.0	

Source: Company Annual Reports.

Exhibit E6.7 *Details of FX Convertibles Issued by Suzlon*

Panel A: FCCB Issues

Instrument Name	Currency/ Amount	Issue Date	Maturity Date	Issue Price	Coupon/ Frequency	Convertible	Conversion Price	Conversion Dates	Floor Price	Redemption at Maturity	Name of Exchange
Convertible bonds	US$35,592.000 Face value US$1,000	May 8, 2009	June 2012	100%	7.50% Semi-annual June 12/ Dec 12	Yes 100% equity shares of par value ₹10	₹. 76.6755 per share	June 18, 2009– June 5, 2012	₹62.0125	150.24% of the principal amount	SGX-ST
Convertible bonds	US$20,796,000 Face value US$1,000	May 8, 2009	Oct 2012	100%	7.5% Semi-annual April 11/ Oct 11	Yes 100% equity shares of par value ₹10	₹76.6755 per share	June 18, 2009– Oct 4, 2012	₹62.0125	157.72% of the principal amount	SGX-ST
Zero-coupon convertible bonds	US$200,000,000 Face value US$1,000	Oct 10, 2007	Oct 11, 2012	100%	Zero coupon	Yes 100% equity shares of par VALUE ₹10	₹1,859.40 per share	Nov 20, 2007– Oct 4, 2012	₹1,102.99	144.48% of the principal amount	SGX-ST
Zero-coupon convertible bonds	US$300,000,000 Face value US$1,000	June 11, 2007	June 12, 2012	100%	Zero coupon	Yes 100% Equity shares of par value ₹10	₹1,800.00 per share	July 22, 2007– June 5, 2012	₹1,102.99	145.23% of the principal amount	SGX-ST
FCCB	US$ 200,000,000	Sept 21, 2007	Sept 22, 2012		YTM 7.55% semi-annual	Yes 100% equity shares of par value ₹10	₹1,859.40 per share			130% of principal	SGX-ST
Zero-coupon convertible bonds	US$ 90,000,000	July 24, 2009	July 25, 2014	104.30%	Zero coupon	Yes 100% equity shares of par value ₹2	₹90.38 per share	Sept 2, 2009– July 18, 2014	₹89.525	134.198% of the principal amount	SGX-ST

Panel B: Stock Market Reaction to Security Issues

Announcement Date	Instrument	Nifty Index Adjusted Return
May 16, 2007	FCCB	−1.04%
September 21, 2007	FCCB	−4.55%
July 21, 2009	GDR	−3.27%
	ZCCB	

Source: Company Annual Reports.

Exhibit E6.8 *Historical (Monthly) Inflation, Interest Rates, and Exchange Rates, 2007–12*

Date	90-day Rupee Lending rate %	90-day Euro dollar rate %	India CPI Inflation rate %	USA CPI Inflation rate %	Fwd Ex Rate 90-day (₹/US$)	Spot Exchange Rate (₹/US$)
Dec-12	8.92	0.3095	11.17	−0.04	55.53	54.99
Nov-12	8.73	0.311	9.55	−0.2	55.27	54.26
Oct-12	8.66	0.3305	9.6	0.24	54.67	53.81
Sep-12	8.81	0.3856	9.14	0.49	53.54	52.86
Aug-12	8.95	0.4323	10.31	0.51	56.42	55.53
Jul-12	9.24	0.4536	9.84	−0.02	56.73	55.65
Jun-12	9.41	0.4656	10.05	−0.03	56.46	55.64
May-12	9.78	0.4665	10.16	−0.13	57.48	56.11
Apr-12	9.64	0.4668	10.22	0.2	53.76	52.74
Mar-12	11.09	0.4733	8.65	0.26	51.88	50.88
Feb-12	10.28	0.5032	7.57	0.21	50.28	49.02
Jan-12	9.91	0.5659	5.32	0.25	50.54	49.46
Dec-11	9.84	0.5557	6.49	−0.02	54.57	53.06
Nov-11	9.63	0.4753	9.34	0.17	52.61	52.21
Oct-11	9.57	0.4065	9.39	0.04	49.49	48.69
Sep-11	9.51	0.3502	10.06	0.23	50.08	48.97
Aug-11	9.5	0.2932	8.99	0.26	46.45	46.1
Jul-11	9.41	0.2499	8.43	0.25	44.57	44.19
Jun-11	9.43	0.2478	8.62	0.03	45.18	44.7
May-11	9.7	0.2607	8.72	0.38	45.59	45.06
Apr-11	9.06	0.2814	9.41	0.49	44.94	44.22
Mar-11	10.15	0.3084	8.82	0.51	45.26	44.58
Feb-11	9.66	0.3119	8.82	0.33	46.02	45.27
Jan-11	9.3	0.3034	9.3	0.29	46.7	45.9
Dec-10	9	0.3027	9.47	0.41	45.3	44.71
Nov-10	8.19	0.2869	8.33	0.24	46.54	45.88
Oct-10	7.85	0.2888	9.7	0.34	44.97	44.43
Sep-10	7.49	0.2914	9.82	0.12	45.4	44.94
Aug-10	6.9	0.3626	9.88	0.15	47.72	47.08
Jul-10	6.53	0.5103	11.25	0.18	47.02	46.41
Jun-10	6.5	0.5369	13.73	−0.01	47.31	46.45
May-10	5.33	0.4585	13.91	−0.04	46.75	46.37
Apr-10	5.01	0.3116	13.33	0.03	44.67	44.37
Mar-10	5.69	0.2684	14.86	0.02	45.12	44.92

(continued)

Exhibit E6.8 *(continued)*

Date	90-day Rupee Lending rate %	90-day Euro dollar rate %	India CPI Inflation rate %	USA CPI Inflation rate %	Fwd Ex Rate 90-day (₹/US$)	Spot Exchange Rate (₹/US$)
Feb-10	4.97	0.2505	14.86	–0.1	46.3	46.08
Jan-10	4.59	0.2501	16.22	0.05	46.46	46.18
Dec-09	4.6	0.2531	14.97	0.05	46.78	46.53
Nov-09	4.44	0.2681	13.51	0.33	46.59	46.51
Oct-09	4.61	0.2831	11.49	0.3	47.51	46.97
Sep-09	4.67	0.298	11.64	0.19	47.96	48.11
Aug-09	4.58	0.4245	11.72	0.33	48.75	48.83
Jul-09	4.52	0.5153	11.89	–0.03	48.19	47.94
Jun-09	4.72	0.6207	9.29	0.83	48.44	47.9
May-09	5.29	0.8166	8.63	0.15	47.45	47.09
Apr-09	5.64	1.1062	8.7	0.1	50.17	50.09
Mar-09	7.64	1.2667	8.03	–0.1	51.69	50.73
Feb-09	7.64	1.2426	9.63	0.36	52.44	51.16
Jan-09	7.83	1.2108	10.45	0.25	49.76	48.88
Dec-08	8.89	1.8294	9.7	–0.82	49.9	48.8
Nov-08	10.43	2.2791	10.45	–1.77	52.32	50.11
Oct-08	11.73	4.0586	10.45	–0.86	51.95	49.46
Sep-08	11.86	3.1217	9.77	0.09	47.63	46.96
Aug-08	11.22	2.8063	9.02	–0.15	44.45	43.94
Jul-08	10.39	2.7921	8.33	0.71	43.13	42.57
Jun-08	9.94	2.7654	7.69	1.05	43.91	43.04
May-08	8.87	2.6924	7.75	0.59	42.32	42.46
Apr-08	8.77	2.7947	7.81	0.23	40.82	40.49
Mar-08	9.82	2.7825	7.87	0.36	40.17	40.12
Feb-08	9.61	3.0876	5.47	0.24	40.13	40.01
Jan-08	8.54	3.9176	5.51	0.34	39.56	39.37
Dec-07	8.56	4.9794	5.51	0.29	39.6	39.41
Nov-07	8.5	4.9621	5.51	0.79	39.9	39.6
Oct-07	7.9	5.1465	5.51	0.31	39.41	39.33
Sep-07	8.45	5.4939	6.4	0.42	39.91	39.85
Aug-07	8.47	5.4837	7.26	0.03	41.4	40.93
Jul-07	7.54	5.3597	6.45	0.18	40.63	40.37
Jun-07	9.31	5.3593	5.69	0.23	40.98	40.72
May-07	9.72	5.3595	6.61	0.41	40.67	40.61
Apr-07	11.12	5.3555	6.67	0.3	41.69	41.18

	90-day Rupee	90-day	India CPI	USA CPI	Fwd Ex Rate 90-day	Spot Exchange Rate
Date	Lending rate %	Euro dollar rate %	Inflation rate %	Inflation rate %	(₹/US$)	(₹/US$)
Mar-07	11.65	5.3479	6.72	0.52	43.61	43.47
Feb-07	10.22	5.3598	7.56	0.39	44.75	44.29
Jan-07	9.19	5.3601	6.72	0.17	44.38	44.18

Source: Bloomberg Database.

Exhibit E6.9 *Stock Price Chart (in ₹)*

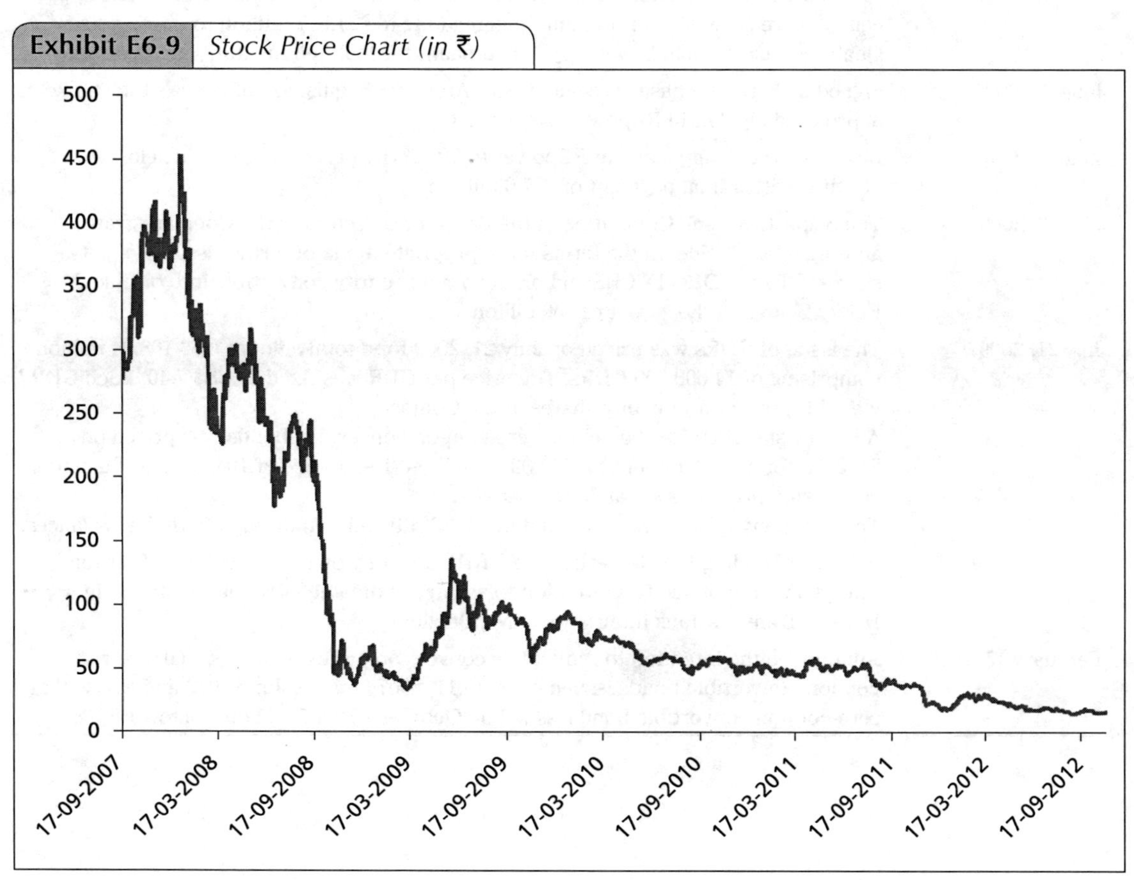

Source: Case Writer.

Exhibit E6.10 *Timeline of Events*[16]

March 2, 2007	Announced the acquisition of REpower Systems AG, Germany
May 16, 2007	Launched US$300 m FCCBs with a tenor of 5 years and 1 day at a conversion premium of 59.59% and YTM of 7.6%
June 3, 2007	Made an offer to acquire the entire outstanding equity share capital of REpower Systems AG to increase the equity stake from 33.85% to 100%
September 21, 2007	Launched US$200 m FCCBs with a tenor of 5 years and 1 day at a conversion premium of 59.59% and YTM of 7.6%
October 11, 2007	Company was awarded the Euromoney and Ernst & Young Global Renewable Energy Award for 'M&A of the Year' for the successful acquisition of REpower Systems AG of Germany
December 20, 2007	Allotted 1,13,86,000 equity shares of ₹10 each for cash at an issue price of ₹1,917 per equity share (inclusive of premium) aggregating to ₹21,827 million to the selected Qualified Institutional Buyers (QIBs) pursuant to Qualified Institutional Placement
June 6, 2008	Signed a share purchase agreement with Areva for acquisition of Areva's total stake of approximately 30% in REpower Systems AG
June 6, 2009	Increased the equity stake in REpower to 90.72% by purchasing shares held by Martifer with a final payment of €87.6 million
July 20, 2009	The Securities Issue Committee of the Board of Directors of the Company was authorized to decide on the terms for appropriate mode of further issue of equity shares, GDRs, ADRs, FCCBS and/or any other security convertible into or linked to Equity Shares to the extent of ₹50 billion
July 21, 2009	The issue of GDRs was priced on July 21, 2009 for a total amount US$ 108.04 million comprising of 14,600,000 GDRs. The price per GDR was fixed at US$ 7.40. Each GDR would represent four equity shares of the Company A fresh issue of US$ 90.00 million zero-coupon convertible bonds was priced on July 21, 2009 for a total amount of US$ 93.87 million (issue price of 104.3%) and the initial conversion price was set at ₹90.38 per share The Company raised a total amount of US$ 201.91 million through both the issuances.
November 19, 2009	AE-Rotor Holding BV, Netherlands (AERH), a wholly owned subsidiary of Suzlon Energy Ltd, announced its intention to sell approximately 35% equity interest in Hansen Transmissions International NV, Belgium
February 15, 2010	Announced the intention to reduce the conversion prices of its US$ 300 m zero-coupon convertible bonds issued on June 11, 2007 and due June 2012 and US$ 200 m zero-coupon convertible bonds issued on October 10,2007 and due October 2012

[16] The time line of events has been constructed by the information contained in company press releases. Available in http://www.suzlon.com/media_center/press_release.aspx?l1=7&l2=31 (accessed on September 13, 2017) on the respective dates.

May 18, 2010	FX Convertible bond holders agreed to: a) Removal of financial covenants b) effect a reduction in (a) the conversion price of the US$ 300 m zero-coupon convertible Bonds due June 2012 from ₹359.68 per equity share to ₹97.26 per equity share and (b) the Conversion Price of the US$ 200 m Zero Coupon Convertible Bonds due October 2012 from ₹371.55 per equity share to ₹97.26 per equity share c) revise the floor price in respect of the US$ 300 m Zero Coupon Convertible Bonds due June 2012 and the US$ 200 m Zero Coupon Convertible Bonds due October 2012 to ₹74.025 per equity share; and d) The fixed exchange rate was set at 1 US$ = ₹44.6000 and replaced the respective fixed exchange rates in the terms and conditions of the US$ 300 m Zero Coupon Convertible Bonds due June 2012 and the US$ 200 m Zero Coupon Convertible Bonds due October 2012
July 6, 2010	Tanti, Chairman and Managing Director, Suzlon Energy Limited was conferred the title, "Wind Visionary of Asia" during an international consultation – 'Quantum Leap in Wind Power in Asia' held at the Asian Development Bank (ADB) headquarters in Manila, Philippines
May 18, 2012	Sought an extension of 45 days to make the interest payment
September 18, 2012	Notices to FX convertible bond holders were sent to grant an extension of maturity dates of each of the series of bonds from October 11, 2012 to February 11, 2013. The meetings of the holders of the bonds were proposed to be held on October 10, 2012
October 3, 2012	Company issued a subsequent notice providing further information in relation to the incentive fee payable to holders of the bonds who consented to the proposed extension
October 10, 2012	Bondholders did not approve extension of maturities. The company announced that it was actively engaged with key stakeholders to find a consensual solution Company defaulted on payment to FX convertible bond holders
October 29, 2012	Initiated discussions with its senior secured lenders to restructure its debt with a maturity period of 10 years under the Corporate Debt Restructuring mechanism, including a two-year moratorium on principal and interest payments on term-debt

Source: Company Press Releases (various dates).

Index